KV-638-730

li WB

AT SPES NON FRACTA

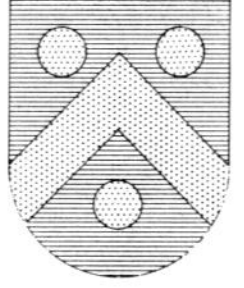

Benjamin West (1738–1820)

The Hope family in 1802
(*Cf. List of Illustrations*)

Museum of Fine Arts, Boston, Mass.
(by courtesy of the owner)

AT SPES NON FRACTA

HOPE & CO. 1770-1815

MERCHANT BANKERS AND DIPLOMATS
AT WORK

by

MARTEN G. BUIST

1974

BANK MEES & HOPE NV

© 1974 by Martinus Nijhoff, The Hague, Netherlands
All rights reserved, including the right to translate or to reproduce this book or parts thereof in any form

ISBN 90 247 1629 2

Printed in The Netherlands

To Jonkheer Wilco Julius van Sminia,
a former partner in the firm of Hope & Co.

FOREWORD

In a so rapidly changing world it seems appropriate sometimes to reflect for a while on the past. Firstly because we should never forget that today's world stems largely from the initiatives of our predecessors. Secondly because it lends a perspective to our present activities and not least as some of the so colourful events in the history of Hope & Co., established in 1762, are worth being recorded for the future.

In the years following the second World War the partners of the banking firm Hope & Co. took the first steps, to sort out for historical purposes the old files and were extremely fortunate in finding Dr. M. G. Buist prepared to accept the challenge and to immerse himself in this work. In the beginning he certainly could not realise what task he took on his shoulders. It soon became evident that a full history of the banking house could not be aimed at; instead he focussed his attention on a comparatively short but highly intriguing period of Hope's 200 years of existence.

The undersigned, who were partners of Hope & Co. and are today active in its successor Bank Mees & Hope are grateful to Dr. Buist for his devotion to this task and the energy and perseverance he has demonstrated.

His book is at the same time a tribute to the founders of the bank and their successors in the period described as well as an inspiration for those who both now and in the future will see to it that Bank Mees & Hope maintains the repute in which it has been and is being held in The Netherlands as well as abroad.

Amsterdam, March 1974

C.P.C.Fabius
H.L.Guldemond
Baron J.G.A.Sirtema van Grovestins

PREFACE

The setting for this study is reflected in the sub-title 'Merchant bankers and diplomats at work.' The aim is to follow the partners in their many and diverse activities: in their relationship towards each other, in their contacts with other houses and in their attitudes towards government officials. Moreover, the author has attempted to show the motives for their commercial and financial actions, where these were discernible. A point of departure such as this implies that the surviving correspondence constitutes the principal source of information. Quantitative data are included, but within this framework their role is subsidiary.

Because this book is intended for various categories of readers, it has been divided into three parts. The introductory chapter, which contains an abridged history of Hope & Co. up to 1815, is intended for those whose interest in the subject is of a more general nature. In the same chapter, a number of main themes such as the growth of foreign loans in the Netherlands and the technique *per se* of issuing loans are discussed, and attention is devoted to some of the problems of trade and to the question whether Hope & Co. should be viewed as merchants or as bankers. In conclusion, an impression is given of the part played by Amsterdam as a financial centre during the Napoleonic era and of the very exceptional position which Hope & Co. occupied at that time.

In the succeeding chapters, the principal themes are examined in detail with the aid of a number of case studies. There is more to the subdivision into Baltic Affairs and Iberian Affairs than appears at first sight: while Baltic Affairs according to the sub-title deals only with loans, and Iberian Affairs only with produce, it becomes clear in the elaboration of the chapters that, in the eyes of Messrs. Hope, mercantile transactions and financial affairs were inextricably interwoven. Accordingly, only in the final chapter do contents and title correspond.

The Notes are intended for researchers who desire to go deeper into certain aspects of this study. This explains their comprehensive nature.

But for the decision taken by Messrs. Hope in 1953 to commission a history of the house, this study would not have been embarked upon. Without the decision of the present-day Board of Bank Mees & Hope to allow the study to continue and to have the result published in book form, the work would not have been completed. The great abundance of data in the Hope archives is illustrated by the fact that, in spite of the length of this book, the author was obliged to limit himself to the period up to 1815.

The author acknowledges with gratitude the interest displayed by the former partners and by the members of the present Board throughout the period during which this book was written. This applies particularly to Jhr. W.J. van Sminia, to whom the book is dedicated. Without his support, mediation and encouragement, this study might well not have seen the light of day.

The author owes a debt of gratitude to his mentor, Jhr. Prof. P.J. van Winter, who brought about the contact between Messrs. Hope & Co. and him, and who, by reason of his exceptionally wide knowledge of the subject matter, has been a source of constant support. Prof. E.H.Kossmann read through the chapters and, drawing on his very great knowledge of literature and wide experience, offered valuable advice which benefited this book and for which the author is most grateful.

Three successive librarians of the University of Groningen, Dr. H. de Buck, the late Dr. S.J.Bouma and Mr. W.R.H.Koops, offered the hospitality of their institution to the Hope archives and to the author for a period of twenty years. The author is greatly indebted to Mr. Koops who, as a friend, allowed him to benefit from his experience as a publisher. The author's thanks are due to the staff of the University Library for their willing assistance and their interest in the advancement of the study.

A search into the history of Hope & Co. would be impossible without data from the municipal archives in Amsterdam. The author is grateful to the archivist, Dr. W.J. van Hoboken, for having made it possible for him to freely carry out his researches, and also to Dr. S.Hart who, with his immense knowledge of economic data, so willingly assisted him in this task.

Many have assisted the author during his investigations, or have aided him in other ways. While it is impossible to refer to them all by name, the author wishes to make an exception in the case of Mr. Derek S.Jordan, the translator of this book, whose critical observations were instrumental in ironing out a number of wrinkles.

Finally, the author is indebted to his family: to his children, who from an early age have shown him every consideration, and above all to his wife, who sustained her husband in the broadest sense of the term throughout the genesis of this book.

INTRODUCTION

THE FAMILY AND THE FIRM

CHAPTER ONE

THE FAMILY AND THE FIRM

SOME OBSERVATIONS ON COMMERCE AND BANKING IN THE LATE 18TH CENTURY

'This is my plan for you, my Lord, and you never had a better opportunity for executing it ... Your Lordship should come over in the beginning of April, spend some weeks with us at The Hague till the end of May, then some weeks at one of my seats in this province from whence we make all our acquaintance to see the country ... Towards the end of the year we may spend some time in Amsterdam, return to The Hague and from thence I give you my word of honour that I and my wife will accompany you to England to make a considerable stay there.' [1]

In this letter, dated 12th March 1776, John Hope, merchant of Amsterdam and a partner in the house of Hope & Co., not only sketched his seigneurial mode of living, but also confirmed his kinship to the recipient, the Earl of Hopetoun, by signing himself 'Your most affectionate cousin.'

John Hope's urge to confirm and maintain his ties with the noble Scottish branch of the family merits closer inspection, for genealogists have so far not succeeded in providing irrefutable proof of the relationship between the Scottish and Dutch branches.

According to the tradition, a certain Jean de Hope travelled from France to Scotland with one of the French wives of James v, the Scottish king. It is improbable that this Jean will have accompanied James's first wife, Madeleine of France, for she died in July 1537, only six months after her marriage. It therefore seems more likely that he accompanied Mary de Guise, whom James v married in 1538.

For those who are inclined to doubt this romantic origin, there is a certain John Hope, who was admitted as a Burgess and Guild Brother of Edinburgh in 1528 or 1529. One thing is certain: in 1560 or there abouts, the son of Jean or John Hope, Edward, played a part in bringing about the Reformation. The succeeding generation included a Henry Hope, who married Jacqueline de Tot or de Jot; they had at least four sons. The French-sounding name of Henry's wife may indicate a Continental link; indeed, an entry in the Edinburgh Roll shows that their son James, a 'factor in Dieppe,' was admitted as a Burgess and Guild Brother in 1619.

Upon the death of James Hope in 1634, his son Henry or Harry took over the business activities. The diary kept by Henry's uncle, Thomas, who received a baronetcy and took the title Hope of Craighall, contains references to his nephew's regular visits to port towns in France. The diary for 1637 also refers to contacts with Holland: 'Saturday 5th August: Harry my nephew went by sea to Calais and given him five twelve pound pieces of gold; and at his return he promised to serve some merchant in Amsterdam.' The visit can not have been of long duration, for on 26th March 1639 Sir Thomas recorded that: 'This night Harry Hope, my nephew, came from France.'

It is tempting to allow this Henry to marry his cousin, Ann, daughter of Sir Thomas, and to let the couple move to Rotterdam in 1660 or thereabouts; this, however, does not correspond to the genealogical facts, added to which it is unlikely that Henry, at his relatively advanced age, would have raised a family in Rotterdam. As a last possibility, there could have been a Henry Hope Jr. who, moreover, might have married the daughter of Sir Thomas's son. No evidence of this is to be found in Edinburgh.[1]

It has, however, been established that in 1664 Henry Hope and Anna Hope (variously written as Hop or Hoop) had their son Archibald christened in the Scottish Church in Rotterdam. They subsequently had other children, three of whom, Bethea, Elizabeth and Anna, reached adulthood.[2]

In the 1680s Henry Hope's business fortunes declined, and eventually he and his family were forced to leave Rotterdam and settle in London. But even there his creditors continued to harass him: on 3rd September 1688, Gilles van Braem, a merchant in Rotterdam, authorized John Schoppens and Samuel Sale of London to recover monies owed to him by Henry Hope.[3]

Shortly after this, it appears, Henry Hope died, leaving his wife and children in impoverished circumstances. In the meantime, however, Archibald had resumed his father's profession in Rotterdam and, as his Wills show, was increasingly successful. In 1694 he married Anna Claus, the daughter of a well-to-do Amsterdam buttonmaker and like himself, a Quaker. Their union was richly blessed with children, of whom eight sons and two daughters reached adulthood. With each new Will, they were more handsomely provided for.[4]

Archibald did not forget his mother and his sisters. Even before his marriage he had brought them back to Rotterdam, where he gave his mother an annual allowance and provided his sisters with capital to start a draper's shop.

A Will dated 1720 shows Archibald to have been the owner of malting houses in Ipswich, Stowmarket and Bury St. Edmunds, and of two vessels used specially for the transport of malt. He also owned at least two other vessels, the 'Henry' and the 'Marlborough,' which were engaged in the trade with England and Ireland.[1]

The ties with Scotland were also maintained. On 22nd February 1701, Charles Hope of Hopetoun authorized Archibald Hope, 'Merchant in Rotterdam, My Cousin,' to collect a debt owed to him by the Rotterdam merchant Cornelis van der Pot. Charles Hope, who owned important lead mines, had supplied Van der Pot with lead ore for which the latter had failed to pay. This authorization is of particular importance because it provides irrefutable proof of the relationship between the Hopes of Rotterdam and the ennobled Scottish family.[2]

Archibald Hope's Will of 1720 stipulated that, upon his death, the merchant house should be carried on by his sons Henry and John. Places in the firm were also reserved for their brothers Isaac and Thomas, who were then under age. The name of the second eldest son, Archibald Jr., does not appear in this connexion, but it is known that in 1720 he lived with his uncle, Warner Lulofs, at a house flanking the Singel in Amsterdam and worked with him as a stockjobber dealing in speculative issues. It was not until 1722 that the name of Archibald Hope Jr. appeared in the Amsterdam Notarial Archives and in the account books of the Exchange Bank in that city.[3]

It is interesting to note that several other Amsterdam merchant houses which played an important role in the 18th century also commenced operations there during the early decades of that century. For example, the distinguished house of Andries Pels & Sons was founded in 1707, while in 1712 Pieter Schout Muilman and Dionijs Meulenaar established a house from which the firm of Muilman & Sons was to evolve fifteen years later. The house of Hogguer, like that of Hope, was not of Dutch origin. At about the time when Archibald Hope was establishing himself, Jacques Christophe Hogguer, on the advice of his father, set up in business in Amsterdam. The Hogguers, who were of Swiss extraction, had settled at Lyons in 1680 or thereabouts and had rapidly achieved a prominent position in banking circles there.[4]

Despite the consolidation and a mild recession in certain sectors of Holland's trade, the Amsterdam of the early 18th century was evidently still so attractive and vital as a centre that enterprising foreigners undertook ventures there – and succeeded.

The notarial archives show clearly that Archibald Jr. followed in his father's footsteps, albeit in Amsterdam, and devoted himself to trade and shipping. He was soon joined by his younger brother Thomas, who evidently foresaw a better future in Amsterdam than in the family business in Rotterdam. On 14th June 1724, Archibald Jr. granted power of procuration to 'His Brother Thomas Hope, also a Merchant of this place,' enabling him, in Archibald's absence, to perform any acts necessary in the interests of the house.[1]

In the absence of accounts for this period, it is difficult to form an opinion of the nature and extent of the business transacted by the Hope brothers. However, the figures for the house's annual turnover with the Amsterdam Exchange Bank are of some value in this context, particularly when they are compared with the turnover of certain other houses. For this purpose we have chosen the aforementioned houses of Muilman, Pels and Hogguer, and in addition the somewhat older houses of De Smeth and Clifford. De Smeth, which, like Hope, was later to earn a reputation as an issuer of loans, had its roots in the Southern Netherlands. After residing for some time in Cologne, Joost de Smeth settled in Amsterdam round about 1650. The Cliffords were by origin British and had arrived in Amsterdam a little later.[2]

The majority of the changes affecting the accounts maintained with the Exchange Bank related to sums transferred to or from other bank accounts. The total of the credits and debits during a period of a year constituted the turnover of the account concerned. The value for our purpose of the sums thus obtained, and reproduced in graph form, is, of course, relative, since we do not know the ratio between the Exchange Bank account turnover of a given house and its total turnover. The ratios may well have varied from year to year and from house to house. Nevertheless, they at least afford a certain indication of the level of business.[3]

If we examine the figures relating to the early years of the Hope brothers' career, the first thing that strikes us is the gradual nature of the growth: in 1728 neither Hope nor Hogguer reached a turnover of two million guilders. In the same year, Muilman and Clifford achieved more than twice this figure, while Pels, with a turnover of twenty million, stood head and shoulders above them all. In 1726, when, in the wake of the adoption by France of the monetary system devised by John Law, French gold and silver coin poured into Amsterdam, Pels had achieved the staggering figure of thirty million guilders. It is clear from the absence of peaks in the graph relating to the turnover of Archibald and Thomas Hope that they did not then deal in specie on a large scale.[4]

The third decade of the eighteenth century saw a change in the house of

106

I Charles Hope of Hopetoun With Consent of My Curators
Undersubscryving have made & Constitute and by these presents Make and
Constitute Archibald Hope Merchant in Roterdam my Cousin Factor and
Procurator for me and in my name to the effect Afterspecified Hereby Giving
and Committing to him my full power and Commission to require Mr
Cornelius Vanderpott Merchant in Roterdam and Company to Make
payment and Satisfaction of the summes of money addebted by them to me
as the pryce of the last years complement of Lead Oar sold by me to them
conform to the Contract thereanent as well in so farr as has been already
delivered to their Order As for what remains of the said Last Years complement
lying att Leith yet undelivered which they had advice of from me & my saids
Curators and others in my name severall moneths agoe And also to require the
said Mr Cornelius & Company to send a ship for takeing in the said remaining
Oar And further to require them to make payment of the Exchange Reexchange
Interest and damnadges sustained by me through their suffering the Bills
drawn by me and my saids Curators or others having our order to be returned
unpayed and protested With certification and intimation and under express
protestation that the said Mr Cornelius and Company forsaid are and shall be
lyable to me not only for the pryce of the said lead oar already delivered But
also for what remains yet undelivered of the said last years complement with
all Exchange reexchange interest damnadges & expence sustained or that may
happen to be sustayned by me by the saids bills being returned protested and by
my want and lyingout of the use of the money And for the charges and
expence of Law & otherways in pursueing the said Mr Cornelius and Company
therefore by and attour the penalties of their Contract incurred by them with
Intimation also to them that if they doe not send a ship with all due expedition for takeing in what remains of the said last years complement of lead oar
that then and in that case it shall be lawfull to me to sell and dispose thereupon
without any breach of the said Contract on my part And upon all and sundry
the premisses to ask and take Instruments in presence of ane Nottar & witnesses
as accords And further with power to the said Archibald Hope my said Factor
and Procurator to prosecute and pursue the said Mr Cornelius and Company
for payment of the haill sumes of money abovementioned according to their
said Contract with all Exchange Reexchange Damnadge Interest and expence
sustayned or to be sustayned by me with the penalties of ye said Contract incurred
by them And yrupon to recover Sentence and decreet and to use all execution
competent in Law And generally all & sundry other things anent the premisses to
doe that I with consent of my saids Curators might doe if wee were personallie
present Promising to hold firm & stable what my said procurator does or
lawfully shall cause be done in the premisses In witness whereof I and my saids
Curators have subscryved thir presents att Edinburgh the twenty second day of
ffebruary One thousand seven hundred & one years Before witnesses
Thomas Pringle wryter to ye Signet & George Keith his servant

Tho Pringle Witnes
Geo Keith witnes
H. Hope Margarett Hope Cha Hope

Power of attorney granted by Charles Hope of Hopetoun to Archibald Hope of Rotterdam, 1701

Hope in Amsterdam. Archibald Jr. died on 28th March 1733. His death occurred in Rotterdam, and the fact that he was buried there–even though he was described as a 'merchant of Amsterdam'–suggests that he had earlier ceased to concern himself with the day-to-day affairs of his business.[1] Prior to Archibald's death, a younger brother, Adrian, had joined the firm, and in 1734 Thomas made him a partner, whereupon the title of the house was changed to Thomas & Adrian Hope.[2]

Of these two, Thomas was destined to achieve the greater reputation as a merchant, and his fame reflected on the firm which bore his name. The house of Thomas & Adrian Hope was renowned for its consistent policy of covering risks and for the high degree of continuity in its commodity trading in the face of changing political circumstances.

The turnover figures at the Exchange Bank confirm this image of solidity and stability. Until the outbreak of the Seven Years' War in 1756, the figures continued to grow slowly but surely, displaying no sensational peaks or troughs. It is notable that De Smeth achieved an appreciably smaller rate of growth, and that Hogguer stood still.

The graphs representing Clifford and Pels display dramatic peaks in the post-1740 period. These are undoubtedly allied to the outbreak of the War of the Austrian Succession, a trial of strength between Prussia and France on the one side, and England and Austria on the other, which afforded exceptional trading opportunities for Holland, a neutral state. But by 1743 the era of record turnover had passed for Pels, and by 1745 the same applied to Clifford. In the latter year, the country's trade commenced to decline under the influence of the war between France and the Dutch Republic.

By the eve of the Seven Years' War, Thomas & Adrian Hope had left Hogguer and Muilman far behind in terms of turnover with the Exchange Bank. They were roughly on a par with De Smeth, and in the period 1750–1755 both houses achieved an annual figure of about ten million guilders. Pels and Clifford were at this time turning over something like twenty million annually, Pels remaining just under this figure and Clifford slightly above it.

In 1747, under the pressure of the French invasion of the southern part of the Netherlands, the stadholdership was restored in the provinces of Holland, Zeeland, Utrecht, Gelderland and Overijssel. The young stadholder, from whom major political reforms were expected, was showered with offices and powers. As an example, he was appointed Director-General and Governor of the *Oost-Indische Compagnie* and the *West-Indische Compagnie* in 1750, but soon afterwards he appointed Thomas Hope and another Amsterdam merchant, Jan van Marselis, to represent him in the latter.[1]

This, however, was not to be the only token of the stadholder's favour. Among the problems facing William IV was the economic decline of the Republic. Concern at the eclipse of Holland as a trading nation by England, and at the increasing competition from France, Sweden and Denmark in the maritime sector, had been expressed during the second decade of the century. In addition, Hamburg was growing into a competitive staple market for colonial produce. In the industrial sector, Dutch firms were suffering increasingly from protectionist measures in the neighbouring countries. Added to all this, the French invasion of the southern part of the Netherlands, as we have seen, had adversely affected the country's trade, and when, following the ending of the War of the Austrian Succession, the anticipated recovery failed to materialize, William commanded that a committee should be established to draw up a plan to revive the commercial and industrial activity.

Jan van Marselis and Thomas Hope were appointed members of this committee, though not without protest. Hasselaer, a powerful burgomaster of Amsterdam, described Thomas Hope as 'the greatest scoundrel of Amsterdam,' and when Gronsfelt, a favourite of the stadholder and a champion of Hope, stood up for him and praised his skill, Hasselaer retorted that this was one more reason for being on one's guard against him. Charles Bentinck, who also enjoyed the stadholder's favour and who was present during the conversation, added that in this respect the Amsterdam Stock Exchange shared Hasselaer's opinion.[2] The immediate causes of these spiteful remarks by Hasselaer and Bentinck, are of secondary importance. In all probability, they stemmed from a combination of envy at Hope's success in business and jealousy of his position as confidant of the stadholder. It is clear that Thomas Hope had become embroiled in a struggle between rival factions at the Court, but this was something which would be repeated when the house undertook loans for countries ruled by despots.

The committee of which Thomas Hope was a member had meanwhile set about its task. One of the focal points of its deliberations was the extent to which import and export duties would have to be reduced if the Republic was again to be attractive as a staple market for the whole of Europe. After lengthy discussions, Thomas Hope succeeded in getting his views adopted. These embraced a limited free trade system in which, in order to provide a measure of protection for traders, farmers and cattle breeders, import duties were retained for a number of competitive commodities. The end of all import duties was in any case not feasible, for the revenue from these was used by the provincial Boards of Admiralty to defray the costs of maintaining the fleet. At the same time, the transit trade had to be given a measure of relief in order to attract more goods to the staple market.

In August 1751 these plans, in the shape of a 'Proposition,' were submitted by the stadholder to the States General of the Republic and the Provincial States of Holland, accompanied by an explanatory document entitled 'Verhandeling over den Koophandel.' A fragment of the draft of the 'Verhandeling' has survived, and as this is in Thomas Hope's own hand it may safely be assumed that he was the author of the document.[1]

The Proposition was ill-fated. The first setback came with the death of William IV a few months after it had been submitted. Added to this, there was disunity among the provinces of the Republic, each of which desired that locally produced goods should be protected by a tariff barrier.

In spite of all efforts by Thomas Hope and his supporters, the Proposition stranded on the rocks of provincial and local particularism. The widow of William IV, the English princess Anne, who ruled as 'Gouvernante' in the minority of her son, was so preoccupied with the maintenance of her own power, and so unfamiliar with relationships in Holland, that she was unable to force a decision on the plan. Furthermore, interest in it began to wane in 1755, when it became clear that the War of the Austrian Succession had been no more than an initial phase in the struggle between England and France for the colonies in North America and India. The Republic, which had maintained close ties with England since the reign of the King-Stadholder William III, faced a new threat of being caught up in the Anglo-French conflict.[2]

In the debate concerning the strengthening of the armed forces, a sharp controversy arose on the question of whether the army or the navy should receive priority. The Gouvernante greatly favoured reinforcing the army, and this led to the suspicion that, as an English princess, she sought to pursue a harsh, anti-French policy. When hostilities commenced in 1756, the issue of higher or lower import duties became one of secondary importance: what mattered now was to preserve Holland's neutrality in order that trade with all the belligerent parties should continue.

Thomas Hope continued to work for the adoption of the Proposition to the bitter end, but after the death of the stadholder he associated himself less closely with the group surrounding the Gouvernante and with her policy of orientation on England. He showed himself to be a supporter of a powerful policy of neutrality in the face of British demands–an attitude which is the more remarkable since he maintained contact with the Hopes of Hopetoun and, through them, with political circles in England. Thomas Hope took the view that ties with a particular party or country of origin ought not to imply unconditional conformity with the opinions prevailing there, and this view was to be shared by his successors.[1]

The information obtained from the Exchange Bank shows that the Hopes' definitive rise to the summit of their profession coincided with the Seven Years' War. From 1755 onwards, turnover rose steeply, reaching 34 million guilders in 1759. A period of diminished growth ensued, but in 1761 turnover again rose, reaching 47 million guilders in 1762. This peak was followed by a sharp decline in 1763 and 1764, when the figures were 42 and 33½ million guilders respectively.

The other houses to which reference has been made also made progress in this period, but with the exception of Pels and Clifford their rate of growth was considerably less spectacular. Pels and Clifford reached maxima of 41 and 34½ million guilders respectively. It is noteworthy that Pels's turnover reached its peak in 1758, after which it declined steadily. De Smeth succeeded in maintaining a level in excess of 20 million guilders from 1758 to 1761, but three years later this had plummeted to just under four million.

The steep rises achieved by Hope, Clifford, Pels and De Smeth indicate that these houses had their share of the greatly enlarged trade in specie. The war served also to stimulate commodity trading, but in this sector large profits could turn into equally large losses in the event of piracy or confiscation.

Despite the risks, the Hopes engaged in commodity trading on a large scale. They had originally concentrated on Great Britain, but by now their activities had for some time been extended to embrace the whole of Europe and even areas beyond, such as North America and the West Indies. By a fortunate coincidence, a member of the family had emigrated to Boston, and was available as correspondent there. Henry, the eldest brother of Thomas and Adrian, had left his father's firm in Rotterdam in 1720 or thereabouts, and had set up in business on his own. But, like his grandfather before him, he had had little success, and his position steadily deteriorated until, round about 1730, he left for America. With the death of Archibald Sr. in 1743, the Rotterdam house had passed into the hands of Henry's younger brothers Isaac and Zachary, and now specialized in the conveyance of emigrants to North America.[2]

During the Seven Years' War the brothers in Amsterdam and Rotterdam maintained a lively correspondence on the subject of trade with the Caribbean. Trade with the islands of the French West Indies, which were cut off from the mother country by the superior English fleet, was maintained via the Dutch colonies of St. Eustatius and Curaçao. This back-door supply route was a thorn in the flesh of England, and it is thus not surprising that the correspondence between the brothers abounds with reports of vessels and cargoes being lost as a result of British naval superiority or the activities of pirates. Nevertheless, the trade with the Western Hemisphere continued, albeit caution was exercised in the traffic with the French colonies.

Isaac and Zachary Hope were among the most enthusiastic supporters of the attitude adopted by the Province of Holland, which was pressing the Gouvernante for a rapid expansion of the fleet and strong action against the English 'piracy.'[1] But the Gouvernante persisted in her view that if the navy was enlarged, the army would have to be also. With this, supporters and opponents of a strong policy against England and supporters and opponents of the Gouvernante began to discover common ground. It was not until Anne's death in 1759 that the conflict abated.

Thomas and Adrian Hope utilized the services of their brothers in Rotterdam for the delivery of coin to France via houses in Brussels and Antwerp. The Amsterdam house also supplied cannon to the French East India Company. These were ostensibly sold to the Hopes in Gothenburg, and the house had them shipped to Amsterdam at their own risk. There, the French East India Company resumed ownership.[2] The timber trade with France and the Iberian peninsula, in which the Hopes engaged on a large scale, also continued, although the number of cargoes declined.[3]

As far as the Hopes were concerned, the trade with, and for the benefit of, France in no way diminished the ties with England. In the financial sector, in particular, there was much for houses such as Hope and Clifford to do. Between 1756 and 1762 the British government was obliged to float loans totalling nearly 50,000,000 pounds sterling to defray the cost of the war, and a substantial portion of these loans were placed in Amsterdam through the medium of Hope and Clifford. Amsterdam also served as the intermediate centre for the transfer of subsidies to Prussia and other allies of Britain on the Continent. For this, the British government issued payment orders to houses like Hope, and these were negotiated in Germany. Subsidies were also paid in gold and silver bullion, most of which passed through Amsterdam.[4]

The incessant calls made upon the money market in Amsterdam led to a scarcity of funds, and this in turn produced a major extension of acceptance credit. The demand for credit did not cease with the restoration of peace in February 1763, and funds continued to be required for purposes such as the restoration of currencies weakened by the war, as in the case of Prussia, or the payment of war levies, as in the case of Saxony. With money so scarce, the greatly inflated circulation in the form of drafts could only be maintained by honouring a matured draft with a draft on another house. This *wisselruiterij* or cross-accommodation system was hazardous inasmuch as a failure anywhere along the line could bring the whole structure tumbling down. To make matters worse, many houses were holding large stocks of colonial produce, the price of which had slumped with the news of peace and the prospect of an early resumption of fresh supplies direct from the colonies.

At the end of July 1763 the ground caved in, and the speculators commenced to drag each other over the precipice. The most startling bankruptcy concerned the house of De Neufville, which had achieved a dubious reputation by indulging with others in practices aimed at debasing the currency in Prussia.[1] Efforts by those at the Stock Exchange, including Hope, to establish an emergency fund failed when Pels backed out. The house of Pels had a reputation for being rigid and conservative (its dwindling turnover with the Exchange Bank in the years after 1758 is an indication of this). Thomas and Adrian Hope had not been in danger for a single moment during the crisis: their cautious and consistent policy of covering risks had stood them in good stead.[2]

It is noticeable that the turnover of all six houses which we investigated declined during 1762, indicating that they reduced the scale of their credit operations before peace was proclaimed. With the exception of De Smeth, who lost more than 400,000 guilders when De Neufville failed, they emerged from the crisis comparatively unharmed.[3]

At this point, let us take a closer look at the Hope brothers. Soon after 1720, Archibald Jr. had moved to a house flanking the Herengracht and situated near the Blauwburgwal. In 1726 he had married Geertruyd Reessen, the daughter of a merchant in the Warmoesstraat. In the following year, Thomas Hope had married Margareta Marcelis, the daughter of an Amsterdam merchant and soap-boiler, and they, too, had settled on the Herengracht, but 'beyond the Bergstraat.' They had one son, John. Thomas's brother, Adrian, who was a bachelor, made his permanent home with them.[4]

In 1758 Thomas purchased a house, with adjacent coach-house and stables, situated on the Keizersgracht, near the Molenpad. This he acquired from Mattheus Levestenon van Berkenrode, who at that time represented the Republic in France. Thomas paid cf 83,000 for the house and its contents. Shortly after the purchase he embarked on a programme of alteration and expansion which was to occupy several years. The first step was the acquisition of houses situated on the Prinsengracht and backing on to Thomas's home. When he had acquired six of these, he had them demolished and replaced by two large warehouses known as Kerkkroon A and B, which were used for storage and stabling. Wagons loaded with goods entered the premises via a narrow street leading past the stables and ending in an inner courtyard which had once been the garden of the house on the Keizersgracht.[1]

It took until 1769 to obtain all the properties needed to make way for the warehouses, and this fact alone indicates that the house must still have handled a large volume of goods. The next step was to join the original coach-house and stables to the house proper; this was probably done for the benefit of Thomas's brother, Adrian.

Conditions in the house on the Keizersgracht are revealed in the diary of Bengt Ferrner, a Swedish professor of astronomy who, in company with the son of the wealthy Swedish manufacturer Lefebure, was touring Europe. Thanks to Lefebure's business connexions, the two were invited to dine with Thomas and Adrian Hope on a day in March 1759. When the company had finished discussing the progress of the wars on the Continent and in America, and the activities of the English pirates, the conversation turned to the swarm of Dutch authors who, Thomas Hope complained, were always trying to dedicate books to him in order to get money out of him.[2]

As one who depended upon the favours of the rich, Ferrner was annoyed by the ease with which Thomas Hope dismissed such authors as 'beggars.' But he went on to remark that the Hopes were recognized as experts *par excellence* in mercantile matters and that both men, especially Thomas, worked like slaves. The latter observation will not have been meant as a compliment, but it does show once again that the 18th-century merchant was not content to sit back and live on his capital.

Ferrner also noted that Thomas Hope was 'a director' of the *Oost-Indische Compagnie*. After the death of William IV in 1751, Thomas Hope had relinquished the post of representative of the stadholder on the Board of the *West-Indische Compagnie*, but in 1756 he was made a director of the much more important *Oost-Indische Compagnie*. From 1766 to 1770 he represented Stadholder William V on the Board of this company, where, as previously, his immense energy and drive soon made him the pivot about which everything revolved. He was the first and only person to attempt to

Amsterdam the 1st. January, 1762.

Sir

Having taken into Partnership with us our Mr. THOMAS HOPE'S son Mr. JOHN HOPE, (now on his travels) and our Nephew Mr. HENRY HOPE; we take the liberty to communicate to you our respective Signatures at foot, (that of our Mr. JOHN HOPE excepted, which will be subjoined at his return,) under our new Firm, commencing this day of HOPE & Company; to which we pray equal respect and credit may be given.

Sensible of your Favours and Friendship to our House, we presume to request the continuance, assuring you that our utmost endeavours will be exerted to merit and acknowledge them.

We have the honour to be with great respect.

Sir

Your most obedt humble Servants

The Signature of Y. M. H. S. THOMAS HOPE,

The Signature of Y. M. H. S. ADRIAN HOPE,

The Signature of Y. M. H. S. HENRY HOPE.

Circular announcing the establishment of Hope & Co., 1762

devise a system of calculating cost prices within the *Oost-Indische Compagnie.*[1]

Towards the end of the Seven Years' War, Thomas and Adrian Hope were joined in the firm by Thomas's son, John, and their American nephew Henry. Henry's father, it will be recalled, had emigrated to Boston round about 1730. In 1735 his wife bore him a son, and five years later a daughter, Henrietta Maria. Henry Jr. was sent to England at the age of thirteen to complete his education, and in 1754 he commenced his commercial career in the house of Gurnell Hoare & Co. of London, with whom the Amsterdam Hopes also were associated.[2] In 1760 he visited his uncles, and such was their opinion of him that he was invited to join the house. Indeed, they were so taken with their nephew that on 1st January 1762 he and Thomas's son, John, were admitted to partnership of what was henceforth to be Hope & Co. In 1763 the property to the east of Thomas's house on the Keizersgracht was purchased, probably for Henry's benefit. John meanwhile continued to live further along the canal.[3]

Of the two new partners, Henry Hope was the better known and without doubt the more able. He may be regarded as the successor to Thomas, although he was less of a public figure than his uncle. This was undoubtedly related to his Anglo-American origin, as a result of which he will have identified himself far less with specific Dutch situations than his cousin, John. When, in the 1780s, contrasting political opinions flared up, Henry Hope observed that because of his civil status (he took no part in administrative affairs) he was not obliged to take sides, and that he therefore maintained strict neutrality in his actions in Amsterdam.[4]

Like Thomas, Henry Hope had pro-Orange sympathies–which he made no attempt to hide–but as an outsider he felt no compulsion to drain the cup of political engagement. Such polarization was not in keeping with his character, which is described to us as 'singularly even, mild, engaging and amiable.' Henry Hope was well known for his concern for his fellowmen, a concern manifested in many ways including liberal donations to charity.[5] 'None ever more perfectly realised the idea of a merchant prince, diligent in gathering, delighted to distribute wherever he could find an object of commiseration and this not thoughtlessly, on the impulse of the moment, merely to relieve the unpleasant sensation of witnessing distress, but with judgement and consideration for the improvement of the sufferer as well as his immediate relief and with all the delicacy of a refined mind, which led him to lessen as far as possible the weight of obligation when his quick tact showed him that it would be oppressive.'[6]

A relative of the authoress of this glowing tribute experienced the extent of Henry Hope's mildness at first hand. A young Cornishman, John Williams, worked as a clerk in a merchant house in Amsterdam. He became seriously ill and, to make matters worse, did not receive the necessary care at his lodgings. News of his plight reached Henry Hope, who immediately took action to assist him, going so far as to have the sick man transferred to his own house. He was so taken by his compatriot–for so must Henry Hope have regarded him–that Williams continued to live in the Hope household.

Henry Hope's sister, Henrietta Maria, had married in 1762. Her husband was John Goddard, an English merchant in Rotterdam. Their eldest daughter, Anne, was the apple of Henry's eye, and he contrived a plan which ended in his niece marrying his protégé, John Williams, in 1782. Simultaneously, the latter was made a partner of Hope & Co.[1] Out of gratitude to his benefactor, he added the name Hope to his own surname.

John Williams Hope is described to us as a 'desk man' who ran the office precisely and with pleasure. He was not a dynamic, enterprising merchant, however, and the manner in which he acquiesced in the otherwise well-intentioned arrangements made by Henry Hope is suggestive of a measure of docility. His wife, Anne, possessed the qualities which he lacked, and according to the stories resembled her uncle both inwardly and outwardly. For a woman with such a strong character, it is not surprising that a *mariage de convenance* ultimately proved to be too much.

With the description of this remarkable episode, we have got somewhat ahead of our story. We have still to concern ourselves with John Hope, the second of the new partners admitted in 1762. In 1737 his father had entered his name in the register of births of the Mennonite Community in Amsterdam, and in doing so had shown that he had not completely abandoned the Quaker sympathies which existed in his parental home. Thomas Hope will therefore not have been a member of the Established (Reformed) Church, and public offices will not have been open to him. But in 1756 John, then aged nineteen, was baptized in the English Presbyterian Church in Amsterdam, probably in preparation for membership of that Church. As the English Presbyterian Church was recognized by the Netherlands Reformed Church on a basis of equality, the way to public office lay open for John Hope.[2] With his marriage in 1763 to Philippina Barbara van der Hoeven, the daughter of a member of the *Vroedschap* of Rotterdam, he took the first step towards membership of the regency class. In 1768, at the intercession of William v, he was made a member of the *Vroedschap* of Amsterdam. In all probability he benefited here from his father's close ties with the stadholder. By now, John Hope had entered upon a process of aristocratization which was gradually alienating him from the everyday affairs of the firm. Lagging appreciably behind his cousin Henry in mercantile skill, he sought satisfaction in official positions and a seigneurial style of living. In 1770, he succeeded his father as a director of the *Oost-Indische Compagnie*. In 1767 he purchased the Groenendaal estate near Heemstede, to which the adjoining Bosbeek estate was added in 1784. Plans to erect new buildings on the land were thwarted by his death in the same year, but these were subsequently implemented by his widow.[1]

In 1774 John Hope acquired Nederhorst den Berg Castle, which lay amid the Ankeveen lakes, near Hilversum, and with it the right to the title 'Master of Nederhorst den Berg.' In Amsterdam, he had assumed occupation of the family home in 1772, but in 1782 he moved again, this time to a house on the Herengracht. In the same year he bought 'a house and adjoining property known of old as Het Tapijthuis' situated on the north side of the Korte Voorhout in The Hague. His duties as Delegate Councillor of Amsterdam in the States of Holland and his connexion with the Stadholder's Court will have influenced this purchase.[2] With this widely scattered property, his life became one of continuous travel from one seat to another, a nomadic existence which was common among the English nobility and was reflected in John Hope's travel plan for his illustrious Scottish relative, with which this chapter opened.

Henry Hope and his relatives in Amsterdam had meanwhile applied themselves to the business, and had achieved some notable successes. From 1765 to 1772, the firm's turnover with the Exchange Bank comfortably exceeded the record levels attained during the Seven Years' War. Between 1768 and 1772, the annual figure was of the order of fifty million guilders, with a peak of more than sixty-five million in 1769. With the exception of De Smeth, the other houses also achieved higher turnover after 1764, but they failed by a substantial margin to match their wartime maxima. Only Muilman and Hogguer, who had profited little if at all from the wartime conditions, achieved a substantially higher figure after 1765 than during the Seven Years' War.

Although commodity trading in Amsterdam began to recover after 1765, the spectacular growth of Hope's turnover with the Exchange Bank must be attributed solely to their considerably enlarged share of the money trade in all its forms. The house had gained experience during the Seven Years' War, and it clearly succeeded in making use of this in the post-war era. At this time also, the house commenced to issue loans for foreign powers, but its activities in this field were not of such magnitude as to constitute an explanation for the sharp increase in turnover with the Exchange Bank.

Hope & Co. was not the first house to issue loans, nor was it the only one to engage in this activity. Loans had been entered into in the Republic during the 17th century, mostly at the request of foreign monarchs and with guarantees provided, from political motives, by the States General. At first, many such loans were issued by collectors of taxes, but with the passing of time they proved to be less than well-suited to the role of bankers, if only because the sums required became steadily larger.[1]

A second line developed directly from the mercantile sector, in which a number of houses succeeded in obtaining a monopoly of the sale of certain articles. When a ruler who had granted a monopoly ran into serious financial difficulty, he would demand larger and longer-term advances on the sale of the article concerned. If the burden of these advances became too great, the house which held the monopoly could at a given moment resort to issuing a debenture loan, and in doing so exchange the role of merchant for that of banker.

A good example of this is provided by the Amsterdam house Deutz, which in 1659 secured a monopoly of the sale of Austrian quicksilver. When, during the wars against Louis XIV, the German emperor faced a financial crisis, a number of loans were issued on the security of quicksilver. These commenced in 1695 and were initially guaranteed by the States General because it was in Holland's interest to ensure that the emperor had the funds to pursue the war against the French. When hostilities ceased in 1715, however, the guarantee was withdrawn.[2]

The next step was to divorce the loan from the delivery of a given article, and instead to require as security a number of specified sources of revenue accruing to the ruler. This applied to two loans, totalling six million guilders, issued by Deutz on behalf of the German emperor in 1734 and 1736, the security for which consisted of revenues from Silesia. This development, however, did not preclude loans on the security of quicksilver or another article being negotiated concurrently or subsequently. Mixed forms also occurred, as will become clear in the chapter describing the Portuguese diamond loan.[3]

Later still, loans carrying guarantees given by another power appeared. This arrangement would be applied in the case of a country with a doubtful financial status, which for political reasons received support from another, e.g. the loan to Poland which was guaranteed by Russia.[4]

As far as can be ascertained from the information at our disposal, Hope's activities in this field commenced in 1768 with the issue of a loan of cf 750,000 on behalf of Sweden. The chapter which deals with that country shows that the affair originated with a request by the *riksdag* that the king should arrange a loan abroad. In the period up to the end of 1787, Hope & Co. issued twelve loans on behalf of Sweden, totalling cf 14,500,000. In 1769 the Company issued a loan of cf 250,000 on behalf of Count Louis of Nassau-Saarbrück. In 1771 the house assisted the Elector of Bavaria with a loan of cf 400,000 at 4% interest, for which the Bavarian crown jewels served as security.[1]

A distinctive variant of the loans which had developed from trade was manifested in the so-called plantation loans, for which plantations in the Caribbean–which in this context covered the West Indian islands and also the coastal area of Guiana–served as security. In the majority of cases, the underlying contract stipulated that all the produce of the plantation should be shipped to the issuer of the loan–who was known as 'the director'–so that the proceeds could be used first and foremost for the payment of interest and principal.[2]

Hope & Co. were concerned in loans to planters on the Danish West Indian islands of St. Croix, St. Thomas and St. John. In 1768 the house of Lever & De Bruine had placed a loan, identified by the letter A, on behalf of planters on all three islands and a second, similar loan, identified by the letter B, on behalf of planters on St. Croix only. These were probably for the benefit of planters who had got into serious financial difficulties as a result of a tornado which had caused damage estimated at more than one million pounds sterling on St. Croix alone. The management of these loans was subsequently transferred to Hope. It may be assumed that this change reflected the close relationship which then existed between the Company and the Danish Court, and which in turn explains the special ties with the Danish West India Company.[3]

Hope & Co. also managed a number of loans to planters on the British West Indian islands of Grenada and Tobago. Under a special law passed in England, foreign bondholders, in the event of non-payment, were entitled to apply to a British court for an order for the sale of the mortgaged plantation. To the greater reassurance of Dutch investors, the payments of interest and principal on these loans were guaranteed by a London house.[4]

In spite of guarantees of this sort, bondholders will all too often have had cause to regret their choice of investment. The planters were easy-going and thriftless, and overproduction, delay in shipment or other setbacks all too soon led to debts. In some cases, the upshot was that the creditors took over a plantation–and with it the attendant commercial risks. We shall see how, in the Napoleonic era, Hope & Co. inherited problems of this nature.

A fresh economic crisis in 1772 brought an abrupt end to Hope's record levels of turnover with the Exchange Bank. The cause of the upset lay in England, where the ending of the Seven Years' War had been followed by lively speculation in shares of the British East India Company. But the high expectations of dividends, which had done much to encourage the speculation, were not fulfilled. At the end of the war, the East India Company was obliged to extend its administrative apparatus to cover a far greater area than before, a task for which it was ill-equipped in both organizational and financial terms. By 1772 the company's debt to the Bank of England reached the point where further credit was withheld. At about the same time, the Bank of England, faced with roaring speculation in goods and shares, restricted the discounting of drafts.[1]

When news of the East India Company's plight became known in London, its shares declined in value, to be followed shortly afterwards by other issues. In the commodity sector, the disclosure put an end to the steady rise in prices.

On the heels of these developments came the sudden bankruptcy of the London house of Neale & Co. It transpired that one of the partners, Alexander Fordyce, had on his own initiative speculated with the firm's capital. Fordyce fled to France, and in the wake of his disappearance twenty other London houses failed.

Speculation in English shares was just as rife in Amsterdam, and acceptance credit there was just as overstrained. The house of Clifford & Sons had indulged so rashly in bull speculations that it was obliged to suspend payments at the end of 1772, ruining a number of smaller firms in the process. In 1773 Andries Pels & Sons went into liquidation, partly, it was said, as a result of losses suffered through Clifford's downfall.[2]

Hope & Co. were involved financially in Neale's bankruptcy. The partners had done a lot of business with Alexander Fordyce, and this had included advancing him monies in association with Gurnell Hoare & Harman of London. A sum of fifty thousand pounds sterling was outstanding when Neale & Co. failed. In addition, Hope had undertaken commissions for Fordyce on the Amsterdam Stock Exchange, involving dealings for the account in shares of the British East India Company.

When the Hopes heard that Fordyce had levanted, they did not await instructions from the receivers but proceeded to liquidate his forward deals. By writing off the proceeds against their claims on Fordyce, they succeeded in keeping their losses within reasonable limits.[1]

Although the Company came through the crisis well, it suffered from the aftermath. The turnover with the Exchange Bank plummeted from more than 50 million guilders in 1772 to 30 million in 1773, thus falling beneath the lows established in 1764 and 1765. It is remarkable that the figures should have remained at this low level, climbing to 38 million only in 1779. The levels of turnover achieved in the 1760s, after the Seven Years' War, were thus by no means equalled during the ensuing decade.

It is not possible to draw comparisons with Pels and Clifford for the 1770s. Hogguer's turnover in this period was generally lower, although the differences were less significant than those applying to Hope. De Smeth and Muilman achieved a higher level of turnover in the 1770s than in the preceding decade, the former by a margin of 9–10 million guilders annually. In assessing these figures, however, it must be borne in mind that the 1760s were exceptionally unfavourable from De Smeth's point of view. It is possible that the firm's share in the issuing of loans for Russia during the succeeding decade tipped the scales.

It is not easy to pinpoint the cause of Hope's lagging turnover. It is known that the crisis of 1772 had a more lasting effect upon the economy than the crisis of 1763. The scarcity of credit also impeded commodity trading, and it was not until 1775 that the curve commenced to rise. If we proceed from the premise that Hope's high turnover figures in the 1760s stemmed principally from financial operations, it is conceivable that the decline in the '70s reflected the diminution of activities in that sphere. One thing is certain: the crises of 1763 and 1772 undermined Amsterdam's position as the centre for billbroking. With its superior credit organization, London gained ground at the expense of Amsterdam, which had neither a central bank nor deposit banks.[2]

The rise in the number of foreign loans issued is also indicative of a decline in exchange dealings. The effect of this was to release money, for which other forms of investment were sought. For Hope & Co. and their correspondents, a decline in mercantile or credit operations automatically led to increased activity in the loan sector.[3]

The loans issued by Hope & Co. in the 1770s included those for Sweden to which reference has already been made, and which between 1770 and 1780 totalled 6 million guilders, and one of cf 2,625,000 for the Republic of Poland, which was negotiated in 1777; the latter is described in detail elsewhere in this book.[4] The loans to planters in Tobago and Grenada also belong to this period.

As we are about to concern ourselves increasingly with Hope's loan activities, it is of value to look more closely into the technique developed by the house over the years.

Firstly, there is the manner in which Hope and the borrowers came into contact. It is probable that the house's *entrée* to the sphere of loans to governments resulted from its own initiatives, since this was an area in which it had yet to earn a reputation. Later, the approach in many cases came from the borrower, but the Company continued to deploy initiatives. In the case of Russia, Hope succeeded in supplanting De Smeth as the issuing house by assisting the Russian Court Banker at a crucial moment, thereby getting him on their side.[1]

The loan negotations were usually conducted in Amsterdam, the monarch in question being represented by his envoy or by a special representative armed with the necessary authority. When agreement was reached, the loan sum, the interest rate, the loan period, the securities, the repayment periods and the commission due to the issuing house were embodied in a contract. This was subject to the approval, by decree, of the monarch, who then signed a principal debenture in which, having set out the undertaking to the lenders in the matter of interest and principal payments, he declared himself officially to be the debtor for the full sum of the loan. Upon receipt of the principal debenture, the house concerned could embark upon the issue of the bonds, which were usually of cf 1,000. All loans entered into in the Netherlands carried the stipulation that interest and principal should be paid in that country and in guilders Hollands Courant. The latter provision meant that bondholders were not affected by fluctuations in rates of exchange – a decidedly important point in view of the fact that debasing of the currency and inflation were common phenomena in the countries which sought capital.

It was customary for British and French loans to be issued in those countries. Interested Dutch investors could purchase bonds of these loans either in the country of issue or through a house in Amsterdam.[2] But then these were countries with a certain reputation for creditworthiness and a well-developed economy, which were thus in a stronger position vis-à-vis the lenders.

Other countries chose Dutch houses for the issue of their loans in order to enhance their credit standing. Most of these were countries in which capital formation was non-existent or, at most, in its infancy. They had a predominantly agricultural, often feudal structure in which the landowning nobility, usually under the protection of an absolute monarch, was omnipotent. Generally speaking, the middle class was small and politically powerless.

The majority of the countries in this category were situated in the 'outer zone' of Europe. They included Sweden, Russia, Poland, Austria, a number of large and small German states, Spain and Portugal. The young United States, a pioneer country with a matching hunger for credit, was a special case, but there, too, the capital formation was inadequate to meet the demand.

On the one side stood those abroad who sought capital, and on the other the Dutch capitalists who, because of the relative fall in the volume of trade and the fact that the Amsterdam exchange market had passed its zenith, were having difficulty in finding suitable objects for investment. The role of an issuing house lay in bringing the parties together through the medium of a loan. The task of actually mobilizing capital in Holland, however, did not fall to the issuing house, but to other, usually smaller, houses which were concerned with selling the bonds. A special broker was in turn engaged to induce these houses to subscribe a given portion of the loan sum–a form of underwriting as we now know it in the world of marine insurance. The names of Ten Kate, Volckmar and Berck, who fulfilled this role, appear on numerous occasions in connexion with the loans issued by Hope & Co. In many cases, two or three such brokers were engaged, their joint services being rewarded with a certain percentage (usually $\frac{1}{4}$%) of the sum subscribed.[1]

In the Hope correspondence, these underwriters are referred to as *entrepreneurs*. While it is realized that this may cause confusion, the title has deliberately been retained: 'stockbrokers' could be equally misleading, for the *entrepreneurs* included merchant houses of substance which on other occasions acted as issuing houses. For example, Weduwe E.Croese & Co., who were among the *entrepreneurs* in the majority of loans issued by Hope & Co., themselves issued loans on behalf of Spain. Similarly, Pieter Stadnitski issued loans on the security of America's domestic debt, while Abraham and Dirk van Vloten acted as trustees for a number of American loans. Nor was there a clear dividing line between brokers and *entrepreneurs*. The brokers repeatedly subscribed to loans which they had helped to arrange, partly for their own account and partly on behalf of others.[2]

Up to the time of the French invasion of 1794, the number of contracting *entrepreneurs* per loan continued to rise. In 1780 there were eight, but in 1792, when a loan was floated for Spain, there were thirty-two. The majority, having once participated, continued to do so. Of the eight in 1780, five were still subscribing to loans in 1792. The increase in the number of houses which engaged in entrepreneurial activities, in this sense,

P. Transp. f 550,000.

Pieter Stadnitski voor tweemaal honderd duyzend Gld. 200000

Wed. Joh. Menkema & Zoon voor honderd en Vyftig duizend Guldens Zegge f 150000

Ketwich & Voombergh voor Honderd duyzend Gl. f 100,000

François Walbeek voor Honderd en Vyftig duiz. Gl. Zegge f 150000

Pieter ten Kate voor Vyf en Zeventig duyzend Guldens Zegge f 75000

Wm. E. Croese & Comp. voor Honderd en Vyftig duyzend Guldens Zegge f 150,000

nog voor Vyftig duyzend Gl. 50,000

[illegible] 50,000

Abraham van [illegible] voor Honderd duyzend Gld. 100,000

Herman Hoogewal voor Vyftig duysend Guld. 50000

[illegible] voor Vyf & Zeventig Duyzend Guldens 75000

Van Heyningen? [illegible] voor Vyf en Zeventig duyzend Guldens 75000

Van Haurik & Willink voor Vyf & Zeventig duyzend Guldens 75000

[illegible] Koopman voor Vyf en Zeventig duyzend Guldens 75000

~~[illegible] & David [illegible] voor honderd duyzend~~ 100000

Anthony Charles voor Vyftig duyzend Guldens Zegge 50000

[illegible] voor Vyf en Zeventig duysend Gld. f 75000

J. E. Guerin voor Honderd Duyzend Guldens Zegge f 100,000

David Berck voor Reek. van de Ondenstaande

Arend van der Werf [illegible] voor Honderd duyzend Gl. Zegge	100,000
[illegible] Vermeulen [illegible] voor Vyf en Zeventig duiz. Gl.	75.000
Wouter Jochems & Zoon [illegible] voor Vyftig duyz. Gl.	50,000
[illegible] Utrecht voor Vyftig duyzend Gl.	50.000
Huybert van [illegible] Utrecht voor Vyftig duyz. Gl.	50.000
[illegible] voor Vyftig duyz. Gl.	50.000
[illegible] Hutteman [illegible] voor Honderd duyzend Gl.	100.000
Strick & van Dyk voor een Honderd duyzend Gl.	100,000
Dirk [illegible] Utrecht voor Vyf & Twintig duyz. Gl.	25.000
David Berck voor een Honderd Vyftig duyz. Gl. Zegge	150.000
	300.0000

Ten Overstaan van My

David Berck

Mak.

Part of the *entrepreneurs'* contract relating to the 8th Russian loan of May 1790 clearly reflects the growing importance to Holland's mercantile houses of the business of floating new issues. Following the French invasion, the volume of this business declined, and with it the number of *entrepreneurs*: in 1807 only four or five subscribed to the loans which Hope & Co. issued.

Most *entrepreneurs*–32 of the 42 known to us from contracts–lived in Amsterdam. The remainder hailed from smaller towns in the provinces of Holland and Utrecht, such as Rotterdam, The Hague, Leiden, Haarlem and Utrecht itself.[1] The principal market for bonds relating to the loans issued by the Company will thus have comprised the three western provinces of the Netherlands. Merchant houses elsewhere in the country–and abroad–ordered bonds from Hope, either directly or through business associates in Amsterdam. We have already referred to the role of the brokers in this context. The Company counted the Austrian-controlled region of Brabant among its most important markets outside the Republic.

When the prospect of a new issue arose, Hope lost no time in ascertaining, via the brokers, which of the *entrepreneurs* would be willing to participate. It often happened that the contract with the *entrepreneurs* was signed simultaneously with the loan contract, or very shortly afterwards. In the case of the Polish loan of 1786, the contract with the *entrepreneurs* actually preceded the loan contract.

If the *entrepreneurs* judged the times to be unfavourable, they reduced their shares, leaving the issuing house to shoulder a larger portion of the burden. In such a situation, there was, of course, little likelihood of the issuer giving an explicit guarantee that the loan would be fully subscribed. But the reverse could also apply: if the issuing house felt that the circumstances were conducive to a quick sell-out, it could reserve a larger proportion of the loan for itself.[2]

Entrepreneurs' contracts usually contained a clause stipulating that the apportionment of the loan to the *entrepreneurs* would be preceded by the opening of a public subscription list at the offices of the issuing house. The sum thus subscribed was deducted *pro rata* from the portions allocated to the *entrepreneurs*, the *douceur* of $\frac{1}{4}$% or $\frac{1}{2}$% granted to public subscribers being deducted from the *entrepreneurs*' commission. If the *entrepreneurs* felt that they could place more bonds than they had contracted to take, they could always obtain the balance by way of the public list, and thus at least earn the *douceur*.

The rate of commission granted to the *entrepreneurs* was not high. Up to 1789, it varied between 1% and 1$\frac{1}{2}$%; thereafter, as the contracts with which we are familiar show, it rose to 2%. This increase probably indicates a strengthening of their position as intermediaries. But even 2% was not overly generous, particularly if one considers that, in order to reach the ultimate investors, it was often necessary to employ middle men, who also demanded their reward. The *entrepreneurs* therefore had to rely upon the volume of their turnover in bonds, and accordingly they aimed not only at the *moyen peuple*, but also at the small saver. Some contracts provided for such widely spaced instalments by the *entrepreneurs* that these extended beyond the date at which interest on the allocated bonds commenced to be paid. This could mean a small bonus for the *entrepreneurs*, and in the vast majority of instances Hope willingly granted this.

Hope's own commission–from which all other expenses had to be met–was naturally higher than that accorded to the *entrepreneurs*, but was subject to wide fluctuation, especially in the '70s and '80s. In the case of the Swedish loans, it ranged from 4% to 9½%.[1]

Why a lower rate of commission was granted at a given moment, is not clear. An obvious assumption is that an abundant money market, in which a loan could be easily placed, tended to produce a lower commission–always provided that the borrower was aware of the state of the market. In return for a high commission on the Swedish loans, the Company was required to guarantee their success.[2] A demand for such a guarantee was normally made only if the borrower was extremely short of funds, or if conditions on the money market were less favourable; in either case, a guarantee was costly by reason of the borrower's weak position. It was customary for an issuing house to require a *courtage* for handling payments of interest and principal; this was in addition to the normal commission. For interest payments, the rate varied from ½% to 1% of the sum paid out, and for principal payments it was usually 1%. The Russian Court was only prepared to pay Hope a commission of 5% on its loans, but subsequently allowed itself to be persuaded to raise this to 6½% on condition that the *courtage* was included. A similar arrangement was stipulated for the great conversion in 1798.[3]

The loan contracts entered into prior to 1794 provided for Hope & Co. to take over the loans at par. In a few instances, the *entrepreneurs* were permitted to pay for their bonds 'at 99% free money,' which implied a profit of 1% if, as was clearly intended, they sold them at par. After 1790, however, contracts with the *entrepreneurs* stipulated a minimum selling price. At first this was 98¾%, but in 1792 it rose to 99½%–probably on account of the abundance of capital in that year. It had apparently become the custom to sell below par, and Hope was anxious to put a stop to this.[4]

In the Napoleonic area, takeovers at par could not be sustained. The majority of the older loans had fallen in price, and new ones had to be competitive if they were to appeal to the investors. Accordingly, the Portuguese loan of 1802 and the Spanish and Neapolitan loans of 1807 were taken over at 90%.[1]

Like the transfer price, the rate of interest was an important factor. Apart from the obvious financial advantage to the borrower, a low interest rate possessed status value: it was a symbol of a country's creditworthiness. It was consequently a personal triumph for Baron Liljencrantz, the Minister of Finance under Gustav III, when, in 1775, he achieved a reduction of the interest on a Swedish loan from five per cent to four. Conversely, Poland's poor credit standing was reflected in the fact that she was obliged to pay 5% for loans in 1777 and 1786, while in those years Sweden paid only 4% and 4½% respectively.[2]

Russia also set great store by equality with other powers in the matter of interest on loans. When Hope & Co. first issued loans on behalf of Russia, the Court, while consenting to an extra ½% for *douceurs sous mains*, was adamant that the interest should not exceed 4%. When the Company raised the rate on its own initiative, it was able to avoid a dispute by pointing to the success of the loan in comparison with one of 4% for Austria, which had not got off the ground. Moreover, Hope pointed out, *douceurs sous mains* might well have tempted the *entrepreneurs* to sell below par, and that would have been highly injurious to Russia's credit standing.[3]

In addition to the prestige and creditworthiness of the borrower, the level of funds available on the market also played a part in determining the interest rate. The loans issued by Hope & Co. between 1767 and 1792 bore interest at rates of between 4% and 5%, but even this variation was sufficient reason for a government to keep a very close watch on the money market in Amsterdam, and to grasp any and every opportunity to convert old, high-interest loans into new ones and thus benefit in terms of its interest burden. One example of this was provided by Sweden, which in 1780 converted a number of 5% loans into 4% issues. Another came in 1792 when Russia, having induced De Wolf in Antwerp to make an offer, used this as a lever to force Hope to effect an identical conversion on her behalf. Sweden performed a similar balancing act, with Hasselgreen & Co. on one side and Fizeaux Grand & Co. and Hope & Co. on the other, and succeeded thus in avoiding overdependence on either.[4]

With the French invasion, the flow of capital diminished and interest rates gradually rose. In 1802 Portugal succeeded in obtaining a loan at 5%, but by 1805 Spain had to pay 5½%, as she was again obliged to in

1807. In that year, the loans for Naples and the Kingdom of Holland were issued at 6%, although this was purely nominal since the takeover price was of the order of 90. If the issuing house and the *entrepreneurs* succeeded in selling bonds at a higher price, the profit was theirs–a speculative element which certainly possessed attractions.

A conversion could also have attractive speculative aspects, especially if it related to old loans which stood low on the Stock Exchange. This is illustrated by the great Russian conversion of 1798, which embraced a number of loans to the Republic of Poland, its ruler and several Polish magnates, on which neither interest nor principal had been paid for many years. By buying up the bonds prudently and in good time, the partners of Hope & Co. made a huge profit. According to the agent of Prussia, Niebuhr, the partners admitted having made six million guilders, but he believed that the true sum was considerably greater.[1]

The Spanish loan of thirty million guilders floated in 1807 similarly afforded opportunities for speculative profit on the conversion of old, low-priced Echenique bonds. But Spain's financial predicament, coupled with political developments in the country, produced an early drop in the market quotation for the new bonds, making them difficult to sell.[2]

Hope & Co. viewed a measure of speculation in bonds as an aid to sales; but excessively large or rapid fluctuations in quoted prices were undesirable and could bring the issue into disrepute. It was with this in mind that Labouchère watched with anxiety the bear speculation on the Russian bonds following Napoleon's invasion of Russia, the principal victims of which were small investors who lived from their dividends. Major price falls were in general pernicious, for they could erode the prestige of borrower and issuer alike, and frighten the respectable investor to death.[3] In 1793 Hope & Co. felt it their duty to purchase Russian bonds in order to support the price, thereby giving investors the certainty of being able to encash their Russian holdings from day to day without incurring losses.[4]

In some cases, instructions for support-buying came from the government concerned. When the price recovered, the bonds so purchased were disposed of at a profit. In addition to the economic motive, considerations of prestige will certainly have played a part in such actions. A significant fall in the price of an issue was a blow to the credit standing of the government, and could adversely affect the placing of subsequent loans.

The prestige element was also of importance to the issuing house. Although its role, once the loan had been fully subscribed, was limited to the payment of interest and principal, the house regarded it as a point of honour to ensure that the conditions of the loan were complied with. The name of Hope & Co. constituted a guarantee for the borrower that the loan would be fully subscribed, and for the investor that the terms on which it was effected would be scrupulously adhered to. Thus, the Company's code of ethics and its business interests compelled it to stand up for the bondholders in all cases where the payment of interest or principal was imperilled. To this end, partners in the firm, or their confidential agents, made repeated visits to Russia and other distant places, primarily in order to defend the interests of bondholders. During the history of the Portuguese loan, no effort was spared to safeguard the interest and principal instalments, while in the case of Spain these payments were financed for as long as possible from the proceeds of the Mexican silver transaction.[1]

Hope & Co. also saw it as their duty to stand up for other houses. When a government which had defaulted in regard to previous loans approached the Company for a new one, it was required to set right its default before negotiations could proceed. This is plainly demonstrated in the Company's handling of the Spanish loan of 1807, when, after long insistence, it succeeded in getting the outstanding Echenique bonds converted.[2] During his journey to Russia in 1797–98, Robert Voûte acted on behalf of a number of other houses, and such was the success which he achieved that Hope was requested to take up the cudgels for the holders of Austrian bonds when, in the early 1800s, the government of that country centralized payments against its loan in Vienna, and proceeded to effect these in depreciated paper money. Two journeys to Vienna for this purpose were rendered fruitless by the prevailing circumstances, but a third, undertaken by Pierre César Labouchère in 1818, brought the long-awaited rehabilitation of the Austrian loans.

The relationship between the issuing house and the borrower government forms a quite separate facet of the business of floating loans. This was always a delicate relationship. After all, nearly all the monarchs concerned were absolutists, and sometimes even despots, who were accustomed to recruiting their ministers and senior civil servants from among the nobility. In their kingdoms, the middle-class citizen was a second-rate figure who, as a provider of funds to the Court and those who surrounded it, might occasionally be raised to the rank of nobleman, but even then continued for long to be regarded as a *parvenu*.

On the other hand, however, the monarch's position vis-à-vis the house was one of a supplicant, and this implied a measure of weakness. Before the loan which he desired was placed, there were down-to-earth questions to be answered concerning the value and dependability of the securities

De Ondergeteekenden in eene talrijke op den 17[den] September 1812 gehouden bijeenkomst van Geinteresseerdens in de Negotiatie ten lasten van het Russiesch Keizerrijk, ten Comptoire van de Heeren HOPE & C°. gevestigd, met en benevens wijlen den Heere WILLEM BORSKI verzogt en benoemd, om dezelve Heeren HOPE & C°. over de gemeene belangens der Geinteresseerden te adieeren, hebben het genoegen gehad te mogen ondervinden, dat dezelve belangens door gemelde Heeren HOPE & C°. met onafgebroken ijver en zorge zijn gade geslagen en bevorderd, en dat de grootmoedige regtvaardigheid van ZIJNE MAJESTEIT DEN KEIZER VAN RUSLAND deze Geldleening heeft terug gebragt in alle hare regten, met eene vergoeding voor den stilstand daarin door de publieke omstandigheden ontstaan.

Bij deze gelukkige uitkomst van zaaken hebben de Ondergeteekenden niet uit het oog mogen verliezen de onkosten door de Heeren HOPE & Comp., in en voor het belang der Geïnteresseerdens gemaakt, en de verpligting van deezen, om dezelve onkosten in eene billijke evenredigheid te dragen, terwijl de Ondergeteekenden zig van de regtmatige denkwijze der belanghebbenden bij voorraad verzekerd hielden, dat niemand zig zoude willen onttrekken aan de zoo ontwijfelbaare verpligting ter dier zaake op hem berustende, en de Ondergeteekenden hebben uit dien hoofde vermeend bij de Heeren HOPE & C°. aanvraage over die onkosten te moeten doen; doch dezelve Heeren zig daarop aan de Ondergeteekenden hebbende gelieven te verklaren, dat, hoezeer hun die aanvrage aangenaam was, en zij daarin met welgevallen bemerkten die erkentenis van gehoudenheid tot schadeloosstelling, welke ook in publieke Geldnegotiatiën op de Geinteresseerdens berust, omtrent de Huizen die zich in buitengewone omstandigheden en op eene buitengewone wijze met de handhaving der algemeene belangens laten belasten, zij Heeren HOPE & C°. echter, ten einde daardoor hunnerzijds bij te dragen, tot vermeerdering van de weltevredenheid der belanghebbenden voor deze uitkomst van zaken, waarin de oogmerken van den verheven Monarch zoo baarblijkelijk doorstraalden, om de Belanghebbenden zoo veel mogelijk schadeloos te stellen voor de vertraging, door de buitengewone omstandigheden te weeg gebragt, in het onderhavig geval, en zonder consequentie op andere gevallen, voor het vervolg, niet verkoozen eenige applicatie van hun regt te maken, en mitsdien de Ondergeteekenden voor alle verdere tusschenkomst daartoe betrekkelijk, dank betuigden.

Zoo is aan de Ondergeteekenden, in de aan hun opgedragene Commissie, niets anders te verrigten overig gebleeven, dan om hunne Committenten van het bovenstaande bij dezen kennis te geven, en aan dezelve tevens te verklaren, dat zij Ondergeteekenden die Commissie thans houden voor geheel afgelopen en ten einde gebragt.

Amsterdam, 22 *December* 1815.

J. van de POLL.

C. van der OUDERMEULEN.

J. BONDT.

J. de BURLETT.

J. van der MANDELE.

Final report of the representatives of the holders of Russian bonds, dated December 1815. This states that Messrs. Hope decline the offer by the bondholders to share in the costs incurred offered – and these could expose particular weaknesses in the system of government. Sometimes guarantees were demanded which struck at the dignity of a monarch. King Stanislaw Poniatowski, for example, refused for this reason to provide a guarantee by his heir, relating to the mortgaging of the king's personal possessions.[1]

In correspondence and personal contact with ministers and senior civil servants, it was necessary to observe the existing rules of respect and even servility, yet at the same time to avoid excess subservience in order not to undermine one's own position. With his eminent amiability, Henry Hope, in particular, must have been a master in the art of balancing on a sharp edge. His action in declining the title offered to him by Empress Catherine II in November 1789 must be viewed as an extremely refined way of showing that the Hopes preferred their citizenship to an obscure barony in one or other Eastern or Northern European country. The noble estate of the Scottish Hopes will certainly have influenced his decision. In this respect, too, the Hopes differed from the Hogguers, the De Smeths and the Hasselgreens.[2]

In their activities on behalf of absolute monarchs, Hope & Co. came in contact with intriguing cliques and Court cabals, which in many cases served to determine the course of government. The difficulties which this produced are clear from the description of Robert Voûte's first sojourn in Russia.[3] The consequences of a shift of power at the Court emerged during Voûte's second visit to that country, when, following the eclipse of the wife of Paul I, the Company had for many years to endure the enmity of the head of the treasury.[4] At the time of the Spanish affairs, Hope suffered greatly from the trouble stirred up by a Spanish confidential agent in Paris, Izquierdo, who regarded Hope as a lackey of Napoleon and equated the house with the speculator-financier Ouvrard. Izquierdo's reports to Madrid repeatedly short-circuited communications between Hope and the Spanish Court.[5]

In his way, Labouchère perpetuated Henry Hope's policy towards foreign Courts. His personal relationship with both French and Russian ministers earned him a position which the Prefect of the Zuyder Zee *département*, De Celles, spitefully summed up as 'an unaccredited agent of a foreign power.'[6] The amicable relationship between his brother-in-law, Alexander Baring, and Sir Arthur Wellesley, later the Duke of Wellington, gave Labouchère an excellent *entrée* in England, a factor which assisted him greatly in his peace mission on behalf of King Louis Napoleon.[7]

Having thus dealt at length with the numerous aspects of the role of an issuing house, let us turn to trade, and in particular to the nature of the organization and the various links which went to make up the chain. According to a treatise which appeared at the beginning of the 19th century, Dutch merchants could be divided into categories, the first comprising maritime traders, the 'first hand,' who were responsible for the supply of wares to the Dutch market and who usually concentrated on particular geographical areas, and the 'second hand' consisting of rich merchants, specialists in particular commodities, who, by storing huge stocks, fulfilled a buffer role between supply and sale. Exports were handled by wholesalers, who distributed them in the various market areas.[1]

This picture earlier attracted criticism on the grounds that it was too rigid and schematic, and that there was very little division of responsibilities in the world of trade in the 18th century.

For Hope & Co., as general merchants, this division was in any case of minor importance, since the house combined all three functions. Nor was there any question of specialization, geographical or in terms of merchandise. Hope's commercial contacts embraced the whole of Europe and north and central America, stretching from Archangel to Asia Minor. As far as wares were concerned, it would be difficult to find an article in which the house did not trade: money, grain, colonial produce, ship's articles, gold, silver, diamonds, drysaltery, ordnance, textiles, tobacco, tea, wine, flower bulbs; in short, anything which could be sold at a profit was traded.[2]

Nevertheless, a distinction between first and second hands did exist: Henry Hope himself employed these terms in 1787, in his description of the cochineal trade in Cadiz.[3] It may be deduced from this that trade was classified, but that the boundaries were neither sharply defined nor generally upheld. We encountered a similar situation when describing issuing houses, *entrepreneurs* and brokers.

As general merchants, the partners of Hope & Co. could not, of course, be *au fait* with the situation in every area with which contact was maintained, or have detailed knowledge of every article in which the house dealt. This know-how resided in the brokers, whose original role as intermediaries in trade in specific articles was at times changed by Hope into one of partners in a transaction. These men were regarded as indispensable, as is evidenced by Henry Hope's remarks concerning Rouen, where all transactions took place between merchants, a practice which was costly in time and, according to Hope, demanded greater knowledge of wares than the average merchant possessed.[4] Robert Voûte, who had started out as a broker in coffee, tea and dyestuffs but, through his personal friendship with the Hopes, had progressed beyond the role of pure middleman, observed during his stay in Moscow that there were no brokers there either, which fact put foreign merchants in an unfavourable position.[1]

Foreign trade was fraught with risks, and houses which engaged in it had to be on their guard not only against their associates abroad, but also against the governments with which they had to deal. Most of the countries with which Hope & Co. were concerned were mercantilistic in their trade policy, and their governments tended to protect their own merchants against foreigners; this was especially true of the economically less developed lands. The protection could take the form of reserving monopolies or specific areas of trade for indigenous houses, or of harassing foreigners. The consequences of the latter policy were clearly demonstrated to Robert Voûte during his first period in Russia.[2]

Governments frequently failed to honour agreements entered into with foreigners. In many cases this can be attributed to ill-will, for attitudes towards strangers were in general grudging; but in others it is conceivable that the Court or a particular minister simply did not have sufficient grip on the often corrupt administrative apparatus. In Hope's case, the official monopoly for the sale of Brazilian diamonds proved to be anything but watertight, while the exclusive right to trade with the colonies in Spanish America was soon breached for the benefit of Court favourites and high officials.[3]

In its dealings with foreigners, too, the house frequently met with unpleasant surprises, and owing to the distances involved it was far more difficult to react adequately to these than would have been the case had another Dutch house been involved. In serious cases, the cause could lie in embezzlement, as occurred with Alexander Fordyce, or the use of funds for purposes other than those for which they had been entrusted. The latter practice resulted in heavy losses for Hope when the house of Sutherland at St.Petersburg went bankrupt in 1794.[4]

Less serious, but equally annoying, was the furnishing of partially or wholly inaccurate trade information. In many instances, the cause lay in ignorance rather than malice. Erroneous information concerning extant stocks of cochineal was among the causes of the failure of Hope's speculation in the article. The ideal solution lay in sending a trusted representative to collect information on the spot, but this could only be justified if the transaction was large and involved a restricted area. In the ensuing chapters of this book we shall find Hope & Co. employing such agents.[5]

A commission having been placed with a foreign house, it remained to be seen whether this was executed with appropriate enthusiasm and business sense. It might involve purchase, as in the case of the cochineal speculation, or selling, as in the case of Operation R.M. following Robert Melvil's departure from Russia.[1] A lack of success could stem from lack of drive or commercial acumen on the part of the correspondent, but it could also result from a counterspeculation undertaken secretly by the agent concerned, for his own benefit, which was given priority over the commission.

The slowness of postal communications could also adversely affect business, the more so where long distances were involved. Instructions issued from Amsterdam on the basis of market information received there had to complete the long journey back, and often a month passed before these reached the correspondent. By this time, the market situation could have changed so drastically that to implement them would have been valueless. The effect of this situation was particularly marked during the cochineal affair.[2]

Should the partners of a house such as Hope & Co. be regarded as bankers? Opinions on this are divided. The crux of the matter lies in the question whether a clear degree of specialization between merchants and bankers had already manifested itself in the 18th century.[3] Strangely enough, while contemporary outsiders repeatedly referred to the Hopes as bankers, the latter seldom if ever applied the term to themselves in their correspondence. During the political troubles of 1787, Henry Hope expressly described himself as a merchant, not as a banker.[4] In the view of the partners, exchange dealing and acceptance credit fell within the scope of trade, and the issuing of loans did not lead to neglect of trading in commodities; on the contrary, where possible the partners attempted to combine trade deals with loan transactions. This mercantile approach to loan business was to continue beyond the period dealt with in this book.

Finally, in this context, we must examine the stature of the firms with which Hope maintained contact, and the stature of the house itself. Needless to say, solidity was a prerequisite for an association with Hope & Co. For the outsider, however, it was difficult to establish the magnitude of a firm's capital and how much of this was committed to transactions. The higher the percentage available in cash or on demand, the greater was the solidity of the house. But those on the outside could do no more than guess. In many instances, outward signs served as a yardstick: a luxurious style of living and dissoluteness in the private sphere were regarded as signs of reduced solidity. Sobriety, a good family life, hard work, knowledge of the trade, prudence and reliability: these were the hallmarks of the first-class merchant. Trading beyond the limit of one's financial resources was regarded as a mortal sin. Financial capacity was of course important, but was not the primary consideration.[1]

The amount of credit which could be allowed to a correspondent was of great importance. In determining this, references were usually sought from more than one house, and these were compared. This information, together with the solidity characteristics already referred to, were entered in separate books. If a change of partners occurred, information had quickly to be obtained concerning the wealth and solidity of the new member or members. Sometimes the death of a partner revealed weaknesses which were capable of bringing a house to the verge of bankruptcy. With the death of the Hamburg merchant Martin Dorner, it transpired that his affairs had been so neglected during his long illness that suspension of payments could not be averted.[2] When James Rowand, a partner in the Moscow house of Thomson Rowand & Co., died in 1791, a seven-year backlog in the bookkeeping was discovered, making it almost impossible to assess the solvency of the firm.[3] Clearly it was possible to struggle on for years without actually coming to grief, and thus we may assume that similar arrears also existed in houses whose affairs were to all appearances in first-class order.

Against this background, the punctiliousness of Hopes' bookkeeping stood out well, and it explains the reputation of the house in this respect. Twice a month, the daily entries in the *journaal* were transferred to the appropriate account in the *grootboek* in accordance with the double-entry system. At the end of the year, the credit or debit balances were entered in the Balance Sheets, from which the Profit and Loss Account was derived. The profit, or loss, was then divided among the partners in the proportions laid down in the partnership agreement. Usually a substantial portion of the profit was allocated to the firm's capital.[4]

In thus describing Hope's exactitude in matters of accountancy, one runs the risk of creating an undue impression that the partners were 'modern' men. They lived in an era of mercantile capitalism which produced a mentality differing from that which we know today. As the considerations and motivations of the partners will repeatedly emerge in the following chapters, mention of one or two specific points suffices here.

In the correspondence at our disposal, where reference is made to the writing off of losses on transactions, there is in no case any trace of a deliberate attempt to calculate the loss as a more or less exact proportion of the capital invested. The sums written off during the cochineal speculation give the impression of having been arrived at arbitrarily. The explanation for this probably lies in the abundance of capital in 18th-century Holland, which made it difficult for the house to find productive investments for all its funds. Moreover, it was the custom for solid houses to maintain substantial liquid assets which usually earned no interest.[1] It is therefore probable that the loss of interest on invested capital was viewed less seriously than it is today.

It is also noticeable that the partners did not seek to make a profit at any cost. Labouchère's admonition to Vincent Nolte, to place honour above profit in establishing business contacts in the United States, is a brief but unmistakable example.[2] This was not an empty gesture for the benefit of the world outside, for Labouchère's instructions to Nolte were confidential. That he did not stop at words became clear when relations with the house of Stephen Girard of Philadelphia were broken off following the latter's discourtesy towards Hope. Nolte, who described the incident in his autobiography, confessed that such a high sense of honour went too far for him, and that he would have given preference to the material advantage.[3] Labouchère and his co-partners were also patently relieved when the detestable Michel the Younger finally went away, taking with him his ill-gotten drafts on the Mexican treasury.[4] This code of ethics in no way precluded keenness in business matters, or the running of risks, but the latter were always of a calculated nature and the margins set were such as to rule out any real danger.

But we digress. We were about to examine the fortunes of the house in the 1780s. That period brought far-reaching changes in the partnership. Thomas Hope had died in 1779, and his brother, Adrian, in 1781. It thus became necessary to inject new blood into the firm, and to this end Nicolas Bauduin, who had been in Hope's employ since 1765, and John Williams Hope, whose acquaintance we have already made, were admitted as partners on 4th July 1782. Their contracts ran for six years, commencing on 1st January 1782, and were subject to one year's notice of termination. One of the opening paragraphs contained the stereotyped sentence: 'that the firm shall engage only in matters of commerce and commissions, and not in any negotiations relating to deposited funds or similar transactions.' This meant that outside capital would not be accepted. The stipulation was probably made because the house was already finding it difficult enough to keep its capital profitably invested. Later, too, considerable reservations were exercised in regard to deposited funds, while on current account interest *à charge* and *à décharge* was charged only where large sums were involved, and even then with reluctance.[5]

A striking feature of the partnership contracts is the care taken to ensure that the assembled capital remained within the firm. In these, the decease of the partners in all conceivable sequences was anticipated, and the manner in which the share of each in the capital was either to pass to the other partners or could gradually be withdrawn by the deceased's heirs was laid down.

In the partnership deed of 1782, Henry Hope took a $\frac{35}{96}$ths share in the capital, John Hope a $\frac{49}{96}$ths share, and the other two partners a share of $\frac{6}{96}$ths each. The sum of the capital at the end of 1782 was cf 8,731,205.0.0. The ploughing-back of profits steadily increased this, with the result that by 1794 it totalled cf 13,435,648.7.8.[1]

With the death of John Hope in 1784, fresh arrangements became necessary. John's sons, Thomas, Adrian Elias and Henry Philip, were still minors, and Nicolas Bauduin had intimated his desire to retire from business upon the expiry of his contract at the end of 1787. To ensure the continuity of the house, Jan Casper Hartsinck Cornelisz., a sheriff or *schepen* of Amsterdam, was admitted as a partner. Pending Bauduin's retirement, he was to have no share in the profits or losses, but would receive a salary of cf 15,000 per annum. The partnership which thereupon commenced was to be for a period of 14 years. Henry Hope's share of the capital was $\frac{37}{96}$ths, John Williams Hope's $\frac{14}{96}$ths, John Hope's children's share $\frac{39}{96}$ths and Hartsinck's $\frac{6}{96}$ths, the portion with which John Williams Hope had commenced in 1782. This contract, too, contained provisions relating to inheritance and to the period for the withdrawal of shares.[2]

The contract, however, was short-lived. Nicolas Bauduin died of a stroke in January 1787, and on 16th November 1789 Hartsinck resigned from the house 'on account of accepting senior government posts,' a probable reference to his nomination to the *Vroedschap* of Amsterdam at the end of November 1787 when, following the intervention of a Prussian army in Holland's domestic troubles, Prince William v dismissed a number of Patriotic regents from the *Vroedschap* and replaced them by his supporters. Hartsinck was zealously pro-Orange, and had taken an active part in organizing those loyal to the prince. Evidently his new office occupied so much of his day that he had no time left for his duties on behalf of the firm. Hartsinck received cf 500,000 from his co-partners by way of compensation, and was given the option of taking this in cash or in bonds at the price ruling on the day. He was obliged to leave the house which he rented from John Hope's widow, and this makes one wonder whether, apart from the demands of his position on the council, his resignation stemmed from differences of opinion with his colleagues.[3]

In a convention entered into at this time, Henry Hope, John Williams Hope and the widow of John Hope agreed to continue the house in the manner prescribed in the event of Hartsinck's death. His share in the capital was divided among John Williams Hope and the three sons of John Hope. The new situation was to become effective on 1st January 1790 and run for the period originally stipulated in the contract with Hartsinck, i.e. until the end of 1801.[1]

The convention referred to the possibility of John Hope's son, Thomas, taking an active part in the firm in due course; however, the surviving correspondence contains no reference to Thomas's role and it must therefore be assumed that he was no more than a sleeping partner. Thomas turned out to be a passionate collector of works of art and a connoisseur of antique architecture, which he studied during his many journeys through the Mediterranean countries. After eight years of travelling about, he settled in Duchess Street, off Portland Place, in London, where he displayed his collection of antiquities, which was as bizarre as it was valuable, in a manner which may be described as ostentatious rather than tasteful.[2]

With the description of this enthusiastic supporter of neo-classicism, we have moved ahead of our story; nevertheless, it shows clearly why there was little to be expected from this member of the family when it came to the day-to-day business of the firm. So, despite all efforts, it had not proved possible to fill the gap in the management which in fact had arisen with the deaths of Thomas and Adrian Hope. This may well account partly for the appearance in the 1780s of a man who was to head major speculations in tea and dyes on behalf of Hope & Co. He was Robert Voûte – known to his friends as 'Little Bob' or 'Swarte Rob' – born the son of a Huguenot emigré, Jean Jacques Voûte, in Amsterdam in 1747. At the age of twenty-four he entered his father's brokerage firm, which specialized in dyes, coffee and tea.[3]

In 1785 and the years which followed, Robert Voûte co-ordinated large-scale speculations in tea and indigo undertaken by Hope. The houses of Thomas Littledale in Rotterdam, and Harman Hoare & Co. and John and Francis Baring & Co. of London were also concerned in these.[4] The cochineal speculation, in which Hope & Co. also availed themselves of Robert Voûte's services, is described in detail in this book. The mercantilistic intervention of governments in the economic life of their countries favoured monopoloid operations of this nature. At the end of 1792 Robert Voûte withdrew completely from the house which bore his name, in order to have time for his hobby, the study of the economy, and for journeys on behalf of Hope & Co.

The leadership which the house needed was to be forthcoming from a young man who entered Hope's employ in 1790. Pierre César Labouchère, the son of a Huguenot cloth merchant, was born in The Hague in 1772. While working in his uncle's merchant house in Nantes, he rapidly distinguished himself to a degree which led his uncle to recommend him to Henry Hope as a clerk. The latter engaged him, and was so impressed with his achievements that after three years he gave Labouchère power of procuration. When the partners moved to England, the day-to-day management of affairs was to rest with him.[1]

Labouchère's contacts with John and Francis Baring & Co. were also to prove of great value for the future. The earliest transactions with this house dated from before 1770, but it was only with the joint speculations that the parties became well acquainted. The Barings almost certainly had their roots in Groningen, in the northern part of the Netherlands. An early ancestor was a Lutheran minister in Bremen, from whence he moved to London. One of his sons, John, opened a cloth mill in Devonshire. Of the ensuing generation, two sons, John and Francis, moved to London, where they bought raw materials for their father's mill and also sold the products of it. Gradually, however, the house dissociated itself from the family business, and by the beginning of the 19th century it had become one of the most important in its field.[2]

Legend has it that the transactions with Hope laid the foundation for Baring's later greatness. The Hope archives do not bear this out. They do, however, show that the strong and fast-growing house of Baring made grateful use of the capital belonging to the partners of Hope & Co. when they fled to England. As the Hopes did not develop any activities there, they needed objects in which to invest, and Barings were an excellent starting point.[3]

Hope's relationship with Barings was closer than with any other house, and this fact can only be explained by a far-reaching similarity in outlook, in both the commercial and private spheres. This naturally did not rule out differences of opinion in matters of business, or personal tiffs, but these did not impinge upon the underlying mutual confidence. Thus was the foundation laid for a friendship which has survived to this day.

Political developments in the Holland of the 1780s also gave rise to countless problems for the partners. The war against England came to an ignominious end in 1784, but this by no means solved the domestic difficulties. The demands by Emperor Joseph II of Austria for the opening of the Scheldt, which the Dutch had kept closed since the outbreak of the anti-

Spanish revolt, served to maintain the tension. The Patriots utilized the situation to widen their influence. Their belligerence towards the Austrian ruler, however, was largely of a verbal nature, France having refused the military support which they sought. Only when an agreement with Joseph II was reached would the French be willing to enter into an alliance with the Republic.[1]

Strengthened by the support of this ally, the Patriots succeeded in weakening the power of Prince William V in Holland to the point where he and his family were obliged to leave the province. The prince embarked on a series of goodwill visits with the aim of strengthening his position in other regions. While these were taking place, an ideological split in the Patriot ranks emerged; this was most serious in Holland and Utrecht. The regents who opposed the stadholder had only one aim, to increase their own power, and they had no desire to share this with radical groups among the populace which, on grounds of historical rights and customs, claimed a voice in municipal and regional government.[2]

The situation became even more complex when foreign diplomats commenced to concern themselves actively with the party conflicts. The British envoy, Harris, proceeded to organize the Orange party and to bribe regents; his French counterpart openly supported the Patriots, albeit only verbally. In the meantime the stadholder, with the aid of his army, had managed to restore his authority in a number of towns in Gelderland. The response of the radical groups was to seize power in several towns in Holland, thereby gaining the upper hand in the States of Holland. Patriot militia, so-called free corps, thereupon crossed the borders of Utrecht to aid their political associates in the provincial capital.[3]

While all this was going on, the Hopes had remained in Amsterdam, although with the radicals in power there they were anything but safe. On 30th May 1787 a full-scale battle developed between the pro-Orange shipwrights, the 'Bijltjes,' and the Patriot militia – an encounter which ended with the siege and capture of the 'Bijltje' bastion of Kattenburg. This Orange defeat was followed by the plundering of the homes of prominent supporters of the prince, some of whom escaped death by fleeing through their gardens. While, according to Harris, 'many of the first commercial families' sought refuge in The Hague, Henry Hope remained at his post throughout this turbulent period. Naturally, the troubles had an adverse effect on trade. For example, an auction of a consignment of tobacco on behalf of the Swedish Crown failed to take place for the simple reason that the brokers stayed away.[4]

In a letter to the French banker Laborde de Méréville, Henry Hope explained that he thus far had been able to stand his ground between the opposing forces 'for, not being obliged either by status or duty to take sides, I have observed strict neutrality.' In this context, we must not overlook his Anglo-American origin.[1]

Hope, devoting himself to 'the neglected issue amid all this confusion, trade,' even managed to set up a speculation in cochineal, details of which appear in a subsequent chapter. At this time he was also deeply involved in the building and furnishing of his country seat 'Welgelegen', which was situated in the wooded area known as the Haarlemmerhout, on the outskirts of the town of Haarlem. He had purchased the farmstead of that name in 1769, and had steadily enlarged the estate by the acquisition of adjoining properties. The farmstead was demolished in 1784, and two years later the construction of a new house commenced.

Henry Hope's country seat was designed by the consul of the Sardinian Court in The Hague, Triquetti, who had modelled it on the Borghese and Albani villas in Rome. When it was completed, in 1788, Hope obtained permission from the municipal authorities to transplant some of the trees in the Haarlemmerhout (at his own expense) in order to obtain an uninterrupted view from the house.

'Welgelegen' is the only example of a *villa suburbana* in the French classic style which exists in the Netherlands. The facade, with its centrepiece of twin Doric and Ionic columns, is characterized by a terrace which extends over the full width and is approached by means of two curved drives. The whole is decorated with reproductions of classic sculptures. The high central hall, overlooked from the balcony with its gilded, wrought-iron balustrade, the library, the circular music room, the reception room and the octagonal dining room are all richly adorned with classicistic ornaments. The three large front rooms on the first floor were for the purpose of housing Henry Hope's collection of paintings and sculptures.[2]

Three catalogues of paintings, which were compiled by insurers following Henry Hope's departure for England, provide an insight into the extent and nature of his collection. The emphasis was on works by Italian and Dutch masters, but Flemish and French painters were also represented. Henry Hope had been careful to spread his purchases, with the result that the collection contained no more than ten works by a single artist. His favourites among the Italian masters were Titian, Guido Reni, the Caraccis and Maratti. Of the Dutch painters, Rembrandt, Willem van Mieris and Gerard Terborch were the best represented, although their works were somewhat less numerous than those of the Italian artists. The collection also contained a substantial number of canvases by Van Dijck and Rubens. Altogether 372 paintings were shipped to England in 1794.[1]

The party quarrels in the Republic had meanwhile reached a new climax. The vacillatory stadholder having funked a military solution to the crisis of authority in Holland, his wife, Princess Wilhelmina, journeyed to The Hague in an attempt to win support for him there. On 28th June 1787, she was stopped by Patriot militiamen near Goejanverwellesluis and forced to abandon her mission.

King Frederick William II of Prussia viewed the detention of his sister as a personal insult, and he demanded full satisfaction from the States of Holland. In this he was supported by the British government, which put heavy pressure on the French Court to withdraw its promise to the Patriots. Throughout the month of August the issue of satisfaction remained in abeyance, but in Prussia itself preparations were made for a punitive expedition. France, which continued to retreat because it was on the rocks financially and dared not risk another war with England, made an abortive effort to persuade the States of Holland to meet the Prussian ruler's demand. When a fresh ultimatum by Prussia was rejected on 13th September, her troops commenced to advance across Dutch soil.[2]

Henry Hope had continued to hope for a peaceful settlement of the conflict. 'We are at present enjoying a large measure of peace locally, and we console ourselves with the thought that the issues between the provinces will soon be settled, in one way or another, without influencing the safety of the individual or the peace of Europe,' he wrote to his correspondent in Marseilles, Councler, on 30th August. With the Prussian invasion, however, his tone became more sombre, and in a letter of 14th September to Baring he said: 'We are still more embarrassed in regard to our own situation, which has become very serious, but we still hope that extremities possibly may be avoided.' The stagnation of trade was an extremely hard blow, particularly as far as the cochineal speculation was concerned, and a Franco-British war could have incalculable consequences.[3]

The last days of the Patriotic resistance were a period of great anxiety for Henry Hope. On 16th September 1787, Prussian troops occupied Utrecht. Two days later, the States of Holland surrendered and consented to the restoration of the prince in all his dignity. Amsterdam alone refused to capitulate, and became a centre for Patriots put to flight elsewhere. The power of political radicalism in Amsterdam became so great that the city refused to bow to demands for submission, preferring to face repeated clashes with the Prussian forces. After three days the city surrendered, but the capitulation was not signed until 10th October.[4]

As it became increasingly clear that the days of the Patriot régime were numbered, Henry Hope made less and less of a secret of his preference for the old government. In a letter of 4th October 1787 to Councler in Marseilles, he said: 'Our internal troubles are at last coming to an end, our fine city having decided to join with others in bringing about the re-establishment of the former constitution, the only means by which we can preserve our commercial prosperity, our existence and our political respect.'[1]

In Amsterdam, however, the revival of the old order was no straightforward matter. The Patriots were still armed, and in spite of an official decree prescribing the wearing of an orange cockade (the colour forbidden by the Patriots), such a demonstration was not without hazard. The Messrs. Hope were to discover at first hand that, as the *Nieuwe Nederlandsche Jaarboeken* expressed it, 'the defeated party did not find it easy to suppress its pain and rancour.'[2]

In pursuance of the decree of the previous day, a number of merchants wearing orange cockades appeared at the Stock Exchange on 12th October. Among them were Henry Hope and John Williams Hope. The *Nieuwe Nederlandsche Jaarboeken* subsequently noted that: 'Some embittered Patriots, incensed by the somewhat larger Orange Cockades worn by the Gentlemen referred to, drew attention to these, made scornful utterances and at last pushed towards them on the Exchange, ostensibly out of curiosity; but they jostled so forcefully that the Gentlemen named were in danger of being crushed and trampled underfoot; assistance was thereupon requested, and a number of officers of the Law hurried to the place, but they were not able to deal with the situation. Thus on the orders of the Government a Company of armed Citizens was sent, whereupon the majority of those present left the Exchange, and the Gentlemen referred to were conducted safely to their homes.'[3]

Messrs. Hope were so angered by the scorn heaped upon the Stock Exchange and 'the slight to which they had been subjected,' that they lodged a protest with the Court of Justice; in anticipation of the outcome, they avoided the Exchange. The court, however, was unable to give them satisfaction until after 15th October, when Amsterdam admitted troops loyal to the prince in order to avoid further Prussian occupation. On the very next day, Messrs. Hope were collected from their homes by the *Schepenen* Van Muyden and Muilman, and taken to the Stock Exchange, where Van Muyden made a 'very polite' speech 'in the presence of many members, as a result of which the wearing of Orange on the Stock Exchange has since become sufficiently general.'[4]

To Baring, Henry Hope wrote only a few sentences concerning the episode. But in another letter he clearly revealed his feelings of bitterness:

'This miserable country, having been devastated and practically ruined during the past ten years by an ambitious faction, is about to take a little rest, but twenty years of economy and industry will not succeed in making good the ruinous losses.' Here, once again, the emphasis is on the economic consequences of the political troubles.[1]

But whereas the confused situations had clearly had an adverse effect on trade, the reverse applied to the activities relating to loans. The events involving Joseph II had been something of an obstacle to the placing of Swedish loans, but by the time the one of 1786 was issued the investment climate in Amsterdam was decidedly favourable. A loan for Poland was floated in the same year, and the principal objection raised by Hope in connexion with this related not to the difficult political situation in the Netherlands, but to King Stanislaw's unsteady position.[2]

The relationship between the stagnation of trade and the ease of placing loans emerged even more clearly in 1787. While drawing the attention of the Swedish government to the effect of political unrest on trade, Hope desired to increase the sum of the loan which had been requested from one to one and a half million guilders. The fact that, under the prevailing circumstances, Hope and Fizeaux together accepted responsibility for two-thirds of this loan indicates that they were confident of being able to place the bonds.[3]

The summer and early autumn of 1787 also saw preparations for the initial loans to Russia. On 9th October of that year, the day preceding the official capitulation of Amsterdam, Henry Hope, in a letter to the Russian Court Banker, made a passing reference to the disturbances; but he clearly viewed the situation as transient. As far as the placing of the Russian loan was concerned, Henry Hope was cautiously optimistic; in the event, he was proved right in a manner surprising even for him: while the brokers had proceeded on the basis of a loan of one and a half million guilders, subscriptions totalled six million within a week.[4] Apart from the slightly higher rate of interest, which was also a factor, Henry Hope attributed this phenomenon to a lessening of 'the general diffidence, which prevented people from placing the large sums which have been accumulating in consequence of the stagnation of trade for so long a time.' In a letter to Baring, he described the success of the loan as 'a melancholy proof of the discredit of our own Government securities.'[5]

Thus we arrive at an economic factor–stagnation of trade, which caused money to be diverted into other channels–and a political factor–an abhorrence of the re-established régime, which led Patriot supporters to subscribe to foreign loans in preference to those issued on behalf of the

Dutch government. A general lack of confidence in the chances of survival of the stadholder's régime, which depended upon Prussian and English support, may also have played a part.

This is not the place to go into the placing of the successive Russian loans (this is dealt with in a separate chapter), but the market, at times easy and at others stressed, more or less clearly reveals a number of general trends. In 1789, fear of a financial debacle in France initially produced reticence on the part of the investors, but when the anticipated catastrophe failed to materialize a relative glut of funds existed, because much had remained uninvested.[1] In 1790, issues became more difficult following the revolt in the Southern Netherlands, which aroused all manner of anxiety concerning international ramifications which, however, did not occur.[2] In 1791 the capital market was easy in the extreme. The principal reason for this must be sought in the *assignats*–paper currency issued in France and secured by confiscated Church property–the value of which began to fall alarmingly in May of that year. The outbreak of the fourth Anglo-Dutch war had caused an appreciable proportion of investors in the Netherlands to switch from English stocks to French, and the results of this were now being felt. As French loans were usually issued in Paris, interest was paid in French currency. With the *assignats* falling in value, a mass flight from French stocks occurred, and this manifestly benefited Hope's Russian loans.[3]

Henry Hope, who described this process in a memorandum, and the house which bore his name soon became the *bête noire* of the French revolutionaries. When, in 1789, southern Europe suffered a general shortage of grain and France purchased large quantities of corn in Amsterdam, the French chargé d'affaires in The Hague, Caillard, circulated a report which suggested that Hope & Co., on instructions from the Dutch government (and probably also from England), was buying up corn in order to block supplies to France and so add to her difficulties.

The facts were otherwise. When, in the summer of 1789, a number of Amsterdam merchants reacted coolly to huge orders from France, the French minister Necker intervened personally, and successfully, with the Company. The *grootboeken* show that Hope & Co. purchased wheat to a value of slightly more than half a million guilders on behalf of the 'King of France.' The house also bought rye and wheat on behalf of the burgomasters of Amsterdam and Haarlem and the magistrate of Liege. When the prices fell, the Company, acting on instructions from its principals, resold the cereals.[4]

In later years, Caillard accused Hope & Co. of having a hand in the fall in the French rate of exchange. Another spokesman asserted that the Company repeatedly drew on Paris with the aim of undermining the rate. It was alleged that when their drafts were returned protested, the partners refused to meet the redrafts, and that by this means they sought to elicit a legal process ending in a ruling that there was no rate of exchange for drafts on France. The only element of truth in this ridiculous story lay in a recommendation to the National Convention that the Hope assets held by the Paris house of Vandenijver should be confiscated.[1]

It is abundantly clear from these stories that radicalism was steadily gaining ground in France. In 1792 the French Legislative Assembly declared war on Austria, a development which brought the revolutionaries dangerously close to Holland, since the war was initially to be fought in the Southern Netherlands. The conditions embodied in the contracts made in 1792 show clearly that the *entrepreneurs* were again experiencing difficulty in disposing of bonds.[2] In the autumn of that year the political situation became decidedly alarming, following the victory of the French general Dumouriez in the Southern Netherlands. It became still worse when the Convention declared war on 'the King of England' and 'the Stadholder of Holland' early in 1793. By March of that year Dumouriez had advanced to the major rivers, but his defeat by the Austrians and his subsequent defection provided a brief respite.

In February 1793, a loan of six million guilders was issued on behalf of Spain. Like the Russian loans, this was in tranches. In May of the same year Hope & Co. contracted for two more Russian loans, each of three million guilders.[3] Subscriptions to these loans continued during the summer, but a major French victory in September brought the flow of funds to a halt. Of the Spanish loan, only the first tranche, of six million guilders, had by then been subscribed. In the case of the Russian loans, which came on to the market later, it proved impossible even to reach the first three million guilders.[4]

Remarkably, Hope's turnover with the Exchange Bank during the eventful years after 1785 reached heights which were not achieved in the preceding fifteen years. Between 1786 and 1790, the annual figure was of the order of 40 million guilders; in 1791 it rose to 52 million, and in the following year the all-time high of 76 million was attained. The factors which contributed to this peak are not immediately apparent. It is very probable that payments arising from the numerous Russian loans negotiated in 1791 played a part. After 1792 the turnover fell sharply, totalling 40 million in 1794. Of the other houses which we investigated, only Hogguer achieved a comparably protracted and significant improvement in the years 1785–1794. De Smeth's turnover declined in this very period, and the figure achieved in 1787 was not repeated until 1791. The growth of turnover by Muilman, while not marked, was consistent.

As the economic history of the Netherlands shows, trade as it were continued to bask in autumn sunshine during the last years of the old Republic.[1] The figures of turnover with the Exchange Bank reveal that Hope & Co. had their full share of this recovery, and more. The revival of trade with Russia will have contributed to this. The Company did a large volume of business in Russian produce with the house owned by the Court Banker, Sutherland, in St.Petersburg. The underlying transactions, which in part were aimed at restoring the rate of exchange in Russia, were undertaken on the instructions of the government.[2] In 1794, Hope & Co. received special permission from Empress Catherine II to import a large quantity of sugar into Russia.[3]

Early in the 1790s Hope also established relations with merchant houses in the United States. They had long ignored these avenues on account of political developments. At that juncture, however, there was no question of the Company becoming involved in America's national finances. Gouverneur Morris, who, as the executive agent of President Washington, was on a tour of western Europe, during which he visited the Hopes, attempted to interest the partners in his country's financial affairs, but without success. The time for such business had not yet come.[4]

It will be abundantly clear from the foregoing that the partners were busy safeguarding life and property against the French armies. In France itself, radicalism had reached its climax in the Reign of Terror, the targets of which included bankers and speculators. In the Southern Netherlands, the French occupation had been followed by a wave of confiscations of property belonging to 'aristocrats', and this boded ill for the North. Shortly after the declaration of war on the Netherlands and England, the Convention, anticipating the victory, declared forfeit the property of the stadholder, 'his friends, his supporters and his willing slaves'–categories which plainly embraced the Hopes.[5]

When Breda fell to the French in February 1793, Henry Hope, sensing imminent danger, fled to England, taking John Williams Hope's family with him. The daily management of the house was left in the hands of his protégé. Although he returned in December 1793 when, following Dumouriez's defection, the situation appeared to be slightly easier, he no longer felt really safe.[6]

The summer of 1794 brought a fresh defeat for the allied armies, and again the future of the Republic was in doubt. Against this background, the partners prepared once more to leave for England. Henry Hope enquired of the British government regarding the possibility of British ports being opened for the goods and chattels of refugees from Holland. The foreign secretary, Lord Grenville, through his envoy in Holland, sought the views of the government there. The *Raadpensionaris*, Van de Spiegel, flatly rejected the idea of permission being granted, as this would be tantamount to a *sauve qui peut*. And he added, bitterly, that an inverse measure would be more appropriate, 'in order to leave to the Hopes and other over-grown capitalists of this country no other chance for saving their property than the giving or at least lending a part of it to supply the wants of the Government.'[1]

While Van de Spiegel's bitterness is understandable, the material and moral bankruptcy of the régime was so complete that there was no justification for condemning Henry Hope's attempt to save himself and those dear to him from almost certain death under the guillotine. An outsider could not know that the Terror had just then come to an end.

Indeed, Henry Hope had given all possible assistance to the government following the restoration of the stadholder in 1787. He had, for example, expressed to Van de Spiegel his readiness to support a loan for the benefit of the decrepit *Oost-Indische Compagnie*. At the same time, he was not willing to throw good money after bad. When the *Compagnie's* debts continued to mount, and the States of Holland maintained support for the *Compagnie* even at the risk of their own financial position, Henry Hope slowly turned away from the government. To make matters worse, the *Compagnie*, in an attempt to recover lost ground, resorted to senseless prohibitions. In 1791 it persuaded the States of Holland to thwart the sale of some parcels of tea imported by Henry Hope, and in 1793 the same thing occurred with a cargo of Javanese sugar consigned by Hope in an American vessel.[2]

When the French had advanced to the river Maas, and a Patriot action group openly took up the cudgels against the sitting regents in Amsterdam, the Hopes considered that their time had come. On 17th October 1794 Henry Hope and John Williams Hope embarked at Hellevoetsluis and crossed to England, where the latter's wife and children had been since the end of August. Thomas, Henry Philip and Adrian Elias fled to Germany.[3]

Before leaving, John Williams Hope had explained the reasons for their departure to the hereditary prince, later King William I. He had pointed to the systematic neglect of the army and the fleet, which was among the causes of the country's hopeless position. Since the outbreak of the war, the Hopes had repeatedly urged the need for compulsory loans, since only by this means could the Patriots be forced to participate. But the government had been both lax and timid in responding to the advice, with the result that the country was now beyond salvation.[1]

Pierre César Labouchère and the young Alexander Baring, a son of Sir Francis who was serving his apprenticeship with the house, remained at their posts until the last minute. A severe frost in mid-December had robbed the major rivers of their value for defence. Early in January 1795 the defeated Anglo-Hanoverian army retreated eastwards. The Dutch army was in disarray, and the civilian population was in the grip of apathy. Holland was there for the taking.

The time had come for Labouchère and Baring to make their escape. But ice, driven by the westerly gales, had jammed the estuaries, making a crossing to England impossible. It was 17th January before the wind moderated and backed to the southeast, freeing the packed ice. On the night of 18th January–at about which time the first French troops were entering Amsterdam–the two embarked at Den Helder.[2]

In London, the Hopes had meanwhile suitably installed themselves. From his distant relative, Lord Hopetoun, Henry Hope purchased a house in Harley Street, off Cavendish Square, to which he added a wing to accommodate the works of art which he had brought from Holland.[3] He also acquired a country seat, the East Sheen estate, near Richmond.

The offices in Amsterdam had been left in the charge of Paulus Taay, 'trusted clerk.' The plan provided for Taay only to liquidate current transactions. There would, of course, be no place under the new régime for a 'maison anglo-orangiste' such as Hope & Co. With this in mind, Messrs. Hope arranged for an advertisement to appear in January 1795, stating that payments by the Company would henceforth be made in London and that drafts on Hope should be sent there.[4]

With the ending of the Terror, however, things in France had changed, and this became apparent after the conquest of the Netherlands. The 'representatives of the people of France,' who had occupied Hope's residence on the Keizersgracht, gave assurances that they would respect the offices, and issued express instructions that the Company was not to be hampered in completing its affairs. Their attitude stemmed not only from the milder political climate in France, but also from a realization that a substantial portion of Holland's wealth, both capital and goods, was highly mobile and could only be enticed back by the right kind of noises.

The new Batavian rulers in Amsterdam were no less forthcoming and they, too, laid emphasis on the peaceful continuation of the business, 'as in that case the Inhabitants of these Countries would not suffer in the matter of the payments to be made to them by that House of Commerce.' Taay optimistically informed the worried correspondents that Messrs. Hope would certainly not have departed if they had known everything in advance, 'since the new order of things has been established here in an indescribably orderly and peaceful manner.'[1]

This unexpected reprieve, however, gave rise to new problems. Now that early liquidation was no longer the primary issue, Taay faced the costly duty to meet incoming claims. Although arrangements had been made with a number of business friends to assist Taay in time of need, they backed out when the stream of demands grew into a flood. At the crucial moment Robert Voûte came to the rescue of the despairing Taay and provided him with the funds necessary to keep the business going. 'If I had not had that good friend, everything would have been in ruins,' a grateful Taay later wrote to London. 'He is a clever chap, and he is always ready to help, day and night.'[2]

The arrangements for the payment of interest and principal on current loans had been made prior to the Hopes' departure. In the case of the Russian loans, the house of Martin Dorner had been appointed to deal with interest coupons tendered by Dutch bondholders. The Hopes dealt with the Spanish loan of 1792/1793 direct from London, because Spain was then at war with France.[3] For the Swedish loans, agreement was reached with Hogguer, who had been associated with Hope & Co. in floating these.

When shortly afterwards trade revived, albeit via Hamburg, it became easier for the partners to meet current liabilities, thus avoiding the bankruptcy of the Amsterdam house. Their energetic associate, Hermann Albrecht Insinger, dealt with the diamonds, which since 1791 had been despatched to Hope by the official Portuguese government contractor in Lisbon.[4] Insinger also handled the sale of coffee which, with Hope's mediation, reached Amsterdam. We can probably interpret this as a means of assisting bondholders of the West Indian plantation loans to obtain their rightful interest. When England and Spain became embroiled in war in 1797, the partners transferred responsibility for the payment of interest on the Spanish loans to Insinger. Official confirmation of Insinger's position as a trusted agent came with the transfer to him in May 1796 of the power of attorney vested in Robert Voûte when the latter was preparing to leave for Russia to intercede on behalf of the holders of Polish and Russian bonds.[5]

The occasion was also used to grant power of procuration to Jan Jacob

Voûte, Robert's eldest brother, whose merchant house, and an account which Robert Voûte maintained there, provided the partners with another avenue through which to continue certain activities on a modest scale. For example, we find settlement accounts relating to tea speculations set up previously. Extensive correspondence with the house of De Coninck & Co. in Copenhagen suggests that the Hopes had a financial interest in the sending of a Danish ship to Batavia.[1] As has been explained, there was no question of the Hopes undertaking any independent activities in England, and such business as there was to be done was channelled via Baring or Harman & Co.

The scale of operations in Amsterdam was deliberately limited in order not to arouse the jealousy and greed of the municipal and provincial authorities. To meet the dire shortage of funds, compulsory loans and levies were rife, and the authorities were very keen to draw the house of Hope & Co. into their net. The partners in London instructed Taay to deny that he had any power to act on behalf of the Company, and to inform the authorities that they need not anticipate any communication on the subject from London. When the pressure on Taay increased, the partners, to the dutiful man's intense dismay, requested him to stay away from the office. The upshot was that Hope's possessions were sequestered.[2]

The confiscation was provisionally a formality and, coming from a moderate administration, was probably aimed at silencing extreme radicals. A moderate policy was to be expected, for Voûte had meanwhile achieved major successes in his efforts on behalf of the holders of Polish and Russian bonds.[3] Under the conventions of 30th June and 29th October 1797, all debts incurred in Holland by the Republic of Poland, its king and the Polish magnates were converted into Russian bonds bearing interest at five per cent. A third convention, signed on 15th January 1798, had the effect of converting all Russian loans issued in Holland and Belgium into the same 5% type.[4]

The implementation of these conventions was entrusted to the house of Raymond and Theodore de Smeth, Hope's erstwhile competitor in matters concerned with Russia's finances. It had briefly looked as if the Company would be able to resume operations in Amsterdam, when the politically very moderate administrators of the province of Holland made tentative proposals for a return by the Hopes. But at the crucial moment the partners broke off the contact, because no absolute guarantees were forthcoming regarding the safety of persons or property.[5] The wisdom of their action emerged in January 1798, when a radical group succeeded in obtaining the French government's approval to carry out a *coup d'état*, in which the moderates were swept from power. For the 'Anglomaniac' Hopes, little good could be expected from the new régime.

Fortunately, the partners were able to render valuable services from their exiled headquarters. When the house of Martin Dorner ran into serious difficulties after the proprietor's death, and the payment of interest on the Russian bonds was jeopardized, Labouchère travelled to Hamburg to put matters right. On his advice, the house of Matthiessen & Sillem was appointed to succeed Dorner. The old connexion which was thus strengthened was later to prove immensely valuable to Hope & Co.[1]

The links with America, which were reinforced at about the same time, were also destined to be of importance to the Company. The American banker and land speculator William Bingham had written to Hope in 1792 concerning the advantages of buying land in Maine. In 1794 he had sent an agent to visit the partners in Amsterdam, but by then they had other problems to contend with and so the man returned to the United States empty-handed.[2]

With the Hopes settled in London, however, things had changed. There was now a need for suitable investments for the capital withdrawn from Holland. Against this background, it is understandable that they associated themselves with a visit to America by Alexander Baring in 1796. The Hopes committed themselves to a three-quarer share in any purchases or other undertakings entered into by Alexander Baring. During his stay, Baring allowed himself to be talked into buying 600,000 acres which Bingham had earlier acquired. The land was situated between the Penobscot and Scodiac rivers, and was valued at nearly 270,000 dollars. The deal brought Bingham release from financial difficulties, and Baring a wife, for he married one of Bingham's daughters. For Baring & Co., the connexion with Bingham meant an introduction to the circles concerned with American government finances, and this was subsequently to prove extremely valuable.[3]

The Hopes were left with a three-quarter share in land which produced nothing but disappointment and expense. The main stream of immigrants entered the United States at more southerly points, and most of them headed west. Year after year, the reports from Hope's agent in Maine, John Richards, echoed the disconsolate theme of drudgery in getting colonization under way and of scarcity of settlers who, moreover, were not an asset but a liability from the financial point of view.[4] The only redeeming feature in the situation was perhaps that it helped to focus Hope's attention on America.

Allusions in the surviving correspondence reveal that in 1797 Alexander

Baring was instructed by the partners of Hope & Co. to attend to their interests in the Caribbean. Because of the war, arrears of payment had arisen, particularly on the part of debtors on the islands of St.Eustatius and Guadeloupe, and these could not be allowed to continue. Baring, however, found no opportunity to undertake this task, and in 1799 Hope's interests in the area were entrusted to William Gordon Coesvelt, who lived on St.Croix. In 1808 and later years we shall find Coesvelt acting as Hope's agent in Spain and, later still, as a manager at the Company's offices in Amsterdam.[1]

The bonds between the houses of Hope and Baring had meanwhile been strengthened by Labouchère's marriage to Dorothea, a daughter of Sir Francis Baring. Legend has it that when his courtship began to develop, Labouchère enquired of the partners of Hope & Co. whether, in the event of his marriage to a Miss Baring, he would be admitted to partnership, and that upon receiving an affirmative reply he went to Sir Francis, to whom he imparted the news and thereby won Dorothea's hand.

This story is probably untrue, for not until the house had returned to Amsterdam do we find Labouchère as a partner. Nevertheless, it is characteristic of his shrewdness in matters of business. In this, he was a match for his friend and later brother-in-law, Alexander Baring.

The lack of progress achieved by England and her allies in their struggle against Napoleon produced a gradual improvement of Hope's chances of being able to return to Holland. Czar Paul I had declared war against France in 1798, but when his armies, after initial successes, suffered defeats at the hand of the French (principally as a result of the lack of Austrian support), he virtually withdrew from the arena. Bonaparte thereupon vigorously attacked Austria, and a series of French victories paved the way for the Peace of Lunéville in February 1801. England, with no continental allies and no prospect of a decisive military success, opened negotiations with France which led to peace preliminaries on 1st October of that year.

For the partners of Hope & Co., the time had come to make serious preparations for the return to Holland, and early in 1801 far-reaching discussions were held with Robert Voûte, who travelled to London for the purpose. The idea of returning was certainly attractive, for during their exile the partners had been obliged to decline requests for a loan for which Brazilian diamonds were to serve as security. Their circumstances had also necessitated turning down an Austrian approach for a new loan.[2]

Robert Voûte proved willing to investigate the feasibility of the proposed move, and was given lengthy instructions regarding the vital issues. First and foremost was an investigation of the state of trade in Amsterdam and the opportunities for the house to resume its activities there. It might be possible for one of the partners to return to Holland ahead of the others to look after the Russian loans, and perhaps also the Austrian. But his presence might not be construed as formal resettlement, and the repatriate would have to receive protection against house-searches or other forms of harassment connected with the fiscal claims against the Hope family.[1]

Upon his return to Holland, Voûte, in conversations with friends and acquaintances, gathered a certain amount of information concerning the economic situation. The prospects were none too encouraging. Behind a facade of prosperity, many Amsterdam houses possessed an inner weakness which, in Voûte's opinion, could not fail to lead to their bankruptcy if the war were to last. 'This country will go to the devil unless it again becomes seventeen provinces, as in the days before William of Orange,' he half-jokingly remarked to a friend. The latter promptly replied: 'Can you persuade England to achieve this? That would be an excellent thing.'[2] A prophetic utterance, which was to be borne out in 1815.

In Voûte's opinion, the lifting of the judicial attachment on Hope's property was a matter of urgency, because it was imperative that the house should be ready to resume its former position when trade revived after the cessation of hostilities. Early in October 1801, Voûte visited The Hague to discuss the matter with the new government, the *Staatsbewind*, which had come to power as a result of pressure exerted by Napoleon. In accordance with Bonaparte's overall effort towards reconciliation, the new rulers were mainly conservatives, both Patriot and pro-Orange. This boded well for Voûte's cause.

In spite of the mutual goodwill, however, Voûte made little progress, and when the first half of November passed without a decision he handed the task over to Insinger. By the end of the month Insinger had managed to achieve a settlement concerning the restitution of the confiscated Hope property, and this was restored to its owners upon payment of a sum of cf 180,000.[3]

In the meantime, the political skies had cleared to the point where Labouchère ventured a brief visit to the Republic. From there he travelled to Portugal to negotiate with the government on a proposed loan against the security of diamonds. As we have seen, the proposal was not new. His mission and its outcome form the subject of one of the chapters of this book.[4]

With the signing of the Treaty of Amiens at the end of March 1802, which finally brought an end to hostilities between England and France, the early return of the partners to Holland became a matter of great importance, not only from the point of view of the impending Portuguese loan but also of the management of the Russian loans. Voûte had revisited England at the beginning of 1802 and had repeatedly referred to this. He had also hammered in the point that the deed of partnership should be amended to cover every conceivable contingency in the event of a new war. A fictitious contract, in which only the names of those partners who would play an active role in the house appeared, should be drawn up for external purposes. Voûte also felt that two domiciles should be maintained, one in London and one in Amsterdam. The London house could bear the title Henry Hope & Co., and the Amsterdam house Hope & Co.[1]

Family quarrels and the failure to obtain permission for the Portuguese loan delayed the signing of the new deed of partnership until the beginning of October, by which time Labouchère and John Williams Hope and their families were on the point of leaving for Holland. The contract itself has not survived, but correspondence and accounts show that the Hopes of London took a five-million guilder share in the Amsterdam house through Henry Hope & Co. Labouchère figured as a partner, but with a relatively small and fluctuating share which by 1808 had grown to cf 700,000; however, he had a $\frac{1}{7}$th share of profits. Earlier plans to admit Alexander Baring to the partnership were not implemented, probably because of the deterioration of relations between England and France. As mentioned in the chapter dealing with the Portuguese loan, Sir Francis Baring considered the possibility of establishing a house in Antwerp. A merger between Hope and Baring also appears to have been seriously considered.[2]

Adrian Elias Hope ceased to be a partner, and his share in the old house was credited to an account held in his name by Henry Hope & Co. It appeared advisable to exclude him from all discreet arrangements because of his strange and unpredictable character.[3]

The action of the *Staatsbewind* in obstructing the Portuguese loan made Henry Hope decide to stay in England. John Williams Hope repeatedly delayed his return to Holland, and this, too, will undoubtedly have been due in part to the opposition to the loan. Weighed down by domestic problems and attacks of gout, this man, who possessed little fighting spirit, was reluctant to exchange the familiar circle of family and friends for an uncertain future in a Holland which had become strange to him.

The re-establishment of the house in Amsterdam, which was announced in a circular dated 5th November 1802, was not without its difficulties. The house naturally resumed control of matters which had been entrusted to others during its exile, and one such matter concerned the Portuguese diamonds, for the sale of which Hope held a monopoly under the terms of the Portuguese loan. At the same time, care was taken not to offend other houses and, in view of the difficult times, to allow them a share in current business. Moreover, the position of the 'Anglomaniac' house was somewhat delicate, and it was therefore in its interest to create a circle of well-disposed business associates. The controversy surrounding the Portuguese loan had amply demonstrated the need for friends.[1]

Accordingly, the sale of Russian bonds was left in the hands of Voûte & Co., and it was not long before tea imports, under government licence, added a new dimension to the relationship between the two houses. Insinger retained a role in the marketing of the diamonds and also became involved in the growing volume of colonial produce which arrived in American ships. Sale of brazilwood, for which Hope & Co. secured the monopoly, were entrusted to the house of Muhl & Van Winter.[2]

In the case of the Russian bonds, the situation was more complicated. Hope's uncompromising enemy, Treasurer Vasilyev, made sure that the house of De Smeth continued to be concerned with the Russian loans even after the Company had resumed operations in Amsterdam. Hope, however, remained the principal agent where the encashment of repurchased bonds was concerned.[3]

In the chapters dealing with the Russian loans, it is explained how transactions in Russia on behalf of the French government were embodied in a loan to the United States to enable that country to purchase the French colony of Louisiana. We also see here that the initiative for that loan stemmed from Alexander Baring. In the light of all that has been written about Baring's American contacts, this is not surprising.

In May 1803, Baring and Hope entered into a convention with the French government concerning the terms of payment by the United States for Louisiana. When, in the same month, war broke out between France and England, Hope as it were automatically came to the forefront in the further negotiations, because they constituted the best avenue for the payment of the loan instalments to the French Treasury.[4]

In a supplementary convention entered into on 21st April 1804, the French government undertook to surrender immediately to Baring and Hope all American bonds which it still held. As a *quid pro quo*, the two houses undertook to substantially accelerate the instalments. The negotiation of this convention was largely the work of Labouchère.[5]

Of the total loan sum of $11\frac{1}{4}$ million dollars, 5 million was payable in Amsterdam and $6\frac{1}{4}$ million in London. The 5 million dollars domiciled in Amsterdam formed the basis for a loan of cf 12,500,000 which bore the title 'Share in a joint property of original American Stocks.' The shares concerned had a nominal value of cf 1,000 and bore interest at $5\frac{1}{2}\%$. As the Louisiana bonds bore interest at 6%, a margin of $\frac{1}{2}\%$ existed, and this was to be used for the purchase of any shares which might come on to the market. Interest accruing on shares thus purchased was to be used for the same purpose.[1] All participants were to share in this reserve fund, the balance of which was to be distributed among them at the end of the 17-year life of the loan. Investors were offered the alternative of original, registered, bonds bearing the full 6%, but the exercise of this option implied forfeiture of a share in the final balance of the reserve fund. The accounts show that 40 participants preferred to manage their own bond-holdings.[2]

The management of the 'Joint Property' was exercised jointly by Hope & Co., Raymond and Theodore De Smeth, and Wilhelm and Jan Willink. Hope had thus deemed it wise to involve competitors in the new loan. The house of Willink had long been concerned in American loans, but had now in fact been supplanted by Hope & Co. De Smeth has already been referred to in connexion with the Russian loans. Alexander Baring had been at great pains to insist that the Company, once re-established in Amsterdam, should become the office for payments for all the old American loans, but the partners had wisely declined this role.[3]

The new management group was domiciled at the offices of Hope & Co., where the official documents relating to the loan were kept in an iron chest secured with three different locks. Each of the participating houses had a key to one of these locks, so that it was impossible for any of them to open the chest independently. Hope made a separate agreement with De Smeth, giving them a one-sixth share in the entire Louisiana transaction. Willink, who was excluded from this, was to receive the mutually agreed commissions, but Hope and De Smeth undertook to renounce their commissions and to enter these only *pro forma* in the books.[4]

The loan was a huge success, and the bonds were very quickly placed. They were even sold to the members of the family and to Willem Borski and his *entrepreneurs* at prices between 102 and 103. Of the $6\frac{1}{4}$ million dollars payable in London, Alexander Baring placed 500,000 dollarsworth in America. The Barings took a one million dollar share, 1.7 million went to Henry Hope & Co. in London and 300,000 dollarsworth of bonds were transferred to Hope & Co. in Amsterdam. This left 2,750,000 dollars to be subscribed in England.[5]

In 1805, with France at war with Austria and Russia, the desire on the

PLAN van Deelgeeving in een gemeenſchappelijk bezit van origineele Americaanſche Fondſen.

Art. 1.

Deeze Americaanſche Fondſen zijn gevestigd tegens den Intrest van 6 pCt. 's Jaars, door het Americaanſche Gouvernement te betaalen binnen Amſterdam, ten kosten en riſico van hetzelve Gouvernement, zoodaanig, dat de Eigenaars deezer Fondſen aan geene verliezen op die Intresſen, het zij uit hoofde van den Wisſel-Cours als anderſints, zullen bloot geſtelt zijn.

Art. 2.

Het Capitaal deezer Fondſen moet door de Vereenigde Staaten van Noord-America worden gerembourſeerd in drie gelijke Termijnen, met Intrest tot de dadelijke aflosſing toe, ieder van een derde part, waarvan de eerſte uitterlijk aanvang neemen zal over 15 Jaaren, te reekenen na primo Januarij 1804, en de anderen in de twee onmiddelijk daarop volgende Jaaren, zoodanig dat het geheele Capitaal zal moeten zijn afgelost en gekweeten — voor of in den Jaare 1821.

Art. 3.

Het Capitaal der voorſchreevene Fondſen, welke onder dit gemeenſchappelijk bezit zullen worden vereenigd, zal niet moogen te booven gaan het beloop van vijf Millioenen Dollars, maar wel tot eene mindere ſomma of bedraagen kunnen worden bepaald, als waartoe de Heeren Bewaarders en Directeuren zich de vrijheid voorbehouden, als meede om in alle voorkomende gevallen te moogen handelen in de uitvoering der na te meldene Articulen, en in alles wat de adminiſtratie deezer gemeenſchappelijk te bezittene Fondſen aangaat, zoo als zij in der tijd ten meesten voordeelen der belanghebbenden zullen vermeenen te behooren.

Art. 4.

Deeze origineele Americaanſche Fondſen zullen worden geſteld ten naame van

de Heeren { HOPE & COMP., R. & TH. DE SMETH, en W. & J. WILLINK,

als Repreſentanten van de Deelhebbers of Geintresſeerdens in deeze Gemeenſchap, en ten behoeve van dezelve onder hunne bewaaring en directie verblijven, tot den uiteinde deezer Deelneeming toe, zullende over zulks de Hoofdſommen deezer Gemeenſchappelijke Fondſen behoorlijk geſplitst, in diverſe Certificaaten, ten naame van voormelde Heeren Bewaarders worden geſteld, en onder hunne directie ten behoeve van, en voor reekening en riſico der gezamentlijke Deelneemers blijven gedeponeerd, met bijvoeging van zoodanige Notarieele Actens, als naar den aard van zoortgelijke Fondſen en Deelneemingen vereischt worden.

Art. 5.

Ieder Aandeel in deeze Gemeenſchap zal groot zijn vier Honderd Dollars Capitaal der gemelde Fondſen, en gereekend worden tegens de Cours van 50 ſt. per Dollar, te repreſenteeren Duizend Guldens Hollandsch Courant geld.

Art. 6.

Uit de Jaarlijkſche Intresſen van het geheele Fonds, zal door Heeren Bewaarders en Directeuren aan de Deelhebbers worden gedaan eene uitdeeling van Vijf en Vijftig Guldens over ieder Aandeel, uitmaakende alzoo over de gerepreſenteerde Hollandſche waarde van Duizend Guldens, eene Intrest van 5½ pCt. 's Jaars.

Art. 7.

Het overige half pCt., het welk de Americaanſche Fondſen Jaarlijks meerder aan Intresſen opleeveren, zal door Heeren Bewaarders en Directeuren Jaarlijks worden beſteed, tot inkoop van zoo veele Aandeelen als daar voor zullen kunnen worden verkreegen, die als dan daadelijk zullen worden gemortificeerd, zullende vervolgens, meede Jaarlijks op gelijke wijze worden gehandeld met het meerder beloop der Intresſen, het welk uit hoofde der vroegere inkoop van Aandeelen zal overſchieten.

Art. 8.

Bij gedeeltelijke aflosſing of remboursſement der Americaanſche Fondſen, zal het beloop van zoodaanige aflosſing worden beſteed tot remboursſement van een proportioneel getal Aandeelen in deeze Deelneeming, daartoe bij Loting te bepaalen, en dit remboursſement geſchieden met de gerepreſenteerde ſomma van Duizend Guldens Hollandsch Courant, voor ieder Aandeel, zullende deeze alzoo gerembourſeerde Aandeelen met een ſtempel die dit rembours aanduid, getekend, en alzoo aan de Houders terug gegeven worden, om te dienen, tot bewijs van hun voortduurend Aandeel in, of proportioneele aanſpraak op het reſultaat deezer Deelneeming, na dat alle de Aandeelen eene gelijke aflosſing van *f* 1000:— Holl. Cour. zullen hebben genooten, of ook voor reekening deezer Deelneeming zullen zijn gemortificeerd.

Art. 9.

Bij de finaale aflosſing van alle de Origineele Americaanſche Fondſen, die tot deeze gemeenſchap zullen hebben behoord, zal het zuiver Reſultaat deezer deelneeming, het welk na de uitbetaaling van *f* 1000:— Holl. Cour. over ieder niet gemortificeerd aandeel, zal aanweezig zijn, over de gezamentlijke niet gemortificeerde aandeelen, gelijkelijk worden gerepartitieerd, en aan de Houders tegens intrekking van de aandeelen zelven worden verantwoord —

Prospectus of the 'Share in a joint property of original American Stocks,' 1803 part of the Dutch investors to find more peaceful havens for their capital increased. To this end, Labouchère enquired of Baring whether a further one million dollarsworth of bonds could be transferred to Amsterdam. But the deteriorating rate of exchange on England made the bonds too costly in Amsterdam, and consequently Labouchère was forced to abandon the idea.[1]

Individual investors, however, did purchase bonds in England. Indeed, N.&J.&R. van Staphorst, Ketwich & Voombergh and Willem Borski went so far as to establish an administrative office to handle joint holdings of Louisiana stock. They themselves probably succeeded in syphoning the bonds, which had a total value of 178,800 dollars, from London to Holland.[2]

Those who participated in the 'Joint Property' at no time had cause for complaint. Even in the difficult years after 1808, the United States continued to meet its obligations promptly. In 1811, coin was sent to Amsterdam on board an American warship in order to safeguard the interest payment. In 1812, there was a threat of stagnation owing to opposition by the French government, but the outbreak of war between England and the United States in that year had the effect of ironing out the diplomatic wrinkles.

In 1819, 1820 and 1821, the loan was redeemed. During the whole period, 1,340 bonds were purchased for the reserve fund, producing for the holders of the 11,128 shares a final bonus of cf 55.75 per share after deduction of expenses and commission.[3]

It is surprising to observe how a merchant house such as Hope & Co., with its manifest ties with England, became steadily more involved in the Napoleonic finances. The process is explained in detail in later chapters, but it is perhaps just as well to preview the sequence of events and the manner in which the various transactions fitted together.

The subject of the loan for Portugal was broached even before the partners returned to Amsterdam. After visiting Lisbon, where he successfully concluded the negotiations with the government, Labouchère went to Paris to plead on Portugal's behalf for an extension of the instalment period for the war levy imposed by the French. His representations to the minister of foreign affairs, Talleyrand, finally achieved the desired result.[4]

Early in 1803, while the house was still occupied with the placing of the Portuguese bonds, Hope and Baring assumed responsibility for the financing of the purchase of Louisiana. The payments which Hope was required to make to the French Treasury in this connexion led on the one hand to large-scale purchases in Russia of shipbuilding materials on behalf of the

French navy, and on the other to dealings with the financier and speculator Ouvrard, who in 1804 commenced to tighten his grip on France's finances.

When Ouvrard went to Spain to recover monies owed to France, and while there succeeded in securing a virtual stranglehold on that country's finances also, Hope became involved in the execution of the gigantic plans which he had devised for Spain.[1] If everything had gone as Ouvrard envisaged, the two could have secured a joint monopoly of the import and export trade of all the Spanish colonies on the American continent, and all the gold and silver accumulated in those colonies would have flowed to Europe via channels planned by Hope. Spain could then have met her commitments towards France, Ouvrard could have replaced the staggering edifice of credit which he had erected around the French Treasury with real money, and he and Hope would together have made profits no less colossal than the plan in its entirety.

The failure of the gigantic project is described elsewhere in this book. When Napoleon purged the French financial system early in 1806, and forcefully eliminated Ouvrard and his associates, he spared the Company. This was wise, for late in 1805 it had opened a loan of 10 million guilders on behalf of Spain, the primary purpose of which was to pay that country's 'contribution' to France. As Napoleon had temporarily shelved Ouvrard's American plan *in toto*, this was one of the few ways to obtain money from Spain in the short term.[2]

Admittedly, the French government, after disposing of Ouvrard, demanded the return of the drafts on Mexico which Hope & Co. still held, but after a time Napoleon also realized that the encashment of these could best be entrusted to the Company. In 1807, the operation which Ouvrard had launched was continued, but now with Napoleon as Hope's partner.[3] The French Treasury fared well under the arrangement, for it received in all 10 million piastres or nearly 40 million francs. Three-fifths of this was in the form of colonial produce, which was shipped to European ports in American vessels.[4]

1807 also saw the opening by Hope & Co. of a new Spanish loan. This was of 30 million guilders and, like the previous one, was for the purpose of meeting Spain's financial commitments towards France. The Company, however, took steps to ensure that older Spanish bonds and overdue interest vouchers were as far as possible rendered convertible so that in the event of the loan being fully subscribed, no more than 10 million guilders would be made available in cash. In the event, the subscriptions totalled only 23 million guilders, and of the sum remaining available only 9 million francs flowed into the French coffers.[1]

These various operations on behalf of Napoleon did not escape the notice of his relatives. Elsewhere in the book it is shown how King Louis Napoleon of Holland withheld permission for a 30-million guilder loan for Spain until Hope & Co., in association with four other Amsterdam houses, had succeeded in placing a loan of 40 million for the Kingdom of Holland.[2]

Hardly had this obstacle been surmounted when King Joseph of Naples approached the house. His requirements were modest, a mere 3 million guilders, but the capital market was tight and the loans for Spain and Holland were a long way from being fully subscribed. The solution which emerged involved the house assuming temporary responsibility for a portion of the loan, the balance being furnished by the king's brothers in France and Holland.[3]

With the Neapolitan loan, the limit had been reached. Overtures by the Prussian agent, Niebuhr, to obtain a loan in Amsterdam for the purpose of financing his government's war levy to France met with a refusal from Labouchère. Similar attempts by a number of small German states and by the Kingdom of Italy met with a similar fate.[4]

The foregoing shows how important a role the Amsterdam money market continued to play within the framework of the Napoleonic régime. In many instances, the calls made upon it related to a form of pre-financing of the war levies and contributions imposed by Napoleon on defeated enemies and allies alike. It is particularly interesting to see how, through a combination of circumstances, it fell to the pro-English house of Hope & Co. to play the principal role and, as a result of this, to achieve a more dominant position than ever in Amsterdam.

Just how closely Hope's mercantile and loan activities were interwoven was again demonstrated during the malaise which accompanied the war. Between 1802 and the end of the Napoleonic wars, the Portuguese loan brought more than 280,000 carats of diamonds to Holland, enabling a degree of continuity in the employment of the polishers in Amsterdam to be maintained. Similarly, the brazilwood monopoly, to which reference has been made, kept trade in this article going.

The transactions with Ouvrard, and later with Napoleon, released a flow of colonial produce which was largely directed towards Amsterdam. This current of trade was accelerated by the payments which the United States faced in Holland, and which stemmed from the Louisiana loan and earlier financial commitments.

In the light of these studies, one may pose the question whether the Napoleonic era did in fact result in such catastrophic losses on the part of holders of foreign bonds as is commonly suggested. This is not the place for a detailed investigation of the matter; but of the loans discussed here, only those granted to Spain had ruinous consequences for the bondholders. France and Sweden arbitrarily reduced their debts by two-thirds, but did not abrogate them altogether. Russia and Austria were in arrears in varying degrees, but both ultimately rehabilitated their former debts, thereby reactivating large sums which had been considered lost. Amsterdam's amazing recovery as a loan centre and the amount of capital invested abroad in the decades after 1815 suggest that the losses suffered previously were limited.[1]

We have already referred to the delicate nature of the relationship between a government which desired to float a loan and a middle-class house such as Hope. In the case of Napoleon and his ministers, the relationship was more difficult in some ways and easier in others.

Napoleon's profound dislike of merchants and speculators is revealed in no uncertain terms in the chapter dealing with the Spanish loans. His treatment of Ouvrard shows that he could translate this dislike into deeds. It is thus the more surprising to find him unreservedly displaying respect for Hope & Co. When on a mission to the house, one of his senior officials, who was later to become Baron Louis, was patently given the cold shoulder by Labouchère, yet no hint of a reprisal was forthcoming.[2]

It is obvious that Hope & Co. enjoyed a position of power. They could have allowed the Mexican transaction to fail without fear of action on the part of the French government. There was also the point that the nucleus of the house was situated in England, and was thus beyond the reach of Napoleon. But there were more factors at work. In spite of his dislike of merchants, Napoleon must have possessed respect for the independence of a man like Labouchère and for the financial strength and integrity of a house which had shown itself to be averse to shady deals and unsound financing. His statement to his ministerial council, that Hope would not be tempted by a sum of 40 million francs to furnish false correspondence, was probably embellished by the spokesman, but it will nevertheless have reflected the essence of Napoleon's opinion.[3] The diplomatic missions subsequently undertaken by Labouchère on behalf of both Louis Napoleon and Bonaparte himself support this view.[4]

Hope's relationships with the ministers and senior civil servants who surrounded Napoleon were generally easier than those with similar officials in countries such as Russia and Spain. Despite the handsome titles bestowed upon them by Napoleon, the majority were of middle-class origin and thus did not suffer from the inhibitions which Voûte and, later, Melvil were to encounter in Russia. Labouchère was even on friendly terms with Talleyrand, an old-style aristocrat, though it must be admitted that the latter's flair for monetary matters will certainly have influenced their relationship.[1]

These sound connexions in Paris were of great importance to the house in Amsterdam. Subordinate police officials in Holland observed Hope's actions with the utmost suspicion, and in their reports to Paris they repeatedly urged that the Company's books and correspondence should be investigated.[2] But thanks to the protection which the Company enjoyed in the highest government circles, such an investigation never took place. In this context, it is piquant to read how, in 1812, Labouchère, who was then at Bad Pyrmont, arranged for his letters to England to be carried by extra couriers detailed to travel on behalf of the Duchess of Rovigo, the wife of the French Minister of Police.[3]

Hope's unassailable position engendered ill-feeling, not only in those countries which had to suffer Napoleon's caprices, such as Spain, but also in Holland itself. The radicals who had been present at the birth of the Batavian Republic found it difficult to stomach a situation in which the Anglo-Orangist house in Amsterdam was not only permitted to go its own way unhindered, but even occupied a position of utter supremacy.

Niebuhr, who as agent of the defeated Prussia had gone to Hope to beg for a loan, and who afterwards felt that he had been treated humiliatingly by Labouchère, wrote with scarcely disguised hate of the 'monopolizing, tyrannical supremacy' of the house. The Amsterdam merchant Brants had earlier intimated to Niebuhr that he could obtain a couple of million from other houses, but that for a loan of 20 million he would inevitably end up 'entre les mains du tyran.'[4] This brings us face to face with a cold, haughty trait in Labouchère's character which had played him false during the negotiations with the *Staatsbewind* concerning the Portuguese loan. Niebuhr, too, would not forget Labouchère's treatment of him.

As the Continental System increasingly paralyzed trade to and from the European ports, the commercial importance of the Amsterdam house declined in the eyes of the partners in London. Personal factors also played a role. Henry Hope was nearing seventy years of age and was taking a steadily less active part in the business. John Hope's sons still displayed a complete lack of interest, and John Williams Hope longed more and more to turn his back on Holland and return to England.

In April 1808 John Williams Hope sold the Welgelegen estate, near Haarlem, to King Louis Napoleon for cf 300,000. In Amsterdam, John Dixon, a former partner in Littledale & Dixon of Rotterdam, was engaged in order to strengthen the day-to-day management. It was also arranged that Henry Hope Jr., John Williams Hope's eldest son, should work in the office. In September 1808, John Williams Hope left for England. His wife was to have joined him after travelling via Germany, but halfway through the journey she turned back and joined her lover, Colonel Von Dopff, with whom she had maintained an association for many years.[1]

Nolte describes in his autobiography how Henry Hope favoured a divorce, but was opposed by John Williams Hope out of sensitivity towards the reputation of his benefactor.

The volume of the *grootboeken* and journals reveals the extent to which business decreased after 1808. The Spanish affairs had got completely out of order since the occupation of Spain by French troops in that year. William Gordon Coesvelt, acting as Hope's special agent, made frantic but unsuccessful efforts to find a way of continuing the interest payments.[2] Even earlier than Spain, Portugal had been occupied by the French, and its Court and government had fled to Brazil. Interest and principal payments on the Portuguese loan could henceforth be expected to emanate from Brazil, and it would be far easier to broach these matters from London than from Amsterdam.[3]

In 1810 Henry Hope Jr., having found that office work interested him little, resigned from the Amsterdam house. Dixon suffered a stroke in the same year, from which he died soon afterwards. In an effort to fill the vacancies, power of procuration was given to one of the foreign correspondents in the office, Pierre Firmin Lestapis.

With the annexation of the Kingdom of Holland to France, a new era in the Company's history commenced. Labouchère by now desired to relinquish the reins of day-to-day management, but the ramifications of the Spanish affair and growing difficulties concerning the Russian interest and principal payments prevented him from doing so.

The gradual disintegration of the Amsterdam house was accelerated by the death on 25th February 1811 of Henry Hope, 'attacked by a disorder which baffled all medical skill.'[4]

Labouchère had already planned a journey to England for consultations on the interest and principal due on the Portuguese loan, and his arrival in London was thus timely from the point of view of the future of the Amsterdam house. After ample discussions with the surviving partners, it was decided that Labouchère should retire at the end of the year. He was given full authority to make arrangements with others for the preservation and continuation of the house. It was agreed that he should continue to sign on behalf of the Company in order that confidence in it should not be undermined, but John Hope–as John Williams Hope had called himself since the death of his great benefactor–undertook to indemnify Labouchère against any adverse consequences arising from the use of his signature. To the outside world, Labouchère thus appeared to be still a partner.[1]

As Labouchère proposed to leave for Russia in June 1811, the matter of the day-to-day management in Amsterdam had to be settled without delay. On 15th June, William Gordon Coesvelt, Pierre Firmin Lestapis and Adriaan van der Hoop appended their signatures to an agreement whereby they became managers.[2]

To Labouchère's vexation, John Hope proved to be obsessed with the idea of liquidating Hope & Co. He insisted that the capital remaining in Amsterdam should be realized as quickly as possible and transferred to London. He quarrelled bitterly with his co-partners, Thomas and Henry Philip Hope, on the subject of money, and his conduct was characterized by avarice and morbid suspicion. His relationship with Labouchère was downright bad, and this was undoubtedly among the reasons which led to the latter's retirement. The steady deterioration of John Hope's health might perhaps be put forward as a mitigating factor.

Labouchère was particularly indignant at John Hope's plans to dismiss the entire staff of the Amsterdam office. Amsterdam was a dead city: there was no work to be found, and this meant that men who had given years of their life to the Company would be reduced to begging. In consultation with the managers and the confidential agent, David Berck, it was decided that John Hope's orders should simply be ignored and that the remaining staff should be kept on.[3] The problems of liquidity experienced by the managers by reason of the short financial rein on which they were kept by John Hope are described in the chapter dealing with the Russian loans.[4] In the case of the Portuguese loan, it took repeated appeals and warnings to persuade him to approve the payment of interest.[5]

John Hope died on 12th February 1813. The tragedy of his life was reflected in the indecent haste with which his widow remarried: two months later she became the wife of Baron Von Dopff. John Hope's death accelerated the process of liquidation which had already commenced. Thomas and Henry Hope had no ties whatsoever with the Amsterdam house, and John Hope's widow was only interested in cash. It was only with difficulty that she was prevented from drawing on Henry Hope & Co.

Herr

Amsterdam, 1° Januar 1815.

Wir haben die Ehre Sie zu benachrichtigen daß durch den Tod der Herren HENRI und JOHN HOPE, Chefs unsers Hauses, und in folge des Entschlußes aller Mitglieder dieser geachteten Familie die Kaufmännische Laufbahn zu verlaßen, die Liquidation der alten Geschäfte, vermittelst Uebereinkunft mit dieser Familie, Herrn PETER CESAR LABOUCHERE einzig überlaßen bleibt. Dadurch wird dieser, nachdem er sich vor drey Jahren aus unserm Etablissement zurückgezogen hatte, der unmittelbahre Besitzer desselben.

Die glücklichen Umstände welche die Befreyung Hollands herbeygeführt haben, und die Aussicht günstigerer Zeiten für die Handlung haben uns bestimmt dem Entschluß einer gänzlichen Liquidation des Hauses zu entsagen. Die seit langer Zeit bestehende Freundschaft zwischen unserm Herrn LABOUCHERE und Herrn HIERONIMUS SILLEM, der in der letzten Zeit Chef des alten und geachteten Hauses MATTHIESSEN & SILLEM in Hamburg gewesen ist, hat diesen bewogen sein Interesse mit dem unsrigen zu verbinden. Wir haben demnach das Vergnügen Ihnen anzuzeigen daß wir uns vornehmen von heute an, unter seiner Direction und derjenigen der Herren A. VAN DER HOOP und P. F. LESTAPIS, die schon unsere Geschäfte seit mehr wie drey Jahren leiten, unsere alten Verbindungen mit unsere Freunden wieder mit aller Thätigkeit anzuknüpfen, welche die Umstände zulassen werden. Wir bitten von ihren Unterschriften Nota zu nehmen, so wie von derjenigen unsers Herrn LABOUCHERE, welche hinführo die einzigen seyn werden, indem unser Freund Herr W. G. COESVELT gewünscht hat dem Antheil, den er bisher an der Leitung unsers Hauses genommen, zu entsagen, unbeschadet indessen den Gesinnungen der Freundschaft und Achtung, die ihn seit so langer Zeit mit allen Mitgliedern desselben verbinden.

Wir wünschen daß Sie uns oft Gelegenheit geben mögen Sie zu überführen daß die Zeit uns weder die Mittel unsern Freunden zu dienen benommen, noch unsern Eifer für Ihr Intresse geschwächt hat.

Genehmigen Sie die Versichrung unserer ausgezeichneten Hochachtung.

Unterschrift von P. C. LABOUCHERE Hope & Co.

Unterschrift von HIERONIMUS SILLEM Hope & Co.

Unterschrift von ADRIAN VAN DER HOOP Hope & Co.

Unterschrift von PETER FIRMIN LESTAPIS Hope & Co.

Circular announcing the re-establishment of Hope & Co. in 1815 in advance of the completion and provisional balancing of the accounts. She had from the outset been on bad terms with her cousins, Thomas and Henry Philip, whom she suspected of planning to cheat her.[1]

On 17th July, the two brothers bought out their troublesome relative. She received the capital which her first husband had possessed according to the balance sheet for 1811, less a share of the losses suffered by the firm as a result of the manipulations of a fraudulent bookkeeper at the Amsterdam office. With accrued interest from 1st January 1812 to the day of John Hope's death, she received a sum of 183,509.2.4 pounds sterling.[2]

This action heralded the complete dissolution of the former partnership. On 3rd September 1813 Thomas and Henry Philip Hope transferred everything relating to that partnership to Alexander Baring, and in return each received three promissory notes to a value of 25,000 pounds sterling, payable on 1st September in the years 1816, 1817 and 1818. Baring accepted responsibility for 100,521.4.7 pounds of the payments to Baroness Von Dopff. He thus paid 250,521.4.7 pounds sterling for the two houses, Hope & Co. and Henry Hope & Co., and the freedom to make of these what he wished.[3]

The ideal for which Sir Francis Baring had striven in 1802 had been achieved. But he did not witness the event, for he had died in 1810. In any case, he would probably not have been pleased by the condition of the new acquisition. After all, Hope & Co. was little more than an empty shell, the facade of which could either be left standing or used to front a new building, at the discretion of the new owner.

Although no immediate decision on its future was taken, thoughts of liquidation receded in November 1813, when the French domination of Holland came to an end and trade revived.

For the house itself, things provisionally continued as before. Alexander Baring approved the payment of current interest and principal instalments, but made his decision regarding the future of Hope & Co. dependent upon the decisions which the Congress of Vienna would take regarding the future of Holland.

With its fate hanging in the balance, the house could make only a limited response to Russian requirements for credit to maintain the armies of occupation in western Europe. In spite of going to the limit of its capability, Hope was more than once obliged to bow to the house of Rothschild, which was only too anxious to demonstrate its financial strength to the allies.[4] The role which Hope & Co. had earlier fulfilled in the loan sector was to pass to Rothschild after 1815.

The protocol of 21st June 1814, in which the allied powers consented to the unification of Belgium and Holland, provided Alexander Baring with the certainty which he desired. A circular was sent to Hope & Co.'s correspondents, advising them that, with effect from 1st January 1815, the affairs of the house would be directed by Pierre César Labouchère, Hieronymus Sillem, Adriaan van der Hoop and Pierre Firmin Lestapis. Sillem had been a partner in the house of Matthiessen & Sillem of Hamburg, of which we learned in connexion with the perilous days of 1798. Sillem had visited Russia in 1812, and while there had skilfully represented the interests of the holders of Russian bonds. Labouchère's role in the new management team was in some ways as theoretical as his partnership under the agreement of 1811, for he had stated emphatically that he no longer wished to bear responsibility for daily affairs. His removal to London served to underline this.[1]

Hope & Co. had thus been reborn, though it was not the Hope & Co. which we have come to know through our researches. But the significance which had become attached to the name with the passing of the years was clearly reflected in the considerable sum which Baring was prepared to pay to acquire it.

Around Hope a silence had descended. All the major houses with whom Hope has been compared in our story had disappeared: Clifford and Pels following the crisis of 1772, and Hogguer, De Smeth and Muilman during the difficult first decade of the 19th century.[2]

Amsterdam's position as the principal financial centre in Europe had passed to London, and the new-style house was destined to operate within a narrower framework. The transactions which had been entered upon in the preceding period provided an outline of the areas upon which the efforts of the reborn Hope & Co. would be focussed: Russia and the United States. The family and the firm had gone their separate ways, but the old business principles remained, and so Hope & Co. in its new framework remained what it had been in the old: the leader in its field; a house with a first-class reputation.

BALTIC AFFAIRS

SWEDISH, POLISH AND RUSSIAN LOANS

CHAPTER TWO

SWEDISH PRELUDE

Sweden lost its position of power in the Baltic at the beginning of the 18th century. When in 1687 Charles XII, then fifteen years of age, succeeded his father, Saxony, Poland, Denmark and Russia considered the moment ripe to deprive Sweden of the areas on the other side of the Baltic Sea which it had conquered during the 17th century. In the early stages of the Great Northern War which ensued, the Swedish king achieved major successes, but eventually the sheer expanse of Russia and the superiority of the armies of Czar Peter proved too much for the limited Swedish forces. At the Peace of Nystad, in 1721, the Baltic states and, with them, the hegemony in the Baltic region passed into the hands of Russia, and from then on Russian influence became a permanent feature there. In the 18th century this unpredictable and expansive country was to exert ever-increasing pressure on its neighbours.

In Sweden, the death of Charles XII in 1718 was followed by a reaction among the nobility which nullified the absolutistic reforms introduced by earlier kings. Sweden again became a constitutional monarchy in which the power of the ruler was insignificant in comparison with that of the *riksdag*. In this body, the nobles dominated the representatives of the other three Estates, the clergy, the burghers and the peasants. The nobles, however, soon disintegrated into two fiercely antagonistic factions: 'the Hats' and 'the Caps.' The Hats favoured a strong foreign policy, which they felt could be best achieved by restoring the old ties with France; the Caps were of the opinion that the country's interests would be best served by a policy of cautious neutrality. Soon opinions were similarly divided in the other Estates.

While the country was recovering from the effects of the long war, the urge for peace triumphed; but gradually a mood of belligerence developed. In 1739 the Hats came to power. Their period in office was marked by a number of ill-conceived wars which produced no gains and brought the country to the brink of financial ruin.[1] From 1741 to 1743 Sweden waged war against Russia, with a signal lack of success, and in the Seven Years' War (1756–1763), at the instigation of France, forces operating from Swedish Pomerania undertook a series of pointless and fruitless campaigns against Prussia. The ruling Hats attempted to meet the cost of these military operations by the simple expedient of printing money. A decree issued in 1745, that banknotes would henceforth not be redeemable in coin, caused this paper money to depreciate to only one-third of its face value.[1] Many suffered hardship from the measure, and for some time there were signs that the *riksdag* of 1760–1762 would put an end to the dominion of the Hats. But by skilful manoeuvres, chief among which was the ending in 1762 of the war against Prussia, they managed to save their political skin.[2]

However, no solution had been found to the confusion which surrounded the nation's finances and, to make a critical situation even worse, a number of disasters occurred. In 1762 the agrarian sector suffered a heavy blow in the shape of an epidemic of rinderpest, and in the following year many Swedish business houses were bankrupted by the collapse of the Stock Exchanges in Amsterdam and Hamburg, which resulted partly from Sweden's inability to meet its liabilities.[3] Efforts to obtain a loan abroad failed utterly.

The bill was finally presented to the Hats during the *riksdag* of 1765–66. The Caps had at last secured a majority of support in all Estates, and they demanded an immediate investigation into the country's financial position. The extent of the mismanagement, extravagance and corruption which the investigation revealed was so great that the *riksdag* was obliged to make drastic cuts in expenditure in all fields and to impose heavy taxes, particularly on merchant members of the Hat party, who were accused of complicity. Because of these measures, the assembly went down in history as the 'Reduktion Riksdag.'[4]

During the deliberations of the *riksdag*, the representatives of the four Estates had approached the king with a request that he arrange a foreign loan. A year later, in 1767, this was negotiated, and on 17th November of that year King Adolph Frederick appended his signature to a document in favour of Hope & Co. providing for a ten-year debenture loan of 750,000 Dutch current florins bearing interest at 5%. Two special collateral securities were provided: first, 'the duties levied on the consumption of imported goods and upon mercantile dealings, the revenues from stamp duties, the surplus revenue of the postal service, the tithes and the duties levied upon iron and the appointed fund for the payment of the State's debts'; secondly, Hope received forty promissory notes of 10,000 rixdollars each, issued by the 'Swedish State Treasury' and guaranteed by the Estates. These were to remain in Hope's possession until the final repayment against the loan had been made. It was these notes which imparted the character of a secured loan to this and subsequent transactions, and with this the title *Negotiaties van belening*, or loans on security.

On 25th February 1768, John Hope, bearing the forty notes, appeared before Cornelis van Homrigh, notary, in whose presence these were deposited in a tin box, which was then wrapped in bleached linen and tied round with a red ribbon to which Hope and Van Homrigh attached their personal seals. The two then journeyed to the Amsterdam Town Hall, where the box was handed to the burgomasters. Their seals were impressed upon the package as well, and it was then taken to the Exchange Bank for safe keeping.[1] Apart from the cumbrousness of the procedure, the reader will have observed that the total value of the promissory notes exceeded the sum of the loan by one-third; it may well be that this reflected Sweden's poor credit standing. Be this as it may, such a margin was not incorporated in subsequent loans.

Despite this loan and another negotiated in Genoa, the new Caps administration failed to balance the budget. In an effort to reduce imports, fines were imposed for drinking coffee and wine, and smoking tobacco, but the savage economies and the over-hasty recall of the paper money caused prices to fall, bringing hardship to large sections of the population. Dissatisfaction grew and was intensified by the action of the Caps in ever more openly turning to Russia, where Catherine II was only too eager to interfere in the affairs of her neighbours.[2] The Hats at that time were strongly supported by France. Everywhere voices were heard for a new *riksdag* to be convened, but not until a serious clash had occurred with King Adolph Frederick (who went so far as to abdicate for a week in order to enforce his will) did the Caps consent to call an extraordinary *riksdag* for April 1769. The ensuing election campaign was fought with immense ferocity and amid repeated interference by foreign powers, notably France and Russia, which liberally distributed funds to the parties of their choice. In spite of dire warnings by the Caps that their defeat would open the way for a Russian intervention, the Hats obtained a majority in all four Estates.[3]

Prior to the election the Hats had given a written undertaking to the French envoy to reform the Swedish constitution in an autocratic sense: it was, of course, as much in France's interest that Sweden should be strong as in Russia's interest that the country should remain weak and disunited.[4] But although moderate, the reform proposal was rejected by the *riksdag* in November 1769, after a protracted debate. The French reacted by cutting off all subsidies to the Hats, thereby placing the government in a difficult financial position–the more so since, as of old, public funds were dispensed lavishly. As in the previous *riksdag*, a solution was sought in foreign loans.[1]

Three loans for Sweden were negotiated in the Republic in the year 1770: in March, a loan of cf 1,250,000 at 5% interest by Horneca Hogguer & Co.; in September one of cf 1,250,000 by Bargum, which was subsequently extended by Van den Sandheuvel & Son and Van Orsoy & Son; and in December a further loan of cf 1,000,000 by Hope & Co. and Horneca Hogguer & Co. The last two also bore interest at 5%.[2]

On 21st December 1770, Adrian Hope and Daniel Hogguer, representing their respective firms, appeared before Van Homrigh carrying two debentures issued by the State Treasury, each in the sum of 200,000 rixdollars. This time the bonds were not lodged with the Exchange Bank via the Town Hall, but were placed by Van Homrigh in an iron chest in his office and one of the keys was given to each of the parties.[3]

The principal debenture did not contain a specification of the goods and revenues mortgaged (this was not surprising after the two previous loans), but as an additional guarantee of payment of the interest it was stipulated that: 'a satisfactory quantity of copper shall be supplied to the lenders by way of security.'[4] Because of the importance of its copper mines, Sweden maintained both silver and copper standards; indeed, copper was the security upon which banknotes were issued. Payment in copper, if other means failed, was thus a logical demand.[5]

In February 1771, Adolph Frederick died unexpectedly. At the time of his death, the Crown Prince, Gustav III, was in France. The government there utilized the opportunity to oblige the young ruler by entering into a new treaty which gave him an annual subsidy of 1,500,000 livres. In an effort to counter Russian intrigues, France despatched her best diplomat, De Vergennes, to Stockholm. Gustav III had meanwhile returned to his capital, where he had become involved in the fierce electoral battle for a new *riksdag*. Thanks to Russian bribes, the Caps had achieved considerable success in all but the noble Estate, and again a change of government was threatened. To avert this, the king did his utmost to have a Hat elected as *talman*, or spokesman for the nobility, but since De Vergennes had arrived in Stockholm empty-handed, the king lacked the funds to attain his goal. Without consulting the French envoy, he drew on Horneca Hogguer & Co. for more than 2,000,000 guilders, offering as collateral only the first instalment of the French subsidies, which did not become due until 1st January 1772. With the funds from Horneca, he succeeded in getting his man elected.[1] No mention of these transactions appears in the books of Hope & Co.: in all probability, the partners viewed financing activities of this nature as being too adventurous and too risky.

Despite this initial success on the part of the king, the Caps gained a firmer foothold, and it began to look as if they would succeed in making Gustav's position as insignificant as that of his father. Gradually, the notion of a *coup d'état* commenced to fix itself in the mind of the king, and this was strengthened by the realization that a Cap government would make the country completely dependent upon Russia. But if he was to act at all, he would have to hurry, for the war which Catherine II was waging against the Turks was progressing extremely favourably from the Russian point of view and could well end soon. Admittedly, the Russians were also occupied with the First Partition of Poland, but there, too, things could change rapidly. On 19th August 1772 the king, with the help of a handful of loyal supporters, succeeded in taking his enemies by surprise. Cowed by the display of military power, the *riksdag* adopted a new constitution on the following day.[2] The hegemony of the nobility was at an end, but the rights of the monarch continued to be somewhat limited by, among other things, the budgetary powers vested in the *riksdag*.

In preparing the coup, Gustav had enjoyed the fullhearted support of the French envoy. De Vergennes had gone so far as to promise him 10,000 ducats, but on the eve of the coup the money had still not arrived. At the last minute, a courier arrived bearing 5,000 ducats borrowed from Grill & Co. of Amsterdam against a guarantee from De Vergennes.[3]

The events which took place in Sweden represented a major setback for Catherine II. Russia could expect little from a powerful Sweden closely allied to France. Indeed, even a resumption of the policy of revenge pursued by the Hats seemed probable. Catherine started to prepare for war with Sweden, but setbacks in the Turkish campaign forced her to postpone her plan–not, however, before she had made secret agreements with Denmark for a future attack against Gustav III.[4]

The restoration of peace, albeit somewhat uncertain, provided Gustav with an opportunity to effect all manner of reforms. Apart from the army and the navy, the country's finances again demanded much of his attention. To avert a threat of bankruptcy, the king appointed the skilful and incorruptible Baron Liljencrantz to the presidency of a newly established Department of Finance. The latter's first act was to implement a much needed and greatly overdue reform of the currency. His initial concern was to abandon the dual standard in favour of a single, silver, standard.

Then, when the rixdollar had been devalued by 50%,[1] the old banknotes (which had become worth only one-third of their face value) would have to be replaced by new ones. Lastly, the new banknotes would have to be freely exchangeable for coin. This last step was dependent upon the *Riksens Ständers Banque*, the historic bank of Sweden, obtaining financial support from the government, and this in turn depended upon, among other things, a foreign loan of 1,200,000 rixdollars. In July 1775, in the face of persistent refusal by the governors of the bank to accept the convertibility of notes, out of fear of a run on the bank, the king intervened personally. He commanded the governors to comply, but agreed to postponement of the operation until the beginning of 1777. The interim period provided Liljencrantz with an opportunity to negotiate the loan abroad, to which end he approached Hope and Horneca Fizeaux & Co., the latter the successor to Horneca Hogguer & Co.[2]

On 26th September and 9th October 1775 Henry Hope and Henri Fizeaux attended the offices of Van Homrigh for the enactment of the protocol and registration of debentures provided by Gustav III. The first, in the sum of 2,000,000 guilders, was dated 6th July and the second, of 1.000.000 guilders, 5th September, 1775. The constituent bonds relating to both were dated 1st November 1775, giving the appearance of a single loan.[3]

The fact that, despite the absence of a guarantee by the Estates, the loan bore interest at 4% instead of 5%, and was of more favourable duration, marked a personal triumph by Liljencrantz.[4] The commission due to the negotiators was admittedly the same as for the 1770 loan, i.e. 4½%, but in neither case could this be regarded as high.

The rewards accruing to the negotiators were scrupulously divided. Commissions, interest payments and principal monies, all were shared down to the last penny. If either exceeded his share as a result of payments, or if the sum of the silver coins, mostly piastres, sent to Sweden was less than one-half of the total, the difference was adjusted at the end of every year.[5]

In addition to the reform of the currency, the national economy demanded Liljencrantz's attention. To cover the deficit over 1776, he obtained at the beginning of that year a 4% loan of cf 3,000,000 from the Amsterdam bankers Jan and Carl Hasselgreen. This greatly embarassed Hope and Horneca Fizeaux, who had then just floated their loan on the market, and in a letter despatched to Sweden they expressed their displeasure in no uncertain terms. If Liljencrantz needed more money and desired to increase the loans, they argued, he should have approached them. What would the public reaction be to a new loan so soon after the other, and one obtained from a different source at that? Sweden's credit would inevitably suffer.[1] Liljencrantz's reply was amicable in the extreme, and from the king the bankers received 'the most flattering assurances of the sustained continuation of His protection and His goodwill.' A severance of relations with Hope and Horneca Fizeaux would not have been in the interest of Sweden, which by spreading its loans over several sources avoided undue dependence on any one. Nevertheless, further loans to Sweden by Hope and Horneca Fizeaux were out of the question for the time being.

After 1775 the government of Gustav III began to lose much of its initial popularity. In response to a proposal by Liljencrantz, distilling, in which the peasants had hitherto freely indulged, was decreed a state monopoly. Efforts to lease to private enterprise the distilleries founded on behalf of the Crown failed. The government, in a mood of anger, proceeded to run them, but soon found its efforts sabotaged by large-scale smuggling and the clandestine production of spirit.[2] The measure was extremely unpopular among the people.

For the government, faced with the collapse of this anticipated new source of revenue, the repayments due against the two ten-year loans taken up in 1770 represented a very heavy burden indeed. If a disastrous drain on the Treasury was to be avoided, steps would have to be taken to extend the period of repayment of the existing loans, or to convert them into new ones. Negotiations were started with Hope & Co. and Fizeaux Grand & Co. (since 1779 successors to Horneca Fizeaux & Co.) for a loan to replace the one of cf 1,250,000 entered into with Horneca Hogguer & Co. on 1st March 1770.[3] On 12th November 1779, 'Monsieur de Heidenstam,' Chargé d'Affaires of the Swedish King at the States General of the Seven United Provinces of The Netherlands, signed, on behalf of his sovereign, a contract with Hope and Fizeaux providing for a twelve-year loan of cf 750,000 bearing interest at 4%. The fact that the sum to be repaid by the Swedish government exceeded the newly negotiated loan by cf 500,000 served to reduce Sweden's debt by this amount. The two banking houses received by way of commission 2% of the principal sum, plus a further 6% 'as a gratification for the brokers and *entrepreneurs* concerned in this operation' and to meet all other expenses.[4]

Having dealt with the loan dated 1st March 1770, the Swedish government was faced with the problem of the one-million guilder loan dated 1st December of the same year. Again they succeeded in obtaining a partial novation. On 14th June 1780, Gustav signed the principal debenture for a 15-year loan of cf 750,000 bearing interest at 4%. As had been

Compte de Liquidation entre Messieurs Hope &
L'Emprunt de Trois Millions de Florins Courants

3000 Obligations
450 Employées en Echange des Anciennes
2550 partagées parmoitié,

1275 Obligations ... Soit	f 1275000.–	
Commission	67500.–	f 1207500.–
La moitié des fraix		10531. 9.–
		f 1218031. 9.–
Payements par HornECA Fizeaux & Comp.		
Traites	875000.–	
Envoys de Piastres	284926. 9.–	1159926. 9.–
La moitié des 6 Mois d'Interets & de La Commission		30600.–
Idem du Solde de f 1007.13.		503.16.8
Fraix Relatifs à cet Emprunt, payés par Horneca Fizeaux & Comp: Suivant la Notte		12451. 4.–
		1203481. 9. 8
à Payer à Messieurs Hope & Comp. pour la demi des f 29099.19. qu'ils ont payés plus que Horneca Fizeaux & Comp		14549. 19. 8
		f 1218031. 9.–

aprouvé Amsterdam le 19 Sep

Horneca Fizeau

[...]Comp: & Horneca Fizeaux & Comp: relativement, á
[...]d'Hollande, pour la Suede, en Novembre 1775 /.

Payements faits par Messieurs Hope & Comp			
Traittes	f 875000.–.–		
Envoys de Piastres	287053. 8.–		f 1162053. 8.–
La Moitie des 6 Mois d'Interets & de la Commission			30600.–.–
Idem ... du Solde ... de f 1007. 13			503.16.8
21 Obligations fourni en échange des Anciennes pour Completter les 471 passées dans le Compte de l'Emprunt		f 21000.–.–	
Interets de 25 Mois sur f 471000: – à 1 p%cent l'An		9812.10.–	30812.10.–
Fraix Relatifs à cet Emprunt payés par Mr Hope & Comp, = Suivant la Notte			f 8611.14.–
			f 1232581. 8.8
deduire			
Pour autant que Horneca Fizeaux & Comp: payent à = Messieurs Hope & Comp le 19 Septembre 1776			14549.19.8
			f 1218031. 9.–

[...]tembre 1776 –

[...]& Comp

Annual settlement between Hope & Co. and Horneca Fizeaux & Co. relating to the Swedish loan of November 1775 the case with the loan of 1st March 1780, bonds relating to the original loan could be exchanged for new bonds; in addition, the holders would receive priority. Any surplus remaining when the public subscription closed would, as usual, accrue to the *entrepreneurs*.[1]

The rate of interest on the new loans was 4%, compared with 5% on those repaid, so that the novation in fact amounted to conversion. Doubtless encouraged by this reduction, the Swedish government decided to repay the loan obtained from Bargum, Van den Sandheuvel & Son and Van Orsoy & Son. Admittedly, this had been entered into for a period of twenty years, but the government had the right to commence repayment after ten years. Conversion into a 4% loan would save the Swedish Treasury 10%, or cf 125,000.[2] At the end of November or early in December, the Swedish envoy signed a contract with Hope and Fizeaux providing for a fifteen-year loan of cf 1,750,000 at 4% interest, commencing on 1st December 1780. In addition to the sum of the repayment, a further cf 500,000 was placed at the disposal of the Swedish government to cover current requirements. Probably as a result of the rapid succession of loans to Sweden, among other factors, Hope and Fizeaux stipulated that they should be free to furnish the monies at a moment 'which is most convenient to us.' In this case, the question of an obligatory period for the repayment of the old loan did not arise. Apart from economic considerations, others of a political nature will undoubtedly have played a role in the cautious wording of the contract as this concerned time. After all, the quarrels between the Patriots and those in the Republic who stood on the side of the prince had a bearing on foreign policy. In the conflict which broke out between England and France concerning the American War of Independence, the Patriots were on the side of the French, while the prince's supporters were in favour of the English. Spearheaded by Amsterdam, the pro-Patriot towns in Holland openly sought a conflict with England, and in 1780 war became almost inevitable. This perhaps explains partly the high rates of commission paid to the negotiators, rates which rose even higher during 1780. In the period November 1779 to early December 1780 these increased from 8% to 9½%.

Just how great was the effect of political developments is shown in an addendum to the contract concluded at the end of November: 'This Contract suspended in consequence of the Rupture between Great Britain and the States General.' On 20th December 1780 England put an end to the uncertainty by declaring war on the Republic. The proposed conversion having thus been rendered impossible, the negotiators limited themselves to furnishing the cf 500,000 for Sweden's immediate needs. On 4th February 1781 a new contract was signed: of the half million guilders, 50% was to be made available immediately, the balance becoming due only after the loan had been floated. The remaining conditions were identical to those of the suspended loan.[1]

It was not until 1782 that Hope and Fizeaux were able to achieve the postponed repayment of the Bargum loan. In the contract entered into with the Swedish envoy on 7th April of that year, they undertook to arrange a loan of cf 1,250,000 by 1st June, the date on which repayment of the loan became due. The *entrepreneurs* were given until mid-June to complete their part, which meant that, if the worst came to the worst, the issuing house would be obliged to advance the principal sum for two weeks. Of this sum, Hope had in any case contracted to furnish cf 400,000, and Fizeaux cf 150,000.[2]

In 1783, bellicose plans on the part of Gustav III necessitated fresh foreign loans to Sweden. Early in that year the king seriously contemplated precipitating a war with his old enemy, Denmark, once Russia became embroiled with the Turks. This, however, did not come about immediately, and it was finally decided to postpone the Danish war until the following year. Liljencrantz, who was the last to be informed of the king's plans, received instructions to obtain the funds necessary to increase the country's armament.[3] In September 1783 King Gustav left Sweden for a political tour of southern and western Europe. Before departing, however, he signed the principal debenture for a new loan from Hope and Fizeaux, this time one of cf 1,500,000 for fifteen years and bearing interest at 5%.[4]

Liljencrantz had succeeded once more and, apart from the higher rate of interest, on terms which were very favourable to Sweden. The contract with Hope and Fizeaux, which was dated 30th September 1783, gave them only 4% commission, compared with 7% on the previous loan, but against this the contracting houses committed themselves only to achieve the completion of the negotiation at the earliest possible moment. Thus, no fixed period for payment was laid down, nor was any guarantee of the success of the loan given.[5] The *entrepreneurs*' commission took the form of '99 per cent free money,' which implied a profit of 1% if the bonds were taken up at par. The *entrepreneurs*, like the issuing houses, were not bound by time limits and were free to accept the bonds 'at the most convenient time or times.' They were also free to accept and subscribe for such additional sums as they might desire, while it was stipulated that the commission paid to brokers and third parties should not exceed $\frac{1}{4}$%.[6] Of the principal sum, the *entrepreneurs* accepted responsibility for no more than one-third–a remarkably small proportion. Volkmar and Ten Kate & Berck, the brokers, jointly undertook to provide half the sum, but it may be assumed that they were acting for principals who did not wish to be named. Hope finally subscribed just over one-sixth.[1]

The terms on which this loan was negotiated reveal a degree of uncertainty and a lack of faith in the prospects for an early placing. The heavy blows dealt to the Dutch merchantmen and to the nation's trade by the English fleet almost certainly contributed to this. Who the brokers' principals were, is not clear; perhaps the issuing houses (or the Swedish government) attempted thus to camouflage a fiasco.

The eighth loan to Sweden, at the end of 1784, was arranged only after many difficulties had been overcome. The principal debenture, for cf 2,000,000 at $4\frac{1}{2}\%$ interest, had already been issued in the name of Hope and Fizeaux when Liljencrantz suddenly demanded that another Amsterdam house (probably Hasselgreen) should be admitted to the consortium.[2] The house concerned had independently offered its services to Liljencrantz, and the minister, who was very well disposed towards Hasselgreen, was anxious to reward the initiative.[3] Hope and Fizeaux, however, stood firm and ultimately got their way. On 25th December a contract was signed with the Swedish envoy, but only for half the sum stipulated in the principal debenture. In correspondence with Liljencrantz, both houses had earlier drawn attention to the thorny situation in which the Republic was placed and which formed an obstacle to the floating of the loan. They were in fact referring to the threatening attitude of Emperor Joseph II of Austria who, as lord of the Southern Netherlands, was demanding the opening of the Scheldt estuary and was prepared to use force if necessary to achieve this. In October 1784 hostilities had broken out near Saeftinge, on the Scheldt.[4]

It was arranged that the one million guilders covered by the contract would be available to Liljencrantz from January up to and including April 1785, by way of 70-day drafts, but Hope and Fizeaux were unwilling to commit themselves in respect of the second million and so the success of the loan as a whole was at the risk of the Swedish king, 'without which reservation we are unable to take this upon us under the present circumstances.'[5] Each of the two houses received 6% commission for the services rendered. Because the contract was not in accordance with the original plan, the royal approval had to be obtained; only when this had been received could the contract with the *entrepreneurs* be signed. The agreement of 28th January was so worded as to suggest that Hope and Fizeaux had undertaken to furnish the floating million, so that responsibility for the 'firmly' contracted million devolved upon the *entrepreneurs*, albeit with the proviso that public subscriptions would be deducted pro rata from the sum of the loan.[1] The terms provided for the bonds to be taken up and paid for within six months of the closing of the period for public subscriptions, 'subject to the payment of Interest up to the time of taking up, at 4 per cent per annum.'[2] No mention was made of the fact that the interest on the bonds up to the moment of taking up would accrue to the issuing houses, who could thereby obtain an interest bonus of ½% in addition to their commission.[3]

On 3rd February–less than a week after the signing of the contract–the *entrepreneurs* empowered the brokers, Volkmar and Ten Kate & Berck, to subscribe on their behalf to the lists held by Hope & Co. and Henri Fizeaux & Co. 'on the same conditions as all other persons, thus benefiting from a *douceur* of ½% and with the obligation to take up forthwith half the sums accepted by us in the capacity of Entrepreneurs, this on condition that the half thus subscribed shall immediately go to reduce our commitment.'[4]

Thus, for a bonus of ½% the *entrepreneurs* were willing to make immediate payment for half their shares, a fact which pointed to an unexpected response to the public subscription. Now, Hope and Fizeaux were assured of cf 500,000 at short notice.[5] Soon a start was made with raising the second million, though this proceeded more slowly than the first. On 9th April the two houses requested Liljencrantz to spread his drawings over a somewhat longer period: drafts of cf 250,000 monthly, commencing on 1st May, would be most convenient.[6]

On further consideration it appeared unwise to allow Liljencrantz to draw on the second million. The first, cf 1,000,000, tranche of the 1775 loan became due for repayment on 1st November 1785; it would thus be folly to allow him to draw a million guilders which he would have to repay to Hope and Fizeaux shortly afterwards.[7] The Swedish minister agreed to the proposed amendment.

The effect of this repayment, however, was to deprive Liljencrantz of the second million, thus leaving a gap which had to be filled by other means. In a letter dated 18th August, the minister advised Hope and Fizeaux that the house of De Weduwe Jean & Martin Smets of Antwerp had offered to negotiate a loan of cf 2,000,000 at 4½% interest. Whether this offer was solicited or not, is not known, but it is clear that the notification of it was designed to goad the Amsterdam houses into action.[8] From the Swedish point of view the result was satisfactory, for early in October Hope and Fizeaux offered to open a new transaction on or about 1st February and formally committed themselves to furnishing cf 1,000,000. As the *entrepreneurs* had not finalized the placing of the previous loan, the new one could not be launched earlier.[1] They advised strongly against arranging a loan in Antwerp, 'not only because there is no certainty that it would be a complete success, but also because it will have a highly adverse effect upon our investors, who would certainly not display any interest in it and who would perhaps not look with favour upon any fresh negotiations which the Court might be contemplating.'[2]

With the abandoning by Joseph II of his plans for the opening of the Scheldt, and his acceptance of an offer of compensation, the investment climate in Amsterdam recovered considerably.[3] In the new situation, Hope and Fizeaux felt justified in offering to guarantee not one, but one and a half million guilders, in addition to which they undertook to furnish the Swedish government with the proceeds of the loan before 10th June 1786. As with the previous loan, they were allowed 6% commission.[4]

Even before the contract with the Swedish king was signed, an agreement was entered into with the *entrepreneurs*. As in 1783, their share was limited to one-third of the principal sum, but it is probable that in this instance the issuing houses did not wish to assign them any more. The contracted shares had to be taken up and paid for by 1st May, and interest on the bonds from 1st February accrued to the issuing houses. The *entrepreneurs* received 1% for their services.[5]

Faith in Sweden's credit had played a major role in the successful negotiation of loans for that country. This faith, in turn, was allied to the great personal prestige enjoyed by Liljencrantz in financial circles. But his days as a minister were numbered. Gustav III was moving steadily towards absolutism, in which there was no place for independent ministers. Liljencrantz's sermons against the extravagances of the Court and his pleas for economy so incensed the monarch that he had Liljencrantz 'promoted' to the Senate. He was succeeded at the end of 1786 by Baron Erik Ruuth, who at the time of the appointment was a protégé of circles well disposed towards the king, and who exercised only nominal authority: before accepting the post, he requested–and obtained–an undertaking from the king that he would not be held responsible for the uses to which the monies which passed through his ministerial hands would be put.[6]

This adverse development did not remain hidden from Hope. A correspondent in Gothenburg kept Hope informed of developments throughout 1786. The man was clearly in great fear of being identified, for he went so far as to erase the place name 'Gothenburg' from his notepaper. In that year the king, partly at Liljencrantz's insistence, summoned a *riksdag* to decide, among other things, upon a number of tax proposals. To the amazement of the royal advisers, opponents of the king secured an electoral majority in three of the four Estates and proceeded to torpedo practically all the proposals. Symbolically, the proposed taxes were all reduced by 1%–a reminder to the king that the *riksdag* held the purse-strings.[1]

According to Hope's correspondent–who is identified in later correspondence as Jacob Andersson–the Estates, in their investigation into the State's finances, ignored the loans obtained abroad on the pretext that the responsibility for these rested solely with the king and that they were nothing to do with the national debt.[2] This did not imply that the Estates were opposed to the repayment of the debts, but rather was a hint to the outside world not to heed future loan proposals from the king. The proceeds of these loans had after all gone to finance theatrical displays which in the eyes of the people of poor, remote Sweden were unnecessary.[3] The nation would thus meet its obligations–not out of love for the king, but only to protect its credit abroad. According to Andersson, Ruuth was a puppet operated from behind the scenes by his father-in-law, Wahrendorff, a Stockholm merchant and a large-scale speculator who had been involved in many an obscure affair.[4]

The commercial transactions undertaken for the Swedish Crown, into which the two Amsterdam houses were drawn by Ruuth, were of the normal type. In 1787 the Amsterdam house of Benjamin Cohen & Son had purchased a consignment of tobacco on behalf of the Swedish Crown and had stored this in its own warehouse. 10,000 or so 'paniers,' or baskets, of the tobacco were sold, via an intermediary in Paris, to the *Fermiers Généraux*, the tax farmers in France, who also controlled the tobacco monopoly, an important and growing source of their income.[5] In June 1787 Hope entered into negotiations with H. Coecq & Son, the Amsterdam agents of the *Fermiers Généraux*, for the sale of the remainder of the stock held by Cohen.[6] At that time, trade in Amsterdam suffered severely as a result of the quarrels between the Patriots and the prince's supporters, which in late May of that year led to a complete civil war. As a result, a long time elapsed before the brokers acting on behalf of Coecq visited Cohen's warehouse to inspect the consignment.[7] In the meantime, a letter arrived from Ruuth containing instructions to sell the tobacco by public auction on 31st July and to advertise the sale in national and foreign newspapers.[8]

With great reluctance, the partners in Hope & Co. set about arranging the auction. Because, in their view, it could serve no useful purpose under the prevailing conditions, they urgently appealed to Ruuth to be allowed to act as circumstances demanded. The confusion reached its zenith a week later with the arrival of a letter from Ruuth stating that Ferdinand Grand of Paris, a brother of the erstwhile partner in the house of Fizeaux, had been empowered to offer the whole consignment to the *Fermiers Généraux* for cf 250,000, and instructing Hope to come to an arrangement with him.[1]

Upon receipt of this information, the partners immediately despatched a letter to Grand, asking how his negotiations were progressing. They meanwhile suspended their discussions with Coecq. The Swedish minister was advised that there could be no question of advertising the sale until such time as a reply was received from Paris. If the effort there failed, it would be necessary to recommence negotiations with Coecq, and the latter would be the more reticent if the plan were to be brought to the notice of the public in advance.[2]

July came and still Coecq was without definite information from the *Fermiers*. Grand maintained a complete silence. Hope expressed to Ruuth a suspicion that the *Fermiers* might well keep everyone waiting until it was too late in the season to sell the tobacco elsewhere, and thus be in a position to dictate their own price.[3] To meet the minister's wishes, steps were taken to arrange a public auction for 22nd August, but the partners repeatedly advised Ruuth to adopt another course. The prevailing circumstances, both political and commercial, gave grounds for believing that the sale would go badly; a consignment of this size, moreover, would deter buyers and this was bound to be reflected in the price. The price limits set by Ruuth were decidedly too high and would have to be revised. Why on earth did the minister not accept Cohen's offer to purchase the whole consignment for cf 200,000? Indeed, Cohen had offered to pay cf 220,000 on certain conditions, namely that he should be allowed to import the tobacco into Swedish ports in lots of fifty to a hundred thousand pounds; to pay import duty on half the imported quantity six months later and on the remainder a year later; and that if there was no market for it in Sweden, that he should be free to ship it abroad again without liability for export tax.[4]

In mid-August Hope received Ruuth's approval of this arrangement, whereupon the sale was negotiated. Cohen was to buy more than a million and a half pounds of tobacco for cf 220,000, payment to be made in cash within six weeks without any discount or deduction for warehousing. Ruuth, for his part, acceded to the import and re-export facilities requested. As a portion of the tobacco had to be excluded on grounds of age or incompatibility with Swedish tastes, Cohen secured the right to replace it with an equal weight of other tobacco. Thus, after many obstacles, the transaction was completed. Hope confessed – not without exaggeration – to Ruuth: 'Of all the operations which we have undertaken, none has brought us so many difficulties and so much sorrow.'[1]

Although the entire transaction was of a commercial nature and was conducted by Hope, it was considered to form part of the loan affairs managed jointly by Hope and Fizeaux. Accordingly, the commission, which amounted to cf 45,096.5.0, was divided equally between the two houses and added to the account with the Swedish Crown.[2]

Despite all the difficulties concerned with the tobacco, the loans were not lost sight of. On 23rd June 1787 Hope and Fizeaux warned Ruuth that the second million guilders of the 1775 loan was due for repayment on 1st November, and that steps should be taken without delay. If the minister wished to prolong the tranche, the two houses should be informed of the fact as soon as possible.[3] When Ruuth reported that the king desired a fresh loan of 1–1¼ million guilders, he was informed that the *entrepreneurs* had rejected the request on the grounds that so small a sum, in addition to the repayment due, would create an adverse impression 'in view of its modest proportions.' In spite of the 'ingratitude of the political situation of this country, which has a dominant influence on trade, especially at a time when the Stock Exchange is experiencing failures which add to the uneasiness and lack of confidence,' the Amsterdam houses favoured increasing the loan to 1,500,000 guilders. With the surplus available after 1st November, it would then be possible to repay to Jan and Carl Hasselgreen the cf 500,000 which the Swedish Court had caused to be advertised for 1st February 1788, 'which will enable us also to reconcile the facilities which are required with the wishes of His Majesty.'[4]

In the opinion of Hope and Fizeaux, what was needed was a loan of 1,500,000 guilders at 4% interest, one half being repayable after twelve years and the balance after fifteen years, in both cases calculated from 1st November 1787. On that date, however, the two houses would be required to furnish only cf 1,000,000 to cover the repayment of the second tranche, while the remaining cf 500,000 would not become due until 1st February 1788. The interest due on the balance over the three-month period would accrue to the negotiators, by whom it was regarded as no more than 'a reasonable incentive in the circumstances existing at the present time.' The king was not disposed to grant an increase in the commission of 6%, and the issuing houses accepted the position even though, in their eyes, this was a mediocre recompense 'in view of the $4\frac{1}{2}\%$ interest which the king then paid, whereas it costs him only 4% today.'[1]

The loan in its entirety was made subject to the right of cancellation 'in the event of the Sovereign imposing a ban on foreign loans in the meantime.' It was unlikely that such a ban would be imposed by Stadholder William V, 'though perhaps appropriate, in the light of the adverse state of the political and financial affairs of this country.' Just how seriously we should take the latter statement is not clear; possibly the houses, for tactical reasons, wished to appear to Ruuth to be disinterested.[2]

Under the agreement with the *entrepreneurs* of 30th July 1787, holders of redeemable bonds were accorded priority until 1st October; the portion thus subscribed would be deducted, pro rata, from the shares taken by the *entrepreneurs*. These would assume responsibility for the remainder of the loan upon payment in cash in the months of November and December, paying to the issuing houses interest from 1st November until the date of taking up their shares. The *entrepreneurs* received a commission of $1\frac{1}{2}\%$, less a $\frac{1}{4}\%$ 'douceur' for the brokers, 'who will arrange for the conversion of redeemable bonds or for subscriptions, these to be paid in cash.'[3] It was further stipulated that cash subscriptions would be limited to a total of half a million guilders up to 1st October, 'and remain open until 31st October for the Balance of the Negotiation, then being finally closed, unless this Negotiation be previously fully subscribed by the Entrepreneurs or other Persons.' Hope and Fizeaux were parties to the contract, jointly accepting responsibility for two-thirds of the principal sum. As in 1786, this high proportion reflected optimism on the part of the issuing houses rather than pessimism among the *entrepreneurs* (it was the latter who had advised increasing the loan to one and a half million and, with a loan which in effect served to postpone two repayments, the risks were comparatively small).

A month after the 'final closure' on 31st October, Hope wrote to Ruuth expressing indignation concerning rumours that the house of Jan and Carl Hasselgreen was about to float a one-million guilder loan for Sweden and, moreover, on terms very favourable to the *entrepreneurs*. The tenor of the reproach was the same as in 1776: why a new loan so soon, from another house and while Hope and Fizeaux still held the greater part of their bonds? Hope and Fizeaux had made it known that the cf 500,000 remaining after the repayment on 1st November would be used to repay a debt to Hasselgreen on 1st February of the following year. It must be clear to the minister, they argued, that any other transaction in this respect could only prejudice the credit of the Crown.[4]

On this note of discord (it is questionable whether we would be justified in saying 'as a result of this discord'), Hope's activities on behalf of the Swedish Crown came to an end. Dissatisfaction with Ruuth's conduct was not in itself sufficient to cause the severance, for, as we have seen, clashes of this nature had occurred previously, but these had been settled. Hope's partner in the Swedish transactions–who since 1st January 1788, had borne the name Hogguer Grand & Co.–did not attach permanent consequences to the affair, and in fact issued further loans for Sweden in 1789, 1790 and 1797.[1]

The true cause of the breach with Sweden must rather be viewed against the background of the commencement of loan negotiations for Russia. On 5th December 1787 Hope & Co. entered into a contract for a loan of cf 3,000,000 to Russia; their partners were the same group of *entrepreneurs* with whom the Swedish loans had been arranged. A second contract for a similar sum was signed on 10th December. With this operation, Hope thus competed directly with its own and Hasselgreen's negotiations for Sweden. And the competition was the more serious by reason of the fact that the Russian loan bore interest at $4\frac{1}{2}\%$ compared with 4% for the two loans to Sweden. In a letter to Ruuth dated 5th January 1788, Hope reported that the Swedish bonds were unsaleable in Amsterdam and Antwerp without sacrifices.[2] They maintained that this was a consequence of Ruuth's dealings with Hasselgreen, but it is obvious that the true cause lay in the higher interest on the Russian loan.

Any prospect which Hope may have entertained of resuming the Swedish negotiations evaporated with the launching by Gustav III of the long-prepared war against Russia in the summer of 1788. We shall not concern ourselves here with the progress of this conflict. After the peace, in 1790, Hope was too much occupied with Russian loans to devote any attention to Sweden.[3]

Looking back on the initial series of loans floated by Hope on behalf of a foreign power, one is moved to enquire why the partners left the Swedish transactions to Hogguer Grand & Co. and proceeded to do business with Russia? The surviving correspondence in the Hope archives does not provide the answer, so that we must be content with a number of assumptions.

Firstly, confidence in Sweden's creditworthiness will have been weakened by the dismissal of Liljencrantz at the end of 1786 and by the comparatively unfavourable information concerning his successor. Increasing opposition to King Gustav III, both in the *riksdag* and beyond, may have played a role insofar as it created uncertainty regarding the approval by that body of fresh loans.

The desire on the part of Hope to act alone in the issuing of loans will also have been a factor in the shift to Russia. With its extensive experience and its financial strength, the firm felt confident to undertake loan negotiations without a partner. With the Swedish loans, Hope had virtually no alternative to continuing with Hogguer Grand & Co. in view of the latter's excellent relations with both the Swedish and French Courts. Later correspondence reveals that the partners in Hope & Co. were not impressed by Hogguer's business methods, but to what degree they were influenced by this is not clear.

It is also conceivable that the partners felt uneasy about the outcome of the clash between Sweden and Russia, the threat of which had long existed. In the Republic itself, the conflict between the Patriots and the supporters of the prince was settled, in favour of the latter, by the intervention of the Prussian army. This development, however, placed the Netherlands in the position of a protectorate of Prussia and England. Would Sweden, poor in terms of population and internally just as divided as the Republic, not face a similar fate if she went to war with Russia?

As the influential position of the Republic declined, it became increasingly important to the capitalists in Holland to find a safe investment for their money, i.e. in countries which could not be swept off the map by a single war and with governments possessing sufficient authority to justify a reasonable expectation that they would honour their commitments.

The extent to which Russia met these requirements is revealed in the ensuing chapters.

CHAPTER THREE

MONEY FOR THE TURKISH WAR

The accession to the throne of Empress Catherine II of Russia in 1762 heralded a resumption of the vigorous territorial expansion which had been set in train during the reign of Czar Peter the Great. The finances of the economically underdeveloped country, however, were inadequate for the waging of lengthy wars, and when, in 1768, Russian intervention in the chaotic domestic situation in Poland led to a conflict with Turkey, the empress found herself in an extremely embarrassing position. The issue of paper money in the form of *assignats*, for which purpose the Assignat Bank was founded in 1768, afforded a certain respite.[1] In addition, Catherine succeeded during the Turkish War in obtaining a number of loans in the Republic of the Seven United Provinces through the intermediacy of the house of Raymond and Theodore de Smeth of Amsterdam. These loans carried interest at 5%.[2]

The treaty of Kutchuk Kainardji in 1774 admittedly gave Russia little territorial gain, but this fact did not deter Catherine in her far-reaching plans in regard to the Turkish Empire. In 1782 she entered into an alliance with Emperor Joseph II of Austria, the aim of which was the division of European Turkey between the two nations. Although the plan provisionally remained on paper the theme of Catherine's policy was clear to see. The loans negotiated with De Smeth in 1781 and 1782–three and a half million guilders at 4½% and five and a half million guilders at 4%, respectively–were said to be required not for purposes of war, but for the colonization of the areas wrested from the Turks and for reform of the administration.[3]

It was not until 1787 that Catherine felt strong enough to embark on the war against Turkey. The latest series of loans, which commenced to become available in 1788, were not, however, in the hands of De Smeth, but of Hope & Co. There was no obvious reason for a change of intermediary, and the fact that one took place merits closer examination. As we have already seen, Hope, in company with another house, had regularly negotiated loans for Sweden since 1768, and relations between Sweden and Russia had long been strained.[4] Furthermore, the firm had severely curtailed its trading interests in Russia in the years prior to 1787 on account of the substantial losses suffered there. In April 1787 Robert Voûte wrote to Hope: 'You told me on the last occasion that Russia had proved fatal for your house, and that this was the reason why your house had ceased to work there.'[1] The *grootboeken* for the years prior to 1787 show that while Voûte exaggerated somewhat, the accounts of the Russian houses which dealt with Hope displayed little activity.[2] Thus, Hope's entry into the area of the Russian state finances stemmed not from a close involvement with the Russian economy, but solely from a rapid, commercial coup which in psychological terms was cleverly prepared. In 1784 Richard Sutherland, with the support of Catherine's powerful favourite, Potemkin, was appointed to the post of Court Banker. Opposition to the appointment in certain circles remained, and during Potemkin's protracted absence from the capital while preparing for the war against the Turks, the intrigues against Sutherland grew.[3] The efforts of Sutherland's enemies to blacken his name among his correspondents abroad and to cast doubts as to his solidity were so successful that in the spring of 1787 De Smeth, Blaauw & Wilkieson and Pye Rich & Co., all of Amsterdam, declined to accept his drafts.[4] His discredit in Amsterdam quickly spread to other centres and threatened to completely undermine his position as Court Banker. At this critical juncture, Henry Hope acted: he accepted *supra protest* the disputed drafts from Richard Sutherland and his brother Alexander Henry in London, and made substantial credits available to the former through his own house.

The relationship between Hope & Co. and the extremely grateful Sutherland rapidly grew in importance. From a sum of cf 78.4.0, which stood unchanged from 1778 to 1787, the account between the two houses rose in the brief period June–August 1787 to cf 715,565.8.0, which sum related solely to the draft transactions.[5] In the trading sector, connexions were established with the firm of Sutherlands & Bock, in which the Court Banker's commercial interests were vested. The firm acted as intermediary for the purchase of Russian iron and sailcloth, and was commissioned by Hope to buy up cochineal, in which large-scale speculation, spearheaded by Robert Voûte,[6] was then taking place. No clear demarcation between banking and mercantile dealings was maintained. As early as 1788, the proceeds of sales to Hope of hemp, iron, ships timber and linen were offset against Sutherland's account as Court Banker, and similar adjustments appear in the records for later years. With these mercantile transactions, which were undoubtedly undertaken on instructions from the Russian government, Sutherland attempted to reduce the outflow of money, and thus to shore up the rate of exchange.[7]

The Russo-Turkish war which finally came in August 1787 brought a greater need for foreign money, and this fact inspired Henry Hope to undertake a detailed examination of Russia's financial position. He attributed the fall in the rate of exchange (which Sutherland had sought to prevent) to the high rate of expenditure by the Court and to the decline in Russian exports to England. This decline he in turn ascribed to the suspension of the 1734 trade treaty between the two countries. Hope saw no prospect of an early recovery of the rate of exchange, first because the war would impose an additional burden on the already inadequate sources of aid and secondly because, in the war situation, the requirements from abroad would increase still further. It was therefore imperative that Russia should obtain, at an early date, 'des retours en dehors'–and a loan in Amsterdam offered the best solution. After all, 'this is the obvious place in which to deposit your funds to meet needs in various parts of Europe.' This would apply particularly to Italy, at least if, as during the previous war with Turkey, the Russian Court despatched a squadron to the Mediterranean. Hope advised the Russians to start by negotiating a loan of 1–1½ million guilders with a target date of February or March 1788 and to repeat this if and when circumstances demanded. The timing of Hope's letter, 9th October 1787, was not very favourable, 'on account of the disturbances which have long ravaged our country, interrupting trade and preventing the circulation of money.'[1] This was a reference to the Patriot disturbances in the Republic (which, in fact, ended on the following day with the complete capitulation of the Patriots in Amsterdam to the Prussian troops).[2] If the situation in Amsterdam shortly returned to normal, and if the Russian armies achieved success against the Turks–'for the credit of a country depends largely upon its success, and, conversely, its success depends upon its credit'–then Hope was certain of being able gradually to float the loan on the market. In consequence of the Turkish war, the last Russian loan from De Smeth, at 4½%, had fallen below par and a further drop was to be expected when news of an extension of the Russian loans was circulated in the Republic. At the outbreak of the previous Russo-Turkish War, the Russian Court had been paying 5% interest on the loans from De Smeth, and substantial discounts had been granted to the *entrepreneurs*; Hope was anxious to limit the interest to 4½% with the aid of bonuses, *douceurs sous mains* or interest facilities.[3]

Hope stressed–not only to Sutherland, but also to third parties–that the house which bore his name had not sought business with the Court Banker; it had even turned Sutherland down after his appointment because, under his predecessor, such business had been conducted with another firm (i.e. De Smeth), so that Hope, 'on grounds of delicacy,' preferred not to interfere. If the Court had at any time changed its policy in this respect, however, he would not have hesitated to undertake the business. Of the acceptance by Hope of Sutherland's drafts, which preceded the new relationship and in which the initiative indisputably came from Hope, there was no mention.[1]

As far as the cochineal affair was concerned, we know that Henry Hope's pessimism regarding the economic circumstances in the Republic at that time was more than an attempt to temper over-sanguine expectations. The signal success of the first loan was the more surprising by reason of the gloomy atmosphere in which it was launched. On 5th December 1787, the day after the arrival of a letter in which the Committee for Foreign Loans in St. Petersburg gave its approval for the negotiation of a loan of 1,500,000 guilders, a contract was arranged with the *entrepreneurs* for a loan of 3,000,000 guilders–twice the sum which Henry Hope had envisaged.[2] The list of subscriptions relating to the contract can be divided into two distinct parts, each of one and a half million. An obvious conclusion is that the brokers had initially proceeded on the basis of a loan of 1,500,000 guilders but that during their soundings the interest on the part of the *entrepreneurs* had proved so great that the sum had immediately been doubled. Of the twenty *entrepreneurs* who subscribed to the first half of the contract, only five applied for a share in the second half, of which their total share was just over a quarter; Hope accepted responsibility for one-half, and the balance was shared among houses outside Amsterdam which had unsuccessfully applied for a share in the first half.[3]

The final bombshell came on 10th December, when a contract for a further loan of 3,000,000 guilders was negotiated with the *entrepreneurs*. This was for twelve years, as against ten for the previous one, but both commenced on the same date, 1st February 1788. To avoid the two becoming confused, and also to give the *entrepreneurs* time to place their initial portion on the market, it was decided that the public subscription to the later loan would not open until 15th January 1788. The *entrepreneurs* were committed to meet their share in three monthly instalments falling due one month after the corresponding shares in the previous loan. Hope ultimately undertook not to float any further loans for the Russians before 1st July 1788 without the prior approval of the *entrepreneurs*.[4]

Greatly satisfied, Henry Hope wrote to Sutherland: 'This operation astonishes everybody and we have received the highest compliments on it.'[5] In Hope's view, the principal reason for the success lay in the interest

BERIGT,

Van een Negotiatie voor Reekening en ten behoeve van het Rusfisch Keizer-ryk, groot DRIE MILLIOENEN Guldens Hollands Courant geld, teegens vier en een half Percent Intrest in 't Jaar, ten Comptoire van de Heeren HOPE & COMP. Banquiers tot Amfterdam, onder verband van alle de Inkomsten van het voorsz. Keizer-ryk, en fpecialyk die van ESTLAND en LYFLAND, beneevens de Tollen en Rechten, van de In- en Uytgaande Goederen der Steden RIGA, PERNAU, REVAL, en NERVA, voor den tyd van TIEN JAAREN, om, na verloop van zes Jaaren, te moogen aflosfen.

De Obligatien, ieder groot *f* 1000 zullen gedateerd zyn 1 February 1788, wanneer ook de Intresfen ingaan, welke Jaarlyks op Coupons zullen worden betaald; dog de Obligatien, dan nog niet gereed zynde, moeten de Fournisfementen provifioneel op RECEPISSEN gefchieden. En zal de Inteekening van nu af aan ten Comptoire van voorsz. Heeren HOPE & COMP. een aanvang neemen.

Berigt of the first Russian loan in 1788, with notes concerning converted bonds rate of 4½%, which was ½% above that of competitive loans and thus attracted ample funds.

Because of this, Hope's own loan to Sweden got off the ground only with great difficulty, and another, for the Emperor of Austria, issued by Goll & Co. of Amsterdam at the end of December, was subscribed only to the extent of one-half.[1] Simultaneous loans for the Emperor of Austria issued in Brussels and Frankfurt, also at 4% interest, were reported to be in similar difficulties.

Hope's triumphant message probably disguised a certain reserve. The permit issued by the Committee for Foreign Loans and the covering letter from Sutherland had both expressly stipulated that the rate of interest should not exceed 4%, and that the difference between this figure and 4½% should go to the *entrepreneurs* in the form of private *douceurs*. Hope had thus unilaterally increased the interest, an act which could incur the severe displeasure of the Committee. In defence of his action, Hope argued that a 4% loan for Russia would have been just as slow in attracting funds as the loans for other countries, so that a higher interest rate would have been demanded for any subsequent issue. Moreover, he maintained, the enormous success of the current loan had enhanced Russia's prestige beyond measure, whereas giving bonuses to the *entrepreneurs* could only have caused the price of the bonds to fall below par, thereby depressing Russian stocks and damaging Russia's creditworthiness.[2] With the arrival of the official documents from St. Petersburg, which proved to be based upon a 4% loan, the tension at Hope & Co. rose. But a week later an express messenger arrived bearing the Committee's approval of the Company's action.[3]

Yet the attractive rate of interest cannot been the sole reason for the unexpectedly abundant flow of capital. Following the signing of the second contract, Henry Hope, who as recently as October 1787 had taken so sombre a view of the situation, wrote to Sutherland: 'We have had an amazing run for our new loan and we now only perceive that the scarcity of money was only apparent and owing to the general diffidence, which prevented people from placing the large sums which have been accumulating in consequence of the stagnation of trade for so long a time.'[4]

In a letter to Baring, Hope described the success of the loan as 'a melancholy proof of the discredit of our own Government Securities.'[5] This was a reference to the aftermath of the disturbances inside the Republic: negotiations for loans for a number of regions had been opened in Amsterdam, but these had made no progress whatsoever. Was it that the pro-Patriot investors avoided domestic loans following the restoration of the House of

Orange, or was the run on the Russian loans a symbol of doubt as to the survival of the Republic as a sovereign state? Hope feared that the unfilled demands for capital at home might well lead to a general ban on foreign loans, as had been the case previously. To avoid precipitating such a step, the *entrepreneurs* concerned in the second contract were bound to secrecy until a date to be decided, and Hope also urged Kalichev, the Russian envoy in The Hague, to keep the affair secret.[1]

Hope's success afforded Richard Sutherland a great deal of support in his struggle against his numerous enemies; it also served to justify the change of hands which he had effected.[2] This change was, of course, painful for De Smeth, a fact which he confessed to Hope 'with his natural candour' when the latter visited him after the first transaction. He added, however, that he did not flatter himself that he could retain the Russian business without having to simultaneously take on extensive and sometimes fearsome Court affairs, which, despite their advantages, were not to be preferred to peace and quiet.[3]

Hope's superior financial strength had once again proved decisive, though it was naturally not unlimited. In his dealings with the Committee, Sutherland had earlier gone too far in his praise of the house of Hope, in its being equal to all possible wants and exigencies both in regard to loans and advances of money, and this mistake was later to come home to roost.[4] The Committee was under the impression that Hope would have no difficulty in negotiating a loan of twenty million guilders by August 1788 and also that the house could furnish any advance which might be required. In a cautiously worded letter aimed at correcting this misapprehension, Hope pointed out that it would be an unpardonable folly for any house, however strong, to measure its strength against the needs of a major country which was in a state of war. Without that qualification, any offer of services would be pointless and ridiculous.[5]

In order not to appear too negative, Hope hinted that it might well prove possible to reduce the period ending on 1st July 1788, within which, under the terms of the contract with the *entrepreneurs*, no loan might be negotiated, and he requested that the relevant debentures and the official instructions of the Court be despatched without delay.[6]

Hope's zeal for the Russian cause was well and truly tested when, early in January 1788, it was learned that the Russian Court proposed to negotiate a loan of three million guilders with the house of C.J.M. de Wolf in Antwerp. In the opinion of the Hope partners, Antwerp was much too close to Amsterdam, so that a loan there would mean competition on Hope's own territory. When the 'Brabanders' had money to invest, they usually looked to Amsterdam. Hope advised the Committee that as far as he was concerned the Antwerp loan could fail, and he expressed the hope (vainly, as it transpired) that De Wolf would not succeed in obtaining the approval of the Austrian government. De Wolf had initially whetted the appetite of the Russian Court with promises of a $3\frac{1}{2}\%$ loan, but the negotiation ultimately commenced on the basis of 4%. When this failed to produce any activity on the market, he succeeded in getting the rate raised to $4\frac{1}{2}\%$, at which figure he came into direct competition with the loans floated by Hope. There was also the fact that the methods of issue employed in Antwerp adversely affected the issue price of loans: there were no *entrepreneurs* and so the loan continued to remain open for public subscriptions. The result was that investors delayed subscribing in the hope of discrediting the loan and so obtaining bonds cheaply.[1]

While the Russian Court was thus busy thwarting Hope–and, by its rash borrowing, creating an impression among investors that it was in dire need of funds–it was knocking on Hope's door for sums of twenty million and more! Hope would have done well to raise twelve million in 1788, but there was no certainty of this 'because of the needs of our neighbours and of this country itself, and because money is scarce.'[2] When Hope wrote this, on 19th February 1788, the easiness on the capital market had largely disappeared. As a gesture of goodwill, Hope asked for debentures for third and fourth loans of three million guilders each for periods of ten and twelve years respectively, commencing on 1st July 1788. The rate of interest could be kept down to $4\frac{1}{2}\%$, although there would be pressure as a result of the scarcity of capital. The proceeds of these loans, however, could not be made available to the Court until they had been publicly announced.[3]

The Hope partners were anything but satisfied with the 'extremely modest nature' of the 5% commission offered. They felt that they were entitled to an additional remuneration, a premium *sous main*, since they could earn so much more by investing their money in other business that undertaking the Russian loans amounted to 'a deed for the sake of glory.' They stated that other Courts allowed 6% and that they desired this from Russia also. It fell to Sutherland to plead their cause with the Committee, and this he of course did in cautious terms, 'on grounds of delicacy.' The ledgers of that time reveal that the request was looked upon favourably; indeed, Hope enjoyed a commission of $6\frac{1}{2}\%$ on these loans.[4]

Sutherland also sought the assistance of Hope in supporting the rate of exchange of the rouble, which showed signs of crumbling. Before agreeing to do so, Hope insisted on knowing the true par value, by which he meant the intrinsic value of the rouble expressed in Dutch or English currency. Hope believed that the exchange rate was 36–38 *stuivers* to the rouble, as against a true par value of 34. Thus the rate of exchange could fall to 34 *stuivers* without adverse consequences for Russia. It would be dangerous to enforce the exchange rate on grounds of needs abroad, for this could lead to a serious financial crisis such as had occurred, for example, in Sweden. 'For,' Hope reminded Sutherland, 'it is an invariable axiom that any nation whose debts exceed the value of its revenues or of its balance of trade will be stripped of its effective in gold or silver, unless it has the wisdom to borrow money, to find ways to defer meeting a deficit and to establish a ratio between the repayment and the annual surplus on its balance of trade.' Thus, instead of offering his support in raising the rate of exchange of the rouble, Hope urged the wisdom of consolidating the national debt.

By mid-March 1788 Hope had reached agreement with the *entrepreneurs* on the third loan for Russia, and he communicated the fact with satisfaction to the Committee.[1] He was obliged to inform the Committee that the date earlier referred to for the fourth loan, 1st July 1788, could not be maintained because the *entrepreneurs* had insisted on a moratorium on fresh issues until 1st September, although, he added, they would probably be willing to reconsider this. Hope viewed the Committee's action in declining loan proposals from the house of Boas in The Hague as very wise in view of the fact that such firms could not hope to succeed in The Hague, added to which Boas's reputation was inadequate for such a transaction.

Russia meanwhile was drawing on other foreign sources of finance, not only in Antwerp, which has been mentioned, but also in Genoa, where a loan was negotiated with the house of Regny.[2] At Sutherland's request, Hope went so far as to seek the opinion of his long-standing colleague Beerend Roosen in Hamburg concerning the prospects for negotiating a loan in that city. If Roosen was open for such a proposition, Hope wrote, he could best adopt the Amsterdam method and work with *entrepreneurs*. The 1% which he would have to pay them out of his commission was vital to the success of a loan such as was proposed, for 'nothing elicits greater activity than self-interest.' 'Without this incentive,' Hope continued, 'the negotiations here would not proceed so smoothly.' He advised Roosen to start with a moderate sum, say one million marks, and if this went well he could consider larger loans. Hope expressed his willingness to take a share of one hundred thousand marks in an initial loan if this would assist in overcoming Roosen's objections. Roosen remained averse to the suggestion, advising Hope that he saw no prospect of raising a loan in Hamburg.

Hope respected his decision, 'in view, inter alia, of your blessed and advanced age.' It would have been very agreeable if a friendly and not too powerful house had seen its way clear to collaborating with the Company, but as Hope recognized – and intimated to Roosen – 'It is far better not to begin than to end in distress.'[1]

As had been the case with the Swedish transactions, Hope's aim was to combine loans with other business. During the previous Turkish War, the Russian Baltic Fleet had penetrated the Mediterranean and had there destroyed the Turkish fleet. Acting on the premise that this might well occur again, Hope made plans. Late in November 1787 – that is to say, prior to the opening of public subscription for the first loan – the Company established contact with the house of Cambiasso in Leghorn with a view to preparing the financial operations which such a naval expedition might demand.[2]

New opportunities arose in March 1788, when the British government prohibited the use of English ships for the carriage of Russian troops and supplies to the Mediterranean. Apprehension concerning the ever more apparent urge for expansion on the part of Catherine the Great, and resentment at the ukases aimed at England's dominant role in Russia's foreign trade, clearly played a part in the decision.[3]

Alexander Henry Sutherland, a London merchant and a brother of the Russian Court Banker, who had been engaged in chartering vessels in England, approached the partners of Hope & Co. with a request that they should take over this activity. The Company consulted J.C. van der Hoop, the Advocate Fiscal to the Admiralty in Amsterdam and confidant of the stadholder in maritime affairs.[4] Van der Hoop was at first very optimistic about obtaining official approval, since this charter business would help to bridge a period of malaise for Holland's merchant fleet.

To Henry Hope's intense dismay, pressure by England on the government of the stadholder resulted in a ban on the chartering of Dutch vessels. Efforts by Hope and the Russian envoy, Kalichev, to secure a reversal of the decision failed. The weak government of the Republic, recently rehabilitated with British support, dared not risk incurring the displeasure of its patron.[5] Hope, with Kalichev's support, made a fresh approach to Van der Hoop in April 1788. The Advocate Fiscal was somewhat more responsive, but he demanded that the Company's activities on behalf of the Russian fleet should have no adverse consequences for relations between the Republic and the Sultan of Turkey or for Holland's trading interests in the Levant.[6]

In order to avoid embarrassing the government, Hope drew up a plan under which the chartering of vessels would *pro forma* be undertaken by a friendly house, De Coninck & Reyersen in Copenhagen. No opposition was expected from the Danish government in view of its close relations with Russia.[1] There are no details of the progress of the plan, but it is known that Dutch vessels were not chartered because the Russian fleet was kept in the Baltic by the outbreak of the Swedish-Russian War.[2]

This new war, which had to be waged alongside the struggle against the Turks, served to increase Russia's financial needs. The expectation voiced by Hope early in March 1788, that it would be possible to proceed with a fourth loan before September, was not borne out, and it was not until the end of the year that agreement was reached with the *entrepreneurs*. This delay, coupled with the increase of the interest rate to 5%, suggested that the scarcity of money, about which Hope had complained in February, had become acute. The loan, like the last and all those which followed, was of three million guilders, and Hope's commission on this and subsequent loans was 6½%.

Simultaneously with the fourth loan, the Russian Court empowered the Company to negotiate a fifth, but the contract between Hope and the *entrepreneurs* was not signed until 3rd April 1789. The tighter conditions on the money market favoured the *entrepreneurs*, who were thereby in a position to extract more favourable conditions for their participation in the fourth and fifth transactions. Their bonus rose from 1% for the first three loans to 1¾% for the fourth and 2% for the fifth, and in addition they now received 'the Interests due in the current month, in which the monies are furnished'–a perquisite which they did not relinquish in subsequent contracts.

The new contract provided for the *entrepreneurs* to meet their obligations in four instalments instead of three, as in the case of the first two loans; the provision for public subscription at the offices of Hope & Co., and the accompanying *douceur* of ½% for private investors, however, was omitted. Hope's share of the fifth loan was cf 870,000, compared with cf 750,000 for the first two.[3]

The increasing political confusion in France will certainly have contributed to the scarcity of capital. After protracted difficulties with his subjects, the French king was finally obliged by lack of funds to recall the legislative body, the *Etats-Généraux*, after an interval of more than a hundred and fifty years. Instead of voting the monies requested, the delegates demanded political reforms; these were refused, and in the summer of 1789 revolutionary movements burst forth both in Paris and in the rural areas.

In spite of the threatening political situation, Hope was able to report to Sutherland on 25th September 1789 that the fifth loan had been placed, albeit with a minor concession to the *entrepreneurs* in the matter of their instalments. Until shortly before the placing, Hope had taken a very pessimistic view of the financial prospects, and although he still feared the consequences of 'a check to the current payments in France' he took the view that it was better to embark on a new loan at that moment than later. If an emergency should arise, a loan which had been launched would fare better than one which was still at the negotiating stage. There was also the fact that Russia had scored a major naval victory over Sweden at Svensksund–and this had to be exploited. Together, these considerations had led Hope to decide to enter into a contract with the *entrepreneurs* for a sixth loan.[1]

The results by far exceeded Hope's expectations. By 13th October, less than a fortnight after the loan had opened, the *entrepreneurs* had placed two million of the three million guilders.[2] In later correspondence, Henry Hope attributed this sudden success to reticence on the part of investors in the early part of the year, at which time there was widespread fear of a catastrophe in France. The failure of this to materialize for the time being had led to large sums remaining uninvested, and these produced 'an unexpected ease in finances.' This situation was, of course, of a temporary nature; nevertheless, Hope was anxious to obtain debentures for seventh, eighth, ninth and tenth loans in order to profit from the circumstances of the moment. Particular care was taken to make each loan appear to be the last and to convince the public that peace between Russia and her enemies would bring the whole affair to an end. The Committee in St. Petersburg had approached the Company on the subject of a separate loan for the Court, but Hope felt that it would be wrong to upset the established pattern and that it would be preferable to embark upon an eighth loan immediately after the seventh.[3] From the loans remaining to be negotiated, a sum would be required by February 1791 to repay a loan obtained from De Smeth in 1781; the remainder would be available for the prosecution of the war. In the event of hostilities ceasing during the coming winter, the loans would be of value 'to restore your numerary' and could be used to curb the large amount of paper money in circulation if the Russian government deemed it wise 'to keep any quantity of it afloat.'

Catherine II demonstrated her satisfaction with the Company's conduct of affairs by presenting Henry Hope with a portrait of herself. She had offered him a title, but this he had declined.[4] In a letter to Sutherland, he expressed, in a manner appropriate to the autocratic empress, his gratitude for the honour which had been bestowed upon him. The portrait, he wrote, was 'a striking instance of the magnanimity and magnificence of the exalted Personage ... Her elevated genius and almost supernatural loftiness of mind ...' Hope instructed Sutherland to give the painter of the portrait a gift of one hundred guineas, and he sent, via the Committee, a letter of thanks to Catharine, to be delivered 'if the etiquette admits it.'[1]

In his references to the Committee, Henry Hope was considerably less flattering. This body had objected to the extension of the time allowed for the payment of instalments of the fifth loan and with this to the 6½% commission paid to the Company. In Hope's view, at least two-thirds of the excess of 1½% over the 5% offered earlier was 'a sine qua non.' The Company denied that Russia was being asked to pay more than any other Court; on the contrary, Spain gave 7% plus 1% for repayment and 2% for the payment of interest; Poland gave 6%, also with 1% for repayment and 2% for the payment of interest; and Sweden had paid the same or more, according to circumstances. Shortly before this, Sweden had offered Hope 8%, but the Company, which since the opening of the first Russian loan had dissociated itself from all other negotiations, had declined this, as it had a Polish request.[2]

With regard to the extension of the settlement date, Henry Hope commented that: 'an indulgence has been given in proportion to the urgency of the times.' In the case of French loans an interval of three months was allowed between the commencement of interest payment and the deposition of monies by the lender, while England, at the time of the American War of Independence, went so far as to pay interest from the time of receipt of the first of twelve monthly instalments. Hope was not disposed to indulge in further correspondence concerning this humiliating problem, and he merely requested that the debentures for the eighth loan, with which the debt to De Smeth would be repaid, be sent to him.[3] No mention was made of the debentures for the ninth and tenth loans to which he had referred a month previously.

Henry Hope refused to give any undertaking regarding either an acceleration of the payments to Russia or an opening date for a new loan. In his view, the 'Brabant Revolution,' the revolt by the people of the Southern Netherlands against the centralist regime in Austria, could give rise to all manner of dangerous, international complications, with unforeseeable consequences for the money market in Amsterdam.

In the event, these complications were of such a mild nature that on 16th February 1790 Hope was able to enter into a contract with the *entrepreneurs* for a seventh loan. This new three-million guilder loan bore interest at 5% and, like all loans since the third, was for twelve years. The *entrepreneurs* received a bonus of 2% and were permitted to pay in four monthly instalments immediately following those relating to the previous loan. The inclusion in the contract of an agreement between the *entrepreneurs* not to sell the bonds at a rate below 98¾% proves that this loan was less easily subscribed. The *entrepreneurs* also bound themselves 'not to permit or to seek any bartering, rebate of interest, commission, variation, premium, indulgence, etcetera, or any advantage whatsoever, large or small, which renders this agreement illusory.' Any change in the rate of 98¾% required the approval of a majority.[1]

The contract for the eighth loan was signed on 13th August 1790, the interest rate again being 5%. The *entrepreneurs* were given the choice of paying in cash or in bonds relating to a loan from De Smeth in 1781 which was due to be repaid at the offices of Hope & Co. on 1st February 1791. The interest on these would accrue to the *entrepreneurs* up to the date on which they were lodged with the Company as payment. Even though this exchange arrangement would in itself make the loan easier to place–the more so since the De Smeth loan bore interest at 4%, making prolongation attractive–the *entrepreneurs* were permitted to settle in five monthly instalments instead of four, as with the previous loan. Clearly, the opportunities for placement had decreased in the course of 1790. The stipulation of a minimum rate of 98¾% and those concerning 'bartering' and other illicit rebates were incorporated without amendment in the new contract, as was the provision for a bonus of 2%.[2]

The slowness with which the 1790 loans were negotiated was matched only by the speed with which those of the following year were arranged. The ninth, for which Hope and the *entrepreneurs* entered into a contract on 6th January 1791, provided yet more evidence of the difficulties in the year which lay behind. On 18th February 1790, the Russian Court gave its approval for the opening not only of the eighth loan, but also the ninth and even the tenth. Thus, the opportunities had up to then remained far below expectations. The terms of the contract for the ninth loan were broadly similar to those of the document of 13th August 1790, although there were no redeemable bonds from De Smeth and the number of monthly instalments had again become four–a sign that the tightness had commenced to ease.[3]

On 28th February 1791 the *entrepreneurs*, who had still to pay the first instalment towards the ninth loan, entered into a contract with Hope & Co. which simultaneously covered the tenth and eleventh loans; this was for six million guilders, which the *entrepreneurs* undertook to furnish in six monthly instalments. In the months of May and June, these ran parallel with instalments of the previous loan.[1] On 18th July the *entrepreneurs* again participated for a further six million guilders, for the twelfth and thirteenth loans, under an almost identical contract. This time the parallel instalments fell due in September and October.[2] On 21st December of the same year they set a crown on their efforts by pledging themselves to furnish monies for fourteenth and fifteenth loans.

While these latest loans bore interest at 4%, compared with the 5% of the ten preceding ones, the *entrepreneurs* undertook to furnish their shares in five months as against six under the earlier six-million guilder contracts. In addition, they bound themselves not to sell at a rate below 99½%, an increase of ¾% on the previous figure.[3] In all, the *entrepreneurs* committed themselves in 1791 to furnish twenty-one million guilders in the space of sixteen months, an average of more than a one and a quarter million per month.

It is obvious that an immense undertaking such as this could only succeed in a money market characterized by abundance. That such ample funds were available in the Republic for investment was largely due to the developments in France. Admittedly, a constitutional monarchy had been established there in September 1791, following a period of intense bickering, but since 1790 the king had been at odds with parliament over the sequestration of Church property and the placing under state supervision of the Catholic clergy.

As security for the confiscated Church property, mortgage debentures or *assignats* were issued, and these soon assumed the role of a paper currency. But lack of confidence in this new tender caused the rate of exchange of the *écu* to fall from about 56 *stuivers* before the Revolution to 50 *stuivers* in November 1790. Between May 1791 and the end of that year it dropped from 44 to 37 *stuivers*.[4] Investors in the Netherlands who, from political motives or in pursuit of profit, had earlier opted for French stocks with their higher rates of interest now had to pay the penalty. This was made heavier by the fact that these investors had purchased the majority of the stock through houses in Paris, the interest being paid in French currency in that city, so that they bore the full brunt of the exchange losses. This development will have caused a mass flight from French government securities, from which Hope and his *entrepreneurs* were able to benefit.[5]

We know from another source that news of the abundance of available capital had reached Russia and that the Committee for Foreign Loans saw in this an opportunity to obtain the long-sought reduction in the interest rate. The Russian Court was due to repay to De Smeth a 4½%

loan of two and a half million guilders in 1792 and wished to obtain a new loan of the same size and with the same rate of interest. In addition, it desired to convert a loan of three and a half million guilders from De Smeth, which still had several years to run, into one of 4%. When Hope declined to reduce the interest rate on his loans, as he had done in 1789, the Committee approached De Wolf in Antwerp, the former competitor of the Company. De Wolf was quite willing to provide the services requested and in the summer of 1791 the house appeared on the market with a loan for Russia bearing a lower rate of interest (probably the desired 4%). In order to avoid incurring Hope's displeasure, it was made to appear that the bonds were issued in St.Petersburg; but the intention was clear to many, including Hope. In the face of angry representations by the Company, the Committee agreed to cancel the loan on condition that Hope negotiated one of six million guilders at 4% to replace it. It is against this background that the lower interest rate on the fourteenth and fifteenth loans must be viewed. In this connexion, it is noteworthy that the contract with the *entrepreneurs* dated 21st December contains no reference to an exchange of De Smeth bonds.[1]

The records also show that the *entrepreneurs* encountered obstacles in placing the fourteenth and fifteenth loans. The abnormally low rate of interest will undoubtedly have been the principal stumbling block, but there was also the adverse effect of the political developments which took place in the early part of 1792. In April of that year the Legislative Assembly in France declared war on 'the King of Bohemia and Hungary,' as it chose to describe Emperor Francis II of Austria. It was plain that the war would be fought mainly in the Austrian Netherlands and on the Rhine, and would thus come dangerously close to the Republic. In the early stages of the war the French armies made little progress; indeed, their setbacks enabled the radical groups in Paris to grow in strength until in August they succeeded, by allegations of treason, in bringing about the suspension of the monarchy. It is obvious that under such circumstances investors were less anxious to subscribe to loans than they had been in the previous year.

The contract providing for the sixteenth and seventeenth loans, to which Hope and the *entrepreneurs* appended their signatures on 6th August 1792, also bears signs of a less plentiful flow of money. The interest rate was 4½%, one half per cent more than in the contract of December 1791, and the *entrepreneurs* were given eight months to pay instead of five. It was agreed that no further loan would be opened until the eight instalments had been paid, in May 1793. The difficulties which faced the *entrepreneurs* in placing the bonds are evidenced in the provision allowing them to subcontract portions of their shares to third parties, provided that not less than cf 50,000 was subcontracted at a time and that the subcontractor became a party to the terms and conditions of the contract. It was even felt necessary to impose a penalty for 'bartering, rebate of interest,' etc.; this took the form of forfeiture of the bonus and a fine of one hundred golden ducats for each offence, 'all to be applied to the benefit of the *Gereformeerde Nederduitsche* Poor Relief Board in this City.' [1]

In the autumn of 1792 the military situation in the Southern Netherlands imposed an increasing threat. Having defeated the Austrian troops in a battle there, the French general Dumouriez proceeded to occupy the whole country. In France, the king, after an interrogation before the National Convention–a new body of deputies elected by universal suffrage–was condemned to death in January 1793. Shortly after this, on 1st February, the Convention declared war on 'the King of England' and 'the Stadholder of the Republic.' By early March Dumouriez had reached the major rivers and it seemed that the Republic was lost. So grave did the situation appear to Henry Hope that he, in company with the wife of John Williams Hope and her children, fled to England. Later in the same month the French general suffered a defeat which forced him to withdraw from the Southern Netherlands. His subsequent desertion to the Austrian side helped to bring to power in Paris extreme radical groups which declared a popular war and acted with vigour against their enemies both at home and abroad.

In May 1793, when the period for settlement of the last loan contract expired, a new contract providing for the eighteenth and nineteenth loans was negotiated. The terms of this are not known, but records show that Hope had to subscribe a considerable sum in order to reach the total of six million guilders. A large sum was also required to support the value of the Russian bonds so that the holders could be sure from day to day of being able to exchange these for cash without suffering a loss.[2] The new loans bore interest at 5%.

The summer came, and in the weeks during which the war against France proceeded favourably subscriptions totalling more than two million guilders were received; but with the defeat of the allied armies at the hands of the French in September, Dutch investors tightened their purse-strings. It was very fortunate that the Russo-Turkish war had ended in the Spring of 1792, for this fact served to reduce Russia's need for loans abroad. The war against Sweden had ended in 1790.

Robert Voûte, the adviser and very close friend of the partners of Hope

& Co. had left Holland in July 1793, travelling in the direction of Russia. Besides the unsatisfactory progress of subscriptions to the latest loans for that country, Voûte had matters to attend to in Poland, where major political changes threatened to endanger the Company's interests.

Voûte's journey in fact marked the end of the initial phase of Hope's loan-raising activities on behalf of Russia, the provision of money for the Turkish war. In the second phase the emphasis would be on consolidation and measures aimed at ensuring regular interest payments and repayment of principal money. Before dealing with this, however, we must concern ourselves with the Company's connexions in Poland.

CHAPTER FOUR

POLISH INTERLUDE

Robert Voûte arrived in Warsaw at half past eleven on the night of 24th July 1793. It was pouring with rain. He had left Berlin on the 19th and, despite the discomforts of the journey, had travelled day and night over roads which had been turned into quagmires by an incessant downpour.[1] But Voûte allowed himself and his companions no more than a day or two's rest before resuming the journey to Grodno, more than 250 kilometres distant. There, the Polish *sejm* had been in session since the 17th. Among the issues facing it were demands from Russia and Prussia for fresh territorial concessions.[2] Hope had a direct interest in this matter, for such concessions would significantly affect the Polish state finances, with which the Company had been concerned for more than fifteen years.

If there was one country which needed the name of Hope to establish its credit and win the confidence of investors, that country was Poland. The 'Republic' was ruled by an impotent king chosen by the nobility–in whom the true power rested. These nobles met in *sejmiki*, or local diets, which sent delegates to the *sejm*, or parliament. Under the Polish constitution, every measure introduced into the *sejm* had to be adopted unanimously; a single dissenting voice was sufficient to send a proposal crashing to the ground. This was the notorious liberum veto. There also existed a 'right of confederation' which gave to an arbitrarily chosen group of gentry the authority to impose their wishes, if necessary by force of arms. Many of these noblemen, however, were in straitened circumstances and were economically dependent upon twenty or so extremely rich landowning families, the magnates, many of whom behaved as if they were sovereign rulers. The remainder of the population consisted of impoverished, uneducated serfs. Towns of any size or with a prosperous middle-class were practically non-existent.

With its form of government, this economically backward country was constantly open to anarchy, a fact of which its more powerful neighbours, Russia, Prussia and Austria, often took advantage in order to interfere in its internal affairs. In 1772 this situation led to the First Partition, the name given to a treaty under which Prussia acquired what later became West Prussia; Russia obtained a part of the Grand Duchy of Lithuania, which was linked to Poland by a personal union; and Austria acquired territories which became Galicia.

This amputation served to revive a reformatory movement to which King Stanislaw Poniatowski–who, on the recommendation of Catherine II, had been elected in 1763–had earlier contributed. The political and financial frameworks were among the objects of reform. The principle of majority decision was introduced in the *sejmiki*, tax reforms were enacted, import and export duties were introduced and a type of budget devised. The *sejm* of 1775 rendered exceptional services in the financial sector. Among its acts was to vote the king a fixed allowance, a necessary step in view of the loss of revenue to the Royal Treasury, in particular following the cession of territory.[1] Owing to a deficit in revenues from taxation, the sums voted to the king could not be paid in full, but in the light of the expenditure by the king of substantial sums in the nation's interest, the *sejm* of 1776, in Warsaw, authorized the monarch to obtain loans abroad to the extent of his claims on the Treasuries of Poland and Lithuania, which totalled nine million Polish guilders (cf 2,625,000). For the repayment of these loans, the king received an annual sum of 50,000 ducats from the newly established Sinking Fund. As security for the payment of interest and repayment of principal money, he was also granted, for a period of ten years, the revenues from the *subsidium charitativum*, the tax on those living in property owned by the Church, amounting to 700,000 Polish guilders annually.[2] The net revenues of the 'oeconomies' of Brest-Litowsk, Kobrin, Olitzka and Szawel served as additional security. An 'oeconomy' was an estate, the revenues from which were destined solely for the Court and the Royal Treasury.[3]

In the opinion of Hope & Co., who were approached by the Warsaw banker Pierre Ferguson Tepper, the sum of these guarantees was inadequate. The Company desired in addition a guarantee from Catherine II, and in this it revealed a realistic view of Poland's dependence upon Russia. The empress expressed her willingness to provide such a guarantee, which she did in a document dated 18th September 1776.[4] The principal guarantor was the Republic of Poland, which in particular was required to guarantee that the 'oeconomies' mortgaged as security for the repayment of the debt would continue to be reserved for this purpose even after the death of King Stanislaw. In the event of the lenders having any complaint whatsoever, Catherine was empowered to take over the 'oeconomies' and to arrange for any arrears to be paid out of the proceeds. On these conditions, the Company negotiated in 1777 a 10-year loan of nine million Polish guilders (cf 2,625,000) bearing interest at 5% and commencing on 1st February of that year.[5]

Nous Stanislas Auguste

par la Grace de Dieu, Roi de Pologne, Grand Duc de Lithuanie &c. &c. &c. a tous ceux qu'il appartient savoir faisons qu'ayant chargé les Banquiers d'ici Pierre Tepper & Compe. de la Negociation de Deux Cents Cinquante Mil Ducats ou Un Million Trois Cent Douze Mil Cinq-Cents florins argent Courant d'Hollande pour le Compte de notre Tresor et pour un fond a servir a l'Amortissement de nos Dettes restantes. Nous authorisons les dits Banquiers Pierre Tepper & Compe. par le present Pleinpouvoir a traiter & conclure cette affaire avec les Sieurs Hope & Compe. Banquiers a Amsterdam, conformement aux Instructions dont ils sont munis, leurs donnant a cet Effet l'Ordre et le Pleinpouvoir de de recevoir des dits Sieurs Hope & Compe. le montant des dits Deux Cents Cinquante Mil Ducats ou Un Million Trois Cent Douze Mil Cinq Cents florins Argent courant d'Hollande et de les en reconnoitre en notre Nom En foi de quoi Nous avons Signé le present de notre propre Main et y avons fait apposer notre Sceau Royal A Varsovie ce 11. Mars 1785.

Stanislas Auguste Roy

Pius Kicinski Secretaire au Cabinet du Roi de Pologne

Authorization by King Stanislaw of Poland to Pierre Tepper & Co. to negotiate with Hope & Co. in the matter of a loan, 1785

In 1784, two years before the period of the loan expired, the *sejm*, meeting at Grodno, voted to renew the allotment to the king of the revenues from the *subsidium charitativum*, totalling 700,000 Polish guilders per annum, for the same period as before and with the freedom to use these as security for a fresh loan abroad.[1] Hope & Co. had by now ceased to be the only potential source of such a loan. King Stanislaw had obtained a loan of cf 1,000,000 from the Amsterdam house of Quirijn Willem van Hoorn in 1781 and in addition maintained financial contacts with Theodoor Gülcher & Mulder, also in Amsterdam.[2]

Early in January 1785 a Redemption Bureau was established on the premises of Ferguson Tepper & Co. in Warsaw; its principal function was the administration of the new loan. It was to this bureau that the Public Treasuries of Poland and Lithuania would pay the approved *subsidium charitativum* of 700,000 Polish guilders per annum.[3] The elimination of the Royal Treasury from the administrative chain was probably aimed at giving the lenders a greater sense of security.

As before, the task of negotiating with Hope & Co. was entrusted to Tepper. He was instructed to negotiate a loan of 250,000 ducats, or cf 1,312,500, but when he put this to the Company he was advised that the sum could, if desired, be increased by 100,000 ducats on condition that part of the proceeds were employed for the accelerated payment of the first three instalments on the Van Hoorn loan. The price of the Van Hoorn bonds had by this time fallen to 94%, indicating a lack of confidence among investors; advancing the repayments would have the effect of restoring the price to par, and this was a prerequisite for the successful launching of the new loan.[4]

In the months which followed, little progress was made in the negotiations. The principal obstacles from the Company's point of view were the absence of a further guarantee by Catherine II and lack of confidence in the stability of Stanislaw's kingship, and even an express declaration by the Public Treasury that the *subsidium charitativum* would continue to be paid after the king's death failed to smooth the path.[5]

Late in 1785 King Stanislaw despatched 'Monsieur de Wickedé, who is charged with safeguarding the interests of the King of Poland in this country,' to Amsterdam with instructions to continue the negotiations with the Company. To the vexation of the king, the new negotiator met with a continued lack of confidence in the continuation of his reign. Stanislaw attributed the mistrust to German newspaper reports suggesting that new stormclouds were gathering over Poland and that he planned to abdicate. The truth of the matter probably lay in an Austrian plan which envisaged the replacement of Stanislaw by the Elector of Saxony, who was less dependent upon Russia.[1] De Wickedé had received instructions to negotiate with other houses in Amsterdam, but it was made clear to him by Hope that the king must choose between dealing with the Company alone or going elsewhere. This was communicated to the monarch, who replied that he had no objection to the Company acting alone in the matter. This decision was accompanied by some flattering comments concerning the partners in Hope & Co., whom the king had 'had the pleasure to meet thirty years ago.'[2] Gratifying as the compliments paid by King Stanislaw to the erstwhile partners, Thomas and Adrian Hope, were, however, the Company remained firm in the matter of guarantees. In addition to the declaration by the Treasury regarding the *subsidium charitativum*, Hope desired a special guarantee from Stanislaw's heir, Joseph Poniatowski, concerning the mortgaging of the king's personal possessions. In the eyes of the king, a private guarantee from his nephew and heir was neither proper nor becoming, and he expressed the view that Hope should respect these 'raisons de délicatesse.' He had no objection to the insertion of the words 'present and future' in the clause relating to the mortgaging of his estate, but he would go no farther than that.[3] If this failed to satisfy Hope, the king was prepared to include his income from the two Treasuries, totalling four million Polish guilders per annum, in the securities; and he added that he did not wish to borrow more than one and a half million guilders altogether.

The loan was finally arranged at the beginning of April 1786. As on some previous occasions, the signing of the contract with the *entrepreneurs* preceded the issue of the principal debenture. The contract was for two million guilders at 5% interest and for a period of 10½ years commencing on 1st June 1786. The contract stipulated that the public subscription to the loan would open at the offices of Hope & Co. fourteen days after the publication of the *Berigt* and that the subscribers would receive a *douceur* of ½%. The *entrepreneurs* were to receive a bonus of 1% on the total sum for which they participated plus one month's interest on this sum, which was equivalent to an extra bonus of $\frac{5}{12}$%. In addition, they were to receive ½% of the sum actually allocated to them following the public subscription. On the assumption that the definitive share would be smaller than that which they had contracted to subscribe, they would thus have received bonuses totalling 2% of their allotted shares.[4]

The principal debenture, which was dated 21st April, and the contract between Hope and De Wickedé reveal that the king had all his own way in the matter of mortgages, for there is no mention of special guarantees by his heir.[1] A notable feature of the loan is the sum, two million guilders, which exceeds by half a million the amount referred to by the king less than two months previously. If, however, we deduct the 6% commission received by Hope and then compare the result with the 350,000 ducats to which Hope desired in 1785 to increase the loan, we arrive at approximately the same figure, namely just over $1\frac{4}{5}$ million guilders.[2] No further mention was made of accelerating the repayment of the Van Hoorn loan, nor of the Redemption Bureau at the house of Tepper; in all probability this did not operate because the administration of the loan was ultimately shared between Tepper and the banking house of Blanc.[3]

Hope was also obliged to yield to the king's demands in the matter of commission on the loan and to accept 6% instead of 7%, Stanislaw having threatened to withhold the 1% on the interest payments and repayment of principal money. It is conceivable that Hope conceded this in order to sweeten the pill of the 5% interest, which was $\frac{1}{2}$% more than the king wished to pay and higher by the same margin than the Swedish loan floated on 1st February 1786.[4] This margin and the difference in bonus paid to the *entrepreneurs*–1% on the Swedish loan as against 2% on the Polish–afford a rough indication of the credit enjoyed by these countries in Amsterdam.

According to the contract between Hope and De Wickedé, the nett proceeds of the loan were to be transferred in four instalments, three of cf 500,000 due on the first day in the months of August, September and October and the fourth, of cf 380,000, on 1st November. Interest, however, was payable on the whole sum as from 1st June, and this Hope kept for themselves. A simple calculation shows this to be worth more than 1%, which means that they were able to give the *entrepreneurs* a bonus of 2% without affecting the remainder of their commission.[5] In December 1786 the king, became aware of the advantage accruing to Hope from the commencement of interest payments on 1st June and, filled with indignation, he commanded De Wickedé to secure a change in the position. Meanwhile the Chamber of Finances took the law into its own hands and remitted only half of the seven months' interest due on 1st January 1787.[6]

Hope's refusal to issue a certificate of payment for the full sum of the interest was met by the withholding of the half-yearly interest due on 1st July 1787. On 25th June the Company had advised King Stanislaw that it was in the extremely unpleasant position of having up to that moment received no remittances in respect of interest or the first instalment of the principal money, while it faced an immediate duty to announce the payment in the newspapers. If the notice failed to appear, the Polish king's credit in the Republic would be at an end. To avoid such a situation, the Company had decided to proceed with the advertisement and, if necessary, to meet the interest and capital repayment out of its own pocket. The arrears of capital were swiftly paid off, but the interest outstanding from 1st January and totalling cf 27,143.15.0 remained a subject of dispute. In January 1788 Hope again wrote on this subject to the king, and also to De Wickedé. Even though the interest computation may have been 'too great a favour,' this fact should have been considered before the contract was signed; the terms of the contract were deemed to have been approved by the king and as such were inviolable. The writer expressed the hope that the king would issue orders on the subject 'which may at once bring an end to our fears for the troublesome consequences of the refusal of His Chamber of Finances.'[1] Despite this appeal, Hope's claim was not met until 1790.[2]

In the request made to King Stanislaw in January 1788, Hope wrote of 'many other, more essential matters' which undoubtedly occupied the monarch's attention. The reference was to a widespread reform movement in Poland which sought to utilize Russia's preoccupation with the wars against Turkey and Sweden to extend the modernization of Poland without risk of Russian intervention. During the 'four years' *sejm*' (1788–92), the task commenced in 1775 was carried a stage farther. New taxes were imposed, the army was strengthened and measures were introduced to improve the lot of the peasants. These efforts were crowned with the constitution of 1791, which converted Poland into a hereditary monarchy and invested the king with executive power. In the new parliament, in which the peasants were represented, decisions were taken by a majority vote and the right of confederation was abolished.[3]

In 1790, Poland had entered into a treaty with Prussia providing for mutual assistance in the event of attack by a third power.[4] This, the Polish government believed, would protect the country against Russian intervention. The true value of the treaty was revealed in 1792 when Catherine II, her hands unfettered by the cessation of the war against the Turks, lost no time in dealing with what to her were displeasing developments in Poland. Under her auspices, a confederation was formed (ostensibly at Targowica, but in fact in St. Petersburg) which protested against the new constitution with its 'pernicious, revolutionary ideas copied from France.' The confederation appealed to Catherine for military assistance, which she of course gladly furnished. The King of Prussia – who had cast covetous eyes on more Polish territory, and who was performing an obscure balancing act between Austria and Russia – left his ally in the lurch, on the pretext that the treaty had lost its validity because of the new Polish constitution.[1] As usual, Stanislaw bowed to the might of the empress and repealed the constitution. But not before Russian troops had commenced to occupy Poland.

Prussia's true nature was revealed in January 1793 with the signing, with Russia, of a second treaty of partition. The effect of this was to deprive Poland, whose wings had already been clipped, of half its territory and a similar proportion of its people.[2] Troops of each of the powers occupied the areas of Poland which they had thus obtained. Under pressure from the occupying Russian forces, elections were held for a *sejm* which was given the task of ratifying the treaty of partition. The newly appointed Russian envoy, Baron Sievers, succeeded by liberal gifts of money in securing the election of the delegates whom Russia favoured. King Stanislaw at first refused to travel to Grodno, where the *sejm* was to assemble, but his financial plight made him so dependent upon Catherine's benevolence that he was finally obliged to yield.

The king's financial difficulties were allied to the total stagnation in monetary transactions in Poland. When news spread of the entry of Russian troops, and soon afterwards of Prussian forces, money ceased to circulate and credit transactions ground to a halt. Support from outside was not to be expected, for the Dutch Republic had just become embroiled in a war against the revolutionary French, and England had suffered a severe financial crisis which was to lead to countless bankruptcies.[3] In Poland, a number of banks and merchant houses were so hard hit by the stagnation that they were forced to suspend payments. Among them were the banking houses of Tepper and Blanc. In February 1793 Tepper informed Baron Sievers that he was owed one and a half million ducats by the king and that if the money was not soon forthcoming he would be obliged to declare himself bankrupt. The king's debts at that time amounted to nearly thirty-four million Polish guilders. In consultation with King Stanislaw, Sievers had Tepper's offices in Warsaw placed under seal in order that the king's financially perilous position should not become public knowledge–and also to prevent any leakage of information concerning the bribes which his predecessor had paid, via Tepper, to numerous members of the Polish gentry.[4]

Naturally, the further payments of interest and capital on Hope's loan were placed in jeopardy by this development. It was with the aim of seeking some clarification regarding these matters that Robert Voûte arrived in Warsaw on 24th July. The prospects were not particularly favourable. Voûte reported that the sum of the commitments of the houses which had been forced to suspend operations was no less than ten million ducats. Tepper's affairs were in a sad state and he would almost certainly go bankrupt; with luck, the assets might be sufficient to meet 50–60% of creditors' claims. Tepper himself was also to blame; his book-keeping was seven years in arrears and the accounts were in such a state that although two senior clerks had been able to systematically rob the firm for years, their crime could not be proven. Tepper was now living in a single room somewhere, on thirty ducats a month, while his son was trying to find a livelihood outside Warsaw. Despite Tepper's demise, Voûte was of the opinion that, in principle, banking in Poland still had a solid foundation, since loans to the gentry were granted only with land as a collateral. The banks also accepted money on deposit, on which they paid interest; but the rapid rise in the number of banking houses in the preceding years had caused the interest rate to rise from 3% to between 5 and 6%.

Blanc & Co. were in a slightly more favourable position, but Blanc himself was ageing and was embarrassed by his circumstances. Voûte reported that Blanc had offended Sievers by failing to offer him loans quickly enough, or of sufficient size, when he arrived in Warsaw and was therefore out of favour with the Russian envoy. Sievers's current favourite was the much younger Jean Meisner, a skilful man possessing great physical strength and thus 'better suited, in all senses, to live among the Poles.'[1] Meisner was closely associated with Hasselgreen of the Amsterdam house of the same name, who, like Voûte, was studying the situation on the spot–and who in Grodno lived completely in the Polish manner. While in Warsaw, Voûte also met Gülcher of Gülcher & Mulder who, like Hope & Co., had negotiated a loan for the Polish king and, moreover, were involved in various loans to Polish magnates.[2]

Voûte was accompanied on the journey by William Porter of William Porter & Co., St. Petersburg. They were jointly authorized to act on behalf of Hope & Co. and Baring & Co. in negotiations with the house of G.Thomson Rowand & Co. in Moscow. Porter's presence was of great value to Voûte, for he spoke the language and was au fait with local conditions. When the visitors arrived in Grodno, the *sejm* had just accepted, amid violent protests, the cession of territory to Russia; but the anger expressed on this issue paled into insignificance alongside the fury and bitterness with which the assembly rounded on the treacherous Prussians and their demands. Sievers, whose work on behalf of Catherine was done, left the Prussian envoy, Buchholtz, to face the tirade of abuse from the livid Poles and did not lift a finger to support him. He thus contrived to demoralize his counterpart to the point where he concurred in the frontiers set out in the treaty and made no further mention of the changes which his government had proposed subsequent to the signing.[1] According to Voûte, the *sejm* was 'bouillante': the noise was deafening. While he was present, a motion tabled by Buchholtz was rejected in favour of a counterproposal calling upon the King of Prussia to first recognize the integrity of Poland; only when this had been done could there be any question of a treaty with that monarch. While this spectacle was taking place, Voûte wrote, the building in which the *sejm* assembled was surrounded on the one side by a Russian army and on the other by a Prussian army, and a battery of Russian 24-pounders was trained on the royal castle. He, Voûte, now realized 'that we in the Republic have been badly informed and have had a very false picture of the behaviour of Russia and Prussia towards Poland.'[2]

Voûte found it strange that the Poles had continued to cling to the republican form of government while they, like the Dutch, suffered under its shortcomings and vices. The situations in the two countries differed greatly, of course, but government in Poland was in the hands of many who, in spite of their differences, had a common aim: to deprive the king of his power–something which had earlier been attempted against the stadholder in Holland. If the tyranny of the minor despots could not be brought to an end, Poland would soon be done for; it would then fall under foreign dominance, 'perhaps the only means of changing the vicious disposition of the inhabitants, a product of the example set by the nobility.' Voûte thus took the view that the failures of the system of government in Poland lay at the root of the partition; in fact, it was the efforts to eliminate those failures which had given rise to the Russian intervention and with it the Second Partition.

Voûte and Porter were the first foreigners to be present at the assembly of the *sejm*, and they accordingly attracted a good deal of attention. News of their presence reached King Stanislaw, who sent a secretary to inquire who they were, and if he, the king, could be of service to them; indeed, this occurred so often that the visitors eventually felt obliged to seek an audience of the ruler. To this end, they enlisted the aid of the British envoy, Gardiner. During the audience, the king asked searching questions concerning the state of trade in England, and also the bankruptcies which had occurred there and which had contributed to Poland's distress. When the audience came to an end, the king drew Voûte and Porter on one side and, 'his face etched with grief,' said he was sure that they could judge the wretched position in which he was placed through his country's serious plight, and he expressed regret at being unable to make their sojourn in

Poland as pleasant as possible. To hear such words from the mouth of a king, Voûte wrote, was indeed unusual, and in his opinion the man was to be pitied because he was not the cause of his country's downfall. The matter of the king's debts had not arisen during the audience, but Voûte was not optimistic on this score. There was little or no doubt regarding the payment of the debts incurred by the Republic of Poland because, among other things, the Russian and Prussian governments would each accept a share; but Voûte had been informed that under the law of Poland the king himself could not incur debts. Moreover, the king had nothing: all his property and revenues had been seized by the Russians.[1] Voûte's only hope lay in a meeting with Sievers, but he was so occupied with affairs relating to the *sejm* that although Voûte and Porter dined at his house they did not see the man at all. The envoy sent them a written apology and enclosed letters of introduction to the governors of Minsk and Smolensk, which would assist them on their journey to Moscow.

On the eve of their departure for that city, early in August, Voûte had another meeting with Hasselgreen, who was anxious that Voûte should read his memorandum to Buchholtz concerning the debts owed by the king, the Republic and the magnates, and who had travelled to Grodno from the Meisner estate near Minsk especially for this purpose. Voûte felt unable to decline so flattering a request, though he feared that, in spite of Hasselgreen's reasoning, the claims by the Dutch against the king and the magnates might well be equated with those of their Polish creditors.

While Poland's future remained undecided, however, nothing could be done about the loans made to the country, so that Voûte and Porter were free to concentrate on the commission which they were to undertake for Hope and Baring in Moscow. When that had been concluded, Voûte proposed to travel to St. Petersburg to raise the question of the Polish loans with the person who wielded the real power, Empress Catherine II of Russia.

CHAPTER FIVE

A DUTCH BROKER AT THE RUSSIAN COURT

Although the problems which occupied Voûte and Porter during their visit to Moscow concerned but one mercantile house, they were in many ways symptomatic of the whole process of trading with Russia. Because of this, and also in the light of a speculative investment in cochineal, which will be described later, it is of interest to examine the house concerned more closely.

Geo.Thomson Rowand & Co. had maintained a business relationship with Hope & Co. for very many years; since 1788, the extent of their transactions had grown rapidly. Following the shipment of large quantities of cochineal to the Moscow house, its account with Hope rose to more than one and a quarter million guilders in 1791, at the end of which year a sum of just over a million guilders in Hope's favour was carried forward to a new account.[1] As this sum included the as yet unsold cochineal, the Company, not surprisingly, kept a close watch on the situation following the death of the senior partner, James Rowand, in the summer of 1791. Shortly before this, Rowand had accepted Thomas Hawes, George Carr and Alexander Grant into partnership. The four were also partners in the house of Rowand Carr & Co. of St. Petersburg, where Carr was responsible for day-to-day management.

In addition to Hope & Co. and Baring & Co., Thomson Rowand's principal correspondents included Raikes & Co. of London, from whom they purchased diamonds and other precious stones. Like Hope, Raikes were liberal in the matter of credit. With the death of James Rowand, uncertainty arose regarding the legal validity of his Will in Russia: would it be accepted, or would the State assume possession of his assets? The effect upon Carr was one of panic. In his anxiety to disengage himself from the house, he wrote alarming letters to Raikes. Their reaction was to refuse further drafts from Rowand and to freeze the house's credit in Amsterdam. This produced a deluge of accusations from Carr and eventually the dispute, which was conducted by correspondence, reached the point where, in May 1792, Raikes refused to have anything more to do with Rowand as long as Carr remained a partner. Carr had earlier found among James Rowand's papers a criticism of himself written by Raikes, by whom he had previously been employed as a clerk, and this merely exacerbated the situation.

Within the firm, Carr was embroiled in a serious conflict with Grant, whom he accused of embezzling funds belonging to the house, even though he had earlier given his approval for these to be used by Grant. By June 1793 the conflict had assumed such proportions that Carr announced his intention to resign. Liquidity problems, which were so acute that only loans from friends saved the house from bankruptcy, probably contributed to this decision, but of these he made no mention. Disquieting reports concerning the house had started to reach Hope & Co. soon after James Rowand's death, and in 1792 the partners deemed it wise to send an observer to Moscow. The warning signals received from this person in the summer of 1793 were among the motives for Voûte's journey.[1]

Voûte and Porter arrived in Moscow on 14th August 1793. They were warmly received by the partners, Grant and Hawes, who offered them shelter at the house of a former partner. At first the visitors were hesitant to accept the offer, but as the purpose of their visit had leaked out (the result, according to Voûte, of Carr's malevolence), they decided that it would be more prudent to do so and thus avoid giving the world outside an impression that things were amiss.

After a cursory examination of the firm's books and correspondence, Voûte expressed the view that Carr's resignation should be accepted, adding that the sooner this was done, the better. Carr's papers, however, should be retained by the other partners in order to prevent him from damaging the reputations of Hope and Baring.[2] Rowand's books, like those of Tepper in Warsaw, revealed an immense backlog of entries, making it difficult to obtain an accurate picture of the firm's financial position. The last occasion on which Rowand had had a balance sheet drawn up was in 1784. Voûte commented sarcastically that this had probably revealed more than enough to Rowand, who had feared to discover more. To obtain a clearer picture, Voûte gave instructions for trial balances to be prepared for the years 1785 to 1792 inclusive. These showed that, while losses had been incurred, the house was financially sound and that it enjoyed a high reputation in Moscow. This reputation was closely linked to the credit obtained from Raikes and other houses, and this in turn was based on confidence in the person of James Rowand. But his death and Carr's rash conduct had undermined confidence in the house, added to which the slowness with which debts were paid gave rise to problems of liquidity. According to Porter, the Russian debtors, with the exception of a few doubtful individuals, were of substance, as were the securities or bonds which they furnished.[1] However, there was no prospect of early settlement, for the Russians viewed the weakness of the rate of exchange, from which they too had suffered losses, as a reason to delay paying their accounts. In April 1793 the weak position of the rouble had led to a drastic reduction of imports, and this also had an adverse effect upon trade.[2]

Voûte devised a plan whereby the firm's creditors would be paid on the due date. Hope & Co. and Baring & Co. alone would be excluded in the sense that they would leave sums of cf 200,000 and cf 100,000 of their claims, totalling cf 1,047,589 and cf 530,805, at the disposal of Thomson Rowand for a period of three years, during which they would receive interest at 4% per annum. Voûte felt justified in proposing this because he was reasonably confident of the abilities of Hawes and Grant. In his opinion, the latter possessed 'esprit,' even genius and a flair for business, and he got on well with the Russians. Hawes was a true office man, quiet, not brilliant but sufficiently intelligent. Both conducted their business affairs as Rowand had done, in the manner which was common to foreign houses in Moscow–and which made such connexions with Russia extremely hazardous. These houses acted as commission agents, and the monies which they earned enabled them to spread their wings ever wider. It was thus easy for them to make their fortune. According to Voûte, they displayed no initiative, nor had they any profound insight into the pattern of trade in Russia; they were concerned only with earning their commission, and paid no heed to the finer points of their business deals.

Thomson Rowand's premises were situated three-quarters of an hour's walk from the trading centre proper (too far in Voûte's opinion) and the Russians who wished to do business with them were obliged to travel the distance. They were received by a Russian clerk, the partners remaining behind their desks and, like their Dutch counterparts, making too few appearances in the warehouse and among the traders and shopkeepers.[3] Such reticence, Voûte considered, was the more serious in Moscow because there were no brokers or other middlemen able to provide information concerning the merchandise, as was the case in Holland, and thus the foreign merchants became even more isolated. In contrast, the Russian merchants–who monopolized the home trade and, insofar as they did not have direct contacts, placed orders for west European goods with houses such as Thomson Rowand–did everything for themselves, saw each other every day, kept each other informed of developments and acted accordingly. Specialist middlemen were consequently less important.

Maintaining direct connexions with Russian merchants seemed to Voûte to be a risky policy, involving as it would incessant parrying of their artifices. But trading in imported goods for one's own account, as in 'the good old days,' would be profitable.[1]

To do this would require a foreigner resident in Moscow, or a foreign merchant who entrusted his interests to a compatriot there. By abandoning the bare role of commission agent, such a merchant would be in a position to secure better payment terms, say, part in cash and the balance in instalments spread over six or twelve months instead of wholly in instalments which dragged on from year to year.

According to Voûte, Moscow was a more important centre for imported goods than St.Petersburg, where the emphasis was on exports. He was greatly impressed by the city of Moscow, with its half a million inhabitants and its innumerable churches, and also by the volume of its trade. The various provinces of the czardom traded with one another in the same way as the nations of western Europe, and from their offices in Moscow, Russian and Armenian merchants conducted business with faraway places such as Persia, Bukhara and China. Most of their business was done in wintertime, when the merchandise could be transported cheaply by sledge. Moscow was bristling with merchants of every nationality, in addition to whom there were innumerable money-changers, who congregated in a particular part of the shopping area. They sat in open-fronted kiosks, the boxes containing the various currencies standing behind and to one side of them. The arrangement, Voûte noted, was similar to that employed in Amsterdam prior to the opening of the Exchange Bank in 1609. The principal dealings involved changing copper coins for silver–a product of the retention by the Russian government of a dual standard.

Trade with China, it was reported, had ceased to be conducted by caravan since the opening of a road linking the two countries. During his stay, Voûte dined with a merchant named Gusyatnikov, who was among Thomson Rowand's debtors and who, with two others, monopolized the trade with China. Voûte extracted from him a promise that he would be allowed to draw samples from his warehouse. Although Gusyatnikov was reputed to be a rich man, he did not pay his debts either to Thomson Rowand or to Amsterdam houses such as Hovy, Hasselgreen and Wilkieson, but kept his creditors on a string with promises of payment in three years time. Here was decisive proof of Voûte's contention that direct associations with Russian merchants were to be discouraged.[2]

Voûte's role as a broker was to prove a sore point in his dealings with houses in Moscow. For example, he was greatly incensed to discover that the house of Muilman in Amsterdam had written to Thomson Rowand saying that 'One Mr.Voûte, a chief broker in the article of teas,' was on his way to Russia and might well stop in Moscow. The house of Tamesz & Co. had so far failed to pay its respects to him and it could well be that they had also been informed of the purpose of his journey and of the fact that he was but a 'chief tea broker.' A sharp attack in the direction of the partners of Tamesz & Co. revealed plainly how deeply he was hurt and how great in his eyes was the social gap between brokership and the profession of merchant, as personified by the Hopes.[1]

Early in September 1793, Carr arrived from St.Petersburg. The impression which he made on Voûte was anything but favourable, and when he began to quibble over the conditions for his resignation from Thomson Rowand, Voûte took a firm hand, with the result that the deed dissolving the partnership was quickly signed. Under the terms of this deed, the house of Rowand & Carr in St.Petersburg would cease to exist and would be wound up by Hawes and Grant.[2]

The signing of the deed providing for the new partnership was not achieved so smoothly, however. Voûte had prepared a draft agreement in which Thomson Rowand would be subject to a form of supervision by the house of Porter in St.Petersburg–to such an extent, indeed, that in the event of the indisposition or death of Grant the house would come under the control of one of the partners of Porter, since Hawes could not manage alone.[3] As an appendix to the deed, Voûte had also drawn up a list of instructions for merchants, showing how and when a balance sheet should be prepared, how the affairs of the house should be conducted and how the securities provided for the debts to Hope & Co. and Baring & Co. should be managed. The complaisant Hawes concurred in both documents, but Grant asked for time to consider them. Grant was evidently digging his heels in; according to Voûte he had previously been employed as a clerk by Porter and, in his heart, still looked up to him.[4]

It is conceivable that Grant adopted delaying tactics because he believed that time was on his side. After all, the agreement was the only item on the Voûte-Porter agenda in Moscow, while all manner of urgent business awaited them in St.Petersburg. In the event, Voûte decided to leave the matter in abeyance, and on 20th September he and his companion departed for St.Petersburg. Grant had meanwhile left for the same destination to close the books of Rowand Carr & Co.[5]

Among the disagreeable matters which Voûte wished to discuss at a high level was one concerning Trosien. In December 1792, the house of Blanckenhagen & Co. in London had been forced by a serious credit crisis there to suspend payments. The house of De Bary & Co. in Amsterdam had thereupon felt obliged to intervene in the matter of drafts drawn by the St.Petersburg merchant Michel Trosien on Blanckenhagen and later assigned by him to De Bary to be further dealt with. The repayment of the advances, however, was not forthcoming despite a series of honeyed letters from Trosien. He even managed to persuade De Bary to extend to him a credit of 150,000 marks banco on Beerend Roosen of Hamburg, for which De Bary stood as guarantor. Trosien, however, continued to find excuses for non-repayment, even after De Bary wrote to him saying that further default would lead to their ruin.

This was no idle threat, for in March 1793 the house was obliged to cease payments. However, their creditors supported them in an approach to the *Schepenen* of Amsterdam with a request that the partners be allowed to continue in control in order that, with the assistance of the trustees in bankruptcy, the firm would be enabled to repay its creditors in full. The trustees, J.C.Hasselgreen, Voûte Bros. and A.Vereul, empowered three houses in St.Petersburg, Amburger & Son, Raimbert & Co. and Rowand Carr & Co., to collect debts totalling cf 307,000 from Trosien. At the same time they arranged, through the Russian envoy in The Hague, for the Vice-Chancellor, Count Ostermann, to be acquainted with the situation. They argued that Dutch merchants had for some time been suffering severe losses as a result of the large number of bankruptcies in Russia and, moreover, were the victims of the evasion by Russian debtors of the law and of the legal processes for its enforcement.[1]

Trosien, stung by these acts against his person, refused to negotiate with the appointed houses in St.Petersburg. He did not like the look of the first; he disliked Frenchmen and he refused to negotiate with an Englishman. And he ignored further correspondence from the trustees.[2]

Much more serious, and of direct interest to Hope & Co., was the shaky position of the house of Sutherland in St.Petersburg. Baron Richard Sutherland (he had been raised to the nobility by the empress) had died in the latter part of 1791, soon after his mighty patron, Potemkin. The enemies who had earlier harassed him now fell with renewed vigour upon the house which bore his name, accusing it of having indulged, under his leadership, in questionable financial practices. The campaign led the Russian government to set up a committee to examine Sutherland's accounts during his period as Court Banker; pending the committee's report, the settlement of his estate was suspended.

Voûte's first act upon reaching St.Petersburg was to visit Sutherland's office and make the acquaintance of the surviving partners, Browne,

Whishaw and Rall. His initial impression of them was mixed: Browne (a son-in-law of Sutherland) he described as 'a man who would not hurt a fly,' of Whishaw he had a higher opinion, while Rall was 'a he-man, an intriguer through and through, restless, possessing the gift of the gab, and destined to make progress in this country.' Sutherland's own son, a degenerate libertine, was ill and could not be present, but Whishaw explained that his condition was improving, 'for Madame Mercury has got him out of trouble.'[1] Whishaw revealed that the house was going through a difficult period pending the settlement of Sutherland's estate and that their drafts were not willingly accepted. From Rall, Voûte learned that the government was disputing the firm's claim to commission on the fourteenth and fifteenth loans, and that bad debts of at least 80,000 roubles would have to be written off.[2]

With all these factors in mind, Voûte deemed it wise to delay broaching the subject of Hope's claims on the house. As far as the Trosien affair was concerned, he proposed to first quietly reconnoitre the ground. He and Porter did, however, obtain an audience with Count Samaylov, the Attorney General, who occupied a central position in domestic affairs, justice and financial matters, but whose powers had been limited during the reign of Catherine II by the influence of the empress's favourite.[3]

The favourite could exert considerable pressure, for good or for evil, and thus it was advisable not to ignore him. In 1793 it was upon Platon Zubov that the empress's favour fell, and after the meeting with Samaylov Voûte obtained an audience with him. He also accorded due honour to Zubov's secretary, Altesti, an Italian fortune-hunter who, within the protection of his master's influential position, maintained his own circle of protégés and who was in a position to furnish an *entrée* to Zubov.

In his reports to Hope & Co., Voûte had difficulty in describing in detail Zubov's position at the Russian Court. He had soon discovered that his letters were opened by the Russian police, and thus he had to be extremely careful in his references to government officials and to the situation at Court. He went so far as to experiment with a code based on key words, but even this failed to provide the required secrecy and in the end he resorted to using the diplomatic bag of a foreign embassy, which was not subject to Russian censorship.[4]

In one such confidential letter, he described Zubov as 'well disposed but of limited knowledge and a man with a heavy burden of debt.' It was reported that he had ousted Bezborodko, the Secretary of State and for many years the true head of the foreign ministry, from his position of power.[5] According to Voûte, Bezborodko was 'the brain behind the whole empire,' but in his private life a degraded individual who was addicted to gambling and abhorred regular work. But when he worked, he did more in a quarter of an hour than others did in a whole day. Markov, his secretary, was equally lazy and degraded; his household was ruled by an actress and several other beauties. He, too, was a gambler, 'but as sharp as a needle' and he was gradually shifting his loyalties to the up and coming man, Zubov. Voûte reported that the Vice-Chancellor, Ostermann, an elderly, tired figure, was head of the foreign ministry in name only, and that he had always been treated like a doormat by his colleagues.[1] Samaylov was good-hearted, but he was a soldier and not a politician; he was ignorant of jurisprudence and disinterested in financial matters. As a brother-in-law of Potemkin, he had risen with him, but after the latter's death in 1791 Samaylov's influence had waned, though he had retained his office. He, too, was a gambler and was thus continually short of money.

Alexander Zablukov, the Imperial Treasurer, struck Voûte as being one of the few respectable people in this environment. He was a man of enlightened views, well disposed towards foreigners and the only one with a normal family life.[2] Voûte also had great respect for Myatlev, one of the senior directors of the state-controlled Assignat Bank, whom he described as 'an unusual man,' adding that he had notions of justice.[3]

This, in Voûte's view, was the principal shortcoming in Russia: each and every one of the courts could be bribed, and in this situation decent people had little incentive to bring actions, with the result that only those who, like Trosien, were up to no good attempted legal proceedings. Voûte was convinced that for fifty thousand roubles he could easily have had Trosien convicted, but his aim was to secure justice and in doing so to set an example. The government's financial needs were limitless, and the Court spent vast sums and paid with cabinet bonds which ran for four years and at times changed hands at 30% below par.

So short of funds was the Russian government that it was unable even to meet its commitments towards its own citizens. As a result, trade was dislocated and private individuals found themselves unable to press their claims in courts of law since the government was ultimately the principal debtor. Voûte reported that this situation lay behind Bezborodko's decision to terminate saltpetre mining on one of his estates. All the organs of government were affected by the dearth of money, and the failure to meet invoices for drugs supplied to the College of Medicine added to Sutherland & Co.'s difficulties. Even the Assignat Bank was living from hand to mouth: it was rumoured that when a lady had called to withdraw 50,000 roubles, the bank was obliged to borrow the money from the St. Petersburg merchant Ritter.[1] All these bodies, Voûte wrote, were headed by military men with no understanding of the job and who earned too little, yet all managed to amass a fortune. They spent more time talking than working, and every day saw decisions taken which conflicted with earlier ones.

The picture which Voûte painted of the foreign merchants in St.Petersburg was just as dismal. In his opinion, Wegelin, of the house of Bonar, and Porter and his partner, Brown, were the only men with honest principles. Bagge, of the house of Bagge & Van Eyssel, was a righteous man but could not be described as a shining light. Ritter, whom Voûte described as a classic example of duplicity, was on excellent terms with Samaylov and Ostermann, and because of this Russia's needs abroad had since Sutherland's death been financed with drafts issued by the house which he headed. Ritter also had a grudge against Hope & Co. which he aired everywhere by saying that the Company had made millions out of Russia.[2] Rall alone was a match for Ritter, because he understood the situation in St.Petersburg and knew just who possessed influence and who did not. Voûte judged that Rall would get very far–a prediction which was later to come true, with extremely unpleasant consequences for Hope & Co. Rall also had connexions with Hasselgreen and, through him, was associated with Meisner and with the financing operations in Poland. In view of the very bad example set by the foreign merchants in St.Petersburg, Voûte concluded that it would be quite wrong to have any illusions concerning the mentality of their Russian counterparts there.

The reports which reached Voûte concerning Richard Sutherland were largely adverse. He was said to have recklessly lent out monies entrusted to him and to have incurred huge losses on exchange operations and exports of goods. He was described as well intentioned but unsuited to his profession. He had frittered away his time and money in chasing after the wife of another merchant, Severin, and had put her above his business interests. Having achieved the position of Court Banker, thanks to protection and to his connexions, he had found it extremely difficult to refuse requests for loans, especially from Potemkin, the mention of whose name was said to have made him tremble. The upshot of this situation was that Potemkin's descendants alone owed him 762,000 roubles. Voûte subsequently learned that, prior to his appointment as Court Banker, Sutherland had incurred debts totalling 450,000 roubles; he had pinned his faith on recovering this sum, and more, through his new office. When, in due course, his position indeed improved, success went to his head and he commenced to fling his money about. Those who had procured the office for him had known of his weakness and indulgence, and had abused them shamelessly. During his lifetime Sutherland had never been called upon to account for his management of the finances, but now that he was dead the vultures, spearheaded by the most unscrupulous profiteers, were tearing at his bones. Voûte observed that the smallness of Sutherland's estate (he left practically nothing) said much for his goodheartedness, but little for his ability as a merchant.[1]

Voûte was nevertheless of the opinion that the shortcomings which he had experienced in the Russian society represented only one side of the story: against the laziness, depravity, corruption and waste must be set the immense resources and the limitless potential of the country, which continued to overawe the observer. It seemed to him that, up to a point, this potential encouraged the fatalism, improvidence and waste, inasmuch as the nation, in time of real need, could always fall back on its untapped reserves which, with only efficient exploitation and strict control, could rapidly enable the largest deficit to be converted into a surplus. 'If we can maintain peace, we will repay all our debts within six years,' Voûte was told. And he believed this.[2]

Russia's natural resources, however, lay open to attack by her redoubtable neighbours, and she was therefore compelled to protect her territory, which she did by expanding her frontiers. Had Voûte been told that: 'The Russians will never enter Constantinople or Peking,' he would have replied: 'They will be there; they can do anything on which they set their minds.'[3] One more war with the Turks would suffice to impart 'a clear structure' to the pattern of trade in southern Russia, because then the links with the Greek archipelago and the whole of the Mediterranean would be firmly established. Voûte commented that a glance at the map of Europe was sufficient to show that Russia's favourable position and the vastness of her territory enabled her government to smash any nation which opposed her. Whatever Sir Francis Baring might say in his letters to Voûte, one visit to Russia would be enough to make him change his views and agree with Voûte that Russia's immense strength was founded on 'the irresistible principle that there is more than enough food to feed the population.' England was also powerful, but her strength was stretched over the seas, whereas Russia could concentrate hers. "If only system and order exist, all must bend.'[4]

Voûte might well conjure up visions of system and order, and dream of the country's inestimable potential wealth, but this in no way detracted from the fact that the reality in Russia was made up of chaotic situations and a desperate scarcity of money. This was brought home to Voûte when, before he had an opportunity to broach the subject of Hope's loan to Poland, he was buttonholed by Rall with a request for a loan for a distinguished Polish lady. At first Rall declined to reveal her name, but later he disclosed that he was acting for the Countess Potocka, who was greatly in favour with Catherine II by reason of her pro-Russian sympathies and of the services which her husband, Count Felix Potocki, had rendered to Russia in organizing the Targowica Confederation.[1] The early messages indicated that the countess desired a loan of 400,000 ducats, security for which would be provided in the form of mortgages on her estates in Galicia and a guarantee from Catherine II herself. The empress had formerly advanced money to meritorious subjects, against the security of estates, but she could no longer do so since the Treasury coffers were empty. Voûte was informed that the valuation of serfs, which was customary in the case of imperial loans, would apply to the loan requested. This would be at the rate of forty roubles per head, a very low figure because women, children, houses and land were totally ignored for the purposes of a mortgage. If the debtor failed to meet his or her obligations, the estate was forfeited and became Crown land – with consequent benefit to the empress. The proposed loan would run for eighteen years – an abnormally long period – and bear interest at 5%. The countess was very rich, but events in Poland had left her short of ready money and she faced the obligation to repay a large sum in Dubno, in Galicia, by 6th January 1794. If she failed to do so, she would be put in an extremely difficult position, and this had to be avoided at all costs. Voûte considered it important that Hope & Co. should provide the loan; after all, the countess ranked high in the favour of the empress and could thus influence, one way or the other, the proposal that Russia should accept responsibility for Hope's loan to Poland. Apart from this consideration, however, it was imperative that the loan be furnished, for: 'The empress must never receive the impression that your house is unable to surmount its difficulties,' and her guarantee would have to suffice to ensure success.[2]

Initially, Voûte assumed that the imperial guarantee had been given only to Countess Potocka, but it later transpired that Countess Alexandra Branicka, a niece and former mistress of Potemkin, had also succeeded in obtaining such a favour. Her husband, Count Xavier Branicki, had been concerned in the Targowica Confederation, where he had rendered services to the empress comparable with those of Count Potocki.[3] Countess Branicka had consulted Ritter, to whom she had intimated her wish that the guarantee be transmitted to Holland as security for a loan to be floated there. Voûte had earlier drawn Samaylov's attention to the adverse effect which incidental, guarantee-backed loans could have upon Hope's latest Russian loans, which had still not been fully subscribed.

When he heard that the guarantee was after all to be transmitted to Holland, Voûte hurried to Zubov's palace, where he was met by Countess Branicka and her husband, Prince Lubomirski, Count Limpicki and Zubov himself. Countess Branicka, whom Voûte described as 'an avaricious virago who tyrannized her husband,' had the most to say. Like Countess Potocka, she desired that Hope & Co. should arrange for an advance to be placed at her disposal at Dubno early in January. Voûte replied that this was easier said than done, since the defeat by the French of the Dutch armies in Flanders had produced a scarcity of credit, making fresh loans impossible for the time being. Furthermore, the ban imposed by the States General of the Republic on foreign loans had to be considered. The best course would be to await further developments; indeed, that was the only advice which he could offer. Voûte added that the guarantee would have to be despatched to Hope, as otherwise the Russian loans could be prejudiced, and that would be contrary to the wish of the empress. The countess ultimately agreed, and even allowed herself to be persuaded to appoint Rall as her agent for the loan. When Voûte reached this point, Prince Lubomirski commenced to calculate how much money the Amsterdam merchant Gülcher had in Warsaw, adding that he would be paying him 25,000 ducats in December. Voûte promptly handed back the guarantee to Count Branicki and observed that the loan would clearly not now be required since Prince Lubomirski could furnish the ducats. This, however, was not in the prince's mind, and the episode ended with the guarantee being returned to Voûte with a request to try to obtain the loan in Amsterdam.[1]

One thing which Voûte did achieve was a reduction of the loan sums: Countess Potocka would now receive no more than 150,000 ducats, and Countess Branicka 100,000; of these sums, 54,000 and 100,000 ducats respectively were required in Dubno before 6th January. He again appealed urgently to Hope & Co. to do their utmost to promote the success of the loan, if indeed there was any chance at all. He proposed that Berck, one of Hope's brokers, should spread the sums over as many *entrepreneurs* as possible, thus reducing individual shares to a minimum. It was believed in Russia that Hope & Co. could achieve anything, and with an eye to other issues it was vital that this impression should be sustained.

Voûte had already discussed the matter of the loan to King Stanislaw with Altesti, Zubov's secretary, and on 21st October, at the latter's request, he set down the details in a memorandum which was to be given to Zubov. Motivated by the guarantees in respect of loans to the two countesses, Voûte made it appear that the loan to King Stanislaw in 1786 formed an extension of the loan of 1777, and that the guarantee given by Catherine II in 1777 therefore also applied to the loan of 1786. He postulated that Hope & Co. had agreed to negotiate these loans only because they stemmed from dispensations granted by the empress to the King of Poland. If the Russian government was prepared to place bonds of the last Russian loan to a value of cf 800,000 at the Company's disposal, it would surrender its claims on King Stanislaw to the empress and, moreover, meet the remaining interest and principal payments in respect of the Polish loan. Catherine could settle the resulting claim on King Stanislaw by assuming direct control of the 'oeconomies' of Brest-Litowsk, Grodno, Kobrin, Szawel and Olitzka.[1] It is remarkable that Voûte should have invoked a non-existent Russian gurantee for the loan of 1786, the more so since the Russian government must have known as well as he did that it did not exist. Moreover, the 'oeconomies' to which he referred served as mortgage security only for the 1777 loan and not for the one of 1786–unless, of course, one wishes to read this into the passage: 'All the wealth and property, present and future, which belongs to us.'[2]

In a memorandum written a few days later and intended for Samaylov, which dealt principally with the Russian loans, Voûte reverted to his conversion plan. After giving an interesting and detailed description of the technique of placing loans in Holland (reference to which has already been made in this treatise), he stated that, following the military defeat in Flanders, the once so abundant flow of money had dried up, with the result that only two million guilders had been subscribed towards the eighteenth and nineteenth loans.

A victory by the armies of the Dutch Republic and its allies, the memorandum continued, would bring an early resumption of the flow. Admittedly, the suspension of the loans to Poland, to King Stanislaw and to the Polish magnates had no bearing on Russia's credit, but it did not enhance the loans as a whole. If the empress would agree to accept responsibility for the balance of cf 800,000, this would undoubtedly have a favourable influence on the Russian loans in the Republic. Such a step would be natural now that Catherine had furnished guarantees for loans to individual Polish subjects, and the Russian government could accomplish this without injury or disadvantage by sequestering the revenues of King Stanislaw and having the interest and principal payments met from these. In his proposals, Voûte thus allied himself completely with the concept of the liquidation of Poland, and in his view the chances of these being accepted were increased by the fact that on 14th October 1793, under severe pressure from 'the venerable and truly great Mr. De Sievers,' the *sejm* had approved a treaty which brought Poland completely under Russian tutelage.[1]

Late in October 1793 Samaylov informed Voûte that the empress had consented to take over the loan to the Polish king; however, she had stipulated that the transfer should constitute a separate transaction in order not to let it weigh upon the bonds of the latest Russian loans. Voûte saw in this an opportunity for speculation: he was willing to buy up Polish bonds at the current low price, safe in the knowledge that either the King or the Republic of Poland would ultimately have to meet the obligation, and that the news that Catherine had assumed responsibility for the loan would send up the price.[2]

During the discussion, Samaylov referred to the lack of success with the eighteenth and nineteenth loans to Russia. He had, he said, been offered six million guilders at 4½% interest, whereas Hope had insisted upon 5%. It was not the half per cent which was worrying him, but rather the fact that he had expected immediate results and had not got them. Voûte attempted to convince him that the prevailing circumstances were responsible for the delay and that if Hope & Co. could not succeed, an inexperienced house would have no chance whatsoever.

To Voûte, Samaylov's offer smacked of one of the many intrigues which had been woven in the latter's circle since the death of Sutherland, against which it was wise to be on one's guard. Voûte was particularly apprehensive of Hasselgreen, who, during a visit to Warsaw, had won over the Russian envoy, Sievers, by means of sizeable loans. Reports indicated that Hasselgreen was at that moment on his way to St.Petersburg, almost certainly with the aim of supplanting Hope & Co. at the Russian Court.[3]

Hasselgreen, however, did not put in an immediate appearance, and Voûte had no cause for complaint about the manner in which he was received into society circles in St.Petersburg. Rall showed his gratitude to Voûte for having involved him in the loan to Countess Branicka by inviting him to a banquet attended by a host of counts and countesses, and Samaylov, in a burst of affability, invited Voûte to a ball which he and his wife gave for the Grand Duke Alexander and his lady, at which all the Russian nobility were present. It was on the grand style, 'les tables splendidement servies et les salles illuminées supérieurement.' It was none the less a convivial occasion, unmarred by sharp distinctions of rank or class: 'It resembled a family rather than a group of people of differing classes;

everyone, from the members of the Imperial family to plain officers, mixed and danced together; there was no trace of etiquette and the rules of procedure were flexible and not in the least restrictive. In short, it was the greatness of Russia showing itself in all its splendour.'[1]

Despite all the friendly gestures by Samaylov, the wearisome wait in Zubov's antechamber and the lengthy discussions with Markov and Ostermann, little progress was made in the matter of the Polish loan. On 3rd December Samaylov promised a decision on the following day, but when this arrived the decision was postponed until the sixth on the grounds that the empress was indisposed. It was later put back to the tenth, and finally, on the fourteenth, the Attorney General announced that Catherine was not favourably disposed towards a settlement because she was greatly displeased with the King of Poland.[2] Her displeasure will have been directed not so much at the king himself as at the growing tide of resistance throughout Poland to the enforced surrender of territory. Voûte declined to regard the rejection as final and remained convinced that the empress would change her mind.

At about the same time, a letter arrived from Hope & Co. saying that the Company could not entertain the proposed loans to the two countesses. The news came as a most unpleasant shock to Rall, who had committed himself to help Countess Potocka, and he appealed to Hope to assist him in keeping his promise. After consulting Voûte, the Company offered Rall a credit of cf 130,000. Voûte was gratified by the fact that the warrants and the guarantees were in the Company's hands, thus preventing the reputation and the credit of the empress being compromised.[3]

Where the loans in Holland were concerned, Voûte's relationship with Samaylov became less pleasant. Hope & Co. needed approximately three million guilders for interest payments on various dates in 1794, but the Russian government had already received more than half of the two million guilders raised towards the eighteenth and nineteenth loans. In a letter written to Samaylov at the end of November 1793, Labouchère explained that the Company, in anticipation of further subscriptions to the loans, was prepared to advance the balance of the sum required. However, he made it clear that the offer did not apply to the million guilders already placed a the disposal of the Russian government.[4]

Later reports from Amsterdam severely diminished Voûte's optimism regarding the chances of completing the Russian loans. The conquest of Toulon by the forces of the revolutionary government in France–'a development which has deeply disturbed me'–could hardly fail to make the money market in Holland even tighter.

The revolts by royalists in the Vendée and in Brittany threatened to collapse, and if the French ceased to be preoccupied in those regions, the full force of their armies would be turned on the allied troops in Brabant, Flanders and Germany; the consequences did not bear contemplation. It was rumoured in St.Petersburg that the Turkish ambassador in London was planning to mediate between France and the allied powers; if he were to succeed in his mission, the Turks would gain a firm foothold in central Europe, but it would make little difference whether they or the French were there: 'the only distinction lies in the manner in which they chop off the heads.'[1]

Voûte had initially reacted with enthusiasm to Henry Hope's return to the Republic early in December 1793, but now he began to think differently. Henry Hope had urged Voûte to appeal to the Russian government to take a strong line with regard to the pro-French tendencies of Denmark and Sweden, but Voûte was careful to avoid the subject: 'that is completely outside my sphere; it is a political matter, and this fact alone would make me avoid it.' He reported that the Russian Court favoured action but that the severity of the Russian winter made it impracticable. 'The climate is a supreme power and as such cannot be trifled with.'[2]

While in the process of writing his letter dated 18th January 1794, Voûte was urgently summoned by Samaylov, who requested him to approach Hope & Co. regarding an advance on the uncompleted eighteenth and nineteenth loans, in the form of gold coins. Voûte referred Samaylov to Labouchère's letter of late November 1793 in order to show that money was too tight to permit any advance, adding that under the prevailing circumstances earlier promises could not be maintained. He went on to point out that a report had just been received, stating that the Duke of Brunswick and General Wurmser had both suffered defeats and that Mannheim had fallen to the French. In this situation, Holland's riches were illusory, for with no money in circulation the Dutch investor was obliged to view his bonds as evidence of money which he had once possessed, and not as proof of money which he still possessed. He stressed that, in compliance with earlier instructions from Samaylov, Hope & Co. had already despatched a sum in golden ducats to Igelström, the Russian envoy in Warsaw. Samaylov conceded this, but requested that the Company should keep available a further sum in gold coins. For the moment he would be content with a draft on Warsaw for 240 ducats, and this Voûte could not bring himself to refuse.[3]

At the end of January 1794, Voûte became seriously ill. 'Une colique continuelle' was how he described it to Hope, adding that Dr.Guthrie, a well-known British doctor in St.Petersburg, had saved him from the grave.[1] Voûte blamed his illness–of which, according to him, there were then a thousand other cases in the city–on the mild winter with its wet snow. He was put on a diet and, because this had to be prepared separately, he was obliged to seek a new headquarters, the Huguet Hotel, even though this cost 60 roubles a month more.

Although Voûte was a sick man, Samaylov summoned him with the utmost urgency to the Court, where, in the presence of the full ministerial council, he informed Voûte that the Russian government required a sum of 200,000 guilders to be placed at its disposal in Frankfurt, and that a decision must be taken within a matter of hours. Voûte, ill and weak, and kept on his feet with Chinese rhubarb, drew the attention of the Court to the large sums owed to Hope & Co. by all manner of merchant houses in Russia and to the two million guilders still owing for interest payments in 1794. Samaylov thereupon offered to give him 160,000–170,000 roubles which he could remit to London or Amsterdam, on condition that the cf 200,000 for Frankfurt was forthcoming. Voûte was requested to give his answer by 6.30 p.m. When he returned, he found that the urgency had evaporated: it later transpired that Ritter had furnished the money in the form of drafts on Melvil & Co. and Hasselgreen of Amsterdam.[2]

This episode gave rise to a discussion between Samaylov and Voûte concerning Russia's finances as a whole, and this was continued on the following morning. The meeting gave Voûte an opportunity to bring up the Trosien case, and he made no attempt to disguise his displeasure concerning the affair. Trosien had used Voûte's presence as an excuse to refuse further contact with the appointed houses in St. Petersburg. He had threatened to bring an action against Voûte, who had thereupon let it be known that he was willing to meet Trosien only in the presence of four or five merchants of good standing and reputation, in order to have reliable witnesses should this be necessary. The case against Trosien should have been heard at the end of November 1793, but owing to slackness, for which Samaylov was partly to blame, no progress had been made up to the time of the discussion, in late January 1794. Voûte made it plain that if people like Trosien were allowed to escape the law, he would have no alternative but to inform his principals that Russia was an abyss in which foreign capital became swallowed up, and as such was not worthy of further credit.[3]

This strong line produced results. Samaylov immediately gave instructions for the merchant Bacharacht to be summoned and, after a conversation between these two, Trosien was ordered to appear before the Attorney

General to explain–in Voûte's presence–his continued default. During this encounter, Voûte was informed that the case would be laid before an arbitration tribunal on the following Friday.

Voûte also succeeded in extracting a number of undertakings in regard to Sutherland's estate. Whereas he had previously got no farther than some vague promises to report to the empress, Samaylov now informed him that the sole obstacle was a report by Bezborodko to Catherine, which he consented to expedite.

In view of the pending hearing involving Trosien, Voûte again delayed his departure for Moscow. At that moment, bringing down Trosien was his prime objective. As he saw it, Trosien would, at the least, be ordered to pay a portion of his debts; if he was unable to do so–and this appeared very likely–his assets would be sequestrated and he would go bankrupt. If all this took place, he, Voûte, would have shown that Trosien had an Achilles' heel, and an action of this sort would be of value in his negotiations with the partners of Thomson Rowand.[1]

Despite all the straight talking, however, Voûte was ill at ease. He was again haunted by the thought of Hasselgreen's arrival in St.Petersburg. Hasselgreen was said to be on very close terms with Ritter, who in turn had a hold over Samaylov, not only by reason of the credit which he had furnished in Frankfurt but also because he had settled some of Samaylov's private debts. It was rumoured that Hasselgreen would make sweeping proposals to the Russian government and, indeed, that numerous undertakings had already been entered into. Voûte would dearly like to see Hope & Co. make an offer to counter the threat. Should the Company advance the monies for the interest payments in 1794, even though the million guilders had been placed at the disposal of the Russian government, or should it not? This very sombre image formed the prelude to Voûte's greatest grievance, namely that Hope & Co. had not given him full powers to act on their behalf.

He decided that the Company would have to make up its mind on this issue: either it gave him full power for a specified period and up to a specified monetary limit, or he would wash his hands of the Russian loan affair.[2] Voûte maintained that he needed this degree of backing in his negotiations with Samaylov, for he did not hesitate to say what was on his mind, and the truth was not always to the liking of the Attorney General. A memorandum from Voûte on the subject of rates of exchange, which was in fact destined for the empress, had lain on Samaylov's desk for more than two months for the simple reason that Samaylov was frightened to pass it on.[3] In this document, Voûte had dealt in depth with the fall in the value of the rouble and the factors which had caused this. In a cautious but unambiguous manner, he had laid the blame at the feet of the Russian government, which had financed its deficits by the inflationary act of creating *assignats*.

Voûte also expressed himself at some length concerning the position of Court Banker, one which was customarily entrusted to a foreigner. He referred in particular to Richard Sutherland who, he said, had established Russia's credit abroad but, by stubbornly believing in a boom in the exchange rate of the rouble even when this continued to fall, had suffered serious losses on exchange operations and the exporting of goods; these losses, he went on, had harmed Sutherland himself, the Russian government and Russian trade as a whole, for the last-named had not been shown where the fault lay. That, in the final analysis, the fault lay with the government and its inflationary policy, Voûte left unsaid.

All ills, it was argued, could be cured by taking a slice of Russia's inestimable natural resources and increasing exports of these. Then why, for example, did the government leave so much copper in the soil? If copper mining were to be greatly expanded, exports of this metal could be increased and silver imported in exchange. With this silver as security, *assignats*, which would have to be freely exchangeable for silver roubles, could be issued. In this manner the exchange rate for the rouble could be restored to its former intrinsic silver value of 36 *stuivers*, with consequent benefit to Russia's trade and to the government itself, which could then meet its commitments for interest and principal abroad at much less cost in terms of roubles. Other mined products such as lead and saltpetre could be dealt with similarly. In later years Voûte was to continue to hammer home the theme of 'the treasures of the bowels of the earth,' and even to achieve temporary success.[1]

Voûte may have refrained from committing any startling truths to paper, but in a conversation with Samaylov he implied that he was well aware that, because they were in debt, those at the top hesitated to do justice to those who sought it. 'He fell silent and appeared embarrassed; a deep sigh which escaped him convinced me that I had touched a sensitive spot.' For this reason, Samaylov was anxious for the case against Trosien to be settled amicably. If Trosien were to be committed to prison, matters which could better remain hidden might well come to light. It seemed to Voûte that the weakness of Samaylov's position enhanced his own influence somewhat: 'Bear in mind that a Russian is proud and haughty when he has the upper hand, but weak and servile when he is at the wrong end of the stick.'[2]

Voûte did not have long to wait for evidence of the weakness of which he suspected Samaylov. Early in February 1794 he received an alarming letter from Hope & Co. concerning a threat of Russian-guaranteed loans to Poland being negotiated through other intermediaries. After adopting the treaty with Russia, the *sejm* at Grodno had discussed the personal debts incurred by King Stanislaw; these were still unpaid, and his creditors, who included Tepper, Blanc and Meisner, faced serious difficulties. In response to Polish complaints on this issue, the Russians had offered to guarantee a loan of 10½ million guilders which was to be raised in Holland against the security of Crown lands; this sum roughly corresponded with the total of the king's personal debts as determined by the *sejm* at its meeting on 9th November 1793.[1]

In Warsaw, Sievers had commenced negotiations with Hasselgreen and Gülcher, who were still in that city; but when, in December 1793, he fell into disfavour–probably as a result of intrigues woven by Zubov–his successor, Igelström, contacted the merchant James Durno from Memel, who, on his instructions, wrote to Hope & Co. on the subject.[2] To the Company, the latest Russian plans came as a bolt out of the blue, and the reply sent to Igelström testified to the shock felt by the partners. A copy of the letter was sent to Voûte with instructions to thrust it under Samaylov's nose. Voûte, who had already heard vague rumours in St.Petersburg concerning the new Polish loan, made for the Attorney General's office, bearing the missive. Samaylov listened to him in stunned silence and then confessed that the guarantee had been given completely without his knowledge. Voûte was inclined to believe him, for it was almost certain that the principal figure in the whole affair was Zubov, of whom it was said that where Poland was concerned he had managed to reduce Samaylov to the role of executor of other people's decisions.[3]

Taking advantage of Samaylov's dismay, Voûte again proceeded to hammer away, both verbally and in writing, at the fundamental issues: an early decision in the Trosien and Sutherland cases, and the conversion of Hope's Polish loan into a Russian loan. A copy of his memorandum was sent to the powerful Zubov, with the advice to look for a new Court Banker so that he might be expertly advised on economic matters.[4] Voûte also discussed this question with Samaylov, advising him to appoint Rall, who had been in charge of the only efficiently run department of the house of Sutherland.[5]

As always, Samaylov was lavish with his promises, but Voûte was gradually losing his faith in these: it was already mid-February and no progress had been made. In matters of finance, the Attorney General repeatedly displayed his utter ignorance. While consenting to raise the matter of the Polish loan with the empress once more, he appeared to have forgotten that the sum involved would be deducted from the proceeds of the eighteenth and nineteenth Russian loans, from which he was anticipating a million guilders in gold in addition to the sum required to pay the interest. When the facts eventually dawned on him, he proposed a new loan of three million guilders, from the proceeds of which the sum of the Polish loan would be deducted and the balance remitted to Russia.[1] When Voûte attempted to point out that it would be folly to embark on a fresh loan while the previous ones were still less than fully subscribed, Samaylov replied that he had been offered twelve million guilders in Brabant prior to embarking on the eighteenth and nineteenth loans with Hope & Co., and Voûte was quite unable to convince him of the absurdity of such an offer from a quarter which bordered on a theatre of war. Samaylov contented himself by saying that the financial sacrifices made by Hope in order to support the price of the Russian bonds on the Amsterdam Stock Exchange would have to be met from the proceeds of the two loans, and that beyond this it was no concern of his.[2]

Against this background, it is no wonder that the partners in faraway Amsterdam found it increasingly difficult to understand the situation, and became more and more impatient with the absence of results. Voûte wrote in lyrical terms about the inestimable riches of Russia and the immense opportunities which existed there, but no progress was made with the conversion of the Polish loan, nor were any of the outstanding debts received.[3] Voûte defended himself by pointing out that the situation in Russia was totally different, that it could in no way be compared with the situation in Holland or in England. He maintained that he approached matters 'in a vigorous manner' because he was convinced that a weak and watery attitude was out of keeping with an atmosphere 'where the severity (of the weather) tones up the muscles better than does our damp climate.'[4] If any of the Hopes had been to Russia, he wrote, his actions would be better understood.[5] It was not surprising that, in this colossal empire, little interest existed in events outside: 'Here, everything must serve to reinforce the coherence and power of the empire; anything which does not do so is of no consequence.' Voûte was himself anxious to exercise the patience which seemed to be required, until such time as the Company cried 'Enough.' But no rapid progress could be expected, for on the day on which he wrote this to Hope, 25th February 1794, the carnival season was beginning and all official departments would be closed for eight to ten days. This would be followed by a six-week period of fasting, which included a number of public holidays, so that Hope's business would be further delayed.[1]

While these events were taking place, the outlook for the house of Sutherland had become steadily more dismal. The committee of inquiry had still not completed its report, and unless and until Sutherland's estate was settled the house could not remain solvent. To make matters worse, the firm's credit standing steadily deteriorated; while on the one hand Alexander Sutherland in London was threatening to return drafts totalling 80,000 roubles, on the other there was the situation that it would take a ukase to make the firm's debtors pay up–and this could only come when the committee had reported on its findings. Voûte reported that the house faced bankruptcy unless a quarter of a million roubles was received from the government at an early date. Both he and Whishaw made desperate efforts to stave off the collapse. Whishaw drew up a plan for dealing with the firm's liabilities, which totalled 876,100 roubles (including 351,000 roubles owed to Hope & Co.). The assets amounted to 700,800 roubles and thus, in theory, were adequate to meet 80% of the debts.

Whishaw was prepared to accept responsibility for this percentage of the commitments on condition that Sutherland Jr. and his brother-in-law, Browne, undertook to meet the balance.

In a memorandum to Samaylov, Voûte pleaded for honourable treatment of the Sutherland affair. He agreed that the late Court Banker owed the government 3,700,000 roubles, but pointed out that this sum included losses of 660,000 roubles on export shipments and 584,000 roubles on exchange operations, both of which had arisen from complying with verbal instructions from the former Attorney General, Prince Vyazemsky, aimed at bolstering up the value of the rouble. In his opinion, the losses on these transactions should be borne by the government. Moreover, the memorandum continued, claims by the house of Sutherland on various government bodies must be deducted, as must the debts incurred by Grand Duke Paul and the late Potemkin, amounting to 200,000 and 762,000 roubles respectively. The balance of the deficit might well be met from the sale of houses and cabinet bonds and the recovery of liquid debts.

Voûte went on to say that while he did not seek to cover up the baron's shortcomings–a cash deficit of 147,000 roubles was a very serious matter–it was only fair that attention should also be focussed on the complicity of those who, knowing Sutherland's weaknesses, had helped him to achieve his office and had then taken advantage of him. It was through Sutherland that Hope & Co. had finally become convinced of Russia's wealth, whereupon the Company had been willing to provide huge sums for the strengthening of the country's army and navy.[1] If Sutherland were to be declared bankrupt at the time of his decease, not only would this mean the end of the house which bore his name, but it would also be a slap in the face of Hope & Co. and would seriously jeopardize Russia's credit.

The die, however, had been cast. Voûte attempted to see Zubov and Samaylov, but Zubov threw the ball back into Samaylov's court, and the latter was adamant.[2] He argued that everyone, inside and outside Russia, knew that the baron had died a bankrupt, and that it was about time the fact was established. Voûte replied that this was the first he had heard about it in all the months of effort, by way of memoranda and audiences, to secure a satisfactory settlement of Sutherland's affairs. He reiterated that Russia's credit standing would be severely harmed if the house of Sutherland, Browne and Wishaw was made bankrupt by reason of the insolvency of the late Court Banker.

This remark incensed Samaylov, who asked what Voûte was driving at; was he trying to compare a mighty country like Russia with republics such as Genoa and Lucca? Sutherland had inflicted great damage on Russia, and his successors must be made to pay. When Voûte repeated his arguments concerning the role of those who had arranged for Sutherland's appointment, Samaylov informed him that the empress had commanded that all who had been concerned in the affair should be punished. Seeing no point in prolonging the argument, Voûte requested a firm decision concerning the estate on 11th March: either the baron had died insolvent, in which case the house which he led would become bankrupt on the 12th, or the successors would receive 250,000 roubles from the estate, in which case Voûte would go to their assistance with a further 100,000 roubles. Samaylov agreed to the proposal and even offered to delay the departure of the courier to Amsterdam until the 12th so that Hope & Co. could be informed of the decision as quickly as possible.[3]

With this, the fate of Sutherland, Browne and Whishaw was in fact sealed. Voûte visited a number of senior officials, but on 11th March 1794 the empress gave her verdict, which corresponded broadly with Samaylov's views, and on the following day the house of Sutherland collapsed.[4] Voûte was profoundly disappointed: this, then, was the outcome of five months' hard work. As for the action against Trosien, that would run its course; he had lost interest in it and had decided to leave for Moscow as soon as possible.[5]

The fact that the empress, as a soothing gesture, had–at long last–consented to the conversion of Hope's Polish loan did little to comfort Voûte. Fortunately, he could not know that even this success was to elude him, for on 12th March, the day on which the courier was to leave with the sad news of the bankruptcy of Sutherland and the good news of the conversion, an anti-Russian revolt broke out at Ostrolenka, in Poland, and this made any early settlement of Poland's debts an impossibility.[1]

However unhappy the Sutherland affair may have been, Voûte now at least had an opportunity to devote himself fully to matters concerning Thomson Rowand–and these certainly required some supervision. The reader will recall that, up to the time he left Moscow, Voûte had been unsuccessful in persuading Grant to sign a deed of partnership which, in fact, would have placed the firm under the supervision of Porter in St. Petersburg. Consequently, no agreement had been reached regarding security for the debts owed to Hope & Co. and Baring & Co. Instead of remitting funds, the partners in Moscow had continued to draw on Hope & Co. and, moreover, had borrowed money against security in Moscow, for which they would be paying at least 10 or 12% interest.[2]

It was for the express purpose of putting an end to these demonstrations of independence that Voûte arrived in Moscow on 25th March, tired and uncomfortable after a journey lasting exactly a week. From St.Petersburg to Novgorod he had travelled through melting snow, but then it had started snowing again and between Twer and Moscow the temperature had fallen to 20 or 25 degrees below zero. Only when they had stopped at Twer had he been able to undress, and then even his hopes of a good night's sleep had been dashed by an uncomfortable bed. But after only two days in Moscow he was sufficiently refreshed to receive Grant and Hawes. Their account had a familiar ring: little of the money owed to them had been received, and they had urgently needed 46,000 roubles to pay for goods which were to be sent to Baring & Co. Voûte gave them a stern lecture, pointing out that if they continued to delay their remittances, confidence on the part of Hope & Co. and Baring & Co. might one day be shaken.[3]

The partners were also warned to take more interest in the domestic trade, particularly that with the Crimea, the Caspian Sea and eastern Siberia.

Voûte was unable to devote a great deal of time to the affairs of Thomson Rowand, for soon he would have to return to his post in St.Petersburg to see what impression he, with the aid of Hope's letters concerning the outcome of the Sutherland affair, could make on Samaylov. Voûte made no mention of the signing of the partnership agreement in Moscow, so we must assume that Grant's policy of obstruction succeeded once more.

On 10th April 1794, in the same changeable weather as had accompanied his earlier journey, Voûte left Moscow. From there to Klin, a distance of fifty miles, he drove through rain, but this gradually turned to snow and on the first night an icy north wind caused the temperature to drop so sharply that Voûte was unable to keep warm despite wearing two fur coats and two pairs of fur boots. During the daytime it became too hot even for one fur coat, but for five successive nights it was bitterly cold. The jolting of the coach over the frozen roads so troubled him that he was no longer able to face bread or meat, and ate only a few apples and oranges which Countess Golowkin had given him in Moscow. The arrival of the frosts made it safer to cross the frozen rivers, but on one occasion Voûte, not trusting the ice, insisted on making the crossing on foot, while the Russians, intrepid as ever, drove the coach-and-six over a staging laid on the hard-packed ice.

The vehicle itself also suffered from the journey, the wheels threatening to disintegrate, the harnessing pole being fractured and the box shaken to the point where it had to be held together with pegs and ropes.

On 15th April Voûte alighted from the coach outside the Huguet Hotel, where he ran into Brown, Porter's partner. Brown, while not expecting him for another three or four days, had nevertheless instructed Huguet to light the stoves in Voûte's rooms. Although his head was swimming, Voûte remained outside to supervise the unloading of his baggage, 'for one must keep a weather-eye open in view of the St.Petersburg ravens, who are less kind than those who attended Elijah.'[1] Once inside the hotel, he briefly lapsed into unconsciousness. When he recovered, he attempted unsuccessfully to take some food, and then retired to bed–for the first time in five days. A few hours later he was awakened by Whishaw, who brought him letters from Hope & Co.; these were dated 25th March, thus prior to the arrival of the fatal news from St.Petersburg. Voûte could think of nothing except the wrath which he knew was being voiced in Amsterdam and of the insult to the Company, and in his own words he became so worked up that sleep was almost impossible; when he got up, he fainted so frequently that Dr.Guthrie had to be called in. His diagnosis was brief but unambiguous: 'You are physically and morally overheated; little medicine, but a lot of rest and quiet will cure you.'[2] A purgative served to refresh Voûte, and after drinking four glasses of port and eating some rye bread to give him strength he returned to his bed.

That evening, Bagge of the house of Bagge & Van Eyssel arrived bearing letters from Hope & Co. of 31st March. The language in which the writer of these had vented his spleen was such that Voûte put them aside and went back to bed. On the following day, 17th April, letters dated 28th March arrived from Amsterdam; the pile was now so high that Voûte spent a large part of the next day reading them. It was not easy to deliver Hope's letter to Samaylov, for it was Maundy Thursday and the Attorney General, together with the other members of the Court, had gone to church at six o'clock in the morning and would not return until four in the afternoon.

During the evening, Voûte developed an acute fever; Dr.Guthrie was called and administered an emetic, but the patient brought up only bile. By the next day his condition had so deteriorated that Dr.Guthrie called in Sir Samuel Rogerson, a Scot and the physician to Catherine II, who diagnosed 'inflammation of the gall bladder, accompanied by fever' and prescribed quinine.[1] This indeed proved beneficial, and by the 24th Voûte was over the worst and his skin had commenced to turn yellow. Guthrie and Rogerson were agreed that only Voûte's strong constitution had saved him. By the 26th of the month the patient had recovered sufficiently to write a letter to Henry Hope; this was given to the English courier and would be posted in Utrecht or Naarden in order to evade Russian censorship.

In this, he disclosed that all of Catherine's ministers had been knocked off balance by Hope's letter of censure to Samaylov, and added that because the recipient had been so stupid as to leave it on his desk, all St.Petersburg was now aware of the Company's rage. The letter had already had some effect, for those of Samaylov's minions who were engaged at Sutherland's offices were now less arrogant, and one had inadvertently mentioned that the final outcome of the affair might be less disagreeable than had at first been thought.[2] It was the custom for those who attended Eastertide church services to embrace each other before going their separate ways. The congregation at the Court chapel had included Grand Duke Paul, who otherwise lived in complete retirement, and after the service he had embraced all except Samaylov and Zubov; to Voûte, this was further proof that the two were hand in glove.

Rogerson had confided to Voûte that the empress's health and intellectual faculties were declining. In contrast, however, it was known that she had in the past fortnight repeatedly voiced her severe displeasure with the course of events in Poland, and that she was particularly rankled by the refusal of the Hollanders to make further loans to Russia. Voûte ascribed the Russian defeat in Poland–the prime cause of Catherine's wrath–to lack of experience on the part of the generals and the total failure of the commissariat, to which had to be added the utter chaos in the State's finances and a lack of ability among its ministers.

Despite the setback, Voûte was sure that the 'Jacobins Polonois' would ultimately be crushed by the sheer physical superiority of Russia and Prussia, and that the Hydra of the revolution would lose even the last of its heads. It was a source of satisfaction to him that the rebels would be given no quarter. After a veiled warning to Hope against 'K' (Kalichev?), he signed the letter 'André Cartier,' reasoning that, with the unsettled conditions in Poland, there was no certainty that the missive would reach Hope & Co. intact.[1]

Voûte's health improved only slowly–to the great consternation of the Russian ministers who, following Hope's letters, feared that the Company would sever its connexions with Russia. They realized that the drastic decree in which the Sutherland affair culminated, and which was published on 28th April, could be equally damaging to good relations with Hope. The decree prescribed that the sum of the monies owed to the Crown should be calculated at the unfavourable rate of exchange ruling at that moment, and not the rate applying when the money had flowed from Holland to Russia. The State would take over Sutherland's house and its contents, the inventory of his office, his mortgages on other houses and his cabinet bonds. At the same time, the government committed itself to pay the debts incurred by the various official bodies, but excluding the sums claimed from Potemkin, and it undertook to take vigorous steps to ensure that private debtors met their obligations.[2]

On the very same day, Sutherland's debtors were pilloried. Zakrewsky, the president of the College of Medicine, and Cley and Dolst, two of the members, faced a charge of having extorted money from Yeames, formerly Sutherland's cashier and the person principally responsible for deliveries of drugs, for passing Sutherland's invoices. Khlebnikov, head of the second department, was charged with failing to exercise adequate supervision of Sutherland and, in 1787, of having neglected to report the protesting of Sutherland's drafts to the then Attorney General, Vyazemsky. Khlebnikov was also ordered to repay 25,000 roubles unlawfully paid to him by Sutherland. Yeames was held responsible for the cash deficit of 147,000 roubles, and Rall was accused of delay in informing the authorities of the true state of affairs following Sutherland's death.[3]

Voûte predicted that Khlebnikov and Yeames would be severely punished, but that Rall had only been dragged in to please Ritter. Rall would certainly emerge unscathed, and in any case Ritter was losing favour now that, on the instructions of the Attorney General, the majority of remittances were being taken care of, not by Ritter but by the Court Broker, Fock. A substantial portion of the monies involved was destined for Hope & Co. to be used for the payment of interest. By this means, the government was trying to get back into the Company's good books.

Samaylov made repeated inquiries regarding Voûte's progress, and made it clear that he would be a welcome visitor when his condition permitted. Voûte replied that he was still far too weak, and that he desired to return to Holland as soon as possible after his recovery. He did, however, visit Zubov at the Tauric Palace, where he received an extremely friendly welcome. During their meeting, Zubov promised to take firm action against Thomson Rowand's debtors. On the advice of Myatlev, the sworn enemy of Samaylov, Voûte, still weak from his illness, painfully drew up yet another memorandum on the Sutherland case; this was to be passed to one of the empress's secretaries so that the matter might be brought directly to Catherine's attention. There were indications that all the earlier memoranda on the subject had failed to get beyond ministerial level. The situation had changed in Voûte's favour inasmuch as Catherine had again taken the reins, and while doing so had administered a severe lecture to her ministers concerning the unsatisfactory developments in Poland. She was understood to have relieved Zubov of control over Poland and to have entrusted this to Bezborodko.[1]

Voûte's recovery was a slow process, and early in May 1794 he suffered renewed attacks of fever accompanied by severe stomach pains. The British ambassador gave him some 'James pills' (a renowned remedy, according to Voûte), but although these afforded temporary relief they did not prevent the fever recurring at regular intervals–and always at four o'clock in the morning. He was obliged to decline a second invitation from Zubov, but the latter so persisted in his enquiries as to the genuineness of Voûte's indisposition that Bagge was eventually obliged to visit him in person to convince him of the fact.[2] Zubov sent a message to Voûte, assuring him that the Trosien affair would be settled to his satisfaction and that other matters would be brought to a similarly satisfactory conclusion. Voûte was moved to observe that his illness had at least served some purpose.

To be ill in Russia at that time was a costly business: the quinine powders which Voûte had to take at hourly intervals in the early days of his illness were expensive, and to these were added the cost of bed and bedclothes, the price of the oranges, lemons and refreshing beverages, and finally the doctors' fees, which were almost as high in St.Petersburg as in London.[3] Voûte's correspondence reveals that Dr.Guthrie accepted banknotes in payment for his services, but that Voûte found it more appropriate to purchase a gift for Sir Samuel Rogerson. Dr.Guthrie advised him to leave St.Petersburg as soon as possible on the grounds that a change of air would assist his recovery. Voûte had proposed to travel overland via Narva, Reval and Riga, but this was impossible in view of the Polish revolution and so he decided to go by sea to Lübeck.[1]

By now, Voûte's health was showing a decided improvement and he was gradually recovering the strength to deal with business matters. The case against Trosien ended as Zubov had predicted, the arbitrators unanimously finding in favour of De Bary and ordering Trosien to pay cf 307,000, in default of which his assets would be seized and he himself imprisoned.[2]

By 29th May, Voûte was well enough to attend an audience with Zubov at Tsarkoye Selo. The most important news imparted by Zubov was that the empress had read Voûte's memorandum and the copy of Hope's irate letter of 31st March and had thereupon stated that she wished to receive Voûte in audience on 5th June. Such an honour was seldom bestowed on untitled persons, and certainly not on those who had not previously been presented to her. Zubov went on to say that he had been instructed to inform Voûte in advance that the empress was completely satisfied with Hope's conduct and that she would uphold the reputation and honour of the Company in every possible way. The favourable verdict in the Trosien case, Voûte learned, had been due to Catherine's personal intervention, and it was she who had instructed Prince Dolgoruky, the Governor General of Moscow, to support Thomson Rowand in their actions against their debtors. Whatever the outcome of their struggle might be, Voûte wrote, it was good that the whole of Europe should know that those who violated the law, as Trosien had done, would be brought to book as soon as their deeds became known to the empress, and that she was always ready to put an end to such unjust practices.[3]

On 5th June Voûte travelled to Tsarkoye Selo for his audience with Catherine, 'a memorable moment in my life.' The empress, he later wrote, was the essence of amiability, and although he had at first been somewhat shy, the conversation had gone easily and smoothly. But in the matter of Sutherland she had refused to budge an inch, saying that the manner in which the Court Banker had abused her trust, and all the things which she had found out concerning the baron's accomplices, had made her decide to end the custom of appointing a Court Banker. Voûte's impression was that the empress wished the Crown's claims upon Sutherland's estate to be placed on the same footing as those of the other creditors. In any case, she was not willing to regard Sutherland as an agent of the Crown in operations which she regarded as having been outside the authorized plan. Catherine went on to say that the credit which Sutherland had enjoyed had been due entirely to the Crown and could thus not be counted among his merits. In spite of this strong condemnation of Sutherland's conduct, Voûte had the feeling that much would still depend upon the manner of the liquidation, as prescribed in the report to be published by the committee charged with investigating the late baron's affairs.

Turning to the matter of Hope & Co., the empress repeated the flattering references which she had earlier made through Zubov. She assured Voûte that she had always met her obligations and that as far as Hope was concerned she would continue to do so. When the issue of Russia's natural wealth arose, Catherine was very modest in describing her role. Since her accession to the throne, she had had more than ten million roubles in gold coins minted, compared with the one million of her predecessors in a similar period; in addition, silver coins to a value of one hundred and fifty million roubles had been minted during her reign. Banknotes, she stated, were only for domestic use (this, Voûte had already discovered). The empress had only very vague notions concerning rates of exchange, but she could not be blamed for this, for she was seated in between three tables, on each of which lay piles of papers and books. It seemed to Voûte that ruling a vast empire like Russia was never-ending servitude. From six o'clock in the morning until after dinner in the evening she was contiously absorbed with the affairs of state–a situation which Voûte had not encountered anywhere else in Russia, 'for cards keep any number of people busy.'[1]

After the audience, which had lasted for more than two hours, Voûte made his way to the office of Zubov, to whom he handed copies of Hope's most recent letters to the Attorney General and the latter's replies to these, and also a list of loans opened in Holland and the relevant *Berigten* in order that Zubov should have a picture of the current situation in that area.

Matters having suddenly taken so pronounced a turn for the better, Voûte was faced with a dilemma: to go, or to stay? If he was to achieve anything in the Sutherland affair, or to round off the case against Trosien, he would have to resign himself to a stay of at least six months. But then it was on the cards that Samaylov and his followers, who had been pushed into the background by Voûte, but only temporarily, would start their intrigues all over again and finally rob him of his goal. Following his sensational audience, Catherine's ministers were eagerly trying to discover what had been discussed, and foreign diplomats, headed by the representatives of Britain and the Dutch Republic, were exceedingly curious. On balance, Voûte decided that it would be better if he departed on the crest of the wave, leaving the strongest possible impression of Hope's influence upon Catherine.[1]

Thus, Voûte reverted to his earlier plan to go by sea. He reasoned that if he were to cross to Lübeck and travel overland from there to Holland via Hamburg, he would have the certainty that his baggage would not be searched and that no one would pry into his papers. The Prussian customs officials were just as inquisitive as the Russian in this respect, and Voûte was determined to avoid trouble of this nature at all cost. Apart from this, reports of the military situation in the southern part of the Netherlands were becoming steadily more disquieting and he was anxious to return home before any danger threatened the Republic.[2] Having taken his leave of Samaylov and had a final audience at Tsarkoye Selo, Voûte left on 18th June for Kronstadt where, having supervised the loading of his carriage, he and his servant embarked.

The voyage was relatively slow and afforded the traveller ample opportunity to review the events of the preceding weeks. Now, he could commit his thoughts freely to paper and, having done so, had no need to sign the letters with the name of André Cartier. In his conversation with the empress, Voûte had carefully avoided any reference to Zubov: 'His physical relationship with Catherine is so intimate that it would be wrong not to assume that his bodily virtues outweigh his moral failings, and that the ageing madonna has a very soft spot for him in her heart.'[3] To Voûte, Zubov was a true Russian–which implied that he was unreliable. This trait was aggravated by his position, for if Catherine should die he would find himself in a serious plight, having no private fortune and, moreover, being saddled with debauched and thriftless relatives. In his memorandum to Catherine, too, Voûte had been at pains not to say anything derogatory concerning Samaylov, Markov or Ostermann, for he knew that the vain Catherine prided herself on her choice of servants, and kept them in their positions in spite of any criticism. Voûte had seen evidence of this when at last he had succeeded in bringing his memorandum and Hope's letters to the attention of the empress. She had received the papers on the Sunday morning, and must have read them after dinner on that day; for the remainder of the evening, he afterwards learned, she had been preoccupied and gloomy. Her first task on the following morning was to summon Samaylov, to whom she gave a blistering reprimand for having kept important matters hidden from her with the result that she was not even aware that Messrs. Hope had sent a representative to Russia and that he was anything but satisfied with what he had found there.

Myatlev was the next to have an audience with the empress, to report on the affairs of the bank. At the mention of Samaylov's name, Catherine snapped angrily: 'Be on your guard for that man, he will deceive you; he has just played me a shabby trick.' She was so incensed that she forcibly pushed away the table which stood in front of her. Myatlev, who contemplated his enemy's disfavour with satisfaction, had later told Voûte that Samaylov had been ordered to lay all matters for which he was responsible before the ministerial council in future, and to adhere to its decisions. Samaylov had thus been placed under supervision – but for how long?

On 5th July 1794 Voûte arrived in Travemünde, where he disembarked and proceeded to Lübeck. When he reached the home of the merchant Blohm there, he found a pile of letters from Hope & Co. waiting for him. These included letters of introduction to Hope's correspondents in the city. To his great satisfaction he read that the partners of Hope & Co. were fully in agreement with his decision to return to Holland. The letters of introduction had an almost magical effect, and Voûte received so many invitations that it would have taken many weeks to pay all the calls. But he excused himself wherever possible, not only because he was anxious to return home quickly but also because he wished to avoid creating obligations towards persons who would in all probability view these as an excuse for seeking additional credit from the Company.[1]

While having a meal at his hotel, Voûte heard that traffic on the route via Hanover was very heavy and that there was consequently a shortage of horses. There were also stories of the great French victory at Fleurus on 26th June and the ensuing retreat of the English and Austrian armies. This news strengthened Voûte's resolve to leave as soon as possible and so put his anxious relatives at ease.[2] He left on 8th July, but it took him a week to reach Amsterdam. The journey took longer than anticipated owing to the looseness of the road surface following a severe drought, and the movement of large numbers of wagons carrying money to Hamburg. The flight of Dutch capital from the advancing French armies had begun. A phase in the history of Hope & Co. was drawing to a close.

CHAPTER SIX

THE GREAT CONVERSION

The departure for England of the partners of Hope & Co. in the latter part of October 1794, and of the managers, Pierre César Labouchère and Alexander Baring, on the night of 18th January 1795, heralded a temporary suspension of the Company's activities on behalf of the Empress of Russia. The invasion by French troops did not come as a surprise to the Company, which some time beforehand had taken steps to ensure that, as far as possible, its assets and property were placed beyond the reach of the French or of any new, revolutionary government in the Republic. Among the consequences of this action was that, for the first time, Hope & Co. were unable to make payments of interest on loans. In response to questions from bondholders, Paulus Taay, Hope's confidential clerk, who remained behind to look after day-to-day matters in the Republic, was obliged to announce that there was as yet no information regarding the payment of interest on the Russian bonds. However, an advertisement placed by the partners informed the holders that the interest vouchers which matured on 1st February and 1st May were redeemable at the house of Martin Dorner in Hamburg, and that subsequent instalments would also be paid via that house.[1] For the Dutch investors, this was a roundabout procedure involving extra expense, but at least it safeguarded the payments by making it impossible for the invaders or the revolutionary government, which by then had taken office, to seize the monies remitted from Russia.

But while the interests of those who had invested in the Russian loans were provisionally safe, the prospects for the holders of bonds relating to the Republic of Poland and its king were a great deal less favourable.

As was explained in a previous chapter, Hope & Co. was not the only house in Amsterdam which was involved; others, such as Quirijn Willem van Hoorn and Theodoor Gülcher & Mulder, had provided loans, not only to the Republic of Poland and King Stanislaw but also to Polish magnates. Raymond and Theodore de Smeth, Pieter de Haan Pietersz. and Hogguer Grand & Co. had also been active in this area. In most cases, the interest and principal instalments on the loans negotiated with these houses had ceased following the financial crisis early in 1793, though a few of the magnates had continued to make payments after that date. During his stay in St.Petersburg, Voûte had done his best in the matter of Hope's loan of 1786 to the Polish king, but the outbreak of the revolt against Russia in the Spring of 1794 had prevented the imperial decision (which was favourable) being implemented.[1]

The loans to the Polish magnates had been granted against the security of all or part of their estates, but the creditors in Holland had no way of enforcing their claims on these properties. In 1795 the territory remaining to Poland had been divided between Russia, Prussia and Austria, and the occupying powers had arbitrarily seized a number of estates. Any creditor insolent enough to attempt to exercise his rights on the spot found himself entangled in a bureaucratic web, as is evident from the correspondence between Pieter de Haan in Amsterdam and his agent in Poland, Jan Abraham Willink, on the subject of the securities provided for the loan to Count Michael Oginski.

De Haan's loan, of cf 1,000,000, to Oginski was covered by a contract signed on 1st February 1791 in The Hague, where Oginski was at that moment serving as special envoy of the Polish monarch. As security for the loan, he mortgaged a portion of his estates in Lithuania, the value of which was put at cf 2,500,000.[2] Interest on the loan was paid up to early August 1793, but the repayments of principal, which initially became due on 1st February 1794, failed to materialize.

The cause lay in Oginski's involvement with the Polish uprising of 1794 and the consequent loss of his property, which was confiscated by Empress Catherine. De Haan was on the point of bringing an action against Oginski when, at the end of April 1795, Prince Nikolai Repnin, the Russian military governor of Lithuania, issued a decree forbidding the courts of law to admit actions against Oginski and his property. On 25th May of the same year, Repnin announced that Oginski's creditors had three months in which to appear before a special committee which sat in Grodno, and which was shortly afterwards given judicial powers. De Haan thereupon instructed Willink to go to Grodno, taking with him the principal debenture and the mortgage deeds for verification by the committee.[3] In spite of all his efforts, Willink failed to obtain a written acceptance by the committee of the validity of his claims. Nor did it help him to extract, by means of a handsel, confidential information from the secretary to the committee, for that body as a whole flatly refused to recognize a memorandum on the subject in Willink's handwriting. In a desperate move, Willink bribed a servant to let him into the house of one of the members of the committee, Brigadier Rusanov, who at that moment had another of the members with him. When Rusanov persisted in his refusal to accept the memorandum, Willink commenced to read the contents in a loud voice; but the commissioners continually interrupted him and finally Rusanov shut himself in his bedroom. Approaches to Count Panin, the civil governor, and, via him, to Repnin similarly produced no result. Repnin went so far as to admit verbally that De Haan's claim seemed well founded, but a written confirmation was out of the question. It must be remembered that the committee had been set up by the empress and was therefore independent of all other authorities; in this situation, Repnin did not even dare to guess what Catherine's purpose might be.[1]

Even more disquieting was the information, obtained unofficially from the committee, that very little property belonging to Oginski was situated in Lithuania, and that Willink would do better to try his luck elsewhere. When Willink continued to press the matter, he was unceremoniously shown the door. Further investigation showed that the committee had been right: of the estates mortgaged to De Haan, only the 'oeconomy' known as Wilnenska was situated in Lithuania–and Oginski had sold most of the land which comprised this oeconomy *after* he had obtained the loan.[2] Much of the land had since been resold and thus it was difficult to discover who it actually belonged to. The majority of the remaining mortgaged property lay in the area which had been ceded to Russia in 1793 and was now under the control of the governor general of Minsk.[3] The fact of the estates being spread out probably made Repnin even more unwilling to give any firm ruling which could bring him in conflict with General Tutolmin, his opposite number in Minsk–where Oginski had similarly realized his assets. There, on the eve of the uprising, he had sold nearly all his estates at far below their true value. What remained had been confiscated by Catherine, who had then given part of it to one of her generals, Count Soltikov.

Throughout the winter of 1795 and the following Spring, Willink made every effort to obtain from the Supreme Court of Lithuania a formal recognition of the validity of De Haan's claims; but he realized that he had little chance of success because, during the Polish uprising, Catherine 'out of mistaken generosity' had held out to her generals and ministers a prospect of rewards which, however, could only be realized by the confiscation of property. Having done this, she had closed the door on the creditors with claims to the confiscated estates. Obtaining the necessary documents was a costly business in Poland, but according to Willink the situation was far worse in Russian-controlled areas, where law and justice had been supplanted by whim and subjugation.[4]

The outlook being so gloomy, De Haan, not surprisingly, began to look for other solutions. He approached other houses in Amsterdam which, like himself, had furnished loans for Poland.[1] If concerted action was to be taken, the holders of bonds of the various loans would have to be informed and their sanction obtained. In consultation with the brokers and *entrepreneurs*, the necessary deeds of authority were drawn up, after which the bondholders were informed by an advertisement that these would be available for inspection and approval at the offices of notary Van Beem between 20th February and 31st March 1796. At the end of this period it was found that a sizeable majority of the bondholders had indicated their approval of the plan. On 11th April of the same year, the Court of Holland empowered the various houses to act on behalf of the interested parties, but it added a rider that those who had not already signed must be given an opportunity to attend the Court in company with the representatives of the issuing houses on the 6th, 9th and 10th May; this was to be communicated to those concerned by means of an advertisement. Anyone who failed to attend would be deemed to have given his consent. On 10th May the Court empowered the houses to jointly send one or more authorized agents to Russia to act on their behalf, and three days later the mission was formally entrusted to Robert Voûte, 'Observing that he has no reason to assume that he will be *persona non grata* for the purpose of dealing with this matter in the appropriate place.'[2] The choice of Voûte was an obvious one in the light of his earlier and relatively successful journey to Russia. As we shall see, the mission covered not only the Polish negotiations, but also Hope's Russian loans.

The sums which Voûte was charged with attempting to recover were quite considerable: nearly 3.6 million guilders for Raymond and Theodore de Smeth and Hogguer Grand & Co.; 3 million for Quirijn Willem van Hoorn and Theodoor Gülcher & Mulder jointly; nearly 2.7 million for Theodoor Gülcher & Mulder severally; and 2.5 million for Pieter de Haan Pietersz. Hope & Co.'s interest concerned their loan of 1786 totalling 2 million guilders. These were all nominal sums, a portion of some loans having been repaid. The capital debts owed by the Republic of Poland and King Stanislaw totalled just over 6 million guilders, while the outstanding claims on the Polish magnates amounted to 5.8 million plus interest, which in most cases had not been paid since the end of 1793 or the beginning of 1794.[3] Hasselgreen had not invested Voûte with authority to deal with his loan but, as we have seen, he personally looked after his interests in Poland and Russia, and thus felt that he did not require Voûte's services.

Immediately prior to accepting the authority to deal with the Polish loans, Voûte appointed Hermann Albrecht Insinger and Jan Jacob Voûte Jr. to act on behalf of Hope & Co. The relevant deed omitted any reference to the powers vested by the Company in Voûte himself, and this was probably done in order to avoid difficulties with the Batavian government, should it conceive the idea of recovering taxes levied on Hope from third parties.[1]

De Haan urged Voûte to travel to St.Petersburg via Wilno and Minsk, in order to investigate the situation there, but he flatly refused. The failure of Willink's efforts had already shown that it would be a waste of time and money to visit provincial towns when all decisions were taken in St.Petersburg. Voûte did not wish to have anything to do with Willink, firstly because the man seemed to him to be totally unsuited to work of this nature, and secondly because he regarded Willink's censorious remarks concerning the corruption and bad justice in Russia as unseemly. Voûte had apparently forgotten his own comments on such matters in 1793 and 1794. As in 1794, he held the view that the causes of the partition of Poland lay with the Poles themselves: 'disorders, intrigues and oligarchs.' The giving away by the empress of one of Oginski's estates was certainly a difficult issue, but Voûte was more afraid of Oginski's actions than of the empress or the committee, which in his opinion had behaved correctly. He was convinced that a calm approach and hard work were the prerequisites for success in dealing with the matters at hand, 'and these qualities are not given to everyone.'[2]

On his way to Russia, Voûte did however visit Berlin, where late in July 1796 he wrote a memorandum on the subject of the Polish loans for the benefit of Kalichev, who in the previous year had exchanged the post of envoy to The Hague for the equivalent post in Berlin. In January 1795, following the suppression of the Polish uprising (in the preceding November), Russia and Austria had reached agreement on the partition of the remainder of Poland, and in October of that year Prussia had perforce become a party to this.[3] The partitioning powers had also expressed their willingness in principle to accept responsibility for the debts incurred by the Republic and its ruler, but consultations on the practical steps, such as the setting up of a joint committee and the apportionment of the responsibility, had yet to commence. Negotiations between Russia and Prussia were proceeding at ambassadorial level, and thus it was logical that Voûte should be anxious to lay his views concerning the Polish debts before Kalichev.

Voûte reasoned that if Russia were to assume responsibility for the loans made in Holland to the king, the Republic and the magnates, and if she were to convert these into Russian bonds, she would for a time be free of the obligation to repay principal money. If, on the other hand, the loans were simply to be divided between the three powers, it was likely that Russia would immediately be confronted with repayments which were either being made or were about to be made. There was also the point that the vast majority of the assets mortgaged by the Polish magnates were situated in Russian Poland, and that their value was greatly in excess of the sums loaned. The magnates were committed to pay interest and principal in Holland in gold or silver coin. The Russian government could either allow this practice to continue, in which case the total of the remittances which it was called upon to make would be smaller, or it could order the payments to be made in Russia and thereby maintain the reserves of precious metals. Voûte's line of thought was not entirely correct, for the new bonds which would be created for the purpose of the conversion would add to the interest burden in Holland, and the increase would have to be deducted from the deferred repayments of principal.

Voûte proceeded to reason that a conversion operation of this nature could also be applied to the Russian loans provided in Holland, the initial repayments against which were due to commence in 1798; however, in view of the extremely unattractive rate of exchange, such a move might well be to the disadvantage of the Russian government. 'The general circumstances in Europe are such that they point to grounds of expediency which would not have been noticed but for these circumstances.'[1] Here, he was probably referring to the French offensives in southern Germany and Italy, which had further inflamed anti-French feeling in St.Petersburg and increased the risk of a Franco-Russian conflict.

Soon after his arrival in St.Petersburg, Voûte suffered a serious setback. Having no children of his own, he took as his companion his favourite nephew, Pierre, the second son of his eldest brother, Jan Jacob. In the early hours of 5th September 1796 a police officer called and arrested Pierre in his bed. Pierre was staying with the Bagge family of the house of Bagge & Van Eyssel, with whom Robert Voûte had been in communication during his earlier visit to Russia. Despite strong protests from Robert Voûte, Pierre and his servant were taken to Kronstadt, where the commandant sent them on to a guard-ship two hours' sailing from the shore. Vessels leaving the port of St.Petersburg were ordered to moor alongside the guard-ship and take the deportees on board. At six o'clock that evening, Pierre and his servant boarded a Danish ship bound for Copenhagen, where they arrived a fortnight later at the end of a stormy voyage.[2]

Robert Voûte, whose whole prestige as an influential figure at the Russian Court now hung in the balance, had naturally not stood idly by. On the day of the arrest, 5th September, he had personally informed the empress of the incident. His protestation resulted in a courier being sent to Kronstadt with an order countermanding the arrest, but this arrived an hour too late. The reason given for the puzzling action on the part of the authorities was that the police had mistaken Pierre for the Amsterdam merchant Gülcher, who had travelled with the Voûtes as far as Warsaw and who was *persona non grata* in Russia. Robert Voûte was so distressed by the episode that he was obliged to rest for a few days–a physical reaction to mental strain which, as we have seen, also occurred during his earlier journey. The authorities, however, made formal reparations. An imperial courier left for Copenhagen in October, and in the early days of the following month he officially escorted Pierre Voûte to St.Petersburg, travelling via Sweden.[1]

Despite the official steps taken to remedy the injustice, there is still something mysterious about the whole affair. Did it stem purely from an administrative error on the part of the police, or did it point to the work of a faction opposed to Hope & Co., personified by Robert Voûte? Why, when Voûte repeatedly assured the police that a mistake had been made, was his word not accepted? Who invented the story concerning Voûte's supposed travelling companion, and why was Pierre Voûte deported with such haste that the mistake could not be corrected? There are no clear answers to these questions, not even in the letters written by Robert Voûte himself–for whom it was doubtless a matter of personal prestige to make the affair appear to be a blunder on the part of the police.

The situation in Russia altered completely with the death, on 17th November 1796, of Empress Catherine II and the succession of her son, Paul. The czar's rule was despotic and thus it was vital for Voûte to get on good terms with him; this, however, was no simple task, for Paul proved to be an extremely fickle and unpredictable ruler. But by good fortune Voûte was looked upon with favour by the empress, Maria Feodorovna, and as she greatly influenced her husband during the early part of his reign, Voûte enjoyed his favour also.[2]

Voûte's chances of succeeding in the matter of the Polish loans rose when, on 26th January 1797, a convention dealing with the division of the debts incurred by the Republic of Poland and its former king was signed by the Czar of Russia and the King of Prussia.[3] The Emperor of Germany also associated himself with this. The convention provided for a committee, the members of which would be nominated from among the three Courts, to meet to verify and liquidate these debts. The debts incurred in Holland by the Republic of Poland (the existence of which had been recognized by the *sejm* held in Grodno in 1793), together with the interest which had meanwhile become due, were divided between Russia, Prussia and Austria in a ratio of 13:13:4. The king's debts, which had been assessed at 40 million Polish guilders, were divided between Russia, Prussia and Austria in a ratio of 2:2:1.[1] The committee charged with realizing the assets of the bankrupt Polish bankers (among them Pierre Tepper, with whom we have already made acquaintance) was to be revived. This body had originally been set up by the *sejm* at Grodno, but had disappeared from the scene during the chaos which accompanied the uprising in Poland.

The convention contained nothing akin to Voûte's notions of a Russian acceptance of the Polish debt in its entirety. Voûte, however, had not been wasting his time in St.Petersburg, for on 30th June 1797 a convention was entered into between Alexei Vasilyev, head of the Treasury, and Robert Voûte, the authorized agent of the creditors of the former Republic of Poland, its king and also a number of citizens of the former republic.[2] The negotiations leading up to this had commenced on 28th April, and progress had initially been slow. Vasilyev and, to a greater extent, the Chancellor, Bezborodko, had opposed Voûte's proposals, and in the end only the direct intervention of the czar had enabled agreement to be reached on 30th June.[3]

Voûte had every reason for satisfaction with the outcome, for this time his ideas–the ideas which he had elaborated to Kalichev in May 1796–had in their entirety been embodied in the convention. Russia accepted responsibility for all the loans made to the Republic of Poland and to its king, and covered by Voûte's powers of attorney, plus overdue interest up to 31st December 1797. Russia also took over the loans made to Prince Alexander, Prince Joseph Lubomirski and Count Michael Oginski, again including the interest due up to 31st December 1797. These were but a few of the loans made to Polish magnates, but Prince Alexander Lubomirski had taken over the estates mortgaged by his brother Joseph, and with these the latter's debt, and had then sold all the mortgaged property to the Russian Crown. The fate of Michael Oginski's assets, the unsold portion of which had been confiscated by Catherine II, has already been explained. Both the last-named cases thus involved loans to Polish magnates against securities which had meanwhile come into the possession of the Russian Crown.

The procedure established for the transfer required that all the original debentures, which were still held by notaries in Holland, be sent to Warsaw for verification by the Russian commissioners appointed to the Mixed Committee for the Polish Debts. Upon the signing of the convention, Pierre Voûte had departed for Holland to attend to this matter.

In addition to the claims with which Voûte was empowered to deal, the convention also embraced a number of personal debentures of King Stanislaw, in all involving a sum of 125,000 ducats, a substantial proportion of which had been borrowed from Carl Hasselgreen and Jean Meisner. Theodoor Gülcher's involvement amounted to only 4,200 ducats. The erstwhile Republic of Poland had issued four *assignats*, totalling 48,500 ducats, in favour of Jean Meisner, and these were also included in the agreement. In all these cases, the loans had been used by the king and the republic to keep on their feet during the second partition of the country. We may safely assume that the agreement came as a great relief to the house of Meisner, which faced certain bankruptcy unless the responsibility for meeting its claims was accepted elsewhere. It may also be assumed that the inclusion of these claims in the convention reflected efforts by Meisner and Hasselgreen rather than by Voûte.[1]

The czar undertook to convert all these loans and the claims thereon, which together totalled cf 12,458,455.5.0, into a loan for the account of the Russian Crown, and to embody this in the loans entered into by Catherine II in the Batavian Republic, as Holland had become known since the French conquest. The rate of interest on the conversion loan was fixed at 5% per annum, commencing on 1st January 1798 and being payable half-yearly at the offices of Hope & Co., in their capacity as bankers of the Crown, or at the offices of any other house whom they might appoint for the purpose. The conversion of old bonds into new was to be effected before 1st January 1798.

The conclusion of this agreement was a major success for Voûte, and thus also for the Company. Thanks to Voûte's efforts at the Russian Court, more than 10 million guilders of Dutch investors' money had not only been saved, but also reactivated after years of dormancy.

The amicable feeling towards Hope & Co. which ensued coincided with an ebb tide in the fortunes of the revolutionary government in the Batavian Republic. The initial enthusiasm among Dutch revolutionaries had been heady, and now many of them were suffering from an emotional hangover. The bill, in the shape of the Hague Treaty, which the French presented for their benefaction was startlingly high. Furthermore, fears regarding the conduct of the active radical wing were growing in the more moderate revolutionary circles. In France, the discovery of the communist plot headed by Gracchus Babeuf had brought about a pronounced swing to the right. Peace negotiations with England were started, and an accommodation between the two states appeared probable. Since the political course in France had a decisive influence on the run of affairs in the satellite states, the change favoured the more conservative body in the Batavian Republic. Some conservative supporters of the old Patriot Party went so far as to establish secret contacts with members of the House of Orange who were then in England and Germany. It is therefore not surprising that the Representatives of the People of Holland, as the States of this province were by now calling themselves, sought to get in touch with the Hopes with a view to discussing the latter's possible return to the Republic. Among the obstacles to such a development was the earlier confiscation of Hope's assets there. In a polite letter, the commissioners who had ordered the confiscation, while defending their action, invited Messrs. Hope to return to the Republic, stating that they were prepared to suspend their claim if the Company could show good reason why they should do so.

But although the partners felt that the time had come to reveal the secret of their associations with Insinger and Voûte, and show openly that they were concerned in the settlement of the Polish debts (as if the public had not long since connected them with this!), they chose not to enter into direct correspondence with the new rulers in Holland and continued to challenge the legality of the sequestration of the Company's assets. The wisdom of their policy was to emerge later.[1]

Although we may assume that Czar Paul, in bringing about a settlement of the Polish debts, was moved by feelings of sympathy towards the Poles (he confessed to Kosciuszko, a hero of the resistance, that he had consistently opposed the partition of the country), the elements of business were not lacking on the Russian side when it came to the signing of the convention between Voûte and Vasilyev.[2] The Russian members of the mixed committee concerned with verifying and liquidating the Polish debts were instructed that the principal obligations which Pierre Voûte brought to Warsaw were to be submitted to the committee for verification like any other documents. This procedure was not expected to produce any difficulties, since the claims had all been recognized by the *sejm* at Grodno. Only the loan of cf 760,000 made to the Republic by Pieter de Haan Pietersz. in 1792 could possibly evoke objections, because the banker Prote Potocki, who had since become bankrupt, had not deposited these funds in the Treasury, but had allowed them to become dissipated along with his own capital. His malversation, however, did not relieve the former Republic of Poland of its responsibilities. Potocki himself faced an inquiry into his conduct by the three Courts.

The Russian members of the committee were also instructed that if, contrary to expectations, their colleagues disputed the debentures and bonds submitted for verification, they were to block further discussion by stating that their Court had already recognized the legality of these and that therefore they were not permitted to indulge in any argument. If the documents submitted were verified, the commissioners were to see to it that interest up to 31st December 1797 was included. When the process of verification and liquidation had been completed, the commissioners were to announce that the czar proposed to deduct the sum of these claims from his share of the debts incurred by the Polish king. These claims together totalled less than the amount which the czar was committed to pay under the terms of the agreement of 26th January 1797. The balance due from Russia could be dealt with within the committee's terms of reference.[1]

As Voûte had earlier explained, the conversion served temporarily to relieve Russia of a series of current or impending repayment commitments; in addition, it brought Russia the political advantage of appearing to the outside world to be the saviour of the creditors of the erstwhile Poland. If Poland's foreign debts had simply been divided, Prussia would in all probability have attempted to convert her share into a new loan, and this could have handicapped the Russians in their own conversion. In the final analysis, the czar had not taken on any commitments beyond those imposed on him by the convention which regulated the sharing of the debts, and thus there was no question of any sacrifices on behalf of Poland.

At the end of October 1797 a further success set a crown on Robert Voûte's mission on behalf of the Dutch creditors. Early in that month the czar had issued instructions to Bezborodko and Vasilyev that the balance of the Dutch claims against the Polish magnates were to be taken over by the Russian Crown. On the 29th, a second *Acte de Cession*, in which the transfer was regulated, was signed. In this, all the loans to Polish magnates which came within the powers vested in Voûte were taken over by the Crown and converted into a Russian loan which, like the last, was incorporated in the other loans obtained in Holland; the interest rate was fixed at 5%. The only loan excluded from the conversion was one of cf 400,000 to the Dowager Princess Jablonowska, and this was probably because the estates which she had mortgaged for the purpose of the loan were situated in areas of Poland which had since come under Prussian and Austrian control.[1] In addition to the loans on which Voûte was empowered to negotiate, a claim by Jean Meisner against the Marquis François Wielopolski for 66,666$\frac{2}{3}$ ducats was included in the conversion, as were six bonds for the account of Prince Dominique Radziwill, a minor. These had been signed by his guardian, Prince Matthias Radziwill, and the principal and arrears of interest totalled more than 120,000 ducats.

These bonds, too, were held by Meisner, for whom their conversion heralded the full restoration of his credit standing. The loans converted under the terms of the second agreement totalled cf 3,449,130.14, which implied that the czar had accepted responsibility for debts of nearly 16 million guilders.[2]

In considering the second convention, one is faced with the question: Why was the czar prepared to assume responsibility for the Polish magnates' debts even though these were not included in the agreement with Prussia and Austria? Voûte partially answered this in his memorandum of 24th July 1796 to Kalichev. Nearly all of the mortgaged estates lay in the Russian-occupied part of Poland; the value of the estates was far in excess of the sums loaned; in the event of default, all the assets of the borrowers could be seized. Czar Paul's action in taking over these loans could be interpreted as a friendly gesture towards the Polish nobility; there is, however, the point that he thereby obtained a financial hold over the magnates, and this will almost certainly have deterred them from acts hostile to the new régime. For the lenders in Holland the conversion brought the solution of a complex problem, namely that the partition of Poland had resulted in the mortgaged estates being on Russian territory, while the laws of Russia prohibited foreigners from holding mortgages on land because these could afford rights relating to serfs.

The Polish affairs having been successfully dealt with, a settlement of the Russian loans in the Republic became a matter of urgency. The earliest of these would become due for repayment on 1st February 1798, and the third on 1st July. But because of the adverse rate of exchange, the Russian government was disinclined–and perhaps hard put–to remit the necessary funds to the Republic.

On 2nd November 1797, a few days after the signing of the second convention, Voûte sent Vasilyev a memorandum which contained a proposal for reconstituting Russia's foreign loans. In this, Voûte went somewhat too far, for the loans which Russia had negotiated in Genoa were not within his domain. He calculated as follows. The loans obtained in Holland totalled cf 53,500,000.[1] To these must be added 3 million guilders which Russia had obtained from De Wolf in Antwerp, the 16 million guilders from the two conventions relating to the Polish debts, 12 million guilders as a reserve, and the commission due to Hope & Co. As far as the last-named was concerned, Voûte proposed $6\frac{1}{2}\%$ on the loans issued by the Company (the figure agreed for all eighteen loans) and 4% on the sums of the Polish conversions and the Antwerp loan. This commission, totalling cf 4,233,803.0.0, would be paid in Russian bonds which, however, would commence to bear interest upon the expiry of the terms of the converted loans and not on 1st January 1798, as was the case with the other bonds.

The reserve of 12 million guilders would serve to meet unforeseen needs, to finance credits for the repurchase of bonds, and to meet other expenses on behalf of the Russian Crown. No interest would be payable on the portion of the reserve not used by the Court, nor would any commission be due thereon. If bonds relating to the reserve were broached, these would bear interest from the date of use, and the full commission of $6\frac{1}{2}\%$ would be payable on the sum involved.

After the expiry of twelve years (a normal period for a Russian loan), i.e. on 1st January 1810, the Court would have to commence the repayment of the balance of the capital; this would be effected in twenty equal instalments, so that the debt would finally be eliminated on 1st January 1830–thirty-two years from 1st January 1798. Accelerated repayment would be permitted. The principal sum, which was nominally cf 88,300,000, would bear interest at 5% per annum. This figure, which had been laid down in the two conventions relating to the Polish debts, implied an increase in the rate of interest on seven of the eighteen loans.[2]

As calculated by Voûte, Hope's commission at first sight appears high. However, if we compare the figure of cf 4,233,803.0.0 referred to in Voûte's memorandum with the cf 76,300,000 on which interest would immediately become payable and which would be repaid (cf 12,000,000, it will be recalled, was provisionally to be kept in reserve), we arrive at a mean commission of $5\frac{5}{9}\%$. In contrast to the commission on Hope's other Russian loans, this would not be payable in cash when the loan was subscribed, but in bonds, which would be handed to the partners. Such bonds, however, could not be sold at par. During the second half of 1797, the average quotation for the Russian bonds did not exceed 90 and the underlying trend was downward.[3] The Hopes themselves held about 2,000 Russian bonds, some of which they had repurchased, and the effects of

documents to the Treasurer at regular intervals. The memory of Sutherland's malpractices was clearly discernible in this stipulation.

Despite this triumphant end to Hope & Co.'s activities on behalf of the Batavian bondholders, it did not fall to the Company to effect the conversion in Amsterdam. At the end of the circular which brought the glad tidings to the investors, Raymond and Theodore de Smeth announced that: 'they had been empowered by Messrs. Hope & Comp., Bankers to His Majesty the Emperor of the Russian Empire, to cause the instructions contained in this *Berigt* to be carried out, and that, accordingly, the exchange of the Bonds, together with the payment of Interests referred to in connexion therewith, will be effected at their *Comptoir*.'

This comeback to the field of Russian loans must have been a source of great satisfaction to the house of De Smeth; for Hope & Co., being prevented by an unforeseen change in the political situation from plucking the fruits of their success was a bitter pill. The change had come in September 1797, when the *coup d'état* of Fructidor brought more radical groups to power in France. They adopted a more stringent policy which included breaking off the negotiations with England. As usual, the Batavian Republic faithfully copied the French example; there, too, the radicals came more and more to the forefront, and the defeat of the Batavian fleet by the British at Kamperduin in October 1797 was eagerly seized upon as an opportunity for accusing the more moderate elements in the government of treason. Eventually the radicals succeeded in gaining the support of the French government for a Batavian 'Fructidor,' and on 22nd January 1798 a *coup d'état* took place which swept the more moderate members of the National Assembly from office. For an 'Anglomaniac' house such as Hope & Co., there was little to be expected from such a radical-revolutionary government, and the partners counted themselves fortunate in having disclosed so little information to the commissioners in Holland concerning their confiscated assets.[1]

The ukase dealing with the loan conversion contained no reference to Hope's commission, but on 18th February 1798 the czar acceded to a request from the Company that a commission of 6½% should be paid on the commission itself.[2] Hope & Co. argued that the commission consisted of interest-bearing bonds and that they were entitled to commission on these. Interest on these bonds was now calculated from 1st January 1798 and not in accordance with the expiry of the period of the converted loans. This additional bonus, which amounted to cf 275,197.0.0, was also derived from the reserve of 12 million guilders and thus consisted of 'activated' bonds–on which the Company was entitled to its 6½%.[3] Hope & Co.'s

Ingevolge het bovenſtaande Berigt geeven R. en Th. DE SMETH hier meede kennis, dat zij door de Heeren HOPE en COMP., Bankiers van Zijne Majesteit den Keizer van het Rusſiſche Rijk, gequalificeert zijn geworden om de beveelen in dit Berigt vervat ter uitvoer te doen brengen; — en dat aldus de verwisſeling der Obligatien, mitsgaders de betaaling der Interesſen daar bij vermeld ten hunnen Comptoire zal geſchieden, waar toe de verdere ſchikkingen nader door de Couranten zullen worden bekend gemaakt.

Announcement by the house of De Smeth, consenting to convert the Russian bonds commission rose by cf 293,000 as a result of this, but was still not exorbitant, as we have already seen; nevertheless, this new concession will have been a thorn in the flesh of Bezborodko and Vasilyev, who were declared opponents of the conversion.[1]

The czar conceived a highly original plan to show his respect for Robert Voûte. On 19th February 1798, Pierre Voûte, José Pedro Celestino Velho and Alexandre François Rall announced that they had formed a company, Voûte Velho Rall & Co., and that the czar had appointed the company to be bankers to the Court and commission agents for foreign trade. The '& Co.' disguised Robert Voûte, who had thus accorded the honour to his favourite nephew while retaining the most influential position for himself.[2]

Thanks to the support of the empress, Voûte succeeded in securing acceptance of his earlier plan to improve the rate of exchange of the rouble by increasing copper exports. The output of copper would be increased from 160,000 poods to 1,200,000 poods, and the foreign exchange thus earned would form the basis for an issue of banknotes to a value of 150 million roubles. Part, at least, of this plan was implemented; the obstacles to its completion will become clear in due course.[3]

Now that the matter of the conversion had been settled in principle, Messrs. Hope felt that a good purpose would be served by giving Vasilyev a few hints. It was of the utmost importance that the interest on the loan should be paid promptly. This would bring about a recovery in the price of the bonds, which had fallen somewhat as a result of the postponement of the maturing date. Vasilyev's plan to effect a principal repayment on 1st January annually, and to announce this in advance on 1st October, seemed to the partners to be very effective. A million guilders annually, commencing on 1st January 1799, was the very minimum acceptable, they said. In extreme circumstances, this sum could be paid in two instalments with an interval of six months. The Hopes also drew attention to the desirability of repurchasing bonds while the price was still low, thus reducing the burden of interest, but they stressed that this must be done discreetly and that De Smeth and their agents must be advised in advance of the sums available for the purpose.

With the appointment of new Court Bankers, the way was now open for the remittances of interest and principal to be spread over the whole year. It fell to the Court Bankers to react flexibly to the fluctuations on the Exchange, by increasing or reducing their purchases of bills of exchange in accordance with the quantity offered. According to Hope & Co., it was a simple task to calculate whether the remittances would have an adverse effect on the value of the rouble: if the value of these exceeded the export surplus shown on the trade balance, the rate of exchange would fall; if it failed to match the surplus, the rate would rise.[1]

Despite all the wise counsel, however, little came of the plans. This was due in part to unforeseen obstacles, but the principal factors were that Vasilyev, an opponent of the conversion from the outset, went out of his way to thwart both Voûte and the Company, and that it was not long before Rall commenced to support him. The methods which were employed will be dealt with in due course.

An unforeseen obstacle, and one which imperilled the continuity of remittances by the Court Bankers, arose in Hamburg. There, the house of Martin Dorner, which since 1795 had been responsible for the payment of interest on the Russian bonds, and which under the new arrangement had been assigned an important role in the remittances to Amsterdam, had run into difficulties following the death of Dorner. When the news that the trustees of Dorner's estate had found it necessary for the house to suspend payments reached the Hopes in London, they despatched their partner, Pierre César Labouchère, to Hamburg with instructions to ensure that, in any circumstances, the bills presented by the Court Bankers would be honoured. A situation which revived memories of the events surrounding Sutherland in 1787 had to be avoided at all costs. Labouchère was also instructed to seek a suitable successor to Dorner.

The collapse of Martin Dorner was a serious setback to the new Court Bankers and also to Hope & Co. Rumours that Dorner was having difficulty in having his bills negotiated and that, old and in ill health, he hardly concerned himself with the business, leaving everything to a partner, had reached the Hopes a year previously.[2] Following his death on 12th April 1798, the suspension of payments by the house which bore his name had caused quite a commotion in Amsterdam, for it brought to a halt the encashment of the Russian bond coupons.[3] As soon as the suspension was announced, the Russian envoy to the *Kreits* of Lower Saxony and the Hanseatic towns, Baron Grimm, set about salvaging the Russian funds; he was assisted in this task by Pierre Voûte, who had been obliged to leave Russia for health reasons in March 1798 and, while en route for England, fortunately happened to be nearby.[4] As a result of their efforts, eight Hamburg houses contributed to a guarantee fund which assured more than a million marks banco. This paved the way for the resumption of the payments on 14th May and for the settlement of the other aspects of the affair.[5]

Upon his arrival in Hamburg, Labouchère discovered that much was amiss with the settlement of Dorner's affairs. For example, creditors were advancing money to the estate against preferential acknowledgements of debt, which they then used to obtain payment of their ordinary claims against Dorner. The effect of this was to shift the risks associated with the liquidation on to the shoulders of creditors such as Hope & Co., who did not enjoy preferential status. Labouchère lost no time in putting a stop to this stratagem, after which he proceeded to have new trustees appointed who treated all creditors impartially.[1] He was particularly impressed by Gabe, the principal partner in J.Gabe & Co., a house which enjoyed the highest credit and an excellent reputation. Labouchère's opinion of other businessmen in Hamburg was poor: to him, the merchants were *parvenus* who, with great ostentation, spent money as rapidly as they earned it. Fortunately, the way of life of the partners in Matthiessen & Sillem, the house which Labouchère had in mind as the successor to Dorner as far as Hope & Co. were concerned, contrasted strongly with this pattern.

Upon his arrival in Hamburg, Labouchère had been warned about Matthiessen & Sillem's pro-French sympathies, and he had resolved to carefully investigate the matter. Grimm also had let slip something to this effect, and it was obvious that he would have written to the Russian Court on the subject. A report of that nature would not have pleased Czar Paul I, for just then he was becoming increasingly prejudiced against France. Labouchère discovered that, some years earlier, Matthiessen had married a Mademoiselle Henriette de Sercey (it was perhaps not without significance that Labouchère spelled her name Circé), a pupil and a relative of the famous *femme de lettres*, Madame de Genlis.[2] That was not all, however. A daughter of Madame de Genlis, Pamela, had married Lord Edward Fitzgerald, one of the leaders of the United Irishmen, a movement dedicated to the violent overthrow–with the aid of a French army–of the British administration in Ireland and the establishment of an independent republic. But shortly before the date appointed for the uprising, Lord Fitzgerald had been arrested; and he later died from a shot wound. Immediately after his arrest, his wife had been compelled to leave Ireland and, still unaware of his death, she had just arrived in Hamburg, where she was lovingly welcomed by her cousin and intimate friend, Frau Matthiessen.

There was thus a danger that the Matthiessen residence would become a sort of headquarters for a Franco-Irish conspiracy–and anything of this nature could compromise the company of which Matthiessen himself was part. During a serious discussion with the partners, however, Labouchère learned that Matthiessen–and to an even greater extent Sillem–was opposed to anything which could support 'le système actuel en France,' and that there was absolutely nothing to fear as far as they were concerned. Matthiessen, who was about forty-five years of age, possessed sound judgement and his heart was in the right place; but, according to Labouchère, he was more interested in science and philanthropy than in business, and it appeared probable that he would soon resign from the firm. Sillem, in spite of being seventy and suffering severely from gout in his arms and legs, had 'an excellent brain and all the nerve required in the spirit of conducting the most difficult business.' His son, Hieronymus, who had recently married, was the key figure in the firm. Labouchère could not speak too highly of the young man.[1] He was 'an incredibly clever fellow' who combined the adroitness required to do business on the hellish market in Hamburg with 'the most refined sense of honour and integrity.' The fourth partner, Texier, who was married to Hieronymus's sister, was a good office-man, but that was all. The thrift and order manifested in the households of these four men compared most favourably with the magniloquence of so many other residences, and this, above all, pleased Labouchère.

Just how solid the house of Matthiessen & Sillem was, emerged during the negotiations concerning an agency for the Russian Court. When Labouchère explained that the Court expected its agents to accord unlimited credit, Matthiessen replied that it was the custom of the house 'never, in any business, to risk more than it could afford to lose without prejudicing either its independence or its freedom of action.' In this case, the house was prepared to go up to 300,000 marks banco. In reply, Labouchère let it be understood that the Court would spread its business if it failed to find a house willing to provide all the facilities which it desired. At this, Sillem Sr. immediately raised the credit limit to 500,000 marks banco; Matthiessen, however, was reluctant to concur. Labouchère hastened to assure the partners that he did not seek to force them to reveal to the Court the limit to which they were prepared to go, but that it was important for him to know this. After all, he reasoned, one could hardly offer the Russian Court anything short of unlimited credit; at the same time, he would certainly have thought badly of the partners had they offered this, for they did not yet understand the Russian government's ways of doing business, so that such an offer would have been extremely imprudent. Thus, the house came through the test with flying colours. Labouchère concluded by assuring the partners that the Court would seldom if ever make use of the unlimited facilities.[2]

The settlement of Dorner's affairs proceeded far more smoothly than had been anticipated. Confidence having been restored by the creation of the guarantee fund, the outstanding debts were speedily collected. By mid-July, 75% of these had been paid and it appeared that not only would complete settlement soon follow, but also that a larger sum would be left for the heirs than had at first been supposed. The monies belonging to the Russian Court which had been in Dorner's charge were consequently transferred to Matthiessen & Sillem without further delay. Dorner had been 'a worthy man,' but had lacked discretion; among his correspondence, Labouchère found confidential letters from the Hopes which should have been burned immediately they had been read–and which, according to Dorner's earlier assurances, had been. And just then the necessity for discretion was greater than ever.

The explanation for this lies in the fact that the British government was working on plans aimed at preventing its nationals from participating in foreign loans, especially those issued in Holland, and at making all correspondence with the inhabitants of a hostile country a treasonable offence. The reason for these measures lay in the extremely critical situation in which England then found itself. In 1797 the country had been struck by a financial crisis of such severity that the convertibility of paper money into coin had to be suspended.[1] At about the same time, a mutiny in the fleet had paralyzed the country's defences–and this just when an open revolt, which would probably be supported by a French army of invasion, threatened in Ireland.

Against this background, Labouchère, who was still in Hamburg, faced the task of organizing the payments of interest and principal on the Russian debt in such a manner that they would proceed smoothly without the need for intervention by, or correspondence with, Messrs. Hope in England.[2] To this end, he introduced, by letter, the houses of Matthiessen & Sillem and Voûte Velho Rall & Co. to De Smeth and Insinger. It was of even greater importance that the new Court Bankers and the agents in Hamburg should become accustomed to each other's ways of working, and to further this Labouchère, in his discussions with Matthiessen & Sillem, repeatedly cited the person of Robert Voûte: 'This is our most intimate friend, whose understanding and integrity we respect the most; you may count on it that this association can only bring you the greatest benefits.' Conversely, as we have already seen, he praised the partners of Matthiessen & Sillem in his letters to Voûte. The last-named was strongly urged to remain in Russia for the time being, because without his support little would come of the house of Voûte Velho Rall & Co. on account of 'the peculiar characters of the respective members of which it consists'; this was an aspect which inspired little confidence among the partners in England.

Pierre Voûte, to whom Labouchère referred derisively as 'Monsieur le Banquier,' was a good-natured young man whose principal trait was that he meekly allowed himself to be swayed by the advice of his uncle, Robert. Velho was an insignificant figure, but Rall was an intriguer and needed constant watching. The correspondence in Dorner's files showed that Rall planned his business operations well; but while he boasted in his letters that he always kept 100,000 roubles in cash for emergencies, he retained monies belonging to Hope with the excuse that he was unable to repay them.[1]

The setbacks suffered by the Court Bankers, such as the Dorner affair and the difficulties with remittances caused by the low rate of exchange, favoured Voûte's former enemies, in particular Treasurer Vasilyev who, in Labouchère's view, had already been far too dilatory in despatching to Matthiessen & Sillem the official guarantee in respect of the Court Bankers' operations.

In the meantime a start had been made with the implementation of Voûte's plans for a large-scale increase in copper exports, and at the end of February Dorner had reported to Voûte that he was prepared to have copper samples from Siberia assayed. Matthiessen & Sillem now took over Dorner's role, going so far as to offer to advance between 500,000 and 1,000,000 marks banco on shipments of copper, provided that the quality was satisfactory.[2] Once copper exports got into their stride, both interest and capital payments could be actively pursued, and it would also be possible to raise the rate of exchange in Russia. In view of the fickleness of the czar, however, it remained to be seen what would come of all these fine intentions.

Labouchère having thus settled the principal issues, there remained the matter of correspondence with England. Vasilyev was requested to enclose letters to the partners in an envelope addressed to Count Simon Vorontsov, the Russian envoy to the English Court. Matthiessen & Sillem received provisional instructions not to write to Hope & Co. unless it was absolutely necessary, and then in such a manner as not to compromise the partners. Reports from De Smeth were to be treated similarly, the date being put on a separate sheet and mention of places or names being avoided. If anything serious or unexpected should occur, De Smeth was to send a letter to Mr. James Smith on the island of St.Croix; as with all other letters, this was to be enclosed in an envelope bearing the address of

Harman & Co. in order, above all, to avoid the name of Hope appearing.[1] Insinger, Hope's principal agent in Amsterdam, was advised that confidential messages should be written in lemon juice at the end of letters, their presence being indicated by a small cross at the top; holding such a letter to the fire caused the invisible writing to appear.[2] Having also settled these matters to his satisfaction, Labouchère was free to return to England.[3]

At about this time, Robert Voûte's position at the Russian Court was seriously threatened by an intrigue which led to the empress being deprived of all political influence. A favourite of the Court, a man of Turkish origin named Kutaysov, who had risen from the position of Court hairdresser to a high office, succeeded in turning the czar against his own wife by insinuating that he allowed it to appear to his people that he was ruled by women. At the same time he provided the czar with a mistress, thereby completing the alienation between the couple. At the beginning of August 1798 the czar forbade his wife ever to concern herself with politics, and shortly afterwards the Princes Kurakin, two ministers sympathetic towards the empress, were dismissed from the government.[4] Others concerned in the intrigue included Bezborodko and Vasilyev, both opponents of Voûte, and after the elimination of his patroness, Voûte faced a cheerless period.

Exactly what took place is not clear, but we do know that early in October Vasilyev, with Rall's collaboration, manoeuvred Robert Voûte into a position in which he was forced to ask for the resignation of his nephew, Pierre, from Voûte Velho Rall & Co. The results of an investigation by Councillor of State Wulff into the firm's financial policy were used as a pretext for the move. Nikolai Rogovikov was appointed Court Banker in place of Pierre Voûte.[5] In this and other ways, Vasilyev made life so intolerable for Robert Voûte that by the end of December 1798 he had no choice but to leave Russia. He journeyed to Warsaw to join his nephew, who at the onset of the difficulties had set off posthaste to return to Russia, but had paused in Poland to await further developments. Early in 1799 the two left Warsaw, bound for western Europe; Robert Voûte's first task was to cross to England to report to the partners of Hope & Co. on the events which had taken place.[6]

Despite the severe damage done to the Company's influence in Russia by Voûte's enforced departure, the conversion of old bonds into new continued undisturbed in Holland; even an attempt by De Wolf in Antwerp to throw a spanner into the works by refusing to send the principal debenture to Amsterdam until such time as the bonds were delivered to him, duly receipted, failed to upset the process.[1] By his action, De Wolf sought to achieve a separate settlement in respect of the Antwerp loan, the effect of which would be that he, and not Hope & Co., received the full commission. When official letters and instructions from Vasilyev failed to dissuade him, and even a visit to Antwerp by De Smeth produced no result, it was decided to proclaim the conversion a success and suspend the payment of interest on the Antwerp bonds. This, it was considered, would spur holders of bonds of the Antwerp loan to bring De Wolf to heel; and indeed this succeeded.[2]

On 10th December 1798, Baron von Stackelberg, the authorized agent of the Russian Court, completed the task of signing and sealing the 88,300 bonds relating to the new loan.[3] Out of consideration for the Court, and also to propitiate its representative, the Hopes had placed their private residence in Amsterdam at Von Stackelberg's disposal. As the envoy firmly refused to accept a gift to mark the occasion, the Hopes decided that the expenditure incurred on behalf of Von Stackelberg and his entourage should be met by the Company as part of the overall cost of the conversion. Such a gesture, the envoy could scarcely decline.[4]

With the end of the conversion now in sight, the time had come to reward the services rendered, and in this the Hopes were usually generous. Pierre de Smeth and Robert Voûte were each given 400 Russian bonds, and Jan Jacob Voûte Jr. received 100. Hope's confidential representative, David Berck, was rewarded with 30 bonds, and the lawyer Schimmelpenninck received 10.[5] Voûte had gained the necessary experience during his first visit to Russia and had already attended to the matter of 'gifts' to the Russian officials concerned, who included Vasilyev.[6]

The political events which took place during 1798 had been anything but favourable from the point of view of the Russian loan. During his advance towards Egypt, General Bonaparte had occupied Malta–to the fury of Czar Paul I, who shortly beforehand had assumed the patronage of the Knights of Malta. The czar increasingly came to regard himself as the spiritual leader of the resistance to the ideas which emanated from the French Revolution, and towards the end of 1798, after difficult negotiations and numerous promises of subsidies from England, a coalition consisting of Austria, England, Russia and Naples was formed to oppose France.

With minor wars breaking out here and there in Europe, and a clear threat of a major conflict hanging overhead, it is not surprising that the reaction of the bondholders was less enthusiastic than the Company had earlier anticipated. The preparations for war which were being made in Russia itself and the financial operations brought about by a war in western Europe combined to steadily depress the rate of exchange of the rouble, with the result that the repayment of principal on 1st January 1799, which Hope & Co. so eagerly awaited–and which was to have made the prolongation of the loans more attractive from the bondholders' point of view–could not take place. This disappointing development was reflected in subsequent market quotations for the Russian bonds. Whereas in the first half of 1798 the price did not fall below 92, Insinger reported on 20th October that it stood at 83–84.[1] The interest payment made on 1st January 1799 put 2½ million guilders into circulation, producing a marginal improvement in the price, but this proved only temporary. The war, which now erupted in full fury in southern Germany and Italy, added to the fear among bondholders that, in spite of the express assurance contained in the principal debenture, Russia might well suspend interest payments in the Batavian Republic, an ally of France.[2]

These fears grew even stronger when, at the end of August, an Anglo-Russian military force landed near Den Helder and then attempted to push southwards. But a lack of energetic leadership on the part of the British component, coupled with the fact that no pro-Orange uprisings were taking place elsewhere in the country, caused the expeditionary force to re-embark in mid-October. The effect upon bondholders of this incursion is clear from the fall in the market price of the converted bonds from an average of 85 during the first half of 1799 to a maximum of 74 during the second half.[3]

Although the outlook in the Batavian Republic was gloomy, the Russian government was in fact doing its utmost to ensure the payment of interest on 1st January 1800; but its efforts were hampered by what Hope & Co. described as 'the astonishing revolution which is making itself felt in the principal areas of currency.'[4] The English subsidies to the Russian and Austrian armies and the equipping of the Anglo-Russian expedition, among other factors, produced a financial crisis which dislocated the rates of exchange and caused the pound sterling to fall so drastically that many English houses were moved to ship gold and silver to Hamburg as a protection against excessive exchange losses. The partners in London acted similarly, sending gold to Matthiessen & Sillem via Harman & Co. in order to advertise the interest payment due on 1st January 1800. This gold, however, could be despatched only in small quantities, for London underwriters had become cautious following the loss of the frigate 'Lutine' off Vlieland, with an extremely valuable cargo of gold, and they were now unwilling to insure gold consignments exceeding thirty to forty thousand pounds in value.[1] As the volume of exchange transactions between Amsterdam and Hamburg had also fallen to zero, it was left to Matthiessen & Sillem to decide whether, in the light of price ratios, it was better to send the gold straight to Amsterdam, or to sell it in Hamburg.

Matthiessen & Sillem were given strict instructions to ensure that the 3.1 million guilders required reached De Smeth before 1st January; in the event of the orders from the Court Bankers in Russia falling short of this sum, the house was empowered to take the necessary action under a personal guarantee from the Hopes. Messrs.Hope were greatly displeased by the fact that the Court Bankers, without consulting them, had made arrangements for remittances to De Smeth; their annoyance was the greater because some of the instructions were pointless. For example, Harman & Co. had been instructed to remit direct to Amsterdam at a time when exchange transactions between London and Amsterdam were impossible. To the immense relief of the partners, the circulation in Hamburg was restored fairly rapidly and sterling became stronger. Added to this, exchange traffic between Hamburg and Amsterdam was revived and thus, despite some anxious moments, De Smeth was able to make the interest payment on time, as a result of which the price of the Russian bonds rose again.[2]

In the latter part of 1799 Czar Paul virtually dissociated himself from the war against France. The fruitless invasion of Holland, coming on top of the defeats suffered by the Russian armies in Switzerland (principally through poor co-operation with their Austrian allies), produced in the impulsive emperor a political *volte face*. Although Russia formally remained at war with France, Paul I informally made increasing efforts towards a *rapprochement* with Napoleon, who in November 1799 had seized power in France. At the same time, Paul adopted a cooler attitude towards England, which he accused of failing to restore Malta to the control of the Knights, and which, because of its great naval superiority in the Mediterranean, constituted a threat to Russia's influence in that area. In December 1800 his anti-British policy was manifested in a Treaty of Neutrality between Russia, Sweden, Prussia and Denmark, the aim of which was to oblige England–if need be, by force of arms–to respect the rights of neutral vessels in international waters. The measures adopted under the treaty included placing an embargo on British vessels and cargoes in Russian ports. In 1801, under the pretext of maintaining neutrality, the Danes occupied Hamburg and the Prussians did the same to Hanover and Bremen. The British answer to these acts included blockading the Elbe and despatching a fleet of warships to Denmark; the latter resulted in the destruction of the Danish fleet at Copenhagen.[1]

Russia having withdrawn, Austria was left alone to face Bonaparte–who prosecuted the war with immense energy. After a series of French victories in southern Germany and Italy, the Austrians were forced to treat for peace with Napoleon. With the signing of the Treaty of Lunéville in February 1801, Austria accepted the new situation in Europe.

For the partners in London, this development implied an intensification of the pressures which, since 1799, had tended to exclude them from matters concerned with the Russian loans. It was becoming increasingly clear that Rall was the evil genius and that his aim was to deal solely with De Smeth, to the exclusion of the partners of Hope & Co. The stagnation of Russia's trade with England, a product of the czar's policies, had an unfavourable influence on the rate of exchange of the rouble, and this, as in the previous year, made it impossible to announce a repayment against the Russian loan. Despite this disappointment for the bondholders, however, the price of the bonds remainded reasonably high; this was probably due in part to the cessation of hostilities between France and Russia and the steady improvement in relations between them.[2]

With these circumstances in mind, the partners in London deemed it wise gradually to dispose of the Russian bonds, which they had received by way of commission, in the Batavian Republic, and to reserve the proceeds for future requirements. To this end, an 'Account X' was opened, ostensibly by Robert Voûte, with the house in Amsterdam which bore his name. The proceeds of the sale of bonds, through the broker Willem Borski, were placed in this account. Borski was instructed to sell only when the bonds were in demand and when the price was over 80.[3] Between 10th October and 31st December 1800, a total of 1,103 bonds were disposed of in this manner at prices which ranged between 82½ and 87½. During the following year a further 3,130 were sold; up to October, in which month England, the sole remaining opponent of France, signed the peace preliminaries, the price fluctuated between 81 and 84, but with the news of peace the figure shot up to 89.[4]

Meanwhile, major changes were taking place in Russia. The caprices of the czar had eventually assumed such proportions that even a clever courtier like Vasilyev could no longer stand his ground. In the autumn of 1800 he had fallen into disfavour and had been dismissed. Prior to his downfall he had succeeded in obtaining a modest loan in Hamburg, but a similar request to Hope met with a firm refusal.[5] Following Vasilyev's dismissal, Voûte was approached by the St.Petersburg merchant J.C.Bergien who hoped, with Voûte's assistance, to have Vasilyev's protégé, Rall, removed from his position as Court Banker. Bergien argued that there was no better way of establishing his reputation than by succeeding where Rall and Vasilyev had failed, and that he accordingly sought Voûte's opinion on the chances of a new loan via Hope & Co.

Before anything definite could be discussed, Russia was thrown into turmoil by the assassination of Czar Paul I on 23rd March 1801. The new ruler, Alexander I, who had known of the plot against his father, chose his ministers from among those who had earlier fallen into disfavour. This meant that not only did figures such as Zubov and the Princes Kurakin become ministers, but also that Vasilyev, who could claim to have been a victim of the previous czar, was rehabilitated. Bergien assured Voûte that Hope & Co. had nothing to fear from the reappointment of Vasilyev, for under the new régime the disregard for the Company would be at an end; after all, one of Alexander's first acts had been to reverse his late father's anti-British policy.[1]

All these friendly gestures were allied to the financial crisis which the Russian government faced as a result of the capricious conduct of the late emperor, and in the circumstances a loan arranged by Hope & Co. would be extremely welcome.[2]

Acting on instructions from the partners, Robert Voûte had meanwhile visited Amsterdam to see whether it would be possible for the Company to re-establish itself there. As far as a new Russian loan was concerned, his findings led him to the conclusion that a portion of the bonds held as a reserve by the Russian government could be sold in Amsterdam at the current market price. This, however, was conditional upon the repayment of at least one million guilders of principal money in the near future.[3] Only thus could the Russian government secure fresh funds, for the *Staatsbewind*, as the new government of the Batavian Republic was known, would certainly not consent to a loan being floated publicly.

Back in London, the partners approached Voûte's proposals with the utmost caution. Labouchère was convinced that the Company ought not to make it too easy for the new Russian government to obtain money, for that would encourage improvidence and extravagance in Russia. As for a Russian loan in England, to which Bergien had also referred, he felt that the chances of success were slim, though they might improve when trade relations between the two countries had been restored.[4]

Such views were anything but welcome to Vasilyev and, faced with little prospect of obtaining a loan, he again allowed the correspondence to lapse.

In the absence of any agreement concerning the reserve, the Russian government had little choice except to find a way to remit the funds needed for the interest payment to Amsterdam. All these transactions took place between the Court Bankers and De Smeth, and did not involve the Company. When the time came for the next interest instalment, however, it would probably be impossible to by-pass Hope & Co. completely, for by this time, December 1801, the plans for a return to the Republic were taking shape. The signing of the Peace of Amiens on 25th March 1802 served to remove the last obstacle to the return of the partners; but owing to the difficulties surrounding the Portuguese loan it was not until October 1802 that John Williams Hope and his family reached Amsterdam.

The sale of Russian bonds via 'Account X' proceeded steadily during 1802 at prices round about 90. The proceeds were used to partly finance the payments due on the Portuguese loan in 1802.[1]

If a complete loss of confidence in the promises made by the Russian government was to be avoided, it was now imperative that a start be made with the repayment of the Russian loan. After a good deal of shilly-shallying, a sum of 263,000 pounds sterling–a balance held in favour of the Russian Court by the British government and stemming from an earlier subsidy–was placed at the disposal of Hope & Co.[2] However, appeals by Harman and Henry Hope to the British Foreign Secretary, Lord Hawkesbury, to release the money before 15th November 1802 became bogged down in the bureaucratic machine, with the result that the maturing date for 2,000 bonds had to be postponed from 1st January to 1st July 1803.[3] When the announcement of the redemption appeared, the price of the bonds rose, reaching 96 at the end of March. During this period Borski carefully fed the market, limiting his sales to fifty bonds or less per day.

The redemption of the 2,000 bonds was the first act which the Company undertook in connexion with the Russian loan after its formal return to Amsterdam; but this return was not without an element of irony. Vasilyev refused to extend the redemption and the preceding ballot to cover the reserve bonds. Redemption of these, he reasoned, would not lighten the burden of interest which rested upon the Russian government; moreover, Hope would be entitled to claim commission on drawn reserve bonds, and this Vasilyev begrudged the Company. Although De Smeth was no longer being involved in the payment of interest, the Court Bankers routed a substantial part of their remittances via that house, and it was also concerned with the repurchase of bonds by the Russian government.

The Hopes were back, and they had taken up the reins of the Russian loan; but the prospects of smooth progress in the loan affair, like those in the political sphere, were anything but encouraging.

CHAPTER SEVEN

'LES TRAITES DU NORD' AND OPERATION R.M.

The general peace in Europe which had enabled John Williams Hope and Labouchère to return to Amsterdam was not of long duration. In May 1803 hostilities again broke out between England and France. Elsewhere on the Continent, however, the situation remained calm–at least temporarily–and this gave Napoleon an opportunity to prepare a large-scale expedition against England. Such an undertaking demanded not only a large army, but also a powerful fleet, and so obviously the period of preparation was accompanied by an extremely urgent need for shipbuilding materials in France. As Russia was the principal supplier, the French equipment programme would necessarily lead to the export of large quantities of material from Russia, and this could only improve the rate of exchange of the rouble. This improvement, in turn, would increase the possibility of repayments against Hope's Russian loans and also immensely facilitate the normal payments of interest.

While this development was in itself of importance to Hope, the Company, as good merchants, could not ignore the French procurement programme, which had got into its stride in June of 1803. In that month, the house of Récamier in Paris, on behalf of its agent, Xavier Farmbacher,[1] approached Hope & Co. with a request for introductions to houses in 'diverses places du Nord.' Shortly afterwards David Parish reported from Antwerp that Récamier had entered into an agreement with the French government for the supply of large quantities of Russian goods, and that Farmbacher, en route for Russia, had arrived in Hamburg and had approached various houses in an effort to obtain sizeable credits on St.Petersburg. As a result of Farmbacher's activities, the drawings on Paris had assumed such proportions that the rate of exchange there had fallen. As Hope had predicted, Farmbacher made little headway in Russia, for besides being unfamiliar with commercial practices there he was unduly restricted by the instructions issued from Paris.[2]

Another major obstacle was the virtual absence of exchange facilities between St.Petersburg and Paris, so that Farmbacher's payments had to be routed via Hamburg or Amsterdam. Thus it is not surprising that the draft on Récamier, which was given to the merchant Jos. Morison of Riga, was presented to Hope & Co.[3]

While Hope & Co. were regarded as suitable intermediaries in the normal pattern of financial traffic, some extraordinary events in France served to emphasize their role. These concerned the sale to the United States of Louisiana by Napoleon. In 1801 Spain, initially under conditions of strict secrecy, had ceded Louisiana to France. The formal acceptance of the territory by France became possible only with the Treaty of Amiens, but in the United States the revelation of the Franco-Spanish treaty produced such unrest that President Jefferson was moved to send an envoy to Paris to negotiate for the transfer of a part of Louisiana to the United States. But before the envoy reached his destination, Napoleon, who regarded a resumption of the war against England as inevitable, decided to sell the whole of the territory on the grounds that it could not be defended. On 30th April 1803 he signed a treaty with the United States providing for the sale to the latter of Louisiana at a price of 15 million dollars. The terms provided for the deduction of 3¾ million dollars representing previous American claims against France. With the signing of the Franco-American treaty, the expeditionary force created for Louisiana and commanded by General Victor, which was standing by for embarkation at Hellevoetsluis, was disbanded.[1]

As the United States was not in a position to effect immediate settlement, it was decided to pay France in 6% bonds on which interest would be payable in London and Amsterdam. This solution was proposed by Alexander Baring, who had been staying in Paris since Christmas 1802 and whose business and family ties (his father-in-law was the American millionaire, Bingham) linked him closely with America's finances. During the negotiations Baring had acted as financial adviser to Jefferson's representative, and thus it is not surprising that on 3rd May 1803–four days after the signing of the Franco-American agreement–he, as a representative of his own company and also of Hope & Co., entered into an agreement with the French Minister of Finance, Barbé Marbois, which resulted in the two houses acquiring the 11¼ million dollarsworth of 6% American bonds for the sum of 52 million francs. It was agreed that when confirmation reached Paris that one-third of the 6% bonds had been handed to a representative of the two houses in America, drafts totalling 17½ million francs would be placed at the disposal of the French government; 6 million francsworth of these would become due in the first month and thereafter 2 million francsworth monthly. When this portion had been paid to the French government, a similar tranche would follow at the rate of 2 million francs per month. As each third of the drafts was placed at the government's disposal, Baring and Hope would receive the following

To all to whom these presents shall come, GREETING:

I CERTIFY, That the annexed Writing is a True Copy of an act of the Congress of the United States, entitled "An act authorising the creation of a Stock, to the amount of Eleven millions, two hundred and fifty thousand Dollars, for the purpose of carrying into effect the Convention of the thirtieth of April, One thousand eight hundred and three, between the United States of America and the French Republic; and making provision for the payment of the same," duly compared with the original Roll deposited, and remaining, in this Office —— " —— " ——

" —— " —— "

In faith whereof, I James Madison —— *Secretary for the Department of State of the United States of America, have signed these presents, and caused the Seal of my Office to be affixed hereto, at the City of Washington, this* Tenth —— *day of* January —— *A. D.* 1804, *and in the* Twenty eighth —— *year of the Independence of the said States.*

James Madison

Certificate issued by James Madison, State Secretary, relating to the text of the Act of Congress which approved the Louisiana loan one-third of the American bonds. The payment would thus occupy two years from the date of arrival in Paris of news of the transfer of the initial batch of bonds.[1]

Ratification of the agreement by the First Consul did not materialize until 22nd May, and it was not until 30th July that Alexander Baring was able officially to hand over the drafts for 52 million francs to the American envoy who, however, was instructed not to release the initial one-third until Alexander Baring had reached America and taken possession of a corresponding portion of the bonds.

But the war against England had meanwhile recommenced, and Napoleon was in dire need of funds. It so happened that President Jefferson had succeeded in persuading Congress to vote a sum of 2 million dollars in order to provide his negotiator in Paris with at least a degree of financial backing. With this security behind them, the Americans in Paris offered to guarantee an advance of 10 million francs, which was to be furnished by Baring and Hope. After all, it was conceivable that the long delay might have caused Napoleon to change his mind, in which case all their work would have been in vain.[2] On 30th July 1803, the day upon which the American envoy accepted the drafts from Baring and Hope, Alexander Baring put his signature to an agreement with the French Minister of Finance, under which the latter would receive 2 million francs in the form of drafts on the house of Willings & Francis of Philadelphia. It is probable that the money was used for the French expeditionary force on the island of Haiti, which at that very moment was in an extremely precarious position.[3] Hope & Co. had earlier made efforts to obtain the balance of 8 million francs, required for French purchases in Russia, in Amsterdam, but the Company had failed to reach agreement with the French government on the rate of exchange, and accordingly this method of payment was abandoned.[4]

Following the signing of the contract between Barbé Marbois and Alexander Baring on 3rd May 1803, Hope & Co. approached Vasilyev in St.Petersburg with a proposal that funds be made available in Amsterdam for French purchases in Russia, but that such purchases should in fact be paid for by the Russian government, which could thus create a credit balance in Amsterdam and thus avoid the necessity for remitting funds – a factor of importance in relation to the highly unstable position of the rouble. Vasilyev reacted by sending Voûte's old enemy, Councillor of State Wulff, 'Contrôleur des Banquiers de la Cour,' to Amsterdam to look further into the plan, but owing to the breakdown of the negotiations between Hope and the French government nothing came of it–probably to the great relief of Vasilyev, who in his discussions with others had earlier revealed his opposition to the whole project.[1]

Bergien, the St.Petersburg merchant, who had got wind of the proposed arrangement and had seen in it an opportunity to advance his own interests at the Russian Court, approached Voûte, and later Hope, presenting himself as the indispensable broker who could manipulate his many important connexions in such a manner as to ensure that Hope's proposals were not rejected out of hand. He reasoned that Hope could expect nothing from Vasilyev, for he was opposed to any suggestions from them. Knowing that Bergien was a sworn adversary of Rall (as was revealed in the previous chapter) and that he did indeed have connexions at the Court, the Company, partly out of consideration for Robert Voûte, opened a credit of cf 50,000 in Bergien's name and persuaded Baring to do likewise. Following Vasilyev's dismissal in 1800, Bergien had assumed responsibility for remittances on behalf of a number of government bodies and it was in Hope's interest to assist him in this matter. Bergien, however, did not use the credit for transactions of this sort, but for speculation in foreign exchange, with the result that he exceeded the limit, and when called upon to repay the excess he did so with drafts on Baring.[2] However useful Bergien may have been, such conduct was inadmissible, and both Voûte and the Company made it plain to him that the credit afforded was for the purpose of remitting funds from the Russian government: it did not constitute an account for speculative purposes, nor would a constant deficit of cf 50,000 be tolerated. In the uncertain political situation, they added, Bergien should exercise caution in his transactions. In addition, Voûte informed him that his reputation was at stake, 'in adopting such a cavalier attitude to the essential aspect of your position as a banker, namely the credit which is accorded to you.'[3]

That Bergien, in spite of his tendency to speculate with other people's money, could be of value emerged at the end of 1803, when he reported to the Company that he had been approached by several Russian ministers regarding the prospects of obtaining a new loan or broaching the reserve of 12 million guilders.[4] This news was anything but welcome to the Company, which had counted on a repayment of principal against the old loan, but certainly not on a request for a new one. Wulff's visit to the Republic had given rise to a host of vague rumours, and the public had got it into its head that his presence was a prelude to a further repayment of principal in the following January. Indeed, the sum of 6 million guilders had been mentioned, and this had caused the price to soar to $97\frac{1}{2}$;

even when the repayment failed to materialize, the demand for bonds continued. Adding to the number available by placing the reserve bonds on the market would certainly cause the price to fall. In a letter to Bergien, Hope & Co. made it clear that the Russian government need not count upon a fresh loan, for with the law passed on 1st June 1802 the *Staatsbewind* had firmly closed the door on the floating of foreign loans in the Republic.[1]

This absolute rejection of Bergien's overtures will not have been entirely dissociated from Hope's anxieties concerning the Louisiana loan. Owing to difficulties and delays in America, the confirmatory report did not reach Paris until late in March 1804. Despite the advance of 10 million francs which Hope and Baring had furnished, Napoleon was still in dire straits. Indeed, such was his need of money that on 21st April 1804 Barbé Marbois put his signature to an agreement which provided for Hope & Co. to receive the remaining two-thirds of the American bonds immediately in return for a substantial acceleration of the instalments. Labouchère signed on behalf of the Company. For anticipating the payments, Hope and Baring were granted a discount amounting to 1,675,000 francs. Among the methods of payment agreed was the establishment by Hope & Co. of a credit of 12 million francs, divided into 8 bonds of 1½ million each, the first of which would mature on 1st May 1804 and the remainder at monthly intervals until the end of the year; the sums which thus became available could be drawn on, up to the monthly limit, by German and Russian merchants holding permits issued by the French Admiralty.[2]

Hope & Co. were no strangers to the Admiralty at that time. The paymaster of the expeditionary force which had been destined for Louisiana had availed himself of their services for a number of minor indents, and when the expedition was abandoned the cash balance was returned to the *Payeurs de la Marine* in Dunkirk via the Company.[3] Shortly before the credit for the 'traites du Nord' was made available, the Minister for the Navy, Decrès, had instructed Hope to charter ten neutral vessels and to place these at the disposal of Morison in Riga for the conveyance of masts to the Emden merchant Philippus Julius Abegg.[4] Six days later, on 16th March 1804, the minister cancelled the instruction, but with the availability of 12 million francs in Amsterdam he contacted the Company fourteen days later.

By the end of March, both Barbé Marbois and Decrès had furnished Hope with the names of the authorized merchants and the limits to which they were permitted to draw on the credit.[1] Labouchère applied to the French envoy in the Republic for a passport for France, but as this was not required until 7th April it must be assumed that the negotiations leading up to the agreement, which was to be signed on 21st April, were conducted by him in writing from the Republic. Of the 12 million francs which Hope & Co. were to make available during the remainder of the year, only 9 million had provisionally been allocated. Half this sum was earmarked for four (later three) merchants in Riga, including Morison; he was to receive just over $2\frac{1}{4}$ million. A number of merchants in St.Petersburg, who were still to be appointed by the French consul general, De Lesseps, would together be granted credits totalling 1,800,000 francs; a house in Hamburg was to be allocated 800,000 francs; a house in Köningsberg 500,000 francs; and three (later two) merchants in Emden were authorized to draw up to 1,400,000 francs.[2]

The sources and merchants from and through which the shipbuilding materials were to be supplied were clearly chosen with care. In Köningsberg and St.Petersburg, only hemp was purchased, while in Riga two houses, Helmund & Son and J.Morison, were charged with the purchasing of timber. Another Riga merchant, Justus Blanckenhagen, concentrated on hemp, and later one-third of the credit originally earmarked for the St.Petersburg houses jointly was transferred to him. The records do not reveal the reason for this change, but it may be assumed that the prices and the stocks available in Riga favoured its selection as the point of supply. The credits granted to the two houses in Emden, Thomas van Cammenga and Claas Tholen, were to cover the costs of handling, neutralizing and re-shipping timber and, to a far lesser extent, hemp from Riga. All shipments from the Baltic to Emden were made in East Frisian vessels flying the Prussian flag. Some cargoes were taken direct from Riga to French ports such as Morlaix, Bordeaux, Nantes and, in isolated instances, Marseilles, and these were carried in Russian or Swedish ships.[3]

The hemp obtained in St.Petersburg was in all cases shipped direct to a French port, Bordeaux and Nantes being the principal destinations. All such cargoes were carried in Russian vessels.[4] It was not long before the credit of 800,000 francs earmarked for Hamburg was allocated to Pehmöller & Droop, who were requested to supply copper.[5]

The costs and commissions relating to the goods shipped varied greatly, both in terms of commodity and source. The costs of handling and shipping timber were particularly high, dues and other charges averaging 70% of the value of the cargo.[6] The figure for hemp was much lower, probably because the transport, storage, loading and unloading charges were considerably less than those for timber. The St.Petersburg houses charged a total of 13% for 'droits, frais, commission, passage de Sund, etc[a].' The commission paid to the houses in Königsberg and in Russia varied between 3% and 4%.[1]

In the case of the hemp and timber shipped to Emden, the costs of neutralization, sometimes supplemented by transshipment expenses, were added to those already mentioned. Van Cammenga's and Tholen's invoices for charges and commission on hemp, timber and copper valued at just over 1½ million guilders and shipped to Emden totalled cf 252,264.3.8, or 16% of the invoice value of the goods. This implies, for example, that timber purchased in Riga almost doubled in price by the time it left the harbour of Emden.

When, in August 1804, news of the blockading of the Channel ports and the arrest by the British of a number of vessels engaged in these operations was received, Decrès gave instructions that future timber shipments were to be consigned to Ryberg & Co. in Copenhagen. This house would undertake the unloading of the ships and would pay the freight and unloading charges.[2] Ryberg's charges on ten cargoes of timber shipped to them by Morison amounted to 34% of the invoice value–more than twice the figure charged in Emden. Hope & Co. eventually received ½% commission on all payments which they effected.[3]

In such uncertain times, the insurance of vessels and their cargoes was difficult. Decrès had initially stipulated premiums of 2% for marine risks and 4½–5% for all-risk cover, but Hope & Co. soon disillusioned him: insurers in Amsterdam were already demanding 5–7% for marine risks, and all-risk cover could not be obtained for less than 8–10%.[4] Upon receiving this information, the minister gave the Company a free hand in the matter on condition that the premium paid covered the voyage to a French port. By the time the letter reached Hope, however, the situation on the Amsterdam insurance market had changed; the report of the arrest by the British of three ships operating for Blanckenhagen and Morison, coming on top of other losses, had made it impossible to obtain insurance against war risks there.[5] In addition, the underwriters were plainly averse to offering cover on damage; the cause lay in the fact that a number of merchant houses who had indulged in speculation, and lost, had resorted to deliberately allowing cargoes to be damaged in order to be able to shift the consequences of their imprudence on to the shoulders of the insurers.[6]

With such poor prospects in Amsterdam, Hope advised Decrès to try his luck in Hamburg. The underwriters there proved to be more flexible in the matter of marine risk cover to French ports, but all-risk insurance on cargoes bound for France had been withdrawn at the beginning of August, and even Decrès's offer of a 10% premium–and later one of 15%–did not tempt the insurers.[1]

In response to an allegation by Decrès that Hogguer & Co. in Amsterdam were offering all-risk insurance on shipments to French ports at 6½–7%, Hope & Co. replied that Hogguer dealt with Swedish vessels, and that Swedish captains inspired more confidence than their Russian counterparts, with whom the Company was principally concerned. The Swedish captains, like the Prussians, were renowned for their skill, knew every inch of the North Sea, the Baltic and the Channel and, moreover, sailed in solidly built ships. The Russian merchantmen were inferior, being built of deal, and easily sustained damage to their cargo–a fact which in the case of hemp, with its susceptibility to moisture, could result in heavy claims upon the insurers.[2] Apart from this, the premiums increased as the season advanced, marine risk cover rising from 6% in August to 7–8% in September and October.[3]

The formalities which the French authorities sought to impose on the commercial transactions constituted an obstacle to the whole operation. According to Decrès's original instructions, the sums corresponding to the invoices were to be drawn only after the loading of the goods. The merchants in the Baltic were required to furnish Hope & Co. with a resumé of the invoice details and a certificate showing the rate of exchange, both bearing the seal of the local French consul or agent. Five days after these documents had been forwarded, the merchant was permitted to draw on Hope & Co., the periods being 70 days for St.Petersburg, 65 days for Riga and 60 days for Königsberg, while those for Hamburg and Emden were governed by local custom. Hope was forbidden to disclose to the merchants the sum of the credits earmarked for them.

Decrès had initially desired that Hope should verify the invoices and, before accepting drafts, satisfy themselves that the drawer had fulfilled his commitments; but the Company, with the support of Barbé Marbois, succeeded in talking Decrès out of this. Hope also advised against the stipulation that the documents which were to accompany the drafts should be stamped or initialled by the French consul in Amsterdam, for this would attract undesirable attention. The Company would consent to no more than the initialling by the consul of the letter of advice, which procedure, it was stressed, would have to be completed rapidly, for in Amsterdam no more than twenty-four hours was ever allowed for the acceptance or protestation of drafts.[4] Furthermore, Hope insisted on the unconditional freedom to accept any draft accompanied by such a document.

In Russia, too, commercial practices proved stronger than Napoleonic regulations. The merchants of St.Petersburg were accustomed to drawing immediately after the despatch of the invoice, and nothing would satisfy them but that De Lesseps should waive the five-day waiting period.[1]

From Hope's point of view, a very disagreeable note was introduced by a request from Van Cammenga of Emden that the Company should furnish ante-dated, false correspondence for the purpose of securing the release of a number of vessels which had fallen into British hands. Labouchère had made it clear to Decrès and his staff in March 1804 that the Company was only willing to allow drafts to be drawn on them, but would have no part in the underlying transactions.[2]

When Decrès began to press the matter, Hope, gambling on the rivalry between two ministers and their departments, enlisted the aid of Barbé Marbois. To the Minister for the Navy, the Company again emphasized that it was acting as banker to the French Treasury, by whom it was required to accept instructions emanating from the Admiralty concerning the funds which it held on behalf of the Treasury, but that its obligations did not go beyond this. From Barbé Marbois's department, Labouchère learned that the minister was fully in agreement with Hope's standpoint, but that he could not admit this publicy, in order not to contradict his colleague.[3] The matter was finally raised in the ministerial council, where Napoleon ruled in favour of the Company. According to Roger, the director of the *Droits Réunis* and a good friend of Labouchère, the emperor said: 'Messrs. Hope, who are accustomed to handling transactions of 80 to 100 million, will not furnish these items for 40 million.' This flattering remark concerning the Company was said to have brought the debate to an end.[4]

In a review of the matter, Hope & Co. pointed out to Decrès that it did not concern a mere formality, but tampering with existing correspondence and the issuing of false statements–actions which would debase the Company in its own eyes and those of others. 'In the profession of merchant, loyalty and strict rectitude are the sole qualifications for earning the respect of the public; it is upon these qualities that we are entitled to the confidence we are honoured with. Only on this basis can it delight us and do we strive for it, beyond all the gains attached to hazardous operations.'[5] For the partners, it must have been very gratifying to be able to teach a French minister a lesson, safe in the knowledge that they had the approval of the highest in the land.

By the end of 1804, this operation on behalf of the French Treasury was virtually completed. The balance of the 9 million francs was used to meet late invoices in 1805, and the unbroached 3 million francs, in the form of drafts issued by the banker Desprez, were transferred to France in December 1804.[1] All in all, the operation was one upon which Hope could look back with satisfaction: it had, indirectly, facilitated the Russian remittances by reason of the drafts on Amsterdam, and, despite the differences of opinion at the end, the Company's prestige in the eyes of the French government had remained unimpaired.[2]

Now that the credit established with the Company by the Treasury for this purpose had been liquidated, the question of financing subsequent expeditions from the Baltic arose. Decrès sought Hope's views on private expeditions to French ports. Hope felt that such a scheme had merit, but recommended that the financial aspect be entrusted to a Paris merchant, to whom the government should supply the necessary funds and who would take over from the Admiralty the task of maintaining contact with the merchants in the Baltic. The Company considered De Bondeville, with whom it had long been associated, a highly suitable intermediary.

Under such an arrangement, all transactions could be carried on between individual merchants, as had been the case during the American War of Independence, when Hope purchased and consigned ships stores for the French Admiralty and was only required to negotiate with Le Chevalier Lambert and Dujardin de Ruzé. For its services on that occasion, the Company had received a commission of 2% on the value of the invoices, plus the customary commission on insurance, freight charges and other services. The French government had had a few of the vessels engaged in that operation neutralized, but had accepted the risks which this entailed.

The Company also expressed the opinion that it would be preferable for the cargoes to be shipped for the account of the Baltic merchants, and offered to cover the shippers' risks at an annual premium of 12%, in the name of and for the account of the Paris house. Hope felt that it would be better if the merchants were not informed that the French Admiralty was behind the transactions, and if they were spared the necessity to furnish certificates concerning the rate of exchange. Too many formalities and excessive secrecy were repugnant to the merchant fraternity. Even if Decrès should decide to place orders direct with the Baltic merchants, Hope would still prefer to have only one house in Paris with which to correspond; this would in future prevent Decrès's time being taken up with petty issues raised by the merchants.[3]

With this elegant ploy, the Company attempted to make it clear that, as a mercantile house, it was not anxious to have direct dealings with a French government department. The reference to Hope's role as a supplier to France during the American War of Independence is noteworthy, for it reveals that even then Henry Hope, a convinced supporter of the House of Orange, separated politics from business. But little came of further large-scale deliveries to the French fleet. In October 1805 that fleet was destroyed by Nelson at Trafalgar, and with its defeat its role as an instrument of power came to an end. Hope & Co. continued to be concerned in the financing of French naval purchases after Trafalgar, but the sums involved were small. Between 1805 and 1811, a six-year period, the entries 'pour le Service de la Marine' totalled cf 1,672,288.15.8, an average of less than 280,000 guilders a year.[1]

The keen demand abroad for Russian goods, among other factors, had resulted in the prompt payment of interest on the Russian bonds at the end of 1804. While the czar continued to be neutral in the matter of the war between France and England, this favourable situation might be expected to continue; but his neutrality was not to last very long. In the eyes of Alexander I, Napoleon was a threat to Europe, and his plan to partition the Turkish Empire conflicted with Russia's interests. Despite the efforts of the British to get the czar on their side after the Treaty of Amiens, he remained uncommitted, although his relations with France steadily deteriorated. In May 1804 the French envoy in St. Petersburg was recalled, a development which threw the exchange rates into a state of confusion. Bergien wrote to Hope that: 'It was another striking example of the extent to which political events imperiously control and influence business.'[2] In the autumn of 1804 the czar signed a treaty with Austria, and in April of the following year he allied himself with England. When, in August 1805, Austria joined the Anglo-Russian alliance, war became inevitable.

The war, when it came, went extremely well from Napoleon's point of view. Early in December 1805 he succeeded in defeating the Austrian and Russian imperial armies at Austerlitz, whereupon Austria sued for peace. Alexander, however, returned to eastern Europe to continue the struggle there. For Prussia, which had still not made up her mind whether or not to join in on the side of Austria and Russia, Austerlitz was a sign to enter into an alliance with Napoleon. Two months later, under French pressure, she closed her ports to English ships. When the Prussian decision was communicated to the British government early in 1806, it retaliated by blockading the entrances to the Eems, the Weser, the Elbe and the Trave, and placed an embargo on Prussian vessels.[3] Shortly afterwards England declared war on Prussia. This situation, however, did not by any means imply that Prussia was now firmly in the French camp: faced with the growth of France's power after her defeat of Austria at Austerlitz, Prussia ultimately decided to challenge Napoleon. But in a lightning campaign the Prussian armies were defeated at Jena and Auerstädt, and shortly afterwards, in November 1806, Napoleon proclaimed in Berlin the Continental System, which prohibited all trade with Britain or her colonies. At about the same time, French troops occupied Hamburg, Bremen and Lübeck.[1]

All these disruptions left their mark on France's trade, and that of her allies, with Russia, and resulted in a growing scarcity of Russian goods.[2] Diminishing stocks and rising prices are a prescription for speculation, and Hope & Co. were not the type to let such an opportunity pass. The partners envisaged particularly high profits on potash, and accordingly a number of orders for this commodity were placed. Bergien was among the recipients, and he was instructed to purchase 4,000 poods at a price not exceeding 46 roubles per pood. When he reported that the price had risen sharply, he was given discretion, and proceeded to purchase a quantity at 54 roubles per pood. But when it came to shipping the potash, fresh problems arose. On 27th April 1806 Bergien wrote to say that the news of the blockade of the Elbe, Weser and Trave had reached St.Petersburg, and that he was in a quandary regarding the choice of flag for the shipment. A month later he reported that the French government had declared all vessels carrying cargoes of Russian origin which might be captured in open waters as prizes of war. In view of this, he wondered whether it might not be wiser to resell the potash in St.Petersburg; but finally he decided to consign it to a house in Lübeck, with instructions to ship it to Hope in a Danish vessel via the Holstein Canal.[3]

Russia also suffered as a result of the stagnation of trade with western Europe. In April 1806 Bergien was already complaining of the inactivity on the commodity markets and the decline in rates of exchange, but by November he reported that things had got far worse. The commodity markets were dead, and in the complete absence of business the value of the rouble was steadily falling–and was in any case purely nominal.[4] The occupation of Hamburg by French troops will certainly have had something to do with the difficulties in that November. After all, Hamburg was an important centre for the financial aspects of Russia's foreign trade. Under normal circumstances, Britain had a deficit in her trade with Russia, while the German territories had a trading surplus with Russia but a deficit with England, so that imbalances in the demand for drafts in these three areas were corrected at the central point, Hamburg.[1] The proclamation of the Continental System and the occupation of Hamburg, however, had eliminated this balancing facility, and Russia was to feel the consequences.

Not surprisingly, there was a degree of pessimism in Amsterdam concerning the question whether the Russian remittances for the interest instalment due on 1st January 1807 would arrive and, if so, whether they would be on time. Fortunately, Matthiessen & Sillem reported in mid-December that Rall and Rogovikov had instructed them to remit the appropriate sum to Hope & Co. Owing to the war situation in eastern Europe, the Russian remittances had had to be routed via Sweden. Matthiessen & Sillem had transferred the funds received from Russia to a place of safety even before the French occupation, but it proved possible to remit to Amsterdam in the normal manner.[2] Hope & Co. were thus enabled to pay the interest on the due date, with consequent benefit to the price of the Russian bonds. Despite the war with Russia, the price had held up excellently, thanks to the prompt payment of interest, and during 1805 and 1806 the six-monthly average had not fallen below 95.[3]

The Russian armies had no more success in 1807 than in the preceding years. While winter held the country in its grip, the battle continued to sway back and forth, but in June Napoleon secured a decisive victory at Friedland. The czar and the King of Prussia sought peace, and this Napoleon gladly granted in order to avoid a risky campaign deep in Russia. During a personal meeting, Napoleon so captivated Alexander that the Peace of Tilsit, signed on 7th July 1807, in fact embodied a Franco-Russian alliance. In the treaty, the czar undertook to declare war on England if that country had not become a party to the general peace by 1st December 1807, and also, in company with France, to force the governments of Denmark, Sweden, Austria and Portugal to adopt the Continental System. Denmark no longer required forcing, for the British government, upon receiving news of the Peace of Tilsit, had anticipated the consequential decisions and had occupied the island of Seeland. After a preliminary bombardment, Copenhagen was captured and the Danish fleet was taken to England intact. Not surprisingly, the Danish government declared war on England, to be followed soon afterwards by Russia.[4]

It is almost superfluous to say that this upset in the political relationships on the continent of Europe had serious consequences for foreign trade, and thus for the rates of exchange in Russia. England now ceased to be the principal buyer of ships supplies, and although this trade link was later to be restored, under foreign flags, a decline was unavoidable. In fact, exports to England continued at the previous level throughout the season of 1807 because British traders, anticipating the severance of relations with Russia following the Peace of Tilsit, laid in the largest possible stocks of Russian goods.[1]

With Russia's trade thus proceeding on relatively favourable lines, the departure in May 1807 of the formidable Councillor of State Wulff for Copenhagen, from whence he attempted to mobilize funds in western Europe for the benefit of the Russian government,[2] did not augur well. In mid-June he approached Hope & Co. regarding the possibility of a loan on the security of bonds. Wulff had been empowered by Vasilyev to negotiate with the repurchased bonds and the reserve of 12 million guilders in order to minimize remittances from Russia at the low rates of exchange which then obtained.[3] The Company replied that it favoured selling the repurchased bonds, adding that the price had risen to 90–92 following the Peace of Tilsit, compared with 85 or thereabouts during the first half of 1807. A loan on the security of bonds entailed certain risks, because it would imply that the Russian government was bound to fixed repayment periods, and with the exchange rate falling this could result in major losses.[4] If Wulff was in urgent need of money, Hope was prepared to advance 2–300,000 guilders on the security of the bonds which the Company held; this would be repayable at a mean annual rate of exchange.

Wulff ultimately chose a compromise between his own plan and Hope's proposals. The Company received instructions to send 2,060 repurchased bonds to Israel Dehn & Co. in Altona, who would then remit to Amsterdam. De Smeth and Hope were each instructed to sell one thousand bonds, but the order to De Smeth was pointedly issued first with the aim of emphasizing Vasilyev's displeasure with Hope.[5] In fact, the instruction to De Smeth was pointless, for upon receiving it the house immediately approached Hope and consented to the whole of the sale being effected via the Company. Hope & Co., in turn, gave instructions to the broker Willem Borski, with whom it was agreed that the bonds should be sold only when the price was above 90. A condition for this was that they should be released gradually and without 'empressement.'[6]

The death of Vasilyev on 15th August 1807 may have freed Hope of a bitter enemy in Russian government circles, but as his successor, Fedor Golubtsov, had little expert knowledge and so relied heavily on Wulff and Rall for advice, little really changed from the Company's point of view. Golubtsov and Count Rumyantsev, the Minister for Foreign Affairs and Trade, together constituted the Committee for Foreign Loans, and in this capacity Golubtsov instructed De Smeth and Hope to sell not 1,000, but

2,000 bonds each.[1] At about the time when this amendment was issued, Hope & Co. reported to Wulff that all of the one thousand bonds held by De Smeth, and about half of the thousand which they had, had been sold at prices ranging from 92 to 92½. With the proceeds of these sales, plus the remittances from Israel Dehn and others from Rall to De Smeth, Hope now had sufficient funds to cover the interest due on 1st January 1808, and under these circumstances the Company enquired whether the government wished for more bonds to be sold.

Early in October 1807 Bergien had put out a feeler to Hope regarding a new loan of 10–12,000,000 guilders with a life of 10 years. In a separate letter he had urged a quick decision.[2] According to Bergien, the Russian government was prepared to take the necessary steps to obtain the approval of King Louis for such a loan. Hope passed Bergien's letter to Robert Voûte, who had accepted the office of Director General of the Treasury under King Louis and could therefore greatly influence the sanctioning of new loans in Holland. Voûte considered Bergien's proposal to be inopportune on the grounds that there was already a heavy demand on the capital market in Holland as a result of a Dutch state loan of 40 million guilders, a Spanish loan of 30 million and a loan to the Kingdom of Naples of 3 million.[3] Hope & Co., who were involved in these loans, had assumed that Bergien was unofficially angling for a loan, and on receiving Voûte's views they fobbed Bergien off with the statement that the Russian Treasury employed far simpler means to obtain funds for interest payments.[4] Only later did the Company discover that Bergien had acted with some authority–and that he had also raised the subject of a loan with Bethmann in Frankfurt.

In his overtures, Bergien had hinted that his government would not be unsympathetic to a request for a quantity of Russian goods as security for part of the loan. This suggestion offered interesting possibilities, for with the value of the rouble at a low level (in November 1807 the rate in Amsterdam had fallen below 20 *stuivers*), large quantities of goods could be bought cheaply in St.Petersburg; if the rate subsequently recovered, these could be sold and the proceeds–including a substantial profit–transferred to Holland.

Another opportunity for profiting from the exchange situation lay in lodging funds in Russia with the aim of withdrawing them when the rate improved. Matthiessen & Sillem, who broached this to Hope, felt that no risk would be involved if the monies were deposited with the Assignat Bank, but Hope argued that any operation of this nature would require a trusted associate, and that they knew of no one to fill the role. The Company had ended its personal connexion with Rall many years earlier and had no reason to think well of his business principles. It had not forgotten the example of Sutherland, Browne and Whishaw–whom it had instructed to deposit money in the Assignat Bank, but who had failed to do so–and was only willing to participate if Matthiessen & Sillem accepted the risk inherent in employing their agent in Russia, for which they would receive a commission of ½% or 1%.[1]

The name of Bergien, as a trusted agent, does not appear anywhere in this letter. The indiscreet manner in which he exceeded the credit afforded to him by Hope has already been described; to make things worse, however, he offered the Company bank debentures, as a collateral for fresh credits, at an exchange rate of 25 *stuivers* per rouble while Hope could obtain them for 18 *stuivers* by having them purchased in Russia and later allowing the buyers to draw on Amsterdam. Once again it was impressed upon Bergien that a collateral, be it money, goods, banknotes or in another form, was required whenever he drew on others. As Hope & Co. were unwilling to allow Bergien to make a remittance at the low rate of exchange then ruling, they agreed to wait until the following Spring on condition that Bergien continued to hold Russian goods to a value commensurate with the security required. There were at that moment good opportunities for purchases and contracts in that sector.[2]

The lack of consistency in the policies pursued by the new Minister of Finance was shown by a letter from the St.Petersburg merchant J.A.Krehmer, of Krehmer Lang & Co., who, almost at the same time as Bergien but entirely on his own initiative, put forward a proposal for a Russian loan–this time, however, one of between 30 and 50 million guilders. Hope & Co. promptly replied that a loan of this size was out of the question since it would interfere with the placing of the bonds of the current loan. The Company suggested that the government would do better to take another look at the proposals which they had put forward in 1803 concerning the making available of goods in Russia by the government as security for the furnishing of guilders in Amsterdam by Hope.[3] In an effort to clarify this highly unusual situation, Hope sent a copy of Krehmer's letter to Bergien. The confusion reached its climax when, on the last day of 1807 according to the Russian calendar, Rumyantsev and Golubtsov sent two letters to Hope, one of which requested a loan of at least 30 million guilders, while the other contained an instruction to place the 12 million guildersworth of reserve bonds on the market![4] Hope's reply was tactical, but unambiguous. No reference was made to the proposed loan, but the letter did refer to the encashment of the repurchased bonds and to the reserve, which, as a result of the raising of Hope's commission in 1798, no longer totalled cf 12,000,000, but cf 11,525,000. It was made plain to both members of the Committee that it was also in the interest of the Court that a start should be made with the sale of the repurchased bonds, since this would not involve the payment of a further 6½% commission, as was the case with the reserve. The entire operation, the letter continued, should be entrusted to a single house, as had been done with the sale of the repurchased bonds. The 2,060 bonds held as security by Israel Dehn & Co. should therefore be brought back to Amsterdam; the money required for their release could be obtained by Hope and De Smeth from the sale of the balance of the bonds. Prior to the commencement of the sale, the two houses had jointly held 9,227 repurchased bonds. Of these, 3,000 had been sold by the beginning of February 1808, so that the balance and the reserve together represented a nominal value of nearly 18 million guilders.[1]

Hope & Co. offered to try to persuade the *entrepreneurs* to take over the bonds in three consecutive transactions, each involving 6 million guilders, the terms and conditions of which could be adapted to meet the rapidly changing situation. The partners were confident that the first of the transactions could be accomplished at a transfer price of 90%, payment being made in instalments between early February 1808 and 1st January 1809, leaving the *entrepreneurs* a *douceur* of 2–2½% in the shape of interest. If the tranches could be disposed of to the *entrepreneurs* in rapid succession, it should be feasible to sell all 18 million guildersworth of bonds to investors during the course of the year. Hope and De Smeth would require ½% commission plus a ¼% brokerage fee on the value of the repurchased bonds; Hope would also be entitled to the deferred commission of 6½% on the reserve. The Company proceeded to say that the Russian Court would naturally appreciate how advantageous such an arrangement would be: at a time when other powers, in spite of offering interest rates of 8% and even 10% on par value, were unsuccessful in their attempts to obtain loans on the market, Russia would succeed for less than 6% of the par value. The opportunity lay solely in the fact that the public at large would not discover that, in fact, a new loan was being floated; but to ensure that it did not, absolute secrecy must be maintained, even towards those 'who seem to have the best opportunity to interfere with it.' That this was a reference to Rall and his associates–and, doubtless, to Bergien and Krehmer also–will have been obvious to the ministers. No one, Hope added, must know of Russia's needs; and if the public were awed by Russia's resources, this would guarantee success.

The Committee had little answer to such a proposal, and after some mutterings to the effect that a new loan would be preferable, Hope's plan was accepted at the end of March 1808, the sole amendment being that the price of 90% should immediately be applied to the whole transaction. It was also expressly stipulated that the sale of the repurchased bonds should be effected in collaboration with De Smeth.[1]

When the time came to agree terms with the *entrepreneurs*, however, developments on the international political scene did not favour the Company. The peace which many had expected to spread through Europe as a result of the Tilsit treaty had still not materialized. Napoleon utilized the breathing space afforded by the alliance with Russia to carry the completion of his dominion a stage farther and to bring more states within the Continental System. Portugal was occupied in November 1807 and was followed a few months later by the Papal State. Meanwhile, military preparations for a French conquest of Spain were being made. In northern Europe, Czar Alexander launched an offensive against Finland in order to force Sweden to adopt the Continental System in accordance with the provisions of the peace of Tilsit.

The clash of arms and the 'combinaisons politiques' together made Dutch investors more cautious, with the result that the price of the Russian bonds fell, while the rate at which the market could absorb bonds declined noticeably. Whereas they had stood at over 92½ in early February 1808, the bonds fell to 91¾ or less during the first few days of March. By the end of that month they had fallen to 90, and it required powerful support by Hope to restore them to 91½ by early April.[2] This recovery was vital if a contract with the *entrepreneurs* was to be achieved. At the end of April the Company was able to report to the ministers that it had succeeded in negotiating an agreement with Borski, 'le principal des entrepreneurs, au nom de tous.'

On 26th April 1808, Hope transferred to Borski Russian bonds to a nominal value of 17 million guilders, at a price of 90%, plus the interest thereon since 1st January. The agreement stipulated that the Russian government should not negotiate any fresh loan abroad before 1st July 1809 without the prior sanction of the *entrepreneurs*. Should the Court do so, the *entrepreneurs* would be entitled to cancel the contract and to claim compensation of 2% of the uncompleted portion. Termination of the contract by the *entrepreneurs* would render them liable to pay Hope & Co. 10% of the uncompleted portion and to forfeit the privilege of the interest.[3]

Observing that Hope had a 6-million guilder share in this operation, it is strange that the Company adopted a critical and reticent attitude towards the Committee in the matter of Borski's contract. In all probability it was forced to take part in a transaction, the feasibility of which it viewed with doubt. After all, the magnitude of the sum and the short period in which the sale of bonds had to be completed made it a risky venture, and if circumstances became unfavourable the parties to the contract might ask to be released from part of their commitments–although in that case they would naturally face a 10% penalty. However, the contract not only assured the interest payment due at the end of the year but also enabled a reserve fund to be created, and this could only be welcome to the Russian government.[1]

Just how welcome this fund was, emerged from the fact that the Russian Court called upon it even before it was created. During the war against France, a Russian naval squadron under the command of Admiral Zenyavin had operated successfully against the French bastions on the Dalmation coast, and also against the Turkish fleet, from bases on the Ionian Islands. These islands were ceded to France under the terms of the Peace of Tilsit, and this meant the ending of the Russian occupation and the evacuation of the Russian flotilla. Because the Turks had blockaded the straits, Zenyavin was obliged to sail via the Atlantic Ocean in order to reach the Baltic.[2] When the flotilla had passed through the Straits of Gibraltar and into the Atlantic, a severe storm blew up, forcing the vessels to put into Lisbon. This event, in November 1807, coincided with Napoleon's orders to General Junot to occupy Portugal. Faced with this threat, the Portuguese government entered into an agreement with England providing for the British navy to convey the members of the Portuguese royal family to Brazil. Almost at the same moment came the news that Russia had declared war on England. The British thereupon blockaded the Lisbon roads, leaving Zenyavin and his men trapped in the harbour.[3] The Russian government now faced the problem of sending money to the flotilla for the purchase of food and other necessities.[4]

On arrival in Lisbon, Zenyavin wrote to Hope saying that he proposed to draw on the Company to meet the costs incurred in maintaining his ships and their crews.[5] During his stay there he drew in all cf 2,550,000. At the end of August 1808, Zenyavin and his British counterpart signed a treaty which provided for the Russian crews to be repatriated at British expense, in return for which Zenyavin would sail his vessels to Portsmouth, where they would be left 'in custody' until the end of the hostilities.[6]

With the Russian government facing such an urgent need for funds abroad, the Committee in St.Petersburg had little option but to approve

goods purchased and 1% on exchange operations. This implies that the Company was willing to pass on to him the whole of the commission which it had requested from the Russian Court.[1] It was laid down that all transactions should be effected through local merchants. Melvil was free to choose these, and it was left to him whether or not he used the houses with which Hope had connexions. He was given letters of introduction to known houses, but these contained no reference to the reason for his presence in Russia or to his relationship to the Company.

Melvil was also given information concerning Hope's association with the above-mentioned houses. He was told that, despite the drawbacks of which we are aware, Bergien could be brought into Melvil's activities, particularly in view of his connexions with the Court. In the light of the long feud between Hope and Rall, Melvil was advised to seek a letter of introduction from another firm, for example Matthiessen & Sillem. Porter & Brown, old and trusted friends of Hope, had, like other British houses, been non-operational since the Russian declaration of war on England, and their assets had been confiscated. Nevertheless, Brown could be an extremely valuable source of information, and it might even prove feasible to involve him in the operation under the name of another house.

Hope & Co. had also had incidental dealings with other firms in St. Petersburg, such as J.C.Meyer (the successor to Thomson Bonar & Co.), Bothlingk & Co., Cramer Smith & Co., Archibald Cramp and Ant.Colombi. In Riga, they had recently corresponded with Jos.Morison, and in earlier years Cumming Fenton & Co. had rendered good service. In transactions for third parties–by which the partners meant the French Admiralty, although it was not necessary for Melvil to know this–the Company had had dealings with Justus Blanckenhagen & Son and Helmund & Son, but of these Hope considered only Blanckenhagen to be suitable as an associate.

Since the termination of the correspondence with Thomson Rowand & Co., Hope had had no correspondents in Moscow; but Melvil was advised that if he required anyone there, Brown could make a suitable recommendation.

As a general rule, Melvil was advised to pay more attention to integrity, skill and drive than to wealth and 'ostensible importance' in his search for the right houses. Influence in government circles, however, was also an advantage, for this would enable matters to proceed much more smoothly.

When Melvil received funds from the Treasury, he was to lodge these with various houses with the aim of putting their goodwill and counsel to the test. He was advised that it would be worthwhile to pay a visit to Riga, and perhaps also to Archangel, even though the results would probably be meagre because, according to reports, the volume of trade had exhausted stocks in these towns, especially the latter. He was in principle free to purchase goods of every nature, provided that they were cheap, possessed sound storage properties and could be sold at a profit. The aim of the operation was to resell the goods locally at a profit, even if this took some time. If, as a result of speculation by others, exchange rates fluctuated widely, Melvil could accept solid drafts on Hamburg, London or Amsterdam and transmit these to Hope. If he made only occasional appearances on the market, other houses would not guess the reason for his presence and would therefore not thwart his plans. Broadly speaking, the best time to invest in commodities was in the Spring, when the stocks from the rural areas reached the port towns and prices were at their lowest.

As far as the Amsterdam end of the financial transaction was concerned, the partners felt that it would perhaps be wise not to make more than three to five hundred thousand guilders available at the outset. If the exchange rate was highly attractive, this could promptly be increased, since the total sum was immediately available in Amsterdam. Melvil was to receive twelve letters from Hope informing him of payments made in Amsterdam, but these would be undated and the space for the amount would be left blank. If the exchange rate seemed favourable, he could fill in the blanks at will in accordance with the formula contained in Golubtsov's letter of 2nd September 1808.[1] To meet the possibility of officials of the Ministry of Finance abusing their knowledge of Melvil's activities and informing other houses, he was instructed to cease operations whenever it might be expected that he was busy, and vice versa. It could be dangerous to complain to the most senior officials about such abuses, but it was best left to Melvil to choose his opportunity. Of the goods which lent themselves to the operation, hemp and flax headed the list. It was not easy to find satisfactory warehouses in which to store them, but Hope was counting on assistance from the Russian government in this matter. It was of great importance that the stocks should be seen as Russian property in all circumstances, including war. It was imperative that the goods be insured against fire, and this could best be arranged in Hamburg now that cover in England had been rendered impossible by political developments. The underwriters in Amsterdam were demanding a premium of 2–2½% on the grounds that the warehouses were timber-built, but the rate in Hamburg was sure to be lower.

Because of its wide sales potential, hemp was the prime commodity for speculation–and the one whose price was most rapidly influenced by political changes. Melvil was instructed to watch these changes very carefully, since a quick reaction could produce large speculative gains. According to Hope, he could assume that clean hemp purchased for 40 roubles per pood, the rouble standing at 20 *stuivers*, could be allowed to depreciate by 20%, the sum of lost interest, warehouse rental, insurance and other charges, over a period of two years and could, in all probability, then be sold at a profit of 20%. When this was discussed, the rouble stood at 16 *stuivers* and clean hemp was fetching between 47 and 51 roubles per pood.[1] If Melvil were to buy at that price and resell when the exchange rate improved, the profit margin of 20% would be assured. Because he would be on the spot, Melvil would have the great advantage of being able to seize every opportunity to resell locally at a profit–a practical impossibility for other major buyers, such as the Americans and the British and French governments.

Flax was a commodity which held little interest for the brokers; in the Prussian ports, however, it attracted a great deal of attention.[2] Melvil was advised that in the event of flax which was of lower quality, but better processed, being offered in other Baltic ports, he could send his drafts on Amsterdam and Hamburg to the port concerned for the purchase of this. Such a procedure, however, was worthwhile only if a substantial profit could be envisaged.

Sailcloth and raven-duck, a fine grade of sailcloth, both of which were made from linen, had been bought in large quantities by the Russian government in order to bolster up the price. As the demand by the Americans for these had also increased in the preceding years, Hope & Co. felt that the price would be too high to justify speculative purchases. But they suggested to Melvil that he should approach the minister with a proposal for a major deal involving all or part of the government-held stock. These materials were very interesting commercially because, not being bulky, they were easy to store and, in contrast to hemp and flax, did not shrink or lose their quality during storage.

As regards tallow, the demand fluctuated continuously and could not be predicted; moreover, tallow deteriorated in store. It might be worthwhile purchasing a quantity on contract for delivery in July 1809, but this would imply speculating on the possibility of selling it locally or despatching it elsewhere in 1810. Iron prices were extremely low, but it might be worth buying large quantities of selected grades. The shipping of iron usually produced difficulties, because the freight charges could only be offset by employing it as ballast, but against this it could be stockpiled for years without losing its value. Potash had become an important product in Holland in the preceding years and, even at the high price which it was then fetching, it could be sold at a profit. It had, however, the drawback that it deteriorated rapidly. Linseed, hare pelts and brushes were also unsuitable as objects of long-term speculation owing to their rapid deterioration, but if they would be purchased at a price which permitted them to be sent overland to Hamburg or Amsterdam, Melvil could consider them.

As France and England were both in the market for masts and hemp, it would clearly be worth trying to obtain licences for these two countries; it would be necessary to apply for an equal number so as to ensure that the same quantity of shipments reached each country. Fortunately, they had until the following Spring to consider this matter.[1]

Melvil left for Russia on 1st November 1808, taking with him credentials which he was to present to Golubtsov, Rumyantsev and Count von Stackelberg, the Russian envoy to Prussia, who at that moment resided in Königsberg and who had been given a certain amount of information regarding the true purpose of Melvil's journey. As Melvil despatched his letters in duplicate, one via Matthiessen & Sillem and the other via Bethmann, both houses were kept simply up to date with developments.[2]

We have seen how Golubtsov was obliged by circumstances to accept Hope's supplementary agreement with the *entrepreneurs*. However, the situation on the bond market so deteriorated that the concessions which he had made became less and less attractive to the hard-pressed *entrepreneurs*. During the month of July, not a single Russian bond was placed, and the price–which was purely nominal–scarcely rose above 86. According to Hope, the market had been gripped by fear and panic. Undoubtedly the investors had a premonition that Europe was heading for another period of major unrest, now that the uprising in Spain was proving so surprisingly successful: for the first time since the French Revolution, an entire detachment of the French army had been forced to surrender. Under these adverse circumstance, the *entrepreneurs* could be persuaded to take only one thousand bonds by 1st August.[3]

In spite of the difficulties which beset the Russian finances, money was shortly required, for on 1st December 1808 the balance of the Russian loan obtained from Regny & Co. in Genoa was due to be repaid. The sum outstanding was nearly $4\frac{1}{4}$ million Genoese lire, which was equivalent to about $1\frac{3}{4}$ million guilders.[4]

Remitting funds to Genoa, however, was no simple matter; indeed, drafts were scarce at all the financial centres in Italy owing to the stagnation of the country's trade. When it proved impossible even to remit via Hamburg, Hope & Co. opened credits in Regny's name at the Paris houses of Babut and Baguenault & Co. However, the acute shortage of drafts on Paris rendered it impossible for these firms to provide drafts to the equivalent value, and in the end Hope & Co. were obliged to send rixdollars, Mexican piastres and bars of silver to cover the deficit.[1]

Viewed against the Russian government's great financial need, the failure of the *entrepreneurs* to meet their obligations under the new agreement was a bad omen. At the beginning of September they were totally in default, and in early October and again in November they took no more than one thousand bonds. The Conference of Erfurt, at which Napoleon had gathered around him the rulers of all the countries which he had subjugated and also those which had allied themselves with his cause, had produced little of substance for the emperor, despite all the outward manifestations of continental unity and the formal expressions of friendship by Alexander I. The Emperor of Austria was absent from the congress, and within his empire vigorous preparations for war were taking place.

Although the circumstances thus hardly favoured a revival of demand for Russian bonds, it was vital that the interest payment due on 1st January 1809 should be assured. The greater part of the funds held by Hope & Co. on behalf of the Russian government had been used up in the drafts for Zenyavin and in payments for the settlement of the debt in Genoa, and so the Company was obliged to enter into a new agreement with Borski before the year ended. Late in November, Hope had got him to the point where he gave a firm undertaking on behalf of the *entrepreneurs* to take 4,109 bonds at a price of 90. Borski was given until 1st July 1809 to decide whether he would take over the balance of 4,000 bonds, and it was agreed that the 10% penalty should apply only to bonds which the *entrepreneurs* refused to take on that date.[2] The payment of interest on these 4,000 bonds proved to be a thorny problem. Borski insisted on receiving the full year's interest on bonds accepted during the course of 1809, but Hope & Co. were only willing to give six months' interest which, however, would be proportionally increased if Borski and his associates accepted the bonds at an earlier date. The obstacle was eventually surmounted when the Company offered the *entrepreneurs* a 'remedy' in the shape of 2% out of the $6\frac{1}{2}$% commission which it was to receive on the bonds relating to the reserve. The *entrepreneurs*, however, complained that their commission was still minimal, because the Russian bonds stood no higher than 88 and thus the *douceur* from Hope served only to bridge the gap between the market price and the acceptance price of 90.[1] While this transaction served to assure the payment of interest on 1st January 1809, it did little to extract the *entrepreneurs* from their predicament. Of the 13,109 bonds which they had accepted, less than 4,500 had been sold, and the political situation did not justify any expectation of an improvement during the first six months of 1809.[2]

In the meantime, Melvil, travelling via Osnabrück and Leipzig, had arrived in Königsberg. His reconnaissance of the market there revealed few opportunities for speculation. Hemp and flax were available only in limited quantities, and the prices were considerably higher than in Russia. Melvil therefore decided to make for Riga as quickly as possible, but poor roads and difficulties concerning his passport resulted in an unwelcome delay. In Mitau, he was obliged to stay for a whole day because the local governor refused to recognize the validity of his passport. When he finally reached Riga, he found that, as in Archangel, prices were higher than in St.Petersburg on account of the large export trade. Exports of flax to England were reported to have been even greater than in previous years. Out of a total of 180,000 ship-pounds of flax exported from Russia –which equalled the level in previous shipping seasons–nearly 80,000 ship-pounds had left from Riga.[3]

As we have seen, the difficulties which confronted Napoleon in Spain served to divert his attention from the rest of Europe. British shippers gladly seized upon this opportunity to send vessels to ports all over the continent, including Russia, in an attempt to make good the shortfall in the first half of the shipping season. The crisis in Anglo-American relations, which centred around the rights of neutral vessels, had not yet led to a conflict, and thus American vessels continued to call at Russian ports.[4]

When Melvil reached Riga early in December, the shipping season had ended and the price of hemp had fallen to a level at which, according to insiders, there were opportunities for speculation. Melvil instructed J.D. Drachenhauer & Co. and B. Zuckerbäcker Klein & Co. each to purchase 500 ship-pounds of hemp for delivery in the Spring, under their own guarantee; payment was to be effected by means of drafts on Melvil & Co. In accordance with advice, Hope & Co. remained completely outside this transaction in order not to betray the connexion, and Melvil accordingly avoided the houses which the Company had recommended[5]. Shortly before his departure from Riga, Melvil purchased a further 1,000 ship-pounds on contract from Hope's former correspondent, Cumming and Fenton. As 30,000 ship-pounds had already been contracted in Riga and the owners of hemp, in anticipation of still higher prices, were hesitant to sell, he decided to suspend further purchases until he reached St.Petersburg.

Melvil left Riga on 13th December 1808, and arrived in St.Petersburg four days later. Golubtsov accorded him a very friendly welcome, but on the subject of the rate of exchange the minister was adamant and refused to depart from the procedure which he had earlier devised. This put paid to the plan for Melvil to apply to Golubtsov for funds whenever he thought fit and then to apply the rate of exchange on the final postday. Moreover, the minister refused to accept a letter from Melvil as the basis for a payment unless a letter referring to an identical sum simultaneously reached the Committee from Amsterdam. Obviously, it had not escaped Golubtsov's attention that Hope & Co. had been vague in their reply on this point. He reasoned, not without justification, that if Melvil's proposal were to be accepted, one party would be aware of the rate of exchange and would secure all the advantages. The fact that Melvil was in a position to offer him half a million guilders on the spot made no impression whatever on Golubtsov. Faced with this situation, Melvil had little choice but to render the blank letters from Hope unusable and to send a mounted courier to Amsterdam with a message urging the Company to send an early report to the Committee concerning the payment of monies in Holland. Only when this had been received could he resume his negotiations with the minister. In the meantime, he would devote his energies to a thorough study of the market in St.Petersburg, and afterwards cautiously embark on the purchase of goods.[1]

In the light of the rumours which were circulating in Riga, Melvil at first found the prices in St.Petersburg somewhat high; but on reflection he had to confess that they were higher still in Riga.[2] There was general anxiety in the Russian capital concerning the disposal of the country's produce in the ensuing year, but this was tempered by the fact that the State Loan Bank provided credits on the security of goods, thus enabling Russian merchants to store their wares, albeit on payment of high charges, until the last moment, thus keeping prices relatively high. Sometimes a merchant would be unable to renew his credit, and when this happened there were bargains to be had. To deposit money in the Assignat Bank, it was first necessary to submit a request in writing, but when the bank accepted funds it issued a simple receipt which, with a blank endorsement, became fully transferable. Upon the change of ownership of a receipt, it was necessary to submit another written request–this time for the account to be transferred to the new owner–but the cost was limited to one day's interest.[1] Despite the fact that money invested in goods earned no interest, it was better to use it thus than to lodge it with the bank, for both the price of goods and the exchange rate offered possibilities for profit.

As far as hemp was concerned, Melvil reported that there were opportunities for speculation in St.Petersburg, but that individual purchases would have to be small. Half the St.Petersburg hemp had already been bought up, and Russian merchants were combing the countryside in search of further stocks and even offering small advances to tempt possible sellers. As a result, the price of hemp in the rural areas, in relation to the current price in St.Petersburg, was higher than normal. The Russians sold only enough to provide funds for their purchases in the country. If the stocks thus being built up were to be taken to the ports in the Spring, and if problems of shipment were to deprive the merchants of their markets, trade in this commodity would entirely collapse.[2]

Flax, Melvil wrote, was not a neglected article, as Hope had thought, but a true object of speculation; accordingly, stocks were held until the commencement of the shipping season. The quantity offered on the market would not exceed 35,000 poods, to which perhaps a further 14,000 poods would be added from the new harvest. But because the additional quantity would not arrive until late in the season, Melvil considered it wise to make purchases of local stocks without delay; this would largely obviate the disputes about quality which tended to occur when forward purchases were delivered. Taken in conjunction with the rate of exchange, the price was low, while the exorbitant prices which flax fetched in England showed that there was an immense demand.[3] Linen, sailcloth and other linen fabrics and calamanco, a woollen material, were also suitable as objects of speculation, Melvil reported; contrary to the information given by Hope, the prices of these had risen only slightly, and stocks were just then arriving in the port towns. The quantities offered in the following season would certainly not be greater, for the Russian government required substantial amounts for the army and the navy.[4] Moreover, it was already evident that prices would be higher by then because, as a result of the fall in the rate of exchange, the labour costs and transport charges affecting these articles had risen. Sailcloth was chiefly sold to North America.

There were also sizeable stocks of tallow. Although the nominal price was high, the low rate of exchange made this commodity well worth considering. Yellow tallow was at least 7 roubles per pood cheaper in

St.Petersburg than in Riga, and could be kept for years without loss of quality. White tallow, which contained mutton fat and thus did not fully solidify, had a much shorter storage life. Melvil preferred Siberian tallow, which was extremely hard and could be kept for very long periods. A large quantity of this was held by a small group of rich merchants.[1]

Iron prices, it was anticipated, would shortly reach their lowest level, reflecting a need on the part of stockholders for money to be sent with their agents to the mines in Siberia to meet all manner of liabilities. The cost of transporting iron would be 60 kopecks per pood, and would add substantially to the overall costs.

Potash, brushes, hides and wax travelled overland, the principal destination being Memel. In spite of the high transport costs, however, Melvil felt that potash offered possibilities for speculation.

If we compare Melvil's findings with the information furnished by Hope & Co., we see how frequently and how seriously the information sent from Holland was at variance with reality. In the case of flax, the Company had clearly been completely misinformed, and the same applied to linen fabrics and calamancoes; similarly, Hope's information concerning the keeping qualities of tallow differed widely from Melvil's findings. The fact that the Company's contacts were regarded as solid and reliable did not, it appears, afford any guarantee against erroneous commercial information. This will certainly have been among the reasons why the Company attached so much importance to having its own agent in making purchases on the scale involved.

Melvil had also made enquiries concerning the merchant houses in St.Petersburg. It was rumoured that Rall had sunk in the government's estimation, not only by reason of his somewhat abrupt manner, but also on account of his 'different system of politics.' His skill and his wealth, however, were not doubted. Just what Rall's political convictions were, we are not told, but as the majority of Alexander's ministers at that time were pro-French, it seems probable that his sympathies were with the English.

Because of its relative displeasure with Rall, the Russian government employed other houses for the purchase of coin abroad. Bothlingk, Stieglitz, Bergien and Severin Bros., were among these. Hope's reaction to the spreading of these orders over several houses was to pray that, faced with hard reality, the Committee would at last realize 'that it is not always in the multitude of counsellors that there is wisdom.'[2] According to Melvil, Bergien was increasingly finding favour and being given all the special assignments. He was particularly friendly with Golubtsov and

Prince Kurakin, while his competitor, Krehmer, was on intimate terms with Rumyantsev. Melvil expressed the opinion that Bergien, like Rall, had a manner which made him extremely well suited to doing business with the truly great men, from whom the merchants in Russia appeared to derive the greater part of their profits. It was sad but true that a Russian house, in order to survive, had to engage in usurious practices of which a Dutch merchant would be deeply ashamed. Just how *bien reçu* Bergien was in high circles became evident when, during their visit to Russia in January 1809, the Prussian royal family, accompanied by their imperial hosts, were entertained at the Bergien residence. Following the death of Rogovikov in February 1809, the post of Court Banker became vacant; it was not, however, given to Bergien, but to Severin Bros., who thereupon joined Rall and formed the firm of Rall & Severin. Observing that the czar was attracted to one of the Mesdames Severin, the appointment can scarcely have been fortuitous.[1]

Of the merchants in St.Petersburg, J.C.Meyer, of the house of Meyer & Bruxner, made the best impression on Melvil. Meyer was prudent, incorruptible and opposed to hazardous draft speculations. Sillem and Bethmann had both expressly recommended him to Melvil, and the last-named was proposing to place a portion of the orders with Meyer and, following his departure, to entrust Meyer with the overall supervision of the operation in Russia, with particular reference to storage and warehouse accommodation. Bothlingk & Co. was a solid, reliable house, and the same could be said of Cramer Smith & Co., which traded mainly with America, in which country one of the partners, Smith, had travelled widely. The firm maintained a cordial relationship with the American consul general, Harris, and this benefited it greatly, for vessels arriving from the United States with cargoes consigned to the house could count on Harris's full co-operation.[2]

Among the German merchants in St.Petersburg, P.J.Blessig and F.W. Kümmel were the most solid. The house of Wolff & Schlüsser, which specialized in trade with Brabant, was also satisfactory. All the British-owned houses, including Rowand & Co. in Moscow, were inactive, and many of the partners were awaiting a suitable moment to leave Russia. Melvil, following Hope's directives, nevertheless proposed to try to involve a few of these houses in the speculation via J.C.Meyer.[3]

Melvil's courier reached Amsterdam on 6th January 1809. After a brief consultation, the partners prepared a reply stating that, in view of the Treasurer's objections to the method of payment proposed by the Company, the operation would be limited to one million guilders, 'as it would be contrary to all rules of prudence and judgement to venture from hence at random, without knowing what variations may have occurred in the interval in the course of exchange or in the prices of produce.'[1] A letter couched in similar terms was sent to the Committee. The partners subsequently advised Melvil that if Golubtsov's proposal were to be accepted, the government would have prior knowledge of the decisive day from the point of view of the exchange rate; in such a situation, it might succumb to the temptation to force up the rate on the day in question.

On 4th February 1809, Melvil reported that he had reached agreement with Golubtsov concerning the exchange rate, which was to be 17⅝ *stuivers* to the rouble, and that accordingly a sum of 1,134,751.77 roubles had been paid to J.C.Meyer.[2] As the highest denomination of the banknotes was 100 roubles, Meyer had to transport a mountain of paper. In accordance with the agreement, he deposited part of the money with a number of houses. Cramer & Smith, Blessig and Wolff & Schlüsser each received 100,000 roubles, the balance remaining with Meyer. All held out the prospect of 5% interest on the deposited funds.[3]

In the matter of the government-owned warehouses, Golubtsov demanded Melvil's written approval of the establishments which had been proposed. As all the hemp warehouses were leased to Russian merchants, Golubtsov offered to have a shed build 'in a proper situation.' In the interests of a smooth settlement of affairs after his departure, and in order to ensure secrecy, Melvil left the matter of the inspection of the buildings entirely to Meyer.[4] The secrecy, however, proved to be a myth. Details of Melvil's operation, even down to the names of interested parties and the extent of their financial participation, were known. The method of payment, however, had not leaked out, and therefore it was anticipated in St.Petersburg that numerous drafts on Hamburg and Amsterdam would shortly appear. Melvil suspected that the source of the leak lay in Holland, for far too many people there knew of the affair. The effect was that every unidentified purchase was attributed to Melvil, who in the eyes of outsiders became a buyer on a fantastic scale.[5]

The minister intimated that he would be pleased to continue the payment transaction with Hope & Co. – but on his terms. He remained amiable and polite, with 'the softest manners,' even though he was fully aware that the assembly of funds by Hope in Amsterdam and the reports sent to St. Petersburg concerning that operation were a complete sham. Melvil reported that he had found Golubtsov looking weak and weighed down by the burden of his office, and that this probably prevented him from making a special study of mercantile affairs.[6] This was almost certainly Melvil's way of telling Hope, in terms which would not offend the censor, that the minister knew nothing of the world of business and the demands which it imposed.

Melvil's relationship with Golubtsov suffered a setback when the latter received a report from Hope & Co. stating that they were not disposed to make any large advances to the Russian Court within the framework of the agreement with the *entrepreneurs*. The minister took the view that this refusal was deliberate and was aimed at forcing him to yield in his dispute with Melvil. His action in broaching the subject to Melvil led to a somewhat fruitless discussion about who benefited most from the payment transaction. Golubtsov offered to fix the rate of exchange for a period of several months, but Melvil declined this on the grounds that it would rule out any possibility of combining exchange rate and commodity price. He, in turn, offered the minister an option on a given offer with the freedom to decide 'from one postday to another.' For example, Golubtsov would receive an offer from Melvil on a Wednesday, based on the previous day's exchange rate, and would have until before the post on Friday to accept or decline. Golubtsov replied that such an arrangement would require the approval of the czar, and that it would take at least ten days to obtain this.[1]

The minister also stated that his colleague on the Committee for Foreign Loans, Count Rumyantsev, who was now back in the Russian capital after a long sojourn in France, was also not enamoured of the contract, and insisted on strict compliance with its provisions. He went on to disclose that Rumyantsev had given an audience to Russian merchants and commercial counsellors who had protested against the contract with Hope. This was a sharp rebuff to the partners, who had fully expected that Rumyantsev, as a good friend of Bethmann, would support the transaction with the Russian government.[2] In order to show Melvil that the government was not dependent upon Hope & Co., Golubtsov dealt at length with French plans to purchase large quantities of Russian produce –of which he had learned on Rumyantsev's return. Melvil–rightly, as it transpired–did not have a great deal of faith in large-scale purchases by France, but the report certainly had an effect on trade.[3] In Riga it caused the exchange rate to rise, and in St.Petersburg it made the merchants even more determined to hold on to their wares. The price of hemp rose by a rouble per pood.

Of the events which took place outside Russia, only vague reports reached St.Petersburg, and these aroused interest only when Russia was involved. The outbreak of war between Austria and France at the beginning of April sent a tremor through the exchange and commodity markets, but when it became clear that the Russian Court was keeping out of the struggle, and that the declaration of war on Austria was merely a formality, the markets quickly recovered. The absence of British reprisals in the Baltic, which had earlier been feared, contributed very greatly to the recovery.

Following the czar's return from Finland at the beginning of April, Melvil was informed that the proposal which he had put to Golubtsov had been rejected. This did not greatly dismay him, for with the approach of the shipping season the prices had commenced to rise, and he would not have known what to do with the money if the government had accepted the proposal.[1] In the light of the declining exchange rates, Hope & Co. concurred fully. The season for buying was past, and the time had come to think about reselling. The partners would have preferred Melvil to manage this personally, particularly in view of uncertainties created by the war between France and Austria, but it had earlier been agreed that he should return to Holland in the Spring and they therefore went no farther than to request him to delay his departure for a few weeks, pending clarification of the political situation in Europe.[2]

In addition to the Franco-Austrian war, the situation in Sweden demanded attention. There, the passionately anti-French King Gustav IV had been deposed in March 1809, and his successor, Charles XIII, attempted to bring the wars against France and Russia to an end. If his efforts led to the adoption by Sweden of the Continental System, this would have repercussions on the attitude of the British Baltic Fleet, which had hitherto found support in Sweden; the outcome of these repercussions, in turn, could affect the possibilities for shipping goods from Russia.

As far as the resale of goods in Russia was concerned, Hope & Co. proposed to instruct Melvil to sell a quarter at 10% profit, a quarter at 15%, a quarter at 20% and the balance at 25%. But Matthiessen & Sillem considered that a larger proportion could be sold at a profit of 10%, particularly if this involved commodities purchased for future delivery and on which there was an immediate saving of handling and storage charges. They also urged greater flexibility in regard to price margins in view of political developments–for example, the revolution in Sweden–and the possible effect of these on trade.[3] Although somewhat reluctant, the partners of Hope & Co. agreed to these suggestions.

The Company desired that the potash–which was eagerly sought in western Europe–should be excluded from the local resale operation. If the route across the Baltic was not free, the potash would be sent by cart to Memel, from whence it could be taken overland to Elbing and finally to Hamburg.[1] Blessig was prepared to supply 2,000 poods immediately from his own stock, on condition that this could be replenished from the quantities purchased by Melvil on contract from Wolff & Schlüsser, which were due to arrive in St.Petersburg by barge from the hinterland between May and July. Hope & Co. stipulated that the cost of transport from St.Petersburg to Memel should not exceed 4 roubles per barrel. They estimated that the journey would take a month. Melvil later learned in Riga that it was a good thing that the order for the transport had been given comparatively late in the Spring, for during the preceding thaw the roads had been in such a terrible condition that many carriers had given up and had simply left goods lying by the wayside.[2] After 200 barrels of potash had been moved by this method, the Company abandoned it on grounds of cost in view of the fact that the movement of vessels to and from the Russian ports during the shipping season of 1809 proceeded almost without hindrance. Accordingly, the volume of cargoes was far in excess of the 1808 figure, and this was reflected in commodity prices. At St.Petersburg, ship arrivals in 1809 totalled 376, compared with 60 in the previous year. In Riga, the number doubled.[3] The majority of the shipments were destined for England, and together these served to restore Russia's trade with that country to the normal level.[4]

Strangely, however, this spectacular revival of exports was not reflected in the parity of the rouble. Under the agreement reached between Melvil and the Russian government on 30th January, this was fixed at $17\frac{5}{8}$ *stuivers*. At the beginning of May it was down to 16 *stuivers* and by the middle of the month had slipped to $15\frac{1}{2}$. Although it recovered to 17 *stuivers* at the end of May, there was nothing to suggest a strong recovery, and indeed the rate of 17 *stuivers* was scarcely attained during the remainder of the shipping season.[5] The absence of a true recovery will certainly have been due in part to the continued creation of paper roubles and to the amateuristic manner in which Golubtsov, with the assistance of a number of houses, obtained coin from abroad. A proportion of this coin was put into circulation, but rapidly disappeared.

With the rate of exchange falling, the Russian government was obviously not disposed to annul the agreement with Hope. Admittedly Golubtsov, in a moment of irritation following Hope's refusal to accept his conditions, had said that there could after all be no question of the government providing warehouses, but he had subsequently rescinded this, albeit not wholeheartedly. He remained polite, but 'in a condescending manner.' Rumyantsev, on the other hand, made no secret of his dislike of the whole transaction and admitted that he was glad it was not being continued.[1] Hope detected in both men 'a little fretfulness at merchants differing from Ministers.' Clearly, the notion of dealing with merchants on a basis of equality was essentially unacceptable to them, and in their hearts they looked down upon Messrs.Hope and their representatives. This attitude had undoubtedly lain at the root of Vasilyev's grim hostility: he had been unable to stomach the mastery of the middle-class Citizen Voûte during the negotiations with Czar Paul I.[2]

Melvil left St.Petersburg on 25th May 1809 and travelled via Riga and Berlin to Amsterdam, where he arrived early in July.[3] On his advice, the Company decided to cease shipping the goods and to concentrate on selling these locally. As English ships were now admitted to Russian ports almost without let or hindrance, while sailings to western Europe continued to suffer from the British blockade, local resale had become much easier and far less risky.[4]

With the return of Robert Melvil, the initial phase of Operation R.M. drew to its close. During his stay in Russia, Melvil had dispensed nearly two and a half million guilders for the purchase of goods. Of this sum, nearly 4% had been invested, through A.Becker of Archangel, in tar, pitch, iron and mats. Purchases of hemp in Riga had accounted for a further 8%, and the remaining 88% had been spent by eight houses in St.Petersburg. Of this, 38% had gone to Melvil's trusted agent, Meyer. Besides his own share, Meyer had purchased hemp on behalf of Porter Brown & Co. and Thornton Cayley & Co. who, as British houses, were debarred from trading but who were thus enabled to obtain a commission. The purchases made on their behalf accounted for 12% of the total sum invested. Next, in order of importance, came Wolff & Schlüsser with 11%, Bergien & Co. with 9%, P.J.Blessig & Co. with 8%, Cramer Smith & Co. (which by now had become Cramer Bros.) with 6%, and Bothlingk & Co. with 4%.

Nearly one-third of the total was invested in linen fabrics, which ranged from coarse linen, sailcloth, raven-duck and Flemish linen to damask, and calamanco. As already mentioned, these were easily stored and suffered scarcely any loss of quality. Hemp, on which Melvil spent more than 28% of his funds, did deteriorate in store, but then it was a readily saleable commodity and, moreover, was in great demand everywhere. Hope had earlier indicated that clean hemp purchased at 40 roubles per pood would afford a substantial profit even at a rate of exchange of 20 *stuivers* to the rouble. Melvil had paid an average price of 45 roubles, and for the purpose of his accounts had taken the rate of exchange to be 17 *stuivers* to the rouble. If we calculate his purchases at this price and exchange rate, we see that an extra profit of one guilder and fifteen *stuivers* per pood could be obtained. Iron, of which nearly 340,000 pood was purchased–and which was again a commodity with virtually unlimited keeping properties–accounted for 23%. The balance of the money was invested in potash (8%), flax (6%), tallow (2%) and linseed and copper (each 1%).[1] If we compare the prices which Melvil was obliged to pay for the various commodities with those indicated by Hope on 27th October 1808, it is clear that in general he was skilful in his purchases.[2]

The choice of houses revealed a degree of concentration. Cramer Bros. and Bothlingk & Co. supplied only linen fabrics; Blessig & Co. and Wolff & Schlüsser supplied linens, calamancoes, potash and tallow; and Bruxner supplied linens, flax, hemp, linseed, iron and copper. Bergien received a contract for a large quantity of iron.

On the sum of the purchases, i.e. cf 2,445,696.10.0, Melvil received the agreed commission of 2%, amounting to cf 48,913.19.0. His commission on the draft transactions, which totalled cf 105,038.17.0, was 1%, so that in all he received nearly cf 50,000.[3] The offer of a $\frac{1}{16}$th share in the transaction was politely but firmly declined.

If the speculation was to be a success, it was vital that the stocks should be sold quickly and at good prices; this, in turn, depended upon the continued freedom of vessels to reach Russian ports. This freedom would also counteract, or at least limit, any further decline in the value of the rouble. And even if this should fall, the loss would not be very serious provided that the brisk shipping trade continued, for then the demand alone would produce higher prices.

The ultimate success of Operation R.M. thus depended upon political developments. The practicability of the contract with the *entrepreneurs*, the promptness with which the interest on the Russian bonds would be paid and the possibility of a resumption of the principal repayments also depended to a very great extent upon events in the political sphere. And in 1809 it was already clear that the prospects in this area were not encouraging.

CHAPTER EIGHT

PER ASPERA AD ASTRA

FROM THE SUSPENSION OF PAYMENTS TO THE ARRANGEMENT OF 1815

In the previous chapter we left the *entrepreneurs*, headed by Borski, in a state of great anxiety. Through their spokesman, they had agreed at the end of 1808 to take a further 4,109 bonds, and they had been given until 1st July 1809 to decide whether or not to accept the balance of 4,000. We also learned that, of the 13,109 bonds which the *entrepreneurs* had accepted up to that point, less than 4,500 had been placed. During the opening months of 1809 the situation was, if anything, even worse. The threat of war in eastern Europe led to a virtual absence of buyers, and the price fell from 86 in January to 82 in April, in which month the conflict between France and Austria finally broke out.[1]

Faced with this situation, Hope & Co. approached the Committee in St.Petersburg with a request that the penalty for bonds not taken up on 1st July be waived. Borski and his associates, the Company wrote, regretted their boldness, for they had been left with a large portion of the bonds which they had already accepted. As there was no prospect whatsoever of the situation improving by 1st July, they would not under any circumstances accept the remaining 4,000 bonds, preferring to pay the 10% penalty–however painful such a course might be for respectable men who owed their sad plight to their blind faith in Hope's persuasion and their long-established preference for everything which came from Russia. The Company, the letter continued, was embarrassed by its role, for it had thus disheartened those who had secured the acceptance of foreign loans on the Dutch capital market and had bred prejudice against the once eagerly sought Russian bonds. Hope blamed the unfortunate situation on political developments, which none of the parties concerned could influence, and on these grounds requested that the penalty clause be waived. If the Russian government acceded to the request, the Company would reconsider its earlier decision not to increase the advances to the Russian Court.[2]

The Committee's reply, dated 23rd June 1809, stated that the czar had refused the submission and that Hope & Co. could recover the advances from the one million guilders which had been placed at the disposal of the Russian government in Amsterdam under the terms of the agreement with Melvil. The managers suspected that this abrupt rejection was allied to the Russian Court's displeasure at the stagnation of Operation R.M.[1] On 4th July, Hope reported to the Russian ministers that the *entrepreneurs* had indeed chosen to pay the penalty. The bond price at this time fluctuated between 82 and 83, and this made it impossible for the *entrepreneurs*–whose number, moreover, had recently declined–to place a further 4,000 bonds. A failure would damage their good name and cause the price to decline even further. As an alternative, Hope proposed that the repayment of the initial $\frac{1}{20}$th of the balance of the loan should be effected early in 1810. This would certainly assist the *entrepreneurs*, who would then be in a position to place the balance of the bonds which they held, and subsequently to accept the remaining 4,000. If the proceeds of the sale were inadequate for the repayment, the *entrepreneurs* might be willing to make good the deficit in exchange for Russian goods due for delivery in the Spring, at day-prices determined by both commodity price and exchange rate.[2]

From Bagnères, whence he had taken his wife for the benefit of her health, Labouchère expressed all manner of objections to this plan. He saw no great likelihood that the Russian government would agree to it, for Operation R.M. had already shown that the Court would have nothing to do with the purchase and supply of goods. How, he asked, was this new transaction to be explained to Matthiessen & Sillem, Bethmann and Borski's associates, the participants in Operation R.M.? This, after all, had only just got under way, and would certainly suffer as a result of the new undertaking.[3] Labouchère also drew attention to the political situation: would France and Russia remain on friendly terms, or would their relationship change? We may assume that the writer, whose journey took him to the French capital, had learned from a reliable source there of the cooling of relations between the czar and Napoleon.

Early in July 1809, Napoleon had won a decisive victory over the Austrians at Wagram, and at the Peace of Pressburg in September of that year he had added the Austrian part of Galicia to the Grand Duchy of Warsaw, a French protectorate. As the nucleus of a new Polish state, this would have a certain attraction for Polish subjects under Russian domination, and could therefore constitute a pocket of unrest on Russia's western frontier. We have already seen how, on the one hand, the rigorous application of the Continental system seriously damaged Russia's trade while, on the other, the admittance of British ships to Russian ports, to which the authorities had closed their eyes since the summer of 1808, was a thorn in the flesh of Napoleon.

Golubtsov having indicated in his reply that he wished for more information concerning Hope's proposals, the managers pursued their theme. The Russian government, they stated, would have to supply such goods as the purchasers desired, and, if required, store these in government warehouses at its own risk and for its own account. Dealing with the balance of the bonds, they expressed the wish to reduce the transfer price from 90 to 80, because the market price in Amsterdam had meanwhile fallen to 81.[1]

It is not clear why the managers in Amsterdam, who were aware of the experience gained from Operation R.M., made such far-reaching stipulations. It may well be that they felt that the minister, wearied by financial worries, would this time give way. The Committee's reply will in any case not have surprised Labouchère: Hope's proposal was rejected in its entirety on the grounds that it was an affront to the dignity of the Russian Court and therefore unacceptable. The managers were requested to cease the sale of Russian bonds and to keep the balance at the disposal of the Committee pending further instructions.[2]

The tone of the letter from Russia was stern, and to Hope & Co. it sounded like a declaration of war. And indeed it was intended as such, as emerged soon afterwards when reports were received that Golubtsov was combing the financial centres of Europe in search of fresh loans. In Paris, his efforts led to a loan being floated by Perregaux Laffitte & Co., but this failed.[3] The reports caused serious disquiet on the Amsterdam bond market, and this caused the price of Russian bonds to fall to 68. Support-buying by Hope & Co. served to restore the level to 75, but this was purely nominal. At the end of 1809 the rouble fell to a new low of 13–14 *stuivers* on the Amsterdam exchange market. Admittedly, the interest on the bonds was paid on the due date, but Hope was unable to answer the many questions concerning the date of the first principal repayment.[4]

Golubtsov had by now made his position as Minister of Finance untenable. By his inept excursions on the European money markets he had not only undermined his own creditworthiness, but also brought the Russian bonds in Holland into discredit and further alienated himself from Hope & Co. The steady decline in the exchange rate of the rouble was closely allied to the increasing quantities of paper money which were being created, and while Golubtsov could not be held solely responsible for this, his purchases of coin abroad–which were as ill-considered as they were ineffective–had exacerbated the exchange position.

In Russia, too, it became clear that things could not go on as they were. On 24th January 1810, Dimitri Guryev reported that the czar had relieved purchase of the goods, and a mean rate of 15 *stuivers* for the post-sale remittances. These figures reflect the order of intelligence–and also perhaps of honesty–of the merchants involved. It is evident from this that, despite all Labouchère's criticism, Meyer was worthy of the confidence placed in him.

The figures also show that the market for linen fabrics was not particularly good; however, their keeping qualities and low storage cost enabled them to be kept in anticipation of better times. Of the stock of iron–also a commodity with a long storage life–only 5% was sold, the gross profit obtained being 11%. By 1st January 1810, cf 955,100, representing 39% of the total sum invested in the various commodities, had been remitted to Amsterdam.[1]

Sales in 1810 were substantially below the 1809 level. As explained earlier, Napoleon made an all-out effort to isolate England economically from Continental Europe, and this included exerting pressure on Russia to take more stringent measures against British ships. Meanwhile, in England itself the abnormal volume of imports from Russia in 1809 had produced a sharp fall in prices, and thus profits were reduced. Remittances to Holland in 1810 totalled only one-seventh of the figure for 1809. The merchants in Russia, however, were doing their best, and the levels of profit on such sales as they did achieve were very reasonable, particularly because rising rouble prices compensated the falling rate of exchange.[2] With linen fabrics, in particular, the merchants were more fortunate than in 1809. Meyer & Bruxner's profit on sailcloth in 1810 was only 9% gross, but Cramer Bros. made 18% and Blessig achieved a remarkable 22½%. Bothlingk & Co., who had contributed nothing to Operation R.M. in 1809, made handsome profits, viz.an average of 20% on Flemish linen and 37½% on raven-duck. It is conceivable that stockpiling by the Russian government had an influence on the prices of these products. In Archangel, Alexander Becker's only success lay in iron, on which he made a net profit of 13%. He suffered a loss of 9% on the sale of four-fifths of the stock of pitch, and fared even worse with tar, of which half the stock was sold at a net loss of 35%.[3]

In September 1810, Meyer sold a further 30,000 poods of the iron lying in St.Petersburg at twice the purchase price. He did not, however, remit the proceeds to Amsterdam, for with the rouble, as stated earlier, standing at less than 9 *stuivers*, remittance would have been uneconomic. After consulting Hope, Meyer deposited the money with the Bank, where it would earn interest at 5%. The plan was to withdraw the capital, plus interest, in the following Spring, by which time the rate of exchange would hopefully have improved sufficiently to justify remittance. Other houses followed this example. Within the Company, a sombre view was taken of the future of the operation, and at the end of 1810 the remaining stocks were written down by cf 200,000–8% of the original investment.[1]

The progress of Operation R.M. during the first half of 1811 served to confirm Hope's pessimism. Despite all efforts, practically nothing was sold; when, at the end of June, Labouchère set off for Russia, the stock of potash was still virtually intact, and 86% of the iron also remained. Of the linen fabrics, nearly all the damask and sailcloth had been disposed of, but of the Flemish linen and the raven-duck, two-thirds was still in the warehouses. Not a metre of the calamancoes or the coarse and plain linen had been sold, but this was due in part to the high import duty in England, the principal market. The Russian merchants together held Hope assets worth 130,000 roubles.[2] Although the Continental System as such had ceased to be effective, strict control of the neutrality of vessels entering the Russian ports made the shipping season of 1811 a poor one. The Americans, who derived the most benefit from the new situation, took Russian goods in exchange for the colonial produce which they shipped in (in large quantities), but Russian exports to England scarcely equalled half the figure for the previous year.[3]

Labouchère lost no time in setting about the task of liquidating the stocks as far as possible. He had the entire stock of potash shipped, stimulated the sale of linen fabrics to the best of his ability, and put pressure on the Russian merchants to remit the proceeds of sales with a minimum of delay. As the exchange rate had eased upwards to 9–10 *stuivers* since the Spring, monies could be remitted without undue losses. By the end of 1811, thanks to Labouchère's efforts, the entire stock of plain linen and calamanco had been disposed of. By the end of November, only one-third of the original stock of Flemish linen remained, and just over half the stock of raven-duck. But of the coarse linen, less than 5% had been sold. In many instances, these articles were bought by other Russian merchants with an eye to speculation. Owing to the rate of exchange, among other factors, these sales were generally effected at a loss, which in the case of the coarse linen and part of the calamancoes reached 14%.[4] Unsold stocks at the end of November were valued, at ruling prices, at more than 1,350,000 roubles, of which iron, the quantity of which had not changed, represented two-thirds and linen fabrics one-third. Labouchère had considered using a portion of the funds available in Russia for a speculation in colonial produce such as cotton and sugar–the prices of which had declined as a result of the large American shipments–but when bonds relating to the domestic loan.[1] All these decisions were confirmed in a ukase dated 28th September 1811.

Even though not everything turned out as Labouchère had envisaged, he was not completely dissatisfied. The Russian Court, he informed the partners in London, still showed evidence of its desire to fulfil its commitments, though this might involve major sacrifices. Therefore, he continued, while it was not his aim to expand the Company's interests in Russia, the creation of the new bonds as an additional security for the whole was justified. We may safely assume that this statement was made in order to forestall certain objections to the new arrangement on the part of the partners in London.[2] The ominous facet of the arrangement lay in the fact that it provided only for the payment due on 1st January 1812, and that fresh negotiations would be necessary during the course of that year. Before leaving St.Petersburg, Labouchère had received a solemn undertaking from the czar that nothing would be allowed to interfere with his decision loyally to meet his obligations, and that Labouchère could set the minds of the Hollanders at rest on this point. The limited time scale of the arrangement, however, indicated otherwise.[3]

Labouchère left St.Petersburg on 18th September 1811 and, travelling via Riga, Berlin, Leipzig and Frankfurt, arrived in Amsterdam on 25th October. While in Leipzig he had a meeting with Hieronymus Sillem, who had travelled from Carlsbad for the purpose, and during this it was finally agreed that Sillem should go to St.Petersburg to supervise Hope's interests there.[4]

Back in Amsterdam, Labouchère set about finalizing the arrangements for placing the new bonds. He informed Guryev that, while the restitution of the cf 400,000 had 'electrified' the *entrepreneurs*, the holders of the earlier bonds were now less inclined to sell, and therefore a contract between Hope and Willem Borski had been signed on 11th December 1811 providing for the latter to take over new bonds to a nominal value of cf 3,200,000, for which he would pay cf 2,400,000 in twelve monthly instalments of cf 200,000 commencing on 1st January 1812. Borski also had the option of paying the instalments in Russian bonds, which for this purpose would be valued at 60. As the new bonds could not be dealt in on the Amsterdam Stock Exchange, Hope undertook to advance a sum of between five and six hundred thousand guilders upon demand, and at 5% interest, on bonds which were not in their year of maturity, for which purpose a price of 80 would apply. Moreover, the Company bound itself to repurchase, if Borski should so wish, bonds to a nominal value of cf 800,000, divided equally over the maturing dates, at a price of 75.[5]

Upon reading the last-mentioned terms, one may wonder why the Company was prepared to commit itself financially towards Borski to such an extent, and whether it would not have been simpler to make the new bonds saleable on the Exchange. Among the probable reasons is that the issue of new Russian bonds would have undermined the price of earlier ones, thereby demolishing one of the pillars upon which the new operation rested. Moreover, deals via the Exchange would have required the prior approval of the French government, and a request for this might well have sparked off an official inquiry into Hope's affairs–something which the Company would not have relished at that juncture. Labouchère, it will be remembered, was planning to retire on 31st December 1811, and John Hope–who had become the senior partner following the death of Henry Hope early in 1811–was pursuing a policy of retrenchment, the safeguarding of funds and the transfer of these to England. In any case, there was no question of actual repurchase because the 4,000 bonds were in the hands of friends.

The agreement with Borski was therefore no more than a smoke screen behind which Hope's funds were transferred to a place of safety. It was agreed between the parties that 2,170,000 guildersworth of the new bonds out of the total of cf 3,200,000, would be in the name of Adrian Elias Hope. More than half this sum was deposited with Willem Borski, in whose name the bonds were registered. The balance was lodged with Berck and Entrop Muller, who administered the affairs of the mentally weak Adrian Elias. But even this amount of camouflage did not satisfy the partners. As Adrian Elias Hope continued to reside in Holland, assets in his name could not be classified as enemy capital, and the partners, who were in England, utilized this situation to safeguard their share in the new bonds. Their action emerged when, at the end of 1812, the initial cf 800,000 of the loan was repaid: $\frac{39}{80}$ths went to John Hope, $\frac{25}{80}$ths to Hope & Co. (i.e. to John Hope and his cousins by marriage, Thomas, Henry Philip and Adrian Elias), $\frac{8}{80}$ths to P.C.Labouchère, and a similar portion to Willem Borski. Whether, and in what degree, Borski acted for others in this matter, it is impossible to say.[1]

In practice, Hope must thus have furnished the greater part of the deficit of cf 2,400,000 which existed on 31st December 1811. The 'payments' made during 1812 were thus purely ledger entries. Nevertheless, the payment of interest and the redemption of 300 bonds on 1st January 1812, which Labouchère had stipulated, had a beneficial effect upon the Russian bonds, the price of which rose from 56–57 in the autumn to 65 and even higher in December and January.[2]

Early in January 1812, Sillem visited Amsterdam for consultations prior to accompanying Labouchère to Paris. Despite the fact that he had retired from Hope & Co., the latter had been approached by a sizeable group with interests in the Russian loan, with a request that he should visit Russia again and personally intervene in the matter of the interest payment due at the end of 1812. Labouchère had planned to take his wife to the south of France again in the summer, but he felt that he could not ignore such a call from the bondholders; he did, however, enquire through his friend Nesselrode, who had meanwhile returned to St.Petersburg, whether his arrival would be agreeable to the czar, and whether he could be certain of obtaining a passport in the event of a radical change in the political situation.[1]

As a journey of this nature also required a special permit from the French authorities, Labouchère journeyed with Sillem to Paris, where, he reasoned, his connexions in the highest circles of government might be of benefit both to himself and his companion. In Amsterdam, Sillem had received ten receipts for deposited interest vouchers to a value of cf 9,550, which were countersigned by Smirnov, the Russian consul general there, and had been instructed to try to encash these when he reached St.Petersburg. On the basis of these, Hope could ascertain whether such a transaction would be sufficiently advantageous. Sillem was also instructed to register in the names of the *entrepreneurs* the metallic bonds given to them as compensation for the cf 400,000 penalty. The share accruing to Strockel & Van Dijk, who had meanwhile left the consortium, was divided equally between Hope and Borski.[2]

At the beginning of February 1812, Labouchère approached the Duke of Bassano, the French Foreign Minister, with a request for a passport for Sillem and his servant with the minimum of delay. He did not ask for one for himself, probably because he wished first to consult Nesselrode, who was due to visit Paris with a special mission. In this matter, however, the political circumstances were very much against Labouchère. Although it had been clear since the end of 1811 that war between France and Russia was not far away, both parties continued to avoid precipitating the conflict. The czar's reasons for staying his hand were that he wished to let Napoleon appear as the aggressor and that he was anxious to sign a peace treaty with Turkey first, in order to have the whole of his army available to meet the French; Napoleon, for his part, was obliged to wait until the roads had dried up and until sufficient forage for the horses had been stockpiled.[3] As part of his game of political chess, the czar kept Napoleon on a line with promises of Nesselrode's arrival in Paris for the purpose of starting talks on the differences between the two governments; but, for mysterious reasons, Nesselrode was repeatedly prevented from leaving St.Petersburg. The postponements were the more displeasing to Labouchère because Guryev had written to say that the emissary was authorized to discuss with him a new financial operation in the interest of the payments due at the end of the year. Even though he failed to realize that the linking of the talks on the interest payment with a vague, specious affair such as Nesselrode's mission was a bad omen, and in spite of the fact that he was still confident about a payment at the end of the year, Labouchère refrained from pressing the matter of his visit to Russia.[1]

While he was waiting, Labouchère bought the contents of Talleyrand's library for 350,000 francs, of which 100,000 francs was paid in cash and the balance in Russian bonds. The purchase was made on behalf of John Hope in London. Painful though this step was, Talleyrand had no option, having suffered serious losses following the bankruptcy of Simons & Co., the house which had contributed to the fall of De Smeth. As neither John Hope nor his cousins by marriage, Thomas and Henry Philip, had any personal interest in the works, which numbered 10,000 volumes, Labouchère was instructed to have the entire library shipped to Harman & Co. in London. Labouchère was moved to enquire whether the English-language volumes, which accounted for a substantial portion of the whole, could not better be sold in France; but John Hope insisted that everything be sent to London, and after considerable argument with French customs officials the books were allowed to be exported.[2] It is surprising that Talleyrand was willing to accept Russian bonds as payment at a time when war with that country was inevitable. He must have been confident of making an exchange profit in the long term; certainly this accords with his political outlook.

Anticipating Sillem's departure, Labouchère wrote letters of introduction for him to Guryev, Rumyantsev and Speranski, the last-named a confidant of the czar. Sillem received comprehensive instructions, and was briefed on the history of the Russian loans. Labouchère impressed upon him the need to make the Court understand that it could not count upon further advances by Hope & Co.: the government must first display a more serious attitude in the matter of remittances. There was already bear speculation in Russian issues, and investors abroad (this reference will certainly have included France) were hoping that the prices would further decline. This could only be averted by prompt or, better still, early repayments of capital. If war between France and Russia came, funds could be remitted to Harman & Co. or Baring Bros. in London. Labouchère took a dismal view of the trading situation. According to him, the losses suffered and difficulties experienced by the Americans in their shipments to Russia had been such that these would not be repeated. But on his arrival in Russia, Sillem was able to send more cheerful news: despite everything, American vessels continued to arrive in large numbers. Early in June 1812, however, the war between England and the United States heralded the disappearance of American vessels from European waters, and thus Labouchère's prediction was ultimately borne out.

Like Robert Melvil, Sillem was given comprehensive information concerning persons with whom he might be involved commercially. Broadly speaking, the information corresponded to that previously communicated to Melvil.[1]

By 14th April matters had progressed to the point where Sillem was able to depart for St.Petersburg–a great favour, as Labouchère subsequently learned, for at that time no other passports were issued. Sillem reported that he had had an extremely unpleasant journey, the roads being in very poor condition following the advance of units of the *Grande Armée*, which was preparing for the attack on Russia. As postal services in Germany were irregular, Sillem and the managers agreed with Hope that their letters would be numbered so that they would know immediately if one went astray. As they advanced, the French commandeered grain for which they paid little and left only a bare minimum for the inhabitants.[2] This occurred not only in Danzig, but also in Königsberg and Elbing.

The nearer Sillem came to his destination, the more obstacles he encountered. At Polangen, his servant was sent back because his name did not appear in Sillem's passport. Deeper in Russia, the roads had just commenced to thaw, and Sillem's coach became bogged down in the mud. It took hours of toil to get him on his way. On 6th May he arrived in Mitau, where he requested a visa, only to learn that such matters were dealt with in Schaulen, twelve miles further on. There he was informed that his passport would have to be sent to Wilno, thirty-six miles away. When his request to be allowed to visit Riga in the meantime, to attend to his affairs there, was refused, Sillem had no choice except to wait, fuming with impatience, for a week until the document was returned. After a lightning visit to Riga, he finally reached St.Petersburg on 28th May. His first act was calmly to take stock of the situation.[3]

Labouchère was annoyed by John Hope's preoccupation with liquidating the current business and his reticence to offer Sillem the prospect of a salary.[4] The bondholders, Labouchère wrote, had offered him 2% of any principal and interest which they received as a result of his efforts, but no such offer had been made to Sillem. It was unlikely that the latter would be keen to run the gauntlet in St.Petersburg on a commission basis; he must at least be offered a salary. During a somewhat acrimonious exchange of correspondence, John Hope allowed himself to be persuaded to offer Sillem cf 20,000, but this he did grudgingly. Relations between the partners took on a decidedly sharp note when Hope began to press for the transfer of the Company's Russian loans to Insinger & Co. He insisted that this should at the latest be accomplished by the time the new partnership came to an end, i.e. late in 1814, but added that the sooner it was done the better. Labouchère replied that such a development would not be well received, either by the public or the managers in Amsterdam. When Labouchère wrote this, on 15th May 1812, war between France and Russia was imminent. He pointed out that if John Hope were to carry through his plan at such a time, the investors would rightly be incensed; moreover, it was by no means certain that Insinger would undertake to manage the loans under the circumstances or, if he did, that he would be able to continue. After all, the price of the Russian bonds had fallen since February from 65 to 50, and it would look as if Hope had abandoned the loan in the hour of danger.

In his reply, John Hope yielded some ground. While he continued to insist upon the transfer of the Russian loan 'or any other concern of ours' to Insinger, he consented to delay the operation until a moment which Labouchère deemed appropriate. The letter ended with the suggestion that Labouchère should broach the subject to both the managers and Insinger.[1]

In the meantime, Sillem had got to work in St.Petersburg, and had secured the acceptance of the receipts bearing the countersignature of the Russian consul general in Amsterdam. However, there were many formalities to be complied with before the Russian customs officials would accept these as payment. Guryev did not wish large numbers of receipts to be tendered at once, for they involved remittances abroad, and a flood of these could adversely affect the rate of exchange.[2] In fact, the risk of an excess of receipts was small, since ordinary bondholders displayed little interest in this form of interest payment. Such vouchers as were tendered nearly all emanated from the Hopes' private holdings, and even if war should break out the family could count on a payment via London. There was also the fact of Smirnov's departure from Amsterdam at the end of May, which followed an 'official visit' to Varel earlier in the month. This meant that receipts could no longer be countersigned by him, and gave the Russian government a formal excuse for refusing to accept any which lacked his signature.[3]

As far as the prime objective of Sillem's journey was concerned, the early signs were favourable. The czar graciously received him in audience and gave the impression that the interest due on 31st December would be promptly paid. Soon however–indeed, before the formal outbreak of hostilities on 24th June 1812–Guryev commenced to express doubt as to the possibility of remitting sufficient funds to Holland, blaming the situation on the inadequate postal service in Germany and the scarcity of sound drafts on foreign capitals. Sillem reported that the latter excuse was not valid, because exports, particularly from the Black Sea port of Odessa, were running at a high level, so that remittances were quite feasible.[1] But the minister continued to funk a direct reply and, in spite of memoranda and audiences, Sillem was unable to obtain clarification. On 5th July, Guryev announced officially that the czar had decided to suspend all payments, both of interest and principal, relating to the loan in Holland. The decision, it was stated, flowed from the outbreak of war between Russia and France.[2]

The conflict brought an early improvement in relations between Russia and England, and on 18th July 1812 this was manifested in a treaty between the two countries. In the negotiations leading to this, Russia had demanded that the British government should assume responsibility for Russian debts in Amsterdam, but this the English negotiators had refused to do. We may assume that Guryev's announcement to Sillem concerning the suspension of the payments followed this refusal.[3] In his formal letter to Sillem, the minister stated that the repayment of the first quarter of the advance of cf 3,200,000 would not be affected and that the instalments of principal already advertised (which covered the period up to and including 1st September) would also be met by the Russian Court.[4]

The decision came as a severe blow to Sillem, and he weighed the respective merits of going to the czar's headquarters at Wilno and approaching him personally, and of sending him a memorandum. In the end he decided on the latter course and despatched the memorandum to Guryev with a request that it be transmitted to the czar. Thus, he reasoned, the ministerial council could not feel that it had been by-passed. On the one hand Sillem wished that Labouchère were present, so that he would be relieved of some of the blame for the way in which matters had gone; on the other hand he realized that Labouchère's presence would make little difference, for there was no question of the czar reversing his decision.[5]

Labouchère, who, with his wife, was staying in Kassel, was the first to receive the sad news. With somewhat forced optimism, he continued for a time to hope that the decision had emanated from the 'collège des finances,' and not from the czar himself. Perhaps 'this piece of kite-flying' was for the purpose of testing public reaction in Amsterdam?[1] For the Company, however, the main issue was what to do next. According to Labouchère, there were two possibilities: either France would soon be in a position to dictate peace terms to Russia, in which case Napoleon would look after the interests of his subjects–interests which he knew extremely well–or the campaign would drag on, in which case the Company would do better not to diminish the legal weight of its claims by dragging them through the mire. With this cryptic utterance, Labouchère probably meant to convey that, in the event of a prolonged campaign, Hope would be well advised not to depend too manifestly and unilaterally upon French support.

Upon examination of the measure announced, Labouchère could not discern any intention hostile to the lenders. He understood the Russian action up to a point, although he could not of course approve of it under any circumstances. At the same time, the decision fell well short of infringing the rights of the lenders or renouncing the obligations towards them. The czar's statements during the last audience before Labouchère's departure had been too specific for anything of this nature. One of the most grievous aspects of the suspension was that many people who lived on their capital would be forced into ruinous transactions which would benefit a handful of speculators. The best course of action seemed to him to be for Borski, Voombergh and a few others to call a meeting of bondholders, at which advice would be given concerning the measures to be adopted. It would be necessary for the meeting to elect a committee with power to act on its behalf; the committee's first task would be to request Hope & Co. to disclose the true state of affairs. It would also be necessary to consider addressing a memorandum to the Duke of Bassano, and to arrange for this to be shown to Napoleon in order that he might display his paternal vigilance for the interests of his subjects. To counterbalance this, it would also be important to send a delegation to London to discuss with John Hope the steps which could be taken by Sillem. Labouchère felt that Willem Borski was best suited to this role. His own advice now counted for little with Hope, and his intervention would probably do more harm than good to the cause. If Borski was unwilling to go alone, Labouchère's brother, Samuel Pierre, might be persuaded to accompany him. The French government would certainly issue the necessary passports.

Under the terms of Hope's contract with Willem Borski dated 11th December 1811, monthly instalments of cf 200,000 had been paid up to and including 1st August. Labouchère recommended that these payments should cease and that the balance of the instalments should be met with Russian bonds at a price of 60. As the transaction affected only Hope and a circle of close associates, the bonds would not have to be physically deposited, but each of the interested parties would retain his share.[1]

To the managers in Amsterdam and to Willem Borski, Guryev's announcement came as a bombshell. The letter containing words of consolation and advice which Labouchère had sent to the managers had not arrived by the time the bad news reached them on 29th August. After prolonged discussions with the confidants, Borski, Berck and Bondt, William Gordon Coesvelt, one of Hope's new managers, was despatched to Frankfurt for consultation with Labouchère, who was then in that city. A report from St.Petersburg prohibiting further ballots for the Russian bonds had already been received in Amsterdam, and this news caused the price of the bonds to fall from 46 to between 38 and 39.[2]

In his talks with Coesvelt, Labouchère reiterated the points of view with which we are already familiar. He added that he had been startled by the 'disposition des esprits à Amsterdam'–a reference not only to the reaction of the investing public, which he described as 'insensée et impolitique,' but also to the state of mind of a man like Borski (to whom he addressed a separate letter of consolation). Borski, he maintained, ought not to be so overcome with dismay; this was not in keeping with his character. He should not bemoan the misery of others, but should do something to help them. He must join with the managers and Bondt and appeal to the public; he must retain the initiative, and not allow the public to take action. Borski would be the ideal person to go to England; Coesvelt and Van der Hoop, another new manager, could not undertake the mission, for that would create the impression of 'une affaire concertée,' and this would produce an even worse situation. Borski should not await Labouchère's return before embarking on the journey; Labouchère no longer desired to play an active role, but longed to retire and 'vegetate,' and devote himself to his ailing wife.[3]

John Hope, however, was not sympathetic towards his partner's desire for inactivity, and continued to press him to go to Russia. Hope countered the wording of Guryev's official announcement–in which it was stated that the czar had commanded that remittances to enemy countries should cease–by asserting that in the principal debenture of 1798, Hope & Co. was referred to as 'actuellement à Londres,' and that this situation again applied since all the partners in the firm now resided there. But neither this somewhat tortuous assertion nor reminders of the Company's earlier services to Russia could alter the czar's decision.[1]

In Amsterdam, the managers and their advisors, aided by Labouchère's moral support, resumed an active role. A dignified letter on the lines set out by Labouchère was sent to Guryev. In this, while naturally protesting against the measure, they expressed confidence in the future, when the war was over. The letter requested the minister to consult with Sillem with the aim of arriving at measures which could at once reassure those living on their capital and prevent speculation.

In accordance with Labouchère's proposal, a meeting of bondholders was called for 17th September 1812. This was extremely well attended, and the announcement of the orders from the Russian Court concerning the cessation of interest payments made a deep impression on the audience. In spite of the shock suffered by the public, the discussion was restrained and not one offensive word was uttered. The establishment of an independent committee was felt to be unnecessary, since all present had the fullest confidence in the Company.[2]

When the meeting drew to a close, the managers received a visit from J.van der Poll, C.van der Oudermeulen, J. de Burlett and J. van der Mandele, representatives of the bondholders present, who, together with Bondt, had come to report on the decisions of the meeting. After reiterating their confidence in the *faits et gestes* of the Company, the bondholders urgently requested that Labouchère should revisit Russia or, if this were not possible, that he should take other action in the matter of the loan. They asked the Company to accept vouchers for the payment due on 1st January 1813 from those bondholders who wished to surrender them, but at the holders' responsibility. The meeting thus sought to contribute, albeit with provisionally non-negotiable paper, to the costs. The announcement caused the bond price to fall from 37 to 32, but compared with the gravity of the measure the decline was modest.[3] Borski and Samuel Pierre Labouchère journeyed to Frankfurt to convey the bondholders' request to Labouchère. It proved relatively easy to persuade him to resume an active part, but he made his co-operation conditional upon both emissaries agreeing to go to England for consultation with John Hope. Borski more than once objected on the grounds that he had never been to sea and that the autumn was anything but a good time to embark on such an adventure, but Labouchère stood his ground. Even Borski's lamentations over his large family, the impossibility of neglecting the management of his affairs, his longing for peace and quiet and his dislike of any interruption of the manner of life to which he was accustomed were of no avail, and in the end he was obliged to submit.[1]

Pierre César Labouchère thereupon threw himself into the task of arranging the two journeys with the minimum of delay. Requests for passports for himself and for Borski and S.P.Labouchère were submitted to the Director-General of Police in Amsterdam, Devilliers du Terrage, and the Minister of Police in Paris, the Duke of Rovigo. In support of the applications, Labouchère wrote to the Foreign Minister, while Robert Voûte–who had been appointed by Napoleon to a senior financial post–added his recommendation in memoranda to Governor Lebrun and Mollien, the Treasury Minister. The request submitted to the Duke of Rovigo was accompanied by a similar document addressed to Napoleon. In this, however, it was explained that the applicants sought to give the Russian government an opportunity to reverse its decision 'even before the end of hostilities brings the inevitable consequence of the success of your campaigns.'[2] This piece of flattery was obviously added for the purpose of reconciling Napoleon to the fact that Hope & Co. already desired contact with the Russian government. When the request was made, on 30th September 1812, the first report of Napoleon's entry into Moscow on the 14th of the month had just reached Amsterdam, and it looked as if the French emperor was in a position to dictate peace terms to the czar.

Sillem's services were invoked for the purposes of the formalities at the Russian end. He was instructed to submit a request to Guryev for a passport for Labouchère. While the passports from the French government were speedily forthcoming, as had been anticipated, Sillem's efforts met with a polite but firm refusal from Guryev. The official reason given was that Labouchère, in his journeys to England, had undertaken semi-diplomatic negotiations on behalf of King Louis Napoleon of Holland and also Napoleon himself, and that a visit by him to Russia could be construed as a diplomatic mission aimed at bringing about a rapprochement between France and Russia.[3] Although couched in elegant terms, the refusal boiled down to the fact that the Russian government had no intention of resuming the payments and therefore did not welcome so 'powerful' a mission.

Labouchère took the refusal philosophically. Because its tone remained extremely friendly towards the Company, he felt that no unfavourable significance need be attached to it as far as the bondholders were concerned. At the same time, he deemed it advisable to cancel the steps taken in Paris in connexion with his passport as quickly as possible and immediately to shift the emphasis to the contact with England.[4]

Developments in the military sphere also pointed in this direction. The conquest of Moscow was followed by a fire which rendered the city unsuitable as winter quarters for the French troops. Moreover, Napoleon wasted a whole month in fruitless efforts to arrive at negotiations with the czar. By the time he had decided on a withdrawal, the Russians had brought up fresh troops and the French were forced to retire along the route which they had plundered during their advance. The unexpectedly early onset of winter added to the ordeal of their disorderly retreat.

Immediately prior to the news of the French setbacks, the price of the Russian bonds reached a new low; on 24th October they stood at 25. Early in November, when reports of the withdrawal began to trickle through from Moscow, the rate rose to 30, and by the end of the month it had reached 35.[1] The sudden change of fortunes, which grew into a catastrophe for the *Grande Armée*, soon attracted speculators. Thanks to the speed with which reports concerning the situation in Russia reached him, Count von Stackelberg, formerly the Russian envoy to the Kingdom of Holland and now occupying the equivalent post in Vienna, was among the first to approach Hope & Co. In October he instructed the Company to purchase ten thousand guildersworth of Russian bonds.[2] He was followed early in December by Moritz Bethmann of Frankfurt, with whom Labouchère was at that moment staying, with an order for fifty thousand guildersworth.[3]

With the cancellation of Labouchère's visit to Russia, Sillem's operations in St.Petersburg became indispensable. The matter of the remuneration for his services again became an issue at the end of 1812 when John Hope changed his mind yet again and refused to pay Sillem a penny unless the other interested parties contributed. In his morbid state of irritability, he despatched a stream of letters urging the early collection of outstanding debts and the sale of any bonds which could not be transferred to England or taken to other places of safety. In Amsterdam, the consequence of this action was to confront the managers with a serious shortage of liquid assets. On 1st August 1812 they had only cf 40,000 in hand, yet faced three monthly payments of cf 100,000 each.[4] Only with the greatest difficulty could John Hope be persuaded to place sufficient funds from his assets in Holland at the disposal of the managers to enable them to meet their current commitments.[5]

In spite of John Hope's refusal, the managers decided at the end of 1812 to pay Sillem a sum of cf 10,000 for his efforts in the matter of the Russian loans during the previous six months. In a letter to John Hope, Berck expressed his great dismay at the former's directives concerning

Sillem; if Sillem had not received any remuneration, he stated, Hope's honour would have been at stake. Berck went on to say that Sillem was too valuable to lose: by obtaining a repayment against the loan of cf 3,200,000 and the metallic bonds relating to the reimbursed penalty during 1812, he had more than justified the expense incurred.[1]

John Hope also strongly opposed the planned visit of Borski and S.P.Labouchère to England on the grounds that 'they can be of no use here on account of the Government.' Harman and Baring were said to have shared this view. Following the approval by the French government of the passport applications, a request for similar facilities, with Harwich or Gravesend as the point of disembarkation, was made to the British authorities via Baring. News of the approval of this request came at the end of February 1813, but now John Hope's letter raised doubts concerning the probable outcome. The managers, supported by Berck, advised against the journey but, at the insistence of the bondholders, Borski and S.P.Labouchère decided to go. By cancelling the agreement entered into with the Company for payment for their journey, they left themselves financially free in their approach to Hope.[2]

The two emissaries left for England early in March 1813. But they were not destined to meet John Hope, for he had died on 12th February. In all probability, his urge for liquidation and the settlement of affairs was prompted by the decline in his already poor health. Faced with this situation, Borski and S.P.Labouchère approached Harman and Baring, but after spending only a few days in London they received an official ultimatum to leave the country without delay. Their expulsion, it appeared, had been motivated by the Russian Court, which desired to avoid fresh claims.[3]

With the suspension of the payments, Sillem's role in St.Petersburg had necessarily become a passive one. The lack of progress in rounding off Operation R.M. also contributed to this situation. Small quantities of iron were sold from time to time, but there could be no question of disposing of the stock of linen until trade with America was restored, and this depended upon a cessation of hostilities between England and the United States.[4] In a review of Operation R.M. undertaken at the end of November 1812, it was established that losses had been incurred on linseed and potash. One ship carrying potash had sunk, and another had fallen prey to Danish pirates. As we have seen, the stock of tar had also been sold at a loss; indeed, the price obtained for the cargo which Becker had shipped to London did not even cover the freight charges. All these commodities had originally been purchased with a view to early resale, and although this failed to materialize, the efforts of Labouchère and Sillem had at least kept the operation alive.[1]

Following the news of the suspension of the ballots, the parties to the agreement with Willem Borski dated 11th December 1811 met their monthly commitment of cf 200,000 on 1st September 1812 in Russian bonds at 60%, as we have already seen. Sillem was instructed to apply to Guryev for the payment of the four remaining instalments, which totalled cf 800,000. The minister was not particularly pleased by the request, but he had earlier approved the agreement with Borski and in the end he was obliged to pay. Sillem received a commission of 1% on the first quarter of the cf 3,200,000 and the four instalments of cf 200,000. In addition, Labouchère left his share of these payments in Sillem's hands for a year in order that he might invest the money and enjoy the interest thereon.[2]

After the signal failure of Napoleon's Russian campaign, Sillem received numerous letters from Holland and France, requesting him to trace missing relatives and provide them with money. This was not a simple task, for the prisoners were spread over a number of provinces and there was no central administration. As a last resort, people took to advertising in the St.Petersburg and Moscow newspapers, but this quickly assumed immense proportions, and for a time such advertisements were banned on superior orders. Finally the czar commanded the provincial governors to draw up lists of prisoners of war in their areas and to send these to St.Petersburg.[3]

For Napoleon, the defeat in Russia was the beginning of the end. Late in February 1813, Prussia signed a treaty with Russia, and Sweden sent troops to Germany. By the Spring of 1813, the French had difficulty in maintaining their position west of the Elbe. However, Napoleon succeeded in assembling new armies, and a number of successes in Saxony enabled him to restore the military balance, at least temporarily. He then requested, and obtained, an armistice, and this took effect on 4th June 1813. To the consternation of England, which, in its struggle against Napoleon, could ill afford to lose the continental armies, the Austrian Foreign Minister, Von Metternich, adopted a policy of neutrality towards France and Russia, thereby threatening the joint military efforts against France. At the Reichenbach Convention on 15th June 1813, England agreed to provide subsidies for Russia and Prussia on condition that both powers fielded armies of a certain strength.[4]

For Russia, the Reichenbach offer implied a grant of $1\frac{1}{3}$ million pounds sterling during the course of 1813, subject to the proviso that the money should be used only for military purposes. England, however, was suffering from a scarcity of cash, and on 30th September 1813 a clause was added to the agreement, providing for a portion of the subsidy to be paid in bills of credit. These bills, which were issued by the Exchequer and bore interest, did not become encashable until one month after the signing of a general agreement ending hostilities.[1]

The political and military developments were reflected in the market price of the Russian bonds. This rose from 35 at the end of November 1812 to 40 at the beginning of 1813, albeit not without temporary relapses. On 20th March, shortly after Prussia declared war on France, the rate briefly reached 50, but on 1st June, following Napoleon's victories in Saxony, it rose no higher than 41. The news of the ceasefire on 4th June, however, brought an improvement to 46.[2] In January 1813, Labouchère had been somewhat nettled by the fact that the bonds had reached 40 and more, a situation which he described as 'just as absurd' as the low of 25 in the previous October. If no interest payment was forthcoming at the end of the year, he predicted, another low was inevitable. On this occasion, however, he was mistaken.[3]

During the ceasefire, peace negotiations took place between Napoleon and the allies. The Company attempted, with the aid of Robert Voûte, who was then in Paris, to have a clause providing for a resumption of the Russian payments incorporated in any peace treaty which might be negotiated, but the breakdown of the talks on 11th August 1813 put an end to these efforts.[4] Hostilities were resumed, and now Austria opposed Napoleon. While the negotiations were still in progress, Von Stackelberg, as usual well informed, instructed Hope to safeguard his funds and securities in Holland against confiscation by entering them in another name in the accounts and holding them at the disposal of a Swiss house. He also instructed the Company to sell his Italian bonds, which in his view would very probably fall sharply in the event of Napoleon's defeat. In fact, the news of the resumption of hostilities alone had caused these to fall to 40 on the Milan Exchange.[5] The news had also caused the Russian bonds to fall to 40 in Amsterdam, but Von Stackelberg made no mention of selling his holding of these. We can but imagine his surprise and anger when, in September, he received news from Hope & Co. that not only the 33 certificates of his Italian bonds, but also his 27 Russian bonds, had been sold, and with this a curt explanation that it had appeared necessary to dispose of the Russian bonds in order to make good the losses on the Italian securities and that he would be receiving a draft on Sillem in St.Petersburg for the sum of the proceeds.[6] Enraged, the envoy wrote to the managers in Amsterdam and to Labouchère in Frankfurt, saying that he had neither asked for his Russian bonds to be sold nor for a draft on Sillem, and that the disposal of the bonds was scandalous because, with the war against Napoleon going so well (the French emperor had been defeated by the allies at Leipzig in a battle lasting from 16th to 18th October), everything pointed to a boom in the price of the bonds.[1]

The solution to this puzzling event was not revealed until the second half of November, after the liberation of Holland. Despite the fact that Labouchère was greatly respected in the highest circles of government in France, the authorities in Amsterdam watched the activities of the 'Anglomaniac' house of Hope & Co. like hawks. In a confidential report to the Minister for Home Affairs in Paris, the Prefect of the Zuyderzee *département*, De Celles, complained that Labouchère, with his quasi-diplomatic journeys to England and Russia and his continual toings and froings between Amsterdam, Paris and Frankfurt, behaved like an unaccredited agent of a foreign power. The present managers in Amsterdam, he continued, were no better: Coesvelt had lived in Spain for years, and at the time of the revolt there had mixed first with the rebels and then with the French armies. It was he 'who gives the orders, after which the Exchange has to toe the line.' Van der Hoop, he wrote, came from a notoriously pro-Orange family, and Lestapis, although a native of Bayonne, had been brought up in England and was an enemy of the French government. Together, these men supported Russia's credit in such a manner that, incredible as it might seem, Dutch merchants, who in other respects were good at arithmetic, valued the issue at 45% even though no interest had been paid in either the previous or the current year.[2]

Faced with a comparatively unfavourable political situation, the French government exercised strict supervision of sales of French and Italian stocks, because such sales could be construed as indicating a lack of confidence in the future of the Napoleonic regime. When Von Stackelberg's instructions had reached the managers, they had sought advice from Labouchère. The settlement of John Hope's estate and the assessment of death duties were expected to involve inspection of the Company's books by the French authorities, and the managers knew that a simulated transaction would be bound to emerge. With the full approval of Labouchère, they thereupon decided to sell both the Italian and Russian bonds and, by means of the draft on Sillem, to make it clear to the French authorities that Von Stackelberg's assets were beyond their grasp.[3]

In the meantime, Czar Alexander had paid a visit to Bethmann in Frankfurt, and Labouchère had availed himself of the opportunity for a meeting with him. The czar repeated his assurance that the interests of the Dutch creditors would be closely watched, but on the subject of a resumption of payments he remained vague. In an effort to expedite the matter, Labouchère handed Nesselrode, who had accompanied the czar, a memorandum addressed to Guryev. In this, Labouchère set out a plan to put the Russian farmers in the devastated provinces on their feet, and at the same time to enable the interest due in 1812 and 1813 to be paid on 1st January 1814. The sum required as interest would be 10% of cf 84,000,000 i.e. cf 8.4 million, or 15,655,555 roubles. Under the plan, a committee would lend each of the million or so stricken farmers a sum of 10–12 roubles for between 5 and 10 years at 5% per annum. On the strength of the certificates of indebtedness, the committee would issue rescriptions which could be exchanged in Amsterdam for interest vouchers maturing on 1st January in the years 1813 and 1814. Redemption in guilders or roubles, at the holder's option, could be effected in five instalments. At the same time it would be necessary to announce the resumption of interest payments during the ensuing year; the first of these, at the end of 1813, would be no problem because, partly as a result of meeting the last four instalments for 1812 in bonds, the Russian government would have at least 1,300 bonds at its disposal, and with the news of the resumption of interest payments these would certainly rise substantially in price and, when sold, provide a portion of the necessary funds. In this way, Russia would be able to pay off the 8½ million guilders over a period of 10 years, while the creditors in Amsterdam would have an incentive to raise Russia's prosperity as far as possible.[1] Even if Labouchère's plan tallied in mathematical terms, it failed to take account of the true situation in Russia. The Russian civil service would have been unable to set up such a detailed administrative system in peacetime, let alone just after an exhausting war and in an area which had been occupied by the enemy.

At the beginning of January 1814, P.C.Labouchère set off for London, travelling via Amsterdam. On his advice, the managers sent Guryev a letter in the spirit of Labouchère's proposals, adding that, during his visit to London, Labouchère could perhaps arrange for the aid, in the form of subsidies, which stood at Guryev's disposal there to be used to meet the commitments in Holland.[2] This new attempt, like others, failed. The Company's letter was ignored, and Labouchère's memorandum was returned to Sillem in March – a clear indication that Guryev did not wish to discuss the resumption of the interest payments.[3]

In December 1813, Sillem had drawn Labouchère's attention to the potential value of the bills of credit as part of a new arrangement for the payment of overdue interest. In February 1814, Guryev and Bethmann both introduced Hope to Councillor of State De Gervais, who had been appointed Russia's representative on the committee charged with issuing the bills of credit, and who would temporarily be residing in Amsterdam.[1] As the British government had specifically stated that the bills might not be sold, but used only as security for advances by merchants, De Gervais enquired of Hope regarding the possibilities in that respect in Amsterdam. In a letter from London, Labouchère explained to De Gervais how the stock of capital in Holland had become depleted as a result of the reduction by two-thirds of the State's domestic debt and the cessation of principal and interest payments on various foreign loans. In addition, the new government had introduced an accelerated tax, the effect of which had been to swallow up such funds as were still available. As if all this were not enough, foreign demands were being made on the Amsterdam money market at a moment when Dutch commerce and industry had scarcely got into motion after a long period of stagnation. Not only was it extremely doubtful whether there would be any money for the Russian and Prussian bills of credit, but there was also the danger that these would become objects of speculation and decline in value out of all proportion, because they would not commence to be redeemable until a month after the signing of peace, and it was anybody's guess when that would come. Such a decline in value would be decidedly unacceptable to the British government. If, however, the Russian Court would agree to accept matured Russian interest vouchers for half its quota of the bills, up to a maximum of eight million guilders, it might yet be possible to launch an operation.[2]

As De Gervais was in urgent need of money, Pierre César authorized the managers to place half a million guilders at the disposal of the Russian commissar. Before doing so, he had sought the views of Alexander Baring, who in fact was the only partner in the Company at that moment, and of Harman, who, together with Baring, had looked after Hope's interests in England and had been co-opted by the British government in connexion with the transfer of subsidies to the Continent.[3] The managers were told that the advances given to De Gervais must as far as possible be financed in Holland–for example, from the funds held by Hope & Co. on behalf of Adrian Elias. As Elias was no longer able to manage his affairs, it would be necessary to consult David Berck, one of his trustees. With the death of Willem Borski on 5th February 1814, a valuable link with the Dutch capitalists had been lost, but it was conceivable that his widow would be able and willing to advance a sum of money. In addition, the managers were authorized to sell, if necessary, 200 Portuguese bonds and the balance of the Russian bonds which they held; the price of the latter had meanwhile risen to 56.[1]

The Amsterdam house must thus generate its own funds as far as possible, and not draw on Baring, because the rates of exchange in England had become extremely unfavourable as a result of the government's subsidy commitments. *Pro forma* drawings on Baring Brothers were allowed, but on condition that the drafts were sent to Alexander Baring, for the account of Henry Hope & Co., the London house which managed the interests of the Hope family.[2]

While De Gervais had yet to present himself to the managers, Samuel Pierre Labouchère, who headed a merchant house in Rotterdam, received news from Harman that shipments of gold consigned to Hope & Co. were on their way. He was instructed to accept these at Hellevoetsluis and arrange for their conveyance to Amsterdam. With the ports still largely blocked by ice after a long and severe winter, and difficulty in moving goods by road, this was not an easy task. Samuel Pierre therefore decided to employ a trusted agent, in the manner of the Jewish money dealers, and to send him to Hellevoetsluis to attend to the inward clearance of the gold and its journey via the offices of the customs agents along the route, at each of which the passport for the gold had to be signed by the excise authorities.[3]

Because De Gervais required cash immediately for the maintenance of the Russian armies, the managers in Amsterdam set about buying gold coin in Holland even before Harman's consignments arrived. Samuel Pierre Labouchère in Rotterdam and, later, Bethmann in Frankfurt were also brought into this operation.[4] Between the end of February and the end of April 1814, more than cf 750,000 in cash was placed at the disposal of De Gervais. In the early stages, the managers recouped their costs by simply retaining equal sums out of Harman's consignments, but De Gervais informed them that he required all the money and that they would have to finance their purchases by drawing on the credit opened in his name with Harman.[5]

The nature of the coinage given to De Gervais varied during the first two months. During February and the first half of March, he received not only *Napoléons d'or* (which were primarily destined for occupied French territory), but also large quantities of guineas and Hanoverian pistoles, of which the last two were in circulation in Germany, especially in Hanover. The British government had minted the pistole in England with a view to its use in Germany, but in the eyes of Pierre César Labouchère the measure served also to circumvent the ban on the export of gold bullion.[1] He was annoyed at the delay in setting up the Mint in Utrecht, the result of which was that in March 1814 there was still no means of converting gold bars into ducats, a form of coinage which had long been in circulation outside the Netherlands. According to Labouchère, government circles in England were amazed by the slowness with which everything was done in Holland, and he maintained that such signs of exhaustion served to diminish foreign interest and willingness to do anything to assist Holland's recovery.[2]

Following the capitulation of Paris on 31st March 1814 and Napoleon's abdication twelve days later, the Russian armies were especially in need of French money. This is reflected in the records of the purchases made by the managers after 1st April, in which French coinage, especially silver Napoleons, predominated. The Napoleons, packed in kegs, were sent to Paris by special courier.[3]

The plan to meet half the bills of credit with overdue Russian vouchers had made little headway in the meantime. Admittedly, Pierre César Labouchère recognized the difficulties. At the end of February 1814, with Napoleon's downfall still in doubt, Labouchère was most anxious to avoid the personal intervention of De Gervais if the question of borrowing on the security of the bills should arise, for 'the name of the Company must not appear.'[4] Collaboration with another house was out of the question for the same reason. Moreover, the supplementary convention to the Reichenbach Treaty, dated 30th September 1813, expressly stipulated that the bills of credit were to be used only for the prosecution of the war, and thus England would probably raise objection to a payment in overdue Russian vouchers. There was also the possibility that the Prussians would complain on the grounds that many of the vouchers had come into the hands of speculators, often at less than half their nominal value. Such men would thus be in a position to offer the bills of credit for sale at 80% or less of their value, and make a handsome profit to boot. Prussia would then be faced with the choice between keeping the bills allotted to her until all those from Russia had come on to the market, or accepting a substantial loss. Added to all this, it was of the greatest importance to England–and not only for reasons of prestige–that the bills should retain their par value. After all, they had been devised in order to assist Russia and Prussia in their struggle against Napoleon, and not to line the pockets of a handful of speculators.[5] These considerations led to the issue of the bills being repeatedly postponed. Guryev's rejection of Labouchère's plan for the Russian vouchers was thus not such a severe blow. The reaction from the czar's headquarters, where Labouchère's proposals had been learned of through De Gervais and Nesselrode, was similarly negative. Just how little the rate for the bills of credit interested the Russian government emerged from Guryev's disclosure to Sillem that any losses suffered on realizing the bills were for the account of the British government, and that he, Guryev, was concerned only with the amount of money which he received.[1]

With the date for the issue of the bills receding, the British government was obliged to seek other ways to meet the urgent needs of its allies. Among these were to allow the foreign powers to draw on London, to transmit money to the Continent, and to send drafts to the head of the British payment office in Amsterdam, Sir George Burgmann, with instructions to hand them to the representatives of Russia and Prussia. The commissary-in-chief, John Herries, who was responsible for providing British troops abroad with funds and supplies–and was therefore concerned with the subsidies for the allies–resorted increasingly to the last of these methods, since this was the only way to prevent the pound sterling declining further under the influence of indiscriminate drawings. The lack of concern on the part of the allies in this respect was also clear from Guryev's remark to Sillem. In his transactions, Herries employed the services of Nathan Mayer Rothschild, who at that time headed the London office of the well-known Frankfurt banking house and who had previously rendered great service to Herries in the financing of the British army in Spain.[2]

Labouchère was convinced of the need for Hope & Co. to give all possible help to Russia, even if no early settlement of the interest payment issue was forthcoming. To this end, the Company must decline all commissions, complete all current affairs as quickly as possible, and in any case maintain 'une caisse bien garnie'–even if the loss of interest thereby incurred should more than swallow up the total commission on the transactions. Labouchère maintained that profit was of less importance than demonstrating goodwill at that moment, and he greatly regretted the fact that the uncertainty concerning the future of the Company was an obstacle to increasing the aid still further.[3]

After Napoleon's abdication and his banishment to Elba at the beginning of May, there remained the question of a peace treaty with France and, allied to this, the encashment of the bills of credit. Under the terms of the convention of 30th September 1813, the bills were to become negotiable one month after the general armistice; but the bills themselves had not yet been issued! Early in May 1814, Herries travelled to Paris to settle these matters. He went by way of Amsterdam, where he had discussions with Sir George Burgmann. Besides De Gervais and the representatives of Prussia and Austria, the visitors to Paris included Pierre César Labouchère, who had journeyed to France with Alexander Baring.[1]

Herries succeeded in extracting promises from the Prussian and Austrian representatives that subsidy funds would no longer be drawn on London without the prior consent of the British Treasury. Instead, they would receive the necessary monies through the Treasury agents in Paris or elsewhere. To seal the agreement, sizeable sums were promptly placed at the disposal of the two countries, an action realized with the assistance of the Rothschilds.[2] De Gervais also consented in principle to the new arrangement, but he added that the final decision rested with Guryev. In view of this, he was not empowered to accept the 200,000 pounds sterling which Herries had placed at his disposal in Amsterdam. To avoid awkward discussions, De Gervais left Paris shortly after this. Before departing, however, he persuaded Pierre César Labouchère to furnish a letter of credit on Baguenault of Paris for one million francs, thus ensuring that the Paymaster-General of the Russian army in France was not without funds. He offered bills of credit for an equivalent sum as security.[3]

The Russian and Prussian governments had sent memoranda to the British Foreign Secretary, Viscount Castlereagh, giving their views on how the bills of credit should be dealt with. Both countries desired that the bills should be directly converted into 6% bonds via Sir George Burgmann's department, thus keeping them out of the hands of third parties. They also asked for a firm date from which the instalments overdue since the signing of the Reichenbach Convention would bear interest. On 15th March 1814, nine instalments were owing (the convention was signed on 15th June 1813), and as Paris had capitulated on 31st March 1814, the first of April seemed a suitable date for the interest to commence. If the British government would agree to make available all matured bills of credit or bonds, Russia and Prussia would undertake not to put them into circulation, but only to use them as security. It would, moreover, please the governments if the bonds could be made negotiable at centres other than Amsterdam alone. Finally, Russia and Prussia wished for the advances already made against the bills to be deducted from the final payment due from the British government.

The Lords Commissioners of the Treasury broadly concurred in these requests, albeit they were only willing to extend the area of negotiability to centres where not less than one million Prussian talers had been advanced on the security of the bonds. They indicated that they wished to settle the matter of the advances not upon the final instalment, but during the ensuing months; moreover, where such advances had been made in foreign currencies, settlement would be made at the rate of exchange ruling on the date of the advance. This, of course, meant that Russia and Prussia would still suffer the exchange losses brought about by their draft transactions.[1]

With the signing on 30th May 1814 of what was later to become the first Treaty of Paris, the bills of credit or corresponding 6% bonds became normal drafts, of which one million Prussian talersworth were negotiable monthly for a period of fifteen months. This implied that, if not freely negotiable, they were discountable and possessed the advantage over normal drafts of bearing interest at ½% per month.[2] Of the total of 15 million Prussian talers, Russia received two-thirds and Prussia one-third.

Even before the treaty was signed, De Gervais wrote to P.C.Labouchère, who was then in London, requesting an advance against the matured Russian bills of credit. In return, he offered seven monthly instalments, totalling 4,666,666⅔ Prussian talers, and, in addition to the monthly interest of ½%, a discount of 1% per month. He asked for the advance to be made in equal instalments in Hamburg, Berlin and Frankfurt or Leipzig. He required the money urgently in order to withdraw the Russian *assignats* with which the German states had become flooded since the entry of the Russian troops. Just how urgent was the Russian government's need of funds became apparent from a letter from De Gervais a week later, in which he offered to raise the discount from 1% to 2% provided the whole sum could be put at his disposal by 1st July 1814.[3]

Labouchère's reaction was cautious in the extreme. The future of the Company had still not been determined, for Alexander Baring had made his decision dependent upon the outcome of the allied rulers' deliberations concerning Holland, and this was still not forthcoming. Under such circumstances, the reserves were inadequate to undertake so large an operation as this, with its attendant risks. In Labouchère's view, the principal obstacle lay in the indeterminate rates of exchange which, by reason of the subsidies and the extent of the British government's financial needs on the Continent, were subject to considerable fluctuation. He therefore declined to go beyond an offer to permit acceptances on Hope & Co. once the maturing dates and rates of exchange of the bills had been established. The best arrangement seemed to him to be to make De Gervais's drafts on the Company payable at Hope's offices one month after the corresponding bill matured. De Gervais would thus be permitted to draw 1 million guilders on Hope, due on 15th August, against the 666,666⅔ Prussian talers which became payable on 15th July. As there was no longer any question of large-scale advances, Labouchère agreed to accept a commission of 2%.[1]

Such a conservative approach, however, was not what De Gervais had in mind, nor did it meet his needs. Fortunately for him, there was another house which, by reason of its extensive transactions on behalf of the British government, had adequate reserves and could influence the exchange rates–the prime obstacle in Labouchère's eyes. The house of Rothschild, which at that time sought to establish relations with as many governments as possible, grasped the opportunity to serve the Russian Court and at the same time to demonstrate its financial strength. On 17th June 1814, De Gervais informed Labouchère that he had entered into a contract covering the first six months' matured bills, and that under this he would receive hard cash in Hamburg, Dresden and Warsaw. While expressing regret that it had not been possible to reach agreement with Labouchère in this matter, he said that clearly the inconveniences which stemmed from the long distances had been against this. De Gervais discreetly refrained from naming the house which had succeeded in bridging these long distances.[2]

Officially, Labouchère could only be relieved by the news that De Gervais had succeeded elsewhere, but privately he was saddened by the thought that the Company had been forced to decline a transaction which it would certainly have accepted in earlier times, when the assets of the Hopes were available. Undoubtedly this reflection added to his annoyance when it transpired that De Gervais was willing to meet Labouchère's advance of 1 million francs in Paris in bills of credit, but refused to repay the credit of cf 500,000 given at the end of February 1814 in the same manner. This, he wrote in bitter tones, was the gratitude for Hope's support of De Gervais's operations at a time when the fortunes of war were uncertain, when no one would accept the bills of credit as security, and when money was so scarce and dear that it was almost impossible to get bills discounted.[3]

Labouchère was equally dissatisfied with the commission of 5% which De Gervais was willing to allow the Company on the advance of 1 million francs made in Paris. In February 1814, when Hope's reserves were fully committed in supporting De Gervais, Sir George Burgmann had offered the Company bills of credit as collateral at 9% interest. Subsequent to the agreement with Rothschild, De Gervais had himself offered the house of Gontard in Frankfurt 7% interest plus 2% commission for an advance against the November 1814 instalment.[1] Despite these protests, however, Labouchère adhered to his standpoint that the interests of the Russian Court were paramount. It was with this in mind that he had declined to speculate in the bills of credit. As far as the single monthly instalment of 666,666⅔ Prussian talers which had been allotted to Hope & Co. was concerned, he wished only to receive the sum in guilders which the Company had originally advanced. Therefore, the credit of cf 500,000 given in February must be debited at par value in the normal manner, plus a bank commission of ½% and interest at 5% per annum.[2] In order to ensure that De Gervais should not distort the facts when he returned to Russia, a comprehensive report on all that had taken place was sent to Sillem in October 1814.[3]

A victim of circumstances, Sillem had achieved little in the matter of the Russian loans. For the time being, his activities remained limited to collecting the annual repayment of cf 800,000 against 3,200,000 guilders-worth of newly created bonds and keeping an eye on the commodity markets in Russia in the hope of opportunities to round off Operation R.M. Sillem had by now become financially interested in the operation, he and P.C.Labouchère each having acquired one-half of Hope's $\frac{7}{16}$ths share. Early in 1813 he reported to Hope that the previous autumn had been bad from the point of view of shipments, because foreign markets were more than adequately supplied with Russian goods. An early end to the war in America should result in a good market for the linen goods, for considerable quantities of linen had been destroyed in the burning of Moscow.[4] Sillem succeeded in selling about 4,500 poods of iron to a ship's master who required ballast for his vessel, and shortly afterwards he disposed of 1,000 pieces of raven-duck and 400 pieces of Flemish linen to the American Company in Russia, which was preparing an expedition. The proceeds of these sales, however, scarcely covered the original cost, let alone the loss of interest or the storage charges.[5]

In spite of this poor result, Sillem was optimistic regarding the future. The reopening of the routes to America was bound to produce a substantial rise in iron prices, for there was no more than 1½ million poods on the market, and with mineowners complaining that selling prices did not even cover their costs, there would be no large-scale deliveries for the time being. The output of the linen mills had fallen for the same reason, and most spinners had gone over to cotton textiles. But the army needed linen goods, and thus peace in America could not fail to produce a boom.[6]

However, the peace from which Sillem expected so much was not to come until 24th December 1814, and so sales of the goods involved in Operation R.M. remained at a very low level. The Spring of 1814 did indeed bring some improvement in linen prices in Russia, but the slow progress which Sillem was able to achieve with Guryev in the matter of the resumption of the interest payments made him decide to leave affairs in Russia where they were for the time being and return to western Europe. As long as the czar remained abroad, no decisions of any magnitude were taken in Russia, and the time had come for Sillem to build for his future. He was anxious first to review the situation in Hamburg and assess the prospects for starting a new house there, and then to cross to England –something which Labouchère had repeatedly urged him to do.[1]

Sillem left St.Petersburg on 3rd May 1814. After a smooth journey he arrived at Altona, from where he travelled on to Amsterdam in early June. There, he discussed the Russian affairs with De Gervais. He did not stay long in Amsterdam, for Labouchère urged him to cross to England without delay, because the czar and Nesselrode were there and it might be possible to obtain an audience to discuss the Russian interest payments.[2] In Paris, Labouchère had approached Nesselrode with a request to be presented to the czar, but the latter, with his peculiar charm, had replied that, as Labouchère was an old friend, there was no question of formal presentation, and that he would invite him to dinner. However, by delaying the invitation, the czar had kept the guest–and his awkward questions–at a distance. Eventually, Labouchère and Alexander Baring had been obliged to return to London, and therefore Labouchère had pinned his hopes on the czar's visit to that country. But once again he was disappointed, for the czar was kept so busy with festivities that there was no time left for a meeting with Labouchère and Sillem. 'Everyone here is so agog with excitement that one does not notice anybody, and nobody is in a mood for anything,' an irritated Pierre César said in a letter to Amsterdam.[3]

On 27th June 1814, Czar Alexander embarked at Dover for the journey back to Russia. En route he visited Holland–probably with the aim of promoting a marriage between his sister, Anna, and the Crown Prince–and during his stay he received the managers of Hope & Co. in audience. To them he repeated the promises which he had earlier made to Labouchère concerning the resumption of the interest payments. In the style of true courtiers, the managers wrote to Guryev, saying that the most enjoyable days of their lives were 'those during which we had the inestimable good fortune to come near to His Imperial Majesty, and to receive from this Grand Monarch himself the most moving assurance of the interest which he still condescends to take in Holland.'[1]

Now that the czar was back in Russia, it was time for Sillem to return to his post in St.Petersburg in case any decisions should be taken there prior to the Congress of Vienna, which was due to open on 1st October 1814. Sillem also faced an important personal decision. Prior to his journey to western Europe, Labouchère had approached him regarding a partnership in a new house of Hope & Co., and during his stay in England this had been among the central issues during three days of talks with Labouchère and Alexander Baring at Tunbridge Wells. It was there that the decision to breathe new life into the Company was taken.[2] In the meantime, the future of Holland–upon which Baring's final decision depended–had been discussed at a ministerial meeting in London, and on 21 June 1814 the allied powers had signed a protocol agreeing to the unification of Belgium and Holland. Nesselrode, on behalf of Russia, had signed subject to the czar's approval, but he later announced that, in return for Russia's support, Alexander desired England and Holland jointly to assume responsibility for Russia's debt in Holland. The final decision on this, however, would be taken in Vienna.[3]

Whereas this declaration in principle by the allied powers had been sufficient to enable Baring to decide upon rejuvenating the Company, Sillem continued to delay his decision regarding a partnership. Early in August he had journeyed to Amsterdam in the company of Labouchère, who remained there to make the necessary arrangements. Only after his return to St.Petersburg in mid-September 1814 did Sillem write confirming his acceptance of Labouchère's offer, in order that they might together continue to serve the Company; he thus explicitly coupled his name with that of Pierre César Labouchère. It is probable that Sillem's decision depended in part on the arrangements which he was able to make in Hamburg concerning his association with the house of Benecke & Co. in the partnership Sillem Benecke & Co.[4]

This new turn of events imposed limits on Sillem's stay in Russia, since it was desirable that he should be back in Amsterdam at the end of the year in order to take his place in the reborn Hope & Co. on 1st January 1815. No fresh negotiations of importance were anticipated in St.Petersburg in the immediate future, for the czar had left for Vienna on 13th September, and in his absence discussions with ministers would be as unfruitful and devoid of commitment as in the past. Furthermore, as already stated, the decision regarding the resumption of the Russian interest payments was to be taken in Vienna and not in St.Petersburg.

It was, however, important that the remains of Operation R.M. should be cleared up before Sillem's departure. As far as the iron was concerned, Sillem, on his own admission, was extremely fortunate. Less than a month after his return, he had sold 200,000 poods to an Armenian merchant, Ivan Gabriel Michailov, who offered him 3 roubles per pood, the rate of exchange for the deal being fixed at 10¼ *stuivers* to the rouble. Sillem could not understand what had moved Michailov to make such an offer at a time when peace between England and America seemed so far away.[1] Remembering that, in fact, it came about at the end of 1814, it seems likely that Michailov was able to look back on a successful speculation, although whether this stemmed from sound political information or pure luck is a matter for conjecture. A fortnight later the remainder of the stock of iron and copper was sold at a slightly higher figure still. The linen goods were far slower to move, and finally Sillem accepted a cash offer from Stieglitz & Co. of St.Petersburg in order to avoid further delay, and also because it had been found that too long a period in storage resulted in a loss of quality.[2]

A closer examination of these final sales reveals that, in contrast to Sillem's optimistic view, the iron was the least profitable. Allowing for the fall in the value of the rouble from 17 *stuivers* or thereabouts in 1809 to 10¼ *stuivers* in 1814, the profit on iron, after deduction of costs, was 2%. Linen and raven-duck, however, produced a net return of 20%.The operation was now five years and four months old. If we put the loss of interest at 5% per annum, we find that ultimately losses of 24⅔% were made on the iron, and 6⅔% on the linen goods. The principal cause of this unfavourable end to the operation will have lain in the war between England and America.[3]

For Sillem, there remained little to do except to give letters of introduction to the new firm of Hope & Co. to the correspondents in St.Petersburg, and to collect the penultimate instalment of cf 800,000. Before leaving, he corresponded with the managers in Amsterdam regarding the houses in St.Petersburg and their respective merits. When Holland was liberated, a number of these had made proposals to Hope concerning financial transactions and the sale on commission of Russian goods, but the Company had declined them all in order to leave itself free for De Gervais's operations. But now these lay behind, and the Company could again think of mercantile matters. According to Hope, hemp, tallow and grain were the only commodities for which a ready market existed in Holland. The demand for tallow probably resulted from diminished stocks; the boom in grain reflected the heavy demands of distillers, who used large quantities of dried rye, in particular.[1]

Sillem left St.Petersburg at the beginning of December 1814 and, travelling via Riga, Berlin and Hamburg, reached Amsterdam at the end of January 1815. A mild winter had left the roads in Russia and Prussia almost impassable, and the river crossings were not without danger. In Amsterdam, Sillem found temporary shelter above the offices on the Doelenstraat, whence the Company had transferred its seat. Upon the death of John Hope, the house on the banks of the Keizersgracht had passed to his widow, and she and her second husband, Baron Von Dopff, were so hostile towards Hope & Co., that it had become impossible for the Company to remain there.[2]

As had been agreed, the question of the settlement of Russia's debts in Holland was again raised at the Vienna Congress. The British cabinet at first showed little inclination to implement the undertakings which Castlereagh had given the Russians on this point. By the end of 1814 the allied camp was rife with dissension, and early in January 1815 England, Austria and France entered into a secret alliance in order to resist, with force if necessary, the Russian and Prussian demands in matters concerning Poland and Saxony. However, Castlereagh had gone beyond the instructions of his government in becoming a party to the alliance, and thus the English delegation was anxious to settle the matter amicably. Among the means to achieve a more moderate approach on the part of the Russians was a proposal that Russia, England and Holland should each accept responsibility for one-third of the debt in Holland. The Dutch delegates, who had no part in the actual negotiations, proposed that Russia should shoulder one half of the burden, and that the other half should be shared between England and Holland. They argued that Russia had earlier made her approval of the unification of Holland and Belgium dependent upon a settlement concerning her debt in Holland. The territory now awarded to Holland was less than had originally been asked for by William I, and thus the *quid pro quo* which Holland was called upon to give could be smaller.[3] In view of the objections on the part of the cabinet in London, to which reference has been made, this line of reasoning suited the British delegation extremely well. Castlereagh thereupon drew up a memorandum on the lines of the Dutch proposal, but he made the payments by Holland and England dependent upon the North and South Netherlands remaining united.

When, on 4th March 1815, news of Napoleon's landing in the south of France reached Vienna, the restoration of unity among the allies became

A V I S.

Les efforts et les sacrifices que la Russie a été obligée de faire non seulement pour repousser en 1812 un injuste aggresseur, mais pour détruire la suprématie que s'étoit arrogée la France et rendre aux autres nations cette indépendance si essentielle à leur bonheur et à leur prospérité, n'ont pas permis à SA MAJESTÉ L'EMPEREUR de toutes les Russies, de continuer avec la même exactitude à remplir les engagemens que ses Augustes Prédécesseurs avoient pris envers les intéressés dans les emprunts de Russie en Hollande.

Les événemens extraordinaires des quatre années qui viennent de s'écouler, sont plus que suffisants pour justifier cette suspension auprès de tous ceux qui sauront calculer les dépenses d'une lutte qui, dans son principe, étoit si inégale, et apprécier les avantages du succès dont elle a été couronnée. La cause de toutes les nations, celle de l'humanité, devoit passer avant tout; mais lorsque la Divine Providence a daigné bénir les armes de SA MAJESTÉ et lui a fait entrevoir l'espérance de la paix, les principes de justice et de magnanimité de cet Auguste Monarque ont porté ses premiers soins à aviser aux moyens les plus convenables d'indemniser les intéressés dans les Emprunts de Russie en Hollande des retards qu'ils avoient éprouvé dans le payement des intérêts qui leur étoient dûs pour les années 1812, 1813, 1814 et 1815.

Cette somme d'arrérages est beaucoup trop considérable pour qu'on puisse songer à l'acquitter en argent effectif. L'état encore languissant du Commerce dans toute l'Europe, en général; la nécessité de pourvoir jusqu'à ce jour à l'entretien des troupes Russes hors de l'Empire, ne permettent point a SA MAJESTÉ IMPÉRIALE de faire effectuer pour cet objet des remises, qui dérangeroient non seulement toutes les opérations de la Trésorerie Impériale mais encore tous les reviremens commerciaux des fidèles sujets de SA MAJESTÉ, et c'est d'après ces considérations, qu'Elle a daigné arrêter le réglement favorable dont M. M. HOPE et C°. ont eu la satisfaction de communiquer préalablement les bases au Public, et dont ils ont soumis en date d'hier tous les détails à M. M. les Commissaires qui, dans l'année 1812, avoient été nommés par les Actionnaires pour se concerter sur leurs intérêts. Ce sont ces détails que M. M. HOPE et C°. croyent devoir porter maintenant à la connoissance du public, en lui annonçant qu'il a plû à SA MAJESTÉ L'EMPEREUR de toutes les Russies, par un Décret rendu à Berlin en date du 14/26 Octobre dernier, d'arrêter et d'ordonner ce qui suit:

Art. 1.

Les intérêts échus les 1er Janvier 1813, 1814 et 1815, et à écheoir le 1 Janvier 1816, accumulés des intérêts de 5 pCt. par an sur les trois premières années d'arrérages, à partir de la date de leur échéance respective, ainsi que les primes de *f* 100,000:-, *f* 75,000:-, *f* 50,000:- et *f* 25,000:-, accordées comme dédommagement du payement en Obligations au lieu d'argent

Announcement of the resumption of interest and principal payments on the Russian loans, dated November 1815 the most important issue. Castlereagh, who had meanwhile returned to England, gave instructions that a written guarantee of the payment by England and Holland of the Russian debt in Holland was to be given to the czar. However, he stipulated that this was not to be handed over until Russia had signed the treaty drawn up at the end of the Congress. It was also agreed–again at Castlereagh's suggestion–that the negotiations on the elaboration of this decision-in-principle should take place in London, in consultation with the British Treasury.[1]

The negotiations opened in the British capital on 30th April 1815. Labouchère who, like the Dutch delegates, had been kept out of affairs in Vienna, now found himself being consulted as an expert by the Russian ambassador to Great Britain, Count Lieven. Labouchère had taken the precaution of having the relevant documents sent to him from Amsterdam, and these he now handed to the ambassador. During a meeting with Count Lieven and Baron Von Nicolai on Sunday, 14th May, Labouchère gave the total figure for the claims on Russia, namely cf 101,486,000.[2] From Lieven and Von Nicolai he learned of the commitments which England and Holland had assumed in regard to the payment of interest. In addition to the fact that both countries were obligated to pay interest on cf 25,000,000, Russia could claim 1% of this sum as a contribution towards the repayment of principal. Indeed, this contribution could be increased to 3% at Russia's request, but in that case Russia would have to pay a similar percentage over her share of the debt.[3]

Labouchère strenuously urged that the payment of interest should be resumed at the end of 1815, but Lieven informed him that neither England nor Holland was prepared to pay immediately, because the war against Napoleon imposed an extremely heavy burden on their financial resources; moreover, it had an adverse effect upon rates of exchange. We may assume that Russia welcomed the delay also. Labouchère made a particular issue of the stipulation that the British and Dutch commitments would lapse in the event of Holland and Belgium being separated.[4] The Sovereign Ruler had proclaimed himself King of the Netherlands after the return of Napoleon, but in Labouchère's judgement the Belgians were only waiting for a sign to throw themselves into the arms of the French once again.[5]

At the moment when Labouchère learned of the stipulations from Count Lieven, the convention remained to be signed, and the strictest secrecy was imposed on him and also on the partners in Amsterdam. Even after the signing on 19th May 1815, the Company was obliged to await an official report from Guryev before making an announcement to the bondholders. Fortunately, the campaign against Napoleon ended soon after the victory at Waterloo, and thus Russia's finances were spared further testing. Under the second Peace of Paris (20th November 1815), a war levy of 700 million francs was imposed on France. From her share of this, Russia could more easily transfer monies to Amsterdam. The czar went so far as to accede to a request by Labouchère that the bondholders should receive an additional *douceur*, by allotting a bonus of cf 250,000 to be distributed, by ballot, among holders of overdue vouchers which had matured in the years 1812–1815 inclusive.[1]

On 9th November 1815, Hope & Co., acting on behalf of the Russian Government, issued a circular giving details of the arrangement for dealing with the overdue vouchers. The matured vouchers, plus interest at 5% per annum, would be capitalized and converted into bonds, which would be identical to those of 1798 and be considered as part of that issue. Commencing on 1st January 1816, all bonds would again bear interest at 5% per annum. On 1st July of each year, beginning in 1816, at least 1,000 bonds would be redeemed by ballot. In the event of war between Russia and Holland, the payment of interest and principal would continue. This new arrangement superseded the ukase of 16th/28th September 1811, in which the interest vouchers assumed monetary value for the purposes of buying Russian land and paying customs duty.[2]

The draw for the bonus on the interest vouchers took place on 9th December 1815 in the presence of Hieronymus Sillem, representing Hope & Co., and Messrs.Jan Bondt, Jan van de Poll, Cornelis van der Oudermeulen, Jan de Burlett and Johannes van der Mandele, representing the bondholders. A few days later, in an official letter on behalf of all with an interest in the Russian loan, these gentlemen expressed their gratitude for all that the Company had done to secure full recognition of the Russian debt, and announced their desire to discuss the matter of recompensing Hope for the costs incurred.[3] Replying on behalf of the partners, Adriaan van der Hoop politely declined any form of recompense because, among other factors, it was the intention of Czar Alexander to compensate all concerned in the Russian negotiation to the greatest possible extent. By circulating copies of all the correspondence, the bondholders' representatives brought Hope's handsome gesture to the notice of those for whom they acted. The decision to do so, they wrote, had been taken 'in the interests of greater satisfaction on the part of all concerned.'[4]

There were indeed sound reasons for this 'satisfaction.' The 'Old Russians,' as the bonds were soon to become known, were the first on which, after a period of stagnation, interest was paid in full. Moreover, the capitalization of the overdue vouchers made good the losses incurred in earlier years. The fact that final redemption had been put back to some time in the distant future was less weighty by comparison, though it did influence the market price of the bonds. During the second half of 1815, the price fluctuated between 66 and 75. In 1816, following the ballot for the bonus and the announcement of the first interest payment on 1st January 1817, it rose to between 82 and 88, but during the next three years it showed scarcely any improvement; not until the second half of 1819 did it exceed 90.[1]

This early, full resumption of interest and principal repayments earned Russia a reputation for creditworthiness and solidity. This in turn ingratiated her with a wide circle of investors in Holland–a situation from which she was to profit until the collapse of the czarist régime in 1917.

IBERIAN AFFAIRS:

SILVER, DIAMONDS AND COCHINEAL

Silver

CHAPTER NINE

EARLY LOANS TO SPAIN

I wish that the house might always have as its motto 'honour and profit'; but if either of these words must be erased, I would that it be the latter.

Pierre César Labouchère to Vincent Nolte, 22nd January 1806.

With the coming to power of the House of Bourbon at the beginning of the eighteenth century, Spain commenced to raise itself from the state of decay into which it had sunk during the preceding century. A start was made with centralizing the machinery of government and reorganizing the civil service on modern lines.[1]

Round about 1760, under Charles III, came the introduction of 'enlightened despotism.' Among the ways in which this was manifested was a well-defined government policy aimed at increasing prosperity. The rise in farm prices and the resumption of growth in the production of silver in Spanish America, where Mexico now emerged as the leading producer of the precious metal, served to boost the Spanish economy.[2]

The favourable circumstances contributed to a growing desire to regain the monopoly of trade with the Spanish colonies. To this end, and on the analogy of England and the Netherlands, privileged trading companies were established for particular areas. At the same time, the monopoly enjoyed by Cadiz in respect of trade with the colonies was gradually dismantled, and by 1778 the principal Spanish ports had obtained access to the majority of the colonies in Central and South America.[3]

This flourishing development was interrupted by the war between the North American colonies and England, in which Spain, in company with France, chose the side of the rebels. But so completely did the English fleet succeed in severing Spain's links with its colonies that the Spanish government faced a severe financial crisis. To meet the deficit, it was decided to issue *vales reales*, a form of paper money which, however, was not legal tender in the retail trade or for the payment of wages.[4]

On the advice of his foremost financial adviser, Francisco Cabarrus, one of the leaders of the 'Enlightenment' in Spain, Charles III established the Bank of San Carlos in 1782. The bank's principal task was to effect a gradual withdrawal from circulation of the *vales reales*, but it was also charged with the discounting of bills and dealing with incoming and outgoing remittances on behalf of the Crown.[1]

The war against England also delayed the ambitious canalization project which was aimed both at reducing the cost of inland transport and providing a source of irrigation. One of the plans, dating from the time of Charles V, was based on a canal alongside the Ebro, the so-called Imperial Canal. By 1778 the stretch from Tudela to Saragossa was complete, but a further extension and the cutting of branches, such as the Tauste Canal, were threatened by lack of funds.

In 1779, 1780 and 1781 the board which controlled the Imperial Canal and the Tauste Canal succeeded in having three loans floated by the Amsterdam house of Echenique Sanchez & Co. Two of these were of two million guilders and ran from 1st May 1778 and 1st January 1779 respectively. The third, which ran from 1st November 1780, was to have been for cf 2,416,000, but the subscriptions totalled only cf 2,298,000.[2]

All three loans bore interest at $3\frac{1}{2}\%$ and were for a period of twenty years; however, the royal letters patent under which they were authorized were so worded as to leave open the possibility that this period would be exceeded. The first of these documents expressly guaranteed the continued payment of interest after twenty years, while the third announced the setting up of a separate fund at the Treasury for the purpose of meeting interest payments. No mention was made of repayment. The terms provided for half the sum of each of the loans to be repaid, if desired, with bonds relating to earlier loans, which would thus be converted. This circumstance may explain the unusual sum of the third loan and also the fact that this was not fully subscribed. In many cases of conversion and repayment, a portion of the bonds was surrendered much too late, or not at all, probably as a result of inadequate notification of holders.[3]

As the war against England dragged on, the financial plight of the government, exhausted by years of fruitless beleaguering of Gibraltar, worsened. Through the intermediary of Cabarrus & Lalanne, Madrid, the merchant house in which Francisco Cabarrus had an interest, the Spanish Court succeeded in concluding a loan of three million guilders at 5% interest with Hope & Co. and Fizeaux Grand & Co., the alliance of Amsterdam houses which at this time was also negotiating loans for Sweden. The date of commencement of the loan was 1st November 1782, and repayment was to be effected in four equal portions in the period 1789–1792. As with the Swedish business, the loan was scrupulously divided between Hope and Fizeaux Grand.[4]

Entries in the *grootboeken* show that while the principal was remitted via

Cabarrus & Lalanne, the interest was received via the Bank of San Carlos. A probable explanation for this procedure is that the Bank of San Carlos did not open its doors until 1st June 1783, so that payments prior to this date necessarily passed through other channels. The fact that Cabarrus was the central figure in the bank and also in the loan transaction does not necessarily imply that the capital furnished was applied for the benefit of the bank. Not only are there no indications in the *grootboeken* and correspondence of Hope & Co. that this was so, but, as experience was soon to show, the Bank of San Carlos had an excessive amount of capital.[1]

After peace had been concluded with England in 1783, the Spanish economy quickly recovered and, strictly in accordance with the agreement, the loan from Hope and Fizeaux Grand was repaid between 1789 and 1792.[2] No fresh loan was negotiated immediately, although the subject was raised in correspondence, and the reason lay in an absence of agreement between the erstwhile partners. In 1788 Fizeaux Grand & Co. had become Hogguer Grand & Co. and, according to Pierre César Labouchère, Hogguer and Hope trod different paths in loan matters. It is conceivable that the partners in Hope & Co. disliked Hogguer himself, but there is the fact that since the Company had concerned itself with loans for Russia it had declined to collaborate with any other house. For a company which felt strong enough to undertake an issue alone, association with another house had little appeal: it halved the profit and frequently doubled the worries.[3]

The Spanish government, however, declined to accept the situation. In the autumn of 1792 the Minister of Finance, Don Diego de Gardoqui, sent his brother, Juan Ignacio, to Holland, and early in the following year a contract was arranged between him and the Company providing for a loan of six million guilders at $4\frac{1}{2}\%$ interest, the rate which had applied to the contract entered into with Russia in August 1792. Repayment, in annual instalments of cf 600,000, was to commence on 1st November 1798 and would thus be completed by 1st November 1807.

As had been the case with Russia, the loan was to be the first of a long series. When the initial six million had been taken up, a further loan for a similar sum would be floated and then a third, bringing the total to eighteen million guilders.[4]

The marked increase in the sum of these loans, compared with the one of 1782, was probably attributable to Spain's urgent need of funds at a time of preparation for war against the French. The course of events in France, particularly the actions against Louis XVI, had not gone unnoticed among the king's kinsmen in Spain; indeed, they had aroused widespread anti-

French feeling. Following the storming of the Tuileries and the imprisonment of the French royal family in August 1792, the Spanish Prime Minister, Aranda, deliberately headed for a conflict.

The declaration of war, however, came from the French side, in March 1793. It followed a similar action against the Stadholder of Holland. The spread of the theatre of war towards the Republic prevented Hope from getting beyond the first tranche of six million guilders. The defeat of the allied armies by the French in September 1793 caused Dutch funds to dry up, just as had occurred at the time of the Russian loans.[1]

In their war against the French revolutionaries, the Spanish fared as badly as the Dutch. At the end of 1792 Charles IV, who had ruled since 1788, replaced his Prime Minister, Aranda, by Manuel Godoy, a protégé of the queen but a man with no political experience. The war against France turned into a fiasco and it was not long before the revolutionary armies penetrated deep into Catalonia. In August 1795 the Spanish government followed the example of Prussia and signed a peace treaty with the French at Basle.[2]

Dislike and fear of England, whose influence was penetrating ever deeper into the Spanish colonies, served to drive the Spaniards into the arms of France, and in August 1796 the two even entered into an alliance. The war with England, to which this alliance gave rise, was even more disastrous for the Spanish economy than the war of 1779. The vital flow of silver from Mexico again ceased and the *vales reales*, of which ever larger quantities were issued, rapidly declined in value. A decree of 1799 imposing an arbitrary rate of exchange of 94% backfired and ultimately the *vales* stood at 25% of their par value.[3]

These financial perils naturally had an effect upon the payment of interest and principal money on the Spanish loans in Holland. Threatened by the advance of the French armies, the Hopes had fled to England at the end of 1794. In 1795, and again in the following year, they succeeded in remitting the interest from London, though the payments from Spain arrived very late and only after repeated requests.

In 1797 the payment of interest in Holland was resumed. By this time England and Spain were at war and it was considered that the operation could more safely be conducted from the newly established Batavian Republic. The matter of the Spanish interest was entrusted to H.A.Insinger & Co. This house had conducted the sale of Portuguese diamonds sent to Hope & Co. prior to 1795 under the terms of a contract with a Portuguese merchant. Correspondence from Insinger to the Hopes in London shows clearly that this firm also found it extremely difficult to obtain remittances from Spain, and how long it was obliged to wait for reimbursement of the advances which it made.[1]

The year 1798 brought fresh distress to the government of Spain in the shape of the need to repay the first loan from Echenique and also the 1792 loan from Hope & Co. As far as the latter was concerned, no further effort was demanded from Insinger because the Spanish Court had in 1798 appointed the Amsterdam house of Weduwe E.Croese & Co. as its bankers. A partner in the firm had travelled to Madrid to seek the appointment and had been supported in his efforts by Valckenaer, the envoy of the Batavian Republic in Spain.[2]

An attempt in May 1798 to float a loan of 3 million guilders at 5% interest via Croese had failed. Despite the added attraction of a lottery with 600 prizes and the possibility to use the 600 redeemed Hope bonds as cash, the reaction of investors was so lukewarm that the loan did not get off the ground. The avoidance of any mention of repayment of the first Echenique loan probably did much to lessen the interest.[3]

In October 1799 Croese, again with Valckenaer's support, succeeded in obtaining a royal patent for a new loan, of which half could be met with Echenique bonds. The 600 bonds from Hope & Co., which were due for redemption on 1st November 1800, could also be used for payment and, indeed, would even carry a bonus of 6%. Holders of bonds relating to the abortive loan of May 1798 were given the opportunity to exchange their holdings for new bonds, and those who did so received a 5% bonus and an extra 4% as compensation for loss of opportunity to win a prize in the lottery. The loan was for 3 million guilders at 5% and ran for eight years from 1st September 1799.[4]

On 1st November 1800 Croese issued a second loan, this time for 2½ million guilders, on practically identical conditions. A dubious feature of this loan was that the house was permitted to resell Echenique bonds accepted for conversion, but not cancelled, at the time of the previous loan, plus those tendered for conversion for the purposes of the new loan, at the market price, provided that this was not below 50%. Clearly the Spanish Court was in such financial straits that it was obliged to sabotage its own conversion loan.[5]

The reasons for its plight were set out in the opening lines of the royal patent dated 17th June 1801, relating to the third loan, namely expenditure arising from the war with Portugal, the high cost of equipping the fleet at Cadiz and the interest which the Court was committed to pay to Holland. This third loan, which was for 4½ million guilders at 5% interest, commenced to run on 1st September 1801 and, like the two previous ones, was for a period of eight years. Once again Croese was given permission to resell converted Echenique bonds provided the price was not below 50%.[1]

According to Labouchère, only 8 million guilders of the nominal total of 10 millions was subscribed to these three loans. Of the 4,000 Echenique bonds which could be converted, 1,000 at the most were redeemed, so that following the floating of the three 'Conversions Espagnoles' more than 5,000 Echenique bonds remained in circulation.[2]

It is true that the Treaty of Amiens in 1802 provided a brief respite and enabled Spain to export large quantities of silver from Mexico, but in May 1803 hostilities again broke out between England and France. Spain was anxious to keep open the lanes of communication with the colonies, but this was possible only if it were exempted from its treaty obligation to provide military assistance to France. Bonaparte was more in need of money than manpower at that moment and thus the parties were able to reach agreement, albeit after some tough negotiations, in October 1803. Spain undertook to pay 6 million francs per month with effect from the outbreak of the war on 20th May 1803. Of this sum, 2 million francs per month were deductable in respect of supplies delivered to France.[3]

But while France was urgently in need of money for armaments, Bonaparte discovered to his intense annoyance that the Spaniards were in no hurry to pay the subsidy. There was little silver in Spain itself, and efforts to obtain loans in Amsterdam, Paris and Hamburg were in vain. In Amsterdam, De Smeth and Hogguer, in addition to the Court Bankers, Croese, were involved in these efforts at the beginning of 1804. The loan proposed was of 10 million guilders for ten years at 5½% interest. To make it more attractive to investors, the issue price was 95% and a bonus of 5% on repayment was offered. Despite these incentives, none of the houses succeeded in obtaining the approval of the government of the Batavian Republic for the loan.[4]

In the meantime the deficits incurred by the French Treasury had reached such alarming proportions that the minister concerned, Barbé Marbois, was forced to contemplate a shortfall of 116 million francs by September 1804. Of the 40 million francs due from Spain in March of that year, only 18 million had been received. Admittedly, bills for the full amount had been lodged with the French Treasury, but while Spain remained in default there was little that Marbois could do with these.[5]

Not knowing what to do next, the minister approached the *Compagnie des Négociants Réunis*, in which the prominent army and naval contractors Ouvrard, Vanlerberghe and Desprez had joined forces. On 4th April

1804 an agreement was concluded between the *Compagnie* and Marbois; under this, Ouvrard was to receive drafts on the Spanish Treasury to a value of 32 million francs, representing eight months' subsidies. Of this sum, half was immediately made available to the minister and the remainder was used to meet outstanding invoices for goods supplied to the army and the navy.[1]

As security, the *Compagnie* accepted obligations entered into by the *Receveurs Généraux*, the collectors of direct taxes. It was their custom at the commencement of each fiscal year to enter into an obligation to the Treasury regarding the total sum which they anticipated collecting in taxes in each month. Their commitment lapsed four months after the taxes in each of the months concerned were considered to have been received in full. Thus, nearly eighteen months passed before the whole of this revenue became available, and to meet this the Treasury had the habit of discounting the obligations promptly at the beginning of each fiscal year. The obligations transferred to the *Compagnie* were entrusted to Desprez.[2]

The preparations for the assault on England increased the French Treasury's need for funds still further, and in June 1804 Barbé Marbois again approached the *Compagnie*, this time with a request for 150 million francs. Ouvrard again agreed to furnish advances but, as previously, after the deduction of sums outstanding for deliveries to the army and navy, then amounting to 48 million francs. In order to deal more adequately with business on such a gigantic scale, the *Compagnie* established connexions with Armand Séguin and the brothers Michel the Elder and Michel the Younger, men of questionable propriety who were later to cause the *Compagnie* no end of trouble.[3]

It will be clear from the foregoing that Ouvrard was the soul of the whole affair. Gabriel Julien Ouvrard, speculator, naval contractor, banker and architect of the most grandiose financial projects, was born at Nantes in 1770. By skilful speculation, he amassed a fortune while the French Revolution was still young. When in 1793, during the Reign of Terror, Carrier was settling his score with the counter-revolutionaries by means of his notorious *noyades*, Ouvrard succeeded in keeping his head above water by joining the republican army which was fighting the royalists in the Vendée. From there he journeyed to Paris to present to the Convention the banners captured from the counter-revolutionaries. Once in Paris he stayed there, using his experience in the Vendée to become one of the most successful contractors to the French fleet. His fabulous riches and his grand style of living made him a textbook example of the *nouveaux riches* from whom the era of the Directory derived its notoriety.[4]

After the seizure of power by Bonaparte in 1799, conditions became less favourable for Ouvrard. The new dictator had an inveterate dislike of *les fournisseurs*, the contractors to the army and navy, who in his view took advantage of the impecuniosity of the government to make scandalously large profits. When Ouvrard presented Bonaparte with an outstanding account for deliveries, the First Consul ordered an investigation of the ledgers with the result that Ouvrard was summarily arrested and ordered to repay one and a half times the sum which he had claimed was due to him.[1]

But Bonaparte could not manage without the connexions and talent for organizing possessed by the *fournisseurs*. Ouvrard and Vanlerberghe, his new partner, accordingly played a significant role in the preparations for the Italian campaign of 1800–1801, albeit they employed a man of straw to submit their tenders. As subsequent events will show, Ouvrard employed this artifice on numerous occasions. For a man such as Bonaparte, this dependence upon persons whom he hated and despised was well-nigh intolerable, and he adopted the policy of delaying payment of accounts from the *fournisseurs* for as long as possible.[2]

Ouvrard was no stranger to Hope & Co. They had been in contact in 1802 in connexion with the *Rescriptions Bataves*, bonds issued by the Batavian government and covering half of the war levy which France had imposed on the vanquished Holland in 1795. In time of war, bonds to a value of 3 million guilders would be redeemed annually; in time of peace, double this sum. Because of its acute financial position, the French government had disposed of these *rescriptions* as quickly as possible. In view of the uncertainty whether the situation was one of war or peace, a highly speculative stock was marketed, and this must have been attractive to a man like Ouvrard.[3]

In 1804 there was very frequent contact between Hope & Co. and the *Compagnie des Négociants Réunis*. As explained elsewhere, Labouchère had signed an agreement with Barbé Marbois on 21st April of that year providing for Hope and Baring to acquire all bonds relating to the Louisiana loan, in return for which they would, *inter alia*, furnish a sum of 5,825,000 francs in Paris and take over French bonds to a value of 15 million francs which became due for redemption in the following September and October. As the *Compagnie*, through the agreements of April and June 1804, had become very closely concerned in French finances, Hope's payments in respect of the Louisiana loan passed directly via Desprez.[4]

After this, however, Labouchère for a time appeared reluctant to become involved in the affairs of the *Compagnie*. He declined a request by Desprez for a credit of between 1 and 2 million guilders against the security of bonds from the *Receveurs Généraux*, giving as his reason that Hope & Co. were wholly occupied with the payments for the Louisiana loan and the Portuguese subsidy to France.[1] According to Labouchère, the demand on the Amsterdam money market from Paris was so heavy that every financial transaction was hazardous. 'People are trying to do too much at once,' wrote the Paris house of Baguenault & Co.; and Labouchère agreed fully with the sentiment. In his view, Desprez could keep his operations going only at the expense of every rate of exchange in Europe.[2]

Early in May 1804 Hope & Co. were approached by the Marquis de la Colonilla, acting on behalf of the Spanish Court. The Marquis, a French banker, had received his title in Spain and headed a firm in Madrid. The aim of his visit was to speed up the payment of the Spanish subsidy to France. De la Colonilla proposed that Hope should negotiate a loan of 5 million piastres at 6% interest, the equivalent of which, in francs, was to be transmitted to Paris. Repayment, in piastres, would be effected in Madrid in three equal instalments in the years 1807, 1808 and 1809; the Spanish authorities would permit the free export of the piastres.[3]

Labouchère's initial reaction was lukewarm. De Smeth, Hogguer and Croese were already active on behalf of Spain, though not with much success; moreover, De la Colonilla had lowered the prestige of the proposed negotiation by hawking it in Paris prior to writing to Hope & Co. Quite apart from the question whether the Batavian government would withdraw its objections to a foreign loan, little response could be anticipated from the Dutch public since many were saddled with large stocks of colonial produce which was very slow-moving as a result of the scarcity of money. Labouchère expressed the view that it might be feasible to start with a small sum, say one million piastres, and to accept as payment the outstanding bonds of Hope's 1792 loan.[4]

Such a proposal did not, of course, fit in with the aims of the Spanish government. In an effort to progress the matter, Labouchère inquired of Alexander Baring whether perhaps the English East India Company would be interested in acquiring piastres in Spain at two-thirds of the current rate of exchange. In England, however, the return to power of Pitt had produced a much more uncompromising policy towards France and her allies, and thus Baring did not respond to Labouchère's overtures.[5]

In the latter part of September 1804, rumours of tension between England and Spain commenced to circulate in Amsterdam. A month later it was reported that English men-of-war, in the absence of a declaration of war, had seized three Spanish frigates which carried nearly five million piastres.

To Labouchère, the only possibility now lay in De la Colonilla initiating expeditions from Spanish American ports to Amsterdam, calling at a port in the United States en route; but he did not press the matter.[1] There was little point in continuing to negotiate with De la Colonilla, for early in 1805 Hope & Co. became involved in the transactions which Ouvrard had meanwhile commenced with Spain.

As we saw in the preceding pages, Ouvrard took over from Barbé Marbois a claim for 32 million francs on the Spanish Treasury in April 1804. At the insistence of Napoleon, who was anxious to see the security of 32 million francs in the form of debentures from the *Receveurs Généraux* returned to his Treasury as quickly as possible, Ouvrard journeyed to Spain at the beginning of October 1804. There he succeeded in winning the favour of the powerful Godoy by quickly satisfying the acute financial needs of the Court, with which an agreement was concluded whereby Ouvrard assumed the role of France as creditor for the sum of the Spanish subsidy.[2] Much greater successes lay ahead of him, however.

On 26th November 1804, a new series of agreements were signed which gave Ouvrard a position of financial power in Spain equal to that which, via the *Compagnie*, he possessed in France. Under these, he first undertook to supply two million quintals of corn to alleviate the famine in Spain. Ouvrard was destined to become a contractor to the Spanish army and navy, and even to meet the immediate financial needs of the State. The latter activity involved the *Caja de Consolidacion*, a sinking fund established for the purpose of withdrawing the *vales reales* but which in practice served as an ancillary source of funds for the government. The Bank of San Carlos was originally established for this purpose, but mismanagement and speculative losses had destroyed much of its credit.

The *Caja* obtained a loan of 10 million francs plus extensive credits from French houses such as Michel the Elder and Michel the Younger. In addition, Ouvrard undertook to float a loan of 10 million guilders in Holland–something which De Smeth and Hogguer had thus far failed to realize. For all these credits, and others which were to follow, Ouvrard received drafts from the *Caja de Consolidacion*.[3]

Ouvrard's crowning glory, however, came with an agreement between himself and Manuel Sixto Espinosa, who as *Contador General* acted as representative of the Spanish Crown. This agreement provided for the establishment, with joint capital, of the house of François Ouvrard & Co.

which, for the duration of the war against England, was given a monopoly of imports and exports in all the Spanish colonies. This included the export of gold and silver.[1]

It must have been a source of satisfaction to the Spanish government, in theory at least, to regain some control of trade to and from the colonies. As we have seen, trade with America was thrown open to all Spanish ports in 1778, but was very expressly limited to Spaniards. With the outbreak of the war against England in 1796, this monopoly ceased to have practical meaning, and in 1797 the Spanish government could do no better than to open the ports in Spanish America for neutral trade, on condition that no prohibited articles such as precious metals were exported and that the vessels plying the trade should call at a Spanish port on the homeward voyage. American ships profited especially from the easier situation, but breaches of the restrictions were so widespread that in 1799 all Spanish American ports were closed to trade except for the import of food. Opposition to this action was so fierce that these ports were reopened in 1801, albeit a system of special licences was introduced. During the brief suspension of hostilities from 1802 to 1804, the Spanish monopoly was restored, but in December 1804 the licensing system was revived. Many of those who were in favour at the Court obtained the right to sell licences, to which end they employed agents. Such an arrangement was, of course, in flagrant contravention of the monopoly granted to François Ouvrard & Co., but at the same time it was characteristic of the general atmosphere of corruption which pervaded the Spanish government machine. The effects of this on Ouvrard's transactions will become clear as our story unfolds.[2]

In a subsequent agreement dated 4th December 1804, Espinosa asserted the rights of his government more emphatically. François Ouvrard & Co. were now compelled to ship goods to and from the American colonies for the account of the Spanish government. In addition, the house's commission on shipments of gold and silver was reduced from 1 % to $\frac{1}{2}$ %.[3]

For Ouvrard, access to the piastres from America, which he had obtained through these agreements, formed the hub of all his transactions with Spain. Only with these could the impoverished Spanish government pay Ouvrard and, through him, France. The French Treasury, too, was interested in the early mobilization of the Mexican silver because its lack of resources was becoming steadily more acute. As Napoleon rejected any form of consolidated national debt and, still mindful of the *assignats*, was equally unwilling to resort to issuing paper money, the arrival of Mexican silver was the only solution to the shortage of funds. Fresh conquests, which could help to fill the state coffers, were as yet not forthcoming. During the absence of this silver–and with the projected loan in Amsterdam still unrealized–Ouvrard, in order to meet his commitments towards Spain, was obliged to fall back upon the French Treasury and the *Banque de France*, via the *Compagnie des Négociants Réunis*, a course which added to France's monetary plight.[1]

Clearly, Ouvrard's financial juggling had to be brought to an end as quickly as possible; but this could only be done if he succeeded in obtaining the English government's approval for the shipment of the piastres. From a purely commercial point of view, there was a chance that he would do so, for the need for precious metals was just as great in England as in France–and if permission were forthcoming at least a portion of the shipped piastres would remain behind in England. Initially, however, Ouvrard's appeal to Pitt fell on deaf ears. Pitt was aware of the financial difficulties which faced Napoleon, and while the French army at Boulogne seriously threatened England's security Pitt was not at all disposed to assist in alleviating Napoleon's difficulties.[2]

Labouchère was kept posted regarding Ouvrard's *faits et gestes* by his Paris correspondents, Baguenault and Hottinguer. To them he expressed his annoyance at the manner in which Ouvrard peddled his plans from door to door. In Labouchère's opinion, Ouvrard's efforts to draw the Americans into the affair was 'an error of judgement' accompanied by talent and even by genius–a situation which could exist only in France. Ouvrard need not think that any Englishman would become a party to such a transaction and thereby compromise himself in the eyes of his own government.[3]

Ouvrard's efforts to arouse American interest in his projected transaction were, however, not original: negotiations with the son of the United States envoy in Paris, Robert L.Livingstone, and his compatriot, the merchant and speculator Daniel Parker, had taken place in the winter of 1803. They offered to purchase 15 million piastres from Spain, deliverable in Vera Cruz, Havana and Montevideo. The equivalent, 57 million francs, would be paid in Amsterdam, Hamburg and Paris in four equal instalments. Despite urgings by the French Foreign Minister, Talleyrand, who was commercially concerned, the projected transaction did not take place. At the last moment Godoy refused to give his consent, partly from unwillingness to pay the subsidy and partly from fear of unfavourable reactions from England.[4]

Early in March 1805 Labouchère received, via Baguenault, a letter from Count de Cabarrus, on whose initiative the Bank of San Carlos had come into being. At the time of the French Revolution he had fallen into disfavour on account of his enlightened views, but now he stood so high in the esteem of the Spanish Court, to which he acted as financial adviser, that he had been raised to the nobility. Labouchère's reply indicates that De Cabarrus had approached him on the subject of getting Mexican piastres to Spain, a transaction of a similar nature to that for which Ouvrard had obtained a monopoly.

Labouchère's reply was cautiously worded, but did not amount to a rejection of the plan. One must naturally be circumspect when putting proposals to one's English connexions, he wrote, but it was quite feasible for the shipments to be routed direct from North America to Amsterdam without by-passing London. Labouchère had sufficient confidence in Baring and his American associates to advance monies against the piastres when news reached him of the receipt by Baring of the funds.

In order to comprehend this somewhat obscure passage, we must bear in mind that a substantial part of the large British exports to the United States were paid for out of the proceeds of American exports to the Continent. There was thus a constant stream of monetary transactions between the principal import centres on the Continent and London, and this could be used for the payment for the piastres. Indeed, Baring & Co. were specialists in intermediacy.

Labouchère, however, was curious about the relationship between De Cabarrus's proposals and the arrangements existing between the Spanish Court and Ouvrard who, after all, had also received drafts on the Mexican Treasury. If such documents were to find their way into various hands, their value would depreciate. Labouchère knew that De Cabarrus had laid his plan before Hogguer, and he did not take very kindly to this: if De Cabarrus, like Ouvrard, knocked on all doors simultaneously, he might find that none was opened.[1]

When Labouchère spoke in such reserved terms about Ouvrard he had already been approached, via Desprez, concerning the great transaction. On 14th February 1805 he reported to Desprez that his company was greatly honoured by the offer, both as regards the piastres and also the licences to trade with Spanish America. Discretion on the part of Hope & Co. was guaranteed, but the lack of secrecy on the other side caused Labouchère to flinch. In some ways there was nothing novel about the operation, for Spain had since 1797 made repeated efforts to arrive at transactions of this nature. The publicity which had surrounded all these plans had made Hope extremely reserved towards them. Even on the highly attractive conditions announced by the Spanish Court in 1800 and

1801, the Company had never dared to offer more than 50% of the value of the piastres for spot purchase. Ultimately a fairly sizeable operation was mounted, but the peace preliminaries of 1801 had thrown a spanner in the works.

The Company was thus well informed concerning the sort of transactions about which Desprez had written, and was willing to accept the offer if agreement could be reached. The advances which Desprez had requested were out of the question, if only because of the attendant publicity, but Labouchère was agreeable to providing one million francs at 6% interest upon the transfer of the drafts on Mexico. Secrecy was of the utmost importance and therefore Labouchère was not disposed to commit details of the affair to paper. He insisted that trusted agents should assemble the funds on the spot and transmit them. If Hope & Co., who were at that moment fully occupied with the payments relating to the Louisiana loan, assumed an active role in the affair a month later, the drafts could be presented in Mexico in four or five months time.

Once the wheels were in motion, the tempo could be adjusted to suit the requirements. Labouchère proceeded on the basis that 'our friends in America' could be in receipt of the first consignment of piastres during the month of September 1805 and that Desprez could count upon remittances from Hope & Co. commencing in October or November. For the completion of the French aspect of the affair, Desprez would have to deal with Baguenault, with whom Labouchère was wont to transact all delicate business in Paris.

If the affair could be kept completely 'American,' the cause of secrecy would be served and the costs reduced. The piastres were the focal point of the transaction, and the use of the import and export licences would have to be made subservient to these. Labouchère feared that excessive sailings to Mexico might attract English cruisers; he therefore proposed that the port of Vera Cruz be temporarily closed to all vessels save those engaged in transporting the piastres.

It is interesting to see how, in this letter to Desprez, the principles for the operation were in fact laid down in the absence of any further contact with Ouvrard. The assertion in Ouvrard's memoirs, that Messrs.Hope almost fell from their chairs when, early in April 1805, he broached the matter to them in Amsterdam, is thus fallacious.[1]

After a month of negotiation the parties reached agreement, and on 6th May 1805 the contract between Hope & Co. and François Ouvrard & Co. was drawn up. The signatory on behalf of Ouvrard & Co. was François Ouvrard, the nominal head of the firm and, in this instance, a figurehead acting on behalf of his brother. Ouvrard had initially proposed that Hope should become a party to his contract with the Spanish Court, but Labouchère declined the opportunity. Hope & Co. thus functioned purely as commission agents, in which role they formally undertook to comply with the instructions contained in the contract. Those instructions, however, were fully in accordance with the draft laid before Desprez by Labouchère in February.

The agreement stipulated that Hope should appoint a general agent in the United States, whose task would be to direct cargoes from Europe to the United States, and from there to the Spanish colonies. The agent would also be responsible for shipments from the colonies to the United States or direct to Europe. In order to carry out these operations, the general agent was permitted to appoint special agents in the various Spanish colonies, insofar as the transactions made this necessary. He was also given discretion to enlist the aid of merchant houses in the United States for the operation. The appointment of merchant houses in the Spanish colonies, however, remained the prerogative of François Ouvrard & Co.

Hope & Co. also undertook to try to obtain guarantees of safe passage from the English government, but with the proviso that their efforts should be circumspect so that in the event of refusal the other operations would not be jeopardized. The maximum sum payable for a safe passage was 4% of the value of the cargo.[1]

A supplementary agreement, in which the commissions to be paid to Hope were stipulated, was signed in September 1805. On their own shipments to Spanish America the Company would receive a commission of 2%, and on shipments for third parties, in either European or American waters, 1%. Return cargoes from America and consigned to Hope would also carry a commission of 2%, and those bound for other European ports 1%. One-half per cent commission would be payable on all insurance. Hope & Co. would be required to pay the general agent's commission out of their remuneration.[2]

The commission on the piastres shipped was remarkably low, a mere ½%. Against this, however, the Company was free to export any desired portion of the piastres for its own account at the price which the piastres would have yielded had they been exported directly for the account of Ouvrard & Co., and also to deduct from this price the costs incurred.[3]

In practice, since François Ouvrard & Co. were unable to export the piastres themselves, this meant that Hope & Co. could do with them as they wished. The price which the Company would be required to pay for the piastres was not stipulated in the contract, but it was agreed between

Labouchère and Ouvrard that this would be 3 francs and 75 centimes for each piastre.[1] On the basis of a nominal rate of exchange of 50 *stuivers* for the piastre, and with the franc standing at just over 9½ *stuivers*, Hope & Co. would thus have made a gross profit of 14 *stuivers* on each piastre.

It was not in Ouvrard's nature to leave this profit entirely to Hope. In addition to the two agreements between the Company and François Ouvrard & Co., a third was concluded which provided that the stipulations relating to the piastres 'rest jointly between Messrs.Hope & Co. and M.Auguste Ouvrard.' Hope & Co. undertook to open an account into which all profits accruing from the aforementioned stipulations would be paid. The balance of this account was to be shared equally between the Company and Auguste Ouvrard. Although somewhat obscure, the wording reveals clearly that Ouvrard, via another brother, obtained his share of the profit made from the piastres.[2]

Before leaving for Paris two days after the signing of this agreement, Ouvrard handed Labouchère drafts on the Mexican Treasury to a value of nearly two million piastres. Hope also received fifty licences for a similar number of expeditions to the Spanish colonies.[3]

Ouvrard took the view, as did Labouchère, that this was but the beginning of a transaction which, if all went well, could be enlarged to any desired scale. An efficient and reliable network of agents was indispensable, and every attention should be paid to achieving this.

A second and no less important aim was the removal of political obstacles, and for this it was necessary to bring Hope's closest business associates, Francis Baring & Co., into the affair.

CHAPTER TEN

THE FRANCO-SPANISH FINANCIAL CRISIS

On 10th May 1805, just two days after Ouvrard had left Amsterdam, Labouchère wrote to Sir Francis Baring concerning the Spanish American operation. It was of the utmost importance that neutral vessels should be adequately protected against arrest by English cruisers, and subsequent confiscation, when carrying piastres and colonial produce from Spanish America to England or an English colony, and on the return voyage British produce.

Baring was requested to lay strong emphasis on the latter operation in his approach to his government. He was to play an important role in the export of produce from England and the import of colonial produce and piastres. The British government, wrote Labouchère, must be interested in thus obtaining the piastres, of which the country was in constant need, and at the same time recovering part of the trade which North America had virtually monopolized in recent years.

Labouchère also pointed out with urgency that the Americans must not be hampered in their trade with Spanish America, in order to avoid 'remarks and jealousy' from a certain quarter, which could bring about the failure of the entire operation. Whether or not he had Napoleon in mind when referring to the 'remarks' is not of major importance; what is important is that he was anxious to keep open a route via the United States in addition to one via England.[1]

Sir Francis Baring did not reply to the letter immediately, so that Labouchère was able to devote all his attention to the establishment of the agency network in North America. First and foremost, the right persons had to be found. The man considered by Labouchère for the post of general agent, David Parish, had been approached at the time of the negotiations with Ouvrard, and agreements had been made with him.[2]

Parish was a younger son of a Scottish merchant, John Parish, who had accumulated a large fortune in Hamburg. David Parish had established his own company in Antwerp following the Treaty of Amiens. A timely piece of advice from Talleyrand, with whom he was on good terms, had enabled him to make a considerable profit from speculation in colonial produce at the time of the renewed hostilities against England. As the war continued, however, business in Antwerp became less and less interesting for him. Labouchère's offer opened up all manner of new prospects in a completely new area. The financial aspects of the deal were also an attraction: 25% of the profit on all transactions which he was instructed by Hope & Co. to supervise. A separate account was to be maintained, showing the profit shares accruing to Hope and to Parish, which would be paid to them out of the account held jointly with Auguste Ouvrard – who quickly appeared as Auguste Ouvrard & Co. in Hope's books.[1] In addition, Parish would be reimbursed for all travelling and hotel expenses incurred by him, and he was permitted to do business for his own account. Labouchère was evidently very keen to recruit this enterprising and astute young man, who was renowned for his engaging manner and his psychological insight, for the new operation.[2]

Labouchère's choice for the agency at Vera Cruz fell on Armand Pierre Lestapis, a native of Béarn in Southern France, who was employed as Spanish correspondent at the office in Amsterdam. He had earlier worked for the house of Juan Planté in Santander. Upon the death of another employee of the house, José Gabriel de Villanueva, his birth certificate fell into the hands of Lestapis. Fearing that the Mexican authorities might raise objections to the arrival of a foreigner, Labouchère persuaded Lestapis to assume the identity of De Villanueva for the journey to Vera Cruz. It was in this name that the application for his passport was made to Madrid.[3]

A third agent was to be stationed at New Orleans. For this post, Labouchère's eye fell on Vincent Nolte, who was employed in his younger brother's merchant house in Nantes, and whose excellent style of correspondence had attracted Labouchère's attention. Nolte had little to do in Nantes and was keen to travel to America. On 13th May, a week after the signing of the contract with Ouvrard, he set out for Amsterdam to collect his instructions.[4]

Early in July 1805 Nolte sailed from Amsterdam in the 'Flora,' bound for New York. Parish had matters to attend to for his firm in Antwerp, after which he journeyed to Paris for discussions with Ouvrard. Lestapis was detained in Amsterdam, problems having arisen concerning his passport for Mexico.[5]

In their role of commission agents for François Ouvrard & Co., Hope ordered a consignment of Silesian linen from their correspondent in Hamburg, Matthiesen & Sillem. Ouvrard was not favourably impressed by the initiative and urged the necessity for caution in view of the probability that the consignment would be delayed by the developing naval war.[1] In April 1805, the French squadron from Toulon had succeeded in eluding Nelson and, together with Spanish naval units, had made for Martinique in the West Indies. The plan was that they should wait there until the squadron from Brest joined them, and thus lure Nelson's ships to the West Indies. If this ruse succeeded, the Franco-Spanish fleet would return with all speed to the Channel to pave the way for the French invasion army to cross to England. Ouvrard's anxiety concerning the situation in the Caribbean was certainly well founded, but there was the additional factor that 'engagements réels' were extremely inconvenient to him because the French and Spanish finances absorbed all his funds.[2]

Besides the preparations for the great American operation, there was the 10-million guilder loan to Spain to consider. Ouvrard had undertaken to float this on behalf of the Spanish Court, but he had failed to reach agreement on this during his meetings with the partners of Hope & Co. in April 1805. In July, Walter Boyd, acting on Ouvrard's instructions, again raised the matter with the Company in a letter sent from Paris.

The warrant or 'cedula' issued by the King of Spain entrusted the negotiation of the loan to the house of Vanlerberghe and Ouvrard. Ouvrard wished the last line of the document to be left blank so that the name of Hope & Co. could be inserted, but the Spanish government was unwilling to accede to the request, probably to avoid offending De Smeth and Hogguer, with whom negotiations had been in progress for longer. Ouvrard had thus been compelled to offer the loan to these houses, but by imposing very severe conditions he had obliged them to decline the business.[3]

Labouchère objected to the appearance of the names of Vanlerberghe and Ouvrard in the warrant on the grounds that this would deter investors, who would find themselves bound up with the common interests of France and Spain. Also, he regarded the issue price of 95% proposed by Boyd as too high; this, he felt, should not be more than 92%. Furthermore, he desired a purely formal relationship with the Spanish government: the Spanish Court must issue an instruction for the proceeds of the loan to be paid to Vanlerberghe and Ouvrard, whose receipt must be recognized by the *Caja de Consolidacion* as official payment. Also, Vanlerberghe and Ouvrard must be the effective owner of the constituent bonds, which Hope & Co., for a commission of 7%, would dispose of. The drafts on Mexico, which totalled nearly 8½ million piastres, should not remain under the control of the *Caja*, he maintained, but should be deposited with a notary in Amsterdam (as had been done in the case of the Croese conversion loans).[4]

The error of allowing the names of Vanlerberghe and Ouvrard to appear on the warrant came home to Boyd, but to the intense annoyance of Labouchère he reacted by writing to Ouvrard in Madrid, requesting a new warrant in which, in addition to Hope & Co., the house of Van der Hoeven & Co. of Amsterdam was mentioned. Labouchère tartly informed Boyd that even though Van der Hoeven might have connexions with Vanlerberghe, their participation would constitute a ground for Hope abandoning the loan. Even after a conversation during which Van der Hoeven expressed his deep disappointment at Labouchère's views, there was no other course open to Boyd than to write to Ouvrard again, this time to request a warrant in the form desired by Labouchère.[1]

Within the context of the new loan, Labouchère raised the matter of the Echenique loans. Strictly speaking, these were perhaps not a matter for the Spanish Court; nevertheless, the king had entered into a lasting guarantee in respect of them. Labouchère's aim was that Ouvrard should persuade the Spanish government to convert the Echenique bonds still in circulation into new 5% bonds and to redeem these on a date ten years after the signing of a peace treaty between Spain and England. The conversion operation could best be undertaken by Echenique and would, moreover, yield a commission of 2% for that house. It might also be possible to obtain drafts on Mexico to serve as security for the new bonds. But this well-meant plan in the interest of the Echenique loans fell on deaf ears in Madrid.[2]

Boyd having had the warrant amended to conform with Labouchère's various wishes, the final text was agreed at the end of September, after which the document was sent from Madrid to Amsterdam. The commencement date for the loan, as prescribed in the principal debenture, was 1st July 1805. The rate of interest was 5½% and repayment of the principal money, plus a premium of 5%, was to be effected over a period of ten years, i.e. the duration of the loan. Security was provided in the form of ten drafts on the Royal Treasury in Mexico, totalling 8,484,375 piastres. The maturing dates of these were so arranged that in the event of non-payment by the Spanish government, the relevant sums could be in the possession of Hope & Co. before 1st July of the year concerned.[3]

The Company received a commission of 5% on the sum of the loan. The official letter from the finance minister referred to 7%, but we may assume that the difference of 2% accrued to Ouvrard. One-half per cent commission was payable on sums of interest, and 1% on principal repayments. The price at which the issue was to be taken over was fixed at 92½%, it being stipulated that the bonds should not be offered to the public at less than 95%.[4]

REAL CEDULA

DE S. M.

Y SEÑORES DEL CONSEJO,

ACEPTANDO LA PROPOSICION HECHA por la Casa de Hope y Compañía, del Comercio de Amsterdam, de poner en la Caxa de Consolidacion de Vales la cantidad de diez millones de florines corrientes de Holanda en calidad de préstamo, baxo las condiciones que se expresan.

AÑO  1805.

MADRID EN LA IMPRENTA REAL.

Real Cedula issued by the Spanish king and relating to the 10-million guilder loan of 1805

While all this was going on, Ouvrard's *Compagnie*, still without the piastres from Mexico, had got into such serious financial difficulties that on 1st October 1805 Boyd humbly approached Hope & Co. with a request that the promised advance of one million guilders be transferred even before the arrival in Amsterdam of the royal warrant.[1] Labouchère replied that the Company could not advance any monies until such time as complete agreement had been reached with the Spanish government. The loan could not be opened until 1st November at the earliest, for on that date Croese was due to pay about a million guilders in capital and interest on the loan provided by Hope in 1793, and it was generally assumed that the greater portion of this sum was being reinvested. Croese had made payments of capital and interest on the three conversion loans on 1st September 1805, but the new loan had not then been finalized and so the opportunity to channel the liquid resources thus released in the direction of the new loan had been missed.[2]

Croese had received drafts on Paris houses early in October, but let it be known that he would not pay the sum due on 1st November unless these were negotiated before that date. There was every reason for this reticence: the *Caja de Consolidacion* was sinking deeper into the financial quagmire, and the situation in Paris gave grounds for anxiety. Labouchère therefore offered to take over the drafts from Croese and provide him with funds to meet his commitment on 1st November. Vanlerberghe and Ouvrard concurred in the proposal and gave permission for Hope & Co. to deduct the sum of the drafts from the proceeds of the loan operation. Labouchère, however, was unwilling to take any risks and he sent the drafts to Baguenault & Co. with instructions not to release them until debentures to an equal value were received from the *Receveurs Généraux* as security. After an agitated exchange of correspondence and the application of the necessary pressure on Croese, the matter was settled at the eleventh hour.[3]

Diplomatic pressure from Paris and a number of hurried visits to The Hague finally combined to secure the approval of the Batavian government for the loan and its opening on the scheduled date, 1st November. During an audience with the *Raadpensionaris*, Schimmelpenninck, it became apparent to Labouchère that the rate of stamp duty on the loan had been increased from $\frac{1}{4}$% to 1%. Schimmelpenninck had informed Ouvrard of this in April, but, to Labouchère's annoyance, the information had not been passed on. In the event, however, Vanlerberghe and Ouvrard agreed to pay the excess.[4]

The pressure exerted from Paris on the Batavian government to sanction the Spanish loan was a by-product of the continuing deterioration of France's financial position. Immediately after the signing of the agreement with the Company in May 1805, Ouvrard had paid another visit to Spain to arrange matters there. The success of the various agreements depended upon the early arrival of piastres from Mexico. Ouvrard's efforts, through the intermediary of the British consul in Madrid, to reach an accord with Pitt in this matter failed, however, and because of this Ouvrard's financial edifice commenced to rock on its foundations.[1]

By the end of June 1805, payments to army and naval contractors had so sapped the liquid reserves of the *Banque de France* that Barbé Marbois was obliged to appeal urgently to the Spanish government for a payment of three million piastres. The money, however, was slow to arrive, with the result that the *Banque's* reserves continued to fall. At the end of September a mere 1,200,000 francs remained.[2]

The exporting of the piastres brought pressure upon the *Caja de Consolidacion* and thus upon the price of the *vales reales*, for the redemption of which it had, of course, been established. When the value of the *vales* began to fall sharply, the Spanish government resorted, as it had done in 1799, to the imposition of an artificial rate. The result was similar: specie disappeared and the *vales* fell to 58% below par.

The depreciation of the *vales* placed the Spanish government's creditors in a very difficult position. This was particularly true of Ouvrard, who faced the prospect of being paid for his purchases of corn and his deliveries to the fleet and the army in a heavily devalued form of tender. To keep his head above water, Ouvrard was forced to bolster up the price of the *vales*, and the only means of achieving this was to suspend the export of piastres.[3]

Deprived of its lifeline, the *Banque de France* sank deeper into the mire; its plight was not lessened by the ever-increasing demands made by the *Compagnie des Négociants Réunis* in an effort to meet the needs of the army. Late in September 1805 Napoleon had embarked on his campaign against the Austrians and the Russians, and this taxed the *Banque* and the military contractors to the limit. Napoleon was aware of the country's financial distress, but in his view a major military victory offered the only solution. As he said to Mollien, the director of the Sinking Fund: 'The financial position is serious, the bank is meeting with difficulties; my task of putting these things in order does not lie here.'[4]

Desprez had meanwhile got into such a predicament that he resorted to the direct collection of monies received by the *Receveurs Généraux*. He had earlier discounted the corresponding debentures from the *Receveurs* with the *Banque de France*, which was thus obliged to meet the cost of redemption in full on the due dates. Increasing the quantity of banknotes in circulation afforded but a temporary alleviation and fanned the growing embers of mistrust. More and more people began to exchange their banknotes for coin and when, at the beginning of November, it became known that the *Compagnie* was in difficulties, a veritable run on the *Banque de France* ensued. Simultaneously Vanlerberghe, acting on behalf of the *Compagnie*, disclosed that there was a deficit of 70 million francs, of which 26 million were owed to the Treasury. The principal cause of the crash lay in Spain's failure to honour its commitments.[1]

In view of the fact that Napoleon's campaign against the Austrians was in full swing, Barbé Marbois continued to support the *Compagnie*, even though the Treasury was in very great straits. On 27th October 1805 he advised Hope & Co. that the Spanish loan–the documents pertaining to which, he stated, were being despatched–had been transferred from Vanlerberghe & Ouvrard to Desprez. Marbois had concerned himself with the matter because the proceeds of the loan, 'en dernière analyse' would accrue to the Treasury. Desprez wrote to Hope on the same day, urgently requesting an advance; but Labouchère would go no further than to remit the drafts from Croese. The emperor had admittedly forced an Austrian army to capitulate at Ulm, but that did not signify the end of the war, and the financial situation continued to be critical.[2]

On 5th November, Barbé Marbois urgently requested that one of the partners of Hope & Co. should visit Paris. Labouchère arrived there on the nineteenth to find a large company assembled; Ouvrard, however, was not present.

With his customary optimism, Labouchère wrote that the situation in Paris was not as serious as the stories which had been circulating had suggested, and that means would be found to overcome the problems expected in the month of December.[3] This did not mean that there were then no difficulties in Paris. Prior to his departure for Spain, Ouvrard had laid the foundations for a large-scale exchange operation or *circulation* between Desprez, the capitals of all the French *départements* and the houses of Doyen, Récamier, Fulchiron and Thornton Power. The basis for the *circulation* was formed by debentures to a value of 12,000,000 francs issued by the *Receveurs Généraux*; these had been discounted by the *Banque de France* and Ouvrard had committed himself to replace them with piastres from Spain in September 1805.

Owing to the catastrophic consequences of the enforced rate for the *vales*, Ouvrard, as we have seen, was unable to honour his promise, with the result that the *circulation* collapsed and Récamier and Fulchiron were forced to suspend their payments.[1]

Even more disturbing were the consequences of the exchange operations set in train by the *Caja de Consolidacion* with the houses of Hervas and Bastide in Paris, Croese in Amsterdam and Meyer Michel David and Van Heyningen & Co. in Hamburg. The *Caja* had furnished drafts on Mexico to a value of two million piastres as security, but when Ouvrard failed to produce funds and the rate for the *vales* collapsed, the Mexican drafts became temporarily worthless.

Logically, in view of all these distressing events, the meeting attended by Labouchère in Paris sent a report by express messenger to Ouvrard in Madrid, and with it a request that he return as soon as possible. He did not, however, arrive until 6th December and even then was unable to offer any comfort. He had the greatest difficulty in keeping his feet and did not think twice about sacrificing the interests of others to save himself.[2] One after the other, those who had participated in the *circulation* by the *Caja* were ruined; first Hervas and Bastide, then Croese and finally David and Van Heyningen in Hamburg. Hervas, who for a time had served as the French Chargé d'Affaires in Spain and, at the request of Napoleon, had been given the title of Marquis d'Almenara, sought a way out of his difficulties by accepting the post of Spanish envoy in Constantinople.[3]

No such opportunity, however, existed for Croese and he was forced to apply to the *Schepenen* of the City of Amsterdam for a twelve-month moratorium. As receivers they appointed Paul Iwan Hogguer, Joan Hodshon and Pierre César Labouchère. The last-named was not particularly keen to undertake the task, but he saw only too well that he could not decline in view of the house's deep involvement with Hope's Spanish interests. Moreover, Hope & Co. were in a better position than any other house to defend Croese's interests before the *Caja de Consolidacion* by reason of the substantial securities which they held.[4] In addition to the business with Spanish America and the loan of 10 million guilders, the Company could also bring into the discussion the 2,590 bales of Spanish wool which Hope and Baguenault jointly had received from Ouvrard for sale on commission. There was also the matter of 2,465 bales of Spanish wool which Ouvrard had had shipped direct to Ball Davis & Vaughan in Bristol, to which, if need be, a claim could be laid via Baring.[5]

With the collapse of his edifices of credit, Ouvrard's position and that of his *Compagnie* began to crumble. To start with, Ouvrard was confronted with the resignation of Desprez, whose role as co-ordinator at the Treasury was transferred to a syndicate of the *Receveurs Généraux*. Next, Barbé Marbois demanded a statement of Ouvrard's account with the Treasury. Payment of his claims against the Ministry of War and the Admiralty was postponed until the account with the Treasury had been examined. Lastly, Ouvrard was obliged to subordinate his claims on Spain and other countries to settling his affairs with the French Treasury – a task which could not be completed before the emperor had returned. Thus, by the time Napoleon arrived in Paris, the activities of the *Compagnie* had largely ceased and the day of reckoning for Ouvrard had dawned.[1]

Labouchère's own dealings with Ouvrard, after the latter's return to Paris, were partially successful. To his great annoyance, Labouchère could make no headway in matters of benefit to Croese, because Ouvrard rejected every compromise. In a letter to Baring, Labouchère wrote of Ouvrard: 'There is in the man's disposition a spirit of distrust and avarice which cannot easily be conceived.' In Labouchère's view, Ouvrard was damaging his own plans by his short-sighted self-interest just when these were about to bear fruit. This was the only occasion on which Labouchère voiced explicit criticism of Ouvrard.[2]

In the matter of the piastre transaction, Labouchère made slightly more progress, though no settlement was reached. On 12th December 1805 a provisional agreement was reached between the two, after which Labouchère offered to take over drafts for between 10 and 15 million piastres at a rate of exchange of 3 francs and 75 centimes. Ouvrard, whose position in France and Spain had been undermined by events, was hesitant about entering into a definitive agreement, and he wrote to Madrid requesting approval. In anticipation of this, Labouchère took back to Amsterdam drafts worth 6½ million piastres. At the end of January 1806, Labouchère made a further attempt to finalize matters, but by that time Ouvrard had other things on his mind.[3]

Napoleon returned to Paris on 26th January. On the very next day he summoned his ministers and demanded from them an explanation for the financial crisis. Mollien, of whom Napoleon was very fond, was invited to be present. Barbé Marbois launched into a lengthy speech about the state of the national finances, but was interrupted by the emperor, who concluded that the *Compagnie*, by means of the resources of the Treasury and the *Banque de France*, had succeeded in meeting the needs of both France and Spain. Since Spain had only been able to promise piastres, France had ultimately paid a subsidy to Spain, instead of the other way round. Napoleon thereupon insisted that Ouvrard, Desprez and Vanlerberghe should be stripped of their possessions, which were to be given to the Treasury, and that Spain should honour its commitments. Marbois was accused of allowing himself to be taken in by the *Compagnie* and of giving Desprez a free hand with Treasury funds. The emperor then relieved him of his office.

After this ominous beginning, Ouvrard, Vanlerberghe and Desprez were summoned and treated to one of Napoleon's notorious verbal broadsides. In the face of threats of imprisonment, and even execution before a firing squad, Vanlerberghe and Desprez burst into tears; but Ouvrard remained absolutely calm.

When the emperor's fury was spent, Ouvrard attempted to convince him that he, Ouvrard, was the best person to carry the complex financial operations, which were conducted via Holland, England and the United States, to a successful conclusion. But such were Napoleon's sense of irritation and his abhorrence of military contractors that he peremptorily gave Ouvrard and his friends the choice between criminal prosecution and the surrender of all their possessions. All three chose the latter. This sweeping reconstruction of France's upper financial echelon was completed by the appointment of Mollien to the post of Minister of the Treasury.[1]

In a decree dated 8th February 1806, it was stated that Ouvrard, Desprez, Vanlerberghe and Michel the Elder together owed the Treasury 87 million francs. As the first instalment of their debt, they were to hand over to the Treasury the proceeds of the Spanish loan negotiated through Hope & Co., drafts on Mexico to a value of 9,802,000 piastres and others to a value of 32½ million francs issued by the *Caja de Consolidacion*. The wool which Ouvrard had shipped to Hope and Baguenault for sale on commission was also declared the property of the French Treasury. Supplies for the army and navy were subjected to a discount of 50%, with a maximum of 18 million francs.[2]

The drafts on Mexico, to a value of 6½ million piastres, which Ouvrard had given to Labouchère during their meeting, but for which no approval had been forthcoming from Spain, were also among the assets confiscated. Mollien instructed Hope & Co. to surrender these to one of his officials, Daumont, who journeyed to Amsterdam in order to receive them. The partners, however, refused to part with the drafts without Ouvrard's permission. Only when he arrived in Amsterdam were the drafts handed to Daumont. The drafts for 5 million piastres which had already been sent to David Parish for collection escaped Mollien's grasp.[3]

Hope & Co. expressed to Mollien their willingness to exchange their draft agreement with Ouvrard of 12th December 1805 for one in the same form with the French Treasury. As regards the drafts which had already been despatched, Hope was prepared to settle with the minister, via Baguenault, when remittances were received. David Parish was instructed not to enter into any fresh transactions until further notice.[1]

Labouchère took advantage of Ouvrard's presence in Amsterdam to settle other matters such as the placing of the balance of the 10-million guilder loan. Dealings with the *entrepreneurs* had commenced in November 1805 at a price of 92½%, but the Franco-Spanish financial crisis and the ensuing bankruptcies had gradually forced the rate down. Hope wished to reserve the right to dispose of the remaining 4,800 bonds at 90%. It was agreed that Ouvrard & Co. would guarantee the interest and principal due on 1st July 1806.[2]

Ouvrard returned to Paris at the end of February 1806. It soon became clear that the power of decision no longer rested with him. Mollien insisted on a price of 3 francs 75 centimes for the piastre with a monthly payment of 1 million francs, commencing on 1st March 1806. The price for the piastres was acceptable to Labouchère, but he was strongly opposed to the idea of fixed instalments, because it was impossible to predict whether the proceeds of the sale of the piastres would arrive with the desired regularity. Mollien yielded to Labouchère's objections in respect of the bills which had already been despatched, but as far as the available ones were concerned he stood firm on minor points, with the result that the negotiations became deadlocked.[3]

For Ouvrard, the heavens grew darker and darker. Mollien had ordered a further investigation of the Treasury's books, which were anything but easy to interpret, and this revealed that the *Compagnie* had debts totalling not 87 million francs, but something approaching 142 million. Its assets amounted to 80 million francs or thereabouts, so that the true deficit was of the order of 60 million. Security for this deficit comprised drafts on Spanish America to a value of nearly 20 million piastres and others worth 32½ million francs issued by the *Caja de Consolidacion.* A substantial portion of the latter drafts had been given by Ouvrard to French houses as security for credits granted to Spain. For example, Michel the Younger held drafts to a value of nearly 11½ million francs, and Armand Séguin held others worth something like 7 million.

Spain, however, had given Ouvrard drafts totalling considerably more than it had received in money and goods. This is understandable because the proceeds of the drafts on Spanish America had still to be received. Now, all the drafts which Ouvrard had held had been transferred to the

French Treasury, and it would be most unfair to make Spain responsible for the payment in full of these.[1]

The man appointed to negotiate on behalf of Spain was Don Eugenio Izquierdo, Godoy's personal agent, who, over the heads of his country's official diplomatic representatives, liaised with the French authorities. Since 1797 Izquierdo had undertaken numerous secret diplomatic missions to France on behalf of Godoy. In 1806 Godoy set out to obtain Napoleon's agreement to a partition of Portugal, whereby he, Godoy, would acquire a kingdom of his own. With this great prize in view, he was prepared to go to any lengths to meet Napoleon's financial demands. An obstacle to an early settlement was the inability of the *Caja de Consolidacion* to honour the drafts drawn on it. Efforts by Izquierdo, with the assistance of Talleyrand's confidential representative, Michel Simons, to negotiate a loan of 30 million guilders with De Smeth in order to provide the *Caja* with much-needed funds, produced no immediate result.[2]

On 10th May 1806, Mollien and Izquierdo finally agreed that the onus which could reasonably be imposed on Spain was limited to the actual deficit of the *Compagnie*, i.e. 60 million francs. This sum was to be paid by means of drafts on Spanish America totalling 10 million piastres, for which a rate of exchange of 3 francs 75 centimes was agreed, and others to a value of 24 million francs drawn on Espinosa. As France already held drafts on Spanish America totalling 20 million piastres and others on Espinosa to a value of 32½ million francs, the balance of 10 million piastres and 8½ million francs, was given back to Spain. It was agreed that the drafts on Espinosa would be met in cash at the rate of 3 million francs per month, commencing on 31st May 1806, and that the governors of the colonies in Spanish America were to be instructed to permit the French Treasury or its agents to freely export the 10 million piastres accruing to it.[3]

In addition to this official agreement with the French Treasury–indeed on the same day–Izquierdo reached a compromise with the *Compagnie*. This concerned the difference between the deficit of 60 million francs which Spain was committed to pay to France and the 34 million francs which the *Compagnie* had actually advanced to Spain. Under pressure from Mollien, Ouvrard and his partners in the consortium undertook to return all drafts from the *Caja* which were in their possession, since these would no longer be honoured by the *Caja*, and also to persuade other holders, such as Michel the Younger and Séguin, to do the same. It was left to the *Compagnie* to settle with them.

The *Compagnie* also undertook to pay the Spanish Treasury a sum of

12 million francs; this would comprise 4 million from the balance of the proceeds of Hope & Co's loan of 10 million guilders, 3 million from the proceeds of the wool shipped to Hope and Baguenault, and 5 million in the form of drafts bearing the joint signatures of the members of the consortium.

The agreements reached on 10th May had far-reaching consequences for Hope & Co. With the protesting of their drafts by the *Caja*, Séguin and Michel the Younger, sensing impending trouble, had taken timely steps to secure the judicial attachment of those assets of Vanlerberghe & Ouvrard which were held by Hope & Co. Fulchiron, another victim of the failure of the *Compagnie*, followed their example.[1]

On the day of the agreement with Izquierdo, Desprez advised Hope & Co. that as far as the loan of 10 million guilders and the consignment of wool were concerned, Izquierdo's instructions must henceforth be obeyed. Having divested themselves of the responsibility for these matters, Vanlerberghe & Ouvrard considered themselves absolved from guaranteeing the payment of interest and principal on the approaching 1st July.[2]

The latter announcement was particularly displeasing to Hope & Co. because they were then on the point of entering into a contract with Willem Borski for the remaining 3,900 bonds at the attractive price of 92%. The terms of the agreement, however, gave the *entrepreneurs* the option of paying with interest vouchers and bonds which became due on 1st July 1806. The news of the withdrawal of Ouvrard's guarantee caused Borski to suspend the negotiations, but a week later he made a fresh offer. In this, he not only reserved the right to effect payment by means of the interest vouchers and bonds which became due on 1st July, but also partly with interest vouchers relating to the Echenique loans, the payment of which had to be advertised by 23rd June 1806 at the latest. It is probably safe to assume that this condition in fact emanated from Labouchère and that its purpose was to remind the Spanish government of its financial commitments.[3]

At the end of May 1806, Hope received a visit from Michel Simons, Talleyrand's confidential agent, who, as we have seen, was busy trying to negotiate a loan of 30 million guilders with De Smeth. As the authorized representative of Izquierdo, he sought control of the Ouvrard assets held by the Company. Labouchère made it plain to him that the Company's hands were tied until such time as the writs of attachment secured by Michel the Younger, Séguin and Fulchiron were withdrawn. Labouchère was quite prepared to allow Simons to take over all the Vanlerberghe & Ouvrard assets held by Hope & Co. on condition that he also accepted responsibility for the claims which attached to them. That, however, was not what Simons had come for: his orders were to obtain money –if possible, 4 million francs from Hope's Spanish loan and a further 3 million from the consignment of wool.

After much discussion, Labouchère consented to advance the 4 million francs from the loan on condition that the interest vouchers and bonds falling due on 1st July and also the vouchers relating to interest on the Echenique loans, which had become due on 1st May but had not been paid, were accepted as part of the sum. In view of the slow progress made with the sale of the wool, Labouchère was willing to advance only 1 million francs on this, and then only after he had obtained the consent of his partner in the consortium, Baguenault.[1] Moreover, his offer was subject to the lifting of the attachment. There was little prospect of this, for Michel the Younger, who had also travelled to Amsterdam, announced that he would make efforts in Madrid to realize his claims and that pending the outcome the garnishment would continue.[2]

The emergence of other figures and the gradual eclipse of Ouvrard constitutes a suitable point at which temporarily to draw a veil over the events on the Continent. Looking back on these, it is clear that the collaboration with Ouvrard produced results quite different from those which the partners in Hope & Co. had envisaged. Thanks to a cautious policy born of sagacity, however, the Company emerged unscathed from the financial crisis of 1805–1806. By insisting on security for all credits, it avoided the fate which befell Récamier, Hervas and Fulchiron. It recognized the dangers attaching to Ouvrard's flimsy financial schemes in good time, and took care not to become too deeply involved in these. Furthermore, the Company remained true to the principle that a country cannot undertake new loans until clear arrangements have been made to repay previous ones.

The operation had got off to a good start, but the financial crises in Spain and France, followed by Napoleon's drastic intervention, had caused the flow of drafts to cease abruptly. By then, however, drafts to a value of 5 million piastres had been sent to Parish and could not be recovered. Under the agreement of 10th May 1806, the Company could at most anticipate drafts for a further 5 million piastres from France. The transfer of these by the French Treasury took much longer than was anticipated. The reason for this will emerge in a subsequent chapter, when we come to deal with the events in England and America.

CHAPTER ELEVEN

ACCOUNT 'X'

At about the moment when Napoleon was putting an end to Ouvrard's plans, the network established in America to carry out those plans commenced to operate. Vincent Nolte had arrived in New York in September 1805, to be followed shortly afterwards by Lestapis. They waited there for David Parish, who arrived early in 1806. Rumours of the transaction had preceded him and this fact made his task decidedly more difficult.[1]

Shortly after he set foot on American soil, Parish received a request from Baring & Co. to hold back the Mexican drafts. There were good prospects for an agreement with the British government, and this would pave the way for the direct shipment of the piastres from Vera Cruz to London. Parish, who had had far-reaching discussions with Sir Francis Baring in London before setting off for America, was content to await further news. After all, Sir Francis was a director of the East India Company and had excellent connections in high government circles, while his son, Alexander, was a director of the Bank of England.[2] But when fresh instructions from Baring & Co. failed to materialize–for reasons which will become apparent–Parish, seeing the time passing, found himself in a quandary. Eventually Lestapis, carrying drafts for a million piastres, left for Vera Cruz with instructions to present them to the Mexican Treasury and to deposit the funds obtained with friendly houses in Vera Cruz for the time being. During his sojourn there, De Villanueva, as Lestapis thereafter became known, acted in conjunction with the houses of Pedro Miguel de Echeverria and Francisco Luis de Septien.

Parish also found it difficult to work with blank licences for trade with the Spanish colonies. During his stay in New York he had succeeded in disposing of three to Archibald Gracie, but the majority of merchants there were highly sceptical, demanding proof of Parish's monopoly of trade with Spanish America before committing themselves to an expedition. In mid-February, Parish decided to move his headquarters to Philadelphia in the hope of finding more takers.[3] But instead of fresh prospects, Parish found competitors there. As we have seen, the Spanish Court, in a flagrant breach of the monopoly granted to Ouvrard, had also given a number of favoured persons and senior civil servants the right to issue licences, and these were sold, via agents, to anyone who would buy them. Espinosa sent Francisco Sarmiento to the United States for this very purpose. Sarmiento was a brother-in-law of the Philadelphia merchant John Craig, who thus obtained six licences for trade with Vera Cruz. Another brother-in-law of Craig, the Baltimore merchant Robert Oliver, also became involved. Robert Oliver and his brother John headed one of the richest and most dependable merchant houses in that city. The Spanish envoy in Philadelphia, the Marquis de Yrujo, was aware of the affair and supported Craig and the Olivers.[1]

To Parish, this complication meant further delay in disposing of the licences which he held. His first act was to send a letter to Madrid, demanding in the strongest terms that the Minister of Finance, Soler, take the necessary action to maintain his monopoly. In the meantime he had to contend with a situation in which others had already prepared five expeditions to Vera Cruz and in which his efforts to obtain the support of the Spanish envoy were without avail.

Lengthy discussions with Craig and Robert Oliver finally led to an agreement in late March or early April 1806. This provided for Craig and the Olivers to take over the licences held by Parish, in consideration whereof they were to pay commissions of 2½%, based on the invoice value of the goods shipped, to Parish himself and 33⅓%, based on the nett proceeds, to his principals. Parish gave a guarantee against confiscation in Vera Cruz, but was not required to bear responsibility in respect of cargoes lost through shipwreck or piracy while bound for Vera Cruz.[2]

Import duties were levied both in the colonies and in Spain. In consultation with the Spanish envoy in Philadelphia, Craig and the Olivers consented to give Parish 20% of the invoice value; he would take steps to ensure that these monies were paid, via Hope & Co., to the *Caja de Consolidacion*. Parish was to receive a further 5% commission for these services.

The nett profit was deemed to be the sum remaining after the deduction of commissions, insurance, freight charges and dues payable in Vera Cruz. In addition to the commissions already referred to, 6¼% of the gross proceeds in Vera Cruz was due to Villanueva and the Spanish house which acted as intermediary for the sale.

The dues levied in Vera Cruz varied during the operation. Import duties ranged from 10% to 20% of the pro forma invoice value, and in one or two instances reached 30%. Other dues, which were sometimes levied and sometimes not, included a consular fee, which ranged from 1% to 5%; war tax, also between 1% and 5%; and an Admiralty tax, which varied

El Rey se ha servido conceder permiso á la Casa
de para que
desde el puerto de pueda despachar
con pabellon y con arreglo á la
Real Orden de 24 de Diciembre de 1804 l
nombrado

Dios guarde á V. muchos años.
á de de 180

Miguel Cayet.º Soler

Blank licence for trade with the Spanish colonies

between 5% and 7½%. The total percentage of dues gradually increased, from 11% in May 1806 to 33% in the second half of 1807, but this varied within such wide limits that no clear line is discernible.[1]

The insurance premium for the round voyage amounted to 12½% of the value of the cargo. To ensure that, in the event of the loss of a ship and its cargo, the insurance premium and the 7½% commission for Parish and Hope would be recovered, the Olivers inflated the estimated value of the cargo.[2]

From the archives of Robert and John Oliver, documents relating to 22 expeditions have survived, and these show the nett profit, of which one-third was due to Parish's principals. This amounted to approximately two-thirds of the difference between the nett value of the cargo when it left Baltimore and the nett proceeds of the sale in Vera Cruz. The remaining one-third represented freight charges, insurance and other costs incurred by the Olivers.[3]

Craig's death, in June 1807, opened the way for a new and very different agreement between the Olivers and Parish. Instead of one-third of the nett profit, Parish had to be content with 37½% of the nett value of the cargo in Baltimore; moreover, the 20% import duty and Parish's own commission were to be paid from this, leaving a mere 15% for other 'compensations.'

For Parish and his principals, the new situation was decidely less favourable than the old. In place of 20% import duty plus 2½% commission for Parish himself and 5% for Hope & Co., all calculated on the nett value of the cargo, plus 33⅓% of the nett profit, there now remained only a bare 15% of the nett value of the cargo. This arrangement, it appears, was applied to eight shipments.

The last two cargoes shipped by the Olivers under licences obtained from Parish were subject to another arrangement. The 37½% of the nett value was retained, but the expeditions were undertaken jointly by Parish and the Olivers. In view of the extremely unfavourable nature of the 37½% system, one may wonder whether the arrangement reached for the two final expeditions did not perhaps apply to the preceding eight. When Craig died, it was more or less a foregone conclusion that someone would take his place. The expeditions in the months of February to May 1807 produced nett profits in excess of the nett value of the cargoes. Parish's commercial insight being what it was, it is extremely unlikely that he would have been prevailed upon to accept such less favourable terms.

In settling their accounts with Auguste Ouvrard & Co. and the *Caja*, the Company maintained the 37½% system, i.e. import duty at 20% and 15%

'compensations', based on the nett value of the cargo, continued to be entered.

However, we know that another, more advantageous method of calculation was employed for 22 of the 32 cargoes shipped by the Olivers. Although there are no details of the commission received by Parish in respect of licences disposed of to third parties, it is clear that the application of the 37½% system to all licences left a highly attractive margin for Parish and Hope.

In order to establish the profits derived from the Oliver shipments, it is necessary to separate the three arrangements. On the first 22 shipments the Company received 33⅓% of the nett profit plus 5% commission on the nett value of the cargo, making in all more than 410,000 dollars, the value of the dollar then being on a par with that of the piastre.[1] On the last ten shipments the Company received a further 15% of the nett value, amounting to 96,000 dollars, in the form of 'compensations.'

If we now apply the method of profit-sharing between the Olivers and Parish to the last 2 shipments only, the question arises: what portion of the profit may be regarded as 'nett profit'? For the first 22 shipments, the proportion, as stated earlier, was about two-thirds. If we apply this to the final shipments, we see that Parish received a further 60,500 dollars, or one-third of the gross profit. On this basis, the proceeds from the preceding 8 shipments would have amounted to nearly 164,500 dollars; as stated, however, this is no more than a hypothesis.[2] In all, thus, the earnings from the expeditions carried out through Robert and John Oliver must have totalled at least 566,500 dollars.

Understandably, the Olivers were anxious to avoid competition from other houses in the trade with Vera Cruz. But, as has been established, Parish, prior to his arrival in Philadelphia, had transferred a number of licences to Archibald Gracie of New York. Nolte had taken 6 with him to New Orleans, where he disposed of them to Amory & Callender, with whom he worked closely. In spite of strenuous appeals from Oliver, Parish reserved the right to grant licences to whosoever he wished, although the quantity concerned was not large. Among the recipients were Isaac McKim and John Donnell, both of Baltimore, who carried out four expeditions, two jointly and two for McKim's account. It is clear from surviving details that one cargo constituted very direct competition with those of the Olivers. Of the other three, one consisted chiefly of military uniforms, dyes and paint, and the remainder, which were shipped in November and December 1807, comprised southern European produce such as brandy, almonds, cork, writing paper and iron and steel. The goods which made up these three cargoes were probably of Spanish manufacture and shipped on behalf of the Spanish government, and as such did not constitute serious competition for the Olivers.[1]

Besides shipping two cargoes for his own account, John Craig participated with the Olivers in four expeditions to Montevideo under the protection of licences furnished by Parish. The house of Robert Gilmor & Sons had an interest in all four, and was supported in two of them by Le Roy Bayard & McEvers and Archibald Gracie of New York. Alas, there are no details of the proceeds of the sale of these four cargoes. Single licences were given to James Brown of New York (who travelled as supercargo) and to Geo.T.Phillips of New Orleans.

Pro forma invoices and final accounts relating to fifteen expeditions by merchants other than the Olivers have survived. The invoices total more than a million dollars. On the basis of the relatively unfavourable $37\frac{1}{2}\%$ system, there would have been a balance of 15%, or nearly 155,000 dollars, for 'compensations.'[2]

Hope & Co's account to Auguste Ouvrard & Co. and the *Caja de Consolidacion* was for the total invoice value of the 53 cargoes, amounting to approximately 2,900,000 dollars. Import duty at 20%, totalling more than 560,000 dollars, was paid to the *Caja*, and the 15% for 'compensations', amounting to 422,000 dollars, less expenses, losses and commissions, was shared between the *Caja* and Auguste Ouvrard & Co.[3] By our calculations, Parish probably received 566,000 + 155,000 = 721,000 dollars, which implies that a margin of nearly 300,000 dollars remained for the Company.

All these items were credited to Account 'X,' the account in which all transactions relating to the Spanish American operation were entered.

The size of the profit on cargoes shipped to Spanish America was, of course, governed by the prices which the goods fetched at the port of unloading. The more closely the cargo was matched to the local requirements, the greater was the profit on its sale. The Oliver archives reveal that goods imported by third parties also occupied an important place. It grieved the Olivers to find that the Spanish government was also undermining Parish's monopoly for the benefit of others. The house of Gordon & Murphy of London, which had received permission to obtain piastres from Vera Cruz on behalf of the Spanish government, also proved to be liberally supplied with trading licences. The only hope of averting the ruination of the market in Vera Cruz lay in co-ordinating the activities of the two houses, and this the Olivers set out to impress upon the London merchants.[4]

In order to arrive at a suitable range of goods for shipment, the Olivers sent an agent to reconnoitre the market in Vera Cruz. He returned bearing a list of items which had been specially recommended by De Echeverria. In place of Silesian linen, 'English Goods' such as fancy chintz, calicoes, corded dimity, cambric dimity and black velvets were specified.[1] These, however, were not readily saleable on the North American market and consequently would have to be specially ordered from England. Throughout 1806 there was talk of peace negotiations between England and France, and if these should be brought to a successful conclusion it would not be advisable to be left with stocks of goods for Spanish America. If peace were to be restored, Spain would certainly close its ports to foreign vessels and the Olivers would be left with the task of disposing of goods which were not in great demand.

Greater care in matching the supply to the demand enabled the anticipated rise in profits to be achieved in the short run. This trend emerged clearly after October 1806, but profits declined in the autumn of the following year. This was partly due to inability on the part of the Olivers to supply a number of current items, but changes in the pattern of demand in Vera Cruz, whereby certain articles went out of favour, was also a contributory factor.[2] Profit margins on the 'loose' expeditions were generally higher in the second half of 1807 than previously, but these shipments arrived in Mexico so late in the year that the prices which they fetched may have been favourably influenced by the United States embargo on foreign trade which had been imposed in the meantime.

From the Company's point of view, the method of transporting piastres on the return voyage from Vera Cruz to the United States constituted another very important facet of the agreement with the Olivers. Archibald Gracie's vessels had already carried piastres to New Orleans, and the first ship despatched under a licence obtained from Parish, the schooner 'Messenger', arrived in Baltimore in June 1806 carrying 133,000 piastres, of which 50,000 had been shipped by Villanueva for Parish's account.

The Olivers objected to this method of shipment on the grounds that, in their eyes, the piastres were the property of the Spanish Crown and as such were a sure prey for British cruisers. The fact that they were really destined for the French Treasury merely increased the danger. To avert this, it was decided that in future the Olivers would only carry piastres which were their rightful property. In pursuance of the decision, they purchased, at a discount of 21%, drafts drawn by Parish on Villanueva. This price applied to a sum of 500,000 piastres, but soon Parish was protesting at the discount, which he considered too high. He succeeded in getting the rate reduced to 17% for subsequent shipments, but even this was excessive in his opinion. When, in October 1806, it became known that vessels in ballast were to be allowed to enter the port of Vera Cruz free of licence, Parish was given the freedom to ship piastres separately from consignments of goods.[1]

Nothing is known concerning the extent of these 'free' shipments, but much can be deduced. In all, some 6,450,000 piastres were exported from Vera Cruz through the agency of Parish. Of these, 1,450,000 were shipped for the account of the Olivers, and thus 5,000,000 must have been exported by other means.

The expeditions to Spanish America and the return cargoes of piastres, however, represent only a part of the activities reflected in Account 'X.' Parish also had the task of getting the piastres to Europe. Various possibilities existed. The most obvious of these was to ship them direct, but little use was made of this method, and according to Hope's ledgers only two shipments totalling 60,000 piastres were undertaken.[2]

By far the greater portion was used to make advance payment to North American merchant houses for goods which they shipped to Europe. The houses then drew on the consignees for the sum of the advance plus interest at 6% per annum. Parish sent the drafts to Hope & Co., who presented them for payment on the due date.

Hope & Co. was not the only house in Amsterdam to be involved in transactions of this nature. Parish also remitted drafts drawn on Couderc & Brants, Daniël Crommelin & Sons, W. and J.Willink, P. and C. van Eeghen, Van Staphorst & Co., Severijn & Hazebroek, Braunsberg & Co., Ruys & Zimmerman and Raymond & Theodore de Smeth. The first five of these had long-established connexions with the United States. The Rotterdam link was formed by Littledale & Dixon, while in Antwerp most of the business was transacted via David Parish & Co. and the remainder via Ridgway & Mertens. Completing the chain were Trotreau & Labouchère, the house controlled by P.C.Labouchère's younger brother, and De La Roche & Co. in Nantes.

This extremely simple and obvious model allowed of variation, each variant affording a given rate of profit according to the relationship between the rates of exchange. For example, Parish could draw on Baring & Co. and remit the drafts to them. As we have established, the United States had a deficit on its balance of trade with England and so negotiable documents on well-established British houses were very much in demand. Baring, in turn, could remit to Hope & Co. drafts which American houses had drawn on their continental consignors and negotiated in London. In some cases Baring remitted direct to Paris–after all, the monies were destined for the French Treasury. But as a general rule Hamburg was preferred for remittances to the Continent because it was on the exchange market there that the deficit in Britain's trade with Russia was adjusted.[1]

The transfer to Paris of funds held by the Company was achieved in part by way of remittances to Baguenault & Co. or by drafts drawn by Baguenault on Hope. In order not to bring the exchange rate for drafts between Amsterdam and Paris under pressure, a system was also employed in which other houses drew on Hope & Co. and themselves remitted to Paris. The houses concerned were Matthiessen & Sillem in Hamburg (who thus were able to deal with remittances from Baring), Littledale & Dixon in Rotterdam, David Parish & Co. in Antwerp and Bethmann Brothers in Frankfurt.

The operations for Account 'X' naturally had a major influence on Hope's own commercial relations with the United States. The initial contacts, which were probably influenced by the Company's relationship with Baring & Co., dated from the early 1790s.[2] But no more than ten consignments per year were involved and the total value of the goods did not exceed half a million guilders. The American consignments ceased after 1795 and the accounts with American houses remained dormant until 1801, when they were all struck off the books.[3]

The years 1802 and 1803 saw a modest revival of the trade, with one or two consignments, but in 1804 the number grew to fifteen with a total value of nearly 2 million guilders. In the following year there were twenty-eight representing a value of 2,340,000 guilders. The records reveal that an upward surge occurred in 1806, when goods to a value of more than $9\frac{1}{2}$ million guilders, distributed over ninety-five accounts, arrived. The climax came in 1807, when the value of goods totalled more than 10,80,000 guilders spread over a hundred and six accounts.[4]

The remittances from David Parish, however, did not match the value of the goods. In 1807, for example, his remittances, including those which passed through Baring & Co., totalled just under 6,800,000 guilders–and this included remittances for consignments to other houses. It may thus be concluded that only a part of the consignments to Hope were a result of Parish's activities. Whether or not the volume of this trade would have increased so sharply without Parish's intervention can no longer be ascertained, but we may assume that, once having discovered Hope & Co., the houses concerned continued to consign cargoes to the Company without prepayment or partial financing. Although incomplete, the reports sent to David Parish concerning the arrival of American vessels in Amsterdam reveal that the consignments to Hope & Co. exceeded those addressed to Couderc & Brants–a firm of importance in its field–by something like 50%.[1]

It is not possible to deduce from the archive material available just which American houses Parish employed for the purpose of his remittances to Europe. But the fact that houses which were concerned in Parish's operations to Spanish America appear on the list of shippers warrants the assumption that they profited from the advance payments in piastres.

Chief among these were Robert and John Oliver; John Donnell, Robert Gilmor & Sons and Thomas Tenant in Baltimore; Archibald Gracie in New York; John Craig in Philadelphia; and Amory & Callender and Geo.T.Phillips in New Orleans.

The Oliver archives reveal that both that house and Craig in Philadelphia had their own 'troops,' merchants to whom they advanced money, on behalf of Parish, for consignments shipped to Europe. The names of these persons and firms indeed appear in the *grootboeken* and on separate accounts in the Hope archives. Examples are: in Baltimore, John Sherlock, Mark Pringle, Smith & Buchanan, Hollins & McBlair, William Patterson & Sons and Lemuel Taylor; in Philadelphia, Willings & Francis, Stephen Girard and Savage & Dugan. But there were others in more distant ports, such as James & Th.Perkins of Boston, Gracie & Andersons of Petersburg, Virginia, and Geo.M.W.Woolsey of New Orleans.[2]

The majority of the cargoes from America consisted of sugar, coffee, tobacco, rice and cotton. In correspondence with Parish, Labouchère complained from the outset about the malaise in the sugar trade, a result of the supply exceeding the demand. The cause of the surplus lay in a substantial expansion of the sugar cane plantations in the non-British areas of Central America, the effect of which had been to bring about fierce competition.[3]

Throughout the Spring of 1806 Labouchère remained optimistic concerning the markets for the remaining commodities, but the knowledge that a British negotiator had gone to France for peace talks brought dealings in colonial produce to a virtual standstill. There were also complaints concerning the merchant houses in Rotterdam, which, 'being always inclined to extremes,' did not sell within a system. By 'system' was meant a mild form of cartel in which a number of large houses would maintain prices at a certain level in order to deter bear operators and profiteers. Such a system, however, could operate to the disadvantage of stockholders; in the case of cotton, for example, the brokers, who were also buyers, banded together to keep prices down. Moreover, there was strong competition in this commodity from the Rotterdam merchants who, using agressive selling methods, covered the German hinterland.[1]

Hope & Co. also complained about the invoices issued by the American houses, which, in terms of the description of the goods, were usually unreliable. Goods were often too highly priced, making their sale at a profit an impossibility and causing good opportunities to be missed.

When, early in August 1806, it was rumoured that the documents heralding peace between England and France had been signed, Labouchère anticipated panic followed by selling at any price. He did his very utmost to interest speculators in the low-priced sugar, but his efforts were thwarted by new customs regulations in western Germany. As part of the redistribution of lands in that area, Napoleon's brother-in-law, Murat, had been assigned the Grand Duchy of Cleves and Berg, which subsequently became part of the Confederation of the Rhine, a conglomeration of satellite states which were closely allied to France.[2]

By 1st October Labouchère had become so pessimistic about the sugar situation that he could scarcely contemplate the recovery of the payments made in advance. It was decided that Parish would have to stay in the United States for a further year at least, in order to give the market an opportunity to recover. Labouchère did not subscribe to the view that peace was imminent. Later in the month of October he reported that none of the current expeditions in sugar and coffee were profitable. Whenever an opportunity arose to dispose of some sugar, there was always a house willing to undercut the price. At times the Company even bought sugar in an effort to halt the panic, but it was only able to resell it in times of political tension, when war threatened and everyone was on the alert. The tension was highest in Germany, where an extremely obscure tug-of-war was in progress; this centred around Prussia, which vacillated between war with France and peace.[3]

The ultimatum of 1st October 1806 by Prussia, which finally chose war, and the breaking off by England of the peace negotiations had the effect of breathing some fresh life into the commodity markets. Coffee was the first to revive, but sugar remained inactive. Even the news of the Prussian defeats at Jena and Auerstädt failed to bring any real improvement, for the further pattern of events was uncertain and, according to Labouchère, uncertainty meant death to trade.[4]

The news of the Berlin Decree of 21st November 1806, by which Napoleon forebade the importation of British goods into all allied or occupied territories, ordered the confiscation of all British goods within his grasp, and even excluded from harbours under his control or in friendly countries any ship which had called at a British port, served to revitalize trade and improve prices. In Holland, the decree was underlined by a regulation covering all incoming vessels: these were allowed to dock only after an authorization had been obtained from King Louis Napoleon, and were required to obtain permission to leave. However, when it transpired that the permit system was applied extremely liberally and that, for Holland at least, the traffic to and from England was scarcely affected, the commodity market suffered a relapse.[1]

Despite the relatively small stocks, prices–particularly that of sugar–remained low throughout the Spring of 1807 in anticipation of large-scale imports during the ensuing summer. The stocks of coffee were not large, but a considerable amount was being smuggled from England; at the same time, consumption was declining under the influence of growing poverty in Holland and the confused situation created in northern Germany by the war between Sweden and France.[2]

At the end of April 1807, Labouchère reported that huge quantities of sugar were being imported from America and England, although no demand existed. Furthermore, substantial amounts were being returned from Brabant because the high French import duty rendered it uneconomic to export sugar to France. Sales in general improved during the months of May and June, albeit sugar prices remained low. In July the market again collapsed in the wake of renewed rumours of peace negotiations between France and England. Moreover, buyers were seen to be awaiting the outcome of the peace talks between France and Russia, which were taking place at Tilsit.[3]

A peace treaty was signed at Tilsit on 9th July 1807, but this did not end the uncertainty, for it was followed by anxiety concerning relations between England and the United States. Late in June 1807 a British man-of-war had stopped the American frigate 'Chesapeake' off the coast of Virginia, overpowered her crew and taken off a number of British deserters. In Amsterdam, fears of an Anglo-American conflict were so great that underwriters refused to insure American vessels. The commodity buyers, gripped by fear and uncertainty, remained inactive. But when the rumours of war increased, they came to life again, motivated by the thought that a conflict would lead to the rupture of communications with the United States and thus force up prices.[4]

Danger also threatened from another direction, however. Following the

Treaty of Tilsit, Napoleon firmly made up his mind to close the whole of Europe to British goods, and he proceeded to apply pressure to Louis Napoleon with the aim of tightening the prohibitive measures in Holland and elsewhere. On 16th September 1807, King Louis issued a new decree providing for the confiscation of any vessel which had called at a British port or which carried a British cargo.[1]

While these developments were taking place, the atmosphere on the commodity market remained lively and prices continued to rise, helped by the action of the American consul in Amsterdam in advising the masters of American vessels to leave as quickly as possible. In spite of the arrival of fresh cargoes from America, the market remained active throughout the autumn.[2]

The end of the boom was nevertheless in sight. On 11th November 1807, partly under pressure from a faction having commercial interests in the West Indies, Orders in Council were issued in England which made it virtually impossible for neutral countries to continue shipments to the Continent. The acceptance of a certificate of neutrality from a French consul would henceforth lead to the confiscation of the cargo concerned. Vessels of neutral states bound for the Continent were required to call at an English port en route and there to pay tax on the goods carried.[3]

Napoleon's reply to this was the Milan Decree of 17th December 1807, which laid down that any vessel which had called at a British port would be declared a prize. The door was finally closed when, on 22nd December, the United States Congress approved a proposal by President Jefferson banning all traffic to foreign ports. With this, American trade with Holland steadily declined. Early in January 1808 four vessels managed to slip in via Texel, but at about the same time six American ships were captured and taken to French ports, where they were later confiscated.[4]

On 23rd January King Louis closed all Dutch ports to foreign shipping. Occasional evasions occurred, but these were of little importance to the Company since it could not base its advice to American merchants on such mere coincidences.

In mid-February 1809 Labouchère informed Parish that not a single pound of sugar, coffee or cotton remained. Examination of the accounts for American imports, however, reveals that, as in his previous report, Labouchère took a somewhat sombre view. In 1808 the value of the goods to which these accounts related was in excess of 5,650,000 guilders, and in 1809 nearly one and a half million guilders, indicating that the decline in the volume of business with America was more gradual than Labouchère suggested.[5] Nevertheless, by early May the Company decided that the time had come gradually to close the American accounts. The era of copious shipments, from which the Company had made substantial profits, was at an end.[1]

While the proceeds from the initial batch of drafts on Mexico were trickling into Europe, in the shape of colonial produce, the Company, in consultation with Baring & Co., was busy devising a more rapid method for the collection of the drafts which were at that moment still held by the French Treasury. Labouchère had first raised the matter in a letter to Sir Francis Baring on 10th May 1805, after which it had lapsed. Late in September of the same year he raised it again. He proposed that two or three American vessels should take cargoes from Spain to that country's colonies and there take on board piastres, which would be unloaded at an English port. If this were not feasible, the operation could be routed via America, for American account.[2]

Baring's reaction was to send his confidential agent, James Richards, to Amsterdam, but when he arrived, late in November, he found that Labouchère had just left for Paris to attend to matters arising from the financial crisis between Spain and France.[3]

The memoranda which Richards–who followed Labouchère to Paris–carried with him reveal that the attitude of the British government towards the projected operations was somewhat inconsistent. On the one hand it was keen to stimulate the export of British goods to the Spanish colonies, to which end it was prepared to allow British traders to export goods from Jamaica to Vera Cruz and from there to import Mexican products and precious metals, provided that such imports were the property of British subjects (this, of course, implied that the Spanish government would have to issue similar trading licences); on the other hand, however, it was opposed to the exportation to England of unlimited quantities of piastres because four-fifths or five-sixths of these would ultimately find their way into the Spanish or French Treasuries and thereby become 'sinews of war.' A limited operation involving, say, five to ten million piastres would be acceptable, though even this was likely to arouse sensitivities, particularly in naval circles.[4]

The affair had clearly been rendered more urgent by the arrival in London of a Spaniard named Saratea, who made efforts, via the house of Gordon & Murphy, to obtain licences for the export of British manufactures to ports such as Lima, Buenos Aires, Caracas and Vera Cruz. He stated that he was in a position to acquire the necessary Spanish licences and also permits for the export to England of unlimited quantities of piastres.[5]

This threat of competition made it vital that Labouchère should obtain the licences requested from the Spanish government without delay. In December 1805 he and Richards held discussions with Ouvrard, following which there was every indication that the matter would soon be settled. In view of Baring & Co.'s desire to participate in future piastre transactions, Labouchère wrote to Alexander Baring in the following January, urging him to come to Holland as soon as possible so that final agreement could be reached with Ouvrard regarding the twelve million piastres which had been offered. Baring replied that there were signs of progress in regard to the affair in England, but that owing to Pitt's illness it was difficult to obtain a decision from the government.[1]

Pitt's death on 23rd January 1806 and the coming to office of the more peace-seeking cabinet headed by Grenville-Fox brought a sudden change in the situation. In France, the dramatic encounter between Napoleon and Ouvrard on 27th January put an abrupt end to the latter's gigantic plans.

The scene thus changed completely. So much more sympathetic did Alexander Baring find the new British government that on 18th February he was able to report optimistically that: 'We are again in a fair way on a new track on this side and can encourage you to move. Our position gives better security than it has ever done.'[2]

Simultaneously, however, Hope & Co. were obliged to surrender their holding of Mexican drafts to the French Treasury, with the result that all the negotiations had to be started afresh. Whereas the urge for peace on the part of the British government had facilitated Baring's negotiations, it formed an obstacle to the Company's efforts to reach agreement with the French Treasury inasmuch as a restoration of peace would render its services as a mediator superfluous.[3]

In March 1806 Labouchère was still optimistic about an early decision, but by April his attitude had become tinged with reservation. We have already seen how Mollien, having abandoned his original demand for fixed monthly payments, refused to yield on minor details.[4]

Despite the slow progress of the negotiations with the French Treasury, Alexander Baring considered the matter of sufficient importance to justify making his long-postponed visit to Amsterdam, where he arrived at the beginning of June 1806. He hoped to be able to take a signed contract back to England, but the French government continued to raise objections, chief among which was that, should peace come, Hope and Baring would make far too large a profit on the terms offered.[5]

A positive facet of the visit was that it enabled the two companies to agree on terms and conditions. Their discussions were based on the premise that both would act as buyers and not as agents. Freight costs, marine risk and other hazards not covered by insurance would be met jointly and equally. In preparation for a final agreement, two contracts were drawn up. In the first of these, Baring Bros. & Co. undertook to pay 3 francs 75 centimes in Paris for every piastre collected. In the second, they promised to pay a sum (which was unspecified) to Hope & Co. in London for each piastre. The latter figure was to be the price at which Baring would sell the piastres. The difference between the two figures represented the profit, and this was to be shared equally by the two houses.

The first draft contract was for external consumption. In it, Hope undertook to deliver, via their agent in Vera Cruz, up to 6 million piastres on board Spanish or neutral vessels, from which they would be transferred to vessels authorized by Baring to load piastres in the Vera Cruz roads. Baring Bros. & Co. were committed to pay 3 francs 75 centimes for each piastre in Paris within sixty days of the receipt of the bills of lading relating to these shipments, up to a maximum of two million francs per month. Sums remaining unpaid after the expiry of the sixty-day period would incur interest at ½% per month.

Hope & Co. also committed themselves to make every effort to obtain guarantees from the French and Spanish governments that no attack would be made on Baring's property, irrespective of the political situation. It was also necessary to ensure that the authorities in Mexico would not impede the movement of the piastres to the waiting vessels, even if these were British warships. The piastres were to be delivered on board free of duty or charges, and vessels used exclusively for the carriage of piastres were to be exempted from all import or export duties.

Baring Bros. & Co. agreed to pay all freight charges and marine risk, but the consequences of arrest by warships or by freebooters flying the flag of France, Spain or a country allied to them were for Hope's account until the piastres were delivered to an American port on the Gulf of Mexico or a port in a British colony, or were put aboard a British man-of-war.

The other draft contract, in which the transaction was approached from the Company's position, provided for the Company to deliver the piastres at a port in the British West Indies or in the United States. Baring Bros. & Co. undertook to accept the piastres thus delivered and, via their authorized agents, to issue receipts for these. Upon presentation of these receipts in London, Baring would pay an unspecified sum per piastre to Hope. A different, and similarly unspecified, sum would be paid for piastres conveyed in a British man-of-war. Baring Bros. & Co. undertook to obtain from the British government a guarantee that the Company would not be hampered in its participation in the transaction and that it would be free to remit abroad the monies accruing to it. Baring also undertook to try to obtain from the British government armed protection for any neutral vessel which Hope might employ for the shipment of the piastres and, if possible, British licences for such vessels. Although the piastres were for Hope's account and at their risk until such time as they were handed over to Baring's authorized agent, Baring agreed to pay to the Company a sum of four shillings and sixpence for each piastre in the event of a ship carrying piastres being arrested and seized by a British man-of-war or by a freebooter, in spite of sailing under a British licence.[1]

Before leaving Amsterdam in July 1806, Alexander Baring was given drafts on Mexico to a value of 1,250,000 piastres for onward transmission to David Parish. Hope & Co. had received these drafts from Ouvrard; they represented the Spanish government's contribution to the capital of François Ouvrard & Co., and as such had been excluded from the drafts restored to Mollien.[2]

From July onwards, little was written concerning the piastre contracts, although the negotiations with the French Treasury were pursued. In mid-November Napoleon inquired impatiently of Mollien how matters stood in regard to the drafts on Mexico. In December he authorized Mollien to sign any reasonable contract, provided the rate of exchange at which he had originally accepted the piastres, i.e. 3 francs 75 centimes, was maintained as a minimum.[3]

Early in February 1807, Councillor of State Louis travelled to Amsterdam, where he had various matters to attend to. Among them was the conclusion of a contract for the Mexican drafts. As Hope & Co. had settled the matter with Baring in the previous July, it did not take long to reach agreement with Louis. The rate of exchange of 3 francs 75 centimes embodied in the draft contract in July served as the basis for an agreement covering in all 5 million piastres.[4] A report of the agreement was sent to Baring Bros. & Co. with a request that they settle matters with the British authorities. When this had been done, Baring Bros. & Co. would be in a position to sign a firm contract with the Company, a copy of which would be sent to Amsterdam.

When Baring Bros. & Co. approached the authorities in search of their approval, they met with an unpleasant surprise. Gordon & Murphy and Reid Irving & Co. had already negotiated a contract to ship 10 million piastres for the account of the Spanish government, and the British government had undertaken not to sanction any fresh operations until this contract had been completed. Gordon & Murphy and Reid Irving & Co. had reached virtual agreement with Saratea regarding the 10 million piastres during the winter of 1805, but the peace negotiations between England and France had caused the Spanish government to hesitate before giving its approval. But the negotiations had been resumed during the French campaign against the Prussians in October, and had ended in agreement.[1]

Nevertheless, Alexander Baring, by reason of his position on the board of the Bank of England, succeeded in negotiating a contract for the delivery of piastres. Alas, his letters to Hope & Co. do not reveal the manner of his success.[2]

The way was now clear for Baring to sign the contract with Hope and send it to Amsterdam. With the countersignature of the document by Hope & Co. on 24th March 1807, the matter was settled–to the immense relief of Louis, who, with mounting impatience, had remained in The Hague to await the completion.[3]

On 17th April, Labouchère received drafts on Mexico to a value of 2,753,170 piastres. He also received drafts on Havana and Caracas, in each case for 700,000 piastres, making a total of more than 4 million.[4]

In correspondence with the Company, Baring Bros. & Co. indicated a desire to extend the contract to cover drafts sent to Parish but which remained uncollected. Hope & Co. had agreed to this in order to avoid the two houses competing with each other in Vera Cruz. Baring was not greatly interested in the drafts on Havana, the value of which was insufficient to warrant despatching a British warship there. The piastres from Caracas were also something of a problem, but it was felt that these could probably be collected at the same time as those in Vera Cruz.[5]

Mollien gave his approval to the extension of the contract on condition that a price of 3 francs 85 centimes per piastre was paid for the most recent drafts–ten centimes above the contract figure. The parties reached agreement on this point, and on 20th July 1807 Hope & Co. and Baring Bros. & Co. signed a supplementary contract. The original contract thus now covered the entire sum of the drafts on the Spanish colonies which the Company held. Parish continued as principal agent, but Baring Bros. & Co. took over control from Hope & Co. with all the attendant dangers and risks.[6]

The agreement with the French Treasury also covered the drafts which Mollien had sent to the French consul general in Philadelphia, De Beaujour, in 1806 with instructions to dispose of them. De Beaujour had offered them to all the merchants in Philadelphia but had found no takers: no one was willing to risk dealing in politically-tainted drafts. In desperation, the consul turned to David Parish, who was perfectly willing to put them through Account 'X.' During the three years 1807–1809, more than a million piastres was paid to De Beaujour.[1]

In the meantime, Baring Bros. & Co. had energetically set about implementing the contract. Late in May 1807 the frigate 'Diana,' with Charles Baring on board as supercargo, had set sail. Unfortunately, the documents sent from Madrid did not include an order for the vessel to be admitted to Caracas and thus this part of the expedition had to be abandoned. The drafts on Caracas were transferred by endorsement to Baring's agents in Jamaica, Atkinson & Co., in order that they could make an attempt to present them at a later date.[2]

On 20th October 1807 Baring Bros. & Co. reported that the 'Diana' had arrived safely at Portsmouth with 3,679,835 piastres on board. The freight charges and attendant expenses had to be repaid to the Bank of England. A sum of 25,780 pounds sterling, representing commissions for Charles Baring and Sir Francis Baring, and incidental expenses, was claimed. The nett proceeds totalled just over 772,000 pounds sterling, which means that the sum paid per piastre was four shillings and twopence.[3] The French Treasury was recompensed at the rate of 3 francs 85 centimes for each piastre received in London plus $\frac{5}{8}$% commission for Hope & Co.'s agents, making approximately 3 francs 90 centimes in all. Assuming the pound to have been equal to cf 11.50 ,and the franc to 48 guilder cents, it can be calculated that Hope and Baring made a joint profit of 52 guilder cents on each piastre. This, however, is only an approximate figure because it is impossible to ascertain the exact rates of exchange applying to these remittances.

While the 'Diana' was loading the piastres off Vera Cruz, another British man-of-war set sail for Malta carrying a cargo of two million piastres for Gordon & Murphy's account. Thus, the deliveries of piastres for the Spanish government continued normally alongside the Hope-Baring operations.[4]

The developments concerning the drafts on Havana to a value of 700,000 piastres were considerably more adventuresome. In September 1807 Parish had sent an agent to Cuba with instructions to present the drafts, but shortly after arriving there the man had died of yellow fever.[5] Parish thereupon requested Nolte to wind up his affairs in New Orleans and take charge of the collection in Havana. The original plan provided for New Orleans to play an important role, both for the shipment of merchandise and the reception of cargoes of silver. But under the subsequent contract with the Olivers the majority of cargoes were shipped from Baltimore and the vessels, laden with piastres, returned to that port. Such silver as did arrive in New Orleans could be remitted only with the utmost difficulty owing to the scarcity of safe drafts on ports in the northeastern part of the country and on England.[1]

When Nolte arrived in Cuba he was faced with an unforeseen problem. The letter of advice from the Spanish Minister of Finance, which accompanied the drafts, referred specifically to payment in silver coin. With the interruption, by the war with England, of communications with Mexico, the golden dubloon had become the sole coinage in Cuba, and thus payment in the stipulated coinage could not be made. Nolte's reaction to this situation was to propose to the Intendant of Cuba, Don Rafael Gomez Roubaud, that the drafts on Havana should be exchanged for drafts on Vera Cruz. At first the Intendant was not sympathetic towards the suggestion, but veiled references to the displeasure of Don Rafael's patron, Talleyrand, and the prospect of a handsel, finally won him over to Nolte's point of view.[2] In exchange for the draft for 700,000 piastres, he received one on Vera Cruz for 945,000 piastres.

Nolte had reasoned that the rate of exchange of the piastre in relation to the dubloon was lower in the United States than in Cuba. He accordingly maintained that in order to collect the required sum in piastres in America, the amount in dubloons would need to be increased by one-sixth. Moreover, because the Spanish government had failed to meet its obligation to effect payment in Cuba, he felt it necessary to include an insurance premium of 25% for the voyage from Vera Cruz to Philadelphia. Even with a surchange of 35%, or 245,000 piastres, it would pay the Spanish government to settle on these terms. In all probability, the handsel of 14,000 piastres was the decisive factor.[3]

At the end of 1807 the draft for 945,000 piastres was sent to Vera Cruz, where it was promptly accepted and paid. For Nolte, the homeward voyage proved to be an anti-climax. The vessel in which he travelled was wrecked on a reef near one of the Florida Keys, and he and the crew were washed up on an uninhabited island. Although they were soon rescued by a fishing boat from Nassau, in the Bahamas, it was mid-March before Nolte reached Philadelphia.[4]

As a result of this unexpected delay, Mollien heard about Nolte's transaction before Hope & Co. The Intendant of Cuba reported on it to Talleyrand, and the letter, carried by a Spanish vessel which evaded the English cruisers, actually reached Talleyrand. According to Mollien, the

Intendant had complained about the manner in which Nolte had dictated the terms.[1]

Faced with this situation, Labouchère could do no more than promise to obtain further information at the earliest possible moment. He did, however, immediately point out that Nolte's action had averted a redraft, which would have added at least 28% to the costs. After receiving Nolte's report, Labouchère offered to pay 4 francs 50 centimes per piastre for the 700,000 covered by the draft, an increase of 60 centimes per piastre on the contracted figure. Mollien, however, persisted in his demand that the amount be paid in full, and eventually Labouchère agreed to this at a price of 3 francs 75 centimes; but a substantial sum was deducted to cover the expenses incurred.[2]

The Havana affair was officially concluded in September 1809 when Nolte (who had meanwhile returned to Europe) and Labouchère together tendered the final account to Mollien. During the meeting, Mollien reiterated the message of gratitude from the emperor which he had earlier conveyed to Labouchère.

With this happy ending, we have anticipated the remainder of our story. Summarizing, it can be said that of the 10 million piastres, in the form of drafts, which remained in French hands, more than 6 million were collected via the United States. The treaty of July 1807, under which the balance of the drafts were entrusted to the care of Baring Bros. & Co., was probably inspired in part by the increasing harassment by British cruisers of the schooners despatched by the Olivers, and the impossibility of obtaining British licences to cover their voyages.[3]

Whether or not Baring Bros. & Co. would succeed in carrying out further expeditions as smoothly as the first, depended to a very great extent upon the political situation. In the following chapter we shall see how a political reversal in Spain completely blocked the piastre affair.

CHAPTER TWELVE

BETWEEN SATELLITES AND NAPOLEONITES

As we saw at the end of Chapter Ten, the winding-up of Ouvrard's business relationship with the French and Spanish governments on 10th May 1806 led to the formal transfer to Spain of the balance of the proceeds of the 1805 loan and also of the wool which Ouvrard had shipped to Baguenault and Hope.

After protracted negotiations with the Company, Michel Simons succeeded in obtaining for Spain an advance of one million francs on the sale of the wool. As the transfer of ownership to Spain had been effected to enable that country to pay off its debts to France, Labouchère instructed Baguenault & Co. to pay the million francs into the French Treasury on 30th June 1806.[1] The placing with the *entrepreneurs* of the balance of the bonds relating to the loan of 1805 had been accomplished sooner than had been expected, so that Hope & Co. were able to make further payments totalling 2,300,000 francs on 31st July and 25th August, for the purposes of which the attachments by Séguin, Michel the Younger and Fulchiron of the Vanlerberghe & Ouvrard funds held by Hope & Co. were suspended.[2]

Where payments for the benefit of Spain were concerned, however, the attachments, and also the Company's claims, were fully maintained. When Espinosa failed to remit the monies to cover the redemption, with interest due, of 1,000 bonds on 1st July 1806, a sum of more than 1,400,000 guilders was debited to Vanlerberghe & Ouvrard's account, and it was made clear that the entry would not be expunged until such time as an official notification was received from the Spanish government stating that the sum might be met from the sale of the wool. Thus, as far as the Company was concerned, Vanlerberghe & Ouvrard's guarantee of the payment due on 1st July remained fully in force, whatever had been stated in writing from Paris.[3]

Spain's continuing, acute shortage of finances necessitated searching for possible new sources in Holland. Simons's efforts to negotiate a loan of 30 million guilders with De Smeth having failed, Izquierdo made a formal approach to Hope & Co. at the end of August 1806. Labouchère's response was cool. Informal discussions had earlier been held with Simons on this subject, but certain conditions put forward by him had thus far made it unlikely that the *entrepreneurs* would be greatly interested.

It was essential that the new loan should serve as a means for the conversion of the outstanding portions of all the previous Spanish loans obtained in Holland, with the exception of the one of 1805. Moreover, measures would have to be taken to put an end to the Spanish habit of reissuing bonds accepted upon conversion–and at lower price at that. This practice had caused more than enough trouble in connexion with the conversion loans issued by Croese.

Labouchère felt that it would be advisable to reduce the rate of interest from the 6% referred to in the royal warrant which Simons brought with him to 5½%, and to lower the premium from 5½ to 5%, thereby matching the conditions of the new negotiation to those of the loan of 1805 and protecting the *entrepreneurs* against losses on 1805 bonds which were still in their possession. He also proposed that the initial repayment should be deferred from the end of the first year to the end of the third, in order to avoid overloading Spain's finances. He made it plain that there could be no question of limiting commission to bonds actually sold: in many instances, it was precisely the initial lots which demanded substantial sacrifices in the shape of reductions, etc. to secure placement. If the Spanish government refused to yield on this point, the loan was unlikely to get off the ground. Finally, it was for Labouchère a *conditio sine qua non* that as yet unhonoured drafts drawn by Croese on the *Caja de Consolidacion* should be met by way of the new loan in order that that house could resume normal business.[1]

Fortunately for Hope & Co., time was not on Izquierdo's side. The French continued to press the Spanish Court for prompt payment of the agreed 3 million francs per month, and the *Négociants Réunis* had protested the drafts for 5 million francs which had been given to Izquierdo on 10th May 1806, with the result that he was unable to fall back on this reserve. Moreover, Mollien had no intention of allowing Spain to share in the 50% discount on supplies to the army and navy which he had forced upon the *Négociants Réunis* for the benefit of the Treasury. Faced with this situation, Izquierdo temporarily sought refuge in chicanery–something which fitted in well with the policy of Godoy, who in the summer and early autumn of 1806 was considering breaking off relations with France.[2]

Following the great French military successes against the Prussians at Jena and Auerstädt, however, Godoy abandoned his plan and devoted himself to the task of getting back into Napoleon's good books. The early negotiation with Hope & Co. of a loan, which would enable the payments desired by France to be effected, was thus of some political importance.

But final agreement with the Company was not immediately forthcoming. Izquierdo had on his own initiative raised the capital sum of the loan to 36 million guilders in order to provide additional monies for payment to France. Labouchère rejected the proposed increase, adding that even 30 million was excessive. In days gone by, an issuing house could enter into contracts with *entrepreneurs* which provided guarantees for the lender of payment at set times; but the majority of the *entrepreneurs* had long since disappeared and now a house could consider itself fortunate if it succeeded in placing a loan in dribs and drabs among the few *entrepreneurs* who remained. Unless the Company received remittances for interest and principal on the 1793 loan on 1st November, there was no hope of floating the new one.[1]

This ultimative conclusion failed to elicit any word from Madrid, but, acting on behalf of Izquierdo, Simons–who had visited Amsterdam in the company of Ouvrard at the end of October–authorized the Company to advertise the payments on 1st November. With this step, a foundation upon which the parties could come to terms was laid.[2] By the 13th November they had agreed to the point where Labouchère was able to apply to King Louis for formal permission to open the loan.[3]

The proposed loan was of 30 million guilders for twelve years, commencing on 1st November 1809. The rate of interest was to be 5½%, and a bonus of 5% would be payable on principal sums repaid. As security for the loan, the Company received drafts on Mexico totalling nearly 28½ million piastres which matured regularly throughout the period, and which could be collected in Vera Cruz in the event of the Spanish government failing to meet its obligations towards the lenders.

Hope & Co. expressed their willingness to take over the loan at 90%. In addition, they stood out for, and secured, a commission of 7% on the value of bonds placed–which implied that Labouchère had acquiesced in the Spanish demands on this point. It was agreed that 1% commission would be payable on principal repayments and ½% on interest. Interest would be payable from 1st November 1806 and a bonus of six months' interest would be paid 'aux preneurs des obligations.' Time would reveal that *preneurs* and *entrepreneurs* were one and the same.

The following were to be accepted in lieu of cash for the purposes of the loan: the balance of the bonds of the Echenique loans, in value totalling more than five million guilders, at the price of 95%; the balance of the Croese conversion loans, totalling 4,300,000 guilders; and the last 1,200 bonds relating to Hope & Co.'s loan of 1793, which fell due in equal portions on 1st November 1806 and 1st November 1807. To these could be added the interest due on all the bonds up to the date of redemption, the interest and principal payment announced by Croese in 1805 (the bonds concerned having been deposited but not encashed) and the proceeds of the redemption of 1,000 bonds on 1st July 1806, with which Hope & Co. had provisionally debited Vanlerberghe & Ouvrard. Finally, it was stipulated that the sum of interest due on 1st November 1808 would be deducted in advance from the proceeds of the loan.

The nett result would be to adjust debts by Spain totalling cf 14,428,000 via the new loan. In addition, the Company reserved the right to use as payment drafts on the *Caja de Consolidacion* totalling cf 1,462,000 which were held by Croese.

After the deduction of the 10% margin on the issue price, Hope & Co.'s commission of 7% and the Spanish commitments totalling cf 15,890,000, just over ten million guilders remained. It was agreed that when the loan had been floated the Company would aim to make 1½ million francs monthly available to the French Treasury, but it was stressed that its ability to do so would depend upon the success of the loan operation. The Company also agreed to try to obtain a reduction, from 5% to 1%, of the stamp duty demanded by the Netherlands government on the 10 million guilders which would actually be furnished. Of this 1% only a quarter would be borne by the Company.[1]

Labouchère had every reason for satisfaction with this loan contract. Thanks to Godoy being in a tight corner, the Company had secured the conversion of all the old Spanish loans–something which had not been achieved at the time of the 1805 negotiation. Furthermore, the Croese affair, which had bothered Labouchère since 1805, would shortly be resolved. From a business point of view also, the deal afforded interesting prospects. The Echenique bonds, which could be converted at 95%, stood at 60% or thereabouts at the end of 1805. A timely purchase of these bonds could thus lead to a very substantial profit; this fact will not have escaped Simons and his patron, Talleyrand.[2]

This hopeful and potentially profitable beginning gave way to immense disappointment. On 18th November 1806 the Dutch Minister of Finance, Gogel, reported that King Louis had decided to withhold approval of the new Spanish loan.[3] Izquierdo, who had meanwhile arrived in Holland, immediately set off for The Hague, where it was made clear to him that the king's decision was less than final. The news cheered him somewhat, but it did little to dispel the problem of meeting the claims by Hope & Co.

for the payments made by them on 1st July and 1st November of that year–claims which he knew the Company would not allow to remain unmet for long. He offered drafts on Mexico to a value of 3,200,000 piastres but these were refused by Labouchère on the grounds that communication by sea had been rendered extremely uncertain by the Berlin Decree of 21st November 1806. The problem was solved by an offer by Auguste Ouvrard & Co. to guarantee the sums advanced. Here, too, the American operations provided the Company with indispensable cover in the back in its dealings with Spain.[1]

In late December 1806 Ouvrard sent Jean Baptiste Ouin to Amsterdam as his agent, for the purpose of settling those of his affairs in which Hope & Co. were concerned. To Labouchère's intense displeasure, a deed stating that Auguste Ouvrard & Co. owed 1¾ million francs to François Ouvrard & Co. was signed in Paris at the same time. Ouin attempted to persuade the Company to pay a similar sum to François Ouvrard & Co. from remittances received from America for Auguste Ouvrard. Such remittances were not to be used for other purposes until such time as the debt to François Ouvrard & Co. had been settled. The effect of this 'milking' of Auguste Ouvrard & Co. would be to devalue that company's guarantee in respect of the advances made by Hope & Co. on 1st July and 1st November 1806 for quite a long time.[2]

Labouchère protested against what he regarded as tampering with accounts, and consented only to discuss Ouvrard's interests privately with Ouin without reference to the Paris contract. At the same time, being mindful of Ouvrard's urgent need of funds to finance his supplies to the French army and navy, he was at pains not to be too inflexible, with the result that Ouin was able to return to Paris in mid-January with an agreement in his pocket. Labouchère, however, made the implementation of the agreement conditional upon the approval of Espinosa, Séguin, Michel the Younger and Fulchiron. He also stipulated that any monies placed at Ouin's disposal would be channelled via Baguenault & Co. in Paris–with the full maintenance of the Company's claims. When, at the end of January, Ouin transferred monies received via Baguenault to Desprez, Labouchère declared that he would have nothing more to do with the arrangement and would in future deal only with Baguenault.[3]

The affair was finalized early in April 1807 by a joint statement by Ouin, Desprez and Vanlerberghe. Labouchère had limited his claim on Auguste Ouvrard & Co. to the sum of the payment made on 1st November and had instructed Baguenault to pay to Desprez the equivalent of the redeemed bonds plus the interest on these. The bonds would thus serve as an additional security. Auguste Ouvrard & Co., however, remained guarantors for the full sum pending settlement by the Spanish Court.[1]

The Company reserved in full its claims in respect of other credit balances on Auguste Ouvrard & Co.'s account, including sums receivable. The drafts for 1,250,000 piastres, which had earlier been handed to Alexander Baring, were specifically referred to in this respect. By carefully avoiding any reference to François Ouvrard & Co., the Company re-emphasized its refusal to recognize the transfer of Auguste Ouvrard's assets.

This statement elicited the formal approval of Michel the Younger and Fulchiron, but no word was received from Séguin or Espinosa. There could thus be no question of unfettered access to the monies placed in Baguenault's charge. For Hope & Co., this arrangement at least had the significant advantage that they were absolved from any further manipulations on Ouvrard's part. Incoming credits for Ouvrard's account were transferred to Baguenault, after which the question of who was to receive the money became one for Ouvrard and his creditors to squabble about. Hope & Co. were required to do no more than exercise formal supervision.[2]

Although dissociating itself from Ouvrard and his affairs, the Company had by no means abandoned him. This became clear to Councillor of State Louis when, during his sojourn in Amsterdam in the Spring of 1807, he haughtily demanded to be allowed to inspect Ouvrard's various accounts. Labouchère replied that the Company was under no obligation to disclose to Louis whether or not it controlled funds belonging to Ouvrard, adding that Louis must be aware of the impropriety of his question. That the rebuke had found its mark was shown by Louis's first letter following his return to Paris: in this, he asked which of his actions in Holland had seemed to Labouchère to be out of place.[3]

Apart from this verbal duel, Louis's contacts with Hope & Co. were valuable and fruitful. As explained earlier, they led to agreement concerning the method of dealing with the drafts on Mexico which remained in the possession of the French Treasury. Moreover, Louis was charged with making a further effort to obtain the approval of King Louis Napoleon for the floating of the Spanish loan. Labouchère, too, made many journeys to The Hague for this purpose, in addition to which the good offices of the French and Spanish envoys were invoked.[4]

The various audiences with King Louis showed that he first wished to see a loan for Holland placed, and that his approval for the loan to Spain depended upon this. When the councillor of state requested the king's final word on the matter, the latter replied: 'I will gladly give it when my loan is assured, but not before.'[1]

Hope & Co. were thus obliged to embark willy-nilly on a negotiation for the considerable sum of 40 million guilders–and this for the benefit of a government of which Labouchère wrote: 'it can attribute its discredit only to its own bad financial policy.' Following the intercession of Robert Voûte, acting in the capacity of Director of the Treasury under the régime of King Louis, a consortium was formed consisting of Hope & Co., Raymond and Theodore De Smeth, W. & J.Willink, J.Hodshon & Son and W.van Brienen & Son, all of Amsterdam. These houses jointly declared their willingness to launch a loan of 40 million guilders at 6% interest. To encourage investors, bonuses and even an additional bonus were offered. The loan was to run from 1st April 1807 to 1st April 1825. A sum of 4 million guilders was to be set aside annually from the taxes collected in Amsterdam, and placed in a sinking fund to be set up for the purpose. All matured but unpaid interest vouchers relating to the national debt, including the debts of the *Oost-Indische Compagnie* which had been taken over by the government, were to be accepted in lieu of cash, as were matured drafts payable by the Receiver General, Daniel Hooft.[2]

It was of the utmost importance to the Company that subscriptions to the loan should be forthcoming speedily and in such a volume that the king could not withhold his approval for the loan to Spain. On 7th April, one week after the loan had opened, 10 million guilders had been subscribed; by the 12th the 15½ million mark was reached. But then the flow ceased. By 19th April just over 18 million had been received, and from that point the total inched upwards, finally reaching 22 million on 11th May.[3]

This point having been reached, Labouchère felt that the market should be left to settle until the end of the month. In the meantime, a start could be made with the Spanish loan, the *Berigt* of which he wished to have published by the 19th. But the death of the king's son and the ensuing Court mourning caused publication to be postponed until the 25th.[4]

This did not mark the end of Hope & Co.'s involvement with Napoleon's family. Early in May 1807 another Napoleonite approached the Company regarding a loan. Acting on instructions from King Joseph of Naples, Gérardin, his equerry, visited the Company's offices bearing a letter of introduction from Louis. The nature of his instructions and the conversations which followed made it clear that King Joseph desired to bring his country to the notice of the capital market in Holland by means of a modest loan.[5]

Labouchère explained the pros and cons of such a loan to Gérardin. Naples was unknown to the Dutch public as a borrower, and thus little interest could be expected from investors, certainly in the beginning. On the other hand, King Louis was well disposed towards the loan which his brother sought; indeed, he was understood to be considering putting part of the 5% reserve on his own loan, which was provisionally blocked, into the loan to Naples.

In view of King Joseph's total lack of experience of loans in Holland, Labouchère made a proposal on the lines current at the time. It would be necessary for the king to furnish a principal debenture for a loan of 3 million guilders; a model for this was given to Gérardin. The loan would be for seven years, commencing on 1st July 1807, and interest, at 6%, would be payable annually on a set date. Repayment, at the rate of 500,000 guilders per year, would commence at the end of the second year, which implied that the loan would be paid off on 1st July 1814. The required security would comprise the revenues of the Kingdom of Naples in general, and those of the domain of Tovegliere, in the province of Puglia, in particular.

Hope & Co. were willing to take over the bonds at 90%, in addition to which they required a commission of 5% on the principal sum. It was stipulated that a commission of 1% would be chargeable on payments of interest and principal, and that stamp duty on the principal sum, estimated to be 1%, would be payable by the Kingdom of Naples. The sum of the interest due on 1st July 1808 would be deducted from the proceeds of the loan and remain in the Company's charge. A similar stipulation had been made in respect of the loan to Spain in order to guarantee at least the initial interest payment and thereby to give the *entrepreneurs* an opportunity to place the loan on the market gradually. As a final condition for the Naples loan, Labouchère insisted that Hope & Co. should be clearly designated agents for King Joseph, and nothing more; in this role, they would not be required to guarantee the success of the loan. On the same day, 13th May 1807, Gérardin accepted Labouchère's conditions and authorized the Company to float the loan. He thereupon departed for Paris, leaving the Company to obtain the formal approval of King Louis.[1]

Labouchère, however, was preoccupied with the Spanish loan. Even before the *Berigt* appeared, Raymond and Theodore De Smeth and Willem Borski had become involved in the matter. Hope & Co. accepted responsibility for half the loan sum, De Smeth for $\frac{3}{10}$ths and Borski for $\frac{2}{10}$ths. All risks attaching to advances to Spain were to be shared in this ratio, as were the subsequent profits.[2]

The *Berigt* appeared in the newspapers on 25th May 1807. On the same day, Hope & Co. and Willem Borski, acting on behalf of an anonymous group of *entrepreneurs*, signed the initial contract for the acceptance of 3,000 Spanish bonds relating to the new loan. Payment was to be effected in four monthly instalments. In addition to enjoying interest with effect from the date of the first instalment, the *entrepreneurs* received a commission of 5% and a bonus of six months' interest, which was equal to an extra commission of $2\frac{3}{4}$%. Half of the sums which comprised the instalments were to be paid in cash, and for this purpose the matured vouchers relating to the Echenique loans and Hope's loan of 1793 would be regarded as cash. The same was to apply to all payments advertised by Croese but not effected because of his moratorium. The *entrepreneurs* were also permitted to meet up to one-quarter of their obligations, or cf 750,000, with Echenique bonds and a similar amount with bonds relating to Croese's conversion loans or Hope's 1793 loan.[1]

This pattern was broadly maintained in all subsequent contracts, albeit the 'cash' portion gradually increased to $\frac{3}{5}$ths and in some cases reached $\frac{7}{10}$ths. In the period up to 1st November 1807, 23,000 bonds were transferred to Borski and his fellow *entrepreneurs*.[2] With this, activity virtually ceased, the *entrepreneurs* merely taking options on 3,000 bonds until 1st January 1808, on 2,000 between 1st January and 1st March 1808 and on the remaining 2,000 between 1st March and 1st May 1808. Izquierdo was advised that the Company's ability to maintain the monthly payments of $1\frac{1}{2}$ million francs to the French Treasury depended upon these options being converted into firm contracts. In no case did this occur, however, and Hope's final payment was accordingly made in November, by which time 9 million francs had been paid over from the proceeds of the loan.[3]

To Labouchère's annoyance, Izquierdo was slow in making his payments to the French Treasury. Immediately after the floating of the loan in June 1807, Labouchère had complained to Mollien that Izquierdo was delaying the payments on purely formal grounds. In July the delay had assumed such proportions that Baguenault & Co. commenced to charge interest on the funds which they had made available but which had remained idle because of Izquierdo's dilatory tatics. Mollien ultimately ordered the attachment of the Izquierdo assets which were in Hope's charge, but this had little effect.[4]

The explanation for Izquierdo's conduct probably lay in his sincere desire to defend Spain's weak financial position against the French, insofar as this lay in his power. Political developments in the second half of

1807 were to prove beneficial to his efforts. In July, following the Treaty of Tilsit, Napoleon demanded of Portugal that it should sever all political and economic links with England. The Spanish government was not told of this in advance, but now that it seemed that Portugal was at last being dealt with, the matter of its partition–and with it Godoy's aspiration after a kingdom of his own–again came up for discussion.[1]

The negotiations on this subject opened in Paris in September. In Napoleon's view, they afforded a suitable opportunity to put pressure on Izquierdo, as Godoy's agent, concerning the arrears in the Spanish payments to France. For Izquierdo, it was an opportunity to repeat his usual excuses about Spain's poverty, but now with added emphasis: if Napoleon wished Spain to mount an army against Portugal, he ought not simultaneously to demand her last resources.

This argument must have convinced the emperor. The *grootboek* entries relating to the Spanish Crown and to the loan of 30 million guilders reveal that on 11th November 1807 a sum of 1½ million francs was placed at Izquierdo's disposal; in contrast to the five previous entries, however, there is no reference to payment of this sum to the French Treasury.[2]

If we examine the accounts relating to this loan in 1807 in their entirety, we observe that the sale of 23,000 bonds yielded something over 20 million guilders. Of this sum, nearly 9 million guilders was subscribed in the form of vouchers and bonds from earlier loans. Of the balance, more than 4¼ million was paid to the French Treasury. Because Spain failed to make any remittances in respect of interest or capital repayments, totalling cf 3,850,000, in 1807, this sum was charged to the new loan. Unmet drafts on the *Caja de Consolidacion* which were held by Croese, and which totalled cf 1,400,000, were also charged to the account. The balance of cf 1,750,000 had been used by Izquierdo himself, who had purchased two thousand bonds of the new loan; but it had been stipulated that these should remain in the charge of De Smeth until such time as all the conditions applying to the loan had been met. This implied the payment in full of Croese's drafts or approval for Hope & Co. to deduct the sum from the proceeds of the loan, the exchange of all old Spanish bonds with payment for overdue vouchers, and the full discharge of Spain's financial commitments to France.[3]

The submission by Hope of the annual account for 1807 concerning the loan produced no response from either Izquierdo or Espinosa, a fact which did not please Labouchère. The silence on the part of the Spanish Court implied the withholding of its approval of the account and a possibility of subsequent objection to certain items. We shall in due course see

BERICHT

Van eene Negotiatie groot DRIE MILLIOENEN GULDENS Hollands Courantgeld, ten Comptoire de Heeren HOPE EN COMP., voor rekening van zijne Koninglijke Majesteit *JOSEPH NAPOLEON*, Koning van Napels, Siciliën &c. &c. onder verband van alle de Inkomften van Hoogstdeszelfs Rijk en Kroon, en Speciaal der Domeinen van Tavogliere in de Provincie van Pouille, dewelke door Hoogstgedachte Zijne Koninglijke Majesteit, Speciaal zijn afgezonderd, tot betaling der Intresfen en der Termijnen van Aflosfing dezer Negotiatie.

De Intresfen zullen à 6 pCt. 's Jaars worden betaald op Coupons, waarvan de eerfte verfcheenen zal zijn 1 Julij 1808.

Deeze Negotiatie zal gerembourceerd worden op de volgende Termijnen:

1 Julij 1809.	*f* 500000:—
1 Julij 1810.	- 500000:—
1 Julij 1811.	- 500000:—
1 Julij 1812.	- 500000:—
1 Julij 1813.	- 500000:—
1 Julij 1814.	- 500000:—

En dat bij loting, daar toe in der tijd voor Notaris en Getuigen te doen, over Reeksfen, ieder van Honderd volgende Nummero's.

De Provifioneele Recepisfen voor de Fournisfementen deezer Negotiatie, door de Heeren HOPE en COMP. uittegeven, zullen zoodra mogelijk tegen Obligatien, met de nodige Intrestbewijzen voorzien, en door den Notaris Mr. W. VAN HOMRIGH, gecontrafigneerd worden ingetrokken en verwisfeld.

Amfterdam 5 October 1807.

Bericht of the loan to Naples, 1807

how a series of events increased Spain's inertia–and how the Company attempted to arm itself against the consequences.

In addition to the Spanish loan, with all its ramifications, there was the matter of the loan to Naples. The moves which led up to an agreement with the representative of the Neapolitan Court at the beginning of May 1807 have already been described. The important thing now was to obtain official sanction for the loan and then to choose a propitious moment at which to float it. The negotiation for Spain and the fitful progress of the Dutch loan temporarily hampered a public subscription, and with this fact in mind Labouchère approached Louis, who had introduced Gérardin to the Company. Labouchère knew from Louis's letters that the emperor was interested in the success of the loan, and he therefore felt that it would be reasonable to expect the French Treasury to contribute a portion of the sum. At the same time, he asked Robert Voûte to find out whether Mollien would be prepared to put up a million guilders towards the Naples loan, adding that, if necessary, the money could be furnished from Hope's monthly payments on behalf of Spain.[1]

Labouchère also inquired of Voûte whether King Louis was still disposed to participate in the loan to his brother and whether he would agree to a million guilders from the 5% reserve relating to the Dutch loan being invested in the one for Naples. He was convinced that unless these contributions were forthcoming, the loan was doomed to failure.[2]

Gérardin and Roederer, the Neapolitan Minister of Finance, did not take kindly to Labouchère's reasoning. His original letter, they argued, had contained no reference to the need for French and Dutch participation, and it looked as if the Company was searching for excuses to delay floating the loan.[3] Their argument was not entirely without foundation, for when permission for the loan was suddenly given, Labouchère sought refuge in the stipulation that a copy of the principal debenture must be sent to the minister of finance. And when this condition was met, he sought to win time by pleading the absence of support by the French Treasury. This could not be anticipated until the emperor returned from Tilsit, where he had negotiated peace.[4]

When Labouchère remained adamant, Roederer suggested limiting the loan initially to 2 million guilders, in the hope that France or Holland would furnish a further million at a later date. The Neapolitan Treasury was in urgent need of cf 300,000 to repay a debt to the house of Falconnet & Co. of Naples, which fell due on 1st July, and Roederer sought to draw on Hope & Co. for this sum. Labouchère consented to this and also expressed his readiness to float the loan on condition that King Louis agreed to furnish 1 million guilders.[1]

A further complication, in the shape of news from Voûte that the king was not prepared to go beyond cf 500,000, caused publication of the *Berigt* to be delayed; but on 14th October Labouchère was able to announce that the loan had opened at a nominal price of 95–96%. It was stated that the bond allocations would be very small indeed, and this implied that the loan would be placed gradually. Labouchère had set his sights on rentiers, who would keep their bonds in portfolio and not use them to play the market.[2]

The issue price of 95% proved too high, but on 5th November Hope & Co., reported the signing of a contract with the *entrepreneurs* for cf 500,000 at 90%, with 5% commission. The bonds did not move far, for Hope, in conjunction with Willem Borski, acted as their own *entrepreneur*. King Louis ultimately agreed to furnish cf 400,000 towards the loan, for which, at the price of 90%, he received 440 bonds; these were transferred to the directors of the sinking fund relating to the 40-million guilder loan.[3]

On 24th December 1807 Hope & Co. advised Roederer that a further cf 500,000 had been placed with the *entrepreneurs* at a price of 90%. Simultaneously Baguenault & Co., acting on behalf of anonymous principals, applied for bonds to a nominal value of cf 500,000. We may assume that they were instructed by Napoleon, who thus acquired an indirect share in the loan. The reason for his secrecy is a matter for conjecture, but it is probable that he did not wish to create an imperial precedent and at the same time desired the freedom to resell the bonds whenever he pleased. He employed the same strategy when, some time later, a Prussian loan was floated in Amsterdam.[4]

With 2 million guilders already secured, Hope and Borski felt justified in jointly providing the remaining million from their own funds, thus completing the obligation towards King Joseph.[5]

During the great political upheaval which took place in the early months of 1808, Joseph exchanged the throne of Naples for the throne of Spain. His departure from Naples was preceded by a number of financial reforms which concerned Hope & Co. Responsibility for the repayment of the loan raised in Holland was transferred to the sinking fund, and Hope & Co. were instructed to deal with its director, Prince De Gerace, on future matters concerning interest and principal payments.[6] On 25th June 1808 Roederer informed the Company that King Joseph had instructed him to transfer 500,000 francs from the proceeds of the loan to Paris for his civil list. This would enable the monarch to bridge the gap between the cessation of one rule and the commencement of the next, and ensure that he did not arrive in his new kingdom, Spain, completely without funds.[1]

The second half of 1807 saw Ouvrard sinking deeper and deeper into the financial morass. In June he had attempted to persuade Hope to shift the overdue commitment for interest and principal repayment in 1806 from his account to the new Spanish loan of thirty million guilders, but had failed. Labouchère informed him politely but firmly that this was a matter between Ouvrard and Espinosa.[2]

In France itself also, Ouvrard's position was becoming steadily more perilous. Louis wrote to Labouchère early in June informing him that Mollien had officially forbidden Ouvrard to leave Paris. The minister was afraid that Ouvrard would go to Amsterdam and there try, to the detriment of his creditors, to lay hands on the funds which Hope & Co. held in his brother's name. Louis could not understand why a man with so high a sense of loyalty and duty as Labouchère should protect an individual like Ouvrard against his legal creditors. All the bitterness felt by Louis concerning his failure to get his way with Hope in February 1807 emerged from his letter.[3]

In his reply, Labouchère flatly denied being on Ouvrard's side. The fact that Ouvrard's assertions were precisely the opposite of Louis's proved this. The Company was willing to be of service to Ouvrard for as long as it believed that his ideas and plans were of general benefit or that, by doing so, harmful operations could be avoided. There was no question of Hope conspiring with Ouvrard to hide funds; everything was duly accounted, albeit the Company maintained its claims on Ouvrard's assets. The Company would never lend itself to operations which conflicted with its 'délicatesse' or with the principles of sound business.[4]

Labouchère in turn complained about a certain Maury, who had called upon the Company bearing a letter of recommendation from Louis. Maury, a partner in Sarraille & Maury, proved to be the agent for Gordon & Murphy. In the letter of recommendation, Louis had indicated that official pressure had been exerted on him to arrange piastre contracts via Maury. It was not clear to Labouchère whether this amounted to a hint to Hope & Co. to co-operate with Gordon & Murphy in the piastre deals; but it was very clear to him that Hope & Co. wanted nothing to do with a person like Maury. Three years earlier Sarraille & Maury had gone bankrupt, and the manner of the bankruptcy had led to criminal proceedings on grounds of embezzlement.

Labouchère had deemed it prudent not to disclose too much information to the visitor, and had parried his questions by saying that Hope and Baring functioned merely as intermediaries. Gordon & Murphy had crossed Hope's plans during the American business; their operations on behalf of Spain had been none too successful and now it looked as if they were going all out to get a foothold in Paris.[1]

Eventually, however, the point was reached at which Labouchère's support could no longer save Ouvrard. In the autumn of 1807 the *Compagnie des Négociants Réunis* ceased payment, and on 31st December of that year Vanlerberghe and Ouvrard had no choice but to follow suit.[2]

A fortnight before he applied for a moratorium, Ouvrard authorized Hope to correspond directly with Espinosa regarding accounts in the name of Auguste Ouvrard & Co. This came as a great relief to Labouchère, for it had long been obvious that the disgrace which attached to Ouvrard in Spain also reflected on Hope & Co. It had vainly been asserted that all funds belonging to Auguste Ouvrard & Co. were intact and that the only payments made from these had been to Spain. In the absence of supporting accounts, Espinosa had ignored the assertions. He had even ordered the seizure of the Mexican drafts to a value of 1,250,000 piastres which Labouchère had given to Alexander Baring in July 1806, of which 1 million piastresworth had meanwhile been collected.[3]

In the light of mistrust in Spain concerning the Company, and the unsatisfactory nature of communications, Labouchère had decided in June 1807 to send a confidential agent to Madrid. His choice fell upon William Gordon Coesvelt, a native of the West Indies, who had previously rendered valuable services to Hope & Co. in connexion with the settlement of long-standing claims on planters in the Western Hemisphere. Labouchère was aware that further piastre shipments were under discussion in Spain and felt that it was advisable to have a man on the spot via whom further steps could, if necessary, be taken. To all intents and purposes, Coesvelt would visit Spain as 'a man of pleasure' and would carry no instructions from Hope. The Company was still sparing in the granting of authority to act on its behalf, especially to agents who had still to prove their worth.[4]

At the end of July Coesvelt received a memorandum giving him the full history of Hope & Co.'s relations with Spain since 1782. His principal task was to inform the authorities in Spain of the true conduct of affairs, and by so doing dispel the erroneous impression to which Izquierdo's actions had probably given rise there. Furthermore, he was instructed to keep an ear open for news of fresh Spanish piastre expeditions and, in a plain but not obtrusive manner, to stress to those concerned the reliability of the Company's system of collection. Coesvelt was warned not to have any contact with Michel the Younger, who, as stated earlier, had gone to Madrid with his drafts on the *Caja de Consolidacion* in the hope of getting them honoured. Thanks to his wife's charms, Michel the Younger had become Murat's confidential agent and go-between in dealings with Godoy, and thus it was on the cards that he would succeed in having his drafts exchanged for others on Mexico.[1]

Coesvelt broke his journey in Paris, where he called on Izquierdo. The latter showed no sign of abandoning his negative attitude. At the end of a lengthy discourse, during which he dealt with all sorts of issues of prestige, he informed Coesvelt that he wished to see an end to the French Treasury's seizure of the Spanish assets held by Hope & Co. Having insisted that all matters should pass through his hands, he then threatened to block them until he got his own way. He also repeated his earlier accusation that the Company favoured the French government at the expense of the Spanish.[2]

Labouchère wrote to Coesvelt, instructing him to collaborate with Adriaan van der Hoop, a partner in Wed.E.Croese & Co., in an effort to settle the matter of the drafts on the *Caja* once and for all. Despite the fact that these had been specifically included in the loan contract, Espinosa persisted in his refusal to recognize the claim. Hope had already paid the sum of the drafts to Croese, but in return had demanded a guarantee of Espinosa's eventual approval. A united effort on the part of Van der Hoop, Coesvelt and the Dutch envoy to Spain, Verhuell, succeeded in breaking down Espinosa's resistance and enabled the matter to be finally disposed of.[3]

Labouchère had a favourable opinion of Espinosa, whom he regarded as extremely loyal to his country, though blind to the fact that his associates and subordinates did not always match him in this respect. If it should transpire that Espinosa was embarrassed by the drafts on Gordon & Murphy, Coesvelt was empowered to offer to take over 100,000 pounds-worth, provided that half of the proceeds were used for the interest and principal instalments due on 1st July 1808.[4]

To Coesvelt, Espinosa poured forth his grievances about the role played by Ouvrard. Labouchère admitted in a letter to Coesvelt that Ouvrard's policies had had adverse effects for Spain, but he remained convinced that Ouvrard had always meant well and that his failings stemmed from inexperience. In Labouchère's opinion, Espinosa would do better to free himself gradually from Ouvrard rather than break off the association abruptly: after all, the contract between the *Caja* and François Ouvrard &

Co. would remain in force at least until the end of the war at sea. As regards the trade with the Spanish colonies–for which, according to Coesvelt, Espinosa was willing to enter into an arrangement with Hope–Labouchère considered the risks at that moment (late December 1807) to be too great. He agreed to re-examine the question in the following Spring, by which time it would be clear whether the Orders in Council and the Milan Decree amounted to anything or not. If Espinosa felt that he would fare better by continuing to deal with Gordon & Murphy in regard to the piastres, he must do so; but under no circumstances would Labouchère consider collaborating with such people.[1]

In his discussions with Coesvelt, Espinosa had also broached the subject of deliveries of Venezuelan Varinas tobacco to the State monopoly in Spain. Labouchère was not averse to a transaction of this nature and he sought information on the subject from Dixon in Rotterdam. Hope & Co. already had 500 hogsheads, making them one of the largest stockholders. The quantity required, 4,000 hogsheads annually, made the affair too risky: Varinas tobacco was traditionally the property of the Crown, and the Governor of Venezuela was hesitant to sell it to American traders. When it was learned that Hogguer had also been approached on the subject of Varinas tobacco, Labouchère lost interest and Coesvelt was instructed to refer Espinosa to Hogguer.[2]

Coesvelt reported with some satisfaction that Espinosa was prepared to remit to Hope the 100,000 pounds sterling in drafts on Gordon & Murphy, and also to allow half the proceeds to remain in Amsterdam in preparation for the payments due on 1st July 1808. The trade decrees had severely restricted traffic to and from England, but Labouchère confidently anticipated that the drafts could be presented via Baring Bros. & Co. He would be very pleased if Coesvelt also succeeded in obtaining permission for the 1,031,250-piastre draft on Mexico, which constituted security for the interest payment due on 1st November 1808, to be met via Hope. Labouchère did not rely greatly on Espinosa's assertion that he would arrange for funds to be remitted from Madrid.[3] Early in February a report reached Amsterdam stating that the Company was free to collect the draft on Mexico, provided that one for 500,000 piastres for the Spanish government was presented with it.[4]

Upon receipt of the news, Labouchère immediately wrote to Henry Hope in London, asking whether he could arrange for the drafts to be sold there. The drafts did not form the subject of any contract with Baring Bros. & Co. and so it was worthwhile trying to keep the profit in the firm. A month later Henry Hope replied that the operation could not be carried out solely for the Company's account as the insurance would then not be valid in law. After investigating the possibilities, he had after all settled on Baring Bros. & Co., who had undertaken to send a warship to Vera Cruz to collect the piastres; the vessel was prepared to remain there for up to thirty days for this purpose. Baring Bros. & Co. would pay 177 pounds 10 shillings for every 1,000 piastres reported to have been placed on board.[1]

In the meantime, the situation on the Iberian peninsula was steadily approaching a climax. The Franco-Spanish treaty providing for the partition of Portugal was signed at the end of October 1807. French troops now had the right to traverse northwestern Spain on their way to the Portuguese frontier. However, they also had the opportunity to penetrate deeper into Spain without attracting attention. When, at about the same time, the French envoy to Spain compromised himself by his involvement in an intrigue aimed at eliminating Godoy in favour of the Crown Prince in the event of the death of Charles IV, Napoleon's thoughts turned increasingly towards the replacement of the weak and unreliable Bourbon regime by a satellite government headed by one of his brothers.[2]

Since the end of December 1807 Labouchère had been perturbed by the developments in Spain, and on more than one occasion he inquired of Coesvelt regarding the movements of the French troops. With the advance of the armies, financial transactions had become perilous: all manner of adventurers followed in the wake of the troops, in search of easy profits, and their operations undermined the rates of exchange. Espinosa could thus scarcely anticipate any early remittances from Amsterdam.[3]

At the end of February 1808 Izquierdo was commanded by Napoleon to deliver an ultimatum to the Spanish government: Spain must cede to France the territory north of the Ebro. Upon hearing of Izquierdo's sudden departure for Madrid, Labouchère instructed Coesvelt to make contact with the Spanish government so that in the event of Izquierdo distorting the facts, the truth could be established without delay.[4]

In spite of the serious nature of Izquierdo's mission and the haste with which this was undertaken, Coesvelt succeeded in arranging a meeting with him in Godoy's presence. Izquierdo lost no time in stating that he was directly responsible to the minister of finance and that he was therefore not obliged to show his accounts to Espinosa. When Coesvelt pointed out that it was the *Caja de Consolidacion* which had the greatest interest in the loan, Izquierdo suddenly produced the letters addressed to him by Hope & Co. and the accounts to which these referred. It was impossible to see much of the contents, for Izquierdo hurriedly put the papers away again. His excuses for not having written to the Company were so vague and incoherent that Godoy ordered him to approve those of Hope's accounts with which he agreed and to write to the Company about matters on which he disagreed, and to do so immediately he returned to Paris. According to Coesvelt, the true reason for Izquierdo's resentful attitude lay in his having been refused interest on the 2,000 bonds deposited in his name with De Smeth.[1]

Soon after this episode the anxieties concerning Spain's financial position were eclipsed by a series of major political events. Amid the general uncertainty, and with rumours of continuing French military advances rife, a popular revolt broke out at Aranjuez on the night of 17th March. This led to the fall of Godoy and his subsequent imprisonment, and to the abdication of Charles IV in favour of the Crown Prince.[2]

Coesvelt and Van der Hoop jointly wrote to Labouchère about the sudden turn of events. Confidence in the new government, they said, was very high, but they wondered whether the pace-by-pace advance of French troops towards Madrid was as innocuous as official circles maintained. The absence from official French statements of any reference to the new monarch, King Ferdinand VII, and his government was to the writers a bad omen. Nevertheless, they were of the opinion that there were opportunities for business. The aura of enthusiasm had changed the fortunes of the *vales reales*, which now stood at nearly 50%. If Labouchère could buy some *vales* drafts on Spain before the great news spread, the Company could make a handsome profit.[3]

In his reply, Labouchère was obliged to disappoint Coesvelt and Van der Hoop. The *vales* displayed little fluctuation in Holland, and offered no opportunities for speculation. Clearly, everyone was waiting to see how the situation in Spain would develop.[4]

In view of Spain's uncertain future, Labouchère impressed upon Coesvelt the importance of steering clear of politics, which did not form part of the Company's area of operation. This, he pointed out, was limited to Spanish financial commitments in Holland.[5]

The warning came at a very opportune moment, for since the uprising in March the situation in Spain had altered with immense rapidity. The change in the monarchy had given Napoleon the opportunity for swift intervention which he had sought. The Commander-in-Chief of the French forces in Spain, Murat, received orders to occupy Madrid. Ferdinand VII was enticed to the northern part of the country and from there to Bayonne, in France. Similar tactics were employed against Charles IV and his wife. When the royal family was reunited on French soil, Napoleon forced

Ferdinand to abdicate in favour of his father. Charles promptly abdicated in favour of Napoleon, who then had his brother Joseph, previously the King of Naples, appointed King of Spain by a council of Spanish noblemen.[1]

On 2nd May 1808, while Charles IV was still officially the monarch, the popular revolt against the French broke out in Madrid. The revolutionaries had little chance against the orderly French troops, but their action was a sign for a campaign of resistance throughout the country. Napoleon at first underestimated the power of the resistance movement, and returned to Paris in June confident that the Spaniards would soon resign themselves to the new order.

With the entry of King Joseph into Madrid on 20th July, Coesvelt's uncertainty ended–at least for the time being. During Ferdinand's brief reign, Espinosa had been replaced as *contador general* of the *Caja* by a directorate consisting of the Marquis de Fuerte Hisar and Don Antonio Cortabarria, both of whom were complete outsiders where financial matters were concerned and accordingly had to be advised from the outset.[2] In the interim period Coesvelt had been forced to mark time, but under King Joseph the situation seemed to be improving. Count de Cabarrus, with whom we have already made acquaintance, was appointed minister of finance and *contador general* of the *Caja*, and this implied that the Company could in future deal directly with the minister of finance on loan matters. De Cabarrus also had close ties with Baguenault & Co., and thus Labouchère hoped to gain access to him via them. In correspondence with Coesvelt, Labouchère stressed that he must concentrate on the payment of interest and principal on the Spanish loans. In the still obscure situation, any vague offers concerning a new loan to Spain with jewels as security, or concerning deliveries of tobacco, must be discouraged.[3]

The wisdom of this advice soon emerged. Eleven days after entering Madrid, Joseph, accompanied by some of his ministers, transferred his seat to the northern part of the country because he no longer felt safe in Madrid. His fears were not altogether without foundation, for on 22nd July a French army had been obliged to surrender to the Spaniards at Baylen, in the south. On 1st August, a British expeditionary force led by Arthur Wellesley landed in Portugal. A month later, Wellesley, aided by Portuguese patriots and units of the Spanish army, forced the French general Junot and his men to capitulate. With this defeat, little remained of French authority on the Iberian peninsula, except in a limited area to the north of the Ebro.

For Hope & Co., this debacle had unwelcome consequences. The payments due on 1st July in respect of the 1805 loan could be met from the available funds, but a question mark hung over the interest and principal due on Croese's conversion loans on 1st September and the interest due on 1st November on the 30-million guilder loan: apart from anything else, there was no confirmation that the drafts on Mexico had been met. Admittedly, De Cabarrus had given Coesvelt permission for the payments on the Croese loans on 1st September, but he had since departed, with King Joseph, to Vittoria, in northern Spain; Coesvelt, however, was still in Madrid, although Van der Hoop and Verhuell had left the city. To support his reasons for staying, Coesvelt could cite the example of the Russian, Austrian and American ambassadors, all of whom still resided in Madrid.[1]

Viewed in the light of the rapid sequence of events, the correspondence from Labouchère at that juncture seems almost unreal. While letters were leaving Amsterdam addressed to De Cabarrus in Madrid, Coesvelt was negotiating with a group of ministers and senior civil servants who had remained in Madrid but were in close touch with the Central Junta in Aranjuez. This body had been set up during Ferdinand's brief reign and now functioned as a sort of Free Spanish Government. Acting in the name of the *Caja de Consolidacion*, the Marquis de Fuerte Hisar instructed Hogguer to secure the attachment of those of Ouvrard's funds which were in Hope & Co.'s charge. Simultaneously, De Cabarrus, who was in Vittoria, instructed the Company to collect all monies owed by Ouvrard and his associates, and at the same time revoked the authority vested in Izquierdo. Both parties inquired of Hope regarding the collection of the million and a half piastres in Mexico.[2]

Labouchère was very concerned about the fate of these drafts. Reports indicated that De Villanueva was preparing to leave Vera Cruz at the end of May 1808, since there was a possibility that the United States embargo and the obstacles to trade in Europe would put an end to the activities of Hope's American network.[3] In September came a report stating that on 19th June (that is to say, after news of the events in Spain had reached that country's colonies) the British warship 'Melpomene' had sailed from Jamaica bound for Vera Cruz. On 7th July she hove to off that port, but after a delay, during which the drafts were refused, she sailed again. On 14th August the vessel again made for Vera Cruz, where the previous pattern was repeated. It became clear from the reports of what was happening in Mexico that De Villanueva had left Vera Cruz in the nick of time. The news of the change of government in Spain resulted in the emergence of popular movements sympathetic towards the former Spanish government, and for Lestapis, to which name he had reverted, such a situation could have been dangerous.[1]

Labouchère meanwhile faced the problem of the interest due on the 30-million guilder loan on 1st November 1808. Although it was stipulated that this should be paid from the proceeds of the loan, no subscriptions to this had been received since 1st November of the previous year. It was then that the value of the claims on Ouvrard's funds became apparent. After some solid pressure had been applied to Ouvrard, Hope & Co. received authority from Auguste Ouvrard & Co. to meet the interest payment from funds held by the Company on their behalf.[2] Labouchère thereupon advised De Cabarrus that he hoped to recover the sum paid out from the sale of the remaining 7,000 bonds. De Cabarrus had earlier made it plain that the payment need not be effected and that he did not desire the sale of further bonds, because a French military victory would naturally enhance King Joseph's credit. Labouchère had ignored these instructions, however; in his opinion, failure to pay the interest due would harm the loan to the point of rendering the sale of the remaining bonds impossible for a long time.[3]

De Cabarrus's indifference in the matter of Spain's obligations towards Hope & Co. was partly a product of his annoyance at the fact that Coesvelt had chosen to remain in Madrid. While apologizing on behalf of the Company for Coesvelt's conduct, Labouchère made it appear that Coesvelt had intended to accompany De Cabarrus to Vittoria but had been prevented by exceptional circumstances from leaving Madrid.[4]

John Williams Hope, who had meanwhile travelled to England via Germany, despatched a strong reprimand to Coesvelt–so strong, in fact, that Labouchère felt obliged to stand up for Coesvelt. He informed Hope that while he also would have preferred Coesvelt to leave Madrid, the fact that he had not done so must be attributed to the fear that the Company might be pushed out by Gordon & Murphy. He explained that Coesvelt had allowed himself to be persuaded to undertake the mission because of his loyalty to Henry Hope, and added that too powerful an 'extinguisher' could have a harmful effect, and might even alienate him from the Company. The relationship with De Cabarrus had not been completely ruined, because contact with him had been maintained from Amsterdam. And anyway Coesvelt was not an official agent of Hope & Co., so the Company could not be held responsible for his actions. In so confused a situation as then existed, the wisest thing was to remain as passive as possible while, of course, covering oneself against all eventualities.[5] This, however, was easier said than done. De Fuerte Hisar, on behalf of the central junta, had authorized Hope & Co. to use the Spanish funds held by Gordon & Murphy and Reid Irving & Co. in the event of the drafts for 1½ million piastres proving unnegotiable in Mexico. At about the same time, a similar authorization had reached the Company from De Cabarrus.[1] Labouchère was temporarily relieved of the necessity to make a painful choice, for the junta's days in Aranjuez were numbered.

Napoleon had not submitted tamely to the capitulation at Baylen and Junot's defeat. Since early November his armies had been on the offensive all over the country, and on 2nd December 1808 French forces marched into Madrid for the second time. The central junta fled to the south, choosing Seville as a temporary residence.[2]

This development came as a relief to Coesvelt. The junta had become increasingly unwieldy and had ultimately assumed control over all sorts of ministries. As far as the loans from Holland were concerned, Coesvelt was dependent upon a committee formed from members of the junta who knew nothing whatever about the matters with which they were supposed to deal, and accordingly failed to reach any decisions.[3] Moreover, thanks to Labouchère's letters, the relationship between De Cabarrus and Coesvelt proved not to have been permanently harmed, and normal contact was soon re-established. At the beginning of January 1809 De Cabarrus finally gave his approval for the payment made on 1st November of the preceding year out of Auguste Ouvrard's funds.[4]

The possibility of further shipments of piastres from Mexico, however, had evaporated. The early days of February 1809 brought news of the definitive protestation of the drafts for 1½ million piastres. Coesvelt and Labouchère were still hoping for a favourable turn of events as a result of a letter which the *Caja* was to send to the Viceroy of Mexico, in which it was to be clearly stated that the protested drafts were for the purpose of meeting a Spanish debt to Holland and that they were in no way concerned with the situation in Spain itself. Labouchère was anxious for Baring & Co. to persuade the central junta in Seville to write a similar letter, thus achieving support from both sides for Hope's case. It was just possible that France would assist financially in order to bolster up King Joseph's prestige.[5]

In a subsequent chapter we shall see whether these optimistic expectations were realized. The prospects were none too favourable. On 14th January 1809 the British government signed a peace treaty with the junta and also undertook to support it in the struggle against Napoleon. This opened the way for silver from Spanish America, which was then still loyal, to reach Seville unhindered.[6]

The situation had indeed altered radically. For Hope & Co. there was no more silver from Mexico, not even in the shape of colonial produce, and it remained to be seen whether they would have free access to Spanish funds held in England. The greater part of Spain was in French hands, but outside the cities a guerilla campaign exploded which almost destroyed the country economically. The practical significance, under such circumstances, of King Joseph's authority and financial position would soon become evident to Hope.

CHAPTER THIRTEEN

THE SPANISH MORASS

With the disappearance of the resources from America, Coesvelt's efforts to obtain funds in Spain itself for interest and principal payments assumed greater importance. Labouchère took the view that France had a duty to relinquish her claim on the proceeds of the remaining 7,000 bonds, and De Cabarrus agreed to write to Mollien on these lines.[1]

Coesvelt was meanwhile busy in his own way. At the end of February 1809 a report was received stating that the junta in Seville had ordered the seizure of the funds held by Gordon & Murphy and Reid Irving & Co. Little could thus be anticipated from London, and so Coesvelt cautiously approached Labouchère with a proposal for a new loan, for which nationalized Church property would serve as security. Labouchère, however, resolutely resisted any precipitate action: Amsterdam had lost three-quarters of its resources and also its influence on the investors. Apart from this, the 30-million guilder loan had yet to be fully subscribed; only then could any new venture be embarked upon. At the time of Labouchère's letter, in March 1809, everyone was anxiously waiting to see whether war would break out between France and Austria, and in such a situation it was pointless to approach the market with a new loan.[2]

Labouchère and his wife planned to visit the south of France during the summer; she suffered from rheumatism and wished to take the waters at Bagnères. The trip would also provide an opportunity to discuss future policy with Coesvelt in person. During Labouchère's absence from Amsterdam, the day-to-day supervision could be entrusted to the managers who had been appointed in 1808, at the time of John Williams Hope's departure for England. They were Henry John Hope Jr., the eldest son of John Williams Hope, and John Dixon, a former partner in Littledale & Dixon of Rotterdam.[3]

Labouchère advised De Cabarrus that the Company was proposing to dispose of a part of the remaining 7,000 bonds to the *entrepreneurs* at 70% (approximately the quoted price) with a bonus of six months' interest. 85% of the purchase price was due in cash or redeemable vouchers, and the remainder in Echenique bonds. This would provide funds for the payments due on 1st July and 1st November 1809, thereby raising the price of the issue and making it possible to dispose of the remaining bonds at a more advantageous price. Coesvelt was under the impression that the emperor had already released the 7,000 bonds, but Labouchère knew better: Napoleon had left for Germany in April in view of the impending war against Austria, and in his absence no decision on this matter could be taken in Paris.[1]

This postponement afforded Coesvelt an opportunity to revert once again to his plan for a loan secured by former possessions of the Church. For this, it would be necessary for the Spanish government to place the property of the Maltese Order in Catalonia at the disposal of the bondholders, who in return would be required to furnish 50 million *reales* in coin and a further 30 million in *vales reales*; for this purpose the *real* was considered to be equal to 2½ *stuivers* or 12½ guilder cents. The *vales reales* stood at 60% below par, and thus the true sum involved was 62 million *reales* in coin. However, interest, at 5% per annum, would be payable on the whole of the 80 million, giving bondholders an effective interest rate of 6¾%.

Bondholders would have the right to sell their share in the land, subject, of course, to surrender of the relevant bonds. The Spanish government would have to undertake to buy back land remaining unsold after four years; this it would do by redeeming the bonds at the market price plus a bonus of 5%. In order not to jeopardize Spain's credit in Holland, 12 million of the 62 million *reales* would have to be retained in Holland to meet the payments due in 1809. Finally, Coesvelt proposed that he should receive a commission of 1%.[2]

Coesvelt's plan offered no solution to De Cabarrus's immediate financial needs, and for this reason the minister authorized the Company to dispose of the remaining 7,000 bonds. No reference was made to permission having been obtained from Napoleon. Subject to the stipulation that 1 million francs remained for the Spanish Treasury–which sum De Cabarrus required immediately–up to 15% was payable in Echenique bonds. The letter was accompanied by a draft for 100,000 pounds sterling on Gordon & Murphy and another for 177,000 pounds sterling on Reid Irving & Co.[3]

Although the British government had blocked these funds for the benefit of the central junta in Seville, De Cabarrus was confident that the junta would recognize the duty to make the payments to Hope & Co. John Murphy, who had just been released from captivity in France, simultaneously wrote to his office in London, supporting the claim.[4]

Labouchère was not impressed by Coesvelt's letter, nor by the one from

De Cabarrus. In his view, a new loan could not succeed. The turnover in shares on the Amsterdam Stock Exchange totalled only 50,000 guilders a day, and business was as dead as it had ever been. There was, of course, no question of accepting De Cabarrus's draft for 1 million francs; as a reason for refusing, the managers could point to the fact that the French Treasury had not relinquised its claim to the 7,000 bonds.[1]

From Brussels, where Labouchère interrupted his journey to allow his wife to recover from an attack of fever, the travellers journeyed cautiously to Paris, where they arrived on 17th May. Labouchère availed himself of a pause in that city to discuss the Spanish affair with Mollien, Louis, Ouvrard and Baguenault. Mollien was ultimately persuaded to consent to the withdrawal by the French Treasury of its claim to the 7,000 bonds, subject, of course, to the emperor's approval.[2]

While in Paris, Labouchère was visited by Colonel Clary, an adjutant of King Joseph and a relative of the queen, who bore a letter from the Spanish monarch. It was clear from this that the sum of 1 million francs was for the king's personal use, and indeed was destined for investment in Russian and American securities. Labouchère took the view that the question of honouring the draft for this sum was best left to the managers in Amsterdam. He did, however, advise them to hold as security any bonds which might be purchased until such time as news concerning the drafts on Gordon & Murphy and Reid Irving & Co. was received from London.[3]

After staying for a week or so in Paris, the Labouchères moved slowly southwards. They frequently travelled at night in order to spare the patient the discomfort of the heat during the daytime. At the end of May, having journeyed via Poitiers and Bordeaux, the company reached Orthez, where the Labouchère family had its origins. There, mail from Amsterdam, Paris and Madrid awaited them.[4]

The managers in Amsterdam reported that they had received a visit from Colonel Clary and that they had made it plain to the young man that there could be no question of yielding to the king's 'personal views' until such time as arrangements were made for the payments due on 1st July and 1st November.[5]

A letter from Coesvelt stated that he would be making for Bayonne with a military convoy which was due to leave Madrid on or about 5th June. During his absence, matters would be taken care of by Sanchez Toscano, a former partner in the house of Echenique. Coesvelt's expectations were not high, for Toscano suffered from consumption and had been at death's door on two occasions during the previous year; moreover, he was a Spaniard and a timid one at that.

De Cabarrus had requested the Viceroy of Mexico to honour the drafts deposited with Hope & Co. as security for the payments due on 1st November 1809. Coesvelt, however, had as little faith in the payment of these drafts as of those for 1st November 1808.[1]

At the end of a long and tiring journey lasting twenty days, Coesvelt arrived in Bayonne on 25th June 1809. Shortly afterwards he joined the Labouchères, who had meanwhile moved to Bagnères.[2] In addition to reiterating his proposal for a loan secured by former Church property, he produced a plan devised by De Cabarrus for a loan coupled with a lottery. In an accompanying letter addressed to King Joseph, De Cabarrus set out to show that of the anticipated total revenue of 92 million *reales*, only 16,300,000 had in fact been collected. In the provinces, in particular, the meagre revenues had been totally absorbed by the cost of maintaining the troops. Then there had been the taxes levied by the French military commander. In Madrid itself, the growth of illicit trading had caused revenues to steadily diminish. The Mint would soon have to cease operations because of the shortage of precious metals, and this while the reserves for expenditure by the Court and by ministers were insufficient for one month.

To meet the deplorable financial situation, De Cabarrus proposed that a lottery loan be entered into; this would cost Spain a great deal of money, but under the circumstances it was the only solution. The loan would be of 6 million *pesos duros* at 20 *reales* per *peso*, half of which would be payable in coin and the balance in *vales reales* at their full nominal value. 10,000 bonds each of 600 *pesos* would be issued, and these would bear interest at 4% and be redeemable within five years. In addition to the fixed interest, annual bonuses, the total of which would have to be increased year by year, would be balloted: these would be necessary in order to attract capitalists who were not interested in the purchase of nationalized Church property. Under this plan, the Spanish government would have to spend 7,856,332 *pesos* in order to obtain 4,200,000 *pesos*. Outside Spain, facilities for subscription would exist at the offices of Hope & Co. in Amsterdam, Chapeaurouge in Hamburg, Paul Maistre in Geneva and Roux Frères in Marseilles. Clearly, the minister anticipated greater results from the provincial towns in France and from the satellite states than from Paris. The plan had still to be approved by Napoleon.[3]

Coesvelt discussed all these plans with Labouchère, after which he outlined the De Cabarrus project with Baguenault; the latter, however, saw little chance of a loan in France succeeding.[4]

His discussions with Labouchère having been completed, Coesvelt left for Amsterdam to submit his plans to the Company's managers. Their reaction, following Clary's visit, was predictable: they rejected the idea of any fresh loan until the old one had been fully subscribed. If Spain failed to meet its commitments on 1st July and 1st November, it could abandon all thoughts of a new loan.[1]

The problems surrounding the payments on 1st July 1809 were formidable. There was still no news from England concerning the fate of the drafts on Gordon & Murphy and Reid Irving & Co. The Company had a claim to assets of Auguste Ouvrard & Co., but as the Spanish American operations had to all intents and purposes come to an end, the remittances in favour of this account were becoming smaller and smaller. Moreover, Ouvrard had just lost an action brought against Vanlerberghe and himself by Séguin, and this had cost him 7 million francs. There was thus all the more reason to view critically the guarantee which Ouvrard had provided on behalf of Spain.[2]

Fortunately, an official report had arrived from Paris stating that the French Treasury had relinquished its claim to the 7,000 bonds. The way was thus clear for a definitive contract with Borski for 2,600 bonds at a transfer price of 70%. As had been the case in the previous contracts, the *entrepreneurs* received a bonus of six months' interest. The interest vouchers which fell due on 1st July 1809 and the bonds of the loan of 1805 which became redeemable on the same date were both acceptable as payment. Bonds and vouchers relating to the loan floated by Hope & Co. in 1793 and those of Croese's conversion loans were also acceptable, as were 160 bonds relating to the Echenique loans; for the last-named, the price was fixed at 95%. In addition, Borski was permitted to exchange 350 Echenique bonds at 95% for a similar number of bonds of the 30-million guilder loan.[3]

In essence, this agreement meant that the *entrepreneurs* exchanged matured bonds and vouchers for new ones. The effect of this procedure (which also applied to a number of older Spanish loans) was to clear up as many old Spanish bonds as possible under the umbrella of the Auguste Ouvrard guarantee. And since Hope & Co. held funds belonging to that company, no risk would be involved even if Spain failed to meet its obligation.

The action of the managers in thus securing breathing space in connexion with the July payment was fortunate indeed, for the plan with the drafts on England miscarried completely. At the end of June 1809, Baring & Co. reported that Reid Irving & Co. had transferred all the Spanish funds which they had held to the junta in Seville. Gordon & Murphy would have followed suit had it not been for the fact that certain of their assets in Mexico had been seized and they were thus retaining the balance on the Spanish account by way of security. In any case, the British government would in no circumstances lift its embargo on these.[1]

After visiting Amsterdam, Coesvelt proposed to cross to England to attend to private business. There would thus be an opportunity for consultation with the partners in London. His journey, however, was anything but straightforward, for on 30th July 1809 a British expeditionary force had landed on the island of Walcheren and had advanced to the outskirts of Bergen op Zoom. In the panic which ensued, the wildest rumours circulated, including one to the effect that a fresh British landing at Den Helder was imminent. This led to an embargo being placed on all Dutch ports.[2]

In addition to other matters, Coesvelt had been instructed to discuss the loan to the Kingdom of Naples with the partners of Hope & Co. The relationship with the director of the Neapolitan Sinking Fund had from the outset been less than satisfactory. There had been no difficulties with the interest payment on 1st July 1808, because the sum involved had been retained out of the proceeds of the loan. De Gerace had clearly been disappointed by Hope's lack of interest in participating to a substantial extent in the Neapolitan Consolidated Debt. This debt, which amounted to 14 million ducats, was for the purposes of buying out the tax farmers and compensating the former owners of Church property which had been nationalized. According to Falconnet & Co., there were good profit opportunities for foreigners, because the shortage of money in Naples had depressed the rates of exchange. This shortage was in turn a product of stagnation of exports under the influence of the Continental System.[3]

Hope & Co.'s reply to this tempting offer was to the effect that the Company might consider participating if Naples made regular remittances for the interest payments due in the following year.[4] It had rapidly become clear that this was not a simple matter, for few commercial contacts had been established between Italy and Holland, with the result that drafts were scarce on the market. Hope & Co. had advised De Gerace to spread the net to embrace Leghorn and Genoa, but this did little to increase the tempo of the remittances.[5]

De Gerace was also anxious to commence repayment of the loan as soon as a sum of any magnitude reached Hope, and it was only with the greatest difficulty that he could be convinced of the irrevocability of the payment date of 1st July laid down in the principal debenture.[6] He thereupon demanded interest on the monies which he remitted, up to the day upon which these were paid to the investors. Even after extremely protracted correspondence De Gerace refused to accept the fact that the Company never paid interest on remittances of this nature and, moreover, that the total stagnation of trade ruled out any profitable investment of the monies concerned.[1]

De Gerace took his revenge by withholding remittances to Amsterdam even beyond the payment date of 1st July, with the result that the Company was repeatedly obliged to make advances. By 1st July 1809, cf 210,000 had been advanced out of a total of cf 692,875. Needless to say, this was a constant source of annoyance. At the same time, De Gerace had no scruples about allowing one of his subordinates, Gennaro Francesconi, to draw on Hope & Co. for his personal requirements, leaving the Company to recover the sums from a firm in Genoa. Later, De Gerace merged his private activities into the commercial operations of Gennaro Francesconi & Co., a mercantile house which was to play an important role in foreign remittances.[2]

Late in July 1809 Labouchère and his wife embarked on their journey northwards. For much of the time he was deep in thought, searching for a solution to the problem of the Spanish payment in November. In his correspondence with Sanchez Toscano, Labouchère continued to toy with the idea of covering the 4 million guilders due on that date by the transfer of the possessions of the La Oliva cloister at Navarre and other ecclesiastical assets in that region; but the weakness of King Joseph's authority outside the towns rendered this plan as illusory as those put forward by Coesvelt.[3] Labouchère hoped that the Napoleonic victory over the Austrians at Wagram and the ensuing armistice of 12th July 1809 would lead to sterner military action in Spain, but as things stood this was tantamount to wishful thinking.

All the plans for the November payment crashed in ruins when De Cabarrus rejected the contract with Borski for the 2,600 bonds; the rejection also threatened the payments due on 1st July 1809. Hope & Co. were even deprived of their authority to negotiate further contracts with the *entrepreneurs*. De Cabarrus had also lost faith in the payment of the drafts on the English houses and those on Mexico, which were to cover the payments on 1st November, and he forbade the Company to incur any further expense in connexion with these.[4]

In their reply, the managers pointed out that De Cabarrus had earlier given permission for the payment on 1st July, and that the contract with the *entrepreneurs* was the only means by which to obtain the money required. They urgently requested De Cabarrus to make such arrangements for the 1st November payment as would ensure that Spain's credit abroad did not collapse suddenly. They stated that the outgoings could provisionally be limited to the payment of interest. The 2,500 bonds which were due to be drawn by lot for redemption could then be used, at the holder's option, for the purchase of Spain's national possessions.[1]

Shortly after the letter was despatched, a later one from De Cabarrus arrived at Hope's offices. In this the minister set forth a plan for a loan of 3 million francs, for which fifty or more paintings from the Escorial would serve as security. The loan would be for three years and bear interest at 6%, and there would be a commission of 2%. Labouchère's reply was that any attempt to raise new money for Spain would be doomed to failure unless the payments due on 1st November were forthcoming. Even if the idea of such a loan were to be entertained, he stated, it would first be necessary to send an expert to Spain to value the paintings.[2] Also, the lenders would probably insist that these be removed from Spain to the safety of Amsterdam.

Startled, De Cabarrus replied that he had envisaged a private transaction with Hope & Co. and not a public one. If the Company was unwilling to undertake this, he would negotiate with 'a few of your capitalists.' The pictures could be given into the custody of the lenders, but would only become their property if Spain defaulted in its repayments.[3]

On his journey back to Amsterdam, Labouchère stayed in Paris. While he was there, Izquierdo made repeated visits to his address, initially without success. Labouchère had not forgotten Izquierdo's failure to reply to all his letters, and had made up his mind 'to be as costive in speaking as Izquierdo (had) been in writing.'[4]

Eventually Izquierdo managed to see Labouchère and to unburden himself. As a loyal servant of Charles IV, he had come to humbly plead for the 2,000 bonds lodged with De Smeth in his name. The interest on these alone would make him a happy man, for his former sovereign was now in Marseilles, poor, ill and overwhelmed by debts following the failure of the French Treasury to pay him his civil list. He had borrowed 230,000 francs from Doyen & Co. and they were now pressing him for repayment.

Labouchère gave no immediate reply to the request but instead inquired why Izquierdo had ignored all the letters from Hope. When the latter commenced to make vague references to 'political reasons,' Labouchère asked what a simple acknowledgement had to do with politics. Izquierdo thereupon embarked on a story about having been afraid of hampering the Company's progress and thereby prejudicing it against himself. Labouchère, mindful of the stories which Izquierdo had told in Coesvelt's presence, let him go on. When at last he spoke, he said that there could be no question of acceding to the request: the 2,000 bonds would remain in De Smeth's keeping, and Izquierdo would not receive the interest.[1] A payment of this nature could be interpreted as a political decision, and the Company could not afford to run such risks.

While in Paris, Labouchère also met Nolte, who, as explained earlier, had gone there to present the final account for the piastre transactions to the French government. He drew Nolte into a plan which Ouvrard and the Minister of Finance, Fouché, had devised and which was clearly inspired by Hope's Spanish American transactions. The plan envisaged the creation of one hundred licences, with the aid of which American or neutral vessels would be able to bring colonial produce into the Neapolitan ports and, in exchange, export goods from the country itself.

Murat, the new King of Naples, had been informed about the plan, but as he was with his armies in Austria the negotiations proceeded slowly. The safety of the inward-bound cargoes of colonial produce constituted a problem: after all, a decree had been issued in Milan prohibiting such imports. Labouchère accordingly insisted that a sum of 2 million ducats be deposited in advance to cover any goods which might be confiscated. As the date of the emperor's return to Paris drew nearer, Murat and Fouché became less and less enthusiastic about the project. When Labouchère left Paris at the beginning of October, nothing definite had been decided. Nolte travelled with him to Amsterdam.[2]

By now, a decision whether or not to make a payment on Spain's behalf on 1st November had become a matter of urgency. When a final appeal to Mollien to save Spain's credit remained unanswered, Hope & Co. placed an advertisement stating that no interest or principal would be paid. The bonds thereupon fell to 50%, but later recovered to 55–56%.[3]

Under the circumstances, the wisest course appeared to be for Coesvelt, who had returned to Amsterdam from England at the beginning of November 1809, to make his way back to Spain and find out what could be salvaged. No communication had been received from De Cabarrus since Labouchère's negative reaction to his proposal for a loan secured by works of art, and it was not clear whether, like his predecessors, he was hiding behind a barrier of silence or whether his couriers had been detained, or even murdered, by guerillas.[4]

At the same time, King Joseph appeared to be more firmly in the saddle following the French military successes. The authority of the junta in Seville had collapsed after the battle of Ocana on 19th November 1809.

The junta withdrew to the Isla de Leon, an almost impregnable peninsula in the vicinity of Cadiz, where, with the support of the English fleet, it was able to maintain its existence.[1]

Late in December, De Cabarrus, no doubt encouraged by these successes, sent Hope & Co. a decree from King Joseph which amounted to no more than an official proclamation of the lottery loan plan launched previously. The decree referred to a loan of 21 million guilders at 6%, a higher rate of interest than had originally been proposed. The sum of the payments due on 1st November 1809 and 1st July 1810 was to be met from the proceeds of the loan, the balance being transferred to Spain. No reference was made to the 4,000 unsold bonds of the 1807 loan.[2]

In the meantime, Coesvelt had travelled via Paris to Bayonne, where he awaited a military convoy to Madrid. While in Bordeaux, he had met Duclerc, De Cabarrus's agent, who had explained the loan plan to him. Coesvelt was fairly optimistic about the success of such a scheme, but with the proviso that the matter of the 4,000 bonds of the 1807 loan would have to be settled first.[3]

Labouchère took a considerably less sanguine view; he found it highly regrettable that Coesvelt had not waited for him in Paris so that they could have discussed the subject in detail. Labouchère had been charged by King Louis with a peace mission to England and this required his presence in Paris. He was opposed to a new loan such as De Cabarrus had proposed. The previous Spanish loan had declined in price to 46%, and in the light of this it was pointless to go to the market with a new issue. The interest due on 1st November 1809, and with it the 5% bonus on the maturing bonds, must first be paid, and this must be repeated on 1st July 1810. The sum of these payments was of the order of two million guilders and this could be obtained through a loan of five million francs, for which Crown jewels and paintings could serve as security; these would be deposited for safe keeping with Cabarrus & Co. of Bayonne, the partners in which were related to the minister. A loan of this nature could be limited to a small circle of investors. If this failed, consideration might be given to the issue of warrants valid for the purchase of national possessions in Spain. It might be possible to find a group of speculators willing to take over warrants of this kind. Also, bonds drawn on 1st November 1809 and 1st July 1810, but not redeemed, could be exchanged for the warrants; holders not wishing to do this could be offered prolongation of their bonds.[4]

Coesvelt remained in Bayonne from late January until early April 1810, during which period he was intensively engaged in correspondence with

Labouchère and De Cabarrus on the subject of new loans for Spain. It became clear that an impasse had been reached: Labouchère was unwilling to undertake any new issue until the arrears of interest had been paid, and De Cabarrus insisted that the arrears should be met from the proceeds of a new loan. Coesvelt was aware that a loan against the security of Crown jewels was out of the question, since these had already been sent to Baguenault in Paris to be sold.[1]

As he contemplated his forthcoming journey to Madrid, Coesvelt was reminded that this was taking him farther and farther away from Amsterdam, where at that moment important decisions were about to be taken. Early in 1810 Henry Hope Jr. had revealed his disinterest in the Company's activities by resigning his directorship and leaving Amsterdam. Some time previously John Dixon had suffered a stroke, and despite a partial recovery he had ceased to take an active part in day-to-day affairs. In order not to leave the Company entirely without management during Labouchère's absence, executive power had been vested in Pierre Firmin Lestapis, a younger brother of Armand Pierre, with whom we have already made acquaintance.[2]

Coesvelt, who eagerly desired a similar position, wrote one agitated letter after another to Labouchère. In these, he repeatedly blamed himself for having journeyed on to so remote a place as Bayonne instead of awaiting Labouchère's further orders in Paris. He was not at all keen to go on to Spain, if only because of the dangers which threatened travellers, and he had lost faith in the idea of a new Spanish loan since he had learned that Spain would be obliged to maintain the French troops stationed on its territory. This, he considered, would ruin the country completely.[3]

It was a very reluctant Coesvelt who, on 9th April 1810, joined a military convoy bound for Madrid. Just before his departure he had received a letter from Labouchère, setting out in some detail the latter's idea of asking the French government to provide funds for the interest and principal payments on 1st July 1810. Labouchère, too, had heard that France proposed to place the full burden of maintaining its garrison in Spain on that country's Treasury, and he took the view that as France would thus save huge sums annually, it could well afford to spend some of this money to restore Spain's credit abroad.

At the end of a journey fraught with privation and peril, Coesvelt arrived in Madrid on 3rd May. There he learned that De Cabarrus had died.[4] His successor was the Marquis d'Almenara, a victim of Ouvrard's Franco-Spanish operations, who is already familiar to the reader. It was, of course, necessary to recapitulate events for D'Almenara's benefit. According to Coesvelt, the change might well prove to be for the better since De Cabarrus 'could not refuse those who were present and . . . forgot his obligations towards those who were absent.'[1]

Coesvelt was received in audience by D'Almenara on a number of occasions, but the results were meagre. They discussed the possibility of France standing as guarantor for the current debt–which was in line with Labouchère's thinking–but no decision on this could be taken in Madrid. The situation had in one respect been simplified by the incorporation of the Kingdom of Holland into the French Empire, which was officially accomplished on 1st July 1810. The people of Holland thereby became direct subjects of Napoleon and as such could count upon him to protect their financial interests.[2]

A long memorandum dealing with the plan followed from Coesvelt, but the first of July 1810 had meanwhile come and gone without payment of interest or principal. Spain had nothing to offer, neither money nor wool, and the king desired to keep the remaining diamonds for private purposes. Coesvelt, however, received an offer of several 'remarkable' paintings as security for a private loan of 250,000 or 500,000 francs, which was to be payable when the paintings reached a safe place. Coesvelt sought the advice of Labouchère and also offered him a half share in the loan. Labouchère replied that nothing would induce him to participate and that Coesvelt would be well advised to have nothing to do with the affair. Amsterdam was the only place where the paintings could be properly valued, and who was to be responsible for any damage which might occur in transit?[3]

Coesvelt's doubts regarding his mission increased when he learned that D'Almenara would be leaving for Paris early in August for talks with the imperial government. Under such circumstances, he saw no point in remaining in a country where utter chaos reigned and the most scandalous forms of cunning were the order of the day. Added to this, Spain's financial resources were in fact controlled by French military men who attempted to collect taxes behind the Spanish government's back. Negotiating with D'Almenara's deputy, Don Francisco Angulo, meant explaining everything from the beginning for the umpteenth time in the knowledge that no decision would be forthcoming. If anything was to be achieved, Labouchère would have personally to raise the matter with D'Almenara and the imperial authorities in Paris.[4]

Labouchère paid little heed to this advice. He had made two journeys to Paris in the space of six months, and the time had come to prepare for his retirement from the Company at the end of the year. The peace mission to

England on behalf of King Louis had failed. He was subsequently approached on the same subject by Ouvrard, who appeared to be acting on instructions from the emperor. Labouchère wrote to Alexander Baring and Lord Wellesley, but made no more progress than on the previous occasion. When news of the correspondence reached Napoleon's ears, he was furious. It then transpired that Ouvrard had not been acting on behalf of the emperor at all but, in company with Fouché, had ventured a private attempt to secure peace. Fouché was dismissed from office, and Ouvrard was returned to the prison from which, thanks partly to Fouché's intervention, he had been released in 1809. Labouchère was summoned to Paris to explain his role, but so well did he succeed in convincing his questioners that he had acted in good faith that he left without a stain on his character. Just how perilous his position was at that moment, however, is revealed in letters from Coesvelt referring to his great anxiety over reports from Paris that Labouchère had been arrested, or was about to be.[1]

Against this background, Labouchère decided that the negotiations with D'Almenara should be conducted by David Parish. Parish had arrived in England early in July 1810 and had crossed to Amsterdam in August to present his report and accounts concerning the Spanish American business. In mid-September he left for Paris carrying letters of introduction to Talleyrand, D'Almenara and numerous French ministers.[2]

Labouchère instructed Parish to test reactions to the idea of disposing of the total Spanish debt in Holland to the United States in exchange for 3% bonds, of which 1% would be redeemed annually. Payment would be required in Amsterdam in guilders, or in dollars at a rate of exchange of 50 *stuivers* per dollar. The United States would thus receive 37 million guilders or 14⅘ million dollars at 5½% interest, plus a 5% bonus on redemption. On the basis of 3% bonds, which then stood at 60%, the whole exchange would cost the United States less than 9 million dollars. In addition there were the drafts on Mexico, which had been calculated at the favourable rate of 32 *stuivers* to the piastre.[3]

To make the deal even more attractive to the United States, it would be necessary for Spain to agree to sell Florida to the United States for the sum of the debt in Holland. The effect of this would be to confront Mexico with the choice between approving the cession of Florida or meeting the Spanish debt; if it chose the latter, the United States would greatly benefit financially. The crux of the matter, of course, was whether Napoleon would agree to such a settlement. If it was true that Florida had declared its independence and had asked the United States for protection, it would almost certainly be to Napoleon's advantage to approve the sale.

At Labouchère's suggestion, Parish also consulted Daniel Parker, the merchant and speculator whose name has already appeared in connexion with the piastre affair. Parker, who had long experience in the sale of land, proposed a shift of emphasis. He felt that it would be feasible to combine Spain's financial requirements and her need to repay her debt in a new loan of 40 million guilders at $5\frac{1}{2}\%$ interest, three-quarters being payable in existing bonds and the balance, 10 million guilders, in cash. The new loan would be redeemable in ten years by the sale of 20 million acres of rich farmland on the shores of the Gulf of Mexico. During the ten-year period, an estimated 2 million acres could be sold at 10 dollars per acre, enabling the loan to be repaid in full. The remaining 18 million acres would fetch 2 dollars an acre, making 36 million dollars. At the conclusion of the loan, every bondholder would be entitled to one forty-thousandth part of this sum, i.e. 900 dollars.[1]

In the matter of the interest payment, Parish and Parker adopted a plan put forward by D'Almenara and the Spanish envoy in France, the Marquis de Santa Fé. This envisaged placing at Hope & Co.'s disposal 30,000 quintals of quicksilver, which lay in Seville, at a price of 100 guilders per kilogram. Half of the proceeds, i.e. cf 1,500,000, would have to be placed at the disposal of the Spanish government, and the balance would serve for the payment of the interest.[2]

Labouchère's initial reactions were unfavourable in the extreme. He was not at all impressed by Parker's ideas about selling land in Florida: 'Nothing would induce the Dutch to invest more money in land in America, whatever people there may think. It will take half a century to erase the consequences of earlier errors from European minds.' This was plain speaking indeed – certainly towards Parish, who had himself indulged in land speculation in America on a large scale.

To Labouchère, the ideas put forward by D'Almenara and De Santa Fé reflected the old misconception on the part of the Spanish Court that its foreign debts constituted a source of new revenue. The ominous rise in the number of bankruptcies throughout the empire ruled out any chance which a proposal of this nature by Spain might otherwise have had.[3]

The 30,000 quintals of quicksilver were nominally valued at 4 million guilders. According to Labouchère, the demand on the Continent did not exceed 20,000 pounds in a year – and there was continuous competition from German and Austrian quicksilver. He took the view that the Company could be well satisfied if it succeeded in selling 10,000 pounds per year, so that it would take three hundred years to dispose of the stock. In Paris, Nicolas Clary was still left with some quicksilver which had been captured in the Tyrol during Napoleon's campaign in 1800.

To achieve larger sales, it would be necessary to export the material to North and South America; but this would require Spanish, French and British licences. If these could be obtained, it would be quite a different matter: if American vessels were used, it might be possible to combine the exporting of the quicksilver with the importing of North American tobacco for the Spanish tobacco monopoly. In considering tobacco imports, Labouchère reverted to an earlier plan; but again he did not go beyond the realm of contemplation.[1]

Early in November 1810 Simons returned to Amsterdam, this time in the role of negotiator for D'Almenara. Once again the familiar issues were listed: the disposal of the remaining 4,000 bonds, the potential use of warrants for the purchase of nationalized Church property, the 30,000 quintals of quicksilver (which might produce some immediate funds) and the possible importation of American tobacco. Only one thing was missing, the thing which interested the Spanish government above all others, namely ready cash.[2]

Simons was thus obliged to return to Paris empty-handed. He arrived there just in time to impart the disappointing outcome to D'Almenara before his departure on 11th November 1810. Simons's own future soon became uncertain, however, for he was obliged to seek a moratorium at the end of November 1810. He carried with him the house of Raymond & Theodore de Smeth, which got into such difficulties that at the beginning of January 1811 it was obliged to cease payment altogether.[3]

For David Parish, the beginning of 1811 coincided with a desire to terminate the association with the Spanish American affair. He had earlier declined a seat on the board of Hope & Co., and now he resigned from his company in Antwerp, though this provisionally continued to bear his name. It was his intention to return to the United States and seek his fortune there.[4]

Account 'X', which Parish had now finally closed, has already been referred to. No good purpose would be served by repeating the estimates of the profits from the various transactions which passed through this account, the more so as the Hope archives do not reveal a grand total from which the level of profit could be determined with certainty. We shall thus have to accept Nolte's estimate, which refers to a profit of 862,250 pounds sterling, or just over 3,800,000 piastres. This figure does not include the profit on the 4 million piastres shipped direct from

Vera Cruz to England. According to our rough calculations, this was just over 830,000 piastres.[1]

The shipments to Spanish America under licences issued by Parish were to have a long and disagreeable sequel. Early in 1809, following the outbreak of the civil war in Spain, Espinosa's agent, Sarmiento, reported that he had received instructions from the *Caja de Consolidacion* henceforth to deal directly with the American merchants concerning the import duties due to Spain. At the same time he demanded from Parish and the Olivers import duties totalling 1½ million dollars, which was equivalent to 50% of the value of the cargoes. Although Sarmiento acted on behalf of Charles IV, it quickly became clear that the demand had originated from the junta in Seville, which thereby attempted to secure funds.[2]

Parish's lawyer in Philadelphia, Charles W.Hare, saw it as his first task to obtain copies of the contracts between Espinosa and Ouvrard and between Ouvrard and Hope. He also proposed that committees of investigation be sent to Europe to interrogate witnesses and, if necessary, summon them to appear in the United States. In Hare's opinion, it was of the utmost importance that Hope & Co. should produce documents showing that all monies transferred by Parish had indeed been remitted to the *Caja*.[3]

The case dragged on for eight years, the hearings taking place in one court after another. In the autumn of 1808 it was the Philadelphia Court of Common Pleas; in 1810 it came on in the Pennsylvania Supreme Court; and finally it reached the United States Circuit Court. Whenever a judge found in favour of Parish and the Olivers, Sarmiento appealed to a higher court.[4]

The questionnaire used by the investigating committees revealed that Parish was suspected of having shipped goods to Vera Cruz on his own initiative and having failed to remit to Hope the duties due on these. Among the other matters investigated were whether Hope & Co. had acted as the agent of the *Caja de Consolidacion* and whether any monies had been paid to the governments of Joseph Napoleon, Charles IV or Ferdinand VII.[5]

In Labouchère's eyes, the matter was a simple one. Hope's principal had been Auguste Ouvrard & Co., and the Company had settled its account with them. If the Spanish king sought to derive extraordinary authority from the decree upon which the trading licences had been based, he should address himself to those to whom the licences had originally been issued, namely Auguste Ouvrard & Co. In pursuance of this view, Labouchère declined to hand over copies of contracts with Ouvrard or to answer the committees' questions. His response to requests to look into the circumstances under which Charles IV and Ferdinand VII had surrendered the Spanish throne to Napoleon, and whether they had been within their rights in doing so, was that these were too ridiculous even to discuss.[1]

However, in the face of an urgent appeal from Alexander Baring to answer the questions, in order not to prejudice Parish's position, Labouchère agreed in June 1811 to issue a brief statement. In this he affirmed that the monies received from Parish had been accounted for to Auguste Ouvrard & Co., but that because the Spanish government had debts in Holland which exceeded the sums received, these had, with the prior knowledge of the Spanish government, been applied to the payment of these debts. The Spanish government, he maintained, had never been concerned in the dealings with Auguste Ouvrard & Co. and Parish.[2]

This, however, did not settle the matter. In 1812 the case was heard by the United States Circuit Court. The prosecution demanded that Parish should furnish a bond of 150,000 dollars, and this was upheld. Parish's lawyers, who also represented the Olivers, submitted that the case should be struck off the list on the grounds that the Court could not put forward a person as the King of Spain unless that person had been so recognized by the government of the United States. This was an embarrassing point and one which the Court, while giving no reason, refused to pursue. After a brief consultation, Parish's counsel decided to withdraw the submission and to concentrate on a complete denial of the prosecution's 'cause of action.' For this, however, counsel required copies of all the contracts with Ouvrard and all accounts relating thereto.[3]

Labouchère viewed the request for documents as indiscreet, to put it mildly. If it were acceded to, details of Hope's transactions, including those which had no bearing on the case, would be revealed to all and sundry. 'Let Sarmiento bring an action against Hope & Co. in a court of justice in London, where Messrs.Hope will gladly address themselves to him,' was his reply.[4] Again Alexander Baring intervened, this time to point out that the court in America would construe a refusal to answer the questions as recalcitrance, and that this would jeopardize a favourable verdict. For the second time, Labouchére allowed himself to be influenced by Baring and furnished the replies requested.[5]

In order to be in as strong a position as possible, Labouchère desired the return of all unmet drafts on Mexico and Caracas. To achieve this, Baring went so far as to write to Echeverria, into whose custody De Villanueva had given the remaining drafts.[6] Early in 1813 the questionnaires, duly completed by Labouchère, and the relevant accounts and authentic copies, all attested by a notary and by the American Consul-General in Amsterdam, Sylvanus Bourne, were despatched to the United States, where a very distressed David Parish awaited their arrival.[1]

In the early weeks of 1814, by which time Holland had been liberated, an American landed in Amsterdam with instructions to obtain fresh answers to the questions. His arrival intensely annoyed Labouchère, to whom the legal battle was as ludicrous as it was irritating. To him, American justice was a riddle: Parish had won his case, yet here was the action being brought again – and without an appeal being entered![2]

The greatest problem facing Parish was that he was unable to prove that the Spanish government had been among the parties to the transaction. This evidence was only forthcoming when Ouvrard re-emerged from the prison into which he had disappeared in 1810. It was not until after the fall of Napoleon that he was released – and indeed this was the excuse which he tendered to the Chief Justice of the Supreme Court for his long silence. Ouvrard himself still hoped to reach a settlement with the Spanish Court, and pending this he was prepared to offer any assistance in clarifying matters. Our sources do not reveal whether or not this clarification was achieved, but we do know that Parish secured a definitive legal victory over Sarmiento in 1816.[3]

After that brief diversion, let us see how fortune was dealing with Coesvelt. We take up our story with D'Almenara's return to Spain in November 1810, still without any promise from Labouchère or Coesvelt regarding fresh loans. In a letter sent other than by the official mail, Coesvelt set out his cheerless view of the situation in Spain. Ministers, he wrote, avoided discussions which might lead to clear conclusions or firm agreements. Not that this was surprising, for Spain was bankrupt and unable to meet its creditors. The only solution lay in the transfer of freely-controlled national possessions and private property to a value equal to the total Spanish debt. This debt would then be soundly consolidated and, with such security, up to 6 or 7 million guilders could be advanced.[4]

Viewed from Amsterdam, Coesvelt's assessment of the situation was unrealistic, for in the economic crisis of 1810–1811 an advance of any magnitude was out of the question. Furthermore, Coesvelt was obliged soon afterwards to report that the custodian of Spain's national possessions had personally stated that, because much had already been sold and because communications with the provinces had virtually been severed by guerilla activities, the possessions which could be assembled would be worth less than 30 million *reales*.[5]

Soon after this Coesvelt gave up the idea of coming to an arrangement in Madrid. Ultimately, he wrote, any negotiations or decisions would have to take place in or come from Paris. It would be best if Spain were to be incorporated into France, for King Joseph's authority was steadily waning. It might be possible to limit the annexation to the area north of the Ebro and, subsequently, to compensate King Joseph in Portugal for the loss of territory. On neither count was there any point in his remaining in Spain, for he was merely being kept on a string.[1]

Indeed, partly as a result of developments within the Company, Coesvelt's stay in Spain was drawing to a close. With the death of Henry Hope in February 1811, new arrangements had become necessary. Labouchère had earlier intimated his wish to retire, and in April of the same year he reached agreement with John Williams Hope, who had changed his name to John Hope following the death of Henry Hope. It was agreed that Labouchère should leave the Company at the end of 1811, but that he should continue to sign documents on its behalf. John Hope undertook to indemnify Labouchère against any consequences arising from the use of his signature. In practice, this meant that Labouchère appeared to the outside world to be still a partner of Hope & Co. but that he was absolved from the financial responsibilities attaching to the position. It was further agreed that Coesvelt, Adriaan van der Hoop and Pierre Firmin Lestapis should be given power of procuration.[2]

In the light of these arrangements, it was of importance that Coesvelt should make his way to Amsterdam as quickly as possible, the more so since Labouchère proposed to go to Russia and wished to settle all outstanding matters before he left. Moreover, he was anxious to speak to Coesvelt before he sought Van der Hoop's reaction to the proposed appointment. Pierre Firmin Lestapis, who was 'always perfectly well disposed,' would concur in any arrangement. Coesvelt left Madrid early in May and arrived in Amsterdam on 10th June. By the 15th, matters had all been settled and the circulars signed.[3]

Before embarking on his duties in Amsterdam, Coesvelt wished to visit England and settle his affairs there. He took with him drafts on Vera Cruz to a value of 50,000 piastres, which were to be sold in London. These had been received from Gennaro Francesconi & Co., the company in which Prince de Gerace had merged his business activities. Drafts for a further 300,000 piastres arrived after he had left, and these were forwarded to him in London.[4]

In spite of these transactions, relations with De Gerace were anything but smooth. On 1st July 1810 the Sinking Fund was still nearly

100.000 guilders in arrears with its payments, and by 1st July of the following year the deficit had risen to nearly cf 150,000.[1] Meanwhile, the squabbling over the date for the payment of interest and principal on the Neapolitan bonds (which was among the causes of the slowness in making remittances) continued.[2] The atmosphere did not improve when, at the beginning of November 1811, Coesvelt returned to Amsterdam with the news that the assets of the drawer of the piastre drafts –whose name was not disclosed–had been confiscated, and that other, similar drafts had been returned protested.[3] De Gerace began by accusing Hope & Co. of having underestimated the premium on the guilders banco. When this allegation was refuted, he cast suspicion on the slowness with which the redeemed bonds were surrendered. Assertions by Hope & Co. that this was a common phenomenon, and was due to poor communications with the bondholders, were treated almost with incredulity.[4]

As if this were not enough, De Gerace also complained that, in dealing with his remittances, the Company did not adhere sufficiently to the due date, with the result that the Neapolitan Court was deprived of a portion of the discount. Hope's managers pointed out that payees of drafts on Italy usually remitted the funds to a third centre and therefore desired some latitude in respect of the due date, but without consequences for the rate at which bills were accepted. They added that, in general, De Gerace benefited by dealing with Hope, because bills bearing the Company's signature were frequently accorded a better rate than those presented by other firms.[5]

By 1st July 1812 the arrears of remittances from Naples had risen to cf 175,000, while the Company, in consequence of the death of Henry Hope and the policy of liquidation pursued by John Hope, was experiencing a steady decline in liquidity. The managers referred this problem to Labouchère, who, with his wife, was at that moment in Bad Pyrmont. Labouchère replied that he was not enamoured of De Gerace's manner, but that he had little doubt that Naples would honour its obligations. In the light of this advice, the managers decided to make the payment due, but at the same time to address a rebuke to De Gerace and to demand immediate settlement of the arrears.[6]

When, following the death of John Hope in February 1813, the Company actually went into liquidation, there was no longer any question of advancing money on behalf of Naples. In March of that year De Gerace was warned that the payment on 1st July would be limited to the sum held by the partners. The majority of the remittances were in the form of bills drawn by Gennaro Francesconi & Co. on Agostino Serra and Giulio di

AMSTERDAM 15 JUNE 1811.

We have the honor to acquaint you that we have granted the firm of our house to our friends Mr WILLIAM GORDON COESVELT, Mr ADRIAN VAN DER HOOP and Mr PETER FERMIN LESTAPIS, who have all long enjoyed our confidence and have had an opportunity of evincing their title to it in various situations of trust in which we have employed them. We add at foot their respective signatures and request that you will be pleased to pay the same attention to them as to those which are already known to you.

We remain with perfect regard,

Your most obedt Servants.

Hope & Co

Signature of Mr W. G. COESVELT. . . . . . Hope & Co

Signature of Mr A. VAN DER HOOP. . . . . . . Hope & Co

Signature of Mr P. F. LESTAPIS. . . . . Hope & Co

Circular of 1811 announcing the granting of power of procuration to Van der Hoop, Coesvelt and Lestapis

Grossi, both in Genoa, and it was virtually impossible to get these accepted in Amsterdam.[1]

On 30th June 1813 De Gerace was advised that there was still a deficit of cf 140,000 and that therefore only 365 of the 500 bonds due for redemption had been drawn. Although this news evoked a response unparalleled in terms of language, a remittance was soon forthcoming, enabling an announcement of the drawing of the remaining 135 bonds to be made on 1st November.[2] There still remained a deficit of cf 25,000, but it was greatly in the interest of the managers not to antagonize the French authorities who, following the defeat at Leipzig, were on edge and easily incensed.[3]

Napoleon's abdication at the beginning of April 1814 cast a shadow over the final payment by Naples of interest and principal, which was due on 1st July of that year. After the rout of the *Grande Armée* in Russia, Murat had hurried off to Naples to seek popularity among his subjects. He had simultaneously commenced negotiations with the British government. He had again fought on the side of Napoleon at Leipzig, but immediately after the defeat there he returned to Naples. In January 1814, Murat signed a treaty with Austria. In this he undertook to help to drive the French out of northern Italy, and in return was given a guarantee of the safety of his kingdom. While Napoleon's abdication remained uncertain, Murat gave only lukewarm support to the Austrians in northern Italy, and when the emperor finally renounced the throne he lost no time in returning to his capital.

As a result of all these events, it was five months before Hope & Co. again heard from De Gerace. In April 1814 another irate letter arrived. In this, De Gerace slated the Company for daring to pay four months' additional interest on the 135 bonds redeemed on 1st November 1813.[4] The remittances to Amsterdam continued, but the amounts were so small that Labouchère, who by then was in Paris, felt it necessary to warn the managers that under no circumstances were payments to exceed the sums received. In view of the size of the remittances, he advised them to limit payments to the interest, and this was done.[5]

The measure produced further angry letters from De Gerace, but the managers were by now accustomed to his outbursts. When he continued to demand restitution of the four months' interest, they informed him that they proposed to lay the matter before Murat himself. The threat had the desired effect. Although he remained convinced that Hope & Co. had kept the additional interest for themselves, De Gerace was obliged to submit and to recognize the right of every bondholder to interest up to the day of redemption.[6]

Fresh remittances from De Gerace enabled 75 bonds to be redeemed on 1st November 1814, but Labouchère continued to warn against granting any advances in view of the uncertainties of the political situation in Naples.[1]

Since the opening of the Congress of Vienna, which was occupied with the redisposition of Europe, Metternich had changed his mind about Murat's position. In northern Italy, which was now controlled by Austria, Murat's presence might well give rise to lasting nationalist agitation. He decided to drop Murat. In January 1815, with the knowledge of the British government, he signed a secret agreement with Louis XVIII of France providing for Murat to be driven out of Naples and for the restoration of the house of Bourbon.

Murat was aware of the plots against him and he therefore moved more and more towards Napoleon, who had been granted the island of Elba as his empire and who, from there, was continuously engaged in preparations for a return to France. As early as mid-November 1814 Labouchère warned of the risk of sudden hostility on the part of Murat, which might lead to the interruption of remittances from Naples to Genoa; in the event, however, it proved possible to redeem 50 bonds on 1st January 1815 and a similar number on 1st April.[2]

With this, matters provisionally came to a standstill. On 1st March 1815 Napoleon landed in the south of France, and on the 20th he again took up residence at the Tuileries in Paris. For Murat, this was the signal to declare himself against Austria and to call upon the peoples of Italy to unite. Early in May 1815, even before the Battle of Waterloo, he was defeated by the Austrians, whereupon the throne of Naples was restored to the Bourbons. A desperate effort by Murat to bring about a revolt in Naples ended with his imprisonment and subsequent execution in the latter part of October 1815. Fortunately for the Company, Ferdinand I of Naples recognized the existence of the loan, so that it was possible for a further 80 bonds to be redeemed on 1st April 1816 and the balance of 245 on 1st June 1818.[3]

With Coesvelt's return to Amsterdam, a silence descended on the Spanish loan. The next reference to it in the Hope archives is a message of congratulation to the *Caja de Consolidacion* on the occasion of the liberation of the two countries, with which was coupled the hope that it would not be long before agreement was reached on the loans granted to Spain.[4]

This was followed by a fresh silence. Eventually Labouchère approached the newly appointed Dutch envoy to Spain, Cambier, who consented to plead the cause of the Dutch bondholders with the Spanish government.[5]

In recognition of Cambier's assistance, Labouchère provided him with letters of credit drawn on Baguenault & Co. in Paris and Sanchez Toscano in Madrid. Cambier's early reports from Madrid were couched in reasonably optimistic terms, but by March 1815 he, too, had lost heart.[1] In a letter sent in August, which for safety was written in Dutch and carried by a private courier, he explained the situation more fully.

'We are making little or no headway in the matter,' he wrote. 'And if we continue to follow the royal path, we shall not easily reach our destination. Two persons of relatively subordinate rank enjoy the full confidence of the Master of the Royal Household and administer its funds, almost to the exclusion of those who appear in the books. It is said they are extremely approachable, with the proviso that one friendship must be repaid with another. This, however, is not unusual and is even found among judges. Since no one is paid, how could it be otherwise?'[2]

This lengthy citation reveals a very great deal about the situation in Spain in the period after 1815–and indeed before that. Weak monarchies, favouritism, corruption and poverty are the hallmarks. While the scope of this treatise precludes us from following step by step the later fortunes of the Dutch loans to Spain, we can, as it were from a distance, envisage the remaining Dutch claims gradually sinking into the Spanish financial morass.

The brief period of liberal government from 1820 to 1823 brought a resumption of interest payments on the debt to Holland. In 1830 and 1831 the loans in their entirety were converted into 5% perpetual *rentes* on which interest was paid until a second conversion was effected in 1834. This conversion in fact amounted to a reduction by one-third: of the 5% perpetuals, two-thirds were converted into a 5% active debt, and the remaining one-third into a passive debt which carried no interest. In the event, the payment of interest on the active debt continued only up to 1836.[3]

Little purpose would be served by recording the progress of this twice-converted debt. Suffice to say that it was not until the end of the 19th century that Spain became ripe for a period of expansion such as took place in the middle of the 18th century, at which point in history our story opened.

Diamonds

CHAPTER FOURTEEN

THE PORTUGUESE DIAMOND LOAN

We have selected this measure as the means to introduce the reestablishment of our House with eclat, by manifesting the most conciliatory disposition and unequivocal proof of our attachment to the interest of the country.

Henry Hope, in a letter to P. C. Labouchère, 3rd August 1802.

The powerful military expansion which took place in France following the outbreak of the Revolution in 1789 had disastrous consequences for Portugal. As members of the first coalition of the European powers against France during the wars of the French Revolution, Portugal and Spain had become involved in the campaign of 1793; but Portugal had been unable to follow Spain's example in suing for peace two years later. To have done so would inevitably have meant a break with England, and this was something no Portuguese government could afford. Since the beginning of the eighteenth century the country had been largely dependent upon England in the economic sphere, and the French Revolutionary Wars had increased that dependence. If the English navy, with its supremacy, were to cut off Portugal's vital imports from the colonies or, worse still, occupy her overseas territories, she would be helpless.

As Spain became more and more a satellite of France, the situation along Portugal's frontiers became more perilous. Added to this, French pirates, operating from Spanish ports, interfered with shipping in Portuguese waters. The consequences were catastrophic: falling revenues and rising expenditure brought the threat of economic collapse.

To meet the situation, the prince regent appointed the energetic Don Rodrigo de Souza Coutinho to the post of Minister with responsibility for the colonies, the navy and the country's finances. This combination of posts was not fortuitous, and by rebuilding the Portuguese fleet and pursuing the war at sea with greater vigour he succeeded in controlling the pirates, thereby enabling shipping to move freely again and thus improving the country's financial position. The modernized Portuguese fleet even operated with success against the French off Malta and in the coastal waters of Egypt.[1]

For Napoleon, the peace treaty with Austria was a prelude to settling accounts with Portugal and simultaneously bringing about the closure of

Portuguese harbours to British ships. Spain had bound herself to assist in accomplishing this, and as a reward had been offered a prospect of additional territory–at Portugal's expense. As British support was limited to a few subsidies, Portugal could offer little resistance to this attack.

The conflict was as brief as it was insignificant. On 6th June 1801 Spain signed a peace treaty with Portugal at Badajoz. The settlement included the cession of some Portuguese territory. Despite the fact that the French envoy to Spain, Lucien Bonaparte, had been a signatory to the treaty, Napoleon refused to ratify the settlement on the grounds that, in his opinion, both his brother and the foreign minister, Talleyrand, had been bribed by the Portuguese. Further negotiations led to the Treaty of Madrid on 29th September 1801–two days prior to the signing of peace preliminaries by England and France. For Portugal, the price of peace included keeping her ports closed to British ships until a final settlement in Europe was negotiated, and the payment to France of a war levy of ten million crusados, the equivalent of more than 11 million guilders.

Faced with this short-term commitment, for which it simply did not possess the funds, the Portuguese government was in an acutely embarrassing position. A loan was the obvious solution, but the chances of obtaining one were poor unless adequate security could be provided. With the possible exception of a tax revenue, no suitable security existed in Portugal. Her colony, Brazil, however, produced an article which was ideal for the purpose, namely diamonds.

The discovery in 1727 of rich diamond deposits in what is now the state of Minas Gerais had made Brazil the world's largest producer of this precious stone. The Portuguese government, realizing the possibilities, had assumed control of mining operations and thereby obtained a virtual monopoly. The marketing of the diamonds was left to merchants, who entered into a contract with the government; in this, they undertook to take a certain minimum quantity during a set period at a fixed price per carat.[1]

The Hope archives reveal traces of the Company's repeated efforts over a long period to secure this 'diamond contract.' In 1765, the Hopes invoked the aid of the Danish Court, with which they maintained good relations. The Secretary of State for Foreign Affairs, Baron von Bernstorff, consented to transmit a memorandum from Hope on this subject to the Danish envoy in Portugal, together with his recommendation, and to instruct the envoy to present it to the government.[2] But the 'balances' relating to the years which followed contain nothing to suggest that the contract was obtained, and thus it must be assumed that this remained in the hands of its possessor, the house of Gildemeester.

In 1777, the fall from grace of the powerful Portuguese minister Pombal brought a fresh opportunity. There was every chance that those who had enjoyed his protection would also disappear from the scene. The house of Thomas Mayne & Co. in Lisbon wrote in most optimistic terms about such a development, even going so far as to give themselves a good chance of securing the contract. If this occurred, Hope & Co. might become Mayne's commision agents in Amsterdam–a disappointing prospect for a house which itself sought the contract! [1]

But there were others with an eye to the main chance. Robert Lewis Cantofer, a Lisbon merchant, informed Hope that, thanks to his contacts in government circles, he would certainly be considered for the contract (although the price per carat offered was also a factor of importance), and in that event he would gladly join forces with Hope. A fixed quantity of 60,000 carats would have to be taken annually, on conditions corresponding to those which Gildemeester had imposed on the Jewish diamond merchants at Amsterdam in previous years. This implied that a fixed quantity would be delivered quarterly at a fixed price and with a six-month advance at 3% interest per annum. Against the 60,000 carats to be delivered, Cantofer wished to draw cf 450,000–about two-thirds of the estimated value–quarterly. The balance would become payable after the principal annual sales.[2]

All these efforts were to no avail, however, for shortly afterwards Mayne reported that Gildemeester's contract would expire in the normal way. In 1787 a further attempt failed, but in 1791 Hope had at least a measure of success.[3] Joachim Pedro Quintella, the new contractor, appointed the Company as his agents in Amsterdam for the duration of his contract, i.e. until the end of 1801.

The correspondence with houses in Lisbon contains numerous references to Hope's wide experience in the diamond trade. This embraced the sale of uncut diamonds in Amsterdam as well as the export of polished stones, especially to Russia and Turkey. The former activity related to commissions from Jewish diamond merchants in London. The earliest surviving 'balance,' which dates from 1763, contains such names as Eleasar Salomons, Gompertz & Heyman, Salomon de Silva and Nathan Salomons.

Perusal of the *grootboeken* for 1770 and the following years shows that the quantities traded varied greatly from one year to another. In some cases the cause can be attributed to political factors, as in 1779–80 and 1793–94, but in others no such influences are discernible. Generally speaking, the annual totals were fairly high: in 14 of the 25 years between 1770 and 1794, more than 15,000 carats were sold.[4]

It is worthy of note that, commencing in 1785, the Company also effected sales on behalf of Jewish merchants in Amsterdam. According to the *grootboeken*, one of these, Ruben Harmsz. Kijzer–who later became Hope's and Insinger's confidential representative–had previously been a diamond merchant in London, and must therefore have moved to Amsterdam later.[1]

The sales made on behalf of Quintella in the years 1791 to 1801 inclusive display the same irregularity as those for the London merchants, but here the cause lay partly in the war. In 1795, following the departure for London of the partners of Hope & Co., diamonds ceased to be consigned via the Company.[2] It is true that a new channel–which led via London and Hamburg to the Amsterdam house of Insinger & Co.–was established in the succeeding years, but that house received so few diamonds in 1798 and 1799 that it was moved to issue a warning to Labouchère. The cessation of supplies in 1795 had already caused serious damage; if the existing situation continued, lasting harm would be done to the diamond polishing industry, and this in turn would have an adverse effect on the market for the gems.[3] Fortunately, supplies were restored at the beginning of the 19th century.

That advancing money against diamonds and lending money on the security of diamonds differed only in degree, became clear round about the turn of the century. Quintella had approached Messrs. Hope in London in the matter of a loan in 1796, and in March 1800 he did so again. On both occasions the partners declined. Since Quintella's first proposal, the demand for diamonds in Holland had risen and sales had improved, but the money market in England was no place for loans on the security of private property.[4] They did, however, offer, jointly with Francis Baring & Co., to advance a reasonable sum for a shorter period–say, 100,000 pounds sterling for two years at 6% interest plus a commission of 5%.

The interest and a portion of the principal could be paid out of the diamond sales effected by Insinger & Co. in Amsterdam; the balance of the debt would be payable by Quintella on the due date, by way of a remittance. As security, Hope would require diamonds totalling 40,000 carats, 'pour notre tranquillité personnelle.' The diamonds, which represented a value of cf 1,765,000 or 147,000 pounds sterling, would be deposited with the Bank of England.[5]

This implies that Hope, in company with Baring, was prepared to advance a sum equal to two-thirds of the value of the security for a period of two years. This differs little from the earlier situation, in which two-thirds was advanced for one year. In their correspondence with Quintella, the partners accordingly kept the whole affair strictly in the sphere of trade by placing the proposed transaction on the same footing as commission sales of wool and silk.[1]

Early in 1801 the Company was approached for the first time, albeit indirectly, by the Portuguese government. The partners' reply was cautious but did not amount to a rejection. They said that, in such turbulent times, there was naturally little incentive to tie up their funds in an article which could only be placed on the market slowly, but that if the Court was prepared to dispose of a high proportion of the diamonds which it held and to refrain from releasing any more on to the market for a given period, a transaction would merit serious consideration.[2] They went to great lengths to recommend the participation of Quintella, since it seemed to them unwise to ignore such a respectable and powerful house.

After the Peace of Madrid, however, the Portuguese government had no time for guarded moves of this nature: it needed money, and quickly, in order to meet its commitment to France. It thus sought a house able and willing to provide immediate advances, and also to float a loan on the English market. As the partners of Hope & Co. had not actively pursued their profession of merchants and bankers since their flight to England, the principal role at this juncture passed almost automatically to Baring & Co., a house which had achieved wartime prominence by the handling of international finance.

During the early days of October 1801, Baring & Co. were approached by John Stanley of Lisbon concerning a loan of 300,000 pounds sterling to the Portuguese Court. It quickly transpired that Stanley, a long-standing business contact of Barings, had close connexions with Jacinto Fernandez Bandeira, a rich and influential merchant who was acting as agent for the Court in the matter of the loan. After a favourable response from Baring, more information was forthcoming. The French government had initially demanded a cash payment of four million crusados, plus diamonds to a value of three million crusados and a similar sum in cotton and sugar. One million crusadosworth of diamonds and a further million in drafts had been given in mid-November. Now, the French were insisting that the balance be paid in cash, and to meet this Stanley proposed that the loan should be increased to 1,200,000 pounds sterling. This would enable the Court to settle its debt to France and also 'to provide at once for all the exigencies of Government for a long time.'[3]

In a 'Plan d'un emprunt' drawn up by Don Rodrigo de Sousa Coutinho on the orders of the prince regent and transmitted to London by Bandeira, the Portuguese government set out the conditions upon which it wished to negotiate. The payment of interest and repayment, over ten years, of the principal could be made from the revenue from the tobacco lease or that from the Crown lands. In addition, the Court was willing to deposit immediately diamonds to a value of 250,000–300,000 pounds sterling with the Bank of England. These would be placed at the disposal of the house which assumed responsibility for the loan, and the proceeds of their sale could be used to repay the principal. The diamond consignments would continue until the final repayment against the loan was made. The Court required the monies subscribed to the loan to be made available in ten monthly instalments, commencing on 1st November 1801.[1]

It may be assumed that the Portuguese Court, in drawing up these conditions, took account of the wishes of Francis Baring & Co., and that this house, in turn, sought the advice of Messrs. Hope, who after all were more experienced in such matters. The deposition of diamonds with the Bank of England – a point raised by Hope in the previous year – points to this. Later correspondence shows also that the proposed loan carried the approval and patronage of the British government. This is not surprising, for prompt settlement of the French claim would mean the restoration of Portugal's freedom of action, and this could only be to England's advantage.[2]

By this time, Labouchère had left for the Continent to make preparations for the re-establishment of the Company in Amsterdam once peace between England and France became a reality. During his stay he had been regularly informed of the position in regard to the Portuguese affairs, and now that the negotiations were beginning to take shape he received instructions from John Williams Hope in London to hold himself in readiness for a journey to Portugal.[3]

The fact that Labouchère was to conduct the negotiations enabled the partners to reconcile themselves to some extent with the subordinate role which the Company had up to then played in the affair. Robert Voûte was negotiating with the government of the Batavian Republic on the conditions for a resumption of the Company's business, but, alas, he had not made sufficient progress to permit an early return to Amsterdam, 'where we might embrace a greater object by participating or dividing the Concern with the publick.'[4] It was agreed that the name of the Company should not be mentioned for the time being; but the major part which Labouchère was to play in the preparations for the affair would certainly become known, and this would naturally draw attention to the Company.

The affair possessed attractive facets from the points of view of both houses: for Hope it presented an opportunity to gain complete control of the diamond trade, and for Baring the prospect of becoming sole agent for the Portuguese Court in matters involving foreign transactions. The respective interest of the two houses were reflected in the agreed ratio of participation, namely five to two, Hope taking the larger share. Both were of the opinion that the sum requested, 1,200,000 pounds sterling, was too large, and initially they were unwilling to go beyond 700,000 pounds, of which 400,000 pounds would be made available on 31st January 1802 and further sums of 100,000 pounds on 30th April, 31st July and 31st October of that year.[1]

Against all expectations, the Company was accorded recognition of the position which it so ardently desired. On the day after John Williams Hope recorded his chagrin concerning the opportunities in Amsterdam which were being missed, it was decided, on the advice of Francis Baring, to transfer the entire Portuguese negotiation to the Batavian Republic. While we can only guess the motives which led to this sudden change of course, it would be safe to assume that the settlement reached with the Batavian government at the end of November, concerning the long-standing claims against the Hope family, had a bearing upon it. Only when this obstacle had been overcome did a return to Amsterdam become feasible, and the move, in turn, was a prerequisite for introducing the Portuguese negotiation. Repatriation and Portuguese affairs thus became interwoven – a circumstance which was subsequently to produce complications.[2]

The news of the momentous decision reached Labouchère in Paris. It was expedient to have the Portuguese affair settled by the time the peace treaty between England and France was signed, whereupon the house would be able to resume operations in Amsterdam. Labouchère was informed that he should therefore depart for Lisbon without delay, leaving matters of secondary importance such as the restoration of trade links with Madrid and Cadiz. If possible, he should charter a vessel in order to avoid the long and circuitous overland journey.[3]

Accompanied by George Baring, the youngest son of Sir Francis, Labouchère travelled via Nantes, La Rochelle and Bordeaux to Bayonne, where both men tried to charter a vessel to take them to Portugal; but their efforts were in vain. Deeply conscious of the need for haste, they hired a train of mules and a driver, by which means they travelled for nine days in bitter winter weather to Madrid, where they arrived on 20th January. The journey was continued at the same tempo, and on 28th January Labouchère was able to report from Lisbon to his principals that he was ready to commence the negotiations.[4]

He was certainly not handicapped by lack of instructions. Mail had preceded him during his journey, and in Lisbon a stack of letters from both Hope and Baring awaited his arrival. In essence, the plans had not altered since mid-November 1801, which implied that the principals adhered to the 'Plan d'un emprunt,' albeit the sum of the loan was limited to 700,000 pounds sterling. Moved by a spirit of caution, John Williams Hope in particular exhorted his negotiator to keep his eyes open and to ensure that the interest payments against the loan commenced on 1st January 1802. Labouchère was advised that the loan instalments should be as widely spaced as possible, since Baring and Hope were about to participate in a loan in England and therefore their liquid resources would be somewhat stretched for a time. In view of the pressure of time, the two houses had agreed to allow Don Rodrigo de Souza Coutinho to draw 100,000 pounds sterling on Hope & Co. in Amsterdam, but they were fervently hoping that Labouchère would reach Lisbon before the sum was drawn.[1] This limited advance reflected a certain fear of competition.[2]

Labouchère's first impressions were wholly favourable. The sovereign and the minister both inspired him with confidence, and the securities which they offered were so solid that nothing in England could match them. The only real hazards lay in the political sphere, for there were clear signs of French intrigue inside Portugal; but provided that the peace congress at Amiens produced the desired results, Labouchère did not envisage any dangers in the current year.

In order not to leave the minister in doubt, Labouchère drew up a 'First Overture to His Excellency,' in which he set out the basis upon which the two houses wished to negotiate. First, they required the minister's approval for the transfer of the loan to Amsterdam. This would be in the interest of the Portuguese Court also, for foreign loans were difficult to place in England and very costly.[3] In Holland, where the house of Hope would resume its activities as soon as peace was restored, the situation was much more favourable, for there loans of this sort had long been commonplace. Although the majority of government bonds yielded more than 6%, Labouchère deemed it wiser to fix the interest on the new loan at 5% and to lower proportionately the price at which the loan would be taken over. If a 6% loan stood at par, a 5% loan should command $83\frac{1}{2}$%. However, 6% Americans commanded 96%, and on this basis the price of the Portuguese loan would be 80. This corresponded to the prices of Austrian, Spanish and even Dutch issues. As a special favour, however, Labouchère offered to place the Portuguese Court on a level with the Russian Court, or even on a higher plane. Thanks to Hope's tireless efforts, the Russian bonds then stood at 88–89, and against this Labouchère offered the minister a takeover price of 90.[4]

The size of the loan was left in abeyance. The minister desired cf 13,000,000, payable in instalments of cf 1,000,000 in the months January to November and a final payment of cf 2,000,000 on 31st December 1802. Labouchère consented in principle to this arrangement, adding that he hoped to be in a position to accomplish the desired increase of the principal sum. This, however, would require consultation with his friends, and pending this it would be necessary to limit the formal contract to cf6,500,000.[1] Of this, cf 4,500,000 would be made available on the signing of the contract and the handing over of the diamonds in Portugal. The balance would follow after the arrival from Brazil and transfer of the diamonds which were available there. In all probability, Hope and Baring were prepared to place a larger sum at the minister's disposal once the contract had been signed.

If we compare the instalments specified by the minister with those in the 'Plan d'un emprunt,' we observe that the number was increased from ten to twelve, and that the date for the final payment was put back from 1st August to 31st December 1802. Labouchère, for his part, made the payments conditional upon the handing over of the diamonds: 4½ million guilders following the signing of the contract and the depositing of 114,000 carats, and 2 million guilders upon the arrival and transfer of the Brazilian portion of the security, which was estimated at about 100,000 carats. Observing that the two deposits of diamonds represented a value of more than 5 million guilders, Labouchère's action in urging his principals to double the sum offered is not in the least surprising.[2]

As Don Rodrigo lacked experience in matters of this nature, it was left to Labouchère to indicate the official documents which had to be prepared. First and foremost was the contract between the minister and Labouchère, as the authorized representative of Hope and Baring, and an allied decree bearing the prince regent's confirmation and approval of the agreement. Two further decrees were required in order to safeguard the sum of cf 1,700,000 needed yearly for interest and principal payments. One of these would serve to mortgage the total output from the diamond mines and transfer it to the two houses during the life of the loan, and the other would give Hope and Baring a yearly payment order for cf 1,700,000 from the tobacco lease. The latter sum was a maximum and would reduce annually by the sum of the proceeds of the diamond sales in the year in question. It would be necessary for the tobacco duty farmers, as a group, to officially accept this payment order and undertake to pay the sum indicated. In addition, each would be required to give a personal guarantee in respect of both the payment order and the undertaking. Lastly, there was the principal debenture.

Interest on the loan was to run from 1st January 1802, and the principal sum was to be repaid within ten years. In the matter of commission, Labouchère asked for 5% on the nominal sum of the loan and 1% on the interest and principal payments, in both cases to be shared between the two houses.

The negotiations were based on these points and proceeded smoothly. There were differences of opinion, but the pressure of time and the urgent need for funds made it almost impossible for the minister to make a stand against the greatly more experienced Labouchère. On the morning of Sunday, 7th February, Labouchère was summoned by the minister and informed that the terms were acceptable. On the following day the two men put their signatures to the contract.

Labouchère's wishes were met on almost all points: the life of the loan, limitation of the formal commitment to half the principal sum requested, and the commission. As if this were not sufficient, the two houses were appointed Court Bankers–Hope & Co. in the Batavian Republic and Baring & Co. in Great Britain. Only the matter of the takeover price remained unresolved: the contract stipulated 92, but the houses retained the right to consult the Portuguese government in the event of it proving difficult to place the bonds at this figure.[1]

The decrees issued by the prince regent relating to the mortgaging of the diamonds and to the payment order for cf 1,700,000 from the tobacco leases were also dated 8th February. Quintella and Bandeira, as agents for the contracting houses, were to receive the diamonds in Lisbon and send them on to London. Stones destined for the polishing industry in Portugal, others which by tradition were reserved for the Court and those which, by reason of their size, might not be sold, were exempted from the agreement. These breaches of the monopoly were later to hamper diamond sales.[2]

Following this rapid success, it took some time to settle the details. A great deal of effort was required to achieve exactly the desired wording of the documents. During the translation into Portuguese, differences of emphasis occurred repeatedly, causing Labouchère to rack his brain in an effort to detect contrasts of word and nuance in a language which was strange to him.[3] On 16th February–by which date all the obstacles had been surmounted–the minister suddenly raised the question of the rate of exchange of the guilder. Nothing less than a specific, written undertaking from Labouchère that the same rate would apply to both the funds to be placed at the disposal of the Portuguese government and the payments of interest and principal would satisfy him. The final document was not

Soares Correa Tabeliaõ que o escrevi = Anselmo Joze da Crus Sobral = Joaquim Pedro Quintella = Jacinto Fernandes Bandeira = Geraldo Venceslao Braamcamp de Almeida Castel Branco = Joaõ Pereira Caldas = Francisco Pedro Quintella = Antonio Francisco Machado = Antonio Joze Ferreira = Jacinto Fernandes da Costa Bandeira = Pedro Cezar Labouchere = Ignacio de Souza Pavia Sardinha Cogominho Vasconcellos = Joaõ Stanley = Luiz Joze de Souza: Eu Sobreditto Antonio Nunes Soares Correa Tab.am de Notas na Cid.e de Lx.a [illegible] pelo Principe Reg.te N. Snr. q D.s G.e este Instrum.to de [illegible] dellas [illegible] escrevi e assinei [illegible]

Em test.o de Ver.de

Ant.o Nunes Soares Correa

Anselmo Joze da Crus Sobral

Joaquim Pedro Quintella

Jacinto Fernandes Band.a

Geraldo Venceslao Braamcamp de Almeida Castel Branco

Joaõ Per.a Caldas

Francisco Pedro Quintella

Antonio Francisco Machado

Antonio Joze Ferr.a

Jacinto Fernandes da Costa Bandeira

Luiz Joze de Souza

P. C. Labouchere

Joaõ Stanley

Ign.o de S.a Pavia Sard.a [illegible]

Acceptance of the payment order for cf 1,700,000 per annum
from the tobacco leases as part collateral for the Portuguese diamond loan,
signed by the tobacco lessees, 1802

handed to Labouchère until 26th February. On 2nd March, Labouchère and George Baring embarked in the Dutch corvette 'Diana' for the voyage to Gibraltar, from whence they journeyed via Madrid to Paris, where they arrived on 17th April.[1]

During the negotiations in Lisbon, Labouchère had promised Don Rodrigo that he would intercede with the French government in an attempt to have the levy on Portugal reduced or, if this failed, to urge that the payments be spread over a longer period. In the event, Talleyrand, the French Foreign Minister, proved unwilling to reduce the sum, but Labouchère eventually persuaded him to extend the period. Under the new arrangement, a cash payment of 3 million livres before 1st June was demanded, and thereafter monthly instalments of 1 million livres, the last of which would fall due on 31st August 1803. (The value of the livre at that time can be put at cf 0.48). These sums, together with the 2 million livres which the French government wished to be paid in Lisbon in connexion with the expedition to the rebellious Santo Domingo (for which sum Bandeira and Quintella had drawn on Hope in March and April), made up the sum of the war levy.[2]

As we have seen, the issue of the transfer price had not been settled. Labouchère had agreed conditionally to a price of 92, but from the outset he doubted whether this could be achieved, particularly in view of the prices of other government issues. The news that the government of the Batavian Republic had floated a 30-million guilder loan at an issue price of 75, and bearing the same rate of interest as the Portuguese loan, added a convincing dimension to his argument. The agreement reached with the French government had the effect of increasing the commitment by Baring and Hope to the full 13 million guilders, and this will undoubtedly have made the Portuguese government more receptive to advice and persuaded it to agree to a transfer price of 90.[3]

As promised in the 'Plan d'un emprunt,' the diamonds which lay in Lisbon were placed at Labouchère's disposal immediately after the signing of the contract. There were 114,342 carats with an estimated value of cf 2,740,000. Bandeira and Quintella had the stones packed in six parcels and sent to London, from whence they were consigned to Insinger & Co. in Amsterdam–the house to which Hope, with a mixture of wisdom and caution, provisionally continued to entrust diamond sales.[4] By the end of 1802, 54,342 carats had arrived in Amsterdam, and of these more than 33,000 carats were sold in the same period. The remaining 60,000 carats were despatched during the first quarter of 1803. By the end of that year, 45,000 carats of the total stock remained.[5]

Now that the wheels were beginning to turn, it was time to prepare for the placing of the loan on the Dutch market. Robert Voûte had also done some spadework in this connexion. He reported that the signing of the Peace of Amiens had distinctly improved the prospects for the Portuguese loan, but added that it should not be placed while the new Batavian loan of 30 million guilders was still on the market.[1] As it was necessary to obtain government approval for foreign loans, Voûte had already had an exploratory discussion in The Hague with the Treasurer-General, De Vos van Steenwijk, whose office was comparable with that of a minister of finance. During their meeting, Voûte made it appear that he had visited Hope in London in January 1802 with the aim of keeping the diamond trade in Holland, and that the Company had subsequently sent a partner to Lisbon. The emissary had achieved his goal, but as a *quid pro quo* a Portuguese loan would have to be floated in Amsterdam. The discussion ended with the Treasurer General indicating his approval and promising to place matters before the *Staatsbewind*–a governing board with twelve members, in which executive power had been vested since the previous year–and to inform Voûte of its decision.[2]

An unforeseen complication arose in the shape of a Bill aimed against the contracting of foreign loans in the Batavian Republic. If adopted by the Legislative Assembly, this would make it illegal for persons living in the Republic to raise money on behalf of foreigners or foreign powers unless such persons were able to furnish security in the form of a mortgage on their own assets to a value of twice the sum to be raised. Voûte proposed to await the arrival in Amsterdam of one of the partners of Hope & Co. before publishing the *Berigt* concerning the Portuguese loan.[3] With this legislative obstacle looming on the horizon (the Bill was due to become law on 1st June), it was important that the arrival should not be unduly delayed. Voûte accordingly urged Labouchère, who was then in Paris, to return to the Republic as quickly as possible. However, the negotiations with the French government took longer than had been anticipated, and it was May before Labouchère was able to free himself from the Portuguese matters. Even then there was no question of him travelling to Amsterdam, for more pressing affairs required his presence in London. The re-establishment of the house in Amsterdam necessitated revision of the deed of partnership, since it was imperative for the house to arm itself against all manner of contingencies and dangers which could threaten it in the event of a fresh outbreak of war.

Upon the completion of the arrangements for the new partnership–to which reference was made in the introductory chapter–Labouchère left

London for Amsterdam, where he arrived early in July 1802. There, he and Voûte jointly drafted the *Berigt*, whereupon the two men journeyed to The Hague to plead their case with the authorities. Voûte, who had contacts in government circles, asked that his presence be made known to Spoors, a member of the *Staatsbewind*, by whom he was received. By the time Labouchère joined them, Voûte had explained the matter and had obtained Spoor's assurance that he would do his utmost to ensure a favourable decision on the difficult issue of the date–which was subsequent to the decree of 1st June. At this point, a discussion arose between Labouchère and Spoors which became increasingly heated and finally deteriorated into an argument. From the somewhat veiled description of the scene in Voûte's handwriting, it appears that Labouchère informed Spoors in a fairly sharp tone that the French government had given its approval to the loan, and that Spoors interpreted this as an attempt to intimidate the *Staatsbewind*. Voûte succeeded in restoring calm, but Spoors sought refuge in officialdom and remained clearly displeased.[1]

Spoor's touchiness was in all probability allied to the failure of the efforts to secure the withdrawal of French troops from the Batavian Republic. Despite its promises, the French government had maintained its occupation of the Republic after the Peace of Amiens. Spoors had recently reached agreement with the French government for the withdrawal of its forces, and, with some pressure, secured the approval of his colleagues in the *Staatsbewind*. But the troops had not departed and thus fresh negotiations would be necessary–a situation which compromised Spoors.[2]

Despite this inauspicious beginning, it was important not to lose any more time. Before the day was out, Labouchère and Voûte, assisted by Hope's lawyer in The Hague, Van Son, had prepared a written request to the *Staatsbewind* and submitted this in person to the president of that body, Van Hoogstraten. The president welcomed them in a most friendly manner, and was very sympathetic towards the matter of the loan. At the end of this emotional day, Labouchère, having no further business in The Hague, returned to Amsterdam.

On 13th July, the request came up for discussion in the *Staatsbewind*. In it, the petitioners stated that the loan had been entered into at the beginning of the year, and that the principal sum had already been advanced. Now that the house of Hope & Co. was proposing to return to Holland, it desired to transfer the loan to Amsterdam. As a token of its loyal disposition, the house was willing to pay a tax of $\frac{1}{4}\%$ on the nominal sum, and to submit to stamp duty on the bonds at the rate of six *stuivers*. The *Staatsbewind* referred the request to the Treasurer-General and the councillors of the Treasury for advice, and they, in turn, requested the petitioners to furnish a facsimile of the proposed bonds and a copy of the *Berigt*.[1]

From the outset, Van Son, Hope's lawyer, was pessimistic concerning the outcome. Voûte did all he could to advance the matter, and this included having a further interview with the Treasurer-General, who again promised his support. After this he, too, left The Hague–not for Amsterdam, but for his newly acquired country residence, Middagten, to recover from the rheumatic fevers which plagued him.[2]

With growing impatience and irritation, Labouchère awaited the outcome of the request; but days and weeks passed without a decision. Voûte had difficulty in restraining him from taking fresh steps. Voûte was of the opinion that it would be better to withdraw the request. How could it be proved that the loan sum had actually been furnished in England? The house could not allow the *Staatsbewind* to inspect its books! The only convincing proof lay in not announcing the loan in Holland; to attempt further action in The Hague could only lead to the conclusion that Hope indeed planned to place the bonds in the Republic. It would be best if Labouchère went his way and left the whole thing to Voûte, who could then say that he knew with certainty 'that matters now rest in England, between your friends and those of Sir Francis.'[3]

Voûte's strategy was obviously aimed at allowing plenty of time for the heated tempers to cool and then broaching the matter afresh. Of course, it remained to be seen whether an issue which had penetrated so deeply into the regions of prestige would emerge from them in the short term. In this context, it was unfortunate that the proceeds of the loan would largely find their way into the French Treasury coffers, for this fact embodied a painful reminder of France's overall superiority. It was doubtful whether the *Staatsbewind* would be in favour of allowing Dutch investors to contribute in any shape or form to the payments. It was all very well for Labouchère to contemplate that rejection of the request would merely imply altering the name 'Amsterdam' on the bonds to 'London,' and that the bonds, in this form, would still appear on the Amsterdam Stock Exchange; for opponents of the loan, this was one more reason for resisting it.[4]

On 5th August 1802, the Treasurer-General and the councillors of the Treasury, after ample deliberation, tendered their advice to the *Staatsbewind*. They recommended that the loan be approved. But in the meantime the president of the *Staatsbewind*, Van Hoogstraten, had joined the opponents (probably under Spoor's influence), and when the matter was referred to a committee–of which Van Hoogstraten and Spoors were members–the future looked bleak for the petitioners.[1] On 20th August, Van Son reported to Voûte that the request had been turned down.

Labouchère did not experience the setback at first hand. On 23rd July, acting on Voûte's advice, he had left for Paris, from whence he had journeyed on 15th August to London.[2] There, his report of the way things had gone produced deep disappointment. Even before the news of the official rejection was received, Henry Hope had expressed his anxiety to Labouchère. If the *Staatsbewind* were to turn down the request, he argued, one of the principal sources of 'circulation and prosperity' in Holland would be blocked and the opportunity to float future foreign loans destroyed for good. A full explanation of all the circumstances surrounding the Portuguese loan ought to have immediately satisfied the Batavian government, 'for we have selected this measure as the means to introduce the reestablishment of our House with eclat, by manifesting the most conciliatory disposition and unequivocal proof of our attachment to the interest of the country.' 'But,' he continued, 'if we are obliged to believe that we are suspected of not dealing in good faith, a regard for the character we have always maintained and which we never will abandon might result in our revising completely the plans concerning ourselves. If those in Holland abandon the vital principle of circulation, neither our capital nor ourselves, nor even the country, will be of any use. And as far as talents and diligence are concerned, these are present in the neighbouring countries in equal, if not greater, measure.' In participating in the loan, at Baring's invitation, Hope also aimed at securing the diamond trade for Holland and for the house, thereby preventing the English developing into competitors in that sector. It had been Hope's idea to transfer the loan to Holland, and it was he who had proposed doubling the principal sum.[3] Holland could surely not object to the houses of Hope and Baring investing part of their idle funds in this relatively small loan? Their action in doing so also showed clearly that they were not proposing to draw capital away from an exhausted country. On the contrary, the return of the Hope family would bring a great deal of money into the country–and without Henry Hope having to sell a single one of the Portuguese bonds which he held. It would, of course, be necessary for a portion of the loan to be placed on the Amsterdam market, if only to arrive at a quotation, and to satisfy the Portuguese Court. But Hope was certain that this 'circulation' would not rise above the sum required annually for interest and principal payments.

In Hope's opinion, it was about time the leading statesmen in Holland got down to considering where the country's true interest lay. And that was clearly in rendering itself 'as much as possible, the general pivot of the World, upon which everything should turn.' Countries like England and France, with their rich resources, could regulate and restrict as it pleased them; for Holland, 'a comparatively nothing,' such a course would be fatal, however. In the artificial situation in which Holland was doomed to subsist for an eternity, circulation would prove to be the basis for trade – not only because trading enterprises were linked to foreign loans and circulation, but also because a healthy circulation had to be founded on capital if it was to beget trade and nourish it. Limiting the use of capital on the grounds of a temporary emergency could destroy the chance of prosperity in the future.

If permission for the loan were to be refused, Barings were prepared to establish a first-class house in Antwerp with the funds which arose from the Portuguese operation. If the diamond contract and an agency for imports from the island of Tobago (and perhaps also one for goods from Martinique) could be added to the loan, the foundations would be laid for a house which could become one of the most important in Europe and which would enjoy the support of the powerful and enterprising firm of Baring & Co. Then the Portuguese bonds would circulate in Holland – only they would bear the name Baring instead of Hope, and Antwerp as the place of domicile instead of Amsterdam!

For Hope & Co., there was little incentive to return to Amsterdam if this implied being limited to trade in Holland. The Company's capital was too great for so small an arena: it had to be free to swell, to flow in any direction and to be invested in, or withdrawn from, exchange transactions, loans or mercantile operations at will.[1]

The manner in which Henry Hope coupled his family's return to Amsterdam with the maintenance of the free movement of capital makes one wonder whether the threat to establish a branch in another country was really so serious. We cannot be certain, though we may assume that Henry Hope's arguments were intended for a wider audience than Labouchère alone, who certainly knew the writer's views and would probably have shared them. One thing is certain: at that time, Sir Francis Baring had plans for a complete merger between Hope & Co. and his own house. Thus the reference to an initiative on his part for the establishment of a branch in Antwerp may well contain an element of truth.[2]

There can be no doubt as to the genuineness of Henry Hope's disappointment. In February 1803 he confessed to John Williams Hope that the failure of the Portugal affair had given his nerves a severe jolt, 'and enhanced on the natural effect of advancing years, so that I find myself unfit for the business ... and absolutely unequal to the shock of any untoward accident in the course of it.' He became steadily less disposed to visit Holland, 'from several causes, not the least of which is the *coup de pied de l'âne* which we have received, which I shall never be able to digest.'[1] This was not the first occasion on which Henry Hope had spoken of retiring from business, as the introductory chapter reveals. Moreover, a return to Holland would mean adapting to totally changed circumstances in that country–an extremely difficult task for anyone of his age. The steadily deteriorating relations between England and France constituted yet another reason for following Voûte's advice to maintain a safe *pied à terre* in England.

There was, however, no question of abandoning the idea of returning to Amsterdam, or even of a lengthy postponement of the move. It was true that capital was mobile, and that talent and diligence were to be found in equal measure elsewhere; but the protection which friends in Amsterdam could offer in time of need was not easily matched. Amsterdam appeared as the place of issue for the loan in all the agreements with the Portuguese government–indeed, it had been especially recommended during the negotiations–and so a unilateral amendment was out of the question. Towards the end of August, Paulus Taay had gone to the trouble of airing and tidying the house in Amsterdam and opening the cases containing the beds and bedding which had been sent from London.[2]

The Labouchères arrived in Holland round about 10th October 1802, to be followed shortly afterwards by Mrs. Williams Hope and her family. John Williams Hope stayed on in England. He was still there on 5th November, the date of the circular informing friends and business associates of the re-establishment of the house in Amsterdam.[3] His reason for putting off his journey becomes clearer if one recalls the opposition to the Portuguese loan. Among the elements of this opposition was a lingering antipathy in radical-patriotic circles towards the Anglo-Orangist 'emigrant house.' In the summer of 1802 a pamphlet was circulated, denouncing those 'who desert the Republic in time of danger, and return in time of peace.'[4] The Portuguese envoy in The Hague, Bezerra, was informed openly that another house would have been given permission to open a loan, and although the truth of this assertion may be doubted, the hostility towards Hope was unmistakable.[5] For this very reason, Voûte advised John Williams Hope that when the moment for his return arrived, he should avoid The Hague at all costs, re-establish himself quietly in Amsterdam and refrain from discussing the Portuguese affair. This could wait until the beginning of November, when Voûte, who was in The Hague, proposed to visit Amsterdam.[6] Under such circumstances, it is

Amsterdam den 1 Julij 1802.

B E R I C H T.

Van eene Negotiatie groot *Dertien Millioenen* Guldens Hollandsch Courant, in dertien duizend Aandeelen, van Een Duizend Guldens ieder, door HOPE & COMP. gedaan, voor Rekening van de Kroon van *Portugal*, voor den tijd van 10 Jaaren, te rekenen van den Eersten Januarij 1802, tegen den Intrest van 5 pCt. in 't Jaar betaalbaar jaarlijks op Coupons.

Ter betaling der Interessen, en tot remboursement van het Capitaal word geäpproprieërd, de somma van Een Millioen zeeven maal Honderd Duizend Guldens jaarlijks, als ruim toereikende, ter betaling van het beloop der Interessen en tot het aflossen van het geheele Capitaal binnen den tijd van tien Jaaren; welk remboursement geschieden zal bij wijze van Looting voor een openbaar Notaris en Getuigen alhier; behoudens de magt door het Hof van *Portugal* aan zig gereserveerd, om de Aflossing te vervroegen of binnen eene kortere tijd te doen. Mits van haare intentie deswegens drie Maanden alvorens kennis te geeven.

Deeze Negotiatie is gevestigd op de origineele Obligatie groot *Dertien Millioenen Guldens*, in dato 19 Februarij 1802, ten behoeven van HOPE & COMP., getekend door den Heere DON RODRIGO DE SOUZA COUTINHO, Secretaris van Staat en Minister der Finantiën, als daar toe gequalificeerd door Zijne Koninglijke Hoogheid den Heere PRINS REGENT VAN PORTUGAL volgens decreet in dato 8 Februarij 1802, bij welke origineele Obligatie den Intrest à 5 pCt. is vastgesteld, de magt tot het uitleeveren der 13000 Aandeelen aan HOPE & COMP. gegeven, met verzekering dat dezelve, van dezelve kragt en te zaamen van dezelve waarde zullen weezen, als de Hoofd-Obligatie, met uitdrukkelijke verzekering nimmer eenige vertraging zoo in de betaling der Interessen als tot aflossing van het Capitaal zal plaats hebben, zelfs niet door Oorlog alwaar het ook onverhoopt met de Bataafsche Republicq.

Tot volbrenging van het geen voorschreven staat, worden door Z. K. H. den PRINS REGENT VAN PORTUGAL in deszelfs Obligatie aan HOPE & COMP. gepasseerd, verbonden alle de Inkomsten van het Rijk van *Portugal* in het algemeen, en specialijk bij wijze van Hijpotheecq eene somma van Een Millioen Zeven maal Honderd Duizend Guldens 's Jaars, voortkomende uit de Inkomsten der Pachting van de Tabak, welke begroot word ten beloope van circa Vier Millioenen Guldens 's jaars, zo mede alle de Diamanten van de Koninglijke Mijnen van Brasil, waar van reeds de waarde van Twee-en Een Half Millioen in handen van gemelde HOPE & COMP. is gesteld en jaarlijks het geen uit Brasil verwagt word, gesteld zal worden. Zo dat het geheele Product der Mijnen gedurende den Loop deezer Negotiatie ter dispositie van gemelde HOPE & COMP. zal wezen, en tot zeekerheid der Deelhebbers bij deeze Negotiatie geïnteresseerd, voor rekening en risico van de Kroon van *Portugal* in de Bank van *Engeland* worden overgebragt.

Het Provenu van gemelde Diamanten naar mate die jaarlijks verkogt en tot geld gemaakt zullen zijn, zal strekken in Mindering of op Afrekening van gemelde somma van *f* 1,700,000 's Jaars; welke somma de Pachters van de Tabak, ten behoeve der geïnterresseerdens in deeze Negotiatie, ter betaling van het Capitaal en Interressen, aangenomen hebben te fourneeren, en waar toe zij, niet alleen in hunne bovengemelde Qualiteit, maar ook ieder in solidum en als voor eigen schuld, hun en hunne Erfgenaamen verbonden hebben: zullende de alzoo resteerende somme aan de Agendarissen van gemelde HOPE & COMP. ter hand gesteld worden, om aan dezelve te remitteeren of ter hunner dispositie te houden.

De principaale Documenten in handen van HOPE & COMP. deeze Negotiatie aangaande zijn de navolgende,

1. Decreet van Z. K. H. goedkeurende het engagement van den Minister DON RODRIGO DE SOUZA COUTINHO met den gevolmagtigde van HOPE & COMP. over gemelde Negotiatie aangegaan.
2. Decreet van Hoogstdeszelfs Z. K. H. ter Hijpothecatie en Uitlevering aan HOPE & COMP. of derzelver Agendarissen van de Diamanten, zoo wel berustende in de Koninglijke Thesaurie te *Lisbon*, als binnen dit en volgende Jaaren verwagt wordende, mitsgaders aanwijzing op de Pachters der Tabak voor de betaling van het geen na aftrek van het Product der Diamanten, die binnen ieder Jaar zullen verkogt worden, te kort mogt komen om de gansche somme van *f* 1,700,000 vol te maaken;
3. Verbintenis der Pachters van de Tabak, waar bij zij zig verpligten aan dezelve punctueelijk te voldoen;
4. Personeele of Solidaire Guarantie der Pachters voor de betaling van de voorschreevene Aanwijzing;
5. Origineele Obligatie op order en in den naam van Z. K. H. den PRINS REGENT voor de Hoofdsomme en Interessen, als te vooren breeder beschreven staat.

Bericht of the Portuguese loan, 1802

understandable that John Williams Hope kept on postponing his return, the more so since he had little desire to return to Amsterdam. To Sir Francis Baring, this hesitant attitude was a source of irritation–to the point, indeed, that, shortly after John Williams Hope's arrival in Amsterdam, Sir Francis tersely informed him that he could perhaps understand his conduct were he proposing to transform the Amsterdam house into a sort of Andries Pels & Sons–by which he meant a house which had the means to do anything, but did nothing. Such behaviour, the letter continued, smacked of weakness and a lack of the energy which was vital if a house was to be kept 'in the real rank of the great and prominent.' [1]

In dealing with the Portuguese loan, however, caution was a more important attribute than energy. The request to the *Staatsbewind* having been turned down, there was little choice except to have the bonds signed outside the Batavian Republic. In order to avoid any risk of giving offence, it was decided that the task should be entrusted to Bandeira in Lisbon.[2] Just how wise this decision was, emerged during a chance meeting between Voûte and Spoors at Bezerra's residence. When 'the affair and the person' (i.e. the Portuguese loan and Labouchère) were mentioned, Spoors flew into a temper, becoming if anything more enraged than on the previous occasion. According to Voûte, some unrepeatable things were said–all in the presence of Bezerra, who, Voûte added by way of consolation, was nonetheless prepared to institute an advertisement concerning the first payment of interest and principal.[3] Indeed, in the closing days of the year, two Dutch newspapers carried an announcement by the Portuguese envoy, stating that the Portuguese Court had furnished Hope & Co., 'Banquiers de la Couronne de Portugal,' with funds to enable it to make a payment of interest and principal, together totalling cf 1,033,000, in respect of the Court's debt to Hope & Co. of 13 million guilders *Hollands Courant*.[4] Simultaneously with this announcement, Bezerra informed the *Staatsbewind* of the payment in a formal note. As neither document bore a reference to the place of issue of the loan, and as Hope & Co. acted only in their capacity of Court Bankers, the announcements produced no reaction from the government.

But although matters appeared on the surface to be proceeding smoothly, the situation backstage was less satisfactory. The tobacco lessees in Lisbon, who were bound by contract to furnish a sum cf 1,700,000 annually (admittedly, less the proceeds from the diamonds sold in the year concerned) for the payment of interest and principal, had been so lax in regard to their commitment that Baring had been obliged to make good the deficit in order that the payment announced could be effected. The men in Lisbon promised to mend their ways in time for the payments in the following year, but Sir Francis Baring deemed it advisable to remind them that their tobacco contract had been renewed only after an express request by Labouchère, and that any further deficit or other shortcoming in their remittances might even at this stage be construed by the Minister of Finance as a reasonable ground for cancelling their contract.[1]

In the early months of 1803, the need to advance monies on behalf of the tobacco lessees was anything but convenient to Barings, for the house stood on the threshold of a major transaction which would probably demand a great deal of capital. Since Christmas 1802, Alexander Baring had been in Paris, where he sought to obtain for his company a share in the financial transactions which would arise in the event of Napoleon deciding to sell Louisiana to the United States.[2]

With all these matters to attend to, Baring's personal participation in the Portuguese loan was extremely limited. By the end of 1802, 3,418 of the 5,000 'sold' bonds had been taken over by the firm of Henry Hope & Co. Of these 3,418, 1,793 had been resold, principally to members of the family, and 942 had been set aside as 'Hope & Co., reserve.' A further 972 had been sold to 'sundry investors,' a term which covered business friends like Voûte and Insinger, members of Pierre César Labouchère's family and clients and acquaintances such as William Gordon Coesvelt, Quintella, Bandeira and the Portuguese envoy in Paris, Don José Maria de Souza.[3] The list reveals that the Amsterdam house was most circumspect in its sales and, as far as 1802 was concerned, had substantiated Henry Hope's view that the magnitude of the Portuguese 'circulation' would not exceed the sum available annually for interest and principal payments.[4]

In 1803, in order to avoid ugly rumours, the partners fell back on their trusted circle of friends in Amsterdam. In that year, 1,000 bonds were transferred to a consortium of *entrepreneurs* headed by Willem Borski at a price of 95. Henry Hope & Co. repeated their purchase of 1802, taking 3,000 bonds, also at 95. Purchases by friends and acquaintances in 1803 totalled 571 bonds.[5] By 31st December 1804, the group headed by Borski held 2,678 bonds; a year later their holding amounted to 3,201.[6]

In spite of prompt payment of the loan instalments by the houses which were parties to the contract, Portugal's financial position remained so serious that eventually the government took the plunge and approached the Company for a fresh loan. If the house would be so kind as to furnish 2 million guilders or, if that was not feasible, then at least 1 million, the necessity to draw on Bandeira or Quintella for the overdue remittances

–a step which would be most inconvenient to the government–could be averted. The balance could be of use in connexion with the establishment, in Lisbon, of a bank in which the Court, as a 'private Person,' desired to associate itself with a number of merchants.[1]

As was to be expected, the reaction of the two issuing houses was one of flat refusal. Sir Francis Baring pointed to the critical political situation and to the danger of being unable to withdraw from such a bank having once become involved in it. In a letter to Hope, he expressed a preference for leaving it to smaller houses to participate, 'whilst we hold the candle.'[2] Labouchère succeeded in making it plain to Bezerra that it was unwise to display special reserves in a situation in which war between England and France could break out at any minute. Perhaps the envoy could tactfully suggest to his government that it would be wise to sell a portion of its silver plate in London. Silver prices were very high at that moment, and to leave the plate lying idle in Lisbon would be to expose it to all manner of hazards–a prediction which was to prove all too accurate. Apart from this, however, Labouchère was unwilling to give even the faintest ray of hope until the diamond shipments from Brazil arrived.[3]

In the threatening political situation, the non-arrival of these diamonds from Brazil was a source of great anxiety. According to the promises made, they should have arrived at the end of 1802; in fact, they were not received until early in May 1803. But the chain of command in Brazil was long, and the civil servants were slow to react. In the case in point, the Viceroy in Brazil, upon receipt of orders from Lisbon, had to instruct the Captain General of the Minas Gerais area to despatch the diamonds to Rio de Janeiro. The latter, in turn, had to pass the order on to the directors of the Royal Diamond Mines at Tijuco. In the event, however, there had been such a muddle that a special messenger had had to be sent from Rio de Janeiro to collect the stones.[4] The reports concerning the size of the consignment varied widely. At first there was talk of 85,000 carats, but later this rose to 120,000 carats. The increase was attributed to the suppression of a gang of mulattoes–'desperate fellows'–who, it was said, had discovered new gold and diamond fields in the interior and had established a lively trade in contraband stones, which were sold in Rio de Janeiro. It was reported that their activities had been brought to a sudden halt, with the result that the output from the mines had been raised.[5]

In Europe, the tension between England and France had meanwhile erupted into conflict. On 12th May, the English envoy, Lord Whitworth, departed from Paris, thereby confirming the breach between the two countries. With this, the onward transmission of the Brazilian diamonds, which, as we have seen, arrived in Portugal at the beginning of May, was in jeopardy. Sir Francis Baring had given instructions that the diamonds were to be shipped aboard a man-o'-war, and had chartered the frigate 'Amazone' for the purpose. She sailed from Portsmouth on 12th July with orders to take the whole consignment–104,000 carats, as it now transpired–on board. But on 13th July the mailboat 'Duke of York' left Lisbon with 15,000 carats on board. This vessel arrived safely in Falmouth on 3rd August. The 'Amazone' arrived in Lisbon on 25th or 26th July. Shortly before this, the mailboat 'King George Packet'–unwittingly in contravention of Sir Francis's instructions–had left for England carrying a further 15,000 carats; this vessel was less fortunate than the 'Duke of York,' for on 1st August, after a fierce encounter, she fell prey to the French privateer 'La Représaille,' operating from Bordeaux.[1]

The whole affair was extremely painful, and if mismanaged could disrupt the delicate intermediary role which Hope and Baring would henceforth have to play in the Portuguese affair. In a letter to the Portuguese envoy in Paris, Sir Francis, in a moment of thoughtful abstraction, suggested that Portugal might withhold the final instalment of her debt to France, thus putting pressure on the French government; but ultimately he decided that it would be wiser to make a protest and leave it at that. Such a protest would have to be based on the premise that the diamonds, although addressed to Barings, were the property of the Portuguese Crown and were in transit to Hope & Co., who had been instructed to sell them in order to recoup advances made to Portugal to meet the war levy due to France.[2] However, the official steps taken by Don José Maria de Souza produced no results, for on 16th September the owners of the privateer had succeeded in obtaining from the Prize Court a 'décision de bonne prise et de possession,' and, as Talleyrand explained to the envoy, such a decision was irreversible.[3]

For Portugal, the consequences of the new conflict between France and England were just as disastrous as those of the earlier one. On 3rd June 1803, in an effort to steer a course between the belligerents, the prince regent proclaimed Portugal's neutrality, but even this feeble attempt at independence was unacceptable to France. The heavy political pressure exerted on the Lisbon government by the French envoy, Lannes, led first to the dismissal of the most powerful ministers, including Don Rodrigo de Souza Coutinho, on a charge of 'Anglomania.' Don Rodrigo's successor, Don Louis de Vasconcellas, was forced to sign a treaty in which France recognized Portuguese neutrality, but in exchange for this exacted a contribution of 1 million francs per month for the duration of the war.[1] Thus, within four months of being liberated from her financial commitments towards France (the final monthly payment had been made on 31st August), Portugal was again obliged to make sacrifices – this time for a neutrality which was fictitious from the outset. But the Treasury coffers were as empty as they had been at the beginning of the year. While the negotiations with France were in progress, Bandeira had sought the views of Hope and Baring regarding the possibility of a supplementary loan, for which diamonds would again constitute a security. Of the two houses, Barings, in particular, were opposed to such an operation – a very understandable reaction in view of the war situation. It was not feasible to destine the diamonds for a second loan while the first had still to be completed. That would shock public confidence and bring both operations into disrepute. It was difficult enough in such times to keep up the price of the Portuguese bonds, even nominally, and thus the government would be well advised to try to meet its needs at home.[2] Labouchère, while concurring in this view, was clearly less opposed to becoming involved in the new Portuguese payments to France and incurring certain commitments, always provided that these were balanced by sound guarantees in case the government's emergency resources failed to flow sufficiently rapidly. He would have liked to see England standing as guarantor, but if this were not possible the tobacco lessees would suffice.[3] Enquiries made by Baring showed that Labouchère's expectations concerning a guarantee by England were illusory. In 1802 the British government had encouraged the Portuguese loan because at that time the prompt payment of the war levy offered a means to lessen French influence on the country. Now, with a new war ahead, London had no desire to stimulate a loan which would pave the way for remittances from a neutral country to France.[4]

In the meantime, the French government had to some extent moderated its demands on Portugal. The open-ended financial demand had been replaced by one for 16 million francs, payable within sixteen months. Even so, it was as much as the Portuguese government could do to make ends meet, and it was not until 19th March 1804 – exactly three months after the signing of the treaty of neutrality – that the parties finally reached agreement. The French negotiators in Lisbon had adhered to the demand for 16 million francs within sixteen months, and had stipulated that the period should run from 1st December 1803. One month after the exchange of the ratification documents, the sum then due had to be paid in Paris, while the Portuguese envoy was required to deposit undertakings, bearing his own signature, in respect of the balance.[5]

The Hope correspondence contains only slanting references to the events in Portugal. The partners made no mention of them in their letters to Don Louis de Vasconcellas, and such news as did circulate emanated from Baguenault, of the house of Baguenault & Co. of Paris. On 18th May, he reported that the payments relating to the contribution would be made via Bandeira and Quintella, and he added a wish that Hope might also be drawn into the process.[1] When Baguenault wrote this, Hope had already decided to assist with the payments which Bandeira was required to make on the instructions of the Portuguese government.[2] There was thus no question of an advance of any kind to the government; the transaction was a purely commercial one between two merchant houses, in which one received payment orders from the other. These formed the subject of a separate account, designated F.R., in which debits and credits were required to balance as far as possible from month to month. The necessary funds reached Hope partly in the form of remittances from Bandeira, and partly from the proceeds of the shipment of produce to French ports, which Bandeira had entrusted to the Hope management. The principal cargo was cotton, which went chiefly to Nantes but also to Caen, Rouen, Dieppe and Marseilles.[3] As far as dealings with Barings were concerned, however, no sharp distinction was made between these trading activities and the Portuguese loan, and in a letter to that house the partners said: 'these concerns ... are connected with our joint adventure as explained verbally to your Mr.Alex. Baring, and will continue in common in the same proportion for profit and loss, till the negociation shall be run off.'[4] Here, as in the case of the Swedish loans, we find mercantile transactions being freely mingled with loan matters.

The transactions entered in Account F.R. in 1804 included one which, while probably allied in origin to the Portuguese payments to France, stood quite apart from these in execution, and was of earlier date. This was related to a contract between Bandeira and Hope for the supply and sale of pernambuco wood, or brazilwood, a dyewood; the Portuguese government had a monopoly of the sale of this wood and, as with diamonds, leased the annual proceeds for a given period of time. If the lessee resided in Lisbon, he could enter into a contract with one or more houses in other European cities.

In October 1803, Hope was approached by Bandeira's confidential agent, John Stanley, who enquired whether the house would be interested in a contract for brazilwood. He explained his offer by saying that the lessee, Bandeira, was dissatisfied with his Amsterdam agents, Tomasachi Marcella & Co., and that as their contract was due to expire at the end of the year he was anxious to make a change.[1] If one realizes that Bandeira himself was at that moment trying to persuade Hope to agree to a supplementary loan for the Portuguese government, one tends to take the motive for the offer with a pinch of salt. Labouchère's reaction was favourable yet cautious, 'as on this score much must depend on political circumstances, which may materially impede our communications.'[2] A week later, however, he again wrote to Stanley, this time dealing at great length with the trade in pernambuco wood – about which he had evidently obtained information in the meantime. In this sector, sound organization was the key to success, and in Labouchère's opinion this had been lacking of late. Markets for dyewood existed in London and Amsterdam, and approximately equal quantities were sold on each of these. Sales in Hamburg were small – about 50–60,000 pounds annually. France obtained supplies direct from Lisbon, and thus sales in that country need not harm the market in Holland, provided that satisfactory price limits were set. But Brabant and Flanders should be included in the territory covered from Amsterdam.[3]

Early in 1804, Hope & Co. took over 160,000 pounds of pernambuco wood from Tomasachi Marcella and became the agent for Amsterdam. In his correspondence with Bandeira, however, Labouchère let it be known that he had higher ambitions, namely to control the whole of the European market for this commodity. He accordingly enquired whether the Portuguese government could supply unlimited quantities of the wood, and whether contractors were required to take any quantity which might be offered.[4]

Bandeira replied that intensive felling in earlier years had increased the distance between the source and the point of shipment, thus adding to the time and cost of transport, and that he therefore anticipated a reduction in the supply. But Labouchère remained sceptical. He reasoned that the stock was virtually inexhaustible, and that if transport from the existing supply areas became a major problem it would be solved simply by drawing on a new forest. What guarantee had he that the Portuguese government, faced with a financial crisis, would not put ever larger quantities on the market? The consumption of pernambuco wood fluctuated widely and was to some extent governed by competition from other dyewoods, which would flood the market if peace were to come. It was also possible that, in the event of traffic between Brazil and Portugal being interrupted, supplies of pernambuco wood would be carried in American vessels, thereby eclipsing the contractors. In all probability, stocks of sufficient size to last for several years – and also to ruin the unfortunate contractor – were already lying in Brazilian ports.

It was a prerequisite for long-term planning that Bandeira's lease contract be extended beyond 1808, the year in which it was due to expire. If this could be done, Hope could simply enter into annual contracts with Bandeira. Provision would have to be made for reduction of the contract price if peace should be negotiated during the year. Naturally, Labouchère wrote, sales would have to be limited to the Company, with the proviso that the Portuguese government could reserve 150,000 pounds for home consumption and for export to Spain–via contraband channels–and the Barbary Coast.[1]

Bandeira's reply to this letter has not survived. Much later, in a report to Barings concerning the 'Portugal Concern' in 1804, Hope wrote: 'The wood concern was intended to embrace the article of Fernambucq wood throughout Europe, but remains limited to this place, where however we hope it will make a satisfactory appearance in this year's account.'[2]

Clearly, Hope's sales efforts were concentrated on Amsterdam. In February 1804, the Company, in a letter to Bandeira, had hinted at the possibility of raising the quantity sold annually to 3–400,000 pounds at 44–45 guilders banco per quintal (1 quintal = 100 pounds), and in the course of that year it proved that it was capable of substantiating this pretentious proposal.[3] On the 9th April 1804, Hope, acting through the broker L.H. Voûte, sold to Messrs. Jacob Muhl and Van Winter 'two hundred thousand Pounds of Whole Fernabuck wood with the original mark R, at the price of forty-five Guilders Banco per Hundred Pounds with Two per Cent Discount.' The sale was conditional upon the buyers being given a monopoly of this wood in the Netherlands and upon a ban on exports of dyewood from Lisbon to Brabant and to French ports north of Dieppe. The buyers took an option on a further 100,000 pounds at the same price, and subject to Hope having this much in stock. The Company, for its part, undertook to store any brazilwood received during the rest of that year, and not to sell to third parties inside or outside the Batavian Republic. It was agreed that further negotiations with Voûte concerning the conditions should take place in December at the latest.

On 4th October 1804, Voûte converted the option for 100,000 pounds into a firm agreement, and on 19th November he purchased 300,000 pounds, which had arrived in the meantime, at the same price.[4] The contract relating to the latter purchase stipulated that the price of dyewood in England should not be lower than that in Amsterdam and that, in the event of a fall in the rate of exchange, the prices in England should be raised proportionately, 'being the adjustment necessary for the success of the article on both markets.' This shows that agreements between parties concerning the establishment of prices were feasible. The fact that the price in London could influence the price in Amsterdam in such a manner is further proof of the close contact which existed in spite of the state of war between the two countries.

L.H.Voûte entered into an agreement with the house of Muhl & Van Winter whereby he took a half-share in the purchase of the dyewood, 'the gradual sale of which they, alone and in their own names, will conduct.' This agreement also applied to all future transactions involving the article. Hope & Co., in turn, confirmed in writing to Voûte that the undertaking, although entered into in the latter's name, related solely to the Company.[1] Once again, circumstances had been turned to the best possible advantage: Muhl & Van Winter continued to pursue their trade, and Hope, unbeknown to all but a select circle, shared in the benefits. The contract was renewed largely on the same terms in 1805, 1806, 1807, 1808 and 1811.[2]

'Voila cette affaire en bon train,' said Baguenault in June 1804, in a letter to Labouchère concerning the payment of the Portuguese 'contribution'; but his optimism was to prove less than well-founded.[3] In the official announcement to Talleyrand, Hope said cautiously that the Company would be pleased to learn which department of the government the monies should be remitted to, 'depending upon the extent to which we are enabled to effect the payments.'[4] By the same post, the Company informed the Portuguese envoy, De Souza, that it held payment orders amounting to only 2 million francs, and urged him in the strongest terms to press the French government to extend the instalment periods.[5] This placed the envoy in a difficult position, for how was he to reconcile this instruction with the terms of the Franco-Portuguese treaty, which stipulated lump-sum payment of all instalments due since 1st December 1803? According to the letter of the treaty, 7 million francs were due at that moment, but only 2 million were available. It is no wonder that Baguenault observed 'une incertitude et vacillation continuelle' on the part of De Souza.[6] To make matters worse, there had been a clear mistrust of the envoy in French government circles since early in 1803, when it had emerged that, on his own initiative, he had suspended payments to the French Treasury.[7] Fresh evidence to show that this mistrust was not entirely misplaced was about to be presented. At De Souza's instigation, Hope's official announcement to Talleyrand of the commencement of the payments to France was delayed for a week, and the 2 million francs held at De Souza's disposal by Baguenault were deposited with the *Banque de France* instead of being paid to the Treasury.

De Souza was no less stubborn in his efforts to avoid signing undertakings relating to the balance of the payments to France.[1] He began by sounding Baguenault regarding the possibility of having Hope's drafts accepted upon Bandeira's responsibility. If that were not feasible, he desired that Hope should guarantee his commitments or, if this were not possible either, that Baguenault should guarantee them for Hope's account.[2] But all these propositions met with a blank refusal from Labouchère; he had resolved to make payments only when the necessary funds had been made available, and had no inclination to depart from this principle. At the same time, he anticipated that, as had been the case with the earlier payments, Talleyrand would be willing to extend the instalment period if the Portuguese Court provided convincing proof of poverty and lack of funds.[3] The ensuing events showed that he had been right, and in the end the French government agreed to accept 2 million francs in cash and the balance in five monthly sums of 1 million francs following the payment of the final instalment.[4]

With all these 'lenteurs diplomatiques,' nearly half the month of July passed without the 2 million francs which Baguenault had deposited with the *Banque de France* being paid over to the Treasury. The French government, incensed by these 'tricks,' demanded immediate payment and the replacement of De Souza.[5] On 14th August, Bandeira instructed Baguenault that in future he should make prompt payments to the French Treasury, and that he was not to accept orders from De Souza in the matter. By the time the letter reached Paris, De Souza had taken it upon himself needlessly to delay the payment of the third million for a week.[6] But the days of his chicanery were numbered, and although he was not recalled until the end of October he was increasingly by-passed in diplomatic affairs.[7]

In spite of all Stanley's exalted stories concerning subdued mulatto gangs and the suppression of smuggling, parcels of diamonds continued to reach Amsterdam through other channels. In its report to the Portuguese Minister of Finance concerning the position of the loan in 1803, the Company had already complained that the market was being ruined by illicit parcels which were offered at cut price.[8] The problem stemmed not only from the consignment of 15,000 carats which had been seized at sea, and which appeared on the market at prices 5–10% below Hope's figure, but also from a stream of large parcels which reached Amsterdam and London direct from Lisbon.[9] Amsterdam houses such as Gildemeester & Co., made offers for parcels of 20,000 carats, the composition and price of which were approximately the same as those handled by Hope. Particularly painful was the discovery that Lorla & Co. in Amsterdam had received a 2,000-carat parcel consisting of exceptionally large and fine stones, and that not only was there a similar parcel in London, but that others were on their way from Lisbon.[1] Labouchère emphasized to Quintella that the situation threatened Hope's sales, and that the tobacco lessees would thus have to transfer larger sums for the interest and principal payments due on 1st January of the following year.

Matters took a much more serious turn when it was reported that the Portuguese Court was attempting to secure a loan of 500,000 pounds sterling in London on the security of diamonds. In a letter to the minister, De Vasconcellas, Labouchère pointed out that this not only undermined the diamond market, but also adversely affected the price of the Portuguese bonds. After all, he reasoned, the value of the bonds was largely based on the security–the proceeds of the entire output from the diamond mines–and if this was jeopardized, the market price of the bonds would inevitably decline. If the loan was obtained in England, it would in any case fall to the Company to sell the diamonds given as security.[2] Quintella replied that the prince regent had been obliged to make a present of an insignificant parcel of large stones a few months previously and, more recently, under pressure of circumstances, to dispose of a fairly large parcel of small stones. The latter was in the hands of the Paris agent, Diogo Dittmer, and was at Hope's disposal; indeed, Dittmer had been instructed to negotiate with the Company concerning the future of these stones.[3] As far as the large stones were concerned, Quintella was obliged to use the gift story, because their sale would have contravened the terms of the mortgage agreement. Regarding the small diamonds, there could be no excuse other than the acute shortage of money from which the Portuguese government suffered in the Spring of 1804. This might even have driven the government to seek a loan in London after it had been refused by Hope and Baring. Quintella, however, flatly denied the suggestion.

In spite of Quintella's convolutions, the affair continued to be depressing. Diogo Dittmer ignored all correspondence, and parcels of diamonds continued to trickle into Amsterdam, where they changed hands at prices below those fixed by Hope. The effect on the market was felt throughout 1804, and in their report to Don Louis de Vasconcellas the partners stated with bitter satisfaction that because of the illicit shipments their sales for the year had amounted to only $4{,}565\frac{5}{8}$ carats.[4]

Although the political situation remained threatening, some time passed before the storm broke over Portugal. With the resumption of hostilities in 1803, Napoleon at first concentrated on his planned invasion of England to the exclusion of all else. When this proved incapable of being accomplished, fresh wars against Austria, Russia and Prussia caused his armies to move to central and eastern Europe.

This, however, did not imply that the emperor had lost sight of other regions on the Continent. In a decree issued in Berlin in November 1806, while the war in the east was still raging, he proclaimed the famous Continental System forbidding all the countries of Europe to trade with England. It was patently obvious that Portugal, which still maintained close economic ties with England, would be among the victims of the system. At the Peace of Tilsit, which brought hostilities between France and the Russo-Prussian alliance to an end in July 1807, Napoleon and Czar Alexander I agreed that Portugal, Denmark and Sweden should be forced to adopt the Continental System. As far as Portugal was concerned, Napoleon did not let the grass grow under his feet. On 12th August 1807, the French envoy in Lisbon handed the Portuguese government an ultimatum demanding an early and complete break with England. By the time the government acquiesced, French troops were advancing on Portugal's frontier, supported militarily by Spain, to whom an area of Portuguese territory had been promised. The *Moniteur* of 13th November 1807 carried an official notice stating that the House of Braganza had ceased to rule.[1]

The report of the deposition brought an end to the protracted hesitation on the part of the prince regent. On 27th November, he and his family embarked in a British naval squadron which lay ready in the Lisbon roads, taking with them their treasures in the form of gold and diamonds. On 29th November the vessels set sail for Brazil. On the following day, the spearhead of the French force, led by General Junot, entered Lisbon.[2]

The partners of Hope & Co. watched the developments in Portugal with rising anxiety. How were the future payments of interest and principal to be realized, now that the Portuguese government had its seat in Rio de Janeiro? The diamonds could presumably be sent direct from Brazil to England and would thus reach Hope, but the government no longer had any control over the vital remittances from the tobacco lessees. Without these remittances, which thus far had totalled about a million guilders annually, it would be impossible for the Court to effect further payments. Urgent requests for information were sent to Stanley, Bandeira and Quintella, and these were followed by even more urgent requests for remittances; but all remained unanswered.[3]

The silence on the part of the tobacco lessees can be attributed in part to the upsurge of unrest in Portugal. On the heels of the revolt by the Spaniards against the rule imposed on them by the French, an uprising broke out in Portugal one month later, in June 1808. Soon the whole country was up in arms, and with the landing on 1st August of a British expeditionary force led by Wellesley, who later became the Duke of Wellington, things began to look black for Junot. Aided by units of the Portuguese resistance and Spanish regulars, Wellesley defeated Junot at Vimeiro and forced him to capitulate with his entire army. In exchange for a safe passage to France, the army withdrew from Portuguese territory. On 18th September the regency council, which had been left behind when the prince regent fled, was restored to power, albeit under the supervision of the British commander-in-chief. Portugal was free again–for a time, at least.[1]

During this highly eventful period in Portugal's history, the remittances from the tobacco lessees had practically dried up. Hope could do little with the 46,500 guilders which had been forthcoming. The Company had succeeded in substantially raising the volume of diamond sales–to 45,000 carats–but there nevertheless remained a deficit of cf 567,606.16.8. This was partially offset by broaching the private accounts of Bandeira and Quintella, and the balance, amounting to cf 194,976.1.8, was met with drafts on the tobacco lessees to the order of Baring.[2]

In May 1809, Bandeira and Quintella replied to the letters addressed to them. They explained that because the war had prevented them from making any payments, they had approached the head of the department of finance, Cypriano Ribeiro Freire, with a request that he should arrange for the deficit to be met. Freire, pleading lack of knowledge of the matter, had asked for time to study the papers.[3] His closing observation that, in the critical situation which then existed, all available funds were needed for defence against the enemy, did not augur well for the request. Napoleon, it must be remembered, had not acquiesced in his defeats on the Iberian peninsula, and had personally led a major counteroffensive in the autumn of 1808. By the beginning of the new year the war had spread to the northern part of Portugal, and now battles were swaying to and fro across large areas of the country. The consequences of the conflict were disastrous for the populace and also for the nation's economy. To all this was added the economic emancipation of Brazil. The decree of 28th January 1808 which opened Brazilian ports to the ships of all friendly and neutral states heralded a sharp decline in trade relations between Portugal and Brazil. Produce from Brazil now travelled direct to its destination, without the ships calling first at Lisbon, and imports into Brazil were handled by foreigners, mainly Englishmen.[4]

Not surprisingly in view of these circumstances, Hope's claims embarrassed the regency council–so much so indeed that it issued a decree forbidding the tobacco lessees to meet the Company's drafts and also suspending their commitment for the duration of the war, on the grounds that this concerned payment to Dutchmen, i.e. enemies.[1] Hope's contentions that the provisions of the principal debenture remained valid in time of war, that Holland was not at war with Portugal, that Hope & Co. had been an English company at the time when the contract was signed, and that the drafts would be collected by Barings, all failed to make any impression on the council.

In spite of all this, however, the payment of interest and principal at the end of 1808 and 1809 took place normally. In 1808, the Company assisted to the extent of about two hundred thousand guilders, but as nearly half the bonds were held by Henry Hope & Co., a proportional amount of the advance was, as it were, merely transferred from waistcoat pocket to trouser pocket. In 1809 the sales of the remaining diamonds, amounting to 54,500 carats, produced nearly one and a half million guilders. This left a deficit of just over a quarter of a million guilders, half of which was covered by funds from the Bandeira and Quintella accounts and the balance by drafts on the tobacco lessees to the order of Baring.[2]

Hope's efforts in Lisbon, which were as numerous as they were fruitless, were viewed with disfavour by Alexander Baring. In his opinion, all these approaches to people who, because of the war, had no money were pointless and even dangerous. The next thing would be that the government in Rio de Janeiro would use the requests from Lisbon as an excuse for not paying. There was only one place to achieve anything, and that was Brazil, where the highest authority lay and where the means of payment existed.[3]

The necessity to make representations in Brazil had not escaped the notice of the partners of Hope & Co. Indeed, they had realized this immediately after the prince regent's departure, but correspondence with faraway Rio de Janeiro, where the situation was still confused and obscure, would certainly be a slow procedure and would in all probability produce little result. To get anywhere, it was vital to have a capable and reliable confidential agent on the spot, who could represent the Hope-Baring interests in person at the Court. In February 1808, Hieronymus Sillem, a partner in the house of Matthiessen & Sillem of Hamburg, put the partners in touch with a man who appeared to possess the qualities required. This was Kieckhoefer, a merchant, who at that moment resided in Hamburg. Kieckhoefer stated that he had lived in Portugal for many years, during which he had learned to speak the language fluently and had met many influential Portuguese. Now that Brazil was open for all foreign trade, he foresaw good opportunities for himself, especially in the trade in Silesian linen, and was planning to emigrate with his family to Rio de Janeiro and to establish a merchant house there. To this end, he was anxious to obtain the support of three first-class houses, in Hamburg, Amsterdam and London, and Matthiessen & Sillem, Hope & Co. and Baring Brothers & Co. seemed to him to be the most reliable.[1]

After lengthy discussions with Kieckhoefer, the partners of Hope & Co. agreed to invest jointly with Barings a sum of 60,000 marks banco in the new house, on condition that Matthiessen & Sillem also participated. In return, Kieckhoefer would have to undertake to represent Hope and Baring to the best of his ability in negotiations with the Portuguese government in Rio de Janeiro.[2] In the latter part of July 1808, Kieckhoefer, travelling on a Russian passport, journeyed via Wismar to Sweden, where he embarked at Gothenburg for the crossing to England. He made a good impression on the Barings, to whom Hope had introduced him, although his plans were considered 'rather premature.' While in London, Kieckhoefer also had a meeting with the Portuguese envoy to England, Don Domingo de Souza Coutinho, a brother of the former Minister of Finance and now, in Rio de Janeiro, the Prime Minister. As they parted, the envoy casually requested him to enquire of Barings regarding the position of the Portuguese loan, but without mentioning his name. Evidently the envoy had reasons for not enquiring himself.[3]

Coutinho's attitude did not bode well for the success of the mission to Brazil. Kieckhoefer and his family arrived in Rio de Janeiro at the end of April 1809 after a voyage lasting fifty-two days. The city was inundated with émigrés who complained loudly of the intense heat and lack of comfort, and Kieckhoefer did not find it easy to obtain accommodation. His first task was to call upon the Prime Minister, who accorded him a most friendly welcome and made a point of asking that his regards should be transmitted to Labouchère. The purpose of these gestures became plain during the ensuing discussion, in which the minister repeatedly touched upon the theme of a new loan, but carefully avoided any reference to diamond shipments for the purposes of the existing one. When, later, Kieckhoefer, ill with malaria, hurried to the Prime Minister's office upon receiving a report that diamonds to a value of one million crusados were to be exported, Coutinho curtly requested him to make an offer for the parcel, adding that he could have the stones in exchange for drafts for half the estimated value. In the absence of instructions from Baring and Hope, Kieckhoefer was obliged to let the parcel go.[4]

Faced with the news that fresh consignments of diamonds would soon be arriving in England, Hope and Baring set about dealing with the problem of how they should react. Consultation between the two had become easier since John Williams Hope's return to England in the autumn of 1808. Alexander Baring felt that it would be best to feign innocence, to simply enquire of the Portuguese envoy whether the diamonds had arrived and, if so, to express readiness to accept them 'and transmit them to their ulterior destination.'[1] He decided against threatening to recoup the overdue payments from the loan which the English government was to make to Portugal, on the grounds that no official support for such an action could be expected.

As usual, Labouchère took a more optimistic view. He pointed out that the necessary steps had been taken to ensure the payment of interest and principal at the end of the year, and that the balance to be claimed was scarcely worth worrying about. Provided that no political difficulties arose, and that agreement could be reached with the tobacco lessees regarding their arrears, he was even prepared to consider a new loan in the following year.[2] There was something fishy about the diamond deliveries, but Labouchère did not regard this as a machination aimed at repudiating responsibility for the loan, but rather as a desperate attempt to obtain funds on the spot. 'Want knows no tie or law,' he wrote. Moreover, he felt sure that the British government, at whose instigation the loan had been arranged, would not permit Portugal to be discredited for the sake of so small a sum.[3]

The consignment of diamonds about which Kieckhoefer had written, and which totalled 50,000 carats, had arrived in England in September 1809, but had remained in the custody of Don Domingo de Souza Coutinho pending a reply from Rio de Janeiro concerning the loan statements which Kieckhoefer had handed to the Prime Minister. Baring offered to open a separate account for the envoy in the meantime, if he was prepared to surrender the diamonds to the house, and even to allow him immediate advances on the stones. When these had been sold, the balance of the proceeds would be placed at his disposal, and he would be free to use all or part of this for Portugal's creditors, according to his instructions from Rio de Janeiro.[4]

Don Domingo declined the proposal, but he offered Baring 25,000 carats which he had had valued and made up into collections, at an average of 3 pounds sterling per carat. He wished to postpone the sale of the other half until the Court's decision became known, but in the event of his receiving permission to sell, Baring would again be given first refusal.[5]

In the view of Alexander Baring, the envoy was asking too high a price. Hope's accounts showed that the carat price in Amsterdam had averaged only 24½ guilders in the preceding months.[1] Sir Francis Baring had earlier informed Don Domingo in writing that in England no absolute valuation could be given for the whole consignment, 'as there is no person in this country who understands the trade sufficiently for the purpose of forming a general assortment, in order to establish an average value; the Jews and Jewellers being very little better than shopkeepers in that respect.'[2] Alexander Baring accordingly refused to advance more than 2 pounds sterling per carat and, moreover, insisted that the stones should be sold by Hope in Amsterdam.[3] The envoy, however, would not go below 3 pounds sterling, and he announced his intention to commence marketing the stones in parcels of 2,000 carats a week later in order to discover the true price. Baring had until then to buy the whole consignment if he wished.[4] An agitated Alexander Baring replied by return of post, warning of the harm which such fragmentary sales would inflict upon the diamond trade. To John Williams Hope, Baring unburdened himself concerning Don Domingo's attempts at intimidation and the tone of his letters, which Baring described as 'civilly impertinent' and 'not a little provoking.' He had, he wrote, been tempted 'to treat him rather roughly,' but, remembering the unfortunate sequel to Labouchère's handling of Spoors, he had decided against it.[5]

Thus, moderation prevailed–temporarily at least, and under pressure from John Williams Hope–and minds were centred on making the best possible showing to the government in Rio de Janeiro.[6] This, however, did not imply that no further steps were taken in England, least of all when it became known that Don Domingo had carried out his threat and had sold half the consignment to the house of Goldsmith in London.[7] John Williams Hope's reaction was to inform the Secretary of State for War and the Colonies, Lord Liverpool, of the situation and to promise to furnish him with a brief summary of the loan affair.[8] Alexander Baring attacked Don Domingo's assertion that no official instructions had been received from Rio de Janeiro. This could not be attributed to the absence of official documents, for his brother in Rio de Janeiro had received them all. There was also the point that the two houses were keenly interested in the future of the small case of diamonds which had reached the envoy a short time before. If Don Domingo dared to allege that Barings had offered only 2 pounds per carat, he would be guilty of a manifest untruth, for 'our offer was to advance to that amount in anticipation, accounting to you for any surplus they might produce.'[9]

In spite of all Alexander Baring's good intentions, the correspondence became so rancorous that on 18th January 1810 Don Domingo was moved to write to Sir Francis Baring, 'of whose friendship and civility to me I have never failed to receive constant proofs.' Much as he regretted it, the envoy said, he would in future be compelled to ignore letters from Barings concerning diamonds unless they bore Sir Francis's signature, since there was someone in that house who signed his letters on behalf of the firm but 'who does not know how to write to me.'

At the moment when the conflict between Alexander Baring and Don Domingo came to a head, the long-awaited instructions from Rio de Janeiro were on their way. Having been kept on a line for some time with the statement that the government was still studying the papers, Kieckhoefer was suddenly informed by the Prime Minister that he had instructed his brother to reach a settlement with Hope and Baring.[1] To have achieved so little after dancing attendance on the government for so long was hard, and Kieckhoefer's letters reveal an unmistakable note of bitterness. In his view, the principal cause lay in the fact that he lacked the status of an official negotiator for the two houses and was thus not in a position to put his foot down at critical moments. The lack of appreciation for all his efforts dismayed him, and he complained of insinuations on the part of Barings to the effect that he had neglected the matter of the loan.[2] It is true that little confidence in the newly fledged linen merchant was forthcoming from that quarter: Alexander Baring described him to John Williams Hope as 'more of an Intriguant than a Merchant,' thereby revealing his fear that Kieckhoefer's tendency to speculate might well result in the rapid disapparance of the loaned capital.[3]

In essence, the outcome of Kieckhoefer's discussions with the ministers was that the latter would deem it a great favour if Baring and Hope would agree to take over the loan of 600,000 pounds sterling which the Portuguese Court had obtained from the British government in April 1810. References to the old loan were limited to a few hollow phrases and vague promises. But the friendly note which had been sounded at the outset was fading, and by 29th May, when Kieckhoefer had an audience with De Souza Coutinho, it had completely disappeared, to be replaced by a tirade against the two houses, especially Hope & Co. Why, the Prime Minister asked, had these gentlemen not used their powerful influence on Bonaparte to have the balance of the loan paid while the French occupied Portugal? He had counted on that, and had acted accordingly. As for the diamonds, in spite of all Alexander Baring's assertions the fact remained that Goldsmiths in London had offered 3 pounds sterling per carat.

He would not dream of handing over the diamonds to Hope, thereby running the additional risk of their being confiscated. It was impossible to do business with Baring, for there had lately been so much evidence of his 'atrocious behaviour' that no government could continue to deal with him.[1]

The Prime Minister's conduct showed very plainly that news of the row between Alexander Baring and Don Domingo had filtered through to Rio de Janeiro. The Lord Treasurer, Count d'Aguiar, showed Kieckhoefer a letter in which Don Domingo stated that Baring planned to use the diamonds solely for the repayment of the old loan, and that they were therefore not to be surrendered to him under any condition.[2] By thus distorting the truth, the envoy succeeded in having a 17,500-carat parcel of fine stones, which were for the purpose of repaying the British government's loan, consigned to him and not to Baring. He was, however, instructed to negotiate with Baring on a new loan of 4–500,000 pounds sterling, the securities for which would be those which served for the original loan.[3]

Following the explosion in January, those in London had come to the conclusion that good relations with the Portuguese envoy had to be maintained at all costs. Sir Francis Baring, to whom so many urgent appeals had already been made, was obviously the best person to initiate a reconciliation. In this he was supported by Labouchère, who, through a fortunate combination of circumstances, was just then heading for England. The semi-independent Kingdom of Holland was viewed with growing disfavour by Napoleon for being insufficiently strict in its implementation of the Continental System. In the autumn of 1809, the emperor summoned his brother to Paris, where he informed him of his plan to annex Holland. Louis Napoleon, whom fear had endowed with ingenuity, developed the theory that the English would go to any lengths to prevent the annexation, and that the mere prospect of it would be enough to bring them to the negotiating table. Napoleon encouraged him in this notion and advised him to bring the issue discreetly to the notice of the English: 'You have an opportunity, for in Amsterdam you have negotiators who are associated with English houses. So take advantage of it, and show the English the threat which hangs over them,' he is reported to have said.[4]

The emperor's utterances were clear beyond any doubt, and it was not surprising that the mission was entrusted to Labouchère, who had both business and family ties with England. On 5th February 1810 he landed at Yarmouth; a month later he returned to Holland, having achieved comparatively little.

From the point of view of a resumption of negotiations with Don Domingo, however, Labouchère's presence in England was of great value. As one who was familiar with the conditions of the loan and its history, he was an ideal partner for Sir Francis in defending the interests of the two houses and straightening out matters distorted by emotions, the more so since he was not handicapped by recrimination. By the beginning of April, relations had improved to the point where serious negotiation on a plan to repay the old debt became feasible.

In the view of Alexander Baring, it would be best if all outstanding claims on the Portuguese Court were incorporated into the loan granted to the Court by the British government. There would then be no problem concerning the arrival of diamonds.[1] As an alternative, Sir Francis Baring suggested that, as previously, the two houses should receive the diamonds and should assume responsibility for payments of interest and principal. If the proceeds of the diamond sales were inadequate for the purpose, the houses could advance the deficit up to the full value of the diamonds deposited with them. In any case, the envoy would have to limit his search for a solution to England, and not look to Holland for a fresh loan.[2]

Early in August 1810 a serious counterproposal from Don Domingo imparted relief to the negotiations. He intimated that he did not wish to concern himself with Hope's existing claims on the tobacco lessees: these were matters for the lessees, the prince regent and the houses concerned to settle among themselves. He was prepared to furnish the monies required for the interest and principal payments due on 31st December 1810 in two instalments, the first on the due date and the second on 31st March 1811. The two houses would be required to effect the final payments in respect of the loan on the due date, 31st December 1811, but they would not be reimbursed immediately. The envoy requested an extension until 31st December 1812 to give time for the repayment to be made from the proceeds of the sale of colonial produce which was to be sold in France and Holland. Baring and Hope were required to approach the British and French governments for licences to import the produce.[3]

Alexander Baring met this with yet another proposal in which great emphasis was placed on the claims against the tobacco lessees in Lisbon. This was important in view of the fact that the prince regent had, at last, ordered the lessees to meet their obligations.[4] Quintella had earlier written to Hope, offering, subject to the approval of the prince regent, to send the remainder of the stock of tea, which had arrived in 1808, in part-settlement of the debt.[5] In May 1810, Labouchère wrote to the French Minister of Home Affairs, the Count of Montalivet, concerning the possibility of importing the consignment, consisting of 2,000 chests, for this purpose.[1]

Regarding the payments due on 31st December of the years 1810 and 1811, Baring expressed his willingness to accept De Souza's drafts on the Portuguese government's London agents, Lucena and De Paiva. The diamonds which had been mortgaged to the two houses would then be placed at the disposal of the Portuguese government.[2] No reply to this proposal was forthcoming. In a letter to Labouchère dated 15th October 1810, Alexander Baring commented: 'Mr. de Souza continues amusing us with plans and projects about the Portugal concern without it having been yet in our power to bring him to anything specific.' He also gave the reason for this galanty show: poverty in Rio, in London, in Lisbon, everywhere. The summer of 1810 had brought Portugal even greater disasters than the previous year. Under pressure from Masséna's offensive, the British commander-in-chief, Wellesley, had gradually withdrawn his troops to prepared positions at Torres Vedras, a little to the north of Lisbon. For the unfortunate populace, this meant being exposed once again to the miseries of war.[3] Under such circumstances, no useful purpose would be served by irrevocably linking the payments at the end of the year to the claims against the tobacco lessees: 'Arguments you know are unavailing where there is nothing,' Baring explained to Labouchère.[4] If the houses simply stood their ground, De Souza would be forced to pay up, because he could not afford to be in arrears at the end of the year and thus gamble his country's creditworthiness. Conversely, it would be wise 'to square our claims at last to his means,' and thus avoid driving the man to distraction; to obtain a fresh admission of the debt and to have it brought to a state of liquidation would be a major step forward.

Baring proved to have been a good judge of the situation, for on 13th December 1810 the envoy, on behalf of the prince regent, signed a new agreement with Hope and Baring. In this, the houses jointly undertook to advance to the Court the sum of the payment due on 31st December, totalling cf 1,700,000. As an earnest for the repayment of the advance, Don Domingo handed over 30,000 pounds sterling and a parcel of diamonds weighing 44–45,000 carats and with an estimated value of 100,000 pounds sterling. The balance of 50,000 pounds sterling was to be met from the sale of diamonds, which were to be consigned exclusively to Hope and Baring until such time as the Portuguese loan and the various sums advanced to the Portuguese government by the two houses had been completely liquidated. The choice of market and method of sale of the diamonds would be matters for De Souza to determine, but it was stipulated that if no instructions were forthcoming from him one year after the arrival of a parcel, the houses would be free to choose their methods of sale. The agreement also provided that Hope and Baring would use their best endeavours to secure licences from the British and French governments for the importation into Napoleon's Europe of colonial produce from Brazil, the proceeds of which would be used for the payment of interest and principal on 31st December 1811. Should this plan fail, the houses would do their best to secure the approval of the bondholders for the capitalization of the final instalment of principal, at an annual rate of interest of 5%. Finally, the agreement upheld in full the guarantee given by the tobacco lessees, and gave Hope and Baring a free hand to obtain the arrears from this source.[1]

It was with justification that Alexander Baring reported: 'We have got more out of de Souza than I expected.'[2] Labouchère, he knew, would be less than satisfied with many details of the agreement, 'but we could not do better.' Indeed, they could not have done better: on one side of the scales lay an advance of 50,000 pounds sterling on 31st December 1810 and the payment of interest at cf 80,350 per annum until the final liquidation of the debt, and on the other the restitution, supported by numerous signatures, of the diamond monopoly.[3] Whether the monopoly would benefit Hope in Amsterdam remained to be seen, for in the second half of 1810 Napoleon had modified his economic strategy against England and now occasionally allowed the import of colonial produce upon payment of a special duty of 50% *ad valorem*. If the diamonds were to be classed as 'colonial produce,' and Amsterdam eliminated as a market, the houses could always fall back on London for the lion's share of the sales, and leave the rest to smugglers. With Portugal in such a piteous state, the re-established guarantee by the tobacco lessees was of greater significance for the future than the present, and it was a good thing that Baring had not made the negotiation of the agreement contingent upon the payments in Lisbon.

The news of Barings' success reached Hope & Co. on Christmas Day 1810, a few days after Labouchère had received a new passport for England from Lebrun, Duke of Plaisance, Arch-Treasurer of the Empire and, since July 1810, Lieutenant General of Holland, now annexed to France.[4] Agreement having been reached with Don Domingo, the urgency of Labouchère's journey to London had diminished and he was free to devote all his attention to the interest and principal payments due on the last day of the year. This was no sinecure, for Amsterdam, like other

European centres, had been in the grip of a serious financial crisis since the autumn of 1810. But in spite of the acute shortage of money, Labouchère succeeded in assembling the funds for the Portuguese payments and others, and on 27th December he wrote with just pride: '... notwithstanding the penury and the shortness of the notice ... the payment is announced to the public together with those for Russia and Louisiana, together seven million florins which must assist the circulation materially.'[1]

By late January 1811, matters had been settled to the point where Labouchère was able to turn his attention to his journey. Finding it impossible to obtain a passage from a Dutch port, he journeyed to France and crossed from there. He was given a passport on condition that he visited Paris on his return and gave the emperor a reliable and unbiassed report on the political situation in England.[2]

In a tragic sense, Labouchère's arrival in England was opportune, for shortly beforehand, on 25th February, the death had occurred of Henry Hope. Much of Labouchère's stay was taken up with discussion of matters relating to the continued existence of the house. Having reached agreement with John Williams Hope (who now called himself John Hope) on the measures to be adopted, he departed for the Continent at the end of April.[3] As agreed, he travelled via Paris to report to Napoleon.

While in Paris, Labouchère took the opportunity to write to the Minister of Finance, the Duke of Gaeta, requesting approval for the importation of diamonds and colonial produce from Brazil. He informed the minister that although he had the emperor's permission to import diamonds into Holland on his homeward journey, the London agents of the Portuguese government had refused to part with the stones because they feared that these would be subject to the high import duty levied on colonial produce. In the letter, he requested total exemption from import duties for this article, 'and to allow us to authorize our correspondents in London to accept them on this basis and to send them over when the opportunity arises.' He also asked for import licences for Brazilian produce such as sugar, cotton, hides and dyewood, the sale of which would provide the funds necessary for the payments due on 31st December 1811. He suggested that the French government would welcome the opportunity thus created to export certain French products to Brazil, 'and of creating there a demand which will imperceptibly make those regions more directly dependent upon France.'[4]

Pending the reply to his letter, Labouchère journeyed to Amsterdam, where he proceeded to reorganize the house in the manner agreed. With the death of Henry Hope and what amounted to aloofness on the part of John Hope, it was necessary to infuse some new blood into the firm, and to this end William Gordon Coesvelt, Pierre Firmin Lestapis and Adriaan van der Hoop were made directors of the firm. Affairs having thus been satisfactorily settled, the ways parted, Labouchère leaving for St. Petersburg to attend to some very urgent matters relating to the Russian loans, while Coesvelt travelled to London on family business and also for the purpose of collecting the diamonds which had been withheld from Labouchère. Although a letter from the French Minister of Home Affairs, stating that diamonds imported into France would be taxed only on the basis of their weight, had arrived on the eve of Coesvelt's departure, Barings sought confirmation of the fact from the house in Amsterdam.[1]

Whereas it was clearly difficult to convince Barings that reliance could be placed on the reduced scale of import duty, it proved an impossible task where the Portuguese were concerned. In spite of all assurances and the production of official French documents, the Portuguese government agents in London persisted in their mistrust. Ultimately a solution was reached in which the two houses purchased the parcel of diamonds then in London at 47 shillings per carat, thereby departing from the customary practice of sale on commission. As all risks were now borne by Hope and Baring, and as it was difficult to obtain cover, the parcel of 24,191 carats in Coesvelt's possession when he left London on 19th October was uninsured. Fortunately he arrived safely in Amsterdam, where the stones were gratefully accepted by Insinger & Co. Despite the scarcity of diamonds at the time, the sale was disappointing. The parcel contained many third and fourth grade stones, whereas the demand was principally for the highest grades.[2] It was obvious, Hope and Insinger both wrote to Barings, that Goldsmiths in London had put their own interests first when sorting the stones.[3] The high import duties levied by the Russians on goods from Napoleon's realm–a symptom of the growing estrangement between the two empires–had brought the export of diamonds to Russia almost to a standstill, while in Amsterdam itself the absence of regular consignments since 1809 had produced a decline in the numbers of cleavers and polishers, and with this a fall in the demand for diamonds.[4]

In the agreement of 13th December 1810, Don Domingo de Souza had made the redemption of the last 1,607 bonds on 31st December 1811 contingent upon the importation into France of colonial produce from Brazil. The request which Labouchère had submitted to the Minister of Finance on this subject, and the subsequent approaches to the government by Baguenault, however, were fruitless, and thus the holders of the bonds had to be content with 5% interest.[1] Early in 1812 Labouchère left for Paris to make a final appeal on the subject to a number of ministers who were well disposed towards him.[2] But this attempt, too, failed, for the emperor rejected the request 'pour des motifs d'une importance majeure.'[3]

Little progress had meanwhile been made in regard to the final settlement of the Portuguese loan. At the end of August, Barings wrote to say that, in the absence of a suitable opportunity, they had not dared to send the diamonds: despite the official French import permit, the house trusted only 'the very best hands.'[4] This news caused immense disappointment in Amsterdam, for Insinger & Co. were rapidly getting through their stock and, in contrast to the previous year, the smaller stones were fetching extremely good prices.[5] In February 1813 Insinger appealed urgently for fresh stocks, adding that the market was 'extremely bare' and that it would be a catastrophe if the polishers, who had so courageously started up again a short time before, should again find themselves without work. According to Ruben Harmsz. Keyzer, Insinger's confidential representative, the firm could easily sell between one and one and a half million guildersworth of diamonds annually.[6]

In the absence of the diamonds, the problem of meeting the interest payment due on 31st December 1812 bore increasingly heavily on the managers in Amsterdam, for John Hope allowed them very little freedom in the financial sense. On 20th October, after repeated requests and on the advice of Alexander Baring, he gave instructions for the interest to be paid. He was, he wrote, relying on the available funds being adequate for the purpose, 'the more so as almost one half of this sum will be credited to us.'[7]

After John Hope's death in February 1813, his heirs transferred the partnership and all pertinent matters to Alexander Baring, upon whom the decision whether or not to pay the interest on the Portuguese loan thus devolved. In reply to a question from the managers in Amsterdam in the autumn of 1813, he consented to the payment, but said that the advertisement should be postponed for a little longer 'for caution's sake.'[8] This circumspection is the more understandable if one realizes that Baring's letter was written on 14th October 1813, a day or two before the Battle of Leipzig, which was decisive for the whole of Europe. At that moment it was impossible to predict Holland's future with any degree of certainty. He did not run a major financial risk, for the diamonds continued to arrive from Brazil, providing him with an equivalent security. In selling them, however, he did not use the services of the Amsterdam house, and such of the stones as found their way to the market there were bought in London by houses such as Braunsberg. The reborn Amsterdam house of Hope & Co., headed by P.C.Labouchère, Sillem and two of the managers of the former firm, A.van der Hoop and P.F.Lestapis, commenced its existence on 1st January 1815, but it was not until 24th November of that year that Baring could bring himself to entrust the sale of the Portuguese diamonds to the new house, which under the arrangement accepted full responsibility for any profits or losses which might ensue from future operations connected with the liquidation of the loan.[1]

Matters having been thus arranged, the partners announced that the remaining 1,607 bonds would be redeemed on 31st December 1815. Shortly before the end of the year the first consignment of diamonds, totalling 20,000 carats, arrived, and this was followed by a parcel of similar size in 1816. For the first time in years it was possible to write down the Portuguese loan.[2] In 1817, the diamond shipments totalled only 20,000 carats, which fact prompted the partners to remind the Ministry of Finance in Lisbon that a reduction in supplies would result in a reduction in the ranks of diamond polishers and thus to a reduction in demand for the gems.[3]

Hope's claims against the tobacco lessees, which dated from the annual accounts for 1808 and 1809, remained outstanding until the end of 1818, when the arrival of a new consignment of diamonds enabled the Portuguese loan to be finally written off.[4] The final accounts for all the diamonds could not be submitted until the following year, the partners wrote, 'but we have grounds for hoping that the result will be such as to move the Court to continue to accord to our market the preference which it has justly acquired above all others by its very organization, by its connexions and its superior avenues for marketing, and by all the other local advantages which it would not be appropriate for us to mention in detail here.'[5]

The fact that, in a period of malaise in Holland, such things could truthfully be written about the Amsterdam diamond market and the branch of industry which was allied to it, was due in large measure to the loan which just then was drawing to a close.

Cochineal

CHAPTER FIFTEEN

COCHINEAL IN THE PATRIOTIC ERA

A SPECULATION WHICH WENT AWRY

'The spirit of emancipation is gaining ground every day and operates in all countries in accordance with the genius of the people,' said Henry Hope in a letter of 9th August 1787 to the French banker Laborde de Méréville. In Hope's view, the French government was still so strong that it had no reason to fear the evil consequences of the development; but in the Republic the picture was gloomier: 'here ... everything has been upset, and it can only end in absolute tyranny, whether by the Prince or by the people–the inevitable outcome of the complete anarchy which reigns today.'[1]

As explained in the introductory chapter, the confrontation between the Patriots and the supporters of the prince reached a climax in the summer of 1787; in Amsterdam, indeed, it led to a complete battle. Surrounded by the tumult of war, Henry Hope had remained at his post and had concentrated on trade–'the neglected issue amid all this confusion'–which had stagnated since the end of the fourth war against England in 1784. Hope, however, consoled himself with the thought that the malaise could not be fatal, for 'trade is frequently ailing, but never dies.'[2]

The truth of this statement was demonstrated by Henry Hope himself when he seized upon the slump to embark on a speculation in a commodity which, in his view, had reached rock-bottom price and, because it was scarce, could be controlled with relative ease. This was cochineal, a valuable carmine dyestuff produced in Mexico by drying the bodies of females of the cochineal insect, which are found on certain types of cacti. The annual harvest or *racolta* was transported from the interior to Vera Cruz and shipped from there to Cadiz, where it arrived between January and the end of June. Anyone who succeeded in tracing and buying up the stock after June could be sure of a free hand until the following year. Cochineal also possessed a high intrinsic value and could be kept for a long time. These factors made it attractive as an investment affording protection against a contingent 'revolution in public affairs, which naturally diminishes the value of landed and funded property.'[3]

According to Henry Hope, the stocks of cochineal throughout Europe amounted to no more than 1,750 bales or seroons, and were distributed as follows:

430 seroons in the hands of large importers or 'first hand' in Cadiz;
433 seroons held by traders or 'second hand' in Cadiz;
450 seroons in London;
437 seroons in Amsterdam.[1]

Users' stocks, he believed, had dwindled almost to nothing, for with prices falling, buyers had covered only their immediate needs. The new *racolta* would be only mediocre, because the continuing low prices of recent years had produced a sharp decline in the breeding and collection of the cochineal insect.[2] Thus, the slightest movement in trade would rapidly send prices upwards. Hope planned to buy as much cochineal as possible–at least three-quarters of the available stock–at the low price. He would place his orders in such a manner that purchases were made simultaneously, thus preventing any warning signals being passed between centres. In this way he hoped to secure 1,200–1,500 seroons without forcing up the price. He estimated the investment at 1½–2 million guilders.

Hope had written to both Laborde de Méréville and his London associates, the house of John and Francis Baring & Co., concerning the speculation, but Laborde showed little interest and so further negotiations were limited to Barings.[3]

There was no element of risk, Hope argued, for the extremely low prices which persisted in the face of low stocks, and which were 'occasioned greatly, at least in this country, by political fears and great scarcity of money and the general depressed state of trade,' afforded the certainty that no losses would result from this enterprise, even though the high expectations were not being fulfilled.[4]

The house in Cadiz which Henry Hope proposed to entrust with the purchases, Thomas Ryan & Co., was 'perfectly au fait of the article'; it could therefore grade the purchased bales according to quality, and send the finest grades, which were suitable for the London market, to Baring and the balance to Amsterdam. If necessary, some could be sent to Marseilles or Rouen.

Henry Hope explicitly sought Baring's views on the speculation as such, and enquired as to the sum which that house was prepared to invest. He also asked for information regarding estimated stocks of cochineal in London and the quantity which Barings felt they could buy up without forcing up the price. The correspondence between the two houses breathes an intimacy which is decidedly lacking in the letter to Laborde. The operations in Amsterdam were to be handled by Robert Voûte, 'our little friend ... and you may be assured they will be executed in character.'[1] Baring could expect to receive a separate letter from him, and Henry Hope was confident that in this Voûte would be able to convince Barings of the solidity of the whole undertaking. Although it was customary for the larger houses to employ brokers in their transactions, and although speculations of this nature were founded on their knowledge of the market and the commodity, it was not usual to accord them so much influence or so great a say. The departure from this principle in the cochineal affair can only be explained by Voûte's exceptional qualities and the friendship which bound him to the partners of Hope & Co.[2]

With the arrival of a letter containing Baring's consent to take a one-fourth share in the speculation, the way was open. Thomas Ryan & Co. received instructions to purchase immediately as much cochineal as they could find. For the ordinary Amsterdam quality, they were empowered to pay 65–67 ducats per arroba (a unit equal to $23\frac{1}{8}$ Amsterdam pounds) and proportionately more for the finer grades, which were suitable for the English and French markets. Of prime importance at the outset were the first hand stocks which, if necessary, could be purchased for cash. Ryan was provided with the necessary funds by way of letters of credit on two Paris houses, although he was not permitted to despatch these until after completion of the purchases.[3] This arrangement ensured that no one would discover the whys and wherefores of the credits until after Ryan had made his move. Urgent letters could be addressed to Boyd Kerr & Co. in Paris, while normal correspondence, in a plain envelope, was to be addressed to the *Administrateur des postes* in Antwerp. This would reduce the delivery time by a few days and also afford greater secrecy.

Hope anticipated that Ryan would complete his purchases in ten to twelve days, and this period was borne in mind when despatching the purchasing orders to Rouen and Marseilles, two markets which, together with St.Petersburg, were brought into the speculation after further consultation.[4] Voûte felt that Baring, in London, should start immediately but act with the utmost caution, 'as your place is the most difficult and most susceptible of sensation on any transaction of moment.' In Amsterdam, 'where a better harvest is more probable than anywhere else,' and where secrecy was so much more easily maintained, the offensive would be opened ten days later, on the 27th.

The choice of purchasing agent in Rouen fell on P. Bournissien Despreaux et Fils, with whom Hope had earlier done business in dyestuffs. The partners of this house were instructed to buy up between two-thirds and three-quarters of the available cochineal in such a manner as not to influence the price. As Hope planned to resell the cochineal in Rouen, the agents were informed that commissions and other charges were to be kept to a minimum.[1] The order for purchases in Marseilles went to Veuve Councler et Fils Ainé. As at Rouen, Hope estimated the stocks here to total 150–200 seroons, although the price limits indicated to Councler were considerably lower, namely 15–15½ livres per pound in Marseilles against 20–21½ livres in Rouen.[2] According to Hope, this was 'as near as possible the pair with 25½ to 26½ in loco.' This was his way of saying that a pound of cochineal costing, say, 15 livres in Marseilles would have to fetch 25½–26½ *schellingen* in Amsterdam in order to cover freight, insurance and other charges. These par values could not be stated precisely, however, for account had naturally to be taken of current prices in the various markets, which in turn were influenced by factors such as demand, turnover and trading customs.[3] As in the plan for simultaneous purchases, the main aim was to prevent speculative sales between markets. The order sent to Ryan on 17th August 1787, it was estimated, would take three weeks and would thus arrive on 7th September. News of Hope's transactions in Rouen and Marseilles would not reach Cadiz until the 22nd at the earliest, so Ryan would have fourteen days in which to complete his purchases. As an added precaution, the letters to Bournissien and Councler were held back until 30th August. If we assume that an urgent letter to Rouen took five to six days, and one to Marseilles ten to eleven days, we see that it was feasible to complete the purchases at those places by 25th September without forcing the market.[4]

In St. Petersburg, the house of Sutherlands & Bock was chosen as buying agent. The principal partner in this firm was Richard Sutherland. He was banker to the Russian Court, but engaged in trading activities through the house which bore his name. Hope estimated that between 300 and 400 seroons of cochineal were available there. After purchasing the stock, Sutherlands & Bock would arrange for storage pending instructions for resale. They were instructed to look first for superior grades, 'such as is in general imported from London,' then for cochineal from Amsterdam, and lastly that from Cadiz.[5]

Sutherland had since the Spring of 1787 increasingly channelled transactions relating to the Russian Crown through Hope & Co. Their connexion formed a most pleasant basis for combining normal business with the cochineal operation. Sutherland, in his role as Court Banker, could take over the drafts which Sutherlands & Bock were to draw on Hope, and use these for his remittances to Hope. This would not only ensure secrecy, but would also bolster up the rate of exchange of the rouble.[6]

In order to complete the circle of market control, it was decided to bring Hamburg into the speculation. As Hope had no knowledge of prices or stocks of cochineal there, instructions were sent to the elderly Beerend Roosen to purchase 'up to the last market price known to you' or, if necessary, up to 4% above this. In contrast to St. Petersburg, preference was to be given to cochineal imported direct from Cadiz, but 'none of that which they adulterate, sift and make up for the Russian market; however, we have nothing against that which has been sent from reputable houses in London, and under no circumstances any from Jews.'[1]

By the beginning of September, all the purchasing instructions which Hope and Baring considered necessary to secure the lion's share of the cochineal available in Europe had been issued. The extent of this share, however, had risen substantially since Henry Hope had launched his plan. Adding the estimated stocks at Marseilles, Rouen, St.Petersburg and Hamburg to the 1,750 seroons already referred to produced a total of 2,650 seroons, of which the speculators needed to acquire nearly 2,000 – an increase of more than 500 seroons. Obviously the preliminary information had not been correct. We are left with the impression that Voûte's intense preoccupation with purchases of tea and his numerous journeys abroad for that purpose adversely affected the preparations for the cochineal speculation.

The stiff resistance put up by the Patriots in Amsterdam, which was referred to in the introductory chapter – and which, as Messrs. Hope were to discover, continued after the capitulation – sorely tried Henry Hope's patience. Trade declined under the influence of the Prussian blockade of all the major roads to Amsterdam, and auctions had to be postponed 'owing to the public unrest which at present occupies minds to the exclusion of business.'[2] Practically no progress was made with the purchase of cochineal either. The rumours of an early outbreak of hostilities between England and France, which radical elements in Amsterdam exploited in an attempt to keep up their spirits, greatly disturbed Henry Hope: 'This event will bring about a very profound revolution in business and will impart an infinite degree of lustre to our speculation, although this was in no way motivated by that consideration; we should be very sorry if it were to owe all its merit to a revolution so distressing to humanity.'[3]

Nevertheless, the prime objective was to get the flagging speculation into motion again as quickly as possible. If the market was to be swept clean in a single operation and without substantial price increases, speed was imperative: the desired two-thirds or three-quarters of the stock must be acquired before the end of September. Cadiz, the fountainhead of the speculation, was the focal point in this respect. On the 22nd of that month – the agreed final date for his purchases – Ryan reported that he had secured 658 seroons and 111 sobernales or half-seroons at prices within the limits laid down.[1] He had done well, although he had let a consignment of 145 seroons held by the Five Gremios slip through his fingers by failing to bid promptly even though the price had been well within his limits.[2] Hope viewed this as 'a terrible check in our speculation' and authorized Ryan to go to 75 ducats per arroba in a final attempt to secure the consignment. Hope found it extremely regrettable that Ryan had ignored 100 seroons of very poor quality cochineal, for 'bad as it may be it may do us much harm, more even than if it was of good quality, as under the name of cochineal it diminishes the nominal quotation.'[3] And why had Ryan not succeeded in securing the consignment from Prasca & Arbore? This was now being shipped abroad, principally to London, where it would have to be bought up at a high price, which implied that others would walk off with a portion of the profit.[4]

Under such circumstances, a rapid completion of the buying programme followed by the 'setting up' of selling prices was an impossibility. It was not until 6th November that Ryan reported that he had secured the 145 seroons from the Five Gremios at 70 ducats per arroba. At this point he held 1,005 seroons and 111 sobernales – almost the whole of the stock in Cadiz, it was hoped, although there was no certainty of this because Ryan's information had earlier proved to be incomplete and at times even contradictory. Altogether the speculators now held twice as much cochineal at Cadiz as they had anticipated buying there, but in spite of this it transpired that more stocks existed in all sorts of unexpected places. In many cases these were held by 'rich and tenacious Spaniards,' and it required long and hard bargaining to persuade them to part with their stocks, not all of which were fresh.[5]

Gradually it became clear that the speculators were busy saddling themselves with a dead stock of cochineal. This was anything but a pleasant discovery, for Hope's plan was based on the assumption that the quantity of cochineal existing in Europe was limited and scarcely covered the annual consumption. Now that the true position had proved to be so different, the dead stock would have to remain dead for the time being. Hope, however, remained confident that the damage which had been suffered would be amply compensated by the profit when sales commenced. 'We think the Chapter of Events is very greatly in our favour,' he wrote to Baring – but without specifying the events to which he referred.[6]

In Amsterdam, too, matters were not going according to plan. On 21st August 1787, Robert Voûte had commenced to purchase 'little straggling parcels' which fell outside the normal trade. The actual purchases in Amsterdam had been entrusted to the brokerage house of De Bruin Abois & De Bruyn, but it was not long before Hope became as dissatisfied with them as with Ryan. At the end of a campaign lasting a fortnight they had secured only half the available stocks, leaving an opening for possible counterspeculation.[1] If Hope had not felt a moral obligation, on grounds of past connexions, to employ De Bruyn, with his narrow mind and limited outlook, and instead had used 'our little friend,' the market would have been emptied in one sweep! Early in September, Hope had got De Bruyn to the point of agreeing to collaborate with Voûte, but owing to the political upheavals the results were still below expectations. Only with the capitulation of Amsterdam did things start to move again. On 12th October–Hope's unlucky day on the Stock Exchange–470 seroons were bought at gradually rising prices.[2] As had been the case in Cadiz, however, small parcels continued to trickle in, and by the end of November Hope's stock in Amsterdam totalled 600 seroons–nearly 50% more than the estimated total stock.[3]

In London, Barings completed their purchases in exemplary fashion. On 4th September, when De Bruyn had with difficulty reached 200 seroons, the figure in London was 364, and by 28th September this had risen to 550. The 'better harvest' which Hope had prophesied in Amsterdam was in fact gathered in London. The phenomenon of the 'lurking parcels' was as apparent there as in Amsterdam, and by the end of November repeated ancillary purchases had brought Baring's stock to nearly 800 seroons.[4]

Meanwhile, in Marseilles, Councler had shown himself to be made of the right stuff. On 10th September, the day on which Hope's letter reached him, Councler was able to report the purchase of 123 seroons, all within the prescribed price limits. Hope duly praised the 'mesures sages et intelligentes' with which Councler had shown that he understood the spirit of the instructions and had been capable of acting in accordance with this. Proof of the wisdom of Councler's conduct lay in the absence of any alarm in Marseilles, where his purchases were seen as an investment or simply as an abortive speculation, 'observing that there is little sign of any boom in this article, which has been almost forgotten by the commercial world.'[5] Councler had expressed some misgivings concerning the port of Genoa, but Hope was able to give him every assurance that no orders had been placed there because he, Hope, had been unable to overcome his deep-rooted prejudice against Italian ports, particularly in the case of an article such as cochineal, which could so easily be tampered with.[1] Councler's decision to continue purchasing beyond the prescribed period, and not to adhere too strictly to the estimated quantity of 200 seroons, similarly earned Hope's full approval. Councler was advised that in the event of cochineal arriving from Leghorn or Genoa, he was free to buy it and to use his discretion in the matter of price. When the market neared exhaustion, he could buy up the balance at up to 20% above the limit, thereby establishing a datum point for the subsequent resale.[2]

Bournissien Despreaux proved to be a weak link in the chain. Rouen was not among the important markets for cochineal, and the stocks there were so widely distributed that individual purchases were limited to very small quantities. By the end of the set period Bournissien had secured only 40 seroons and, moreover, had gone above the limit for the greater part of this.[3] Worse still, these purchases, small as they were, had quickly sparked off rumours elsewhere. Sources in London, for example, were so well informed as to be able to tell Hope exactly what had been bought and what instructions the principals had given to Bournissien. This leak added to the difficulties confronting Hope's brokers in Amsterdam: several stockholders who had initially been willing to sell at the ruling price of 26 *schellingen* per pound now withdrew in anticipation of further developments.[4]

As had been the case in Cadiz, Hope was unable to discover just how much cochineal existed in Rouen. As the correspondence with Bournissien progressed, the quantities–and the prices–steadily increased. Reports reaching Hope from another source referred to a counterspeculation in Rouen. This, it was said, had been based on the outbreak of hostilities between England and France, and when this failed to materialize the holders had tried to get rid of their stocks to Hope at the best possible price. In a letter to Baring, Hope voiced the suspicion that Bournissien might be tempted to indulge in double-dealing, and might even have been involved in the counterspeculation.[5]

According to Sutherlands & Bock, Hope's information regarding the stocks of cochineal in St.Petersburg was inaccurate. There were, they said, no more than 83 seroons, and the price was above Hope's limits. Hope raised the limit, albeit with some reticence, but the relevant letter crossed one from Sutherlands & Bock reporting a steady rise in prices in St.Petersburg, the effect of which was to exceed Hope's limits once again. Hope's initial reaction was to refuse a further increase, 'as we only wish them a happy riddance of what they have on hand at such prices,' but as it would doubtless benefit the resale operation 'to set up that market,' he finally consented. At the same time he expressed to Sutherlands & Bock his surprise at such price increases 'when the article is in disgrace in every other place.'[1] But an even greater surprise was in store: in mid-November, Sutherlands & Bock reported that they had purchased 93½ seroons, two-thirds of which had been obtained at less than the lowest price limits.[2] There was now practically no more cochineal in Moscow, for 65 seroons or thereabouts had been sent to Astrakhan in exchange for raw silk. The Russian markets were principally transit points for cochineal, much of which found its way from them to the Islamic countries in Central Asia where, in accordance with the Koran, only dyes made from scale insects were used for dyeing fezzes and tarbooshes.[3]

The unexpected extension of the speculation, both in time and volume, made it difficult to close off the account and draw up a resale plan. When the original buying period expired at the end of September, 1,415½ seroons had been acquired; by early November the figure had risen to 2,288½, and by the end of the month it was 2,860–1,000 seroons more than the total stock originally thought to exist in Europe and twice the amount which the speculators had anticipated purchasing. Baring's misgivings about 'the final success of the undertaking' are understandable if one reflects that by the end of November some 5 million guilders had been invested in the speculation.

Details of the sales plan were discussed with Voûte, 'as it will be chiefly directed by him.'[4] Voûte expressed the view that the stocks held in Marseilles and Rouen should be shipped to Amsterdam and London, and those from Cadiz to Marseilles, 'to keep up the circulation and augment the appearance of demand.' This, he maintained, could not be done if the cochineal was resold where it lay. Voûte advised delaying the sale because, France having capitulated in the struggle involving the Patriot party, small consignments from all manner of sources would be coming on the market at the beginning of November. If the speculators were to emerge simultaneously, it would appear that they, too, had gambled on a war, and this would inevitably depress prices. Under these circumstances, he advised buying up any cochineal offered at a reasonable figure and then waiting, even though this implied a risk that the new *racolta* from Mexico would meanwhile reach the market in Cadiz, 'which we must not lay ourselves open to the effects of but on the best grounds.'[5]

The exporting of cochineal from France in the manner which Voûte had envisaged was fraught with difficulties. Hope had instructed Councler to transfer half of the 250 seroons purchased into barrels and send these by road to Amsterdam. But the *Chambre de Commerce* in Marseilles protested at what it described as 'ransacking the local market.'[1] As the regulations governing sea cargoes were less stringent, Hope made efforts to charter vessels to take the bales to Amsterdam, but this, too, proved far from easy, for sea transport in the stormy winter season was costly and dangerous, added to which there were few regular sailings to Marseilles from either Amsterdam or London.[2] Meanwhile, Councler was instructed to commence repacking the cochineal, and was told that if the Chamber of Commerce raised an alarm he could simply offer a quarter of the stock at 24 livres per pound; he was also authorized to give an assurance that parcels of 25–50 seroons could be ordered from Cadiz as required.[3] Towards the end of December, in response to an urgent plea from Councler, Hope abandoned his export plans. It is probable that rising costs and growing stocks had made him more receptive to Councler's argument that 'drawing on the one hand and stocking up on the other' was costly, and that it would be wiser to allow Councler to meet the substantial demand for cochineal for export to the Greek archipelago, Turkey and the Levant from his stock. There was also the point that transport by sea would not be possible until February.[4] Similar considerations led to Bournissien being allowed to retain his stock, and to Rouen being designated 'un dépôt pour fournir tous les environs.'[5]

The events in France having rendered Voûte's stock transfer system impracticable, it became necessary to ship the cochineal lying in Cadiz direct to London and Amsterdam. At first Voûte proposed sending 200 seroons of the best quality to London and a similar quantity of the lesser quality to Amsterdam, but later he decided that Rotterdam would make a better central storage point, since it could be shipped from there to other ports at comparatively low cost. Voûte maintained that, in contrast to Rotterdam, cochineal could not be imported into London 'without éclat' and that as the quantity held by Baring was more than sufficient to meet consumption in England, news of such a large stock on hand might well have an adverse effect on the latter's sales. But Baring was not to be convinced by this line of reasoning and in the end Voûte had to agree to ship 400 seroons to Rotterdam and 200 to London. The fact that trade in the Republic was in the doldrums will almost certainly have had a bearing on this arrangement.[6]

As far as actual sales were concerned, Voûte's advice at the beginning of November had been to wait. The resulting delay had played a role in the drawing up of the plans. Before conceding to the pressing desires of the houses in France and Spain to commence selling, it was necessary to establish the price ratios to be maintained between the four principal markets, namely Cadiz, London, Amsterdam and Marseilles. The prices in Amsterdam were relatively the lowest, and thus it was expedient to raise these. Hope thought in terms of an increase from 31 *schellingen* to 33–34 per pound, but this was contingent upon the return of Voûte, 'whose animating genius is extremely necessary.'[1] Following his return on 13th December, 'the parr of the markets' was determined. The point of departure was a given price per arroba in Cadiz, from which each of the houses arrived at the selling price on its market. On this basis, Councler was permitted to sell 25 seroons at the equivalent of 98 ducats in Cadiz, while Bournissien's price for 12 seroons had to be based on 100 ducats. Ryan was initially given permission to sell 100 seroons at 90 ducats per arroba, but this was subsequently reduced to 25 seroons at 100 ducats with the proviso that sales were limited to three or four buyers. Baring was given a price indication of 95 ducats.[2] The two French houses received sound marketing advice from Hope. It was very important not to force matters, but to wait for the emergence of demand. As sales progressed, efforts would be made to raise the price, but the increase had to be natural and a product of demand. In some instances it would be possible to assist Nature by fixing a *prix général* on which a discount could be given to any buyer who took a certain quantity. This incentive would attract the commission agents, who in turn would stimulate individual buyers.[3]

The sales plan was thus complete, but no actual sales materialized. Trade was slack in the winter, and such demand as there was for cochineal could provisionally be met from other sources. The speculators were well aware that the impending arrival of the new *racolta* was among the factors responsible for the lack of demand, and this filled them with anxiety. The main questions were how much would arrive from Mexico, and when? Hope wrote that the new *racolta* would be 'regular but not abundant,' totalling 1,500–1,600 seroons, but this was not confirmed and the uncertainty was reflected in the prices quoted in Cadiz. Despite all Ryan's assurances that there was no cochineal whatsoever on the market, prices there refused to rise above 72 ducats per arroba. And while Cadiz remained low, Voûte's 'parr of the markets' would have no significance.

As we have seen, the cochineal price in Amsterdam was also low. In the latter part of December 1787 the brokers had with difficulty succeeded in reaching 36 *schellingen*, but on 1st January 1788 they were obliged to drop to 32, albeit with the idea of gradually climbing back to 36. This level was indeed achieved for the odd bale or retail sale during January, but with the news of the arrival in Cadiz of part of the new harvest from Mexico, the price again fell to 32 in mid-February.[1]

Early in January Hope, dissatisfied with the situation in Cadiz, decided to employ another house there. His eye fell on Bohl Bros. & Co., an extremely solid and capable house, 'for many years devoted to us.' Ryan had rendered good service in the purchase of cochineal, but he was not the right man to keep the price up in Cadiz, 'for lack of bold and animated conduct.' The unexpected arrival in London of 63 seroons, of which Ryan had made no mention, was the last straw.[2] After a thorough dressing down in which Hope, in veiled terms, accused him of taking part in a counterspeculation, Ryan was to all intents and purposes dropped.[3]

In the instructions issued to Bohl, priority was given to raising the price of cochineal in Cadiz. The speculators had lost two months as a result of bungling on the part of Ryan, who had failed to buy up the remaining parcels of cochineal at 80–90 ducats and thus block any underspeculation on the other markets. This delay made it imperative for Bohl to be informed as quickly and accurately as possible regarding the consignments expected from Mexico, the vital issue being whether the greater part would arrive during the first two months of the year or between March and June. Enclosed with the letter to Bohl were three sealed envelopes containing instructions. The first of these was to be opened if 4–500 seroons arrived in January and February, with the anticipation of a further 700–1,000 seroons in June; the second in the event of the bulk of the harvest arriving first and the balance later; and the third if only a couple of hundred seroons arrived during the first six months and the balance thereafter.[4]

The tactics differed in the three letters of instruction, but always the aim was to buy as few arrobas as possible at the highest possible price and to take an option on the balance of the stock. This kept up expectations among the sellers, while giving the speculators time to dispose of their stocks elsewhere at good prices. If the cochineal market were to fall again at the end of the year, the speculators could replenish their stocks at low prices. In this manner, large investments in the article could be avoided.

A westerly wind in the Atlantic favoured the ships, but played havoc with Hope's support plan. Almost at the same moment as the instructions to Bohl were being written, four vessels arrived in Cadiz with more than 500 seroons of cochineal on board. They had completed the voyage from Havana in the unusually rapid time of 45 days.[5] At that moment no house in Cadiz held orders from Hope to support the price, and the result was that a considerable amount of cochineal changed hands at 72 ducats per arroba–three ducats below the minimum price for which Hope was aiming.

When the first report of the arrival of the vessels was received, Hope had ordered Bohl to carry out Instruction Number One, but when it became clear from the second letter, which was dated 21st February, that the position was virtually irretrievable, Bohl was given greater freedom of action.[1] Hope expressed deep regret at his inability to entrust 'the management of this important concern' to Bohl at an earlier date, and added that this was not 'a mere speculation, but rather an investment of money in a branch of trade which will be continued.' However, the letter bore a postscript replacing the greater freedom of action with an instruction to cease all buying until further notice, 'as it would be idle now to attempt to force the prices above their strength, which would be only favouring the late low priced purchases.'[2]

The extent to which the slowness of the post hampered merchants and made it impossible for them to react adequately to certain market developments is evidenced by the time which elapsed before Bohl received instructions matched to the situation. Hope's original instructions of 7th January did not reach Bohl until the end of the month. On the 29th, Bohl wrote to Hope, giving details of the adverse developments in Cadiz since 7th January. Meanwhile, Hope had received Bohl's letter of the 8th announcing the arrival of the four cochineal ships. In reply to this, Hope instructed him on the 31st to implement Instruction Number One. Bohl's letter of the 29th January reached Hope on or about 20th February, and in the reply to this the execution of Instruction Number One was replaced by a ban on further purchases. This did not reach Bohl until the middle of March and thus more than six weeks elapsed before he was in possession of corrected instructions. During this period Bohl, acting largely on his own initiative, had cautiously bought small quantities; in this he was supported by Ryan who, at his own risk, bought up all the small parcels which came on the market, intending to offer them to Hope later at a higher price.[3] Ryan's parcels were declined, but Bohl's action in continuing to buy met with Hope's full approval even though it conflicted with the directives of 21st February, which probably stemmed from a fear of unbridled stockpiling. Now that Bohl had shown himself to be made of the right stuff, the reins could be slackened–the more so since his actions had been successful and prices in Cadiz were recovering well.[4]

The speculators had extricated themselves as best they could from the difficulties in Cadiz, but it was clear that their escape was temporary and that the difficulties still existed. Hope confessed to Baring that he was at a loss to know what to do: 'We have a great share of timidity and little faith even in the arguments we have used' (i.e. towards Bohl). If only they could be sure that 1,000–1,200 seroons would be sold before the bulk of the new *racolta* arrived, and had even a rough idea how much would arrive and when, 'we should have sufficient strength of mind to give pretty haughty orders to Cadiz.' But in the absence of even a rough idea, Hope found himself in a most unpleasant situation of uncertainty and indecision which was aggravated by the urgent need for a firm plan. Did Baring perchance have a plan? If so, Hope would gladly consider it.[1]

In spite of the anxieties and doubts which beset him, Hope was obliged to maintain an optimistic tone in his correspondence with others concerning the speculation. This was necessary because the events in Cadiz had not left the other markets untouched, particularly since the instruction 'sell, sell large quantities' had been issued. In Marseilles, relatively close to Cadiz, Councler was having an exceptionally difficult time. It was at his insistence that Hope had agreed to leave the bought stock there, and he felt honour bound to sell it quickly and profitably. But all his efforts were thwarted by the arrival of small parcels from Italy and Cadiz. The par price which had originally been indicated to Councler was far too high in view of the fall in prices in Cadiz, and had a reverse effect. Councler began by buying up as many as possible of the parcels which appeared on the market at this price, but when these continued to flow in he lost courage. A further reduction of the par price had no effect whatsoever and in the end he was instructed to sell at one or two ducats beneath the Cadiz price, provided that this was still profitable.[2] Hope instructed him to cease buying for the purpose of supporting the price: 'ce serait la mer à boire'; if no more were purchased, these imports would dry up. Councler would be well advised to ignore the criticasters who predicted that the speculation was destined to fail; if it succeeded, they would alter their tune.[3] Hope gratefully seized upon reports of more stable prices in Cadiz to revive Councler's spirits, although to Baring he confessed to fears that speculative purchases might well have played a significant part in the recovery.[4] It was perhaps this fear which led him to instruct Councler to cease selling if the bottom were to fall out of the market. In that case he was to wait, while at the same time doing all in his power to get the price rising again.

Councler succeeded in selling a few parcels of between 2 and 4 seroons, but over February and March the total amounted only to about 30 seroons and this made little impact. To cheer him up, Hope hinted, as he had done to Bohl, that although it was not proposed to perpetuate the operation, this could well span several years. In all probability a political development–for example, the war against the Turks–would favourably influence the speculation, though Councler should not bank too heavily on this but should meanwhile try to sell as much as possible. Hope conveyed the impression that the speculators were able to influence prices in Cadiz, 'comme il convient au bien de la chose.' In view of the extremely limited nature of Bohl's brief, this was a bold assertion.[1]

In Rouen, sales were practically nil and even a gradual decline in price levels produced little or no improvement. Hope, in a somewhat bitter mood, implied that Bournissien had earlier asked for a depot for cochineal, but was unable to justify the central position which he claimed in the sales plan. Bournissien had initially attributed his lack of success to the high par price which, he maintained, had resulted in buyers ordering direct from Cadiz and thus supporting prices there. This argument, however, had ceased to be valid following the price reductions, for buyers in Cadiz were now reported to be paying 78–80 ducats per arroba and Bournissien could scarcely have difficulty in competing with this in Rouen? Bournissien had repeatedly made vague references to a war, and anything of that nature could certainly influence sales. Hope did not relish the idea, but if Bournissien had any information, those in Amsterdam would like to know about it as soon as possible. War did not seem very probable to Hope, 'in view of the disorderly finances of the Sovereign Courts and of the strange tricks they play.'[2] War or no war, the fact remained that there was no demand in Rouen for Hope's cochineal. On 27th March, in a burst of optimism, Hope wrote to Bournissien saying that he had read somewhere that the 'fabriques' in France were showing signs of revival. On 7th April he lamented that the stagnation in trade could not last for ever.[3]

The tone of the correspondence with Baring at the beginning of April concerning the policy to be followed was if anything more pessimistic than that of a month earlier. The primary aim of the speculation–to corner the market in cochineal while prices were low and to sell when prices subsequently rose–had not been achieved. Hope was unable to put his finger on the exact causes of the failure, but one thing was clear: wherever the speculators had assembled stock, there had been a refusal to buy. The later observer is less convinced of the existence of a boycott and is more inclined to attribute the absence of demand to the economic malaise of the time, from which France in particular suffered. There was certainly a threat of war, which could have forced prices upwards, but it did not occur and this fact was a disadvantage rather than an advantage to the speculators because, in the prevailing uncertainty, buyers became even more reticent. The war which did take place, between Russia and Turkey, added to the difficulties, because the hostilities in the border areas impeded the cochineal trade with Asia.[1]

Baring took a much more optimistic view of the future than his partner in the speculation. The London house felt that attention should continue to be focussed on Cadiz, 'to keep up a certain spirit there as the spring of every other,' and this required that one-third or one-fourth of all the cochineal which arrived in Cadiz be bought up by the speculators. The result would be to keep up the price of the remaining stocks, and this in turn would assist prices elsewhere to the benefit of the speculators, whose sales, Baring was convinced, would greatly exceed their additional purchases in Cadiz, so that on balance the 'stock on hand' would diminish. He added that the issuing of instructions to Bohl was a matter of some urgency if they were not to be too late for the arrivals in June.[2]

Hope and Voûte regarded Baring's view as far too optimistic. In the light of 'the general combination which seems formed against us,' they saw little possibility of a surplus of sales, and in addition they had no inkling of the quantities which would arrive from Mexico. It could well be that, following the report of improved prices in Cadiz, all the manpower available in Mexico had been directed to the collection of cochineal insects and also that every scrap of old stock would also be put on the market. If Bohl was stimulated prematurely or on too large a scale, the speculators might soon find themselves saddled with a further 1,000 seroons merely in order to keep up the price, while it might be necessary to change the policy altogether if such colossal stocks actually arrived on the market.[3] It therefore seemed prudent to Hope and Voûte to await further news before issuing fresh instructions to Bohl.

Hardly had this letter been written when Hope received news from Bohl that the frigate 'The Confidence' had arrived in Cadiz with 295 seroons of cochineal and that the 'Mentor' and the 'St.Raphael,' together carrying 400–500 seroons, were expected shortly. Hope's letter instructing Bohl that no more purchases were to be made had reached him at about the same time as 'The Confidence' arrived. Faced with this order, Bohl had made no move, with the result that several parcels had gone to other buyers at 76 ducats per arroba. Bohl added that he would continue to support prices of between 76 and 80 ducats and hoped that these would be maintained. Ryan wrote to say that he would purchase for his own account any cochineal offered at 74 ducats.[4]

Thus the time lag between Hope's instructions and the market developments in Cadiz was repeated in March, and it looked as if the same situation would arise when the 'Mentor' and the 'St.Raphael' arrived. On 24th March, Hope had despatched fresh orders to Bohl, authorizing him to make limited purchases and instructing him to support prices at the level which he had thus far maintained. But although Hope assumed that the letter would reach Bohl before the arrival of the two vessels, it will certainly not have done so.[1] In a letter to Baring, the partners in Amsterdam showed that they knew where the crux of the problem lay: 'In fine everything turns out for the best, tho we are really much indebted to good luck for it, as we have continued to be too late in our orders.'[2]

Whether or not all came right in the end, the letterbooks of the day do not reveal. The last letter concerning the cochineal speculation bears the date 16th April 1788, and later surviving correspondence bears no reference to the subject. We are, however, in possession of details of the 'Cochineal Account' covering the years 1788 to 1793 and this shows that the speculation fared badly. At the end of 1793, 3,368 seroons and 124 sobernales, which up to that moment had cost cf 6,128,341.4.8, including warehouse rental, freight, insurance and other costs, stood on the debit side. Against this stood sales of 2,435 seroons, 27 sobernales and 904 pounds, totalling cf 4,010,748.14.0. This implies that a loss of more than two million guilders, or one-third of the purchase price plus costs, was incurred. Hope had written off cf 300,000 'for losses' from his three-quarter share in 1788, and a further cf 100,000 in 1791.[3] Against the debit balance, however, stood a stock of unsold cochineal totalling 911 seroons and 88 sobernales which, on the basis of the Amsterdam market quotation of 28 *schellingen* per pound in December 1793, was worth cf 1,603,400. But this was a theoretical value, for more than three-fifths of the stock lay in Russia and a further fifteen per cent or so in Marseilles.[4]

In the interest of clarity, the details of the 'Cochineal Account' are reproduced in three summaries, which the reader can consult.[5] It should be noted that these statistics possess only relative value, for whereas Table F-1 shows that cochineal sales in 1788 were limited to Amsterdam, we know from the correspondence in the period January–April of that year that parcels had also been sold in London and Marseilles. In all probability Hope entered these sales in 1789, and it may be assumed that similar overlaps also occurred in later years, though it is not clear to what extent. The summaries do, however, provide answers to the questions: How did the sales progress subsequently, and what were the prices obtained?

At first sight, one is struck by the extremely disappointing results achieved in Amsterdam, both in terms of quantities sold and price. In

1794 even the original stock remained unsold, while the 500 seroons transported from Cadiz had in fact been sent on to St.Petersburg and Moscow (see Table F-III).[1] It was natural that Hope should do this, because losses had been suffered on 504 of the 568 seroons sold in Amsterdam, and these had increased as the years went by.[2] A remarkable aspect and one which defies immediate explanation is the difference between the prices obtained for the cochineal in Amsterdam in each of the years and the average market quotations for the years concerned as shown in Posthumus's *Nederlandsche Prijsgeschiedenis.* Whereas the difference in 1789 was 19 cents per Amsterdam pound, it had risen to cf 3.15 by 1793.[3] This is the more remarkable because the prices paid by Hope during the buying period corresponded exactly to the average monthly market quotations; moreover, the efforts to set up the price can all be traced: 31 *schellingen* or cf 9.30 in December 1787 and 36 *schellingen* or cf 10.80 in January 1788, with a fallback to 32 *schellingen* or cf 9.60 in February.[4]

The results achieved in London were also unsatisfactory. While it was true that virtually the whole of the stock on hand was disposed of, 60% was sold at a loss of between cf 1.33 and cf 2.42 per pound, based on the average purchase price there. Admittedly about a quarter of the bales sold had come from Cadiz, where they had been bought at a favourable price, but this did not prevent an adverse balance in the end.[5] Indeed, if one considers the higher purchase price, the results obtained in London were even worse than those in Amsterdam. One gets the impression that the speculators were anxious to reliquidate their investment and, if necessary, were prepared to accept a substantial loss. In all probability the lower-priced grades of cochineal were not marketed until a later date; if so, this would partly explain the crumbling of the prices.[6]

The consignments from Cadiz more than doubled Councler's stock in Marseilles. By 1794 he had succeeded in selling 80% of the total, albeit at steadily declining prices and steadily greater losses but nearly always at levels above those achieved by Hope in Amsterdam, while the purchase prices at the two centres had been practically the same.

Probably under the influence of the growth of radicalism in revolutionary France, 106 seroons were shipped at the speculators' expense from Marseilles to various ports in Asia Minor and the Levant.[7] These shipments produced no profit, for the 61 seroons which Councler sold in 1793 fetched as much per pound as the 41 sold in Constantinople and Smyrna.

In St.Petersburg and Moscow, the speculators were unfortunate in the extreme. Of the total stock of 628½ seroons at these two places, no more than 11 seroons had been sold by the end of 1793. Furthermore, two of the three houses to which the cochineal had been consigned ran into serious difficulties in that year. Richard Sutherland had died in 1792, and an investigation had revealed that his affairs were in a state of chaos. The Russian Court demanded 3,700,000 roubles from his heirs as compensation for serious neglect of the interests of the Court. Robert Voûte, who had visited Russia in 1793 on behalf of Hope & Co. in connexion with Polish and Russian loans, sought through the personal intervention of Empress Catherine II to prevent Sutherland's merchant house becoming involved in the debacle, but he had no success. Sutherland was declared bankrupt in March 1794, Hope & Co. being involved to the extent of 351,000 roubles; it is probable that this sum included a claim relating to cochineal consignments.[1]

The difficulties which concerned G. Thomson Rowand & Co. in Moscow were fortunately of a less serious nature. Like many others, the house had been hit by the acute scarcity of money in Russia, a product of the disruption of trade in western Europe by the French wars of conquest. Voûte submitted a claim on Hope's behalf in which a sum of cf 586,404 relating to the cochineal account figured, but it proved possible to save the house from collapse.

Hope's fortunes in the matter of this claim fall outside the scope of this story. Suffice to say that Pierre César Labouchère, during a sojourn in St.Petersburg in 1811, disposed of the claim on Thomson Rowand & Co. to another debtor to Hope & Co. in order to be rid of the worry.[2]

Thus ended a speculation which certainly caused Messrs. Hope a great deal of anxiety and undoubtedly brought heavy losses. The failure of the house of Sutherland and the delay in settling the claim on Thomson Rowand & Co. will have necessitated the writing off of further sums. Nevertheless, this unsuccessful affair fits into the general picture of the house of Hope & Co., for in the world of business one must continually take risks, and if the house had not done so it would never have achieved eminence. But it was characteristic of the policy of the partners that the cochineal speculation, like other ventures, was a calculated risk; the house could permit itself to undertake this investment. While millions of guilders were tied up in cochineal for years on end, Hope & Co. embarked upon one Russian loan after another without ever incurring problems of liquidity. Nevertheless, the cochineal affair was a source of anxiety, especially in the early stages. In the letter books which we consulted, the letters referring to the speculation outnumbered those dealing with the Russian loans by more than five to one. And it was at this very time that the first Russian loans were being floated.

Let us examine the causes of the failure of the speculation. Chief among these was the incompleteness of the information regarding the stocks of cochineal in Europe. The true figure will have been more than double the 1,750 seroons to which Henry Hope referred at the outset, and these stocks were far more widely distributed than was thought. If we ask ourselves who was primarily responsible for the incompleteness, we are forced to the conclusion that it was Robert Voûte. He was the broker with specialized knowledge of dyestuffs; it was he who, prior to the commencement of the speculation, supplied information concerning potential sales in Russia; and he helped to draw up the entire plan. His too numerous absences and his preoccupation with other matters are bound to have had an adverse effect on the execution of the plan. This opinion, however, is not expressed in the correspondence, and, in spite of the unhappy note on which the undertaking ended, Voûte continued to enjoy the confidence of the partners, who called upon his services in many important matters.

The lack of demand for cochineal on the various markets greatly vexed the speculators, particularly as they were powerless to alter the situation. In planning the speculation, they proceeded from the premise that, in spite of the malaise, a revival of demand was inevitable, and when the inevitability of this was not borne out they became obsessed with the notion of a plot.

Besides the malaise in the French textile industry, which has already been mentioned, the factors leading to the failure of the speculation included the system of par prices, the effect of which was to cause holders of parcels of cochineal to either foist these on to the speculators or their agents, or sell them to third parties at a fraction less than the par price. The overextended buying period also played a role. This was in part allied to the underestimation of the existing stocks, but political factors beyond control of the speculators were also among the causes. For example, the disturbances involving the Patriots in Amsterdam and the aftermath of these demonstrably slowed the buying programme in that city, while the subsequent appearance on the market of stocks released by disappointed war speculators hampered its completion. The time-consuming work necessitated by a lack of drive on the part of some agents, such as Ryan and Bournissien, was yet another factor.

The slowness of communications with distant ports such as Cadiz was also a major obstacle. This, after all, made it impossible to issue orders in time to meet the fluctuating market situation. The cry 'too late' echoed repeatedly during this episode. Amsterdam, which by its sales record so sadly demonstrated its fall from the position of central market, was no exception in this respect. Whereas Voûte expected the 'better harvest' to be reaped in Amsterdam, the purchases in London were 40% greater. In terms of sales, the contrast was sharper still: compared with Baring's total of 1,222 seroons, only 563 were sold in Amsterdam. Viewed against this background, the financial strength of Hope & Co. becomes even more impressive.

ILLUSTRATIONS

Gerard Sanders (1702–1767)

Dulwich College Picture Gallery, London
(by courtesy of the owner)

Archibald Hope, merchant at
Rotterdam (1664–1743)

Cosmo Alexander (1724–1772)

National Gallery of Scotland, Edinburgh
(by courtesy of the owner)

Adrian Hope (1709–1781)
at the age of fifty-four

Mezzotint by C.H.Hodges (1764–1837)
after a painting, now lost,
by Sir Joshua Reynolds (1732–1792)

Bank Mees & Hope N.V.,
Amsterdam

Henry Hope (1735–1811)
at the age of forty-one

Cosmo Alexander (1724–1772) Owner unknown

John Hope (1737–1784)
at the age of twenty-six

Angelica Kauffmann (1741–1807) Bank Mees & Hope N.V., Amsterdam

John Williams Hope (1757–1813)

Angelica Kauffmann (1741–1807) Bank Mees & Hope N.V., Amsterdam

Anne Goddard (1736–1820),
wife of John Williams Hope

Jacques Henri Sablet (1749–1803)

Lords Cricket Gallery,
Marylebone Cricket Club, London
(by courtesy of the owner)

Thomas Hope (1769–1831)
playing cricket with friends in the Italian countryside

By an unknown artist Bank Mees & Hope N.V., Amsterdam

Pierre César Labouchère (1772–1839)

Lithograph by H.W.Couwenberg (1814–1845) J.A.Sillem, The Hague

Hieronymus Sillem (1768–1833)

Mezzotint by J. Ward (1769–1859)
after a painting by
Sir Thomas Lawrence (1769–1830)

Bank Mees & Hope, N.V.,
Amsterdam

The partners of John and Francis Baring & Co.
From left to right: Sir Francis Baring, John Baring
and Charles Wall, a son-in-law of Sir Francis

Sir Thomas Lawrence (1769–1830)

Baring Bros. & Co. Ltd., London
(by courtesy of the owner)

Alexander Baring (1774–1848)

By an unknown artist — Voûte Vereniging, Amsterdam

Robert Voûte (1747–1823)

Miniature on ivory by an unknown artist J.L. Insinger, Laren (N.-H.)

Hermann Albrecht Insinger (1757–1805)

The Hope residence, Keizersgracht 444–446, Amsterdam.
The building now houses the Municipal Public Library

The warehouses Kerkkroon A and B,
Prinsengracht 659–661, Amsterdam

Engraving by Benjamin Comte (circa 1760–1845)
after a drawing by H.P.Schouten (1747–1822)

Bank Mees & Hope N.V.,
Amsterdam

'Welgelegen,' Henry Hope's country seat in Haarlem, drawn in 1791.
Henry Hope owned this property from 1788 to 1808

'Welgelegen' as it is today. It is now the centre of local government for the province of Noord-Holland

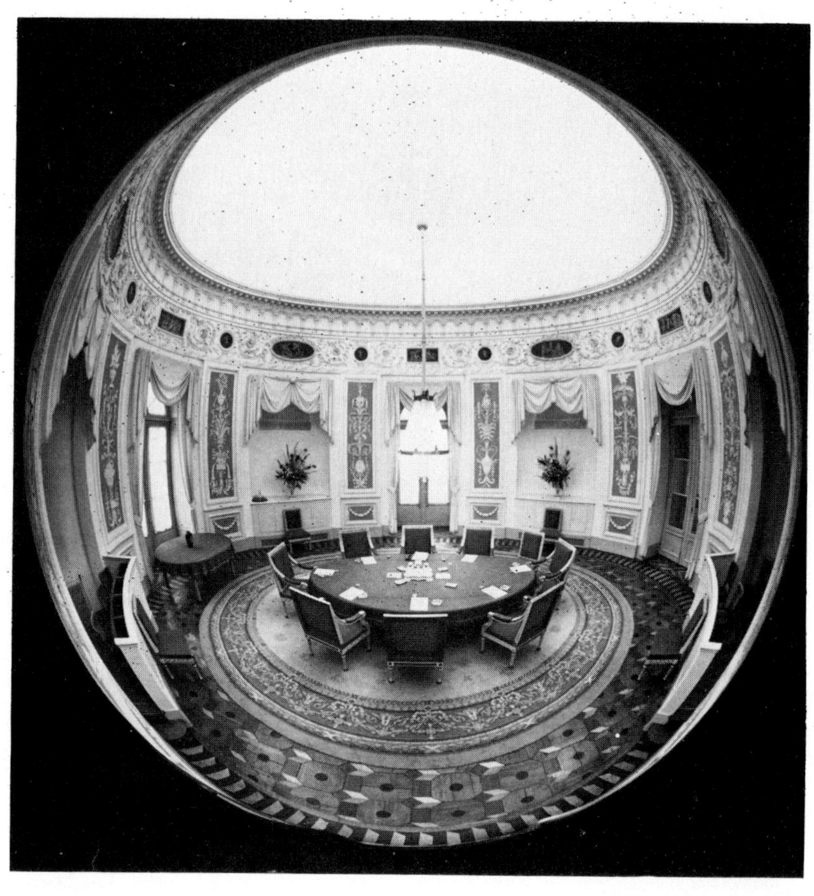

Fish-eye view of the circular music room at 'Welgelegen.'
This is now used for the meetings of the Executive Committee
or *Gedeputeerde Staten* of the province of Noord-Holland

Nederhorst den Berg Castle.
The property of John Hope and
his heirs from 1774 to 1803

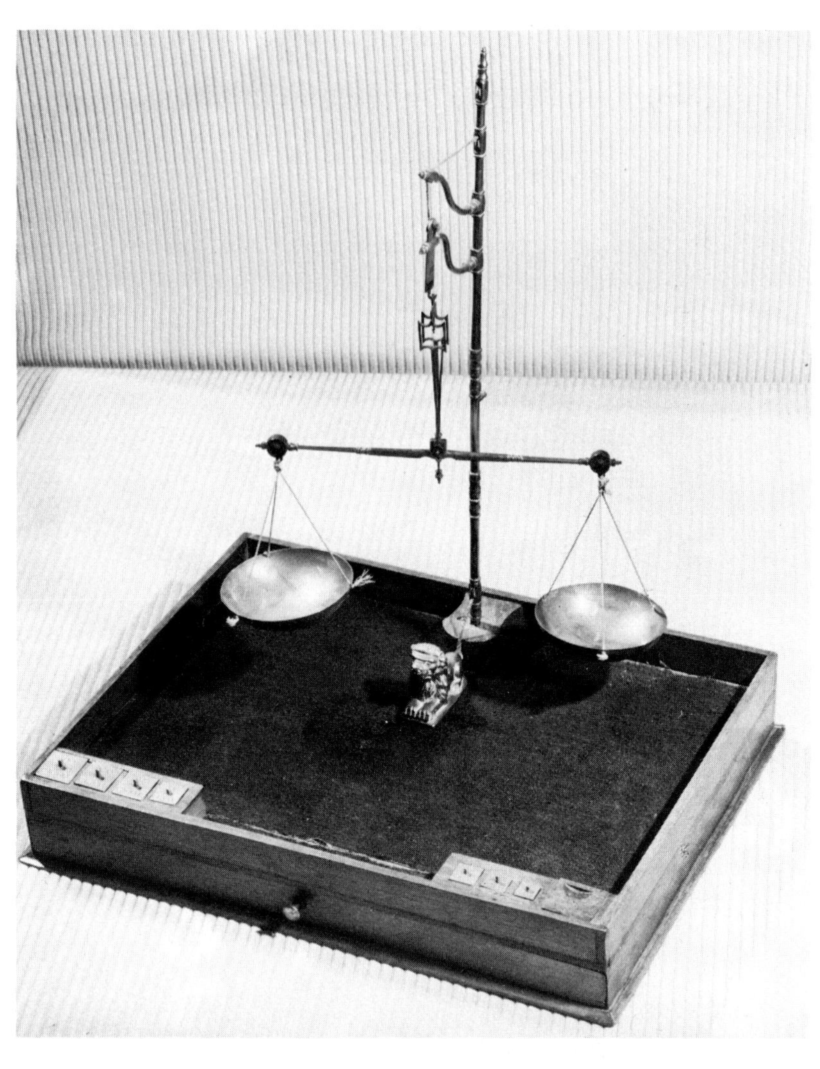

Scales with weights in carats.
Now in the possession of Bank Mees & Hope N.V.

APPENDICES

A. ANNUAL TURNOVER

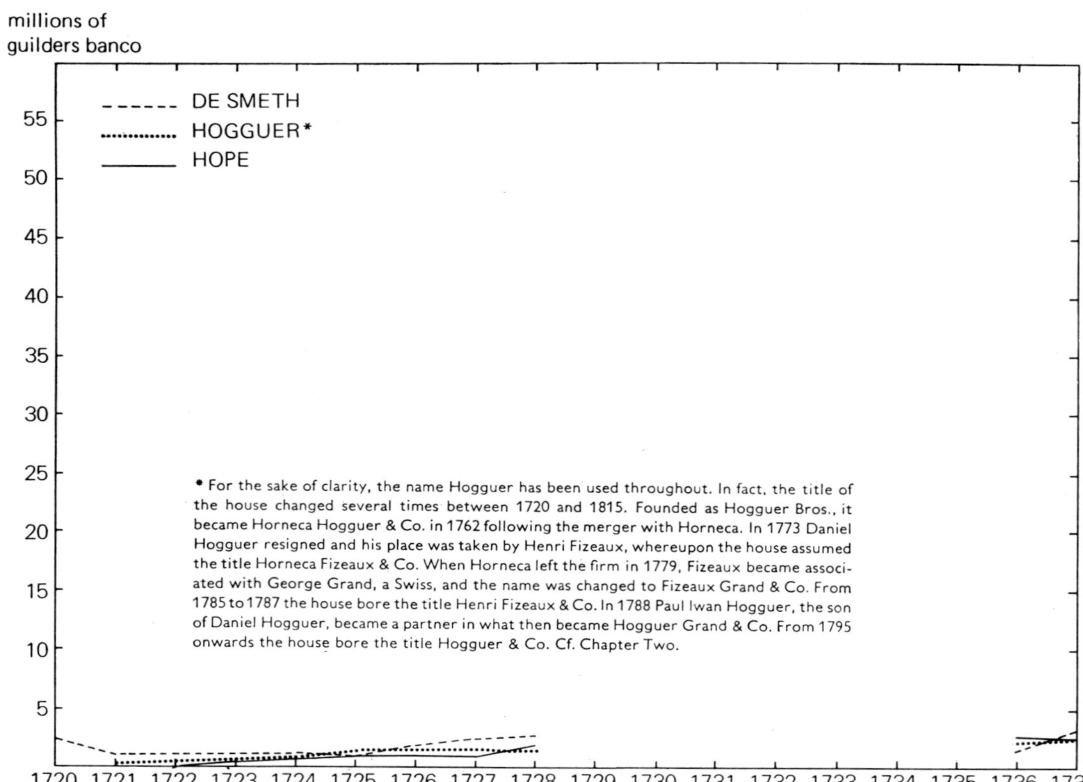
millions of
guilders banco
DE SMETH
HOGGUER*
HOPE
55
50
45
40
35
30
25
20
15
10
5
1720 1721 1722 1723 1724 1725 1726 1727 1728 1729 1730 1731 1732 1733 1734 1735 1736 1737
* For the sake of clarity, the name Hogguer has been used throughout. In fact, the title of the house changed several times between 1720 and 1815. Founded as Hogguer Bros., it became Horneca Hogguer & Co. in 1762 following the merger with Horneca. In 1773 Daniel Hogguer resigned and his place was taken by Henri Fizeaux, whereupon the house assumed the title Horneca Fizeaux & Co. When Horneca left the firm in 1779, Fizeaux became associated with George Grand, a Swiss, and the name was changed to Fizeaux Grand & Co. From 1785 to 1787 the house bore the title Henri Fizeaux & Co. In 1788 Paul Iwan Hogguer, the son of Daniel Hogguer, became a partner in what then became Hogguer Grand & Co. From 1795 onwards the house bore the title Hogguer & Co. Cf. Chapter Two.

A-I. Annual turnover with the Amsterdam Exchange Bank of the houses of Hope, Hogguer and De Smeth, in the period 1720–1737

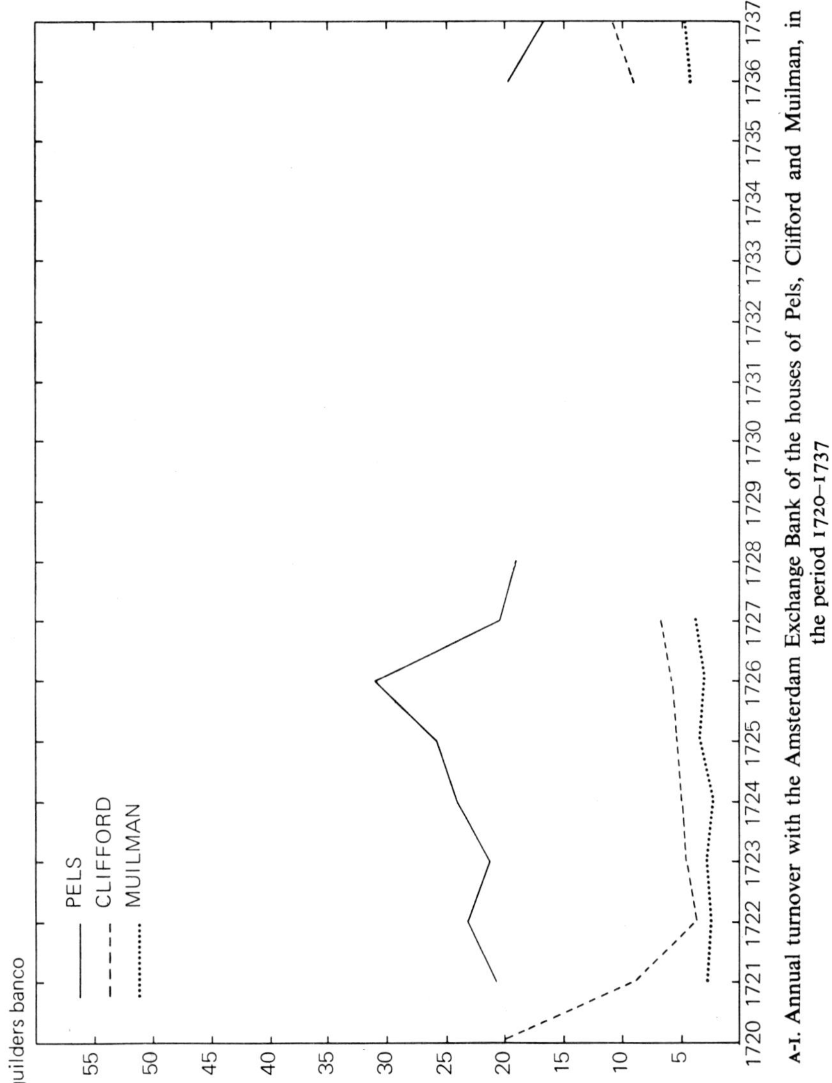

A-I. Annual turnover with the Amsterdam Exchange Bank of the houses of Pels, Clifford and Muilman, in the period 1720–1737

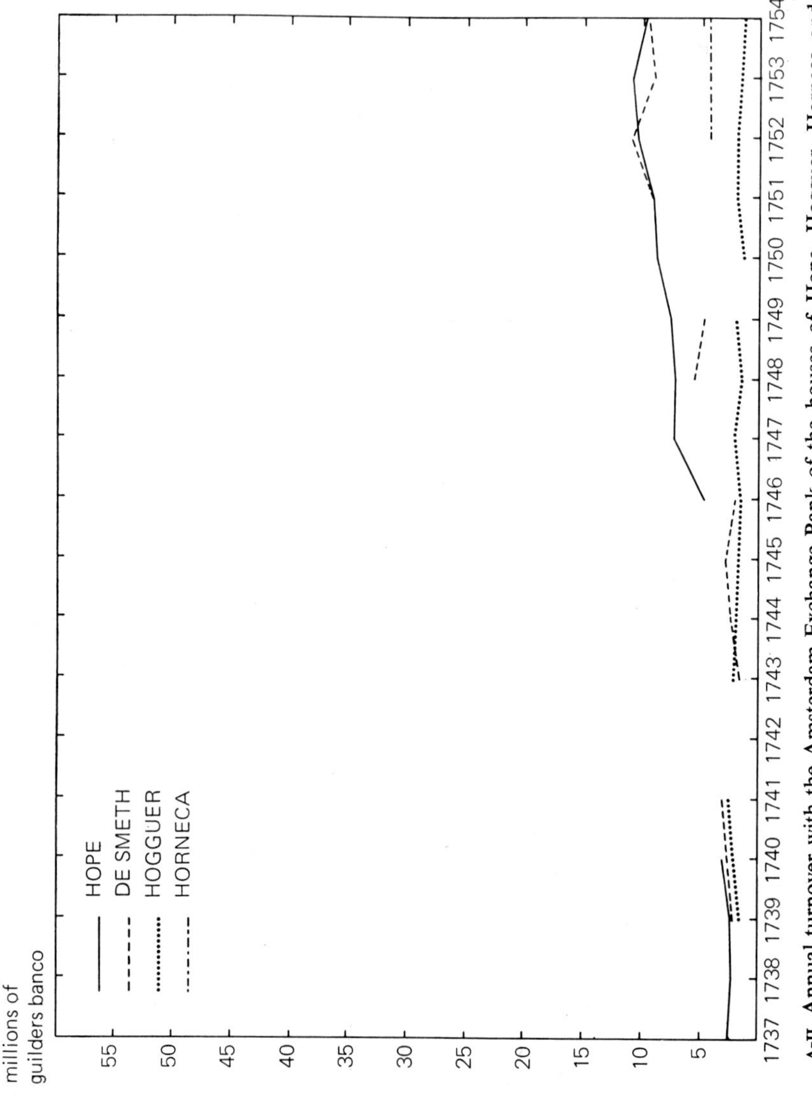

A-II. Annual turnover with the Amsterdam Exchange Bank of the houses of Hope, Hogguer, Horneca and De Smeth, in the period 1737–1754

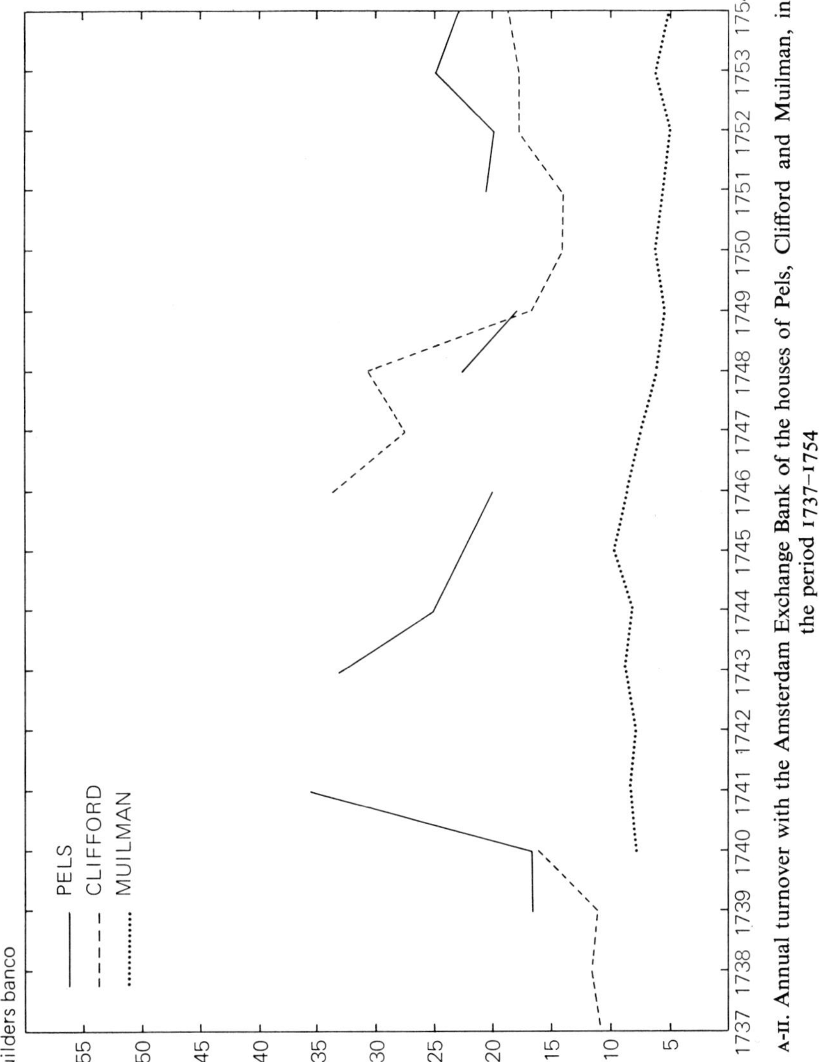

A-II. Annual turnover with the Amsterdam Exchange Bank of the houses of Pels, Clifford and Muilman, in the period 1737–1754

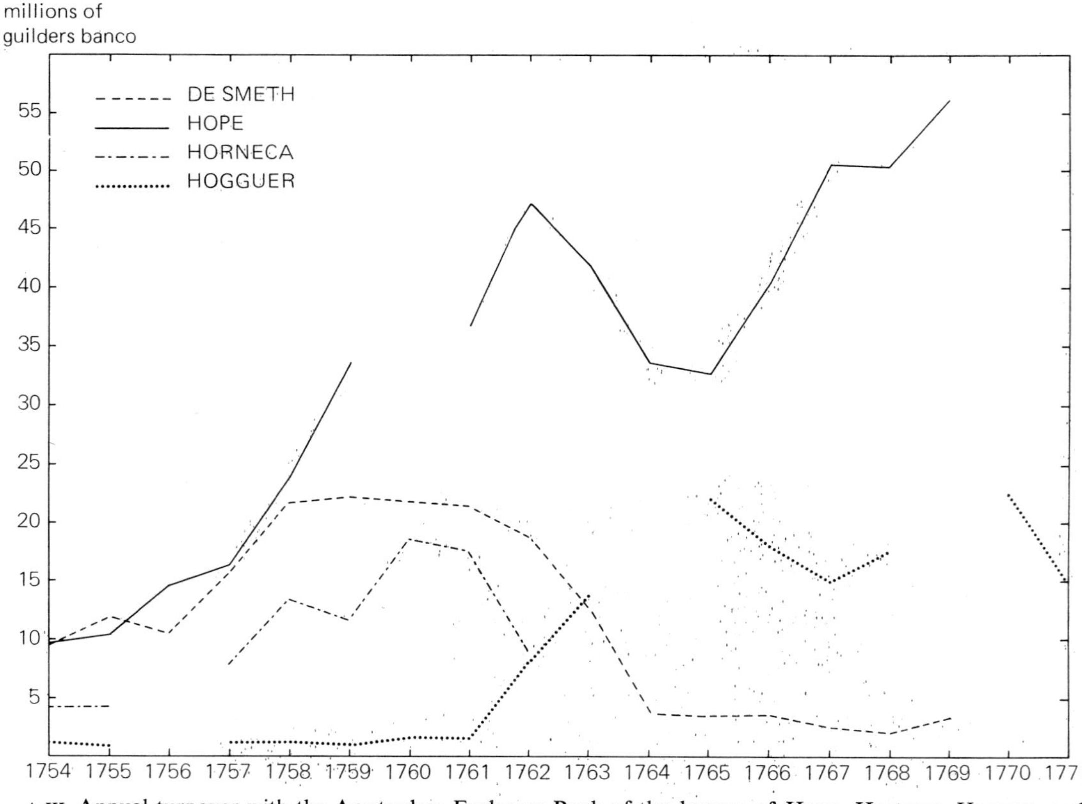

A-III. Annual turnover with the Amsterdam Exchange Bank of the houses of Hope, Hogguer, Horneca and De Smeth, in the period 1754–1771

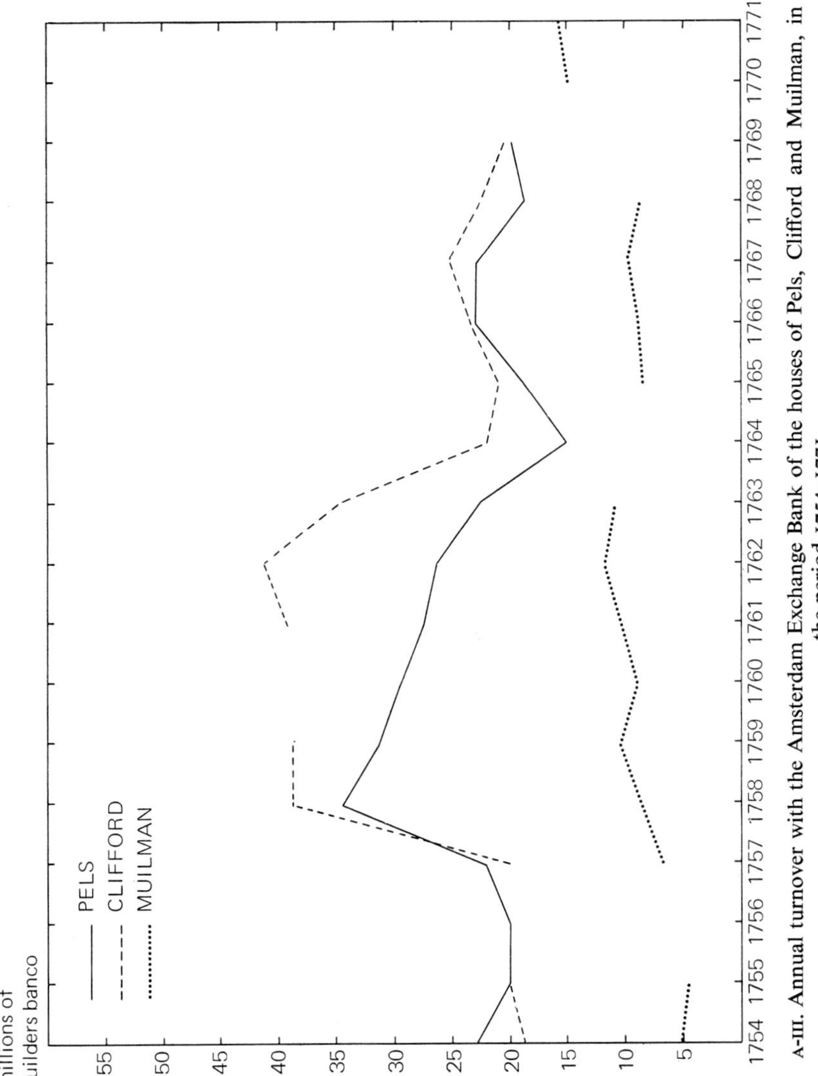

A-III. Annual turnover with the Amsterdam Exchange Bank of the houses of Pels, Clifford and Muilman, in the period 1754–1771

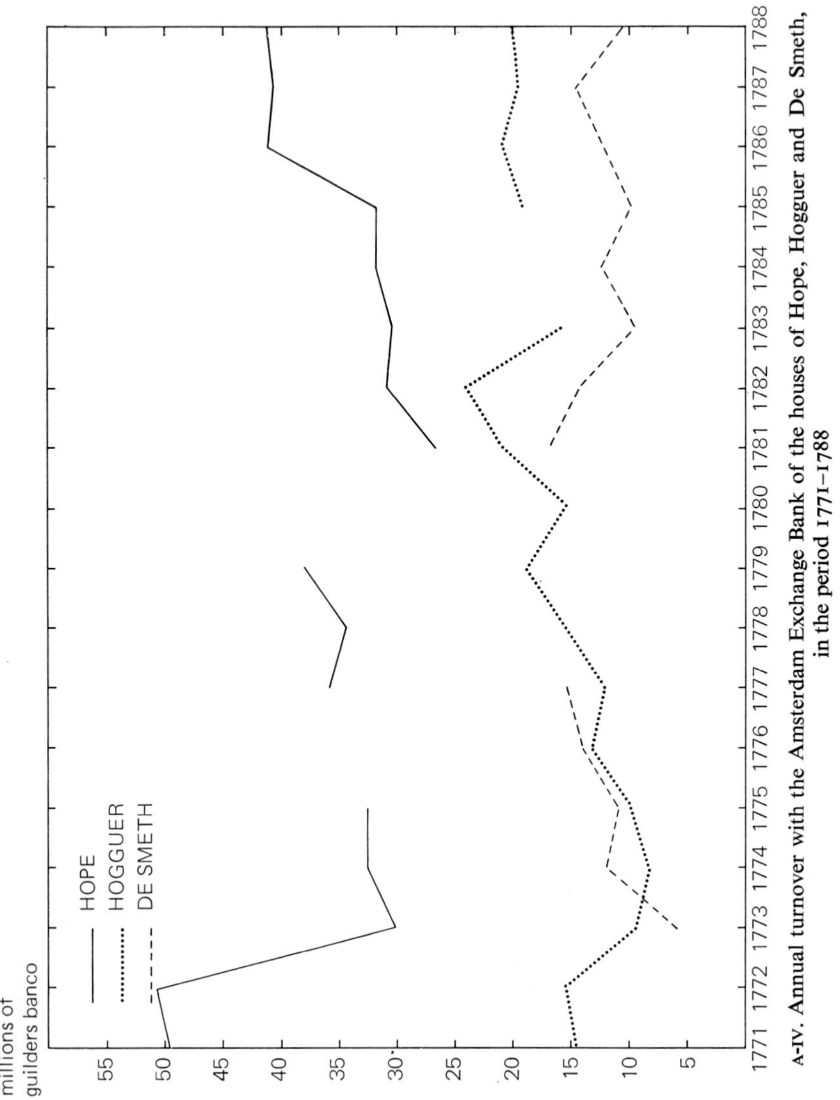

A-IV. Annual turnover with the Amsterdam Exchange Bank of the houses of Hope, Hogguer and De Smeth, in the period 1771–1788

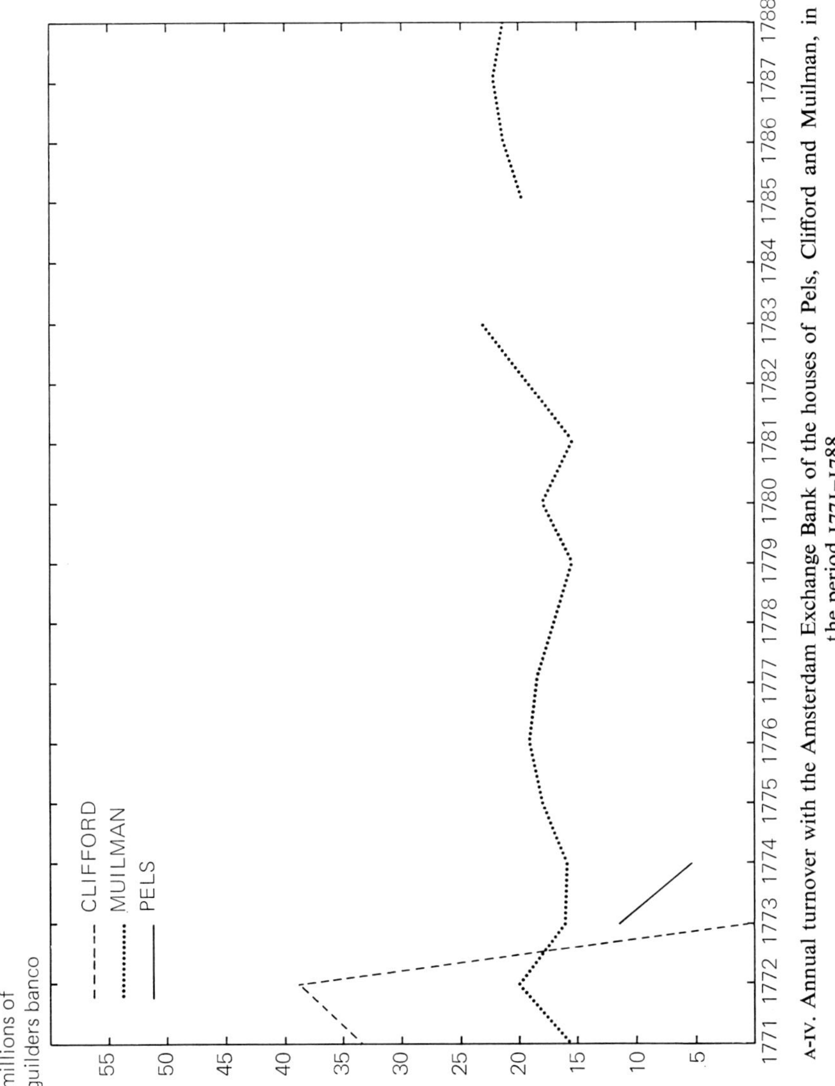

A-IV. Annual turnover with the Amsterdam Exchange Bank of the houses of Pels, Clifford and Muilman, in the period 1771–1788

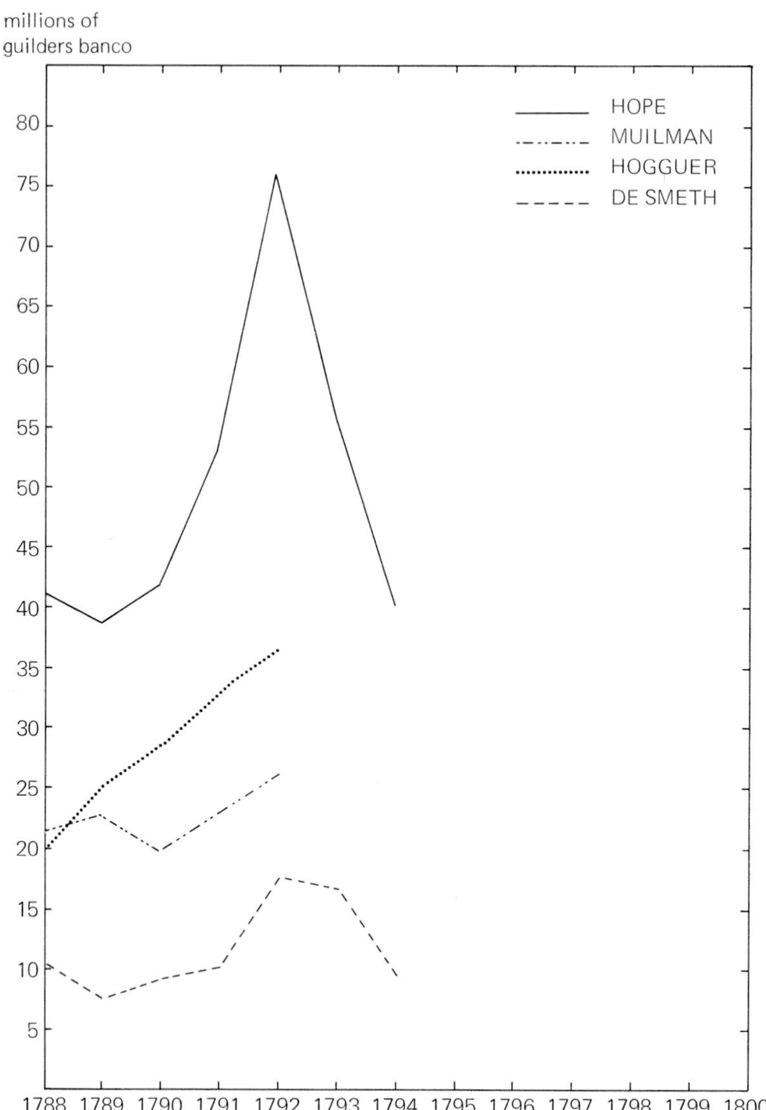

A-V. Annual turnover with the Amsterdam Exchange Bank of the houses of Hope, Hogguer, De Smeth and Muilman, in the period 1788–1800

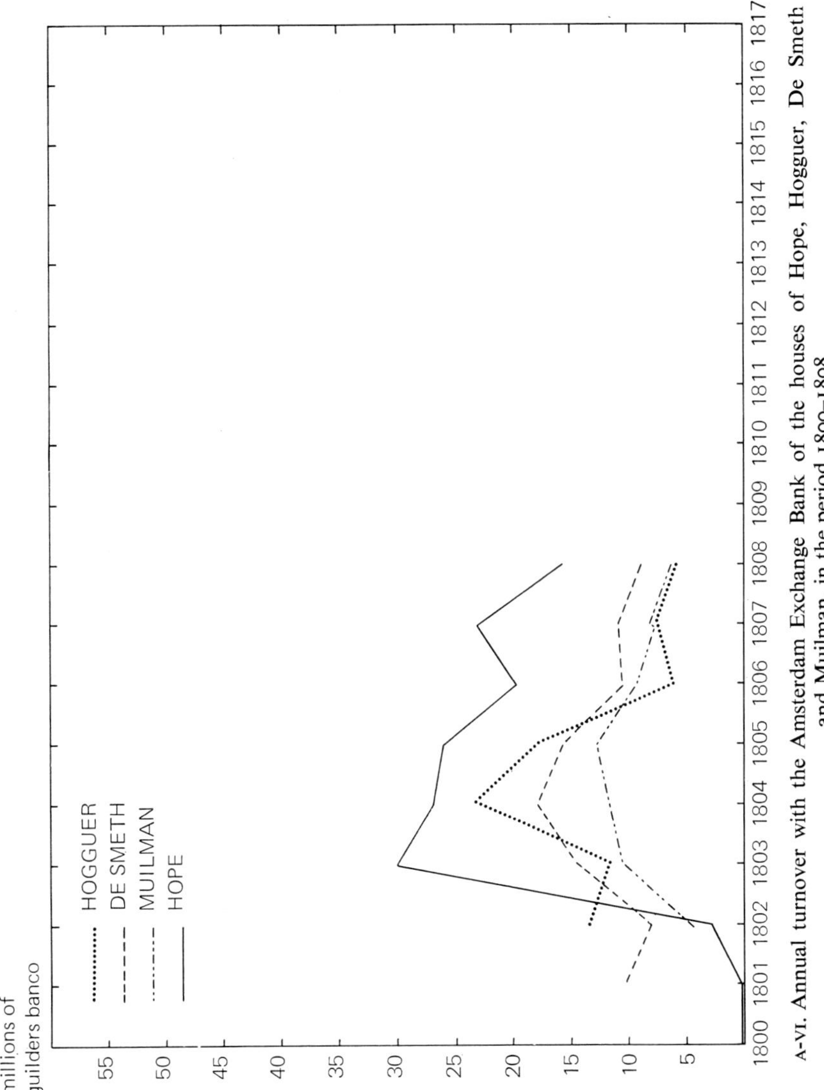

A-VI. Annual turnover with the Amsterdam Exchange Bank of the houses of Hope, Hogguer, De Smeth and Muilman, in the period 1800–1808

B. THE HENRY HOPE COLLECTION OF PICTURES

CATALOGUE A

OF PICTURES IN THE HOUSE NO. I THE CORNER OF HARLEYSTREET, BELONGING TO MR. HENRY HOPE, ON WHICH IS ENSURED TWELVE THOUSAND POUNDS

Master	*Subject*	*Value in £*
Albano	Diana & Acteon	160.—
Do.	Bacchus & Ariadne	160.—
Do.	The Fortune Teller	50.—
Bolognese	2 Landscapes	100.—
Lud.Backhuysen	View on the Maze	200.—
Bassano	The Saviour comforted	40.—
N.Berghem	Landscape	120.—
Do.	Do.	100.—
Bloemaert	A Patriarch	40.—
Bourdon	Jacob & Laban	10.—
Breughel	Stable in Bethlehem	20.—
Ch.le Brun	Family of Jabach	1,000.—
Do.	Allegorical	50.—
Do.	Do.	100.—
Lod.Caracci	Birth of Bacchus	50.—
Do.	A Saint comforted	20.—
Do.	Holy Family	80.—
Do.	Diana & Acteon	500.—
Do.	St.John in the Wilderness	200.—
Do.	Hercules & Cacus	300.—
Guido Canachi	Susanna & Elders	100.—
C.Cigniani	Virgin & Child	50.—
Do.	Woman & three Children	40.—
Corregio	Ascension of the Virgin	100.—
Do.	Holy Virgin	100.—
Do.	Two Children	160.—
Seb.Concha	Virgin & Child	10.—
Cocci	Diogenes & Alexander	20.—
Pedro de Cortona	A Bible Composition	100.—
Do.	Herodes' Cruelty	100.—
Do.	Holy Family	100.—
Crocci	Holy Family	60.—
Crespi	Jupiter & Semele	20.—
Cuyp & v.d.Elst	Landscape & Figures	110.—

Master	*Subject*	*Value in £*
B.Denner	Portrait	40.—
Do.	Do.	20.—
Do.	Young Elector Palatine	20.—
And.del Sarto	Holy Family	120.—
Do.	Do.	100.—
P.Dorner	Roman Charity	10.—
Domenichino	Susan & Elders	300.—
Doudijns	Allegory	20.—
Carlo Dolci	A Magdalen	50.—
Do.	Head of the Virgin	70.—
Do.	Dying Magdalen	40.—
Dufresnoy	Achilles discover'd	100.—
Van Dyck	Two Children	20.—
Do.	Portrait, half length	100.—
Do.	Paris	150.—
Do.	Portrait	40.—
Do.	Do.	40.—
Do.	Dr.de Vos	150.—
Do.	D.his Wife	150.—
Do.	Full length portrait of Gaston de Foix	300.—
Elsheimer	Toby & the Angel	20.—
van der Elst	Portrait	40.—
Do.	Do.	40.—
Verelst	Do.Flemish Woman	10.—
Dom.Faeti	Dedalus & Icarus	150.—
F.Fery	Landscape	40.—
Do.	Do.	40.—
Do.	Joseph sold	40.—
Do.	Jacobs departure	40.—
Franceschini	Holy Family	20.—
Do.	Landscape & figures	40.—
Giorgione	Christ triumphant	150.—
Do.	Warrior	50.—
Goltzius	Susanna & Elders	50.—
Do.	Magdalen's head	50.—
Guido	Angel Gabriel	50.—
Do.	St.John & the Lamb	60.—
Do.	Magdalen	60.—
Do.	Ecce Homo	500.—
Do.	St.John	60.—
Do.	Virgin & Child (oval)	20.—
Do.	Magdalen treading underfoot the Vanitas of this world	700.—
Do.	Cleopatra dying	500.—
Guercino	Virgin & Child	150.—
Grimaud	Portrait, half length	20.—
Hamilton	Death of Lucretia	150.—

Master	*Subject*	*Value in £*
Hobbema	Landscape	100.—
Cs.v.Harlem	Christ crucified	50.—
Fs.Hals	North Holland Woman	20.—
J.van Huysum	Landscape & figures	20.—
L.Jordano	The hot & cold blower	100.—
Ph.Laura	A Charity	20.—
G.de Lairesse	Narcissus	45.—
Do.	Allegorical composition	100.—
C.Lorain	Landscape	500.—
Do.	Do.	500.—
Do.	Do.	150.—
C.Maratti	A Madonna	50.—
Do.	Holy Family	50.—
Do.	Parce somnum sumere	300.—
Do.	Theseus & Ariadne	50.—
Do.	Titan & Aurora	70.—
Do.	Venus rising from the Sea	70.—
Do.	Venus & Adonis	150.—
Do.	Virgin & Child	50.—
Metsu	A Woman at Supper	20.—
Rap^{hl} Mengs	St.John	100.—
v.Mieris	Boy blowing bubbles	50.—
Do.	A Boors family	100.—
Moucheron	Landscape	40.—
F.Mola	Mary Magdalen	20.—
Murillo	Holy Family	550.—
Do.	St.Ignatius	100.—
Mancini	Female Saint with Holy Ghost	40.—
Miereveld	Van Tromp	30.—
Le Nain	Adoration of the Shepherds	50.—
Ostade	Landscape	220.—
Palma	Peters Apostasy	40.—
Palma the young	A Nymph pursued by Satyrs	20.—
Pagi	Venus & Cupid	50.—
Parmeggianino	Holy family	300.—
Do.	Do.	150.—
Do.	Do.	100.—
Perino del Vaga	Holy family	200.—
Poelenburgh	Two Seasons	20.—
Do.	Do.	20.—
Do.	Landscape & figures	50.—
Poussin	Jupiter & Antioche	600.—
Do.	Allegory	50.—
Do.	Venus & Satyrs	100.—
Do.	Holy family	200.—
Do.	Ascension, sketch	50.—
Do.	Phocion	300.—

Master	*Subject*	*Value in £*
Do.	Do.	300.—
Rembrandt	Family piece	500.—
Do.	The Saviour & Mary Magdalen	50.—
Do.	Family piece	300.—
Do.	Landscape (oval)	100.—
Raphael	Holy family	60.—
Do.	Virgin & Child	100.—
Ricci	The Saviour suffering	40.—
Julio Romano	Mars & Venus	100.—
Romanelli	Virgin & Child	20.—
Do.	Holy family	40.—
Sal.Rosa	Landscape	520.—
Rottenhammer	The Muses	20.—
Do.	Landscape & figures	20.—
Do.	Do.	20.—
Do.	Do.	20.—
Rubens	Woman taken in Adultery	700.—
Do.	Christ triumphant over Sin & Death	500.—
Do.	Deluge of Philemon	500.—
Do.	Landscape	100.—
Reynolds	Venus & Cupid	100.—
Siro feri	Holy family	20.—
Sassoferrato	2 Madona's	60.—
Schedoni	Holy family	100.—
Eliz.Sirani	Magdalen	150.—
Spagnoletta	Roman Charity	80.—
Le Sueur	Cupid stealing the thunder of Jupiter	100.—
Do.	Abraham & Hagar	100.—
Do.	Allegorical Composition	150.—
Do.	Death of Dorcas	300.—
Van Teelden	Nessus & Deianira	50.—
David Teniers	Landscape	500.—
Titian	Lucretia	20.—
Do.	Venus & Cupid	100.—
Do.	The Woman cured by touching the Saviours Garments	100.—
Do.	Holy family	150.—
Do.	Full length portrait Duchess of Parma	500.—
Do.	The Graces	500.—
Tintoretto	Madonna & Child	70.—
Trevisani	Death of Adonis	70.—
Do.	Apollo & Marsias	70.—
Wm van de Velde	A Stormy Sea	300.—
Ale^{r} Veronese	Loth & his Daughters	40.—
Do.	Hercules & Omphale	220.—
Do.	Samson & Dalila	100.—
P^{l} Veronese	Rebecca	50.—

Master	Subject	Value in £
Do.	Mars & Venus	100.—
Do.	Marriage in Cana	300.—
Velasquez	Family portrait	300.—
Van der Werff	Loth & his Daughters	40.—
Do.	A Magdalen	100.—
Do.	Nymph & Satyr	200.—
West	Landscape & figures	150.—
Do.	Fable	70.—
Do.	Do.	80.—
Ph.Wouwermans	Landscape with Warriors	20.—
De Witte	Lisera & Jahel	20.—
Zuccarella	Joseph sold	50.—
		24,915.—

London 17 December 1795
(signed)
Henry Hope

CATALOGUE B

OF PICTURES IN THE HOUSE NO. I THE CORNER OF HARLEYSTREET, BELONGING TO MR. HENRY HOPE, ON WHICH IS ENSURED TEN THOUSAND POUNDS

Master	Subject	Value in £
Alexander	Mary Queen of Scots	20.—
Antonissen	Landscape	20.—
Do.	Do.	20.—
Do.	Do.	20.—
C.Bega	Inside of a Boors house	10.—
Do.	Boors housekeeping	10.—
L.Backhuysen	Sea piece	200.—
Do.	Do.	100.—
Do.	View of a Warehouse in India	40.—
Beschey	Boors house with figures	40.—
N.Berchem	Landscape with buildings	140.—
G.Berckheyde	14 views of Dutch Towns	140.—
Breughel	View in Brabant	10.—
J.& A.Both	Landscape & Waterfall	300.—
B.Breenbergh	St.John preaching in the Wilderness	30.—
H.de Cort	View of a City	30.—
A.Cuyp	Landscape, Cattle & Herd	300.—
Dusart	Boor housekeeping	20.—
Ger[d].Dou	Dutch Kitchenmaid	1,000.—

Master	*Subject*	*Value in £*
Do.	Woman asleep by a Candle	50.—
Dirk van Deelen	Inside of a Church	25.—
Van Dijck	Ascension of the Virgin	400.—
J.van Elst	Flower piece	10.—
P.Ghijsels	City view full of action	30.—
Do.	Game, still life	10.—
B.Graaf	Nymphs bathing	10.—
R.Greffier	3 views on the Rhine	30.—
Goltzius	Vertumnus & Pomona	10.—
J.van der Heyden	View of a Village & Church	90.—
Van der Heyden & Van de Velde	View of a Convent & great Church	150.—
Do. & Do.	View of the Harlem p[t]. in Amsterdam	100.—
Huchtenburg	Shock of Cavalry	10.—
Do.	Do.	10.—
Holbein	Portrait	40.—
Hamilton	Copy of Titian's sleeping Venus	60.—
M.Hondecoeter	Poultry	40.—
Do.	Landscape with Do.	50.—
Do.	Landscape with Poultry	60.—
Van Huysum	2 Landscapes	50.—
Do.	A Flower piece	300.—
Do.	Fruit	400.—
Do.	Arcadian Landscape	200.—
De Hoog	Inside of a Room with figures	35.—
Janson	Landscape with figures	20.—
Do.	Do. with Cattle	20.—
Ch.du Jardin	Do. falcon chase	250.—
Do.	Do. a horse & two Oxen	40.—
Ph.Koning	Inside of a house	10.—
Limburg	The Infant Ajax	30.—
Do.	Ariadne	30.—
J.Lingelbach	2 Italian Markets	80.—
Lentz	Historical	100.—
Do.	Minerva	30.—
G.de Lairesse	Death of Cleopatra	80.—
Metsu	Appartment a Man & a Woman	160.—
Do.	Dutch Appartment	150.—
Do.	A Man writing	110.—
Do.	A Woman writing	80.—
F[s].v.Mieris	The Old Shrimp Eater	450.—
Do.	Gentleman & Lady	300.—
W[m].v.Mieris	Judgment of Paris	50.—
Do.	Vertumnus & Pomona	50.—
Do.	A Woman with Grapes	50.—
Do.	Lady, Maidservant and Dog	50.—
Do.	Chandlers Shop	20.—

Master	*Subject*	*Value in £*
Do.	Green Shop	20.—
F[s].Milé	Landscape	80.—
Moucheron	Do.	20.—
Do.	Do.	20.—
F[s].v.Mieris Junr.	Women playing with bones	30.—
L.de Monié	A fortune teller	10.—
Do.	2 Fish boors (a pair)	10.—
J.de Maubeuge	Virgin & Child	40.—
Netscher	Lady with a Parrot	60.—
Do.	Young Man in a niche	20.—
A.van Ostade	Landscape & Boors	30.—
Do.	Conversation	50.—
Do.	Landscape & Boors	250.—
Poelenburgh	Offering of the wise men	20.—
Poelenburgh	Glaucus on the Sea Shore	15.—
Paul Potter	Stable with horses	150.—
Do.	Landscape, Oxen & Sheep	120.—
Do.	Do. 3 Standing & One resting Oxen	150.—
Rembrandt	Sea piece	500.—
Rottenhammer	Ascension of the Virgin	40.—
Do.	Feast of the Gods	20.—
Rottenhammer & Breughel	A repose in Egypt	50.—
Schouman	Birds	10.—
Do.	Inside App[t]. & 3 Figures	10.—
Schalken	Man lighting his pipe	30.—
B.v.Slingeland	A Woman in a Niche with a brass kettle	40.—
Saftleven	View on the Rhine	20.—
B.v.Staveren	Hermit reading	50.—
Stork	Sea piece	10.—
Do.	Do.	10.—
Jan Steen	Flemish lying in visit	50.—
Do.	Flemish fair	50.—
Do.	Flemish family	40.—
G.Terborch	Lady and Guitar	50.—
Do.	Corps de Guard	100.—
Do.	Gentleman writing	120.—
Do.	Lady at Toilet	50.—
Do.	Lady and Gentleman	50.—
David Teniers	Corps de Guard }	300.—
Do.	Do. }	
D.van Tol	Boor Schoolmaster	20.—
Uchterveld	Violin player	10.—
Van der Ulft	Roman Market	30.—
Do.	Italian Seaport	50.—
W[m].van de Velde	2 Seapieces	220.—
Do.	1 Do.	400.—

Master	Subject	Value in £
A.van de Velde	View in the Hague	300.—
Do.	Landscape with Cattle	200.—
Do.	Do.	50.—
Do.	Do.	50.—
P[l].Veronese	Bathseba	80.—
manner of Do.	Diana and Nymphs	150.—
Verkolje	Susanna & Elders	20.—
Do.	Bathseba bathing	90.—
Do.	Do.	20.—
J.Weenix	Poultry	60.—
Do.	Architecture & Still life	40.—
Do.	Game still life & barking Dog	60.—
A.v.d.Werff	St.Thomas	350.—
Do.	Magdalen reading	250.—
P.Wouwermans	A rich Landscape	350.—
Do.	Falcon Chase	150.—
J.Wijnants	Landscape, Mountainous	80.—
R.Xavery	Entry into the Arch	10.—
		12,515.—

London 17th December 1795
(signed)
Henry Hope

CATALOGUE C

OF PICTURES IN THE HOUSE NO. I IN THE CORNER OF HARLEYSTREET, BELONGING TO MR. HENRY HOPE, ON WHICH IS ENSURED FOUR THOUSAND POUNDS

Master	Subject	Value in £
Bassano	Christ array'd before the People	50.—
Berghem	Falcon chase	300.—
Berger	Achilles & Briseis	20.—
Bolomey	2 Portraits	50.—
Giov.Bellini	Salvator Mundi	100.—
F.Bartholomeo	Monk in devotion }	40.—
Do.	St.Sebastian }	
Lod.Caracci	Dying Magdalen	150.—
Aug.Caracci	Holy family	100.—
Corregio	Virgin & Child	150.—
Do.	Magdalen repenting	300.—
Denis	Landscape	20.—
Demarez	Lucretia receiving Tarquin	40.—

Domenichino	St.Cecilia	150.—
Do.	St.Thomas	50.—
Ducos	Landscape, Water Colours	20.—
A.del Sarto	Holy family	50.—
Do.	Jonas & the Whale	50.—
Gauffier	Achilles discover'd	30.—
Do.	Repose in Egypt	20.—
Geminiani	Travellers to Emaus	50.—
Giorgione	Judith with the head of Holofernes	100.—
L.Giordano	Womans head	20.—
Benven.Garofalo	Holy family	100.—
Guido	Ecce Homo	50.—
Do.	Ariadne & Bacchus	150.—
Do.	Magdalen repenting	100.—
Guercino	St.John & the Lamb	100.—
Do.	Apollo with the violin	150.—
Lentz	Venus chastising Cupid	50.—
O.Lorain	Landscape	100.—
A.Martigna	The Saviour scourged	50.—
F.Mola	Peter repenting	50.—
Pannini	Campo vaccino	50.—
Palma vecchio	Venus & Cupid	50.—
Parmeggianino	Stable in Bethlehem	100.—
P.Peregrino	Maria & Child	50.—
Poligraphick	Landscape (C.Lorain)	10.—
Sal.Rosa	The Hermit bound	50.—
Do.	View of Castellamare	100.—
Do.	(on paper) Warriors	20.—
Do.	Jonas & the Whale	50.—
Julio Romano	Hell in uproar	50.—
Reynolds	2 Portraits	50.—
Rubens	Travellers in Emaus	150.—
Do.	View in Ancona	40.—
Sablé	Moon Shine	50.—
Do.	Roman rural Composition	20.—
E.Sirani	Nessus & Deianira	50.—
after Schalken	Womans head	10.—
Titian	Ecce Homo	100.—
Do.	The Saviour betrayed	150.—
Tintoretto	Madonna & Child	100.—
		4,010.—

London 17 December 1795
(signed)
Henry Hope

D. RUSSIAN LOANS

D-I. LOANS ISSUED BY HOPE & CO. ON BEHALF OF RUSSIA BETWEEN 1787 AND 1793

No.	*Amount*	*Interest rate*	*Life*	*Date of loan*	*Date of authorization*	*Nos. and qty. of bonds*
1	cf 3,000,000	4½%	10 yrs.	1- 2-1788	24-12-1787	6, A-F.
2	cf 3,000,000	4½%	12 yrs.	1- 2-1788	24-12-1787	6, G-M.
3	cf 3,000,000	4½%	10 yrs.	1- 7-1788	22- 3-1788	6, N-S.
4	cf 3,000,000	5%	12 yrs.	1- 2-1789	13-12-1788	6, T-IJ.
5	cf 3,000,000	5%	12 yrs.	1- 5-1789	13-12-1788	6, AA-FF.
6	cf 3,000,000	5%	12 yrs.	1- 9-1789	9- 5-1789	6, GG-MM.
7	cf 3,000,000	5%	12 yrs.	1- 1-1790	9- 5-1789	6, NN-SS.
8	cf 3,000,000	5%	12 yrs.	1- 5-1790	18- 2-1790	6, TT-IJIJ.
9	cf 3,000,000	5%	12 yrs.	1- 8-1790	18- 2-1790	6, ZA-ZF.
10	cf 3,000,000	5%	12 yrs.	1-11-1790	18- 2-1790	6, ZG-ZM.
11	cf 3,000,000	5%	12 yrs.	1- 2-1791	23- 9-1790	6, ZN-ZS.
12	cf 3,000,000	5%	12 yrs.	1- 9-1791	7- 4-1791	6, ZT-ZIJ.
13	cf 3,000,000	5%	12 yrs.	1-11-1791	7- 4-1791	6, AZ-FZ.
14	cf 3,000,000	4%	12 yrs.	1- 2-1792	17-12-1791	6, GZ-MZ.
15	cf 3,000,000	4%	12 yrs.	1- 2-1792	17-12-1791	6, NZ-SZ.
16	cf 3,000,000	4½%	12 yrs.	1- 6-1792	17- 5-1792	6, AH-AN.
17	cf 3,000,000	4½%	12 yrs.	1- 6-1792	17- 5-1792	6, AO-AT.
18	cf 2,500,000	5%	12 yrs.	1- 8-1793	22- 6-1793	5, TN-TR.

D-II. NUMBER OF ENTREPRENEURS AND NUMBER OF LOANS IN WHICH THEY PARTICIPATED

No.	*Loans*	*Int. rate*	*Principal sum*	*Entrepreneurs' commission*	Johs Menkema & Son	Pieter du Montier	Abr.v.Broeck	Isaac v.Eyck	Jan Koning	Abr.v.Vloten	A.v.Ketwich	Francois Walbeek	P.v.Hogenhuysen Jr.	Wed.E.Croese & Comp.	[illegible]
1	Sweden, 1-3-1780	4%	cf 750,000	1½%	x	x	x	x	x	x	x				
2	Sweden, 1-12-1780	4%	cf 750,000	1½%						x	x	x	x	x	x
3	Sweden, 1-3(6)-1782	4%	cf 1,250,000	1%	x		x	x	x			x		x	x
4	Sweden, 1-12-1783	5%	cf 1,500,000	1%	x		x	x	x	x		x		x	
5	Sweden, 1-12-1784	4½%	cf 2,000,000	1½%	x		x			x		x		x	x
6	Sweden, 1-2-1786	4½%	cf 1,500,000	1%	x		x	x		x		x		x	x
7	Sweden, 1-11-1787	4%	cf 1,500,000	1½%	x			x		x		x		x	x
8	Poland, 1-6-1786	5%	cf 2,000,000	2%			x	x		x	x	x		x	x
9	Russia, 1-2-1788 (I)	4½%	cf 3,000,000	1%	x			x		x	x	x	x[2]	x	x
10	Russia, 1-2-1788 (II)	4½%	cf 3,000,000	1%	x			x		x	x	x	x	x	x
11	Russia, 1-5-1789	5%	cf 3,000,000	2%	x			x		x	x[1]	x	x	x	x
12	Russia, 1-9-1789	5%	cf 3,000,000	2%				x		x	x	x		x	x
13	Russia, 1-1-1790	5%	cf 3,000,000	2%				x		x	x	x		x	x
14	Russia, 1-5-1790	5%	cf 3,000,000	2%	x			x		x	x	x		x	x
15	Russia, 1-8-1790	5%	cf 3,000,000	2%	x			x		x	x	x	x	x	x
16	Russia, { 1-11-1790 1-2-1791	5%	cf 6,000,000	2%	x			x		x	x	x	x	x	x
17	Russia, { 1-9-1791 1-11-1791	5%	cf 6,000,000	2%	x			x		x	x	x	x	x	x
18	Russia, 1-2-1792	4%	cf 6,000,000	2%	x			x		x	x	x	x	x	x
19	Russia, 1-6-1792	4½%	cf 6,000,000	2%	x			x		x	x	x	x	x	x
20	Spain, 1-11-1792	4½%	cf 6,000,000	2%	x			x		x	x	x	x	x	x

1 Hereafter V.Ketwich & Voomberg.
2 Hereafter V.Hogenhuysen & Visser.
3 Hereafter Albert Strockel.
4 Hereafter Strockel & V.Dijk.
5 In this contract, A.H.Vermeulen, W.H.Dreux.
6 Hereafter Stadnitski & Son.
7 Hereafter V.Zwijndregt & Gossiaux.
8 Hereafter Pieter ten Kate.
9 Hereafter V.Maarseveen & Le Jolle.
10 In these contracts the words 'for Jacob de Kempenaer' were added.

Anthony Charles	D.W.v.Vloten, Utrecht	Pieter Stadnitski	Wouter Zeelt	N.Ad.Goetzee	Herman Hoogewal	v.Maurik & Willink	Samuel & David Saportas	Arend v.d.Werf, Dordrecht	Adriaan Maint, Westzaan	D.Huttemans, Haarlem	Huybert v.Vloten, Utrecht	J.Gossiaux	Albs.Brinkman	Herman ten Kate	H.J.Koopman & Co.	N.Ad.Gockel	H.v.Maarseveen	v.Vloten & de Gijselaar	W.Jochems & Z., Den Haag	Pama de Kempenaer	J.E.Guérin	Vlaer & Kol, Utrecht	Paschier Soetbrood, Leiden	W.C.Tack & Son	Euke Siblesz	Donker & Son	Johs.Bouman	I.D.Croese, Utrecht	Hope & Co.
																													x
x	x																												
		x																											x
	x	x																											
	x	x																											x
	x	x	x	x	x	x	x	x	x	x																			x
	x	x	x		x		x	x																					x
x	x	x	x	x	x	x	x	x		x	x	x																	x
x	x	x	x	x	x	x	x	x		x	x	x	x																x
x	x	x	x	x	x	x	x	x		x	x	x[7]		x	x	x													x
x	x	x	x	x	x	x	x	x		x		x			x		x	x	x										x
x	x	x			x	x	x	x		x		x			x		x[9]	x	x										x
x	x	x			x	x	x	x		x	x	x		x[8]	x		x		x	x	x	x	x						
x		x			x	x	x	x		x	x	x		x	x		x	x	x	x[10]	x	x	x						
x	x	x		x	x	x	x	x		x	x	x		x	x		x	x	x	x[10]	x	x	x						x
x	x	x[6]		x	x	x	x	x		x	x	x		x	x		x	x	x	x	x	x	x	x					x
x	x	x		x	x	x	x				x	x		x	x		x	x	x	x	x	x	x	x	x	x			x
x	x	x		x	x	x	x	x		x		x		x	x		x	x	x	x	x	x	x	x	x	x	x		
x	x	x		x	x	x	x			x		x		x	x		x	x	x	x	x		x	x	x	x	x	x	

D-III. NUMBER OF SUBSCRIPTIONS BY THE ENTREPRENEURS AND MEAN, LOWEST, HIGHEST AND TOTAL SUMS SUBSCRIBED

No.	*Name of house*	*Number*	*Total*	*Mean*	*Lowest*	*Highest*
1	Wed.E.Croese & Comp.	19	cf 3,525,500	cf 186,000	cf 25,000	cf 400,000
2	François Walbeek	19	cf 2,775,000	cf 146,000	cf 25,000	cf 250,000
3	Abraham van Vloten	19	cf 1,992,000	cf 105,000	cf 25,000	cf 200,000
4	Rijk Strockel	18	cf 4,147,500	cf 230,000	cf 25,000	cf 500,000
5	Isaac van Eyck	18	cf 3,812,500	cf 212,000	cf 25,000	cf 500,000
6	Pieter Stadnitski	17	cf 4,295,000	cf 253,000	cf 25,000	cf 675,000
7	Johs Menkema & Son	17	cf 1,995,000	cf 125,000	cf 25,000	cf 200,000
8	A.H.Vermeulen, Rotterdam	17	cf 1,012,500	cf 60,000	cf 25,000	cf 75,000
9	J.Bourcourd	16	cf 1,587,500	cf 99,000	cf 25,000	cf 200,000
10	D.W.van Vloten, Utrecht	16	cf 950,000	cf 53,000	cf 25,000	cf 150,000
11	A.van Ketwich	15	cf 1,825,000	cf 122,000	cf 50,000	cf 300,000
12	Samuel and David Saportas	14	cf 1,625,000	cf 116,000	cf 25,000	cf 250,000
13	Herman Hoogewal	14	cf 975,000	cf 70,000	cf 25,000	cf 100,000
14	Van Maurik and Willink	13	cf 1,375,000	cf 106,000	cf 25,000	cf 200,000
15	Anthony Charles	13	cf 650,000	cf 50,000	cf 50,000	cf 50,000
16	J.Gossiaux	12	cf 1,500,000	cf 125,000	cf 25,000	cf 250,000
17	Arend van der Werf, Dordrecht	12	cf 1,175,000	cf 97,000	cf 25,000	cf 150,000
18	Daniel Huttemans, Haarlem	12	cf 1,100,000	cf 92,000	cf 25,000	cf 150,000
19	P.van Hogenhuysen Junior	10	cf 1,292,500	cf 129,000	cf 30,000	cf 200,000
20	H.J.Koopman & Comp.	10	cf 950,000	cf 95,000	cf 50,000	cf 150,000
21	N.Ad.van Goetzee	10	cf 900,000	cf 90,000	cf 25,000	cf 150,000
22	H.van Maarseveen	9	cf 1,625,000	cf 181,000	cf 50,000	cf 300,000
23	Wouter Jochems, Den Haag	9	cf 650,000	cf 72,000	cf 50,000	cf 100,000
24	Herman Ten Kate	8	cf 1,000,000	cf 125,000	cf 75,000	cf 200,000
25	Van Vloten & De Gijselaar	8	cf 650,000	cf 81,000	cf 50,000	cf 100,000
26	Huybert van Vloten, Utrecht	8	cf 475,000	cf 59,000	cf 50,000	cf 75,000
27	I.E.Guérin	7	cf 1,100,000	cf 157,000	cf 100,000	cf 200,000

No.	Name of house	Number	Total	Mean	Lowest	Highest
28	Pama de Kempenaer	7	cf 900,000	cf 129,000	cf 75,000	cf 150,000
29	Paschier Soetbrood, Leiden	7	cf 450,000	cf 65,000	cf 50,000	cf 75,000
30	Wouter Zeelt	6	cf 625,000	cf 104,000	cf 25,000	cf 150,000
31	Abraham van Broek	6	cf 437,500	cf 73,000	cf 25,000	cf 150,000
32	Vlaer & Kol, Utrecht	6	cf 350,000	cf 58,000	cf 50,000	cf 75,000
33	W.C.Tack & Son	4	cf 500,000	cf 125,000	cf 50,000	cf 150,000
34	Donker & Son	3	cf 500,000	cf 167,000	cf 100,000	cf 200,000
35	Euke Siblesz	3	cf 200,000	cf 67,000	cf 50,000	cf 100,000
36	Jan Koning	3	cf 162,500	cf 54,000	cf 50,000	cf 62,500
37	Johs.Bouman	2	cf 100,000	cf 50,000	cf 50,000	cf 50,000
38	Pieter Du Montier	1	cf 125,000	—	—	—
39	I.D.Croese, Utrecht	1	cf 100,000	—	—	—
40	Adriaan Maint, Westzaan	1	cf 25,000	—	—	—
41	Albs.Brinkman	1	cf 25,000	—	—	—
42	N.Ad.Gockel	1	cf 25,000	—	—	—

D-IV. ASSESSMENT BY WILLIAM PORTER OF THE SOLIDITY OF THE DEBTORS OF GEO. THOMSON ROWAND & CO.

KALUSTOV
Four brothers, two of whom are named Martin and two Avet. The most prominent Armenian merchants. Trade in cochineal, cloth and all manner of other articles, which they barter in Astrakan, principally for Persian silk which they sell to merchants in Moscow. They are quite rich, and would have been more so had they not suffered exchange losses.

ZAKHAREV and REBININ
Trade in pots and pans and knives. The leaders in their field. Nevertheless, they are in difficulties as a result of exchange losses and the new edict prohibiting the import of all manner of articles. Retailers are not buying, on the one hand because they are still trying to liquidate their stocks, and on the other because they are of the opinion that the importation and sale of these goods will be prohibited on 1st January 1794. If, however, the ban does not materialize, these debtors will be able to sell their stock at a large profit.

MANUSHIN
Trades under the name of the previous debtors. Zakharev's son-in-law. Deals in woollen goods, which he sells mainly in the Ukraine. Has suffered heavy losses, but continues to be regarded as safe.

SHOROKOV
A young house. Has suffered heavy exchange losses by issuing drafts in foreign currencies.

P.NASHOTKIN
Little capital, active, deals in India price goods.

P.UVAROV
Russian jeweller, reliable, old customer of Thomson Rowand.

IVAN GREBENSHCHIKOV
Moscow retailer dealing in cloth. Very rich, but has applied for moratoriums for 1, 2 and 3 years. Thomson Rowand holds assets of his as security, though these are probably inadequate.

STRAPOZHNIKOV
Wholesale grocer in Moscow. Highly reliable.

ZHIGAREV
One of the China traders; a general merchant; considered worthy of a credit of 3–400,000 roubles.

GUBIN
A wealthy man, but has taken too much money out of his business and invested it in land.

KIRYAKOV
Safe. A brother-in-law of Gubin, with whom he is not on good terms.

PLONKIN and SIROTIN
Plonkin has earned a lot of money by trading with Leipzig. He has bought land and has largely retired from business. Sirotin is now running the house; safe.

M.KOLOSOV
Owner of a silk mill in Yaroslavl'. Not particularly rich, but industrious and honest.

K.GORBUNOV
One of the most reliable shopkeepers. Importer, wholesaler and retailer of cloth.

The principal debtor, GUSYATNIKOV, is not referred to in this summary.

D-V. POLISH LOANS TAKEN OVER BY THE CZAR OF RUSSIA ON 30TH JUNE AND 29TH OCTOBER 1797

a: *30th June 1797*

Name of debtor	*Issuing house*	*Loan sum*	*Int. rate*	*Opening date*	*Principal outstanding*	*Interest overdue since*	*Total taken over*	*Deed enacted by*
The King of Poland	Hope & Co.	cf 2,000,000	5%	1- 1-1786	cf 700,000	1- 1-1794	cf 840,000	C.v.Homrigh
The King of Poland	Q.W.van Hoorn and Th.Gülcher & Mulder	cf 1,500,000	5%	1- 3-1791	cf 1,500,000	1- 9-1793	cf 1,815,000	A.v.Beem
Republic of Poland	Hogguer Grand & Co. and	cf 2,100,000	5%	1-11-1790	cf 2,100,000	1-11-1793	cf 2,538,000	A.v.Beem
	R. & Th.de Smeth	cf 955,555		1- 1-1791	cf 955,555	1- 1-1794	cf 1,146,666	
Republic of Poland	Pieter de Haan P.Zn.	cf 3,500,000 of which cf 760,000 subscribed	5%	1- 6-1792	cf 760,000	1-12-1792	cf 953,166	C.v.Homrigh
Prince Alexander Lubomirski	Th.Gülcher & Mulder	cf 525,000	5%	1-10-1787	cf 330,000	1- 4-1794	cf 391,875	A.v.Beem
Prince Alexander Lubomirski	Q.W.van Hoorn and Th.Gülcher & Mulder	cf 1,500,000	5%	1- 1-1792	cf 1,300,000	1- 1-1794	cf 1,560,000	A.v.Beem
Prince Joseph Lubomirski	Th.Gülcher & Mulder	cf 1,000,000	5%	1-12-1789	cf 760,000	1-12-1793	cf 915,166.$\frac{3}{4}$	A.v.Beem
Count Michael Oginski	Pieter de Haan P.Zn.	cf 1,000,000	5%	1- 2-1791	cf 1,000,000	1- 8-1793	cf 1,220,833	C.v.Homrigh

b: *29th October 1797*

Name of debtor	*Issuing house*	*Loan sum*	*Int. rate*	*Opening date*	*Principal outstanding*	*Interest overdue since*	*Total taken over*	*Deed enacted by*
Prince Stanislaw Lubomirski	Th.Gülcher & Mulder	cf 315,000	5%	15-12-1781	cf 158,000	15-12-1793	cf 189,929	A.v.Beem
Prince Adam Czartoryski	R. en Th.de Smeth and Hogguer Grand & Co.	cf 535,000	5%	1- 1-1793	cf 535,000	1- 1-1796	cf 588,500	A.v.Beem
Prince Antoine Barnabe Chrisostom de Pruss Jablonowski	Th.Gülcher & Mulder	cf 525,000	5%	1-10-1787	cf 158,000	15- 1-1794	cf 189,270	A.v.Beem
Counts Ignace and Jean Potocki	Th.Gülcher & Mulder	cf 525,000	5%	1- 8-1786	cf 210,000	1- 2-1793	cf 261,625	A.v.Beem
Count Vincent Potocki	Th.Gülcher & Mulder	cf 787,000	5%	1- 1-1792	cf 787,000	1- 1-1793	cf 983,750	A.v.Beem
Matthew and Michael Sobanski	Pieter de Haan P.Zn.	cf 350,000	5%	1-12-1791	cf 245,000	—	cf 245,000	C.v.Homrigh

D-VI. ESTATES MORTGAGED BY POLISH MAGNATES IN CONNEXION WITH THEIR LOANS IN HOLLAND

PRINCES ALEXANDER and JOSEPH LUBOMIRSKI
Prince Joseph Lubomirski sold to his brother, Alexander, the land which he had provided as security against his loan. This, together with lands given by Alexander himself as security for two loans, comprised the Poberéje estate, which Alexander ultimately sold to the Russian Crown.

COUNT MICHAEL OGINSKI
Supra, page 156, note 2.

PRINCE STANISLAW LUBOMIRSKI
The estates of Konstantinow in Wolhinia, Wiśniez and Greezezin (the reference to the last of these bears a note 'Imperial'). Prince Stanislaw had died. His widow, the Dowager Princess Lubomirska, née Czartoryska, lived at Lançut.

PRINCE ADAM CZARTORYSKI
Klerwan and Zuckow in Wolhinia, in the Luck district, and Konenskowola in the province of Lublin (marked 'Imperial').

PRINCE ANTOINE BARNABE CHRISOSTOM DE PRUSS JABLONOWSKI
Annopol, Pluzne, Krzywin and Kilikijow, in Wolhinia, in the Luck district, and Krzemincec.

COUNTS IGNACE and JEAN POTOCKI
The county of Sidra in the wojewodztwo Troki, in the Grodno district, and the Radzyn estate in the wojewodztwo Lublin, in the Luckow district (marked 'Imperial').

COUNT VINCENT POTOCKI
The town of Niemierow and 40 villages, situated in the wojewodztwo Braclaw, in the Winnica district.

MATTEUS and MICHAEL SOBANSKI
Obodowka, situated in the wojewodztwo of Braclaw, together with 22 bailiwicks known as Slobada, Josefowka, Cybrolowka, Pisanowka, Ruska, Klemibowka, Sciana Pisanowka Woloska, Krzykliwiec, Ruskiy Woloski, Howe Pole Palow, Palowka Maydan, Torkanski, Torkanowka Katazyn, Zabokruyeska, Pictkowka Balanowka and Dimedowka, together incorporating 19,961 'Ames chrétiennes' and 3,690 farm cottages.

D-VII. CREDITS ALLOCATED TO HOUSES IN THE BALTIC AREA BY H.E.MONSIEUR BARBÉ MARBOIS, MINISTER OF THE FRENCH TREASURY, AS SET OUT IN HIS LETTER OF 27TH MARCH 1804

J.Morison, Riga	Frs. 2,400,000
Helmund & Son, Riga	Frs. 300,000
Justus Blanckenhagen, Riga	Frs. 1,400,000
Melchior Tromposky, Riga [1]	Frs. 400,000
Toussaint Bros, Königsberg [2]	Frs. 500,000
Various merchants in St.Petersburg, upon a visa issued by Citizen De Lesseps, Consul General of the French Republic in St.Petersburg [3]	Frs. 1,800,000
Senator Meyer, Hamburg, upon a visa issued by Citizen Ollivier, Agent of the Minister for the Navy in Hamburg [4]	Frs. 800,000
Three as yet unnamed merchants from Emden [5]	Frs. 1,400,000
	Frs. 9,000,000

at a rate of exchange of Fr. 2.15
for cf 1.00 = cf 4,186,046.10.0.

1 Tromposky was subsequently removed from the list, and his credit was transferred to Blanckenhagen.

2 Toussaint Bros, were later replaced by Schwink & Koch, alsof of Königsberg, for the purchase of 3,000 ship-pounds of hemp.

3 These were F.W.Isenbeck, Ant.Colombi, Rd.Mitton and Blandow & Co. The lastnamed went bankrupt during the operation.

4 Senator Meyer's place was later taken by Pehmöller & Droop.

5 These were Thomas van Cammenga, Claas Tholen and Philippus Julius Abegg. Abegg's name was subsequently removed from the list.

D-VIII. 'PAPIERS CONCERNANT L'OPERATION R.M.' RECORD OF PURCHASES AS AT 10TH JULY 1809

RIGA

500 ship-pounds	Clean hemp at $16\frac{3}{4}$ Albertustalers per ship-pound
500 ship-pounds	Clean hemp at $17\frac{1}{4}$ Albertustalers per ship-pound
1,000 ship-pounds	Clean hemp at $17\frac{1}{2}$ Albertustalers per ship-pound

ARCHANGEL

9,000 barrels of tar	(forward, August delivery) 285 kopecks per barrel
6,000 barrels of tar	(forward, June/July delivery) 300 kopecks per barrel
15,000 barrels of tar	for forward delivery
6,000 poods	(forward, August delivery) 67 kopecks per pood
4,000 poods	(forward, June/July delivery) 70 kopecks per pood
10,000 poods	for forward delivery
15,000 large mats	(forward, June/July delivery) Ro. 130 per 1,000
30,000 poods iron	spot at 165 kopecks per pood

ST. PETERSBURG

Flax	*Spot*
11,000 poods	Ro. 60 per pood
3,000 poods	Ro. 61 per pood
14,000 poods	
	Forward
5,000 poods	Ro. 59 } all for cash
6,000 poods	Ro. 63½ } all for cash
2,000 poods	Ro. 65 partly for cash
13,000 poods	
Clean hemp	*Spot*
14,000 poods	Ro. 49
2,000 poods	Ro. 46
5,000 poods	Ro. 45¾
16,436½ poods	Ro. 45½
2,500 poods	Ro. 45¼
24,920 poods	Ro. 44
64,856½ poods	
	Forward
26,500 poods	Ro. 45 } partly for cash
23,000 poods	Ro. 45½ } partly for cash
4,000 poods	Ro. 44¾ all for cash
2,000 poods	Ro. 44½ } all for cash
3,000 poods	Ro. 44 } all for cash
3,000 poods	Ro. 43½ } all for cash
61,500 poods	
Hemp, low-grade	
1,940 poods	spot Ro. 42
7,000 poods	forward Ro. 40 partly for cash
5,000 poods	forward Ro. 38½ all for cash
13,940 poods	
Hemp, semi-clean	
1,000 poods	forward Ro. 34½ all for cash
3,507¼ poods	spot Ro. 36
440 poods	spot Ro. 37
4,947¼ poods	
Yellow tallow	
7,000 poods	forward Ro. 57 Siberian soap tallow, all for cash
2,600 poods	forward Ro. 51 Soap tallow, all for cash
2,000 poods	spot Ro. 52 all for cash
11,600 poods	

Potash

25,000 poods	forward Ro. 43	all for cash
10,000 poods	forward Ro. 43½	all for cash
2,000 poods	forward Ro. 44	all for cash
7,500 poods	forward Ro. 46	
44,500 poods		

Linseed

1,500 chetverts	forward Ro. 9	1 chetvert = 2.09 hectolitres
1,500 chetverts	spot Ro. 10	all for cash
3,000 chetverts		

Copper

989 poods	spot Ro. 26½

Iron

70,000	poods forward	Kop. 210	1st Old Sable Iron	all for cash
22,500	poods forward	Kop. 180	Old Sable P.S.F.	25 kopecks cash
127,500	poods forward	Kop. 175	Old Sable P.S.F.	25 kopecks cash
20,000	poods spot	Kop. 165	Old Sable P.S.F.	
15,744	poods spot	Kop. 170	Old Sable P.S.F.	
20,000	poods spot	Kop. 165	Guryev's iron	
62,636.11	poods forward	Kop. 170	Broad Iron	
338,380.11	poods			

Calamancoes (also known as drillings)

400/2 pieces	Kop. 40 per arshin (1 piece = approx. 35 arshins)
2,489 pieces	Kop. 41 per arshin
1,450 pieces	Kop. 42 per arshin
4,339/2 pieces	

Diaper (a type of damask)

54,832 arshins	Ro. 225 per 1,000 arshins	Broad Diaper
1,933 arshins	Ro. 175 per 1,000 arshins	Narrow Diaper
6,000 arshins	Ro. 170 per 1,000 arshins	Huckaback
62,765 arshins		

Sailcloth

350 pieces	Ro. 30½ per piece
600 pieces	Ro. 30 per piece
1,949 pieces	Ro. 29 per piece
1,309 pieces	Ro. 28½ per piece
1,054 pieces	Ro. 28 per piece
450 pieces	Ro. 27½ per piece
2,250 pieces	Ro. 27 per piece
410 pieces	Ro. 26½ per piece
1,600 pieces	Ro. 26 per piece
1,000 pieces	Ro. 23½ per piece
10,972 pieces	

Flemish Linen	
96 pieces	Ro. 28 per piece
560 pieces	Ro. 27½ per piece
1,400 pieces	Ro. 27 per piece
300 pieces	Ro. 26¾ per piece
400 pieces	Ro. 26½ per piece
780 pieces	Ro. 26 per piece
420 pieces	Ro. 25½ per piece
1,100 pieces	Ro. 25 per piece
620 pieces	Ro. 24¼ per piece
350 pieces	Ro. 23½ per piece
500 pieces	Ro. 22½ per piece
6,526 pieces	

Raven-duck	
704 pieces	Ro. 18 per piece
1,300 pieces	Ro. 17½ per piece
9,880 pieces	Ro. 17 per piece
1,000 pieces	Ro. 16½ per piece
266 pieces	Ro. 15½ per piece
72 pieces	Ro. 15¼ per piece
350 pieces	Ro. 14½ per piece
13,572 pieces	

Crash (a coarse linen fabric) *and linen*		
200,000 arshins	Ro. 110 per 1,000 arshins	Crash
50,000 arshins	Ro. 105 per 1,000 arshins	Crash
140,000 arshins	Ro. 115 per 1,000 arshins	Crash
50,000 arshins	Ro. 120 per 1,000 arshins	Crash
440,000 arshins	Crash	
20,000 arshins	Ro. 115 per 1,000 arshins	Linen
27,000 arshins	Ro. 175 per 1,000 arshins	Linen
6,000 arshins	Ro. 195 per 1,000 arshins	Linen
4,037¼ arshins	Ro. 330 per 1,000 arshins	Linen
10,000 arshins	Ro. 350 per 1,000 arshins	Linen
12,000 arshins	Ro. 380 per 1,000 arshins	Linen
79,037¼ arshins	Linen	

D-IX. ROBERT MELVIL'S TRAVELLING EXPENSES

Coach	cf 884.16.
Wages of travelling servant for 8½ months at 10 louis d'or (cf 11.14) per month	cf 994.10
Expenses on outward journey via Leipzig	cf 1,600.00
Expenses on return journey via Berlin	cf 1,400.00
Lodging expenses in St.Petersburg	cf 2,867. 3
	cf 7,746. 0.9

INVESTMENT PER HOUSE BY ROBERT MELVIL

In Riga

Sum of drafts for purchases of hemp		
J.D.Drachenhauer & Co.	8,359.15 rixdollars	
B.J.Zuckerbäcker Klein & Co.	47,669.13 rixdollars	
Cumming Fenton & Co.	17,412.47 rixdollars	
	73,441.75 rixdollars	cf 183,603.15

In St.Petersburg and Archangel

St.Petersburg:		
Meyer & Bruxner	Ro. 1,103,252.18	
Porter Brown & Co.	Ro. 227,328.25	
Thornton Cayley & Co.	Ro. 113,690.26	
Bothlingk & Co.	Ro. 104,068.71	
Cramer Bros.	Ro. 167,611.—	
Wolff & Schlüsser	Ro. 312,500.01	
P.J.Blessig & Co.	Ro. 238,965.51	
100 barrels of potash, transported overland	Ro. 20,290.87	
Bergien & Co.	Ro. 268,980.—	
Archangel:		
Alex.Becker	Ro. 104,598.82	
	Ro. 2,661,285.61 at a rate of exchange of 17 *stuivers*	cf 2,262,092.15
		cf 2,445,696.10

D-X. ASSESSMENT OF VARIOUS MERCHANTS IN ST.PETERSBURG BY P.C.LABOUCHÈRE, EARLY 1812

MOLLWO BROS
Solid and pleasant to deal with.

MEYER & BRUXNER
An excellent house. Meyer is an annoying person; Bruxner is rich and not happily married.

LIVIO
A wealthy and solid house. The man himself is tiresome and sentimental.

CRAMER & SMITH
An active house; has done a great deal of business with America. Cramer himself is somewhat too animated and jolly.

COLOMBI
Spaniards; reputed to be solid.

CAYLEY
Formerly the house of Thornton; excellent people.

BLESSIG
A good reputation. Looks sly, but appears to be honest. Good company.

VENNING
In association with Fischer. A reasonably sound firm.

SCHLÜSSER
A sombre, boring firm. The man is rich but lacks finesse.

BAGGE & CO.
A good firm. The manager, Tesche, has a pleasant wife.

PICHLER & CO.
Former partner of Livio. The proprietor now holds a position related to the Sinking Fund. Has a large family, and is not at home to anybody.

KIRCHENER
A poor head for business; the czar has lent him 400,000 guilders. His debts are said to run into several million. A nice man. His wife is one of the most remarkable and striking women in St.Petersburg.

E. THE PORTUGESE DIAMOND LOAN

E-I. QUANTITIES, IN CARATS, SOLD ON BEHALF OF LONDON DIAMOND MERCHANTS

Year	*Quantity*	*Year*	*Quantity*	*Year*	*Quantity*
1770	7,324	1778	19,411$\frac{1}{4}$	1786	18,269$\frac{1}{16}$
1771	2,532	1779	3,116$\frac{6}{8}$	1787	17,252$\frac{1}{8}$
1772	1,753$\frac{3}{8}$	1780	5,325$\frac{9}{16}$	1788	11,694$\frac{3}{4}$
1773	8,864$\frac{1}{8}$	1781	17,007$\frac{7}{8}$	1789	21,055$\frac{7}{8}$
1774	34,605	1782	22,345$\frac{5}{16}$	1790	15,727$\frac{1}{2}$
1775	21,713$\frac{15}{16}$	1783	21,598$\frac{7}{16}$	1791	17,189$\frac{3}{16}$
1776	8,752$\frac{15}{16}$	1784	19,866$\frac{21}{32}$	1792	16,675$\frac{5}{8}$
1777	8,921$\frac{1}{2}$	1785	23,437$\frac{1}{2}$	1793	782$\frac{7}{8}$
				1794	1,224$\frac{7}{8}$

E-II. QUANTITIES, IN CARATS, SOLD ON BEHALF OF QUINTELLA

Year	*Quantity*	*Year*	*Quantity*
1791	30,349$\frac{7}{8}$	1797	17,378$\frac{13}{16}$
1792	18,721$\frac{7}{8}$	1798	2,041$\frac{3}{8}$
1793	23,023	1799	3,976
1794	30,860$\frac{13}{16}$	1800	10,961$\frac{1}{6}$
1795	—	1801	19,170
1796	12,458		

E-III. SUMMARY OF QUANTITIES, IN CARATS, OF DIAMONDS (A) RECEIVED IN LONDON BY BARING BROS. & CO. (B) ACCOUNTED FOR TO THE PORTUGUESE COURT BY HOPE & CO.

Year	*(A) Received by Baring*	*(B) Accounted for by Hope*	*Sum*
1802	114,000	33,000	cf 821,390. 4.0
1803	75,000 per 'Amazone'	36,000	cf 936,383. 0.8
	15,000 per 'Duke of York'	4,500	cf 99,607. 3.0
1804			
1805	30,000 per 'Pomona'	35,000	cf 840,881. 4.0
1806	9,500 per 'St.Margarita'	20,000	cf 455,009. 6.0
1807	—	30,000	cf 768,848.12.0
1808	15,000 per 'Lively'	45,000	cf 1,110,586.17.0
1809	—	54,500	cf 1,496,970.17.8
1810	—	—	—

In addition to the official diamond account with the Portuguese government, Hope maintained one headed 'Diamonds for our account' in which settlements for small quantities were entered each year.

E-IV. DIVISION OF THE PORTUGUESE BONDS INTO VARIOUS CATEGORIES, 1803–1805

	1803	*1804*	*1805*
Unredeemed	10,882	9,743	8,548
Henry Hope & Co.	4,205	3,907	3,421
Relatives and friends	1,377	1,264	1,032
'Reserve Hope & Co.'	928	894	894
'Concern' (unsold)	3,372	1,000	—
Borski and associates	1,000	2,678	3,201

E-V. QUANTITIES OF BRAZILWOOD TAKEN BY THE HOUSE OF JACOB MUHL & VAN WINTER

Year	*Date*	*Quantity*	*Price per quintal*
1804	—	600,000 pounds	f 45. banco
1805	28th January	100,000 pounds	f 45. banco
1805	10th December	300,000 pounds	f 40. banco
1806	20th November	150,000 pounds	f 40. banco
1807	28th May	150,000 pounds	f 40. banco
1807	14th September	300,000 pounds	f 45. banco
1808	3rd December	200,000 pounds	f 72.50 banco
1811	4th December	130,000 pounds	f 85. banco

E-VI. METHOD OF PAYMENT OF INTEREST AND PRINCIPAL ON THE PORTUGUESE DIAMOND LOAN

Year	*Transferred from diamond account*	*Received from the tobacco lessees*	
1802	cf 585,939.15.0	cf 1,113,890. 5.0	
1803	cf 715,694. 6.8	cf 984,489. 3.8	
1804	cf 581,424. 0.0	cf 1,122,103. 6.0	
1805	cf 637,388.14.0	cf 1,061,582.16.0	
1806	cf 696,681. 2.0	cf 1,008,321. 5.0	
1807	cf 821,615. 2.0	cf 878,769.18.0	
1808	cf 1,086,330. 6.8	cf 46,498.17.0[1]	
1809	cf 1,444,794. 9.8	cf 256,816.16.8	in drafts on the tobacco lessees
1810	cf —	cf 1,713,063. 8.0	in drafts on Baring Bros. & Co.

1 A deficit of cf 567,606.16.8 remained after the payment of these sums. This was met with drafts on the tobacco lessees.

F. COCHINEAL

F-I. SALES, PER YEAR AND PER MARKET, IN SEROONS, SOBERNALES AND POUNDS

Year	*Amsterdam*	*London*	*Cadiz (Bohl)*	*Marseilles*	*Rouen*	*St.Petersburg*	*Hamburg*	*Total*
1788	62	—	—	—	—	—	—	62
1789	201	140	10	87	—	—	—	438
1790	142	486	—	50	16	5	—	699
1791	52	555 and 94 pounds	—	164	—	6	—	777 and 94 pounds
1792	104	—	—	131 and 25 sob.	79 and 2 sob.	—	—	314 and 27 sob.
1793	2	41 and 810 pounds	—	102	—	—	—	145 and 810 pounds
Total Sales	563	1,222 and 904 pounds	10	534 and 25 sob.	95 and 2 sob.	11	—	2,435 27 sob. and 904 pounds
Total Purchases	628[1]	866	1,282 and 59 sob. (Ryan and Bohl)	308 and 3 sob.	111	91 and 61 sob.	60 and 1 sob.	3,346 and 124 sob.[2]

1 During 1792, 22 seroons were purchased for the purpose of replenishing other bales. These cannot, of course, be included in the sales.
2 Adding the 22 bales bought in 1792 brings the total to 3368 seroons and 124 sobernales.

F-II. AVERAGE SELLING PRICES FOR COCHINEAL IN EACH YEAR ON EACH MARKET, EXPRESSED IN GUILDERS AND SCHELLINGEN PER AMSTERDAM POUND[1])

Year	*Average quotation*[2] *at Amsterdam*	*Amsterdam*		*London*		*Cadiz*		*Marseilles*		*Rouen*		*St.Petersburg*	
		cf	*sch.*	*cf*	*sch.*	*cf*	*sch.*	*cf*	*sch.*	*cf*	*sch.*	*cf*	*sch.*
1788	9.66	9.76	32½	—	—	—	—	—	—	—	—	—	—
1789	8.44	8.25	27½	7.98	26⅗	7.93	26½	9.53	31⅘	—	—	—	—
1790	8.15	7.60	25⅓	9.44	31½	—	—	8.31	27 3/10	11.29	37⅔	11.14	37 1/10
1791	8.35	7.87	26⅕	7.94	26½	—	—	8.00	26⅔	—	—	9.60	32
1792	8.25	6.55	21⅚	—	—	—	—	7.42	24 7/10	5.91	19 7/10	—	—
1793	8.93	5.78	19 3/10	6.89	23	—	—	7.35	24½	—	—	—	—
Average purchase price on market		8.54	28½	9.31	31	7.75	25⅚	8.58	28½	9.75	32½	11.32	37 7/10

1 The average selling prices have been calculated from the 'Cochineal Account,' the entries in which relate to Hope's three-quarter share. The seroon was taken to be 200 Amsterdam pounds, and the sobernal 100.

2 According to N.W.Posthumus, *Nederlandsche Prijsgeschiedenis*, I, p. 422.

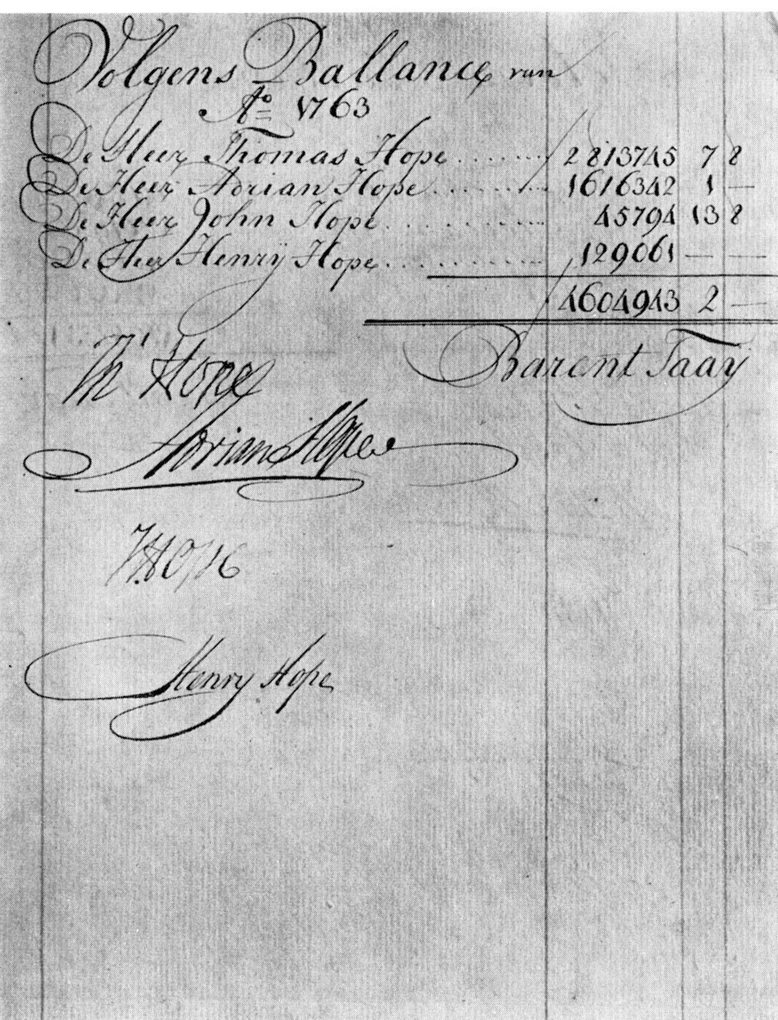

Volgens Ballance van A° 1763

De Heer Thomas Hope	2813745	7	8
De Heer Adrian Hope	1616342	1	—
De Heer John Hope	45794	13	8
De Heer Henry Hope	129061	—	—
	4604943	2	—

Barent Taay

Th. Hope

Adrian Hope

J. Hope

Henry Hope

Page from the *Ballance bookje* of Hope & Co.

F-III MOVEMENTS OF COCHINEAL BETWEEN THE VARIOUS MARKETS IN THE PERIOD 1788–1793 (QUANTITIES IN SEROONS AND SOBERNALES)

	Amsterdam		*London*		*Cadiz (Ryan)*		*Marseill[es]*	
1788	Stock	628	Stock	866	Stock	1,158	Stock	
	from Cadiz	400	from Cadiz	200	to A'dam	400	+ 1½ (sob	
	to London	26	from A'dam	26	to London	200	from Cadiz	
	Sold	62			to Mars.	50		
1789	Stock	940	Stock	1,092	Stock	508	Stock	
	from Cadiz	100	from Cadiz	100	to A'dam	100	+ 1½ (sob	
	from H'burg	54	Sold	140	to London	100	from Cadiz	
	Sold	201			to Mars.	308	Sold	
					Ryan's stock	0		
					Bohl's stock	124		
					+ 29½ (sob.)			
					Sold	10		
1790	Stock	893	Stock	1,052	Stock	114	Stock	[illegible]
	to St.P.	102	from A'dam	3	+ 29½ (sob.)		+ 1½ (sob	
	to London	3	Sold	486			Sold	
	Sold	142						
1791	Stock	646	Stock	569	Stock	114	Stock	[illegible]
	to Moscow	215	from Cadiz	25	+ 29½ (sob.)		+ 1½ (sob	
	Sold	52	Sold	555½	to London	25	Sold	[illegible]
1792	Stock	379	Stock	45	Stock	89	Stock	[illegible]
	to St.P.	6	+ ½		+ 29½ (sob.)		+ 1½ (sob.	
	to Moscow	110					to East.	
	Sold	104					Med.	1[illegible]
							Sold	1[illegible]
							+ 12½ (sob	
1793	Stock	159	Stock	45	Stock	89	Stock	1[illegible]
	to St.P.	85	+ ½		+ 29½ (sob.)		Sold	
	Sold	2	Sold	45				
rem. at end of 1793		72		½	+ 29½ (sob.)	89		[illegible]

1 In 1788, at Hope's request, Beerend Roosen in Hamburg had placed orders with Rey & Brandenburg, Bohl Brothers & Co. and Ellerman Schliepen & Co., all of Cadiz, for 6, 5 and 6 seroons respectively, for the purpose of supporting the price in Cadiz.

…uen	*St.Petersburg*	*Moscow*	*Hamburg*
k 111	Stock 91 $+30\frac{1}{2}$ (sob.)		Stock 43 $+\frac{1}{2}$ (sob.) from Cadiz 17 (support purch.)[1]
:k 111	Stock 91 $+30\frac{1}{2}$ (sob.)		Stock 60 $+\frac{1}{2}$ (sob.) to A'dam 54
ck 111 d 16	Stock 91 $+30\frac{1}{2}$ (sob.) from A'dam 102 Sold 5		Stock 6 $+\frac{1}{2}$ (sob.)
›ck 95	Stock 188 $+30\frac{1}{2}$ (sob.) Sold 6	Stock – from A'dam 215	Stock 6 $+\frac{1}{2}$ (sob.)
›ck 95 ld 79 2 (sob.)	Stock 182 $+30\frac{1}{2}$ (sob.) from A'dam 6	Stock 215 from A'dam 110	
›ck 15	Stock 188 $+30\frac{1}{2}$ (sob.) from A'dam 85	Stock 325	Stock 6 $+\frac{1}{2}$ (sob.)
15	273 $+30\frac{1}{2}$ (sob.)	325	6 $+\frac{1}{2}$ (sob.)

2 In 1793, Paul Thoron and M.W.Qm.Salomon Fua sold 24 and 4 seroons respectively in Constantinople, while I.B.Geraud & Co. of Smyrna sold 13 seroons.

G. CAPITAL AND PROFIT

G-I. CAPITAL OF HOPE & CO. AND THE SHARE OF THE PARTNERS THEREIN, IN 'GULDENS COURANT,' IN THE PERIOD 1762–1785

Year	*Capital*[1]	*Thomas Hope*	*Adrian Hope*	*Henry Hope*	*John Hope*
1762	4,279,000.16.8	2,733,657.11.8	1,489,005. 9.8	57,326.15.8	
1763	4,604,943. 2.0	2,813,745. 7.8	1,616,342. 1.0	129,061, 0.0	45,794.13.8
1764	4,801,855.18.8	2,469,417. 2.8	1,701,929.17.0	174,186. 8.8	456,322.10.8
1765	5,088,126.15.0	2,567,873. 3.8	1,815,805.10.8	229,546.13.0	474,901. 8.0
1766	5,420,954. 3.8	2,681,567. 2.8	1,939,409.15.8	286,398,11.8	513,578.14.0
1767	6,033,320.18.8	2,900,567. 7.0	2,170,621.17.8	392,401,19.0	569,729.15.0
1768	6,448,212.16.8	3,051,751.19.0	2,326,403.15.8	463,482.18.0	606,574. 4.0
1769	6,815,487.16.8	3,190,554. 2.8	2,457,971. 0.0	518,874. 3.0	648,088.11.0
1770	7,253,232.18.8	3,357,637.14.0	2,631,526. 3.8	576,390. 7.0	687,678.14.0
1771	7,647,772. 6.8	3,537,317. 8.8	2,733,587.12.8	631,008.16.8	745,858. 9.0
1772	7,827,364. 5.0	3,613,629. 4.0	2,824,807. 4.0	642,414.14.8	746,513. 2.8
1773	8,037,999. 3.0	3,697,550.10.0	2,918,158. 4.8	668,537.16.8	753,752.12.0
1774	8,086,819. 5.0	3,725,985.19.0	2,999,720. 1.0	687,743.17.0	673,369. 8.0
1775	8,385,834. 4.0	3,849,196.12.0	3,114.438. 2.0	730,628.14.0	691,570.16.0
1776	8,762,299.15.8	3,997,201.17.8	3,252,453. 3.8	778,653,10.0	733,991. 4.8
1777	9,189,353.14.0	4,164,877.18.8	3,414,792.11.0	831,749. 8.0	777,933.16.8
1778	9,629,990.17.0	4,320.818. 2.0	3,586,492. 4.0	884,555. 9.0	838,125. 2.0
1779	10,055,063. 7.8	4,488,803.14.8	3,753,909.15.0	938,315.16.8	874,034. 1.8
1780	10,333,858.16.8		3,929,618.10.8	977,418. 8.0	5,426,821.18.0
1781	9,056,172.11.0			2,376,573. 1.0	6,679,599.10.0

Year	*Capital*	*N. Bauduin*	*J. Williams Hope*	*Henry Hope*	*John Hope*
1782	8,731,205. 0.0	30,543. 1.8	15,919. 2.0	2,223,787.11.0	6,460,955. 5.8
1783	9,174,575. 5.8	69,095.17.8	50,662. 0.0	2,420,691.10.8	6,634,125.17.8
1784	9,911,548. 9.0	208,139.13.8	90,100. 3.8	2,728,786.12.8	6,784,521.19.8[2]
1785	10,777,177.17.8	318,243.19.8	294,439. 5.8	2,943,118.11.8	7,213,734. 0.0[2]

1 A guilder is divided into 20 *stuivers* each consisting of 2 *groten*. As one *groot* is made up of 8 *penningen*, it is represented in the accounts by the figure 8. The number of *stuivers* and *penningen* appear on the right of the guilder amounts, e.g. cf 715,694. 6.8.

2 'John Hope's heirs.'

G-I. PROFITS AND THE SHARE OF THE PARTNERS IN THESE, IN 'GULDENS COURANT,' IN THE PERIOD 1762–1785

Year	Distributed profit	Thomas Hope	Adrian Hope	Henry Hope	John Hope	Remaining in credit (c/f)
1762	412,766. 0.0 [1]	206,388. 0.0	137,588.13.0	68,794.17.0		
1763	461,124.13.0 [2]	153,708. 4.0	153,708. 4.0	76,854. 2.8	76,854. 2.8	
1764	309,895. 6.8	103,298. 9.0	103,298. 9.0	51,649. 4.8	51,649. 4.8	
1765	365,661.15.0	121,887. 5.0	121,887. 5.0	60,943.12.8	60,943.12.8	
1766	394,638. 9.8	131,546. 3.0	131,546. 3.0	65,773. 1.8	65,773. 2.0	
1767	720,906. 4.0	240,302. 1.0	240,302. 1.0	120,151. 1.0	120,151. 1.0	
1768	514,457.14.8	171,485.18.0	171,485.18.0	85,742.19.8	85,742.19.8	
1769	487,234.13.8	162,411.11.0	162,411.11.0	81,205.15.8	81,205.15.8	
1770	565,660.19.0	188,553.13.0	188,553.13.0	94,276.16.8	94,276.16.8	
1771	619,935. 3.0	206,645. 1.0	206,645. 1.0	103,322.10.8	103,322.11.0	
1772	300,000. 0.0	100,000. 0.0	100,000. 0.0	50,000. 0.0	50,000. 0.0	225,243. 4.8
1773	331,916.14.8	110,638.18.0	110,639.18.0	55,319. 9.0	55,319. 9.8	400,000. 0.0
1774	300,000. 0.0	100,000. 0.0	100,000. 0.0	50,000. 0.0	50,000. 0.0	289,981.19.0
1775	400,000. 0.0	133,333. 6.8	133,333. 6.8	66,666.13.8	66,666.13.8	194,294.17.0
1776	500,000. 0.0	166,666.13.0	166,666.13.0	83,333. 7.0	83,333. 7.0	135,698.16.0
1777	540,000. 0.0	180,000. 0.0	180,000. 0.0	90,000. 0.0	90,000. 0.0	138,439. 9.0
1778	560,685. 3.0	186,895. 1.0	186,895. 1.0	93,447.10.8	93,447.10.8	
1779	508,710. 8.0	169,570. 2.8	169,570. 2.8	84,785. 1 8	84,785. 1.8	
1780	542,935.18.8 [3]		180,978.13.0	135,733.19.8	226,223. 6.0	
1781	504,000. 0.0 [4]			210,000. 0.0	294,000. 0.0	71,832. 2.8
Year	**Distributed profit**	**N.Bauduin**	**J.Williams Hope**	**Henry Hope**	**John Hope**	**Remaining in credit**
1782	480,000. 0.0 [5]	30,000. 0.0	30,000. 0.0	175,000. 0.0	245,000. 0.0	147,051. 7.8
1783	672,000. 0.0	42,000. 0.0	42,000. 0.0	245,000. 0.0	343,000. 0.0	140,299. 3.8
1784	768,000. 0.0 [6]	96,000. 0.0	96,000. 0.0	280,000. 0.0	296,000. 0.0 [12]	56,674. 0.0
1785	975,000. 0.0	120,000. 0.0	120,000. 0.0	350,000. 0.0	370,000. 0.0 [12]	56,179.13.8

For footnotes, see page 525.

G-II. CAPITAL OF HOPE & CO. AND THE SHARE OF THE PARTNERS THERE IN, IN 'GULDENS COURANT,' IN THE PERIOD 1786–1801

Year	*Capital*	*J.C.Hartsinck*	*J.Williams Hope*	*Henry Hope*	*John Hope's heirs*
1786	11,152,807. 6.0	1,333. 6.8	406,386.15.0	3,077,042. 4.8	7,668,045. 0.0
1787	11,705,850. 9.0	743.16.8	599,692. 9.8	3,058,186.10.0	8,047,227.13.0
1788	11,338,146.11.8	9,372. 3.0	641,233.19.8	2,736,758.16.8	7,950,781.12.8
1789	11,298,262.10.8		652,867.18.0	2,672,493. 5.8	7,972,901. 7.0

Year	*Capital*	*Thomas Hope*	*J.Williams Hope*	*Henry Hope*	*Adrian Elias and Henry Philip Hope*
1790	11,796,570. 1.0	2,785,133.15.8	728,273. 1.0	2,819,741.10.0	5,463,421.14.8
1791	13,023,649.10.8	2,970,204.15.0	939,302.15.0	3,268,533.16.0	5,485,608.14.8
1792	13,367,527.11.8	2,915,823.14.0	1,031,942.17.8	3,396,879.15.8	6,022,880. 4.8
1793	13,462,222. 4.0	2,847,612.16.0	1,103,329. 3.8	3,460,352. 3.0	6,050,928. 1.8
1794	13,435,648. 7.8	2,941,817.11.0	1,156,920. 2.0	3,466,605.13.8	5,870,305. 1.0

Year	*Capital*	*Thomas Hope*	*J.Williams Hope*	*Henry Hope*	*Adrian Elias and Henry Philip Hope*
1795	13,650,499. 8.0	3,014,463. 2.0	1,229,588. 3.0	3,444,065.10.0	5,962,382.13.0
1796	13,697,487. 4.0	3,061,968. 9.8	1,274,374.14.0	3,410,659. 0.0	5,950,485. 0.8
1797	14,080,063.18.8	3,147,982. 9.8	1,353,422. 1.0	3,568,116.19.0	6,020,542. 9.0
1798	14,649,647. 2.8	3,233,802, 3.8	1,464,130.16.0	3,793,432.18.0	6,158,281. 5.0
1799	14,913,048.14.8	3,214,233.12.8	1,575,533.16.0	3,992,503.18.8	6,130,777. 7.8

Year	*Capital*	*Thomas Hope*	*J.Williams Hope*	*Henry Hope*	*Adrian Elias Hope*
1800	15,229,568.13.8	3,214,535. 7.0	1,678,544.17.0	4,194,377. 3.8	3,354,083.10.0
					Henry Ph.Hope
					2,788,027.16.0
					Adrian Elias Hope
1801	16,561,849.14.0	3,305,350.15.8	1,942,730. 4.0	4,759,761. 2.0	3,589,888. 8.8
					Henry Ph.Hope
					2,964,119. 4.0

G-II. PROFITS AND THE SHARE OF THE PARTNERS IN THESE, IN 'GULDENS COURANT,' IN THE PERIOD 1786–1801

	Distributed profit	*J.C.Hartsinck*	*J.Williams Hope*	*Henry Hope*	*John Hope's heirs*	*Remaining in credit (c/f)*
(1785)		15,000. 0.0				
1786	1,058,390. 0.0[7]	15,000. 0.0	130,423.17.0	443,803. 7.0	469,163.10.0	
1787	918,528. 1.8[8]	15,000. 0.0	225,881.19.0	329,411. 5.0	438,234.17.8	
1788	480,000. 0.0[9]	30,000. 0.0	70,000. 0.0	185,000. 0.0	195,000. 0.0	3,269.15.8
1789	378,000. 0.0[10]		58,800. 0.0	155,400. 0.0	163,800. 0.0	

	Distributed profit	*Thomas Hope*	*J.Williams Hope*	*Henry Hope*	*Adrian Elias and Henry Ph.Hope*	*Remaining in credit*
1790	720,000. 0.0[11]	127,500. 0.0	112,500. 0.0	277,500. 0.0	202,500. 0.0	
1791	1,457,376. 0.0	258,077. 0.0	227,715. 0.0	561,697. 0.0	409,887. 0.0	30. 6.0
1792	720,000. 0.0	127,500. 0.0	112,500. 0.0	227,500. 0.0	202,500. 0.0	406. 7.8
1793	526,080. 0.0	93,160. 0.0	82,200. 0.0	202,760. 0.0	147,960. 0.0	277. 5.0
1794	560,000. 0.0	99,167. 0.0	87,500. 0.0	215,833. 0.0	157,500. 0.0	16,777.14.0

Year	*Distributed profit*	*Thomas Hope*	*J.Williams Hope*	*Henry Hope*	*Adrian Elias and Henry Philip Hope*	*Remaining in credit*
1795	560,000. 0.0	99,167. 0.0	87,500. 0.0	215,833. 0.0	157,500. 0.0	119,416. 7.0
1796	465,280. 2.8	85,000. 0.0	75,000. 0.0	185,500. 0.0	135,000. 0.0	14,219.17.8 (*too much distributed*)
1797	624,000. 0.0	110,500. 0.0	97,500. 0.0	240,500. 0.0	175,500. 0.0	8,661. 3.0
1798	840,000. 0.0	148,750. 0.0	131,250. 0.0	323,750. 0.0	236,250. 0.0	8,336. 1.0
1799	840,000. 0.0	148,750. 0.0	131,250. 0.0	323,750. 0.0	236,250. 0.0	11,909. 1.0
1800	840,000. 0.0	148,750. 0.0	131,250. 0.0	323,750. 0.0	*Adrian Elias Hope* 118,125. 0.0 *Henry Philip Hope* 118,125. 0.0	77,835.13.0 (*too much distributed*)
1801	1,920,000. 0.0	340,000. 0.0	300,000. 0.0	740,000. 0.0	270,000. 0.0 *Adrian Elias Hope* 270,000. 0.0	41,381. 5.8

For footnotes, see page 525.

Year	Capital	Henry Hope & Co.	P.C.Labouchère	Adrian Elias Hope	J.Williams Hope
1802	5,180,928.14.8	5,000,000. 0.0	180,928.14.8		
1803	5,232,382. 3.0	5,000,000. 0.0	232,382. 3.0		
1804	5,276,211.13.0	5,000,000. 0.0	276,211.13.0		
1805	5,360,211. 9.8	5,000,000. 0.0	360,211. 9.8		
1806	5,496,114.10.0	5,000,000. 0.0	496,114.10.0		
1807	5,601,308. 3.8	2,000,000. 0.0	601,308. 3.8	3,000.000, 0.0	
1808	5,710,834.14.0	2,000,000. 0.0	710,834.14.0	3,000.000. 0.0	
1809	5,485,717. 7.0		485,717. 7.0	3,000.000. 0.0	2,000,000. 0.0
1810	5,403,700. 6.8		403,700. 6.8	3,000.000. 0.0	2,000,000. 0.0
1811	2,443,700. 6.8		443,700. 6.8		2,000,000. 0.0
	'Oude Boeken'				*John Hope*
1812	378,000. 0.0[1]				378.000. 0.0
	'Nieuwe Boeken'				*John Hope*
1812	1,000,000. 0.0[2]				1,000,000. 0.0
	'Oude Boeken'				*Henry Hope & Co.*
1813	1,000,000. 0.0				1,000,000. 0.0
	'Nieuwe Boeken'				*Henry Hope & Co.*
1813	1,000,000. 0.0				1,000,000. 0.0

Year	Capital	A.Baring	Henry Hope & Co.
1814	1,433,019.14.8	433,019.14.8	1,000,000. 0.0
1815	1,750,000. 0.0	1,750,000. 0.0	

1 Carried forward to the account of Hope & Co., London, in 1813 as 'Debt owed by John Hope.'

2 Credit.

Year	Distributed profit	Henry Hope & Co.	P.C.Labouchère	Remaining in credit (c/f)
1802	1,161,300. 0.0 [13]	995,400. 0.0	165,900. 0.0	408.17.0
1803	840,000. 0.0	720,000. 0.0	120,000. 0.0	14,004.18.0
1804	574,000. 0.0	492,000. 0.0	82,000. 0.0	1,048. 0.0
1805	980,000. 0.0	840,000. 0.0	140,000. 0.0	1,296.10.0
1806	1,190,000. 0.0	1,020,000. 0.0	170,000. 0.0	650. 2.8
1807	910,000. 0.0	780,000. 0.0	130,000. 0.0	3,092. 6.0
1808	938,000. 0.0	804,000. 0.0	134,000. 0.0	918. 3.0
1809	735,000. 0.0 [14]	615,000. 0.0	120,000. 0.0	15,875.17.0
1810	44,100. 0.0	36,900. 0.0	7,200. 0.0	2,483.17.8
1811	245,000. 0.0	205,000. 0.0	40,000. 0.0	
1812	212,715.18.8	(loss, charged to Henry Hope & Co. in 1813) ('Oude Boeken')		
1812	18,421. 9.8	(loss, charged to Henry Hope & Co. in 1813) ('Nieuwe Boeken')		
1813	41,350.14.8	(loss, 'Oude Boeken')		
1813	59,454. 5.0	(profit, 'Nieuwe Boeken')		
1814	106,223.18.0	(profit)		

	Distributed profit	H.Sillem	A.v.d.Hoop	P.F.Lestapis	A.Baring	Remaining in credit
1815	220,000. 0.0	55,000. 0.0	27,500. 0.0	27,500. 0.0	110,000. 0.0	3,022.14.0

1 In 1762 the profit was shared as follows: Thomas Hope $^{3}/_{6}$ths, Adrian Hope $^{2}/_{6}$ths, Henry Hope $^{1}/_{6}$th.

2 From 1763 to 1779 the shares were: Thomas Hope $^{1}/_{3}$rd, Adrian Hope $^{1}/_{3}$rd, Henry Hope $^{1}/_{6}$th, John Hope $^{1}/_{6}$th.

3 In 1780 the shares were: Adrian Hope $^{1}/_{3}$rd, Henry Hope $^{1}/_{4}$th, John Hope $^{5}/_{12}$ths.

4 In 1781 the shares were: Henry Hope $^{5}/_{12}$ths, John Hope $^{7}/_{12}$ths.

5 In 1782 and 1783 the shares were: Henry Hope $^{35}/_{96}$ths, John Hope $^{49}/_{96}$ths, Nicolas Bauduin $^{6}/_{96}$ths, John Williams Hope $^{6}/_{96}$ths.

6 In 1784 and 1785 the shares were: Henry Hope $^{35}/_{96}$ths, John Hope's heirs $^{37}/_{96}$ths, Nicolas Bauduin $^{12}/_{96}$ths, John Williams Hope $^{12}/_{96}$ths.

7 In 1786 the shares were: Henry Hope $^{35}/_{96}$ths plus $^{35}/_{72}$nds of $^{12}/_{96}$ths, John Hope's heirs $^{37}/_{96}$ths plus $^{37}/_{72}$nds of $^{12}/_{96}$ths, John Williams Hope $^{12}/_{96}$ths.

8 In 1787 the shares were: Henry Hope $^{35}/_{96}$ths, John Hope's heirs $^{37}/_{96}$ths, John Williams Hope $^{24}/_{96}$ths.

9 In 1788 the shares were: Henry Hope $^{37}/_{96}$ths, John Hope's heirs $^{39}/_{96}$ths, John Williams Hope $^{14}/_{96}$ths, J.C.Hartsinck $^{6}/_{96}$ths.

10 In 1789 the shares were: Henry Hope $^{37}/_{90}$ths, John Hope's heirs $^{39}/_{90}$ths, John Williams Hope $^{14}/_{90}$ths.

11 From 1790 to 1801 the shares were: Henry Hope $^{37}/_{96}$ths, John Williams Hope $^{15}/_{96}$ths, Thomas Hope $^{17}/_{96}$ths, Adrian Elias and Henry Philip Hope $^{27}/_{96}$ths (in 1800 and 1801 their joint share was divided into two equal sums).

12 In 1784 and 1785 'John Hope's heirs.'

13 From 1802 to 1808 the profit was shared as follows: Henry Hope & Co. $^{6}/_{7}$ths, P.C.Labouchère $^{1}/_{7}$th.

14 From 1809 to 1811 the shares were: Henry Hope & Co. $^{41}/_{49}$ths, P.C.Labouchère $^{8}/_{49}$ths.

It is clear from the profit figures shown above that the Hope millions did not stem from profits on the firm's capital. This becomes the more evident if one reflects that the growth of this capital was achieved by consistently ploughing back a substantial portion of the distributed profit. The real profits were made on private transactions financed by the partners from their private accounts.

SOURCES AND A LIST OF WORKS CITED

SOURCES

The most important source of information for this study was, of course, the Hope archives, which are at present kept at Messrs. Mees & Hope's offices in the Coolsingel in Rotterdam. These archives have not yet been put in order, and in view of this the references to archival sources in the Notes are as comprehensive as possible, thus simplifying the task of tracing them when the whole has been placed in its correct sequence.

As regards the accountancy details, all the Journals and *Grootboeken* from 1770 onwards are available. In the case of the *grootboeken*, the alphabetical registers for the years 1776–1794 inclusive are missing, with the result that it takes considerably longer to obtain information from these sources. The Balance Sheets date from 1763, but those for the periods 1777–1785 and 1800–1808 have not survived. There are also smaller account books and single account sheets, most of which relate to specific transactions and afford more detailed information about these than do the *grootboeken*. They are denoted by a certain name, letter or number in the Notes.

The correspondence can be divided into incoming and outgoing. As stated above, the references to incoming letters are as complete as possible. The majority of the outgoing letters were copied in the letter books, of which the following are still in existence:

15th January 1795–18th April 1800: 'Letter book for Replies.' This contains copies of correspondence between Paulus Taay, in Amsterdam, and Hope & Co.'s business associates on the Continent. This letterbook is numbered A XXIV in the Notes.

15th May 1798–22nd November 1803: Letter book of the partners in London, numbered VI.

22nd November 1803–9th May 1805: Letter book of the partners in Amsterdam, numbered A II.

2nd Januari 1807–24th January 1809: Letter book of the partners in Amsterdam, numbered VII.

24th January 1809–31st December 1811: Letter book of the partners and managers in Amsterdam, numbered A XXVII, Nos. i and ii.

2nd January 1812–30th December 1814: Letter book of the managers in Amsterdam, numbered A XXVIII.

7th October 1802–8th March 1809: Letter book of Henry Hope & Co., London, numbered A I.

16th March 1809–30th June 1823: Letter book of Henry Hope & Co., London, and their bookkeeper, numbered A V.

3rd June 1803–25th July 1806: Letter book of Henry Hope, London, numbered A III.

19th September 1806–6th February 1811: Letter book of Henry Hope, London, numbered A XXVI.

In addition to these general letter books, there are a number which relate to specific transactions or to correspondence with particular persons. On some occasions when the subject matter was too confidential to appear in the general letter book, a separate book headed 'Private correspondence' was maintained. Of these special letter books, the following have survived:

19th June 1787–31st December 1787: Private correspondence concerning the cochineal speculation and the Swedish, Polish and Russian loans. This also contains copies of letters to Vandenijver Frères & Co., in Paris. Abbreviated in the Notes to P.C. '87.

1st January 1788–18th April 1788: Private correspondence concerning the cochineal speculation and the Russian loans. Abbreviated in the Notes to P.C. '88 and numbered A XXIII.

25th May 1798–26th June 1798: Letter book of P.C. Labouchère during his visit to Hamburg in connexion with the Martin Dorner affair. Numbered A XXV.

5th December 1805–30th April 1807: Letter book containing correspondence from the partners in Amsterdam to David Parish. Designated D.P. I.

6th May 1807–22nd November 1808: Letter book containing correspondence from the partners in Amsterdam to David Parish. Designated D.P. II. The letters are numbered from VI-ha-34 to VI-ia-13.

4th October 1805–10th November 1807: Letter book of the partners in Amsterdam relating to Franco-Spanish loan and silver transactions. Designated O.E. I and numbered A IV.

14th December 1807–2nd November 1810: Letter book of the partners in Amsterdam relating to Franco-Spanish loan and silver transactions. Designated O.E. 2 and numbered VIII.

1st October 1807–16th June 1808: Letter book containing correspondence from the partners in Amsterdam to William Gordon Coesvelt. Designated W.G.C. I and numbered A XXXII, i.

30th June 1808–17th November 1810: Letter book containing correspondence from the partners in Amsterdam to William Gordon Coesvelt. Designated W.G.C. II and numbered A XXXII, ii.

5th August 1811–25th May 1812: Letter book containing correspondence from

P.C.Labouchère and the managers in Amsterdam to Hieronymus Sillem and Russian officials. The letters are numbered from VI-ga-92 to VI-ha-11.

There are also loose copies of letters. Many were clearly written in haste and are difficult to read, particularly those in the handwriting of P.C.Labouchère.

The Hope archives also contain information books, in which details concerning other houses and obtained from third parties were recorded. Four such books exist, covering the periods 1779–1787, 1791–1803, 1803–1811 and 1811–1819 respectively.

There are also books containing the texts of contracts, letters, memoranda, deeds of procuracy, receipts and brief notes on accountancy matters. The three largest of these bear the title 'Diversen Documenten.' 'Diversen Documenten laast van 1700-begin 1800' covers the period 1770–1805 and 'Diversen Documenten 1802 en later,' numbered VI-da-7, the period 1802–1808, while 'Diversen Documenten,' numbered VI-da-8, deals mainly with matters current in 1802 and 1803. A smaller book, numbered VI-ea-73, contains similar material and covers the period 15th November 1805 to 31st December 1811. In a continuation of this, which runs from 1st January 1812 to 9th July 1816, the contents are individually numbered from VI-ea-73 to VI-fa-84. Correspondence and accountancy data relating to Operation R.M. are to be found in the book marked 'R,' in which the individual documents are numbered from VI-fa-87 to VI-ga-34.

The information contained in the municipal archives in Amsterdam is of importance in compiling a history of Hope & Co. This applies particularly to the Notarial Archives and those of the Amsterdam Exchange Bank. In the former, the deeds enacted by the notaries Adriaan Baars, Cornelis van Homrigh Sr., Cornelis van Homrigh Jr., Willem van Homrigh, Jan Barels the Younger, Daniel van den Brink and Pierre Fraissinet Jr. are of value in this context. The most important of these deeds were enacted by Adriaan Baars and the Van Homrighs.

Other sources included the register of births of the Mennonite Community and the baptismal registers of the English Presbyterian Church and the English Episcopal Church in Amsterdam. The registers of banns and of deaths were also examined during the investigations. The *Quytscheldingen* (Debt Remissions) provided interesting data relating to the purchase and sale of houses. Information obtained from 'Handel en Nijverheid' ('Trade and Industry') was of importance in relation to the loans. Details of the early correspondence from Archibald Sr. and Isaac Hope of Rotterdam and Archibald and Thomas Hope of Amsterdam are to be found in the Brants archives, under reference numbers 1620 and 1638. Facts concerning Thomas Hope's years as a director of the Dutch East and West India Companies can be found in the 'Heerenboekje' and in the *Particuliere Notulen* of Mr. Pieter Rendorp.

The Rotterdam municipal archives provided information concerning the earliest generation of Hopes in Holland. Here, too, the Notarial Archives constitued the principal source, the deeds enacted by the notaries Philips Basteels, Jacobus de Bergh, Gommer van Bortel and Johan van Weel being of importance in relation to the Hopes. Also in Rotterdam, the baptismal register of the Scottish Church and the register of births of the Mennonite Community were consulted, as were extracts from the registers of deaths.

In the municipal archives in The Hague, the register of conveyances was consulted in connexion with the purchase of 'Het Tapijthuis' by John Hope. The Notarial Archives were consulted for a single deed enacted by the notary Adrianus van der Wijck.

In the General State Archives, in The Hague, the Hope Collection (number 8468) revealed details of Thomas Hope's activities as a director of the Dutch East India Company. Facts relating to the loan floated by the Kingdom of Holland in 1807 are to be found under the heading 'Financiën.'

The Voûte archives, which are at present in the custody of Mrs. A. G. Voûte-Esser in Amsterdam, also contain information which is of importance for the history of Hope & Co.

In Edinburgh, Mr. Gavin M. Goodfellow consulted the Roll of Burgesses and the Marriage Register of that city and also the Hopetoun Papers, which are preserved at Hopetoun House.

A LIST OF WORKS CITED

Nederland's Adelsboek, XXXI, XL. The Hague, 1933 and 1942.

Altamira, R. *A History of Spain*. New York, 1949.

Alting Bösken, J.A. *Over geldleeningen hier te lande door vreemde mogendheden aangegaan*. Utrecht, 1864.

Amburger, E. *Geschichte der Behördenorganisation Russlands von Peter dem grossen bis 1917*. Leiden, 1966.

Andersson, I. *A History of Sweden*. London, 1955.

d'Angeberg, V.A. *Recueil des Traités et Actes diplomatiques concernant la Pologne*. Paris, 1862.

Baasch, E. *Holländische Wirtschaftsgeschichte*. Jena, 1927.

Balfour Paul, J. ed. 'The diary of Sir James Hope 1646–1654,' in: *Publications of the Scottish History Society*, Second Series, Vol. XIX, Miscellany III, 97–168.

Baumgarten, H. *Geschichte Spaniens vom Ausbruch der französischen Revolution bis auf unsere Tage*, I. Leipzig, 1856.

Baumgarten, S. *Le Crépuscule Néo-Classique: Thomas Hope*. Paris, 1958.

Baumgarten, S. 'Emprunts de Suède à Amsterdam.' *Tijdschrift voor Geschiedenis*, LXXVII (1964) 439–47.

Nouvelle Biographie Générale, 46 vols. Paris, 1855–1866.

Dictionary of National Biography, 63 vols. London, 1885–1900.

Blauw, K. 'Het Provinciehuis van Noord-Holland'. *Haerlem* 1958 (1959).

Blauw, K. 'Van 'Hofstede' tot 'Paviljoen' Welgelegen.' *Haerlem* 1962 (1963).

Blok, P.J. *Geschiedenis van het Nederlandsche Volk*, 2nd ed.. Leiden, 1912–1915.

Blum, K.L. *Ein russischer Staatsmann. Des Grafen Jakob Johann Sievers Denkwürdigkeiten*, III. Leipzig and Heidelberg, 1858.

Boxer, C.R. *The Portuguese Seaborne Empire*. London, 1969.

Bruchey, S.W. *Robert Oliver, Merchant of Baltimore, 1783–1819*. Vol. LXXIV, i of *The John Hopkins University Studies in Historical and Political Science*. Baltimore, 1956.

Brugmans, I.J. *Paardenkracht en Mensenmacht. Sociaal-economische geschiedenis van Nederland 1795–1940*. The Hague, 1961.

Buijnsters, P.J. 'Swedenborg in Nederland.' *Tijdschrift voor Nederlandse Taal- en Letterkunde*, LXXXIII, iii (1967).

Burke's Genealogical and Heraldic History of the Peerage and Baronetage, the Privy Council and Order of Precedence. 99th ed. of 1949, London.

Butterfield, L.H. ed. *Diary and autobiography of John Adams*, IV. Cambridge, Mass., 1961.

Buys, J.T. 'De Nederlandsche staatsschuld sedert 1814.' *Werkzaamheden van de Afdeeling Koophandel der Maatschappij onder de Zinspreuk Felix Meritis te Amsterdam*, (1857).

Carter, A.C. 'Dutch foreign investment, 1738–1800.' *Economica*, XX (1953).

Casanova, G. *Mémoires*, II (1756–1763), texte présenté et annoté par Robert Abirached. Paris, 1959.

Channing, E. *A History of the United States*, IV. New York, 1917.

Colenbrander, H.T. *De Patriottentijd*, 3 vols. The Hague, 1897–1899.

Colenbrander, H.T. *De Bataafsche Republiek*. Amsterdam, 1908.

Colenbrander, H.T. ed. *Ontstaan der Grondwet*, II. Rijks Geschiedkundige Publicatiën, Kleine serie, VII. The Hague, 1909.

Colenbrander, H.T. ed. *Gedenkstukken der algemeene geschiedenis van Nederland, van 1795 tot 1840*. I–IX. Rijks Geschiedkundige Publicatiën, I, II, III, IV, V, VI, XI, XII, XIII, XVI, XXIII, XXV, XXVII, XXX, XXXI, XXXVII. The Hague, 1905–1917.

Colenbrander, H.T. *Schimmelpennick en Koning Lodewijk*. Amsterdam, 1911.

Colenbrander, H.T. *Inlijving en Opstand*, 2nd ed.. Amsterdam, 1941.

Colenbrander, H.T. *Vestiging van het Koninkrijk*. Amsterdam 1927.

Corti, E.C. Conte. *Der Aufstieg des Hauses Rothschild*. Leipzig, 1927.

Crouzet, F. *L'économie britannique et le blocus continental (1806–1813)*, 2 vols. Paris, 1958.

Crouzet, F. 'Groupes de pression et politique de blocus: remarques sur les origines des Ordres en Conseil de novembre 1807.' *Revue Historique*, 86, CCXXVIII (1962).

Damme, A. van. *De buitenplaatsen te Heemstede, Berkenrode en Bennebroek*. Haarlem, 1903.

Dillen, J.G. van. 'Eenige brieven der firma Hope & Co.'. *Economisch-Historisch Jaarboek*, I (1915).

Dillen, J.G. van. 'Honderd jaar economische ontwikkeling van het Noorden' in: *Algemene Geschiedenis der Nederlanden*, VII. Utrecht, 1954.

Dillen, J.G. van. *Mensen en Achtergronden. Studies uitgegeven ter gelegenheid van de tachtigste verjaardag van de schrijver*. Groningen, 1964.

Dillen, J.G. van. *Van rijkdom en regenten. Handboek tot de economische en sociale geschiedenis van Nederland tijdens de Republiek*. The Hague, 1970.

Ehrenberg, R. *Grosse Vermögen, ihre Entstehung und ihre Bedeutung*. Jena, 1902.

Elias, J.E. *De Vroedschap van Amsterdam*, 2 vols. Amsterdam, 1903–1905.

Enno van Gelder, H. *De Nederlandse munten*. Utrecht, 1965.

Fugier, A. *Napoléon et l'Espagne, 1799–1808*, 2 vols. Paris, 1930.

Gerhard, D. *England und der Aufstieg Russlands*. Munich and Berlin, 1933.

Golovkine, F. *La cour et le règne de Paul Ier*. Paris, 1905.

Grandmaison, G. de. *L'Espagne et Napoléon*. Paris, 1908.

Hamilton, E.J. 'The foundation of the Bank of Spain.' *The Journal of Political Economy*, LIII (1945).

Hamilton, E.J. *War and Prices in Spain*. Vol. LXXXXI of *The Harvard Economic Studies*. Cambridge, Mass., 1947.

Heckscher, E. *The Continental System*. Oxford, 1922.

Heckscher, E. *An economic history of Sweden*. Cambridge, Mass., 1954.

Heertje, H. *De diamantbewerkers van Amsterdam*. Amsterdam, 1936.

Herr, R. *The Eighteenth-Century Revolution in Spain*. Princeton, 1958.

Heyliger, R.V. *De Nederlandsche wetgeving op de vreemde geldligtingen.* Leiden, 1854.

Memoir of the Public Life of the Right Hon. John Charles Herries, in the reign of George III, George IV, William IV and Victoria, by his son Edward Herries, C.B., I. London, 1880.

Hidy, R.W. *The House of Baring in American Trade and Finance.* Cambridge, Mass., 1949.

Hoekstra, P. *Thirty-Seven Years of Holland-American Relations, 1803–1848.* Grand Rapids, 1916.

Hogendorp, D.C.A. van, ed. *Mémoires du Général Dirk van Hogendorp.* The Hague, 1887.

Hovy, J. *Het voorstel van 1751 tot instelling van een beperkt vrijhavenstelsel in de Republiek (propositie tot een gelimiteerd porto-franco).* Groningen, 1966.

Nieuwe Nederlandsche Jaarboeken, 1787. Leiden and Amsterdam, 1787.

Japikse, N. *De geschiedenis van het Huis Oranje-Nassau*, II. The Hague, 1948.

Jong-Keesing, E.E. de. *De economische crisis van 1763 te Amsterdam.* Amsterdam, 1939.

Kannegieter, J.Z. *Geschiedenis van de vroegere Quakergemeenschap te Amsterdam: 1656 tot begin negentiende eeuw.* Amsterdam and Haarlem, 1971.

Kannegieter, J.Z. 'Een stoomwerktuig op de buitenplaats van een Amsterdams regent in het jaar 1781.' *Amstelodamum*, LXVI (1973).

Karmin, O. 'Autour des négociations Anglo-Prusso-Russes de 1813.' *Revue Historique de la Révolution et de l'Empire*, XI–XII (1917).

Katzenelsohn, P. *Zur Entwicklungsgeschichte der Finanzen Russlands*, I. Berlin, 1913.

Kernkamp, G.W. 'Bengt Ferrners dagboek van zijne reis door Nederland in 1759.' *Bijdragen en Mededeelingen van het Historisch Genootschap*, XXXI (1910).

Kooy, T.P. van der. *Hollands Stapelmarkt en haar verval.* Amsterdam, 1931.

Labouchère, G. 'P.C. Labouchère, un financier diplomate au siècle dernier.' *Revue d'Histoire Diplomatique*, XXVII (1913).

Lacour-Gayet, G. *Talleyrand*, II. Paris, 1930.

Laing, D., ed. *A Diary of the Public Correspondence of Sir Thomas Hope of Craighall. From the original in the library at Pinkie House.* Printed for the Bannatyne Club. Edinburgh, 1843.

Lanzac Laborie, L. de. *Le monde des affaires et du travail.* Paris, 1910.

Lasky, H. 'David Parish: a European in American Finance. 1806–1816.' (unpublished Ph.D. dissertation, University of Ann Arbor).

Law, H.W. and Law, I. *The Book of the Beresford Hopes.* London, 1925.

Lesage, C. *Napoléon I, créancier de la Prusse.* Paris, 1924.

Lévy, A. *Un grand profiteur de guerre sous la Révolution, l'Empire et la Restauration: G.J. Ouvrard.* Paris, 1929.

Livermore, H.V. *A New History of Portugal.* Cambridge, 1966.

Lobanov-Rostovski, A.A. *Russia and Europe, 1789–1815.* Duke University Press, 1947.

Lord, R.H. *The Second Partition of Poland.* Cambridge, Mass., 1915.

Lord, R.H. 'The third partition of Poland.' *Slavonic Review*, III, i (1925).

Lüthy, H. *La Banque Protestante en France de la Révocation de l'Edit de Nantes à la Révolution*, II. Paris, 1961.

Manger jr., J.B. *Recherches sur les rélations économiques entre la France et la Hollande pendant la Révolution Française 1785–1795*. Besançon, 1923.

Mansvelt, W.M.F. *Rechtsvorm en geldelijk beheer bij de Oost-Indische Compagnie*. Amsterdam, 1922.

Marion, M. *Histoire financière de la France depuis 1715*, I. Paris, 1914.

Martens, F.de. *Supplément au Recueil des Traités*, v, *1808–1814*. Göttingen, 1817.

Meischke, R. 'Het Kasteel Nederhorst Den Berg.' *Amstelodamum*, XL (1957).

Meulen, A.J.van der. *Studies over het ministerie van Van de Spiegel*. Leiden, 1905.

Meulen, W.W.van der. 'Beschrijving van eenige West-Indische Plantageleeningen. Bijdrage tot de kennis der geldbelegging in de achttiende eeuw.' *Bijdragen en Mededeelingen van het Historisch Genootschap*, XXV (1904).

Mollien, Comte. *Mémoires d'un ministre du Trésor Public, 1780–1815*, I. Paris, 1898.

Morris, A.C. ed. *Diary and Letters of Gouverneur Morris*, I. London, 1889.

Nicolson, H. *The Congress of Vienna, a study in allied unity, 1812–1822*. New York, 1946.

Nierop, L.van. 'Henry Hope te Boston.' *Amstelodamum*, XXVI (1939).

Nierop, L.van. 'Over het huis Thomas en Adrian Hope te Amsterdam.' *Amstelodamum*, XXVII (1940).

Nisbest-Bain, R. *Gustavus III and his contemporaries*, II. London, 1894.

Nisbet-Bain, R. *Scandinavia*, Cambridge, 1905.

Nolte, V. *Fünfzig Jahre in beiden Hemispheren*. Hamburg, 1853.

Ouvrard, G.J. *Mémoires sur sa vie et ses diverses opérations financières*. Paris, 1826.

Posthumus, N.W. *Nederlandsche Prijsgeschiedenis*, 2 vols. Leiden, 1943–1964.

Pribram, A.F. and Fischer, E. 'Ein politischer Abenteurer (Karl Glave Kolbielski, 1752–1831).' *Akademie der Wissenschaften in Wien, philosophisch-historische Klasse, Sitzungsberichte*, Band 216, Abhandlung V (1937).

Ramon, G. *Histoire de la Banque de France*. Paris, 1929.

Renier, G.J. *Great Britain and the establishment of the Kingdom of the Netherlands, 1813–1814: a study in British foreign policy*. The Hague, 1930.

Roosegaarde Bisschop, W. *De opkomst der Londensche geldmarkt 1640–1826*. The Hague, 1896.

Rutkowski, J. *Histoire Economique de la Pologne avant les partages*. Paris, 1922.

Sarrailh, J. *L'Espagne éclairée de la seconde moitié du XVIIIme siècle*, Paris, 1954.

Sautijn Kluit, W.P. *De Amsterdamsche Beurs in 1763 en 1773*. Amsterdam, 1865.

Schäfer, H. *Geschichte von Portugal*, v. Gotha, 1854.

Schöffer, I. 'De vonnissen in Averij Grosse van de Kamer van Assurantie en Avarij te Amsterdam in de 18de eeuw.' *Economisch-Historisch Jaarboek*, XXVI (1956).

Seton-Watson, J. *The Russian Empire 1801–1917*. Oxford, 1967.

Sillem, J.A. *Het leven van Mr. Johan Valckenaer*, II. Amsterdam, 1876.

Soloveytchik, G. *Potemkin*. London, 1938.

Staring, W.C.H. *De binnen- en buitenlandsche maten en gewichten van vroeger en tegenwoordig; met hunne onderlinge vergelijkingen en herleidingen*. Schoonhoven, 1902.

British and Foreign State Papers, edited by the Librarian of the Foreign Office, I. London, 1838.
Stavenow, L. *Geschichte Schwedens, 1718–1772*. Gotha, 1908.
Stavenow, L. 'Der aufgeklärte Absolutismus des 18en Jahrhunderts in Schweden.' *Bulletin of the International Committee of Historical Sciences*, v, iii, 20 (1933).
Thiers, A. *Histoire du Consulat et de l'Empire*, I–II. Brussels, 1845–1846.
Trende, A. *Barthold Georg Niebuhr als Finanz- und Bankmann. Forschungen zur internationalen Finanz- und Bankgeschichte*. Berlin, 1930.
Treue, W. *Wirtschaftsgeschichte der Neuzeit*. Stuttgart, 1962.
Vandal, A. *Napoléon Ier et Alexandre Ier*, 3 vols. Paris, 1891.
Vicens Vives, J. *An Economic History of Spain*. Princeton, 1969.
Voûte-Esser, A.G. *Robert Voûte als zakenman en financier*. Amsterdam, by the Author, 1969.
Vreede, G.W. *Mr.Laurens Pieter van de Spiegel en zijne tijdgenooten (1737–1800)*, IV. Middelburg, 1877.
Vries, J.de. *De economische achteruitgang der Republiek in de Achttiende Eeuw*. Amsterdam, 1959.
Waliszewski, K. *Autour d'un trône: Cathérine II de Russie, ses collaborateurs*. Paris, 1894.
Waliszewski, K. *Le fils de la grande Cathérine, Paul Ier*. Paris, 1912.
Waliszewski, K. *Le règne d'Alexandre Ier*, I. Paris, 1923.
Walters, P.G. and Walters jr., R. 'The American career of David Parish.' *The Journal of Economic History*, IV (1944).
Watkin, D. *Thomas Hope 1769–1831 and the Neo-Classical Idea*. London, 1968.
Webster, C.K. *The foreign policy of Castlereagh, 1812–1815*, I. London, 1931.
Weeveringh, J.J. *Handleiding tot de geschiedenis der staatsschulden*, 2 vols. Haarlem, 1852–1855.
Weill, G. 'Le financier Ouvrard.' *Revue Historique*, XLIII, 127 (1918).
Westermann, J.C. 'Beschouwingen over de opkomst en den bloei des handels in de Gouden Eeuw' in: *Zeven Eeuwen Amsterdam*, ed. A.E.d'Ailly, Amsterdam, s.a.
Westermann, J.C. *Kamer van Koophandel en Fabrieken voor Amsterdam, Gedenkboek*, I. Amsterdam, 1936.
Wilson, C.H. *Anglo-Dutch Commerce and Finance in the Eighteenth Century*. 2nd ed.. Cambridge, 1966.
Winter, P.J.van. *Het aandeel van den Amsterdamschen handel aan den opbouw van het Amerikaansche gemeenebest*, 2 vols in: *Werken van het Nederlandsch Economisch-Historisch Archief*. The Hague, 1927–1933.
Winter, P.J.van. 'Lousiana gekocht en betaald' in: *Verkenning en Onderzoek*. Groningen, 1965.
Winter, P.J.van. 'De Amerikaanse zaken van C.J.M.de Wolf.' *Mededelingen van de Koninklijke Vlaamse Academie voor Wetenschappen, Letteren en Schone Kunsten van België. Klasse der Letteren*, XXXII, ii (1970).
Wolff, O. *Die Geschäfte des Herrn Ouvrard*. Frankfurt a. Main, 1932.
Nieuw Nederlandsch Biografisch Woordenboek, 10 vols. Leiden, 1911–1937.
Wijnman, H.F. *Historische gids van Amsterdam*, 2 vols. Amsterdam, 1971.

NOTES

ABBREVIATIONS

A.R.A.	*Algemeen Rijks Archief* (General State Archives)
G.A.	*Gemeente Archief* (Municipal Archives)
Not.Arch.	*Notarieel Archief* (Notarial Archives)
V.A.	*Voûte Archief* (Voûte Archives)

CHAPTER ONE

PAGE 3

1 Letter of 12th March 1776 from John Hope, The Hague, to the Earl of Hopetoun. Hopetoun Papers, Hopetoun House. With grateful acknowledgement to Mr.Gavin M. Goodfellow, who conducted investigations in Edinburgh to establish the Hopes' Scottish origin.

PAGE 4

1 Johan E. Elias, *De Vroedschap van Amsterdam*, II (2nd ed.; Amsterdam, 1963), 941. *Nederland's Adelsboek*, XXXI (The Hague, 1933), 301. *Ibid.*, XL (The Hague, 1942), 632–633. *Burke's Peerage Baronetage and Knightage* (99th ed.; London, 1949), 1032. H.W.Law and Irene Law, *The Book of the Beresford Hopes* (London, 1925), 16. Also investigations by Mr.Goodfellow of the Roll of Edinburgh Burgesses and the Edinburgh Marriage Register. We did not succeed fully in elucidating the origin. As the are many contradictions, we proceeded from the fact that the generations as a rule followed each other in the Roll of Edinburgh Burgesses and the Edinburgh Marriage Register at intervals of thirty years. Assuming that the first John Hope was admitted as a Guild Brother in 1528, his sons could have followed him in 1560 or thereabouts (allowing the necessary margin). In the following generation, Henry Hope, who married Jacqueline de Tot (or de Jot), would have been eligible round about 1590. Indeed, he was appointed a Burgess and Guild Brother in 1588. Thirty years later – in 1619, to be precise – Henry's son, James, became a Guild Brother. James died in 1634, leaving a son, Henry or Harry, who was probably then still a minor. The keen interest which Sir Thomas Hope of Craighall displayed in his nephew points in this direction. D.Laing, ed., *A Diary of the Public Correspondence of Sir Thomas Hope of Craighall. From the original in the library at Pinkie House.* Printed for the Bannatyne Club, (Edinburgh, 1843). Henry or Harry became a Guild Brother of Edinburgh in 1642, a logical step since his father had died and he himself had for some time carried on the profession of merchant. In 1646 he married Catherine Jonkin. He was thus very young to be a husband and father, but not too young. The daughter of Sir Thomas Hope of Craighall, Anna, was married in 1653 to William Cochrane, and can thus not have been the wife of Henry Hope of Rotterdam. J.Balfour. Paul, ed., 'The diary of Sir James Hope 1646–1654,' in: *Publications of the Scottish History Society*, Second Series, Vol. XIX, Miscellany III, 97–168.

2 G.A. Rotterdam. Baptismal Registers of the Scottish Church. 7th December 1664: Arch(i)bald.

Father: Hendry Hop. Mother: Anna Hop. In these registers, the mother appears under her maiden name. Margaret and Henry, born on 23rd January 1667 and 20th January 1669, presumably died young.

3 G.A. Rotterdam, Not. Arch., 1137–56.

4 G.A. Rotterdam, Not. Arch., 926–401, 927–164, 1498–164, 1508–352.
J.Z.Kannegieter, *Geschiedenis van de vroegere Quakergemeenschap te Amsterdam* (Amsterdam, 1971), 52, 154.

PAGE 5

1 G.A. Rotterdam, Not. Arch., 2091–612.

2 G.A. Rotterdam, Not. Arch., 1487–106. At the time of the authorization, Charles Hope of Hopetoun was no more than twenty years of age. His father had lost his life in a shipwreck in 1682. This probably explains why the authority was signed by his mother, Margaret. Charles Hope was made the first Earl of Hopetoun in 1703. Burke, *Peerage*, 1230.

3 Kannegieter, *Quakergemeenschap*, 155 note 3, 165, 166.
G.A. Amsterdam, Not. Arch., 8592–492.

4 Concerning Pels: Elias, *Vroedschap*, II, 813–817, 1062. Like Archibald Jr., Andries Pels, who in 1707 established the very well known house which bore his name, was not a self-made man. His father, Jean Lucas Pels, had already established a reputation as a merchant in Amsterdam.
Concerning Muilman: Elias, *Vroedschap*, II, 864–870. Like Pels, Muilman and Meulenaer came from well-to-do merchant families and thus had adequate capital from the outset.
Concerning Hogguer: Elias, *Vroedschap*, II, 979–985, 1054–1058; Herbert Lüthy, *La Banque Protestante en France de la Révocation de l'Edit de Nantes à la Révolution*, II (Paris, 1961), 331–342.

PAGE 6

1 G.A. Amsterdam, Not. Arch., 8598–709.

2 Concerning Clifford: Elias, *Vroedschap*, II, 880–886, 1045–1046.
Concerning De Smeth: Elias, *Vroedschap*, II, 796–800. Clifford and De Smeth were also among the leading houses at the time when Archibald Jr. commenced business in Amsterdam.

3 *Infra*, Appendix A.

4 J.G.van Dillen 'Bloeitijd der Amsterdamse Wisselbank, 1607–1701,' *Mensen en Achtergronden* (Groningen, 1964), 397–398.

PAGE 8

1 G.A. Rotterdam. Extracts from registers of deaths.

2 G.A. Amsterdam, Not. Arch., 8613–1726. The earliest deed bearing a reference to Thomas and Adrian Hope is dated 1735.
G.A. Amsterdam, Not. Arch., 8726–884.

PAGE 9

1 J.Hovy, *Het voorstel van 1751 tot instelling van een beperkt vrijhavenstelsel in de Republiek* (*propositie tot een gelimiteerd porto-franco*) (Groningen, 1966), 253.

2 *Ibid.*, 334.

PAGE 10

1 *Ibid.*, 397–408.
2 *Ibid.*, 622–628; Van Dillen, *Van Rijkdom en Regenten. Handboek tot de economische en sociale geschiedenis van Nederland tijdens de Republiek* (The Hague, 1970), 531–533.

PAGE 11

1 Hovy, *Propositie*, 336. E.E.de Jong-Keesing, *De economische crisis van 1763 te Amsterdam* (Amsterdam, 1939), 19–20.
2 Letter of 4th December 1730 from Henry Hope, Boston, to Messrs. Archibald and Thomas Hope, merchants in Amsterdam, in *Amstelodamum*, XXVI (1939), 160. As early as 1720, Archibald and Isaac Hope in Rotterdam were concerned with the conveyance of passengers to the United States: G.A. Amsterdam, Brants archives, number 1638; letter of 4th January 1720 from Archibald and Isaac Hope, Rotterdam, to Simon Bevel, Haarlem. During the War of the Austrian Succession, Thomas and Adrian Hope traded, via St.Eustatius, with Thomas Hancock of Boston. This trade was illegal and therefore quite risky: Discoveries made by Dr.Leonie van Nierop in the John Hancock Papers (1728–1761) in the Library of the Massachusetts Historical Society, *Amstelodamum*, XXVII (1940), 47 et seq.

PAGE 12

1 Letters of 29th July, 22nd, 29th and 30th August, 2nd, 4th and 8th September, 31st October, 6th, 9th, 10th and 12th November, 2nd and 21st December 1758; 2nd, 11th, 14th, 23rd, 24th, 25th and 28th January, 1st, 3rd, 24th and 26th February, 3rd, 6th, 15th and 16th June, 14th, 16th, 17th and 25th July, 18th, 29th, 30th and 31st October 1759, from Isaac and Zachary Hope, Rotterdam, to Thomas and Adrian Hope, Amsterdam.
2 Letters of 14th August 1759 from La Compagnie des Indes, Paris, to Thomas and Adrian Hope, Amsterdam; 23rd November 1759 and 31st October 1760 from P.F.Goossens, Paris, to Thomas and Adrian Hope, Amsterdam. Lüthy, *La Banque Protestante*, II, 322.
3 I.Schöffer, 'De vonnissen in Averij Grosse van de Kamer van Assurantie en Avarij te Amsterdam in de 18de eeuw,' *Economisch-Historisch Jaarboek*, XXVI (The Hague, 1956), 108–109. De Jong-Keesing, *Crisis 1763*, 19, note 2.
4 *Ibid.*, 43–45. Van Dillen, *Rijkdom en Regenten*, 601.

PAGE 13

1 De Jong-Keesing, *Crisis 1763*, 121–129, 159–172. Van Dillen, *Rijkdom en Regenten*, 605.
2 De Jong-Keesing, *Crisis 1763*, 121, 159–160. Van Dillen, *Rijkdom en Regenten*, 605. With Baring, the name Pels was still a byword for lack of action and flexibility in 1802. *Infra*, 402.
3 De Jong-Keesing, *Crisis 1763*, 110, 123. Elias, *Vroedschap*, II, 799, note q.
4 G.A. Amsterdam, register of banns: Archibald Hope Junior and Geertruyd Reessen, 20th December 1725; Thomas Hope and Margareta Marcelis, 11th December 1727. Elias, *Vroedschap*, II, 937–939.

PAGE 14

1 G.A. Amsterdam, Quytscheldingen, C 6, 66 of 17th January 1758. H.F.Wijnman, *Historische Gids van Amsterdam*, II (Amsterdam, 1971), 410.
Elias, *Vroedschap*, II, 942, note ss.

2 G.W.Kernkamp, 'Bengt Ferrner's dagboek van zijne reis door Nederland in 1759,' *Bijdragen en Mededeelingen van het Historisch Genootschap*, XXXI (1910), 367–368. Ferrner noted that the Hopes had an office staff of 26, which at that time must have been large. The Hopes had earlier received special or famous visitors from abroad. According to his memoirs, Casanova was received in Amsterdam by a banker whom he identified only by a single letter (d'O.), and who is assumed to have been Thomas Hope. However, the story of the mysterious Esther, the daughter of his host, with whom Casanova had his umpteenth affair, renders it improbable that Thomas Hope was the banker concerned, for he had only a son. The innocence, bordering on naivety, with which Casanova's host is said to have allowed himself to be persuaded to take part in a sort of spiritualistic séance is very much out of keeping with other descriptions of Thomas Hope: G. Casanova, *Mémoires*, II (1756–1763). Texte présenté et annoté par Robert Abirached (Paris, 1959), 134–147, 160–161, 166–167, 170. Henry Hope continued the tradition of receiving eminent foreign guests, for example Benjamin Franklin. Emanuel Swedenborg, the famous Swedish scientist, philosopher and theosopher, frequently dined with Henry Hope, who also looked after his financial affairs: P.J.Buijnsters, 'Swedenborg in Nederland,' *Tijdschrift voor Nederlandse Taal- en Letterkunde*, LXXXIII, 3 (1967), 200.

PAGE 16

1 G.A. Amsterdam, 'Particuliere Notulen van Mr.Pieter Rendorp. Aanteekeningen wegens de deliberatien en Resolutien genoomen bij Burgemeesteren, 1st July 1750'.
G.A. Amsterdam, Heerenboekje 1760.
A.R.A., The Hague, Hope Collection, 8468. Extract from 'De resolutien van de O.I. Comp. ter Kamer Amsterdam van 7 April 1766 en van 13 September 1770'.
W.M.F.Mansvelt, *Rechtsvorm en geldelijk beheer bij de Oost-Indische Compagnie* (Amsterdam, 1922), 106 note 1.

2 *Nederland's Adelsboek*, XXXI, 302.

3 Circular dated 1st January 1762. G. A. Amsterdam, Not. Arch., 12358–193.

4 Letter of 9th August 1787, to Laborde de Méréville, Paris, P.C. '87, 83.

5 Obituary in 'The Times' of 5th March 1811.

6 H.W. and I.Law, *Beresford Hopes*, 272–273. The reference is to the diary of a cousin of John Williams Hope, Loveday Sarah Gregor.

PAGE 17

1 Partnership contract entered into by H.Hope, J.Hope, N.Bauduin and J.Williams Hope, enacted in the presence of C.van Homrigh, notary, on 4th July 1782. Elias, *Vroedschap*, II, 936, 942. Vincent Nolte, *Fünfzig Jahre in beiden Hemispheren* (Hamburg, 1853), 46, 193.

2 G.A. Amsterdam, Baptismal Register of the Mennonite Community, 14th February 1737, Nos. 298, 162. Baptismal Register of the Presbyterian Church of England, 13th June 1756, Nos. 137, 153.

PAGE 18

1 Elias, *Vroedschap*, II, 933–934, 940–941. John Hope had a fire engine built for his country estate. This was a type of steam engine, and was used to pump water into the ponds. It attracted a great deal of attention. The pump, or a copy of it, is to be found at the entrance to Groenendaal Park in Heemstede. The business correspondence of the Hopes contains no reference to the steam engine as a source of power in industry. J.Z.Kannegieter, 'Een stoomwerktuig op de buitenplaats van een Amsterdams regent in het jaar 1781,' *Amstelodamum*, LXVI (1973), 27–29. A.van Damme, *De buitenplaatsen te Heemstede, Berkenrode en Bennebroek* (Haarlem, 1903), 53, 56.

2 G.A. The Hague, Register of Conveyances. Conveyance of 'Het Tapijthuis,' situated on the north side of the Nieuwe or Korte Voorhout, from Jhr.Carel Bigot, Burgomaster of Stavoren and Deputy of the States of Friesland, to John Hope. R.Meischke, 'Het Kasteel Nederhorst Den Berg,' *Amstelodamum*, XL (1957), 90. John Hope also acquired the title 'Master of 's Graven-Ambacht:' Elias, *Vroedschap*, II, 934.

PAGE 19

1 Van Dillen, *Rijkdom en Regenten*, 457–458.

2 *Ibid.*, 458–459. Elias, *Vroedschap*, II, 1046–1050. E.Baasch, *Holländische Wirtschaftsgeschichte* (Jena, 1927), 194, 201–203.

3 Elias, *Vroedschap*, II, 1050. *Infra*, Chapter Fourteen.

4 *Infra*, 112.

PAGE 20

1 *Infra*, 74–90. Elias, *Vroedschap*, II, 1059. G.A. Amsterdam, Not. Arch., 12403–263. The loan to Count Louis of Nassau-Saarbrücken must have totalled cf 250,000, for 50 bonds were redeemed annually in the period 1770–1774.

2 W.W.van der Meulen, 'Beschrijving van eenige Westindische Plantage-leeningen,' *Bijdragen en Mededeelingen van het Historisch Genootschap*, XXV (1904), 509–510.

3 Elias, *Vroedschap*, II, 1059. Ch. Wilson, *Anglo-Dutch Commerce & Finance in the Eighteenth Century* (2nd ed., Cambridge, 1966), 182–183. Van der Meulen, *Westindische Plantage-leeningen*, 521. Van Dillen, *Rijkdom en Regenten*, 587.

4 G.A. Amsterdam, Not. Arch., 12404–468; 12410–447; 12413–1010, 1011. Wilson, *Anglo-Dutch Commerce*, 183–184. The loans concerned were those made to Patrick Maxwell and John Balfour, the security for which consisted of plantations on Tobago; to Charles Irvine and John Leith, also against the security of plantations on Tobago; to Alexander Campbell, against the security of plantations on Grenada; and finally to Robert Tuite, for which plantations on St.Croix served as security.

PAGE 21

1 W.P.Sautijn Kluit, *De Amsterdamsche Beurs in 1763 en 1773* (Amsterdam, 1865), 65–67, 71–72. Wilson, *Anglo-Dutch Commerce*, 170. Van Dillen, *Rijkdom en Regenten*, 609–610.

2 Van Dillen, *Rijkdom en Regenten*, 611–613. Wilson, *Anglo-Dutch Commerce*, 187. J.de Vries, *De economische achteruitgang der Republiek in de Achttiende Eeuw* (Amsterdam, 1959), 77–78.

De Jong-Keesing, *Crisis 1763*, 72 note 1. Adrian Hope was appointed trustee following Clifford's bankruptcy: Sautijn Kluit, *Amsterdamsche Beurs*, 98.

PAGE 22

1 Letters of 4th, 15th, 18th and 22nd May, 1st and 3rd June 1770 from Alexander Fordyce, London, to Hope & Co., Amsterdam.
Letter of 9th November 1770 from Henry Neale & Co., London, to Gurnell Hoare & Harman, London.
Letter of 11th June 1772 from Gurnell Hoare & Harman, London, to Henry Neale & Co., London.
Letter of 25th December 1772 from J.Harman, London, to Hope & Co., Amsterdam.
Letter of 16th February 1774 from Cust, Ward & Matthews, London, to Gurnell, Hoare & Harman, London.
Memorandum of 16th June 1775 concerning the Fordyce affair.

2 De Vries, *Economische achteruitgang*, 78–79. Wilson, *Anglo-Dutch Commerce*, 182, 187. Van Dillen, *Rijkdom en Regenten*, 608.

3 Letter of 30th January 1807 from Matthiessen & Sillem, Hamburg, to Hope & Co., Amsterdam.

4 *Infra*, 112.

PAGE 23

1 *Infra*, 94.

2 During the fourth war against England, Hope, in association with the Paris houses of Pourrat Frères and Vandenijver Frères & Co., floated French annuity loans on the Amsterdam market. The number of loans and the sums involved vary from one source to another. Lüthy quotes sums of cf 3,000,000 in 1782 and cf 1,100,000 in 1784 (Lüthy, *La Banque Protestante*, II, 522, 534, 546). The Notarial Archives in Amsterdam contain only the deeds relating to one loan on behalf of Pourrat Frères and one on behalf of Vandenijver Frères & Co., the sums being cf 282,000 and cf 1,100,000 respectively (12463–345, 12474–631). The *grootboeken* refer to a loan of cf 2,100,000 and not cf 1,100,000. *Grootboek* 1785, 83, 92, 94. Hope was at this time also engaged in the movement of shipbuilding materials for the benefit of the French fleet, *Infra*, 197.

PAGE 24

1 Memorandum of 24th October 1793 from Robert Voûte, St.Petersburg, to the Attorney General, Samaylov, St.Petersburg, *Infra*, 135.

2 P.J.van Winter, *Het aandeel van den Amsterdamschen handel aan den opbouw van het Amerikaansche Gemeenebest*, II (The Hague, 1933), 466–468, 470, 472.

PAGE 26

1 *Infra*, Appendix D-II.

2 *Infra*, 86.

PAGE 27

1 *Infra*, Appendix C-I.

2 *Infra*, 79, 82.

3 *Infra*, 100, 167–168.

4 *Infra*, 116–117.

PAGE 28

1 *Infra*, 340, 345, 394.
2 *Infra*, 78, 112, 115.
3 *Infra*, 98.
4 *Infra*, 82, 84, 107–108.

PAGE 29

1 A.Trende, *Barthold Georg Niebuhr als Finanz- und Bankman. Forschungen zur internationalen Finanz- und Bankgeschichte* (Berlin, 1930), 51. Niebuhr later achieved fame as a historian. *Infra*, 136.
2 *Infra*, 336.
3 *Infra*, 249.
4 *Infra*, 109.

PAGE 30

1 *Infra*, Chapter Five, *passim*; 126–136, 240–242, 247–248, 253–255, 258, 266, 268–270; Chapter Thirteen, *passim*; 413–427.
2 *Infra*, 334–336.

PAGE 32

1 *Infra*, 115.
2 *Infra*, 104–105. Henry Hope's Anglo-American origin, and with this his English nationality, will probably have influenced his refusal of the Russian title.
3 *Infra*, Chapter Five, *passim.*
4 *Infra*, 178, 182, 184–185, 190–191, 201.
5 *Infra*, 341–342, 347–349, 350–351, 364–365.
6 *Infra*, 257.
7 *Infra*, 366, 369, 420.

PAGE 33

1 T.P.van der Kooij, *Hollands Stapelmarkt en haar verval* (Amsterdam, 1931), 18–26.
2 J.C.Westermann, 'Beschouwingen over de opkomst en den bloei des handels in de Gouden Eeuw,' *Zeven Eeuwen Amsterdam*, ed. A.E.d'Ailly, II (Amsterdam, undated), 98. Wilson, *Anglo-Dutch Commerce*, 11. De Vries, *Economische achteruitgang*, 34. Van Dillen, 'Honderd jaar economische ontwikkeling van het Noorden,' *Algemene Geschiedenis der Nederlanden*, VII (Utrecht, 1954), 278–279.
3 *Infra*, 432.
4 *Infra*, 433, note 1.

PAGE 34

1 *Infra*, 125.
2 *Infra*, 127–128, 139–149, 150–151.
3 *Infra*, 289, 311–312, 411–412.
4 *Infra*, 144–145, 448–449.
5 For example, Lestapis, Nolte and Parish in connexion with the Mexican silver transaction, Coesvelt for the Spanish loans, Robert Melvil for the purchase of Russian produce, and Hieronymus Sillem for the sale of this produce. *Infra*, Chapter Eleven, *passîm*; 347–356, Chapter Thirteen, *passim*; 210–214, 216–226, 242–248, 252–254, 266–267, 269.

PAGE 35

1 *Infra*, 237–239.
2 *Infra*, 443, 446–447, 450.
3 De Vries, *Economische achteruitgang*, 70. De Vries treats the subject cautiously here. The investigations which formed part of our study point towards the development of certain principal facets in the activities; however, this was not accompanied by the relinquishing of other activities. As in the various branches of trade, there were dividing lines, albeit these were obscure and were repeatedly disregarded. A far-reaching quantitative investigation of the journals and *grootboeken*, to which the data obtainable from the correspondence would have to be related, would undoubtedly throw more light on this.
4 *Infra*, 431.

PAGE 36

1 De Jong-Keesing, *Crisis 1763*, 72–78. The picture presented in this book accords with the findings from the Hope archives.
2 *Infra*, 173.
3 *Infra*, 124.
4 *Infra*, Appendix G.

PAGE 37

1 *Infra*, 177. Labouchère describes here how Rall of St.Petersburg prided himself on having a cash reserve of 100,000 roubles. Hope maintained a balance at the Exchange Bank, the size of which grew as the number of debits increased. In 1752, the half-yearly balance stood at cf 175,000, while the debits totalled approximately 700 per half-year. De Jong-Keesing, *Crisis 1763*, 70.
2 Letter of 22nd January 1806 from P.C.Labouchère, Amsterdam, to Vincent Nolte, B.I. 12.
3 Nolte, *Fünfzig Jahre*, 178–182.
4 *Infra*, 348, note 1.
5 4th July 1782: Partnership agreement between H.Hope, J.Hope, N.Bauduin and J.Williams Hope.

PAGE 38

1 *Infra*, Appendix G.
2 12th May 1785: Partnership contract between H.Hope, Nicolas Bauduin, J.Williams Hope and J.C.Hartsinck. 3rd April 1765: Contract wherein Nicolas Bauduin bound himself to Messrs. Hope & Co. for a period of twelve years, commencing on 1st January 1765. As a 'clerk,' Bauduin was to receive 5,000 carolus guilders per annum. On 1st February 1772 his salary was raised to 10,000 carolus guilders.
3 16th November 1789: Deed of resignation of J.C.Hartsinck. 29th November 1789: Receipt signed by J.C.Hartsinck. On 13th March 1787, the remaining partners paid to Paul Degalz, the executer of Nicolas Bauduin's Will, a sum of cf 304,252.10.8 representing Bauduin's share in the capital of the firm. Bauduin's share of the profit from 31st December 1785 until his death on 18th January 1787, totalling cf 33,578.1.8, was also paid. Elias, *Vroedschap*, II, 1015.

PAGE 39

1 16th November 1789: Convention between Henry Hope, J.Williams Hope and the widow of John Hope.

2 S.Baumgarten, *Le Crépuscule Néo-Classique, Thomas Hope* (Paris, 1958), 25, 31–40. H.W.Law and I.Law, *Beresford Hopes*, 19–26. On Thomas's activities as a collector and patron of the arts: D.Watkin, *Thomas Hope 1760–1831 and the Neo-Classical Idea* (London, 1968).

3 A.G.Voûte-Esser, *Robert Voûte als zakenman en financier* (Amsterdam: By the Author, 1969).

4 *Grootboek* 1785: 252; *grootboek* 1786: 224; *grootboek* 1787: 82, 141, 146.

PAGE 40

1 Nolte, *Fünfzig Jahre*, 47–48. As in other instances, Nolte's account is not entirely reliable.

2 R.W.Hidy, *The House of Baring in American Trade and Finance* (Cambridge, Mass., 1949), 3–13.

3 Hidy suggests that the relationship between Hope and Baring was based on an exceptionally rapid and profitable sale of drafts by Baring on behalf of Hope (p. 14–15). The oldest surviving *grootboek*, which dates from 1770, contains an account in the names of John and Frederick Baring of London. In some later years, however, no entries were made in the account, and it was not until the mid-1780s, when the houses jointly engaged in speculations, that really large sums appeared. At the same time, Hope's letters to Francis Baring reveal that a large measure of confidence and deep respect for Baring's judgement already existed in 1787. *Infra*, 432.

PAGE 41

1 H.T.Colenbrander, *De Patriottentijd*, (3 vols, The Hague, 1897–9), I, 324–332, Chapter VIII, and II, Chapter I.

2 *Ibid.*, II, 116–117, 121, 128–139.

3 *Ibid.*, II, Chapter IV, and III, Chapter II.

4 *Ibid.*, III, 205–206, 207, note 1; *Infra*, 88, 431–432.

PAGE 42

1 Letter of 9th August 1787 to Laborde de Méréville, Paris, P.C. '87, 83.

2 K.Blauw, 'Het Provinciehuis van Noord-Holland,' *Haerlem, jaarboek 1958* (Haarlem, 1959), 69–83.
K.Blauw, 'Van "Hofstede" tot "Paviljoen" Welgelegen,' *Haerlem, jaarboek 1962* (Haarlem, 1963), 53–64.

PAGE 43

1 *Infra*, Appendix B. Henry Hope's great liking for the Italian baroque painters is evidenced by the fact that he had copies of works by Guido Reni and Annibale Caracci mounted in the skylight above the staircase of 'Welgelegen.' Blauw, 'Het Provinciehuis,' 78.

2 Colenbrander, *Patriottentijd*, III, chapter VI.

3 Letter of 30th August 1787 to Vve. Councler & Fils Ainé, Marseilles, P.C. '87, 120.
Letter of 14th September 1787 to J. & F.Baring, London, P.C. '87, 143.

4 Colenbrander, *Patriottentijd*, III, 282–283, 285, 287.

PAGE 44

1 Letter of 4th October 1787 to Vve. Councler & Fils Ainé, Marseilles, P.C. '87, 173.
2 *Nieuwe Nederlandsche Jaarboeken 1787* (Leiden and Amsterdam), 5374.
3 *Ibid.*, 5376, 5380. Colenbrander, *Patriottentijd*, III, 288.
4 *Nieuwe Nederlandsche Jaarboeken 1787*, 5381.

PAGE 45

1 Letter of 18th October 1787 to Bournissien Despreaux & Fils, Rouen, P.C. '87, 200. Letter of 23rd October 1787 to J.&F. Baring, London, P.C. '87, 208.
2 *Infra*, 86, 114–115.
3 *Infra*, 90.
4 *Infra*, 95–96.
5 *Infra*, 98–99.

PAGE 46

1 *Infra*, 104.
2 *Infra*, 105.
3 *Infra*, 107.
4 J.B. Manger Jr., *Recherches sur les relations économiques entre la France et la Hollande pendant la Révolution Française, 1785–1795* (Besançon, 1923), 67–68, 70. Colenbrander, *De Bataafsche Republiek* (Amsterdam, 1908), 33. Van Dillen, 'Eenige brieven der Firma Hope & Co., medegedeeld door Dr.J.G.van Dillen,' *Economisch-Historisch Jaarboek*, I (The Hague, 1915), 267–268. Van Dillen, *Rijkdom en Regenten*, 621. Alice Carter, 'Dutch foreign investment, 1738–1800' *Economica*, Vol. XX (London, 1953), 329, 338–339. *Grootboek* 1789: 248, 264, 271, 281.

PAGE 47

1 Manger, *Recherches*, 75–77.
2 *Infra*, 108.
3 *Infra*, 109, 281–282.
4 *Infra*, 109.

PAGE 48

1 Van Dillen, *Rijkdom en Regenten*, 618–620.
2 *Infra*, 94, 141.
3 Letter of 4th October 1808 to the Committee for Foreign Loans, St.Petersburg, VII, 498. Letter of 27th October 1808 to R. Melvil, Amsterdam, R.I.
4 *The Diary and Letters of Gouverneur Morris*, I, ed. by Anne Cary Morris (London, 1889), 303.
5 Colenbrander, *Bataafsche Republiek*, 24, 27.
6 Colenbrander, *Gedenkstukken der Algemeene Geschiedenis van Nederland van 1795 tot 1840*, I (The Hague, 1905), 473.
Infra, 109, 138.

PAGE 49

1 Colenbrander, *Gedenkstukken*, I, 475–476.
2 A.J.van der Meulen, *Studies over het ministerie van Van de Spiegel* (Leiden, 1905), 342–344, 375–376.
Van de Spiegel visited Henry Hope at 'Welgelegen' in 1788. In 1790 Henry Hope

received the stadholder, William v, there. H.W. and I.Law, *Beresford Hopes*, 272. Van Winter, *Aandeel*, I, 125, note 2.

3 Letter of 21st October 1974 from A.Caxtier to J.Williams Hope, London. Letter of 11th November 1794 from I.Eckhardt, to J.Williams Hope, London. On 21st August 1794 Thomas Hope advertised seven horses and two carriages for sale in the 'Amsterdamsche Courant:' Baumgarten, *Crépuscule*, 25–26. There is no truth in the story that Mrs.Williams Hope stayed in Amsterdam, or returned there, in order to defend Hope's property: Letter of 17th June 1797 from Hope & Co., London, to J.J.Voûte Jr., Amsterdam.

PAGE 50

1 12th July 1794: unsigned letter headed 'My Lord.' 11th October 1794: unsigned letter to 'Monsieur le Baron.'

2 Letter of 19th January 1795 from Jacob Hoogland, Den Helder, to Paulus Taay, Amsterdam.

3 H.W.Law and I.Law, *Beresford Hopes*, 272. On 28th March 1799, Henry Hope, John Williams Hope, Thomas, Adrian Elias and Henry Philip Hope, partners in the firm of Hope & Co., informed the Office of Commercial Commissioners that 8,000 pounds sterling constituted 10% of their income. This 10% income tax was levied annually as a special contribution for the prosecution of the war.

4 Colenbrander, *Gedenkstukken*, I, 366.

PAGE 51

1 Letter of 26th February 1795 from P.Taay, Amsterdam, to Vilmain, Nantes, A XXIV, 14.

2 G.A. The Hague, Not. Arch., 3893–48. Letters of 3rd/6th and 19th May 1795 from P. Taay, Amsterdam, to Hope & Co., London. Taay gave a moving description of the difficulties which faced him: 'In order to uphold your noble honour and house, I was obliged to go and beg from one or other good friend, a task which came very hard to me. The one was deaf and could not grasp my meaning, another wanted to help but was in great straits himself, a third had no money to hand, and so on and so forth. When a bill of yours is protested, I am consumed with anxiety and get the fever. I am already so ashamed that I do not dare to show myself in the street during the daytime ...'

3 *Infra*, 282.

4 Hermann Albrecht Insinger was born on 6th January 1757 in Bückeburg. In 1768 he moved to Amsterdam, where on 19th August 1787 he married Anna Maria Swarth. He initially traded under the name of Insinger & Prins, and later as Insinger & Swarth. On 30th December 1800 he founded the house of Insinger & Co., which has retained the name up to the present day. Insinger probably visited the Caribbean, and is said to have been shipwrecked there. Such a visit would explain his numerous contacts with plantation owners in the area. Data obtained from the Insinger archives and furnished by Mr.J.Nauta, adviser to Insinger & Co.

5 *Supra*, 51, note 2. *Infra*, 282.

PAGE 52

1 Letters of 26th November 1796, and 4th, 17th, 20th and 21st January, and 20th February 1797 from J.J.Voûte, Jr., Amsterdam, to Hope & Co., London. An

attempt was made in association with the Swedish East India Company to set up a speculation in tea, but this probably failed to materialize.
Letters of 11th and 18th June, and 16th July 1796 from De Coninck & Co., Copenhagen, to Voûte & Co., Amsterdam.
Letters of 18th and 21st June, and 9th July 1796 from Voûte & Co., Amsterdam, to De Coninck & Co., Copenhagen. De Coninck's correspondence shows also that the plantation owners on St.Croix sent produce to Copenhagen to be sold, in order to provide funds for interest and principal instalments. At the end of May 1798, Insinger paid Taay a sum of cf 8,000, which was debited to the account headed 'St.Croix negotiations A and B.'
Letter of 2nd June 1798 from H.A.Insinger, Amsterdam, to P.C.Labouchère, Hamburg.

2 Letters of 25th March, 28th April and 17th June 1797 from Hope & Co., London, to J.J.Voûte Jr., Amsterdam.
Letters of 13th April, 28th June, 4th and 5th July 1797 from J.J.Voûte Jr., Amsterdam, to Hope & Co., London.

3 *Infra*, 162–163, 165–166.

4 *Infra*, 168.

5 *Infra*, 163–164.

PAGE 53

1 *Infra*, 173–176.

2 Van Winter, *Aandeel*, II, 367 note 1. Van Winter, 'Louisiana gekocht en betaald,' *Verkenning en Onderzoek* (Groningen, 1965), 380–382. We are indebted to Prof.van Winter for allowing us to consult the revised edition of his book *Aandeel van den Amsterdamschen handel aan de opbouw van het Amerikaansche Gemeenebest* which is to be published in English.

3 Van Winter, 'Lousiana gekocht en betaald,' 382–383. Hidy, *House of Baring*, 28–30.

4 Henry Hope, John Williams Hope, Thomas Hope and Henry Philip Hope each shouldered a quarter of the cost. The Hopes acquired 445,334¼ acres, for which they paid 48,126 pounds sterling. Expenses up to 1804 totalled 5,360.12.6 pounds sterling against which stood revenues totalling 3,067.9.10 pounds sterling. VI-ba-8 ('America.')

PAGE 54

1 Letter of 12th June 1799 to William Gordon Coesvelt, St.Croix.
Letter of 4th April 1800 from Friderici, Paramaribo, to Mr.Hope, London.

2 *Infra*, 387. Letters of 16th and 24th March, 15th and 17th August 1799, and 20th May 1800, and 11 undated letters from Count Starhemberg, London, to Messrs. Hope, London.
Letters of 14th June, 16th and 19th July, 2nd and 6th August 1799 from J. Schubach, Hamburg, to Hope & Co., London; of 16th July, 2nd and 23rd August 1799, from Count von Pergen, Hamburg, to Hope & Co., London; and of 1st October 1799 to J.Schubach, Hamburg, VI, 118.
Letter of 12th April 1800 from Count von Pergen, Vienna, to Hope & Co., London.

PAGE 55

1 30th April 1801: Memorandum to Robert Voûte.

2 Letter of 30th June 1801 from R.Voûte, Amsterdam, to Hope & Co., London.

3 Letter of 8th November 1801 from R.Voûte, The Hague, to H.Hope, London. Letter of 5th December 1801 from R.Voûte, Utrecht, to H.A.Insinger, Amsterdam. The total value was then put at cf 825,000.
4 *Infra*, Chapter Fourteen.

PAGE 56

1 Early July 1802: 'Circumstances,' written by Robert Voûte, Middagten, to Hope & Co., London.
2 Letters of 4th May 1802 from R.Voûte, The Hague, to J.Williams Hope, London, and 22nd May 1802 from R.Voûte, Middagten, to J.Williams Hope, London. *Infra*, 399, note 2.
3 Letter of 6th November 1802 from Henry Hope, London, to J. Williams Hope, Norwich.

PAGE 57

1 *Infra*, 396, 402.
2 *Infra*, 407–410.
3 *Infra*, 201–202.
4 *Infra*, 188–190.
5 *Infra*, 192. 'Propositions faites au Ministre du Trésor Public par M.Labouchère, associé de la Maison Hope & Cie. d'Amsterdam.' Labouchère received from the minister drafts from F.Baring & Co. to a value of 34½ million francs. These were dated 3rd May 1803 and had been accepted by Hope & Co. In exchange for these, Hope was required to furnish: 1) drafts issued by the *Receveurs Généraux* and totalling 15 million francs, of which 5 million fell due on 30 Fructidor of the year 12 and 10 million on 30 Vendémiaire of the year 13; 2) eight bonds involving in all 12 million francs and falling due at monthly intervals from 1st May 1804 to the end of that year; these were to be used for credits opened by the French Admiralty; 3) a sum of 5,825,000 francs in the form of six bonds from Hope & Co., payable in Paris; these payments, however, would not be made until the remaining two-thirds of the bonds had been surrendered to Hope, and pending this the Company would pay ½% interest per month on the sum remaining unpaid. In recognition of the acceleration of the payments, Baring and Hope were allowed a discount of 1,675,000 francs.

PAGE 58

1 Van Winter, *Aandeel*, II, 387–388.
2 *Ibid.*, 388. VI-ba-8 ('America').
3 Van Winter, 'Louisiana gekocht en betaald,' 386–387.
4 1804: Contract between Hope & Co. and R.&Th.de Smeth.
5 VI-ba-8 ('America').

PAGE 60

1 Letter of 15th February 1805 from P.C.Labouchère, Amsterdam, to A.Baring, London. Because of the poor rate of exchange, an issue quoted at 98 in London came out at 105 in Amsterdam. The nominal price there was 107, but the arrival on the market of a large number of bonds would have rendered this unattainable.
2 Van Winter, *Aandeel* (revised edition).
3 Van Winter, *Aandeel*, II, 388, note 5. 'Louisiana 6%, Staat van Deelneeming in

Americaansche Fondsen,' 1805–1821. The 1,346 bonds purchased would each have grossed the participants cf 120.

4 *Infra*, 394.

PAGE 61

1 *Infra*, 292–294.

2 *Infra*, 306–309.

3 *Infra*, 327–328.

4 *Infra*, 331.

PAGE 62

1 *Infra*, 335–336, 340–342.

2 *Infra*, 338–339.

3 *Infra*, 339–340, 344–346.

4 MECKLENBURG-SCHWERIN: Letter of 26th May 1808 to Van Herzeele, Amsterdam, VII, 384. BADEN: Letters of 23rd September 1808 and 31st January 1809 to Gronovius, Karlsruhe, VII, 491. GRAND DUCHY OF WARSAW: Letter of 15th January 1808 to Jean Ant.Noffolk, Warsaw, VII, 282. PRUSSIA: Letters of 5th January and 16th February 1808 to Niebuhr, Berlin, VII, 261, 315; of 10th and 19th February 1808 from Niebuhr, Berlin, to Hope & Co., Amsterdam; and of 7th April 1808 from Hope & Co. to R.Voûte, Utrecht, VII, 342. Ch.Lesage, *Napoléon I, Créancier de la Prusse* (Paris, 1924), 232. DENMARK: Letter of 5th February 1811 from P.F.Lestapis, Amsterdam, to P.C.Labouchère, Antwerp. KINGDOM OF ITALY: Letters of 17th July and 4th August 1809 to Rougemont de Löwenberg, Paris, A XXVII, 127, 141; of 24th July 1809 from Rougemont de Löwenberg, Paris, to Hope & Co., Amsterdam, and of 18th August 1809 from Nic.Hubbard, Geneva, to P.C.Labouchère, Amsterdam.

PAGE 63

1 In a 'report concerning the foreign policy of the Netherlands' dated 23rd January 1829, the sum of the capital invested in foreign loans was estimated to be cf 640,000,000. Colenbrander, *Gedenkstukken*, IX; (The Hague, 1917), 474. In October 1829, O.J.A.Repelaer van Driel, director of the *Algemeene Maatschappij* in Brussels, put the figure at cf 1,600,000,000, a difference of 1,000 million guilders. Colenbrander, *Gedenkstukken*, IX, ii, 913. In the Netherlands, the heaviest losses were incurred on domestic loans. In 1814 the national debt amounted to 1,250 million guilders, of which only one-third bore interest, which was at the rate of 2½%. Of the interest-free portion, four million guilders, later to be increased to five million, was to be transferred annually to the interest-bearing debt. In 1841 the interest-free debt, which then totalled nearly 900 million guilders, was converted to an interest-bearing loan; the conversion rate was 6.8% and the interest rate 2½%. J.T.Buys, 'De Nederlandsche staatsschuld sedert 1814,' *Werkzaamheden van de Afdeeling Koophandel der Maatschappij onder de Zinspreuk: Felix Meritis te Amsterdam* (Haarlem, 1857), 112, note 1, 156–157. J.J.Weeveringh, *Handleiding tot de Geschiedenis der Staatsschulden*, I (Haarlem, 1852), 214.

2 *Infra*, 338.

3 *Infra*, 196.

4 *Infra*, 366, 368–369, 420, 424.

PAGE 64

1 *Infra*, 336, note 2.
2 *Infra*, 257.
3 Letter of 13th August 1812 from P.C.Labouchère, Pyrmont, to A.v.d.Hoop, Amsterdam. The French campaign against Russia had dislocated postal communications in Germany.
4 A.Trende, *Niebuhr*, 40, 46, 47 note 71, 50, 55. As a precondition for any loan to Prussia, Labouchère stipulated that a settlement be reached in the matter of a loan granted to Austria against the security of revenues from Silesia, which Prussia had seized from Austria in 1742. No interest had since been paid on the loan, and the principal repayments had ceased immediately following the seizure. The loan sum was cf 4,800,000. Niebuhr also feared that Labouchère, by reason of his contacts with Talleyrand, was fully aware of Prussia's extremely vulnerable position vis-à-vis France.

PAGE 65

1 Letter of 1st December 1808, from Hope & Co., Amsterdam, to J.Williams Hope, London.
2 *Infra*, 357–360, 366–368, 374–375.
3 *Infra*, 413–415.
4 Obituary of Henry Hope in 'The Times' of 5th March 1811.

PAGE 66

1 Letters of 3rd April 1811 from John Hope, London, to Mr.Shadwell, London, and 14th and 15th April 1811 from John Hope, London, to P.C.Labouchère, London.
2 *Infra*, 375.
3 *Infra*, 246–254. Letters of 28th September 1812 from John Hope, London, to Hope & Co., Amsterdam, A V, 142, and of 28th February 1813 to John Hope, London.
4 *Infra*, 253.
5 *Infra*, 426.

PAGE 68

1 Letter of 23rd March 1813 to Mrs.J.Hope, London, A V, 170–171.
2 Agreement of 17th July 1813 between Mrs.Anne Hope of the one part, and Thomas and Henry Philip Hope of the other part.
3 Deed of assignment and transfer by Thomas and Henry Philip Hope to Alexander Baring, dated 3rd September 1813.
4 *Infra*, 265.

PAGE 69

1 *Infra*, 246–248, 252, 254–255, 266–267, 268–270.
2 Concerning Hogguer: Elias, *Vroedschap*, II, 1058.
Infra, 91, note 3. Concerning De Smeth: *infra*, 235, 371. Concerning Muilman: Elias, *Vroedschap*, II, 869 note n.

CHAPTER TWO

PAGE 73

1 Ingvar Andersson, *A History of Sweden* (London, 1955), 261.

PAGE 74

1 Eli F.Heckscher, *An Economic History of Sweden* (Cambridge, Mass., 1954), 197.
2 L.Stavenow, *Geschichte Schwedens, 1718–1772* (Gotha, 1908), 350–359.
R.Nisbet-Bain, *Gustavus III and his contemporaries*, II, (London, 1894), 30–31
3 Stavenow, *Geschichte Schwedens*, 364.
Van Dillen, 'Bloeitijd der Amsterdamse Wisselbank,' 309.
4 Stavenow, *Geschichte Schwedens*, 368–378.
Nisbet-Bain, *Gustavus III*, II, 30–31.
R.Nisbet-Bain, *Scandinavia* (Cambridge, 1905), 355.

PAGE 75

1 G.A. Amsterdam, Not. Arch., 12380–100, 155. The State Treasury or *Comptoir Royal d'Etat*, in turn, was dependent upon the revenues of the kingdom. The extraordinary security pertaining to these notes lay in the fact that they became negotiable in the event of Sweden failing to pay.
2 Stavenow, *Geschichte Schwedens*, 388.
3 Nisbet-Bain, *Gustavus III*, II, 49.
Stavenow, *Geschichte Schwedens*, 395–396. The English and Danish envoys also supported the Caps.
4 *Ibid.*, 396.
Nisbet-Bain, Gustavus III, II, 49. While the *riksdag* was in session, units of the Danish and Russian fleets were cruising off the Swedish coast. Stavenow, *Geschichte Schwedens*, 401.

PAGE 76

1 *Ibid.*, 403. Request to the king by the *riksdag*, dated 17th November 1769, to negotiate a loan abroad, in G.A. Amsterdam, Not. Arch., 12395–136.
2 Elias, *Vroedschap*, II, 1057. Cancelled contract between the Swedish king and Hope & Co. and Fizeaux Grand & Co., late November- early December 1780.
3 G.A. Amsterdam, Not. Arch., 12394–889.
4 *Supra*, 76, note 1.
5 As coins of relatively high value were also minted from copper, these were met in the form of blocks of the metal weighing up to nearly 20 kilograms. Because copper coins

were costly to transport, a severe fall in the value of paper money was necessary to bring about a flight of capital in coin. Heckscher, *Economic History*, 88, 197.

PAGE 77

1 Nisbet-Bain, *Gustavus III*, II, 64. This transaction does not seem to have resulted in a public loan.

2 Stavenow, *Geschichte Schwedens*, 427–433; Nisbet-Bain, *Gustavus III*, II, 105–140.

3 Nisbet-Bain, *ibid.*, 117. The name of Grill & Co. also appears in the deeds of settlement issued by Hope to the Swedish government in later years. In the 18th century the Dutch silver ducat was commonly used in trading circles in the Baltic. It was equal in value to 2½ guilders and for this reason was also referred to as a rixdollar. H.Enno van Gelder, *De Nederlandse munten* (Utrecht, 1965), 149, 225, 259–260.

4 Nisbet-Bain, *Gustavus III*, II, 159.

PAGE 78

1 Nisbet-Bain, *ibid.*, 166–167; Hecksher, *Economic History*, 198; Stavenow, 'Der aufgeklärte Absolutismus des 18en Jahrhunderts in Schweden,' *Bulletin of the International Committee of Historical Sciences* V, iii, 20 (1933), 766.

2 Daniel Hogguer resigned from the firm in 1773, whereupon Jan Jacob Horneca entered into a partnership with Henri Fizeaux under the name of Horneca Fizeaux & Co. Elias, *Vroedschap*, II, 1057.

3 G.A. Amsterdam, Not. Arch., 12426–725, 765.

4 The first million guilders were repaid after 10 years, the second after 12 years and the third after 15 years. The 1770 loans, like those negotiated in 1767, ran for 10 years.

5 *Vide* photo of the annual settlement. The text reveals that the bonds could be obtained in exchange for others dated 1767, which were redeemable in 1777. This implied a profit to Sweden of 1% on conversion for the year 1777.

PAGE 79

1 Letter of 1st December 1787, from Hope & Co. to Baron de Ruuth, P.C. '87, 297; Nisbet-Bain, *Gustavus III*, II, 169.

2 Nisbet-Bain, *ibid.*, 170 et seq.

3 Horneca resigned from the firm in April 1779. Fizeaux formed a new partnership with George Grand, a Swiss. Elias, *Vroedschap*, II, 1057. At the time of the seizure of power by Gustav III, Grand was living in Stockholm. It was at his house that De Vergennes met the leaders of the conspiracy, and in recognition of his services he was given a title by the King of France. It was thus extremely appropriate that he should become part of a firm concerned with negotiating loans for Sweden. *Diary and autobiography of John Adams*, edited by L.H.Butterfield, IV (Cambridge, Mass., 1961), 64–65.

4 The term commenced on 1st March 1780. Three debentures, each of 100,000 rixdollars, issued by the State Treasury were given by way of special security. The principal debenture dated from 13th September 1779. In: G.A. Amsterdam, Not. Arch., 12451–24.

PAGE 82

1 Diversen Documenten, laast 1700–begin 1800, 23.

2 Div. Doc., 25.

PAGE 83

1 Div. Doc., 26–28; the bonds relating to this loan were dated 7th February 1781. They were, however, numbered from 751 to 1250 and thus corresponded to the bonds of the loan of 1st December 1780. The debentures issued by the State Treasury bore the date 14th June 1780, the date of the bonds relating to the suspended loan. The principal debentures of the two loans also bore the same date, namely 10th November 1780.

2 Div. Doc., 28–29; Hope and Fizeaux received a commission of 7%, of which 1% was passed on to the *entrepreneurs*. The latter, however, were not required to pay interest for the period 1st–15th June on that part of their share which had not been claimed and paid up. The loan was for 16 years commencing on 1st March 1782, and bore interest at 4%. The interest for the period 1st March to 1st June accrued to the Swedish king. Of the Bargum loan, cf 125,000 had been repaid by 1781.

3 Nisbet-Bain, *Gustav III*, II, 258–259. The political situation in Europe in 1784 also did not favour a war with Denmark.

4 G.A. Amsterdam, Not. Arch., 12469–658.

5 Div. Doc., 32. Hope and Fizeaux had negotiated a 5% loan for Spain in 1782.

6 *Ibid.*, 33.

PAGE 84

1 Volkmar subscribed cf 250,000, Ten Kate & Berck cf 500,000 and Hope cf 275,000.

2 G.A. Amsterdam, Not. Arch., 12476–83. Dr.Sandor Baumgarten, 'Emprunts de Suède à Amsterdam,' *Tijdschrift voor Geschiedenis*, LXXVII (1964), 439–440.

3 Baumgarten, *ibid.*, 440. Regarding Liljencrantz's preference for Hasselgreen, see letter of 27th December 1786, from J. Andersson, Gothenburg, to Hope & Co., Amsterdam.

4 P.J.Blok, *Geschiedenis van het Nederlandsche Volk*, III (Leiden, 1914), 585.

5 Div. Doc., 50–51. The principal debenture bore the date 20th October 1784; the loan was for 15 years, commencing on 1st December 1784. The public were to be invited to subscribe during the month of February, and the loan was officially opened on 1st March 1785. The interest due on the bonds in the period 1st December 1784 to 1st March 1785, accrued to the Swedish Crown.

PAGE 85

1 The floating million was thus also included, so that the deductions from the shares taken by the *entrepreneurs* diminished.

2 Div. Doc., 49.

3 Div. Doc., 49. The *entrepreneurs* thus enjoyed a respite until 1st September.

4 Div. Doc., 49–50. The contracts with the Swedish Crown reveal that Fizeaux Grand & Co. became Henri Fizeaux & Co. on 1st January 1785. The change escaped the notice of Elias. (Elias, *Vroedschap*, II, 1057–1058).

5 Hope and Fizeaux's first instalment to Liljencrantz, of cf 250,000, was not paid until 10th March 1785, at the earliest.

6 Baumgarten, 'Emprunts de Suède,' 442. The text 'Nous appliquerons d'ailleurs au remboursement en question votre assignations sur nous ...' and, previously, '... et en les dirigeant, comme pour le premier million ...' shows clearly that we are concerned with the second million.

7 Baumgarten, *ibid.*, 442. Cf. previous note.

8 Baumgarten, *ibid.*, 442.

PAGE 86

1 Baumgarten, *ibid.*, 443.
2 Financial relations between the Swedish Crown and the house of Smets in Antwerp certainly existed in 1787.
3 The peace preliminaries were signed in Paris on 20th September 1785. Blok, *Geschiedenis van het Nederlandsche Volk*, III, 589.
4 The principal debenture was dated 12th December 1785. The loan bore interest at 4½% and was for a period of 15 years, commencing on 1st February 1786. G.A. Amsterdam, Not. Arch., 12481–9. The principal sum was to be furnished in four equal instalments during the months of January to April inclusive and was payable by 70-day drafts. Div. Doc., 68–69.
5 The contract with the *entrepreneurs* was signed on 31st December 1785. Div. Doc., 129–130.
6 Nisbet-Bain, *Gustavus III*, II, 5.

PAGE 87

1 Nisbet-Bain, *ibid.*, 289.
2 To the letters in 1786 Hope appended the name J.von Jacobsen. Letters in the same handwriting and dated 1788 and 1789, however, bear the signature of Jacob Andersson.
3 27th September 1786. J.Andersson, Gothenburg, in a letter to Hope & Co., Amsterdam.
4 Letter dated 27th December 1786, from J.Andersson, Gothenburg, to Hope & Co., Amsterdam.
5 M.Marion, *Histoire Financière de la France depuis 1715*, I (Paris, 1914), 31. The name of the intermediary in Paris was De Montessuy.
6 The balance consisted of 12,520 'paniers' or 1,513,793 Amsterdam pounds. The letter book refers to 1,252 paniers, but this is presumably due to an error in transcription since paniers weighing 600 kilograms do not exist. A weight of 60 pounds, however, is normal. (Information supplied by T.H.Kimm, Curator of the Niemeyer Netherlands Tobacological Museum, Groningen). Letter of 14th Augustus 1787 to Baron de Ruuth, P.C. '87, 86.
7 Letter of 19th June 1787 to Baron de Ruuth, P.C. '87, 4.
8 Letter of 19th June 1787 to Baron de Ruuth, P.C. '87, 4.

PAGE 88

1 Letter of 23rd June 1787 to Baron de Ruuth, P.C. '87, 6. Ferdinand Grand was also banker to the United States. Butterfield, *Diary of John Adams*, IV, 64.
2 Hope foresaw a fall in prices if the auction were publicly announced in advance.
3 Letter of 14th August 1787, to Baron de Ruuth, P.C. '87, 86 et seq. Four days later Hope wrote to say that a report had been received from Grand stating that the *Fermiers* had broken off the negotiations and had even refused to bid at the public auction. This auction had meanwhile been cancelled (letter of 18th August 1787 to Baron de Ruuth, P.C. '87, 95).
4 Letter of 7th July 1787 to Baron de Ruuth, P.C. '87, 26.
Letter of 17th July 1787 to Baron de Ruuth, P.C. '87, 43, 46 and 47.

PAGE 89

1 Letter of 14th August 1787 to Baron de Ruuth, P.C. '87, 90.

2 'La Couronne de Suède, S/Cte Courant de Tabac.' The account totalled cf 393,604.7.8. After deduction of Hope's costs, including those concerned with arranging the auction, the sale netted cf 210,801.5.0 for Cohen. The advantage to the latter lay in the fact that the import duty did not become due until the tobacco had been sold, thus avoiding a substantial loss of interest on the (high) *ad valorem* duty. Moreover, because tobacco was subject to a rapid loss in value (estimated at between 4% and 8% between the moment of importation and the moment of sale), the fact that the duty, *ad valorem*, did not become due until the time of sale was an advantage in itself. Cohen's ultimate plan was to supply much larger quantities of tobacco to Sweden. His correspondents there would store the tobacco in the Crown warehouses at the various ports during the period of freedom from duty, and would sell it from there in the presence of a customs officer, who would collect the duty from the purchasers. The plan misfired. Cohen was obliged to pay immediately and was later reimbursed. Faced with this situation, he declared that he could not compete with the tobacco smugglers. Letter of 16th February 1788 to Baron de Ruuth, P.C. '88, 162–164.

3 Letter of 23rd June 1787 to Baron de Ruuth, P.C. '87, 9.

4 Letter of 28th July 1787 to Baron de Ruuth, P.C. '87, 60–62. The repayment to Hasselgreen probably concerned the loan of 1776 (*vide* page 78).

PAGE 90

1 Letter of 28th July 1787 to Baron de Ruuth, P.C. '87, 62–63.

2 The conditions referred to here were incorporated, without modification, into the official contract dated 25th August 1787 (Div. Doc., 239). The principal debenture bore the date 8th August 1787. G.A. Amsterdam, Not. Arch., 12487–452. On 7th August, De Ruuth reported that the king had agreed to the conditions. Letter of 25th August 1787 to Baron de Ruuth, P.C. '87, 111.

3 Div. Doc., 235. The commission to be paid to the *entrepreneurs* was based on the sums converted or provided by them.

4 Letter of 1st December 1787 to Baron de Ruuth, P.C. '87, 298–299. This letter was despatched to Sweden by express messenger on the same day. A copy was sent by ordinary post on 4th December. Following publication of the *Berigt* (Report) of the loan by Hasselgreen, Hope repeated their objections. Letter of 3rd December 1787 to Baron de Ruuth, P.C. '87, 316.

PAGE 91

1 *Infra* Appendix C-II.

2 Letter of 5th January 1788 to Baron de Ruuth, P.C. '88, 15.

3 Elias, *Vroedschap*, II, 1058. In 1798 the outstanding portions of all Swedish loans floated in the Netherlands were merged into a single fund totalling cf 15,000,000, the interest on which was raised to 5%. The management of the fund was entrusted to the erstwhile competitors, Hogguer & Co. (successors to Hogguer Grand & Co.) and Jan and Carl Hasselgreen. The terms provided for half a million guilders of the fund to be repaid annually. The loans arranged by Hope and Fizeaux in the years 1784, 1786 and 1787 were embodied in the fund. When, in 1808, Sweden again became embroiled in a war with Russia, the Swedish government suspended the payment of interest and principal money on the fund in the Netherlands. The country's foreign loans were

reduced by two-thirds by the *riksdag* held at Orebrö in 1812, and the balance was subsequently abrogated. In 1814, following the Napoleonic wars, steps were taken in the Netherlands with a view to recouping the debt and the accumulated interest. A memorandum on the subject was sent to the Netherlands envoy in Stockholm. In this, the sum owing was stated to be cf 14,700,000. However, many bonds had been purchased for Swedish account since 1808 – at a low price, of course. Whether these had been bought by the Swedish government or by private investors was not clear. Of the managers of the fund in 1798, little remained: Hogguer & Co. had been completely liquidated, and Jan and Carl Hasselgreen had, according to the memorandum, 'lost all credit and substance, so that it cannot be anticipated that the public would willingly support the continuation of this intermediary.' In 1815 a meeting of those with interests in the Swedish loans was held, and this led to G.van de Poll being despatched to Sweden with instructions to plead the cause of the Dutch bondholders. He succeeded in moving the authorities to recognize one-third of the debt, repayment of which ensued in 1816. His efforts to obtain the interest owed failed, however: J.J.Weeveringh, *Handleiding tot de geschiedenis der Staatsschulden*, II (Haarlem, 1855), 781–783. Cf. instructions sent to 'Mr.de Zuylen' in Stockholm, 12th November 1814.

CHAPTER THREE

PAGE 93

1 Weeveringh, *Geschiedenis staatsschulden*, II, 708 et seq.
2 According to Elias (*Vroedschap*, II, 798 and 800), cf 4,000,000 was borrowed in 1769; cf 500,000 in 1770; and cf 1,000,000 in 1774. P.Katzenelsohn, *Zur Entwicklungsgeschichte der Finanzen Russlands*, I (Berlin, 1913), 104–105, quotes the following amounts: 1769, cf 500,000 at 3%; in 1773 and 1774 a total of cf 4,000,000 at 5%.
3 Katzenelsohn, *Entwicklungsgeschichte*, 105.
4 *Supra*, 77, 83.

PAGE 94

1 Letter of 9th April 1787 from R.Voûte to Hope & Co., Amsterdam.
2 *Grootboek* 1783: 219, 246, 270, 295, 314, 25, 39, 48, 84, 152, 156.
Grootboek 1784: 15, 24, 37, 45, 133, 146, 197, 229, 259.
Grootboek 1785: 24, 33, 34, 40, 45, 47, 87, 135, 145, 192, 263, 274, 292, 354.
Grootboek 1786: 7, 25, 33, 55, 47, 89, 134, 180, 179, 232, 260, 282, 318.
This summary appears more impressive than it really is. The majority of these accounts consisted merely of small balances left over from earlier transactions. These 'dead' accounts were carried forward year after year. In fact, business of significant proportions mainly related to a few houses in St.Petersburg, e.g. Thomson Peters Bonar & Co. and William Porter & Co. In Moscow, the only connexion of importance was with Thomson Rowand & Co. Voûte advised Hope to spread his business over a number of houses, so that if one should become bankrupt the loss could be made good out of profits from the other transactions; after all, 'the object of commission and interest on monies should be a sure profit.'
3 Letter of 18th December 1787 to Alexander Henry Sutherland, P.C. '87, 351.
4 Journal for 1787: 384, 427, 673, 696. Decree by Alexander Nicolayvich relating to the Sutherland affair, 28th April 1794.
5 Journal for 1786: 1934. Journal for 1787: 694, 696, 774, 783, 794, 848, 878, 907, 909, 916, 934, 938, 989, 1001, 1005, 1047, 1062, 1082, 1089, 1109, 1125, 1144.
6 *Infra*, 432–433.
7 *Grootboek* 1788: 74, 227, 288.
Grootboek 1789: 196.
Grootboek 1790: 161.
Grootboek 1791: 46, 275.
Grootboek 1792: 46, 328.

PAGE 95

1 Letter of 9th October 1787 to Richard Sutherland, 'Banquier de la Cour,' St.Petersburg, P.C. '87, 184.

2 *Infra*, 435.

3 Letter of 9th October 1787 to Richard Sutherland, St.Petersburg, P.C. '87, 186.

PAGE 96

1 Letter of 9th October 1787 to Richard Sutherland, St.Petersburg, P.C. '87, 187.

2 The members of the Committee for Foreign Loans in 1787 were: the Attorney General, Prince Vyazemsky; the Vice-Chancellor, Count Ostermann; the Director of the Assignat Bank, Count Shuvalov; and the President of the Board of Trade, Count Vorontsov.

3 The *entrepreneurs* were permitted to furnish their shares of the 5th December loan in three equal instalments in the months of March, April and May 1787. The names of the *entrepreneurs* were almost identical to those concerned with the contract of 30th July 1787 for a loan to Sweden (*supra*, 91). Interest payments were scheduled to commence on 1st February 1788; no capital repayments were permitted during the first six years. The debentures took the same form as those relating to the earlier loans made by De Smeth, and the securities provided were the same. Members of the public who purchased bonds from Hope & Co. received a commission of ¼%, but this was not deducted from the 1% bonus paid to the *entrepreneurs*. Hope commenced to accept investments on 5th December.

4 The conditions of the second loan largely corresponded to those of the first. The Company sent 'plans' of both loans to the Committee. A remarkable feature of these is that they refer to four monthly instalments by the *entrepreneurs*, whereas in fact the period was three months. Thus, the *entrepreneurs* were enabled to place both loans more quickly than was disclosed to the Committee by Hope. It may be that this stratagem afforded Hope some latitude in meeting their commitments to the Court, but whether or not this was its purpose is not known because the contracts between Hope and the Russian Court have not survived. 'Plan' for the first loan, letter of 6th December 1787 to R.Sutherland, St.Petersburg, P.C. '87, 314. 'Plan' for the second loan, letter of 11th December 1787 to Committee for Foreign Loans, St.Petersburg, P.C. '87, 331.

5 Letter of 11th December 1787 to R.Sutherland, St.Petersburg, P.C. '87, 329.

PAGE 98

1 Letter of 21st December 1787 to R.Sutherland, St.Petersburg, P.C. '87, 359.
The loan obtained from Goll was of cf 2,500,000 and was secured by debentures issued by the Bank of Vienna (Elias, *Vroedschap*, II, 1052). The first loan in this sum succeeded; a second, for the same amount, is reported to have been withdrawn owing to lack of interest. Letter of 22nd January 1788 to Beerend Roosen, Hamburg, P.C. '88, 94.
In correspondence with Sutherland, Hope referred to their Swedish loan of cf 2,500,000. In fact, this loan was for only cf 1,500,000, while Hasselgreen was in the market with a loan of cf 1,000,000 (*Supra*, 90). This suggests that Hope was unwilling to admit to Sutherland that another house was also busy with a loan for Sweden. Letter of 21st December 1787 to R.Sutherland, St.Petersburg, P.C. '87, 359.

2 Letter of 6th December 1787 to R.Sutherland, St.Petersburg, P.C. '87, 311.

Letter of 21st December 1787 to R.Sutherland, St.Petersburg, P.C. '87, 359.
Letter of 8th December 1787 to Kalichev, The Hague, P.C. '87, 317.
Letter of 11th December 1787 to the Committee, St. Petersburg, P.C. '87, 331.

3 Letter of 15th January 1788 to the Committee, St.Petersburg, P.C. '88, 53. The receipt of the approval was acknowledged in a postscript.

4 Letter of 11th December 1787 to R.Sutherland, St.Petersburg, P.C. '87, 329.

5 Letter of 18th December 1787 to J. and F.Baring, London, P.C. '87, 352.

PAGE 99

1 Letter of 6th December 1787 to the Committee, St.Petersburg, P.C. '87, 319.
Letter of 11th December 1787 to the Committee, St.Petersburg. P.C. '87, 331.
Letter of 11th December 1787 to Kalichev, The Hague, P.C. '87, 334.
The silence imposed on the parties to the contract will also have enabled the public subscription to the first loan to be completed smoothly, leaving minds free to concentrate on the second.
Van der Meulen, *Ministerie Van de Spiegel*, 349.

2 Letter of 18th December 1787 to A.H.Sutherland, London, P.C. '87, 351. Sutherland will also have had opponents among the members of the Committee for Foreign Loans. Vyazemsky was known to be opposed to loans from abroad. Katzenelsohn, *Entwicklungsgeschichte*, 106.

3 Letter of 8th December 1787 to Kalichev, The Hague, P.C. '87, 317.

4 Letter of 6th December 1787 to R.Sutherland, St.Petersburg, P.C. '87, 311.

5 Letter of 6th December 1787 to the Committee for Foreign Loans, P.C. '87, 319.

6 Letter of 21st December 1787 to R.Sutherland, St.Petersburg, P.C. '87, 359.

PAGE 100

1 Letter of 14th January 1788 to C.M.J.de Wolf, Antwerp, P.C. '88, 44.
Letter of 15th January 1788 to R.Sutherland, St.Petersburg, P.C. '88, 50.
The loan issued by De Wolf was ultimately fully subscribed. The proceeds were remitted to Hope & Co. and subsequently placed at Sutherland's disposal.
Grootboek 1788: 101, 222, 303; letter of 14th March 1788 to the Committee, St.Petersburg, P.C. '88, 252.
P J.van Winter, 'De Amerikaanse zaken van C.J.M.de Wolf,' *Mededelingen van de Koninklijke Vlaamse Academie voor Wetenschappen, Letteren en Schone Kunsten van België. Klasse der Letteren*, XXXII, ii (1970), 10, 14.

2 Letter of 19th February 1788 to R.Sutherland, St.Petersburg, P.C. '88, 171.

3 Letter of 19th February 1788 to R.Sutherland, St.Petersburg, P.C. '88, 171.

4 Letter of 15th January 1788 to R.Sutherland, St.Petersburg, P.C. '88, 50.
Letter of 15th January 1788 to the Committee, St.Petersburg, P.C. '88, 53.
Grootboek 1788: 133,322. *Grootboek* 1789: 56,265. *Grootboek* 1790: 113,312. *Grootboek* 1791: 90. Hope & Co. thus received a gross commission of 6½% which included 1% on the shares taken by the *entrepreneurs* (whose remuneration later rose to 1¾% and, later still, to 2%), ½% on the value of public subscriptions and ¼% for the brokers. Hope's share of both the first and second loans was cf 750,000. There are no details of the contracts for the third and fourth loans, and thus the Company's share in these is not known.

PAGE 101

1 Letter of 14th March 1788 to the Committee, St.Petersburg, P.C. '88, 252. The loan was for 10 years and the rate of interest 4½%. The interest was to be payable from 1st July 1788 and to accrue to the *entrepreneurs;* they were committed to furnish their portions of the loan in three equal instalments on 15th July, 15th August and 15th September. The *entrepreneurs* thus enjoyed a *douceur*. Cf. 'Plan' for this loan, enclosed with letter of 14th March to the Committee.

2 The name of Regny was mentioned in letters addressed by the Committee in St.Petersburg to Hope & Co. on 28th August and 8th September 1808. Sutherland's efforts to borrow money in Genoa had the approval of Hope, provided that the rate of interest did not exceed 4½%. Letter of 19th February 1788 to R.Sutherland, St.Petersburg, P.C. '88, 171.

PAGE 102

1 Letter of 25th March 1788 to Beerend Roosen, Hamburg, P.C. '88, 285.

2 Letter of 23rd November 1787 to J.Cambiasso, Leghorn, P.C. '87, 262. Cambiasso shrank from undertaking any business in which Sutherland was involved. Hope attributed this reticence to a lack of financial strength on the part of those who had acted for Sutherland in Amsterdam. In this, he was probably referring to De Smeth.

3 Letter of 22nd March 1788 to Kalichev, The Hague, P.C. '88, 280. J.Seton Watson, *The Russian Empire 1801–1917* (Oxford, 1967), 46–48.

4 Letter of 24th March 1788 to Kalichev, The Hague, P.C. '88, 283.
In addition to occupying the office of Advocate Fiscal to the Admiralty in Amsterdam, Joan Cornelis van der Hoop was a member of the Council appointed to assist the stadholder-admiral-general. He was on intimate terms with the partners in Hope & Co., and his son, Adriaan, became a partner in the Company in 1815. *Nieuw Nederlandsch Biografisch Woordenboek*, VI, 801–802.

5 Letter of 25th March 1788 to Kalichev, The Hague, P.C. '88, 284.
Letters of 25th and 28th March 1788 to J.&F. Baring, London, P.C. '88, 287, 296.
Letter of 29th March 1788 to J.C.van der Hoop, The Hague, P.C. '88, 392. Hope was fobbed off with references to 'the interests of the State.'

6 Letters of 2nd and 7th April 1788 to Kalichev, The Hague, P.C. '88, 310, 323.

PAGE 103

1 Letters of 29th March and 1st April 1788 to De Coninck & Reyersen, Copenhagen, P.C. '88, 301, 309; 4th April 1788 to Kalichev, The Hague, P.C. '88, 319.
A rate of 16½ shillings per ton per month had earlier been agreed in London; in the Republic this would be equal to about eleven guilders per last (of two tons). Insurance on the London market would cost ¾% per month. At the outset, when there seemed little prospect of obtaining the approval of the Netherlands government, Hope thought of proposing to De Coninck & Reyersen that they should purchase vessels in the Republic and sail them under the Danish flag. De Coninck & Reyersen supplied the Russian squadron with hardtack.

2 Nisbet-Bain, *Gustavus III*, II, 14–16.

3 The fifth loan ran for 12 years from 1st May 1789, and bore interest at 5%. The settlement period for the *entrepreneurs* commenced on 1st May and ended on 1st August. Hope undertook not to place any further loans before 1st September 1789 without the consent of the *entrepreneurs*.

PAGE 104

1 Letters of 25th and 29th September 1789 from H.Hope, Amsterdam, to Baron Sutherland, St.Petersburg. The *entrepreneurs* were thus two months in arrears according to the terms of the contract, which provided for payment in four monthly instalments in the period November to February. They received a bonus of 2 %. The loan was for twelve years commencing on 1st September 1789, but provision was made for repayment after seven years. Hope's share was cf 590,000, nearly one-third of the total sum.

2 Letter of 13th October 1789 from H.Hope, Amsterdam, to Baron Sutherland, St.Petersburg.

3 Letters of 10th and 24th November 1789 from H.Hope, Amsterdam, to Baron Sutherland, St.Petersburg.

4 Letter of 10th November 1789 from H.Hope, Amsterdam, to Baron Sutherland, St.Petersburg.

PAGE 105

1 Letter of 4th December 1789 from H.Hope, Amsterdam, to Baron Sutherland, St.Petersburg.

2 Letter of 25th December 1789 from H.Hope, Amsterdam, to Baron Sutherland, St.Petersburg. Count Vorontsov, in particular, objected to the commission paid to Hope. The contracts between Hope and the Russian Court are missing, so we do not know whether the figure of 6½ % included commission on interest and capital payments. This seems probable, however, because Hope here compares the Russian commission with the Polish figure of 6 % plus 1 % for interest payments and 2 % for repayments of capital (the last figure is incorrect: Hope received only 1 % on capital repayments). Even if the commission paid to Hope by the Russians did not include remuneration for such payments, the comparison would be unfortunate. We must assume that the total comprised 5 % on the sum of the loan, 1 % on capital repayments and ½ % on interest payments.

If a separate commission of 1 % on capital repayments had been granted, this would have been payable only from the eighth to the twelfth years – assuming that the loan was for twelve years with provision for repayment after seven years. On the basis of a five per cent loan, payment of the commission on the repayment of capital at the commencement of the loan, instead of after the eighth year, would have given Hope a profit on interest of ½ %. For a 12-year loan, the half per cent on the interest payments, if paid on the principal sum, is equal to something like 1½ % on the interest due if this were paid annually. The *grootboeken* contain no reference to commission on interest paid; capital repayments were then not yet due. Hope's reasons for not undertaking any loans except those for Russia are self-explanatory: the Company worked with a fixed group of *entrepreneurs* who could only place a certain number of bonds and, as our story shows, were kept busy enough doing that.

3 Letter of 25th December 1789 from H.Hope, Amsterdam, to Baron Sutherland, St.Petersburg. As the preceding note shows, we have no information concerning the terms of payment agreed between Hope and the Russian Court. It is conceivable that Hope requested indulgence when the *entrepreneurs* got into arrears with their payments for the fifth loan. A similar indulgence in respect of the sixth loan would largely have benefited Hope because, under the relevant contract, the *entrepreneurs*

were committed to pay interest on their shares 'beyond the Month previously laid down, in which the monies are to be furnished.'

PAGE 106

1 Contract for the seventh loan dated 16th February 1790. The period of the loan commenced on 1st January 1790. The *entrepreneurs* were obliged to furnish their shares in the months of March, April, May and June. Provision was made for repayment after seven years. Hope, whose share amounted to cf 800,000, undertook not to negotiate any fresh loans before 1st July 1790.

2 Contract for the eighth loan, dated 13th August 1790. The period of the loan commenced on 1st May 1790. The period for settlement by the *entrepreneurs* ran from October 1790 to February 1791 inclusive. Hope undertook not to float further loans until 1st March 1791. Provision was made for the loan to be repaid after seven years. Hope did not have a share in this loan.

3 Contract for the ninth loan, dated 6th January 1791. A 12-year loan, this commenced officially on 1st August 1790, which fact reveals that it had been arranged some time before. Here, too, repayment was allowed only after seven years. The *entrepreneurs* had from March to June inclusive to furnish their shares. No fresh loan might be floated until 1st July 1791 without the approval of the *entrepreneurs*. The interest rate was 5%.

PAGE 107

1 Contract for the tenth and eleventh loans, dated 28th February 1791. Both were for twelve years, the tenth loan commencing on 1st November 1790 and the eleventh on 1st February 1791. It appears that the second portion remaining from the previous year was linked to a new loan. Repayment was possible after seven years. The *entrepreneurs* had from May to October inclusive to meet their commitments. The loans bore interest at 5%. No fresh loans were permitted before 1st November 1791 without the approval of the *entrepreneurs*. Hope's share of these loans totalled cf 325,000.

2 Contract for the twelfth and thirteenth loans, dated 18th July 1791. These were for 12 years, the twelfth commencing on 1st September 1791 and the thirteenth on 1st November 1791. Provision was made for repayment after seven years. The period for settlement by the *entrepreneurs* ran from September 1791 to February 1792, inclusive. The interest rate was 5%. Hope undertook not to float any new loans until 1st March 1792 without the approval of the *entrepreneurs*. Hope's share was again cf 325,000.

3 Contract for the fourteenth and fifteenth loans, dated 21st December 1791. Both were for twelve years commencing on 1st February 1792. Repayment after seven years was provided for. The *entrepreneurs* had from 1st February to 30th June to meet their commitments. The loans bore interest at 4%. Any fresh loan by Hope before 1st July 1792 was made subject to the approval of the *entrepreneurs*. Hope's share of these loans totalled cf 600,000.

4 Manger, *Recherches*, 69–71.

5 G.W.Vreede, *Mr.Laurens Pieter van de Spiegel en zijne tijdgenooten* (*1737–1800*), IV (Middelburg, 1877), 386. This reference concerns a memorandum from Henry Hope to Lord Auckland, British envoy in The Hague.

PAGE 108

1 Van Winter, *Aandeel*, II, 156, 157, 161. The fact that the American diplomat Short knew about the fourteenth and fifteenth loans on 28th December 1791 (page 157, note 1) was not so surprising, since the contract had been signed on 21st December. The commencement of the official period of the loan on 1st February 1792 was not of major significance.
Van Winter, 'Zaken C.J.M.de Wolf,' 15.

PAGE 109

1 Contract for the sixteenth and seventeenth loans dated 6th August 1792. Both were for a period of twelve years commencing on 1st June 1792, with provision for repayment after seven years. The period for settlement by the *entrepreneurs* was from September 1792 to April 1793, inclusive. The loans bore interest at 4½%. The minimum selling price was fixed at 99½% for these loans also. Hope did not participate financially.

2 24th October 1793, Memorandum from R.Voûte, St.Petersburg, to Count Samaylov. St.Petersburg.

CHAPTER FOUR

PAGE 111

1 27th July 1793, Letter from R.Voûte, Warsaw, to J.Williams Hope, Amsterdam.
2 R.H.Lord, *The Second Partition of Poland* (Cambridge, Mass., 1915), 460.

PAGE 112

1 J.Rutkowski, *Histoire Economique de la Pologne avant les partages* (Paris, 1922), 232.
2 Constitution of the *sejm* held in Warsaw in 1776, entitled 'L'assurance de Nos dettes royales.'
3 Rutkowski, *Histoire Economique de la Pologne*, 26, 231–232.
4 G.A. Amsterdam, 'Handel en Nijverheid,' N 12.16.03.
5 *Grootboek* 1777: 299, 421. Cf. ordinance by King Stanislaw for the loan of 1786. The *grootboeken* for the years 1777 to 1787, inclusive, reveal that interest and capital were duly paid.

PAGE 114

1 Constitution of the *sejm* held in Grodno on 4th October 1784, entitled 'Etablissement du fonds pour payer le reste de Nos dettes royales.'
2 Elias, *Vroedschap*, I, 333–334. The Van Hoorn loan bore interest at 5%. For the 1786 loan, the Court Bankers furnished Hope with drafts in favour of Gülcher & Mulder; this house, as we shall see, also negotiated loans for the Polish magnates.
3 From the protocol of the *Commission Economique du Trésor de Sa Majesté*, dated 5th January 1785.
4 Excerpt from the proceedings of the session of the Chamber of Finances of the King held on 22nd April 1785.
5 Declaration by the Treasury Committee, made at the request of the Economic Committee of His Majesty, on 13th August 1785.

PAGE 115

1 Lord, *Second Partition*, 71, 72.
2 Letter of 31st December 1785 from King Stanislaw, Warsaw, to De Wickedé, Amsterdam. As a young man, the king had travelled in western Europe.
3 Letters of 15th February and 19th March 1786 from King Stanislaw, Warsaw, to De Wickedé, Amsterdam.
4 Contract dated 7th April 1786. The *entrepreneurs* were committed to settle in three equal instalments on 1st August, 1st October and 1st December. If, on 15th May, the principal obligation was not properly signed, or the contract with De Wickedé was

not in order, the *entrepreneurs* were to be relieved of their obligations and Hope was to pay them ¼% of the sum subscribed, by way of compensation for the risks borne by them. The latter provision clearly served as a lever in the negotiations with De Wickedé. In the event, the contract with him was not signed until 5th May 1786. Hope's share of the loan was cf 500,000.

PAGE 116

1 The mortgages in the principal debenture dated 21st April 1786 now comprised:
1. The *subsidium charitativum*, amounting to seven million Polish guilders;
2. 'All the wealth and property, present and future, which belongs to us';
3. The income paid to the king by both Treasuries, amounting to four million Polish guilders per annum.
Repayment was to be effected in 20 half-yearly instalments, commencing on 1st July 1787.
2 350,000 ducats at cf 5.5.0 (the rate of exchange of the ducat for the purpose of the loan of 1777): cf 1,837,500
94% of cf 2,000,000, less 1% of 7 months' interest (on 1st January 1787): cf 1,871,167.
3 *Grootboek* 1787: 128. Also Receipt dated 3rd June 1786, from Tepper and Blanc for the proceeds of the 1786 loan.
4 Letters of 15th February and 19th March 1786 from King Stanislaw, Warsaw, to De Wickedé, Amsterdam.
5 Hope suffered a small loss in connexion with the terms of settlement for the *entrepreneurs*, but this was more than compensated by the favourable interest computation.
6 Letters of 24th and 25th June 1787 from Hope & Co., Amsterdam, to De Wickedé, Amsterdam, P.C. '87, 9, 11.

PAGE 117

1 Letter of 25th June 1787 to King Stanislaw, Warsaw, P.C. '87, 13.
Letter of 4th January 1788 to King Stanislaw, Warsaw, P.C. '88, 10.
Letter of 4th January 1788 to De Wickedé, Amsterdam, P.C. '88, 11.
2 *Grootboek* 1790: 177.
3 Rutkowski, *Histoire Economique de la Pologne*, 232–233.
4 Lord, *Second Partition*, 125.

PAGE 118

1 *Ibid.*, 287.
2 *Ibid.*, 391.
3 W.Roosegaarde Bisschop, *De opkomst der Londensche geldmarkt 1640–1826* (The Hague, 1896), 98–99.
4 K.L.Blum, *Ein russischer Staatsmann: des Grafen Jakob Johann Sievers Denkwürdigkeiten*, III (Leipzig and Heidelberg, 1858), 59–60, 109–110.

PAGE 119

1 Letter of 27th July 1793 from R.Voûte, Warsaw, to J.Williams Hope, Amsterdam.
2 Letter of 19th August 1793 from R.Voûte, Warsaw, to J.Williams Hope, Amsterdam.

PAGE 120

1 Lord, *Second Partition*, 474–475.

2 Letter of 19th August 1793 from, R.Voûte, Moscow, to J.Williams Hope, Amsterdam.

PAGE 121

1 Voûte was mistaken about this. As we saw earlier, the instalments of interest and principal were guaranteed by the *sejm:* in other words, by the Republic itself. Subsequent events also conflict with Voûte's statement.

CHAPTER FIVE

PAGE 123

1 *Grootboek* 1788: 32 and 322; *grootboek* 1789: 32, 102; *grootboek* 1790: 28, 291; *grootboek* 1791: 28; *grootboek* 1792: 28, 156; *grootboek* 1793: 28, 167, 372. Besides cochineal, Hope & Co. shipped sugar, diamonds, tea, indigo, madder and drugs to Thomson Rowand, the cost of which was remitted. Thomson Rowand did not ship goods to Hope. This underlines the latter company's role as importers, reference to which is made on pages 125–126.

PAGE 124

1 Documents and correspondence between the partners in Thomson Rowand & Co. and those of Rowand Carr & Co., and correspondence with Raikes & Co. All were enclosed with Voûte's letter of 30th August 1793 to John Williams Hope. Hope's confidential agent, Le Chevalier, who had obtained foreign experience while working for De Coninck in Copenhagen, offered to join Thomson Rowand & Co. as a clerk. Letter of 2nd January 1792 from T.Le Chevalier, Suyderwoude, Monnikendam, to Hope & Co., Amsterdam.

2 Letter of 26th August 1793 from Robert Voûte, Moscow, to J.Williams Hope, Amsterdam.

PAGE 125

1 *Infra*, Appendix D-IV.

2 Letter of 4th January 1794 from R.Voûte, Moscow, to Hope & Co., Amsterdam. Letter of 9th January 1794 from R.Voûte, Moscow, to G.Thomson Rowand & Co., Moscow.
W.Treue, *Wirtschaftsgeschichte der Neuzeit* (Stuttgart, 1962), 279. Under the ukase of April 1793, goods already in Russia were allowed to be sold until the end of January 1794. The Russian merchants were afraid that they would not be able to dispose of their stocks in time, and they used this as yet another excuse for not paying their debts on the due date. An edict issued at the beginning of January 1794 increased the list of prohibited articles, but extended the sale period until March (in his letter of 9th January, Voûte states that the extension was up to 1st July 1794).

3 Letter of 16th September 1793 from R.Voûte, Moscow, to J.Williams Hope, Amsterdam.

PAGE 126

1 In the light of the considerably more favourable assessment of the Moscow

merchants contained in Appendix D-IV, Voûte's opinion in this case seems extremely pessimistic.

2 Letters of 26th and 29th August 1793 from R.Voûte, Moscow, to J.Williams Hope, Amsterdam.
On 9th September, Voûte reported to John Williams Hope that he had extracted from Gusyatnikov a promise to meet the claims of his Amsterdam creditors over a period of four years, during which they would receive interest at 5% per annum on the sums owed. Voûte is believed to have acted also for the house of Braunsberg & Co. of Amsterdam in this matter.

PAGE 127

1 Letter of 2nd September 1793 from R.Voûte, Moscow, to J.Williams Hope, Amsterdam. The disparaging remarks concerning his profession were the more hurtful to Voûte because not only had he withdrawn from his own firm, Jan Jacob Voûte & Sons, at the end of 1792, but, indeed had abandoned the profession of broker early in 1788 in order to devote himself to financial and economic matters. According to Voûte, one of the partners of Tamesz, a man named Pipping, had gone bankrupt in St.Petersburg and had then become a broker, before finally being admitted to the firm through the influence of his father-in-law, Bacharacht. The house seemed to Voûte to be an 'intrigue continuelle.' Voûte's vanity at times took on a childish note. For example, on 28th December 1793, he wrote to John Williams Hope: 'Mr.Van de Spiegel (the Grand Pensionary) wrote to Hogguer (the Republic's envoy in St.Petersburg) saying that he was vexed to hear that I had departed without taking leave of him, and he appears to have said a lot of nice things about me.'

2 Letter of 12th September 1793 from R.Voûte, Moscow, to J.Williams Hope, Amsterdam. Deeds dated 11th September 1793. Carr would continue to receive expenses until 1st October, in addition to which he would receive from Rowand Carr & Co. a sum of two thousand roubles; this would either be paid in cash or deducted from any sum which he might owe to that house. He was also empowered to conclude for his own account a number of Rowand Carr's deals which he had personally handled. Carr purchased the furniture and fittings of the St.Petersburg house for 2,500 roubles. The company coach became the property of Hawes and Grant. Carr's allowance for household expenses was 5,000 roubles per annum.

3 Letter of 19th August 1793 from R.Voûte, Moscow, to J.Williams Hope, Amsterdam.

4 Letters of 16th, 19th and 28th September 1793 from R.Voûte, Moscow, to J.Williams Hope, Amsterdam. Grant's recalcitrance served to lower Voûte's opinion of him. Grant, he said, still possessed 'genius,' but his principles were not particularly high; his father had been 'un mauvais sujet,' and such an example always rubbed off.

5 Letters of 29th August and 12th September 1793 from R.Voûte, Moscow, to J.Williams Hope, Amsterdam.
Letter of 28th September 1793 from R.Voûte, St.Petersburg, to J.Williams Hope, Amsterdam. It was a fortunate coincidence that Voûte's departure from Moscow was delayed, because just then the new Turkish ambassador passed through that city on his way to take up his appointment following the conclusion of peace between the Porte and Russia. Because of the size of his entourage – 'sa cohorte détestable,' as Voûte described it – the ambassador needed 1,000 horses at every staging post,

which meant a total of 22,000 for the journey from Moscow to St.Petersburg. Porter proved to be an agreeable travelling companion except when he became involved in arguments about payment for the horses, for then his parsimony could be positively embarrassing.

PAGE 128

1 'Stukken aangaande de vordering op M.G.Trosien' (Documents relating to the claim against M.G.Trosien). 18th April 1793: Power of attorney granted by J.&C. Hasselgreen. A.Vereul and the Voûte brothers of Amsterdam to Messrs. Amburger & Son, Messrs. François Raimbert & Co. and Messrs. Rowand Carr & Co., all of St.Petersburg (Voûte archives). These houses reported to the creditors that they could anticipate receiving the remaining 50% of the monies owing to them when the greatest single debtor in Russia, i.e. Trosien, met his commitments. It is thus clear that a 50% payment had been made.

2 Letter of 4th June 1793 from the agents appointed by De Bary & Co., Amsterdam, to M.G.Trosien, St.Petersburg.

PAGE 129

1 Letter of 30th September 1793 from R.Voûte, St.Petersburg, to J.Williams Hope, Amsterdam. Mercury was already being used for the treatment of syphilis.

2 Voûte wrote concerning the commission on the 13th and 14th loans. These, however, do not constitute a pair, for the contract for the 13th was dated 18th July 1791 and that for the 14th was entered into on 21st December 1791. The commission, however, was disputed on the grounds that Sutherland had died prior to the official date of authorization for the two loans; this applies to the 14th and 15th loans, but not to the 13th. (*Infra*, Appendix D-1).

3 Letter of 30th September 1793 from R.Voûte, St.Petersburg, to J.Williams Hope, Amsterdam.
E.Amburger, *Geschichte der Behördenorganisation Russlands von Peter dem grossen bis 1917* (Leiden, 1966), 20, 75, 132.
K.Waliszewski, *Autour d'un trône, Cathérine II de Russie, ses collaborateurs* (Paris, 1894), 15, 231.
G.Soloveytchik, *Potemkin* (London, 1938), 40, 66, 100.
While Voûte, in his correspondence, usually referred to Samaylov, he occasionally spelled the name Samoylov. The former spelling has been used in this chapter.

4 Letter of 10th October 1793 from R.Voûte, St.Petersburg, to J.Williams Hope, Amsterdam.
Letter of 6th February 1794 from R.Voûte, St.Petersburg, to Hope & Co., Amsterdam.

5 Letter of 28th November 1793 from R.Voûte, St.Petersburg, to J.Williams Hope, Amsterdam.
Waliszewski, *Autour d'un trône*, 158–165.
Amburger, *Geschichte Behördenorganisation*, 85–86.

PAGE 130

1 Concerning Markov: Waliszewski, *Autour d'un trône*, 20 et seq., 27.
Waliszewski describes Ostermann as 'une nullité absolue' (12, 21, 40). In F.Golovkine's *La cour et le règne de Paul Ier* (Paris, 1905), Ostermann is referred to as 'un chef pompeux et pédantesque.'

2 Amburger, *Geschichte Behördenorganisation*, 229.
K. Waliszewski, *Le fils de la grande Cathérine, Paul Ier* (Paris, 1912), 145.
Alexander Zablukov is described in both works as the president of the 'Manufacturers College,' a State Commission. According to Amburger, he held the office from 1797–1798 and again from 1799–1800. Voûte obviously received a hospitable welcome from Zablukov. On 16th October 1794, Bagge Van Eyssel & Co. of St.Petersburg informed Voûte, who by then was back in Holland, that Zablukov's eldest daughter hoped that the French would invade Holland, because then 'Mister Voot' would return to Russia.
3 Letter of 15th March 1794 from R.Voûte, St.Petersburg, to Hope & Co., Amsterdam.

PAGE 131

1 Letters of 8th and 29th January, 6th February and 15th March 1794 from R.Voûte, St.Petersburg, to Hope & Co., Amsterdam. According to Voûte, Ritter received 5,000 roubles for his services. A week later, however, he approached the bank with a request for the repayment of the sum which he had advanced, at the rate of 10,000 roubles per week. 'And to think that this was the man who asserted that Hope & Co. had made millions out of Russia,' Voûte scornfully added.
Letter of 31st January 1794 from R.Voûte, St.Petersburg, to Hope & Co., Amsterdam.
2 Letter of 28th November 1793 from R.Voûte, St.Petersburg, to J.Williams Hope, Amsterdam.
Letter of 6th February 1794 from R.Voûte, St.Petersburg, to Hope & Co., Amsterdam.

PAGE 132

1 Letter of 28th November 1793 from R.Voûte, St.Petersburg, to J.Williams Hope, Amsterdam.
Letter of 15th March 1794 from R.Voûte, St.Petersburg, to Hope & Co., Amsterdam.
'Considerations favourable to Baron Sutherland,' dated 7th March 1794, paragr. 7.
Sutherland was said to have left only 230,000 roubles.
2 Letters of 23rd October and 28th November 1793.
According to Voûte, little was done during the brief summer to lay in stocks for the winter.
3 Letter of 10th December 1793 from R.Voûte, St.Petersburg, to J.Williams Hope, Amsterdam.
4 Letter of 28th December 1793 from R.Voûte, St.Petersburg, to J.Williams Hope, Amsterdam.

PAGE 133

1 Letters of 30th September and 4th October 1793 from R.Voûte, St.Petersburg, to J.Williams Hope, Amsterdam.
Golovkine, *Le règne de Paul Ier*, 373 note 1.
Blum, *Sievers*, III, 98.
2 Letter of 4th October 1793 from R.Voûte, St.Petersburg, to J.Williams Hope, Amsterdam.
3 Letter of 28th October 1793 from R.Voûte, St.Petersburg, to J.Williams Hope, Amsterdam.

Waliszewski, *Autour d'un trône*, 396.
Soloveytchik, *Potemkin*, 168–169.
Blum, *Sievers*, III, 99.
Count Branicki had lost 65,000 ducats when Tepper went bankrupt.

PAGE 134

1 Letter of 28th October 1793 from R.Voûte, St.Petersburg, to J.Williams Hope, Amsterdam. The ducat was to be valued at 108 *stuivers* for the purpose of the loans. Voûte was wrong about the ban imposed on foreign loans; such a measure was considered, but did not become law. Van der Meulen, *Ministerie Van de Spiegel*, 399–400.

PAGE 135

1 Memorandum dated 21st October 1793 from R.Voûte for the benefit of Count Zubov.
2 *Supra*, 116, note 1.

PAGE 136

1 R.H.Lord, 'The third partition of Poland,' *Slavonic Review*, III, 9 (1925), 480.
Letter of 23rd October 1793 from R.Voûte, St.Petersburg, to J.Williams Hope, Amsterdam.
2 Letter of 30th October 1793 from Voûte, St.Petersburg, to J.Williams Hope, Amsterdam.
3 Letter of 31st October 1793 from R.Voûte, St.Petersburg, to J.Williams Hope, Amsterdam.

PAGE 137

1 Letter of 3rd/4th December 1793 from R.Voûte, St.Petersburg, to J.Williams Hope, Amsterdam.
2 Letters of 3rd, 6th, 10th and 14th December 1793 from R.Voûte, St.Petersburg, to J.Williams Hope, Amsterdam.
3 Letters of 14th and 28th December 1793 from R.Voûte, St.Petersburg, to J.Williams Hope, Amsterdam. These loans appear in the *grootboeken* of Hope & Co., thus proving that the Company did finally undertake them.
Letter of 13th May 1794 from R.Voûte, St.Petersburg, to Hope & Co., Amsterdam.
4 Letters of 13th and 27th November 1793 from R.Voûte, St.Petersburg, to J. Williams Hope, Amsterdam.
Letter of 25th December 1793 from R.Voûte, St.Petersburg, to J. Williams Hope, Amsterdam.
Letter of 18th January 1794 from R.Voûte, St.Petersburg, to Hope & Co., Amsterdam.
Because Labouchère's handwriting was scarcely legible, Samaylov instructed one of his subordinates to make a copy of Labouchère's letter.

PAGE 138

1 Letter of 18th January 1794 from R.Voûte, St.Petersburg, to Hope & Co., Amsterdam.

2 Letter of 10th December 1793 from R.Voûte, St.Petersburg, to Hope & Co., Amsterdam.

3 Letters of 18th and 22nd January 1794 from R.Voûte, St.Petersburg, to Hope & Co., Amsterdam.

PAGE 139

1 Letter of 22nd/23rd January 1794 from R.Voûte, St.Petersburg, to Hope & Co., Amsterdam.
Concerning Guthrie: Waliszewski, *Le fils de la grande Cathérine*, 208.

2 Letter of 29th January 1794 from R.Voûte, St.Petersburg, to Hope & Co., Amsterdam.
Chinese rhubarb possessed laxative properties and was widely used as a medicine at the time of Voûte's sojourn in Russia. It was brought from China, in the dried state, by caravans. The state had a monopoly on its sale (information supplied by Dr.J.H.Zwaving, senior lecturer at the *Laboratorium voor Farmacognosie en Galenische Farmacie* of the University of Groningen).

3 October and November 1793: Two memoranda (one of which is in the handwriting of R.Voûte) concerning De Bary & Co.'s claims against M.G.Trosien.
Letters of 29th January and 6th February 1794 from R.Voûte, St.Petersburg, to Hope & Co., Amsterdam.

PAGE 140

1 Letter of 31st January 1794 from R.Voûte, St.Petersburg, to Hope & Co., Amsterdam.

2 Letters of 31st January and 6th February 1794 from R.Voûte, St.Petersburg, to Hope & Co., Amsterdam.

3 'Essay sur les Variations survenues dans le cours du change de la Russie avec la Hollande et l'Angleterre et ses suites,' dated 3rd December 1793.

PAGE 141

1 For example, in a letter of 6th February 1794 from R.Voûte, St.Petersburg, to Hope & Co., Amsterdam.
Letters of 18th and 22nd February 1794 from R.Voûte, St.Petersburg, to Hope & Co., Amsterdam.
It is open to doubt whether the principles underlying Voûte's argument were entirely original. The idea of expanding the exploitation of the mineral wealth was also developed by William Porter in two of his letters, one of 1st October 1793 to John Williams Hope and the other of 29th October 1793 to Sir Francis Baring.
Voûte also championed the cause of the serfs. He recommended that they be given the certainty of some property, however little, because they would till the soil better if they could be sure of sharing in the fruits of their labours.

2 Letter of 6th February 1794 from R.Voûte, St.Petersburg, to Hope & Co., Amsterdam.

PAGE 142

1 Blum, *Sievers*, III, 475–480. The king's debts totalled 34 million Polish guilders, which was equivalent to cf 10 million. Thus, one Dutch guilder can be said to have been worth 3.4 Polish guilders.

2 Letter of 19th August 1794 from Charles de Glave Kolbielski, Amsterdam, to Thomas Christie, London. A.F.Pribram and E.Fischer, 'Ein politischer Abenteurer (Karl Glave Kolbielski, 1752–1831),' *Akademie der Wissenschaften in Wien, Philosophisch-historische Klasse*, *Sitzungsberichte*, Band 216, Abhandlung v (1937). Sievers is believed to have fallen from favour because he was too lenient towards the growing anti-Russian demonstrations. Meisner and his associate, Hasselgreen, who had had close ties with Sievers, temporarily lost some of their influence following Sievers's dismissal. The consignments of ducats from Hope & Co. served to keep Igelström out of Meisner's hands for quite a long time, but when a consignment of 30,000 ducats from the Company failed to materialize in time, Igelström was forced to fall back on Meisner. Letters of 8th, 10th, 12th and 26th February 1794 from R.Voûte, St.Petersburg, to Hope & Co., Amsterdam. Concerning James Durno, British Consul in Memel: Dietrich Gerhard, *England und der Aufstieg Russlands* (Munich and Berlin, 1933), 299, note 77.

3 Letters of 6th and 12th February 1794 from R.Voûte, St.Petersburg, to Hope & Co., Amsterdam. Voûte also delivered to Samaylov and Zubov memoranda in his own handwriting on this subject (both were dated 10th February). After the failure of the transaction with Hope & Co., Igelström sent Charles de Glave Kolbielski, a politico-financial adventurer in the service of the Polish government, to Holland in the hope of achieving a resumption of the negotiations. The Polish rebellion, however, brought these discussions to an end (Pribram and Fischer, 'Politischer Abenteurer,' 36). Kolbielski asserted that he had played a major role in the negotiation of the loans to the Republic of Poland and to its king, and of many Dutch loans to Polish magnates (*ibid.*, 30, 31, note 13). In a letter to Thomas Christie in London, Kolbielski referred specifically to the loan of cf 3,055,555 to the Republic of Poland through Hogguer Grand & Co. This was negotiated in 1790. In August 1794 we find Kolbielski in England, where he approached Thomas Christie on the subject of a loan to Russia. He proposed a loan of 12 million guilders, half to be furnished in cash and the balance in Dutch bonds relating to loans to Polish magnates, which had fallen to 30–40% below par as a result of the political situation and could thus be bought cheaply. The Russian government, which was in a position to sequestrate the mortgaged estates at any time, would have to accept the bonds at their par value. Under Kolbielski's plan, Hope & Co. would float the loan, half of the sum of which would ostensibly be subscribed by dummy investors in St.Petersburg, who would then privately exchange their Polish bonds for Russian bonds. Hope would receive the normal commission on the loan, but the conversion of the bonds relating to the Polish magnates would have to be effected without the intermediary of the Company. The necessary capital would have to come from English investors, and Kolbielski and his associates (who were probably senior officials) would be content with a small percentage.

Christie rejected the plan on the grounds that loans to foreign countries were not very popular in England where, moreover, there was general abhorrence of Empress Catherine for her policies towards Poland. Christie also felt that the proposal was unfair to Hope & Co., who would only be in nominal control of a transaction of which the salient details remained hidden from them. He was sure that Hope's friends in London would not accept such a situation. At the precise moment at which Christie wrote this, the Company was engaged in transferring the focal point of its operations from Amsterdam to London.

Letters of 16th September, 20th and 31st October 1794 from Thomas Christie, London, to Charles de Glave Kolbielski, Kassel.

4 Letter of 12th February 1794 from R.Voûte, St.Petersburg, to Hope & Co., Amsterdam.

5 Letters of 14th and 19th February 1794 from R.Voûte, St.Petersburg, to Hope & Co., Amsterdam.

PAGE 143

1 The sum to be converted was now estimated at cf 700,000. The account relating to the 1786 negotiation for the Polish Crown contains an entry dated 1st July 1793 covering a principal repayment of cf 100,000. This payment passed via Meisner; *grootboek* of 1794: 87 and 331. A half-year's interest was paid on 1st July, also via Meisner.

2 Letter of 19th February 1794 from R.Voûte, St.Petersburg, to Hope & Co., Amsterdam. The subscriptions were so slow in coming that the *entrepreneurs* were unable to meet their commitments to Hope & Co.

3 Letter of 22nd February 1794 from R.Voûte, St.Petersburg, to Hope & Co., Amsterdam.

4 Letter of 25th February 1794 from R.Voûte, St.Petersburg, to Hope & Co., Amsterdam.

5 It follows from this that, in contrast to the current versions, Henry Hope did not personally visit Russia to bring about the initial loan to that country. A somewhat obscure version appears in Elias, *Vroedschap*, II, 986.

PAGE 144

1 At the time of Voûte's sojourn, the Russians still used the 'old style' Julian calendar, which between 1700 and 1800 lagged eleven days behind the 'new style' Gregorian calender then in general use in western Europe. Under the Russian system of dating, the carnival began on 14th February. Except where otherwise indicated, the dates referred to in this chapter are in accordance with the 'new style.'

PAGE 145

1 Sutherland, Browne and Whishaw were said to have failed to comply with an earlier instruction from Hope & Co. to invest certain funds in bank debentures, with the result that the sum involved came to be among Hope's claims following the bankruptcy. Letter of 20th October 1807 from Hope & Co., Amsterdam, to Matthiessen & Sillem, Hamburg.

Letter of 7th March 1794 from W.Whishaw, St.Petersburg, to Hope & Co., Amsterdam.

Letter of 7th March 1794 from W.Whishaw, St.Petersburg, to R.Voûte, St.Petersburg.

7th March 1794: 'Avis au sujet de la prétention de la Couronne sur la masse du feu Baron Sutherland.'

7th March 1794: 'Considerations favourable to Sutherland' (in Voûte's handwriting).

2 Letter of 7th/8th March 1794 from R.Voûte, St.Petersburg, to Hope & Co., Amsterdam.

3 Letter of 8th/9th March 1794 from R.Voûte, St.Petersburg, to Hope & Co., Amsterdam.

4 Letter of 11/13th March 1794 from R.Voûte, St.Petersburg, to Hope & Co., Amsterdam.

Letter of 11th March 1794 from W.Whishaw, St.Petersburg, to Hope & Co., Amsterdam.

5 Letters of 13th and 15th March 1794 from R.Voûte, St.Petersburg, to Hope & Co., Amsterdam.

PAGE 146

1 Letter of 5th March 1794 from R.Voûte, St.Petersburg, to Hope & Co., Amsterdam. Lord, 'Third Partition of Poland,' 482.

2 Letters of 13th March and 2nd May 1794 from R.Voûte, St.Petersburg, to Hope & Co., Amsterdam.

3 Letters of 31st March, 7th and 9th April 1794, from R.Voûte, Moscow, to Hope & Co., Amsterdam.

PAGE 147

1 Letter of 17th April 1794 from R.Voûte, St.Petersburg, to Hope & Co., Amsterdam. In a moment of aberration, Voûte wrote: 'the prophet Elisha.' 1 Kings, 17:6.

2 Letter of 17th April 1794 from R.Voûte, St.Petersburg, to Hope & Co., Amsterdam.

PAGE 148

1 Letter of 18th April 1794 from R.Voûte, St.Petersburg, to Hope & Co., Amsterdam. Concerning Sir Samuel Rogerson: Golovkine, *Le règne de Paul Ier*, 200–201.

2 Letter of 26th April 1794 from R.Voûte, St. Petersburg, to Hope & Co., Amsterdam. Letter of 26th April 1794 from R.Voûte, St.Petersburg, to Henry and J.W.Hope, Amsterdam. Whishaw reported that 20% could be paid out in May and a further 20% two or three months later. Letter of 5th May 1794 from W.Whishaw, St.Petersburg, to Hope & Co., Amsterdam.

PAGE 149

1 Letter of 26th/27th April 1794 from André Cartier, St.Petersburg, to Hope & Co., Amsterdam.

2 Decrees of 28th and 30th April 1794 issued by Alexander Nikolayvich, pertaining to the Sutherland affair. Concerning Voûte's recovery: letter of 2nd May 1794 from R.Voûte, St.Petersburg, to Hope & Co., Amsterdam.

3 Decree of 28th April 1794.

PAGE 150

1 Letter of 7th May 1794 from R.Voûte, St.Petersburg, to Hope & Co., Amsterdam. It was said that Zubov would have been made a prince had it not been for his handling of the Polish situation.

2 Letters of 13th and 16th May 1794 from R.Voûte, St.Petersburg, to Hope & Co., Amsterdam.

3 It is not immediately apparent which illness Voûte was suffering from. The yellowing of his skin and the 'bilious fever' might indicate jaundice, but the beneficial effect of the quinine powders and the regular recurrence of fever point to a form of malaria. (Information supplied by Dr.C.Russchen, specialist in internal medicine, of Zwolle).

PAGE 151

1 Letter of 20th May 1794 from R.Voûte, St.Petersburg, to Hope & Co., Amsterdam.

Concerning the objections to travelling overland: letter of 21st May 1794 from André Cartier, St.Petersburg, to Hope & Co., Amsterdam.

2 Letters of 23rd and 30th May 1794 from R.Voûte, St.Petersburg, to Hope & Co., Amsterdam.

Trosien was in fact declared bankrupt in 1796, and his goods and chattels were sold on the orders of the court. A.G.Voûte-Esser, *Robert Voûte als zakenman en financier* (Amsterdam: by the Author, 1969).

3 Letter of 30th May 1794 from R.Voûte, St.Petersburg, to Hope & Co., Amsterdam.

PAGE 152

1 Letter of 6th June 1794 from R.Voûte, St.Petersburg, to Hope & Co., Amsterdam.

PAGE 153

1 Letter of 26th June 1794 from R.Voûte, in the Gulf of Finland, to Hope & Co., Amsterdam.

2 Letters of 10th and 14th June 1794 from R.Voûte, St.Petersburg, to Hope & Co., Amsterdam.

Letter dated 1st July 1794 from R.Voûte, then 10 miles past the island of Gotland, to Hope & Co., Amsterdam.

Porter had been inconvenienced by inquisitive Prussian customs officials.

3 Letter of 1st July 1794 from R.Voûte, then 10 miles past the island of Gotland, to Hope & Co., Amsterdam.

PAGE 154

1 Blohm was determined to show Voûte by his welcome that he was worthy of Hope's recommendation, 'for there was no house for which he had so deep a regard.'

2 Letter of 6th July 1794 from R.Voûte, Lubeck, to Hope & Co., Amsterdam.

Letter of 13th July 1794 from R.Voûte, . . .lder, to Hope & Co., Amsterdam.

CHAPTER SIX

PAGE 155

1 Letter of 2nd May 1795 from Maria Hoogland, Den Helder, to Paulus Taay, Amsterdam.
Letter of 28th May 1795 from Paulus Taay, Amsterdam, to Maria Hoogland, Den Helder.

PAGE 156

1 *Infra*, Appendix D-v.

2 Breakdown of the loan to Oginski, furnished by P.de Haan Pietersz. to R.Voûte:

The 'oeconomy' of Wilnenska, in the wojewodztwo of Wilno	Pol. f. 3,300,000
Rakow and Isabelin in the wojewodztwo of Minsk	Pol. f. 3,000,000
Chozow, Wigowice, Puzeli, Oborek and Bielew in the Osmiana district	Pol. f. 2,000,000
	Pol. f. 8,300,000

At an estimated 18 Polish guilders to one ducat, Pol. f. 8,300,000 was equivalent to cf 2,421,000. In Lithuania the courts of law valued estates at twenty times the estimated annual yield. Letter of 11th April 1796 from Willink's agent in Grodno to J.A.Willink, Warsaw.

3 Jan Abraham Willink was the son of Willem Willink, of the house of Willem and Jan Willink in Amsterdam.
V.Winter, *Aandeel*, II, 268, 491.
Concerning Repnin: Amburger, *Geschichte Behördenorganisation*, 392.

PAGE 157

1 Letter of 9th January 1796 from J.A.Willink, Warsaw, to P.de Haan Pietersz., Amsterdam.

2 Letter of 11th April 1796 from Willink's agent in Grodno to J.A.Willink, Warsaw. Oginski had bought the 'oeconomy' of Wilno from the princes Charles and Hieronymus Radziwill on 14th January 1790 for 3,400,000 Polish guilders. It had been given to the vendors in heriditary ownership by the *sejm*, in settlement of half their claim against the Republic, which totalled 4,000,000 Polish guilders. After mortgaging the 'oeconomy,' Oginski sold all the estates of which it consisted, with the exception of one, Garne, which was valued at 250,000 Polish guilders; in June 1795 this was awarded to Mme.Derkassowa in settlement of her claim of 150,000 Polish guilders against Oginski.

3 Of the estates in Minsk, Rakow was confiscated by the empress and given to General Soltikov, while between January and March Oginski sold to various persons Isabelin for 250,000 Polish guilders, Chozow for 120,000, and Wigowice and Bielew for 77,000. Puzeli and Oborek had been confiscated and were administered by the Treasury.
4 Letter of 24th March 1796 from J.A.Willink, Warsaw, to P.de Haan Pietersz., Amsterdam.

PAGE 158

1 De Haan instructed Willink to dismiss his agent in Grodno on the grounds that he was too expensive, but Willink persisted in his view that negotiations in St.Petersburg could only bear fruit if a document from the Supreme Court in Lithuania, which proved the validity of De Haan's claims, could be produced. As late as 30th July 1796, by which time Voûte was already on his way to Russia, Willink sent memoranda on these lines to Repnin and to the empress. He probably did so in an attempt to obtain at least part of the bonus which was threatening to elude him.
Letter of 6th May 1796 from J.A.Willink, Warsaw, to P.de Haan Pietersz., Amsterdam. 'Emprunt d'Oginski,' May (?) 1796.
2 G.A. Amsterdam, Not. Arch., 15145–139.
Voûte had earlier been empowered by Hope & Co. to act in the matter of the Polish loan of 1786.
3 *Infra*, Appendix D-v. Details of the various loans also appeared in the procuratorial deed dated 13th May 1796.

PAGE 159

1 G.A. The Hague, Not. Arch., 3893–48.
2 'Emprunt d'Oginski,' May (?) 1796. 'Mémoire pour Monsieur Robert Voûte,' undated. (Both are in De Haan's handwriting).
Remarks (undated) made by R.Voûte to P.de Haan Pietersz. with reference to J.A.Willink's letter of 24th March 1796.
3 Lord, 'Third Partition of Poland,' 494, 498.

PAGE 160

1 24th July 1796. Memorandum to Kalichev, Berlin, in Voûte's handwriting, V.A. The first loan, which ran for 10 years, dated from 1st February 1788.
2 Story of the life of Robert Voûte by J.H.Veldhuyzen, V.A.Robert Voûte had also received an extremely warm welcome from Bagge during his first journey to Russia.
Letters of 16th and 18th October 1794 from Bagge & Van Eyssel, St.Peterburg, to R.Voûte, Amsterdam.

PAGE 161

1 Story by J.H.Veldhuyzen, V.A. The Russian envoy in Copenhagen prevented Pierre Voûte from travelling on to Hamburg. It is not clear whether he did so on his own initiative, or whether he acted on instructions.
Letter of 6th September 1796 from Robert Voûte, St.Petersburg, to Hope & Co., London, V.A.
Letter of 6th September 1796 from Robert Voûte, St.Petersburg, to P.F.Voûte, Amsterdam, V.A.

2 Story by J.H.Veldhuyzen, V.A. According to the author, Maria Feodorovna played an active role in the settlement of the Polish debts. She is said to have informed Voûte in a letter in July 1797 that Vasilyev had reported to the czar on the discussions and that the czar, as an expression of his satisfaction, had commanded that the 'souvenir' (gift?) from Voûte be accepted. The empress consulted Voûte regarding the newly established – more accurately, the newly equipped – School of Commerce in Moscow, with which Count Sievers had also been concerned. The aim was said to be to modify the curriculum to bring it more into line with practice; such a change fitted in well with Voûte's views as he had expressed these in Moscow back in 1793. Voûte's friendship with Maria Feodorovna continued until his death.
Blum, *Sievers*, IV, 472, 475, 477. Amburger, *Geschichte Behördenorganisation*, 163.

3 15th/26th January 1797. Convention between the Czar of Russia and the King of Prussia, to which the German emperor became a party. V.A.d'Angeberg, *Recueil des Traités et Actes diplomatiques concernant la Pologne* (Paris, 1862), 403.

PAGE 162

1 The sum of the king's debts was fixed at 34,000,000 Polish guilders in 1793. To this had meanwhile been added 3–4 years' interest at 5% per annum.

2 30th June 1797. *Acte de Cession* between Alexei Vasilyev, Imperial Treasurer, and Robert Voûte, authorized agent of the creditors of the former Republic of Poland and a number of private individuals residing in the former Republic.

3 Letter of 8th November 1801 from R.Voûte, The Hague, to H.Hope, London. Concerning the positions of Bezborodko and Vasilyev: Amburger, *Geschichte Behördenorganisation*, 128, 210. Others also resented the influence which Robert Voûte was able to exert by reason of the support of the empress. On 12th November 1797, Count Rostopshin wrote to Vorontsov in London concerning 'Woot, premier commis de Hope. Il est très protégé par l'Impératrice.'
Golovkine, *Le règne de Paul Ier*, 158, note 1. In 1802, members of the Committee for Foreign Loans in St.Petersburg gave Bergien, a merchant in that city, to understand that at the time there had been great opposition to Voûte's activities, and that he had been able to continue these only 'par la Douairière,' i.e. with the support of Maria Feodorovna. Czar Paul was by then dead. Letter of 18th February 1802 from J.C.Bergien, St.Petersburg, to R.Voûte, The Hague.

PAGE 163

1 Two orders for payment dated 30th March 1792, for 7,500 and 7,000 ducats respectively, at 5% interest, issued against the king's 'oeconomies' in Lithuania and accepted by Marcin Bedeni in his capacity of authorized agent for Prince Stanislaw Poniatowski, leaseholder of these 'oeconomies,' together with interest due since 1st August 1794. A draft dated 30th May 1792 issued by King Stanislaw in favour of Jean Meisner, in the sum of 23,000 ducats, together with overdue interest since 30th May 1793. An acknowledgement of indebtedness by King Stanislaw to C.A.Hasselgreen dated 30th November 1794 in the sum of 81,329 ducats, payable over a period of 4 years and bearing 5% interest. No interest had been paid. An acknowledgement of indebtedness by King Stanislaw to Theodoor Gülcher dated 26th September 1793 in the sum of 4,200 ducats et 6% interest, payable by the *Chambre des Finances;* no interest had been paid. Four drafts dated 10th September 1793 issued by the Republic of Poland in favour of Jean Meisner and signed by R.de Glogowa, Grand Treasurer

of Poland, and J.Okeczki and D.Kamieniecki, both commissioners of the Treasury, together amounting to 873,096.16 Polish guilders. Meisner owed 21,000 ducats to De Smeth and 5,000 ducats to Hasselgreen; other claims against him amounted to some 175,000 ducats. The transfer of these debts and also those embodied in the second *Acte de Cession* (*infra*, 165–166) enabled Meisner to settle with his creditors.

PAGE 164

1 Letter of 30th August 1797 from Hope & Co. London, to H.A.Insinger, Amsterdam.
2 A.A.Lobanov-Rostovski, *Russia and Europe, 1789–1815* (Duke University Press, 1947) 16–17.

PAGE 165

1 Special instructions issued to Baron d'Asch, Privy Councillor, and Divov, a member of the Chancellery, both of whom were empowered by the czar to verify and liquidate the debts incurred by the Polish king and the former Republic of Poland. S.a., V.A.

PAGE 166

1 The loan to the Dowager Princess Jablonowska, amounting to cf 400,000 at 5% interest, was negotiated in January 1792. Interest had been paid up to 1st January 1794. Repayment, at cf 40,000 annually, should have commenced in January 1795. The security provided for the loan comprised the estates of Siemiatycesk in the Drohi district of the wojewodztwo of Podlachie (which became Prussian territory following the partitions of Poland), and Kockesens in the wojewodztwo of Lublinsk, which passed to Austria under the partition. The securities provided for the other loans by Polish magnates are listed in Appendix D-VI.
2 29th October 1797. *Acte de Cession* between Alexei Vasilyev, Imperial Treasurer, and Robert Voûte, relating to the debts of a number of Polish gentlemen. With the two *actes*, the czar accepted responsibility for debts totalling cf 15,907,585.19.0 Meisner's claim of 66,666⅔ ducats or 1,200,000 Polish guilders against Marquis François Wielopolski had been transferred to Voûte by the creditor. Interest on this debt had been paid up to 31st December 1797. The six bonds relating to Prince Dominique Radziwill bore interest at 7%. The principal totalled cf 523,953.17, and the arrears of interest from 27th April 1793 to 31st December 1797 amounted to cf 171,463.17. After the signing of the convention on 29th October, Voûte continued to correspond at length with the Sobanski brothers, who had always paid the interest on their loan but had fallen into arrears owing to difficulties in remitting two instalments of principal. Through Voûte they requested, and obtained, permission from Vasilyev to continue to pay principal and interest to De Haan, who would remit the sums to De Smeth. As there were no facilities whatsoever for monetary transactions between Obodowka, where the brothers lived, and St.Petersburg (in fact, Amsterdam was nearer), they were given the option of making payments to the Court Bankers in Russia by means of drafts on Odessa, Riga or Moscow. In August 1798 the Sobanskis complained to Voûte that the local authorities were threatening to sell their property under an execution on the grounds that they had been dilatory in providing details of the income derived from the property. Voûte raised the matter with Vasilyev and succeeded in having the action of the local authorities brought to an end.
Letters of 18th November 1797, 1st and 3rd February and 29th September 1798 from

R.Voûte, St.Petersburg, to the Sobanski brothers, Obodowka; and of 10th December 1797, 16th January, 2nd February, 12th April, 5th May and 22nd August 1798 from the Sobanski brothers, Obodowka, to R.Voûte, St.Petersburg.

PAGE 167

1 2nd November 1797. Eleven articles, in Robert Voûte's handwriting, concerning the method of 'reconstituting' Russia's foreign loans. Subscriptions to the 18th loan floated by Hope & Co. ultimately totalled cf 2,500,000.
2 The converted Polish loans all bore interest at 5%. Of the converted Russian loans, 15 million guildersworth bore interest at 4½%, and 6 million guildersworth at 4%. The rate of interest on the cf 3,000,000 loan from De Wolf in Antwerp was also 4½%.
3 Weeveringh, *Geschiedenis Staatsschulden*, II, 848, quotes the following average market prices for bonds during the second half of 1797: Russian 5% bonds: 93; Russia 1788, 4½%, with 1, 2 and 3 coupons: 94; Russia 1792, 4½%: 86. Thus the mean for the three types of loan was still just below 90.

PAGE 168

1 'Consideration relating to the commission granted to Hope for regulating Russia's former debts,' 1803. The matter of rewards to third parties is dealt with on page 179.
2 15th January 1798: Ukase issued by Czar Paul I concerning Russia's foreign debts. The sums involved in the 'arrangements' totalled cf 15,892,414.1.0, which included Hope's commission of cf 3,892,414.1.0. To the latter must be added cf 330,000 in respect of repurchased bonds and cf 11,388,19.0 in cash, bringing the total of the commission to cf 4,233,803.0.0 – the sum to which Voûte had earlier referred in his memorandum to Vasilyev. Letter of 15th May 1798 from Hope & Co. Amsterdam, to Vasilyev, St.Petersburg, VI, 1.
3 Amburger, *Geschichte Behördenorganisation*, 452.

PAGE 170

1 Letter of 30th August 1797 from Hope & Co., London, to H.A.Insinger, Amsterdam. Letter of 22nd June 1798 from P.C.Labouchère, Hamburg, to R.Voûte, St.Petersburg. Two members of the new government, Van Langen and Vreede, did not, however, regard it as beneath their dignity to visit Amsterdam to investigate the possibilities for a trade agreement with Russia, 'which, it had been suggested to the Government, could be realized through the influence of the citizen Voûte of Petersburg (who was held in high esteem by the Court), or alternatively to secure for our trade any commercial advantages, but this proved impossible to obtain ...'
Memorandum from Van Langen, Colenbrander, *Gedenkstukken*, II, 613.
2 18th February 1798: Order from Czar Paul I to Chancellor Bezborodko and Treasurer Vasilyev concerning the payment of interest on Hope's commission.
3 The commission now became cf 4,233,803 plus 6½% interest thereon (cf 275,197) plus 6½% on this sum (cf 17,887.7.0), making cf 4,526,887.7 in all. Letter of 15th May 1798 to Vasilyev, St.Petersburg, VI, 1.

PAGE 172

1 Count Golovkin, in his memoirs, described the conversion as 'un désastreux projet' (Golovkine, *Le règne de Paul Ier*, 157). In *Le fils de la grande Cathérine, Paul Ier*, Waliszewski refers to 'Woot, un agent de la maison Hoop, théoricien chimérique

ou filibustier adroit' (p. 258). Waliszewski, however, appears not to have seen through the nature of the conversion. On the one hand he refers to the conversion of the old Russian debts (p. 255), while on the other (p. 257) he states that Paul I negotiated a new loan of cf 88,300,000 in Amsterdam in January 1797 (this should be 1798). As a result, the picture which he seeks to give of Russia's finances under Paul I is completely distorted. According to the merchant Bergien, Vasilyev's hostility towards the Company stemmed from dissatisfaction with the size of the gift presented to him and his wife. Letter of 18th February 1802 from J.C.Bergien, St.Petersburg, to R.Voûte, The Hague. Bearing in mind Voûte's previous experiences at the Russian Court, the cause is more likely to have lain in intrigue and corruption on the part of others – for example, Rall.

2 Story by J.H.Veldhuyzen, V.A.

3 Waliszewski, *Le fils de la grande Cathérine*, 258 (1 pood was equivalent to 16.3 kilograms).

Golovkine, *Le règne de Paul Ier*, 158. Waliszewski states that the entire plan was abandoned; but here he is mistaken, for a part of it was implemented (*vide* page 177). According to Golovkine, Voûte was the spiritual father of a plan to establish an aid bank, the function of which would be to protect the nobility against usurious practices. This it could do by giving loans on security of estates, and the interest and principal payments could be effected in interest-bearing bank paper issued by the aid bank. Waliszewski states that Bezborodko copied Voûte's ideas.

Blum, *Sievers*, III, 121, describes Prince Alexei Kurakin as the *auctor intellectualis* of the project, and states that the bank was actually established on 18th December 1797. It is said to have commenced operations on 1st March 1798 and to have issued bank paper to a value of 500 million roubles in the space of a few months. An unwarranted issue of bank paper such as this, however, is so contrary to Voûte's ideas in this field that we are moved to cast doubt upon his role as the initiator of the proposal for the bank. His correspondence at that time contains no reference whatever to the matter.

PAGE 173

1 Letter of 15th May 1798 to Vasilyev, St.Petersburg, VI, 1.

2 Letter of 15th May 1798 to Vasilyev, St.Petersburg, VI, 1.

Letter of 13th April 1797 from J.J.Voûte, Jr., Amsterdam, to Hope & Co., London.

14th May 1798: Printed announcement by the Dorner heirs that payments, suspended on 3rd May under the moratorium, were to be resumed.

3 Letter of 8th May 1798 from H.A.Insinger, Amsterdam, to Hope & Co., London.

4 Letter of 25th June 1798 from P.C.Labouchère, Hamburg, to Vasilyev, St.Petersburg, VI, 28. Story by J.H.Veldhuyzen, V.A.

5 11th May 1798: List of houses which accepted responsibility for the credit of the house of Martin Dorner. Johannes Schubach, B(anco) M(arks) 150,000; J.P.Averhoff, BM. 100,000; J.Parish, BM. 100,000; Sieveking, BM. 50,000; Pierre Voûte, 'für Voûte Velho Rall & Co.,' BM. 300,000. The example set by these five houses was quickly followed by others: Joh.Gabe, BM. 50,000; M.J.Jenisch, BM. 50,000; Matthiessen & Sillem, 'für einen Freund' (namely Hope & Co.), BM. 150,000; B.Roosen, BM. 50,000. In a letter to Hope, John Parish claimed that the initiative for the subscription had emanated from him. Letter of 11th May 1798 from J.Parish, Hamburg, to Hope & Co., London.

PAGE 174

1 Letter of 12th June 1798 from P.C.Labouchère, Hamburg, to H.A.Insinger, Amsterdam, A xxv, 61.
Letters of 15th and 29th June 1798 from P.C.Labouchère, Hamburg, to R.Voûte, St.Petersburg, A xxv, 20, 32.
Insinger reported that gossips in Amsterdam were saying that Labouchère had gone to Hamburg purely in order to obtain preferential treatment of Hope's claims. Letter of 5th June 1798 from H.A.Insinger, Amsterdam, to P.C.Labouchère, Hamburg.

2 Labouchère described Gabe, who had commenced his commercial career in Portugal, as a man like Insinger, except that he too easily allowed himself to be persuaded by those whom he trusted; this, however, did not detract from his solidity. Gabe could fill the role of liaison man between Baring, in London, and Amsterdam in the matter of the loans on the security of plantations on the island of St.Croix, which were referred to by the letters A and B, thus enabling interest on these loans to be paid in the Republic. As it was, Hope had entrusted the supervision of these loans to Insinger in Amsterdam.
Letter of 19th June 1798 from P.C.Labouchère, Hamburg, to R.Voûte, St.Petersburg, A xxv, 21.
Lawaetz was rich and reliable, but he was more interested in acquiring a title than in recruiting new correspondents. Chapeaurouge owed his immense fortune to his connexions with the French Republic, and was now concerned to find a safe place for the money which he had earned in the face of such enormous risks. Letter of 19th June 1798 from P.C.Labouchère, Hamburg, to H.A.Insinger, Amsterdam, A xxv, 66. Concerning the events surrounding Frau.Matthiessen: Letter of 19th June 1798 from P.C.Labouchère, Hamburg, to R.Voûte, St.Petersburg, A xxv, 21. Concerning Pamela Fitzgerald and her husband: *Dictionary of National Biography*, XIX (London, 1889), 110–111, 142–143. Insinger described Matthiessen & Sillem as 'being somewhat too deeply involved in French affairs.' Letter of 5th June 1798 from H.A.Insinger, Amsterdam, to P.C.Labouchère, Hamburg.

PAGE 175

1 Letter of 19th June 1798 from P.C.Labouchère, Hamburg, to R.Voûte, St.Petersburg, A xxv, 21. Sillem Jr.'s forename generally appears as Jerôme, but this is a later Frenchification.

2 Letter of 19th June 1798 from P.C.Labouchère, Hamburg, to R.Voûte, St.Petersburg, A xxv, 21.

PAGE 176

1 Letter of 12th June 1798 from P.C.Labouchère, Hamburg, to H.A.Insinger, Amsterdam, A xxv, 61.
Letters of 15th, 26th and 29th June 1798 from P.C.Labouchère, Hamburg, to R.Voûte, St.Petersburg, A xxv, 20, 31, 32.
Letter of 25th June 1798 from P.C.Labouchère, Hamburg, to Vasilyev, St.Petersburg, VI, 28. When Hope's account with Dorner was closed on 31st December 1798, there remained a credit of cf 908.15 in favour of Hope. Thus matters had straightened themselves out completely. The Russian Court ultimately proved to owe a small sum to Dorner. *Grootboek* 1798: 15.

Roosegaarde Bisschop, *Opkomst Londensche geldmarkt*, 104–105.

2 In England, where the Company was not active, it availed itself of the services of Harman & Co. and Sir Francis Baring & Co.

PAGE 177

1 Letter of 30th June 1798 from P.C.Labouchère, Hamburg, to Matthiessen & Sillem, Hamburg, A XXV, 15. In his correspondence with Voûte Velho Rall & Co., Labouchère sketched Voûte as the man who had a great deal of influence with the emperor and who was completely *au fait* with Hope's thinking. To Baron Von Nikolai, Czar Paul's former tutor, Labouchère also sang Voûte's praises, emphasizing his important role in the firm of Court Bankers and the fact that he, 'homme d'affaires, sans prétentions, instruit, intègre et indépendant,' exerted an influence on the Court in spite of the fact that he lacked the manner which characterized the 'courtisan achevé.' Letter of 5th June 1798 to Voûte Velho Rall & Co., St.Petersburg, VI, 24. Letter of 5th June 1798 to Baron de Nikolai, St.Petersburg, VI, 25.

2 Letter of 29th June 1798 from P.C.Labouchère, Hamburg, to R.Voûte, St.Petersburg, A XXV, 32.
Letter of 30th June 1798 from P.C.Labouchère, Hamburg, to Matthiessen & Sillem, A XXV, 11.

PAGE 178

1 Gabe's correspondence from Hamburg regarding the St.Croix loans was also to be addressed to James Smith. The St.Croix loans A and B were to be referred to as 'Account A' in correspondence with Insinger, and Hope was to be known as 'our friend.' J.J.Voûte Jr. was instructed to remit the interest on 100 Russian bonds to A.I.v.d.Hoeven of Rotterdam, an uncle of Thomas Hope. Voûte was to retain the coupons pertaining to these bonds, but to send the relevant certificates to Matthiessen & Sillem. This procedure would make it impossible for the Batavian government to seize the bonds, while ensuring that V.d.Hoeven received his interest. Letters of 30th June 1798 to J.Gabe, Hamburg, A XXV, 80, and of 29th June 1798 to J.J.Voûte, Jr., Amsterdam, A XXV, 90.

2 Letter of 29th June 1798 to H.A.Insinger, Amsterdam, A XXV, 70. As Robert Voûte had been in 1795, Insinger was instructed to furnish Taay with advice and funds whenever he might require these.

3 Letter of 12th June 1798 from P.C.Labouchère, Hamburg, to H.A.Insinger, Amsterdam, A XXV, 61.
Letter of 6th July 1798 from P.C.Labouchère, Bremen, to J.J.Voûte, Jr., Amsterdam, A XXV, 90.
Letter of 25th September 1798 from P.Voûte, Amsterdam, to Hope & Co., London. Pierre de Smeth took his brother-in-law, Willem van de Poll, into partnership with effect from 1st January 1799, a step which, in Hope's opinion, would afford De Smeth the long-desired 'tranquillité de l'esprit' and 'loisir' – a need for rest which, as we have seen, was also present in the firm in 1788. In August 1799, Hope congratulated De Smeth on his safe return to Amsterdam after a long holiday. Letters of 5th October 1798 and 13th August 1799 from Hope & Co., London, to Pierre de Smeth, Amsterdam.

4 Golovkine, *Le règne de Paul 1er*, 174.

Waliszewski, *Le fils de la grande Cathérine*, 202.
Character sketch of Paul I in Robert Voûte's handwriting, V.A.

5 Story by J.H.Veldhuyzen, V.A. Letters of 7th December 1798 and 22nd January 1799 from Hope & Co., London, to R. and Th.de Smeth, Amsterdam, VI, 51, 55.
Letters of 17th February and 23rd March 1801 from R.Voûte, London, to J.C.Bergien, St.Petersburg.
Following Pierre Voûte's resignation, the title of the firm was changed to Velho Rall & Rogovikov. Robert Voûte's difficulties with Vasilyev and Rall resulted in his becoming ill; the circumstances of his indisposition were thus similar to those which had felled him in 1794 and 1796.

6 Letter of 8th March 1799 from Hope & Co., London, to Matthiessen & Sillem, Hamburg, VI, 66.

PAGE 179

1 Letters of 30th May and 25th June 1798 from Hope & Co., London, to Vasilyev, St.Petersburg, VI, 9, 28.
Letter of 23rd November 1798 from Hope & Co., London, to David Berck, Amsterdam, VI, 47.
Letters of 7th December 1798 and 22nd January 1799 from Hope & Co., London, to P.de Smeth, Amsterdam, VI, 51, 55.
Letter of 25th January 1799 from Hope & Co., London, to the Committee for Foreign Loans, St.Petersburg, VI, 63.

2 Letters of 4th June and 26th July 1799 from Hope & Co., London, to Vasilyev, St.Petersburg, VI, 75, 92.
Letter of 14th June 1799 from Hope & Co., London, to P.de Smeth, Amsterdam, VI, 76.
Letter of 26th July 1799 from Hope & Co., London, to the Committee for Foreign Loans, St.Petersburg, VI, 96. On 25th June 1799, Vasilyev wrote to say that the principal debenture had been received from De Wolf. Hope thereupon received 4% commission plus 6½% commission on the 4%, i.e. cf 120,000 + cf 7,800. On 5th July 1798, the principal debenture was entered in the Register of Private Deeds kept by the Town Clerk of Amsterdam (folio 66v). It was exempted from stamp duty or 'Kleinzegel' by a decree of 23rd March 1798 issued by the National Assembly, which at that time was known as the Constituent Assembly. The bonds bore a 6-*stuiver* stamp.

3 Deed enacted before W.v. Homrigh, notary, on 10th December 1798.

4 Letters of 12th and 16th March, 14th June and 13th August 1799 from Hope & Co., London, to P.de Smeth, Amsterdam, VI, 67, 72, 76, 100. Hope wished to give a ring costing between ten and fifteen thousand guilders. As the original plan provided for Von Stackelberg to stay on in Amsterdam, perhaps for between one and two years, the offer to assume responsibility for his domestic expenses involved a sum of 10–15,000 guilders, i.e. the same as the cost of the ring. However, the circumstances of war forced Von Stackelberg to leave Amsterdam in November 1799. Letter of 22nd November 1799 from Hope & Co., London, to P.de Smeth, Amsterdam, VI, 136.

5 Letters of 7th December 1798, 12th March, 14th June and 13th August 1799 from Hope & Co., London, to P.de Smeth, Amsterdam, VI, 51, 67, 76, 100.
Letter of 13th August 1799 from Hope & Co., London, to D.Berck, Amsterdam, VI, 107.

Letter of 26th August 1799 from Hope & Co., London, to R.Voûte, London, VI, 112.

6 Notary van Beem was dissatisfied with the seven thousand guildersworth of bonds intended for him. His reaction was extremely unpleasant for the partners, who wished to satisfy all concerned. Their desire will certainly have been allied to the delicate position in which the Company then found itself. The correspondence and copy files which we have examined contain no reference to a reward for Insinger, but this can scarcely have been less than the 100 bonds given to J.J.Voûte, Jr. According to later accounts, Vasiliev's feud with Hope was exacerbated by the 'gift' which, in Vasilyev's opinion, was too small (*supra*, 172, note 1).

PAGE 180

1 Letter of 5th October 1798 from Hope & Co., London, to P.de Smeth, Amsterdam, VI, 38.
Letter of 5th October 1798 from Hope & Co., London, to Vasilyev, St.Petersburg, VI, 40.
Letter of 23rd November 1798 from Hope & Co., London, to D.Berck, Amsterdam, VI, 47.
Letter of 20th October 1798 from H.A.Insinger, Amsterdam, to Hope & Co., London.
Weeveringh, *Geschiedenis Staatsschulden*, II, 848, dealing with the three types of Russian loan which were individually quoted during the first six months of 1798, gives the following prices: 5 per cent, 92; 4½ per cent, 86; 4 per cent, 84. This author states that during the second half of 1798, when, following the conversion, only the 5% type was quoted, the average price fell to 86, a decline of 6%. Insinger refers to an even sharper fall.

2 Letters of 22nd January and 26th March 1799 from Hope & Co., London, to P.de Smeth, Amsterdam, VI, 55, 72.
Letter of 25th January 1799 from Hope & Co., London, to the Committee for Foreign Loans, St.Petersburg, VI, 63. The interest totalled cf 2,492,462.10.0.
During the Spring of 1799, the prices of the Russian bonds fluctuated madly. In a letter of 26th March to De Smeth, Hope & Co. referred to a fall to 70, which they attributed mainly to the failure of the Russian government to make a repayment of principal. The Swedish bonds, which were previously lower than the Russian, recovered to 96 following the announcement of a modest principal repayment.

3 Weeveringh, *Geschiedenis Staatsschulden*, II, 848.

4 Letter of 5th November 1799 from Hope & Co., London, to P.de Smeth, Amsterdam, VI, 123.

PAGE 181

1 Early in November 1799, Matthiessen & Sillem received gold to a value of 150,000 pounds sterling. The gold shipped by Harman travelled first to Copenhagen and thence to Hamburg. Harman probably played a part in the transfer of British subsidies to the Continent. Matthiessen & Sillem were instructed that in the event of their being unable to remit the full amount of the interest to De Smeth before 1st January 1800, they were to advise De Smeth that the money was indeed available. This would enable De Smeth to advertise this news and thus put the public's mind at ease. Letter of 5th November 1799 from Hope & Co., London, to Matthiessen & Sillem, Hamburg, VI, 125. Harman furnished Matthiessen & Sillem with 133,000

pounds sterling in silver in December 1799; of this sum, 100,000 pounds belonged to the British government and was in Hamburg. It is conceivable that, following the signal failure of the Russo-Austrian campaigns, the British government had decided to dispose of the reserves of silver built up to finance subsidies. Harman despatched a further 50,000 pounds in silver in January 1800. Letters of 13th December 1799 and 24th January 1800 from Hope & Co., London, to Matthiessen & Sillem, Hamburg, VI, 149, 154.

2 Letter of 22nd November 1798 from Hope & Co., London, to Matthiessen & Sillem, Hamburg, VI, 134. Other correspondence on this subject appears on pages 125, 131, 133, 140, 142, 144, 145, 147, 149, 151, 157 and 160. The interest totalled cf 3,828,750.0.0.
Letter of 22nd November 1799 from Hope & Co., London, to P.de Smeth, Amsterdam, VI, 136.

PAGE 182

1 Early February 1801: Description by De Coninck of the events in Copenhagen, addressed to Hope & Co.
Lobanov-Rostovski, *Russia and Europe*, 63–65.

2 Weeveringh gives mean quotations for Russian bonds of 81 during the first half of 1800, and 84 during the second half of the year.

3 30th April 1801: Memorandum from Hope & Co., London, to Robert Voûte.
Letter of 27th April 1801 from R.Voûte, London, to Hope & Co., London.

4 The account headed 'Bonds chargeable to the negotiation for His Imperial Majesty the Czar of Russia, negotiated by ourselves' contains an entry, dated 31st December 1799, in respect of 4,528 bonds at 80% (*grootboek* 1799: 20). The commission to date totalled cf 4,526,887.7.0. On 31st December 1801, 346 bonds remained on this account. In the interim period a further 51 bonds had been purchased or accepted as payment. In a letter of 27th April 1801 to Hope & Co., Voûte stated that he had no claim to the funds which stood to his credit in the Republic. When he wrote this, he was on the point of leaving for the Republic.

5 Letters of 17th February, and 13th and 23rd March 1801 from R.Voûte, London, to J.C.Bergien, St.Petersburg.

PAGE 183

1 Letter of 24th March 1801 from J.C.Bergien, St.Petersburg, to R.Voûte, London.

2 Letter of 17th April 1801 from J.C.Bergien, St.Petersburg, to R.Voûte, London. The Company rightly anticipated that the rehabilitation would lead to a resumption of the earlier difficulties. Memorandum of 30th April 1801 from Hope & Co., London, to Robert Voûte.

3 Letter of 30th May 1801 from R.Voûte, Amsterdam, to J.C.Bergien, St.Petersburg.

4 Letter of 12th June 1801 from P.C.Labouchère, London, to R.Voûte, Amsterdam.

PAGE 184

1 The transfer to the Portuguese Government of the proceeds of the diamond loan involved payments of cf 1,000,000 in each of the first eleven months of 1802, and cf 2,000,000 on 31st December of that year. A sum of cf 500,000, allocated from the proceeds of the sales of Russian bonds during 1800 and 1801, had been transferred to Insinger by way of advances on consignments of diamonds.
Infra, 403.

2 Memorandum of 30th April 1801 from Hope & Co., London, to Robert Voûte. This still refers to a sum of 463,000 pounds sterling which stood to the credit of the Russian Court.

3 Lord Hawkesbury became Foreign Secretary in February 1801. He will thus not have been aware of the Russian subsidy credit. *Dictionary of National Biography*, XXIX (1892), 311–312.

CHAPTER SEVEN

PAGE 187

1 Letter of 17th June 1803 from J.Récamier, Paris, to Hope & Co., Amsterdam.

2 Letter of 27th July 1803 from D.Parish, Antwerp, to P.C.Labouchère, Amsterdam. In Hamburg, Chapeaurouge, Matthiessen & Sillem and Israel Dehn & Co. were said to be acting on Récamier's behalf.

3 Letter of 23rd September 1803 from Jos. Morison, Riga, to Hope & Co., Amsterdam. Morison received an advance of 50,000 albertustalers against a contract for masts valued at a far greater sum. Morison was not permitted to draw until shipment was effected, after which the 50,000 albertustalers would be deducted from the sum of the final shipments. In an attempt to turn this situation to good account, Hope proposed to Porter Brown & Co. in St.Petersburg that they should remit to the Company in the event of Farmbacher's purchases leading to drafts being drawn on Paris, and thus to a rise in exchange rates in Russia.
Letter of 12th August 1803 to Porter Brown & Co., St.Petersburg, VI, 521.

PAGE 188

1 Van Winter, *Aandeel*, II, 377–379.
Letters of 5th May and 9th June from A.Peyrousse, The Hague, to P.C.Labouchère, Amsterdam.
Letters of 16th March and 16th May 1803 to A.Peyrousse, The Hague, VI, 423, 479.

PAGE 190

1 Van Winter, *Aandeel*, II, 383–385.
Van Winter, 'Louisiana gekocht en betaald,' 43–44.

2 Van Winter, *Aandeel*, II, 386.

3 Napoleon had sent his brother-in-law, Leclerc, to Haiti in 1801 to subjugate the negro dictator, Toussaint Louverture, and restore French control on the island. The expeditionary force achieved successes initially, but was later so stricken with yellow fever that it was forced to withdraw at the end of 1803.

4 At this point, the sums were deposited in the Treasury. On 1st December 1803 an agreement was signed between Barbé Marbois and Labouchère providing for the former to receive drafts totalling 8 million francs.

PAGE 191

1 Letter of 7th July 1803 to De Stackelberg, The Hague, VI, 497.
Letter of 1st August 1803 from A.Baring, Paris, to Hope & Co., Amsterdam.

Letter of 29th December 1807 to J.A.Krehmer, St.Petersburg, VII, 253.
The Russian envoy to the Batavian Republic in 1803 was Gustav Ernst von Stackelberg. According to the list of envoys contained in Amburger's book, this Von Stackelberg was not the one who had signed the bonds in 1798–1799. Amburger, *Geschichte Behördenorganisation*, 446, 452, 569.

2 Letter of 14th July 1803 from J. Bergien, St.Petersburg, to R.Voûte, The Hague.
Letter of 12th August 1803 to Bergien & Co., St.Petersburg, VI, 519.
As an additional precaution, Hope made enquiries of Porter Brown & Co. regarding Bergien's status, in particular his prudence.
Letter of 12th August 1803 to Porter Brown & Co., St.Petersburg, VI, 521.

3 Letter of 20 August 1803 from R.Voûte, Middagten, to Bergien & Co., St.Petersburg.
Letter of 8th November 1803 to Bergien & Co., St.Petersburg, VI, 593.

4 Letter of 4th December 1803 from Bergien & Co., St.Petersburg, to Hope & Co., Amsterdam.

PAGE 192

1 Letter of 9th January 1804 to Bergien & Co., St.Petersburg, A II, 54.

2 21st April 1804: 'Propositions faites au Ministre du Trésor Public par Mr.Labouchère, associé de la Maison Hope & Co. d'Amsterdam.'
Van Winter, *Aandeel*, II, 386–387.

3 Letters of 13th May and 9th June 1804 from A.Peyrousse, The Hague, to P.C.Labouchère, Amsterdam.
Letter of 20th June 1804 from A.Peyrousse, Amsterdam, to P.C.Labouchère, Amsterdam.
Labouchère had placed Peyrousse under an obligation by meeting a few of his private commitments from the war fund, thus sparing him from difficulties during the audit.

4 Letter of 10th March 1804 from Decrès, Paris, to Hope & Co., Amsterdam.
Letter of 16th March 1804 to Decrès, Paris, A II, 150.

PAGE 193

1 Letter of 23rd March 1804 from Roger, Paris, to Hope & Co., Amsterdam.
Letter of 27th March 1804 from Barbé Marbois, Paris, to Hope & Co., Amsterdam.
Letters of 30th March, 6th April, 11th June and 6th August 1804 from Decrès, Paris, to Hope & Co., Amsterdam.
Letters of 5th April and 31st May 1804 to Barbé Marbois, Paris, A II, 177, 221.

2 'Opérations relatives à divers crédits assignés à diverses maisons du Nord sur nous, par S.E.Mr.Barbé Marbois, Ministre du Trésor Public de France etcetera.'
A detailed breakdown of the credits will be found in Appendix D-VII.

3 Timber to the following values was shipped from Riga:

Helmund & Son	cf 183,799.04.0
J. Morison	cf 1,380,360.14.0
	cf 1,564,159.18.0

Morison thus handled 88% of the consignments of timber. These were carried in 32 vessels, of which 18, all flying the Prussian flag, sailed to Emden; 10, of which 9 flew the Swedish flag and 1 the Prussian flag, to Copenhagen; 2, under the Russian and Swedish flags, to Morlaix; 1 under the Prussian flag to Marseilles; and 1 under the Russian flag to Bordeaux.

Helmund & Son shipped the timber which they purchased in 12 vessels, of which 9 sailed to Emden under the Prussian flag, and 3 to Marseilles under the Swedish flag. Justus Blanckenhagen shipped hemp to a value of cf 901,716.5.0., which represented 46% of the total shipments of this commodity. He employed 20 vessels for the purpose, 5 of which sailed to Morlaix, 5 to Emden, 3 to La Rochelle, 3 to Nantes and 1 to Bordeaux. The destinations of the remaining three are unknown, as are the nationalities of all the vessels which he employed.

4 The hemp shipments from St.Petersburg were divided as follows:

F. W. Isenbeck	cf 416,850. 0.0
Ant. Colombi	cf 244,953. 2.0
Rd. Mitton	cf 20,948. 6.0
Blandow & Co.	cf 42,478. 3.0
	cf 725,229.11.0

F.W.Isenbeck chartered 9 vessels, 4 of which sailed to Bordeaux, 2 to Nantes, 1 to Morlaix and 1 to an undisclosed port; the ninth ran aground.
Ant.Colombi chartered 4 vessels, 2 for Bordeaux, 1 for La Rochelle and 1 which ran aground before reaching its destination.
Rd.Mitton chartered one vessel for Dieppe or suitable alternative port, and Blandow & Co. one for Nantes.

5 Pehmöller & Droop shipped seven cargoes of copper valued at cf 124,535.11.0 to Emden. Schwink & Koch of Königsberg shipped hemp to a value of cf 306,030.13.0 in four vessels, 2 bound for Emden and 2 for Amsterdam; 3 of these flew the Prussian flag and 1 the Hamburg flag. The vessels themselves came from East Friesland. Morison and Helmund received a further 4% commission on the value of the cargoes plus the 70% overheads.

6 Helmund's charges were somewhat lower, but this firm had received part-payment in 1803. Morison's charges varied between 53% and 83% of the value of the cargo.

PAGE 194

1 All the merchants in St.Petersburg charged 13%, covering commission, charges, etc. The only exception was Rd. Mitton, who charged 16% for one shipment. We have no details concerning the commissions paid to the St.Petersburg houses; however, if we take the 3% paid to Schwink & Koch of Königsberg as a basis, we may assume that transport charges, dues and storage in St.Petersburg will have totalled about 10%.
Pehmöller & Droop charged 2% commission on the shipments which they undertook. The actual cost of preparing the shipments did not exceed $\frac{1}{3}$–$\frac{2}{5}$%.
Schwink & Koch supplied 16% of the hemp shipped in the operation, the total value of which was cf 1,932,976.9.0.

2 Letters of 16th July and 20th August 1804 to Decrès, Paris, A II, 282, 343. Letter of 17th August 1804 from Barbé Marbois, Paris, to Hope & Co., Amsterdam. 'Opérations relatives' etc., 15, 17. The vessels arrested were the 'Vrouw Hermina' and the 'De Jonge Onnen Pieters Brouwer,' both of which were carrying cargoes from Blanckenhagen, and the 'De Generaal Von Blücher,' with a cargo from Morison on board. The bills of lading and 'Opérations' reveal that all three were bound for Emden. But, as the story will subsequently show (page 196), the three ships underwent neutralization and then made for France, where they were stopped.

3 The invoice value amounted to cf 503,914.5.0.
Ryberg's charges on this totalled cf 171,000.
4 Letter of 11th June 1804 from Decrès, Paris, to Hope & Co., Amsterdam.
Letter of 11th June 1804 to Barbé Marbois, Paris, A II, 228.
Letter of 2nd July 1804 to Decrès, Paris, A II, 253.
5 Letters of 9th and 16th July 1804 to Decrès, Paris, A II, 275, 282.
6 Letter of 23rd July 1804 to Decrès, Paris, A II, 292.
Letter of 30th July 1804 to Bergevin, Paris, A II, 303.

PAGE 195

1 Letters of 6th and 13th August 1804 to Decrès, Paris, A II, 317, 321. Hope advised Decrès to consult Pehmöller & Droop in regard to the insurance in Hamburg. In Amsterdam, the premium for marine risks alone was 6% in August 1804, and this even applied to cargoes bound for Marseilles.
2 Letter of 23rd August 1804 to Decrès, Paris, A II, 346. While Hope & Co., in spite of putting heavy pressure on the insurers, were obliged to pay a premium of at least 8% for hemp carried in Russian vessels, other houses paid only 4% for shipments of tar and timber.
3 Letters of 30th August, and 10th, 13th and 17th September 1804 to Decrès, Paris, A II, 358, 373, 380, 387.
4 Letters of 23rd and 27th March 1804 from Roger, Paris, to P.C.Labouchère, Amsterdam.
Letter of 29th March 1804 to Roger, Paris, A II, 164.
Letter of 30th March 1804 from Decrès, Paris, to Hope & Co., Amsterdam.
Letters of 5th and 19th April 1804 to Decrès, Paris, A II, 175, 188.

PAGE 196

1 Letter of 30th July 1804 to Decrès, Paris, A II, 304.
2 Letter of 23rd March 1804 from Roger, Paris, to P.C.Labouchère, Amsterdam.
Letter of 27th September 1804 to Decrès, Paris, A II, 399.
Letter of 22nd October 1804 to Aug.Bergevin, Paris, A II, 433. Bergevin was 'Commissaire Principal de Marine.'
3 Letters of 29th October and 7th November 1804 to Roger, Paris, A II, 442, 457.
Letter of 29th October 1804 to Barbé Marbois, Paris, A II, 444.
4 Letter of 9th November 1804 from Roger, Paris, to P.C.Labouchère, Amsterdam.
5 Letter of 12th November 1804 to Decrès, Paris A II, 465.

PAGE 197

1 Letter of 26th November 1804 to Roger, Paris, A II, 487.
Letter of 29th November 1804 to Barbé Marbois, Paris, A II, 492.
2 Letter of 14th February 1805 to Barbé Marbois, Paris, A II, 551. Napoleon had voiced his satisfaction with the services rendered by Hope.
3 Letters of 22nd March, and 11th and 29th April 1805 to Decrès, Paris, A II, 583, 598, 606. Decrès approved the proposal regarding De Bondeville, but the name of this house does not appear in the accounts. It would thus appear that no intermediary was appointed in Paris.

PAGE 198

1 Data obtained from 'Opérations relatives,' etc.

2 Letter of 4th June 1804 from Bergien & Co., St.Petersburg to Hope & Co., Amsterdam.
3 F.Crouzet, *L'économie britannique et le blocus continental (1806–1813)*, I (Paris, 1958), 165.

PAGE 199

1 *Ibid.*, I, 211.
2 Stocks of ship supplies in Amsterdam were extremely limited at the beginning of 1807. These consisted of 200,000 pounds of clean hemp from Königsberg, at cf 120–121 per ship-pound; 10,000 pounds of clean hemp from Riga, at cf 116–120 per ship-pound; and 300,000 pounds of semi-clean hemp from St.Petersburg at cf 48 per ship-pound. One ship-pound was approximately 150 kilograms. The Russian ship-pound or *berkovich* was equal to 10 pood, the latter being 16.3 kg. The shortage greatly encouraged speculation in hemp. Letter of 6th May 1807 to Decrès, Paris, VII, 75.
3 Letters of 13th, 20th and 23rd February, 27th April, 15th, 18th and 28th May, 1st June and 28th October 1806 from Bergien & Co., St.Petersburg, to Hope & Co., Amsterdam. When the potash was delivered, it was found to be below specification in terms of quality. Bergien thereupon offered to compensate the Company. As will become evident (page 213, note 2), lack of certainty regarding the quality of the Russian products was a common complaint.
4 Letters of 27th April and 13th November 1806 from Bergien & Co., St. Petersburg, to Hope & Co., Amsterdam.

PAGE 200

1 Crouzet, *Blocus continental*, I, 128, note 5.
2 Letters of 16th, 19th and 26th December 1806 from Matthiessen & Sillem, Hamburg, to Hope & Co., Amsterdam.
Crouzet, *Blocus continental*, I, 216, note 8.
3 Weeveringh, *Geschiedenis Staatsschulden*, II, quotes the following prices: 1805, first half 98, second half 97; 1806, first half 95, second half 96. In Hamburg, the link between the stagnation of trade and the floating of loans again became apparent. To provide an outlet for capital unemployed because of the blockade, Matthiessen & Sillem had floated two small loans in Hamburg in January 1807. Letter of 30th January 1807 from Matthiessen & Sillem, Hamburg, to Hope & Co., Amsterdam.
4 In his letters, Hope's correspondent in Copenhagen, De Coninck, gave an eye-witness account of the events. To assist De Coninck, Hope granted him a credit of cf 100,000. Letter of 29th September 1807 to De Coninck & Co., Copenhagen, VII, 173.

PAGE 201

1 Crouzet, *Blocus continental*, I, 253–254.
2 Letter of 16th/28th May 1807 from Rall & Rogovikov, St.Petersburg, to Hope & Co., Amsterdam.
Letter of 17th/29th May 1807 from Vasilyev, St.Petersburg, to Hope & Co., Amsterdam.
3 Letter of 4th/16th June 1807 from J.Wulff, Copenhagen, to Hope & Co., Amsterdam.
4 Letters of 21st July and 11th August 1807 to J.Wulff, Copenhagen, VII, 133, 149. In

August the price rose briefly to 94. Weeveringh quotes an average figure of 85 for the first and second halves of 1807.

5 Letter of 15th/27th October 1807 from J.Wulff, Altona, to Hope & Co., Amsterdam.

6 Letter of 11th August 1807 to J.Wulff, Copenhagen, VII, 149.
Letter of 2nd November 1807 to De Smeth, Amsterdam, VII, 208. Strangely enough, Wulff also suggested that Hope might consider buying bonds. It is not clear how funds could have been mobilized in this manner, unless Wulff was thinking of a speculation based on an exchange profit on resale.

PAGE 202

1 Letter of 23rd October 1807 to J.Wulff, Altona, VII, 204.
Letter of 2nd/14th November 1807 from Th.Golubzov, St.Petersburg, to Hope & Co., Amsterdam.
Amburger, *Geschichte Behördenorganisation*, 26, 208.

2 Letters of 20th September/2nd October and 24th September/6th October 1807 from Bergien & Co., St.Petersburg, to Hope & Co., Amsterdam.

3 Letter of 2nd November 1807 from R.Voûte, Utrecht, to Hope & Co., Amsterdam.

4 Letter of 10th November 1807 to Bergien & Co., St.Petersburg, VII, 215.

PAGE 203

1 Letter of 20th October 1807 to Matthiessen & Sillem, Hamburg, VII, 202.

2 Letter of 29th October/10th November 1807 from Bergien & Co., St.Petersburg, to Hope & Co., Amsterdam.
Letter of 15th December 1807 to Bergien & Co., St.Petersburg, VII, 237.

3 Letter of 29th December 1807 to J.A.Krehmer, St.Petersburg, VII, 253.
Letter of 29th December 1807 to Bergien & Co., St.Petersburg, VII, 256. According to Bergien, Krehmer did not act on the basis of any authority. Bergien and Krehmer were said to have collaborated initially in the loan proposal, but later to have disagreed, whereupon each went his own way. Both houses – and in particular Krehmer – subsequently pestered Hope & Co. with proposals for the purchase of Russian goods, ostensibly on a fifty-fifty basis but in reality with Hope advancing the whole of the sum required. The Company parried these advances with polite but noncommittal replies at a distance.
Letters of 13th/25th, 17th/29th March, 15th/27th May, 2nd/14th June, 18th/30th, 19th/31st August 1808 from J.A.Krehmer Lang & Co., St.Petersburg, to Hope & Co., Amsterdam; 29th April and 12th July 1808 to J.A.Krehmer, St.Petersburg, VII, 367, 439; 27th March/7th April, 29th May/9th June 1808 from Bergien & Co., St.Petersburg, to Hope & Co., Amsterdam. It later transpired that Krehmer had already purchased substantial stocks at his own risk and sought to use the Company to supplement his liquid assets. With the market still in a listless state, Krehmer was hoping and praying that Rumyantsev's negotiations, which were aimed at achieving peace between England and France, would succeed. The restoration of peace would benefit the prices of Russian products. The conditions for negotiations with England had been drawn up at Erfurt in October. Letters of 16th/28th October, 13th/25th November 1808 from J.A.Krehmer, St.Petersburg, to Hope & Co., Amsterdam.
Albert Vandal, *Napoléon Ier et Alexandre Ier*, I (Paris, 1891), 474–475.

4 Letter of 31st December 1807/12th January 1808 from N.Rumyantsev and Th.Golubtsov, St.Petersburg, to Hope & Co., Amsterdam.

PAGE 204

1 Letter of 9th February 1808 to the Committee for Foreign Loans, St.Petersburg. On 1st January 1807, Hope & Co. held 4,525 repurchased bonds, and De Smeth 4,702.

PAGE 205

1 Letter of 10th/22nd March 1808 from Golubtsov and Rumyantsev, St.Peterburg, to Hope & Co., Amsterdam.
2 Letters of 5th February, 4th, 15th and 29th March, 1st and 5th April 1808 to Golubtsov, St.Petersburg, VII, 299, 324, 335, 339, 340, 341.
3 26th April, 1808. Deed of transfer of Russian bonds to a value of 17 million guilders from Hope & Co. to W.Borski. Borski received a commission of ¼%.

PAGE 206

1 Letter of 29th April 1808 to the Committee for Foreign Loans, St. Petersburg, VII, 368.
Letter of 1st December 1808 from P.C.Labouchère, Amsterdam, to J.W.Hope, London.
Letter of 17th December 1811 from W.Borski, Amsterdam, to Hope & Co., Amsterdam.
Hope subscribed cf 6,000,000, Borski cf 3,000,000, Strockel & Van Dijk cf 3,000,000, D.J.Voombergh cf 3,000,000, N. and J. and R.Staphorst cf 1,000,000 and W.&J.Willink cf 1,000,000.
2 Lobanov-Rostovski, *Russia and Europe*, 128–132.
K.Waliszewski, *Le règne d'Alexandre Ier*, I (Paris, 1923), 191–192, 198, 239.
3 Lobanov-Rostovski, *Russia and Europe*, 132, 162.
Zenyavin left part of his fleet at Porte Ferrajo, on the island of Elba.
Waliszewski, *Règne d'Alexandre Ier*, I, 248, 260.
4 Jean Calamai of Leghorn, to whom fell the role of providing funds for the fleet on Elba, preferred to draw on Hope. even when, subsequently, he received instructions to recover advances from the Russian envoy in Vienna, Prince Kurakin.
Letter of 20th November 1807 from Jean Calamai, Leghorn, to Hope & Co., Amsterdam.
Letter of 11th December 1807 to Jean Calamai, Leghorn, VII, 232.
To meet the needs of vessels at Trieste, Cesare Pellegrini, a merchant in that city, was permitted to draw on Hope & Co. During 1808 his drawings totalled cf 399,454.12.8. Accounts of the Russian Crown, 1808.
5 Letter of 12th December 1807 to J.Wulff, Altona, VII, 236.
6 Letter of 31st July/12th August 1807 from Golubtsov, St.Petersburg, to Hope & Co., Amsterdam.
Lobanov-Rostovski, *Russia and Europe*, 132. Calamai drew on Hope for approximately cf 115,000. On 28th June, he reported that the squadron at Porte Ferrajo had sailed. The destination later proved to be Toulon.
Letter of 22nd July 1808 from J.Calamai, Leghorn, to Hope & Co., Amsterdam.
Letter of 30th August/11th September 1808 from Zenyavin, Lisbon, to Hope & Co., Amsterdam. One vessel, the corvette 'Spitsbergen,' remained at Vigo. It was left to the Russian consul-general in Lisbon, A.Dubatshevskoy, to meet the expense occasioned by her stay, and also to settle Zenyavin's accounts. Zenyavin sailed for Portsmouth on 12th September, and five days later Dubatshevskoy drew on Hope for

cf 202,688.5.0. Such were the sums drawn on the Company for the benefit of the Russian men-of-war that by 1st July 1808 no more than cf 326,000 was left to meet other needs on the part of the Russian government. Letter of 1st July 1808 to the Committee for Foreign Loans, St.Petersburg, VII, 413. Just how saddened the French government was by Zenyavin's position in Lisbon was revealed by rumours which circulated in Paris, to the effect that France had purchased Zenyavin's entire fleet for 16 or 18 million francs.
Letter of 26th February 1808 to J.A.Krehmer, St.Petersburg, VII, 321.

PAGE 207

1 Letter of 29th May/9th June 1808 from the Committee for Foreign Loans, St.Petersburg, to Hope & Co., Amsterdam.
2 Letter of 1st June 1808 from R.Voûte, Amsterdam, to Hope & Co., Amsterdam. Letter of 2nd June 1808 to R.Voûte, Amsterdam, VII, 385.
3 4th July 1808. Supplement to agreement with W.Borski and associates dated 26th April 1808.

PAGE 208

1 Letter of 5th July 1808 to the Committee for Foreign Loans, St.Petersburg, VII, 415.
2 Letter of 18th/30th January 1808 from J.A.Krehmer, St.Petersburg, to Hope & Co., Amsterdam. Hope viewed Wulff's passing as a severe blow to the Ministry of Finance, 'as this gentleman had the clue of all transactions of the late minister.' Letter of 26th February 1808 to J.A.Krehmer, St.Petersburg, VII, 321.
3 Letter of 4th December 1807 from Bergien & Co., St.Petersburg, to Hope & Co., Amsterdam.
Letter of 29th December 1807 to J.A.Krehmer, St.Petersburg, VII, 253.
Letter of 13th/25th March 1808 from J.A.Krehmer & Co., St.Petersburg, to Hope & Co., Amsterdam. There were rumours that France was prepared to furnish Russia with up to 200 million francs in subsidies, in exchange for substantial quantities of Russian produce. This should probably be viewed as an attempt to bind Russia to France in the economic sphere as well as in others, and thus to drive a wedge between her and England. Similar rumours emerge in later correspondence (see, for example, page 222), but there is no evidence that any such plan was carried through.

PAGE 209

1 Crouzet, *Blocus continental*, I, 292–293.
2 Letter of 21st August/2nd September 1808 from Th.Golubtsov, St.Petersburg, to Hope & Co., Amsterdam.
3 Letter of 21st October 1808 from J.Sillem, Hamburg, to Hope & Co., Amsterdam. Letter of 25th October 1808 to J.Sillem, Hamburg, VII, 516.

PAGE 210

1 Sillem, who had been to Carlsbad and Egra for his health, returned in mid-October 1808 or thereabouts. The mere fact that he could afford to be away from Hamburg for five months is an indication of the depressed state of business in that city. Sillem was indeed little disposed to undertake a fresh journey.
Letter of 21st October 1808 from J.Sillem, Hamburg, to Hope & Co., Amsterdam.
2 Letter of 27th September 1808 to Matthiessen & Sillem, Hamburg, VII, 489.

3 Letter of 10th October 1808 from R.Melvil, Amsterdam, to P.C.Labouchère, Amsterdam.

PAGE 211

1 Letter of 4th October 1808 to the Committee for Foreign Loans, St.Petersburg, VII, 498. Somewhat to the surprise of Hope & Co., Golubtsov wrote on 5th November to say that the Russian government had agreed to the 2% asked for.
Letter of 12th October 1808 to R.Melvil, Amsterdam, R. 1.

PAGE 212

1 *Supra*, 209.

PAGE 213

1 On 27th October 1808, Hope & Co., in briefing Melvil, quoted the following prices, in roubles per pood, as being current: hemp, clean, 47–51; second-grade 40–44; hemp, semi-clean 40–43; flax, twelve-headed, 50; potash 51; beeswax 27; tallow, yellow, 62; tallow, white, 54; soap tallow 52; Russian leather 18; hemp oil 4; brushes 22; linseed 10–11.

2 Shortly before he left for London in 1794, Hope had bought large quantities of flax for shipment to ports in Spain, France, Italy and Portugal. Trial shipments were undertaken following his return to Amsterdam, but widespread complaints from the consignees concerning the quality of the material led the Company to abandon the trade. *Supra*, 199, note 3.

PAGE 214

1 Letters of 12th and 27th October 1808 to R.Melvil, Amsterdam, R. 1 et seq.
Letter of 25th October 1808 to J.Sillem, Hamburg, VII, 516.

2 Melvil also carried letters of recommendation addressed to Schickler Bros. in Berlin, Cumming & Fenton and J.Blanckenhagen in Riga, Bagge & Co., Bothlingk & Co., Livio Bros. & Co., Arch. Cramp and Porter Brown & Co., all of St.Petersburg, and Brandt Rodde & Co. and R.van Brienen & Sons in Archangel. Generally speaking, all were houses which Hope considered suitable to be involved in the transaction. Melvil also received letters of credit for other houses, most of which were in Germany. These were Fred.Hoffmann & Son of Düsseldorf, Jean Walter de Becke of Cologne, H.H.Kalm & Son of Brunswick, J.H.Pottgeisser of Coblenz, N.Turkheim of Mainz, Bethmann Bros. of Frankfurt, Mich.David & Son of Hanover, J.Brentano of Kassel, Dufour Bros. of Leipzig, Bassenge & Co. of Dresden, Benecke Bros. of Berlin, J.A.Noffolk of Warsaw, Toussaint & Co., of Königsberg, J.D.Drachenhauer & Co., of Riga and Bergien & Co., of St.Petersburg. All the letters bore the date 28th October 1808. During his visit to Hamburg, Melvil received from Matthiessen & Sillem a number of letters of recommendation and credit from this house. In order to prevent fraud (the credit, after all, was unlimited), Melvil was required to provide 16 specimens of his signature, which were then sent to the houses at which a credit had been opened in his name.
Letter of 4th November 1808 from Matthiessen & Sillem, Hamburg, to Hope & Co., Amsterdam.

3 Letter of 2nd August 1808 to the Committee for Foreign Loans, St.Petersburg, VII, 462.

Letter of 12th August 1808 to Golubtsov, St.Petersburg, VII, 468.

4 Letter of 28th August/2nd September 1808 from the Committee for Foreign Loans, St.Petersburg, to Hope & Co., Amsterdam. The accounts show that the Genoese lira, one-fifth of a piastre, was then worth just over 8 *stuivers* (41 guilder cents).

PAGE 215

1 Letter of 14th February 1809 to the Committee for Foreign Loans, St.Petersburg, A XXVII, 29.
Letter of 11th April 1809 to Golubtsov, St.Petersburg, A XXVII, 56.
The consignment consisted of 10,000 rixdollars and 110,000 piastres, together valued at cf 283,331.10.0, and bars of silver to a value of cf 25,000.

2 Letter of 29th November 1808 to the Committee for Foreign Loans, St.Petersburg, VII, 553.
Letter of 29th November 1808 from W.Borski, Amsterdam, to Hope & Co., Amsterdam.
Letter of 29th November to W.Borski, Amsterdam, VII, 581.
Letter of 10th January 1809 to the Committee for Foreign Loans, St. Petersburg.

PAGE 216

1 Letter of 1st December 1808 from P.C.Labouchère, Amsterdam, to J.W.Hope, London.
Letter of 29th November 1808 to W.Borski, Amsterdam, VII, 581.

2 Interest at 5% was paid on 82,300 bonds, making a total of cf 4,115,000. In 1803, 2,000 bonds were redeemed, and the interest on the 4,000 was provisionally held on deposit. Hope initially referred in correspondence to 5,000 bonds, but on 10th January 1809 the Committee in St.Petersburg was advised that there were in fact only 4,000.

3 Letter of 22nd November 1808 to R.Melvil, St.Petersburg, R. 32.
Letter of 24th November 1808 from R.Melvil, Königsberg, to Hope & Co., Amsterdam.
Letter of 7th December 1808 from R.Melvil, Riga, to Hope & Co., Amsterdam.

4 Crouzet, *Blocus continental*, I, 371. According to Melvil, 80 American vessels arrived at Russian ports during 1808; they were admitted without difficulty upon the production of evidence that they had come from neutral ports.

5 Letters of 7th and 10th December 1808 from R.Melvil, Riga, to Hope & Co., Amsterdam. Drachenhauer charged 16¾ albertustalers per ship-pound for his services. Zuckerbäcker Klein & Co. charged 17¼ albertustalers per ship-pound.

PAGE 217

1 Letter of 8th/20th December 1808 from R.Melvil, St.Petersburg, to Hope & Co., Amsterdam.

2 Letter of 9th/21st March 1809 from R.Melvil, St.Petersburg, to Matthiessen & Sillem, Hamburg.

PAGE 218

1 Letter of 8th/20th December 1808 from R.Melvil, St.Petersburg, to Hope & Co., Amsterdam. Monies deposited with the Bank gathered no interest for the first three months. After a year the interest was added to the capital.

2 Letter of 22nd January/4th February 1809 from R.Melvil, St.Petersburg, to Matthiessen & Sillem, Hamburg.

3 Crouzet, *Blocus continental*, I, 380.

4 Letters of 26th February/9th March and 2nd/17th March 1809 from R.Melvil, St.Petersburg, to Matthiessen & Sillem, Hamburg. The Russian government's requirements for coarse linen were put at 7 million arshins per annum (1 arshin was equal to 0.71 metres). This was somewhat at variance with the information supplied by Hope, who viewed the government purchases as a means of supporting prices. On 17th March, Melvil reported that the government had contracted to purchase 15 million arshins of coarse linen at 130 roubles per thousand arshins. The house of Stieglitz specialized in flax.

PAGE 219

1 Letters of 3rd/15th January 1809 from R.Melvil, St.Petersburg, to Hope & Co., Amsterdam, and 29th January/9th February 1809 from R.Melvil, St.Petersburg, to Matthiessen & Sillem, Hamburg.

Letter of 15th/27th December 1808 from R.Melvil, St.Petersburg, to Hope & Co., Amsterdam.

'Old sable iron,' the highest grade, was supplied by Nicolai Demidov, but his prices were then too high. Most of this iron was exported to England. A lower grade, known as P.S.F., was available in large quantities. The principal markets for this were North America and the European continent. Yakovlev was unable to manage his affairs owing to mental illness, and his firm, which owed money to the government, had been taken over. More than a million poods of iron lay in the stockyard of his factory, and some of this would certainly be sold to meet his debts to the government.

Letter of 15th/27th December 1808 from R.Melvil, St.Petersburg, to Hope & Co., Amsterdam. Demidov was asking 235 kopecks per pood for his iron. Melvil ultimately purchased, for cash, 70,000 poods at 210 kopecks per pood. The commissars who managed Yakovlev's business had earlier declined an offer of 160 kopecks on the grounds that the mines could not operate economically at such a price. Melvil was of the opinion that iron from Siberia could be transported more cheaply to a port on the Black Sea. Eventually he bought just over 185,000 poods of P.S.F. iron, of which 150,000 poods was ordered through Bergien. For spot quantities he paid 165–170 kopecks per pood in cash, and for forward purchases 175–180 kopecks with an earnest of 25 kopecks. On 25th August 1809, Bergien offered Melvil a consignment of 1,900,000 poods from the government-controlled Yakovlev stock at 195 kopecks per pood. Hope's reaction to this was to offer to establish a 'combinaison générale' in the form of a public loan, subject to the approval of King Louis Napoleon. The absence of any mention of the matter in the later correspondence (letter of 29th September 1809 to Bergien & Co., St.Petersburg, A XXVII, 17) suggests that the royal approval was not forthcoming. The 185,000 poods of iron which Hope & Co. bought from the Yakovlev stock had been manufactured while Yakovlev was still of sound mind. It was reported that the quality of the iron produced by the firm deteriorated after the owner had ceased to exercise control. The stock in question took two years to travel from the mines to St.Petersburg.

2 Letter of 27th May 1809 to Matthiessen & Sillem, Hamburg, A XXVII, 93.

PAGE 220

1 Letters of 12th/24th and 16th/28th February 1809 from R.Melvil, St.Petersburg, to Hope & Co., Amsterdam. Amburger, *Geschichte Behördenorganisation*, 206. The Severin brothers – whose name appears as Severeyn on a number of occasions in the Hope accounts – were brothers of the widow of Velho, the erstwhile partner in Voûte Velho Rall & Co. She was in dispute with Rall concerning her share in the firm. In Hope's view, Rall & Severin was not an attractive house, 'entreprenant beaucoup par delà ses forces,' and while Rall continued to be a partner there could be no question of good relations. The wife of one of the Severin brothers was among the czar's mistresses. Waliszewski, *Règne d'Alexandre Ier*, I, 451.

2 Letter of 15th/27th December 1808 from R.Melvil, St.Petersburg, to Hope & Co., Amsterdam.

3. Letter of 15th/27th December 1808 from R. Melvil, St. Petersburg, to Hope & Co., Amsterdam. Letter of 29th December 1808/8th January 1809 from R.Melvil, St. Petersburg, to Hope & Co., Amsterdam. The founders of the houses of Bagge & Co. and Archibald Cramp were by now dead. Both houses continued under new management, but only in the case of Bagge & Co. was Melvil satisfied on the score of reliability. The house of Ant. Colombi, a Spaniard, was also widely respected. Stieglitz & Co., 'formerly Jews,' appeared to be wealthy; this firm maintained relations with Matthiessen & Sillem. In Archangel, Melvil chose the house of A. Becker, whom he had met in St.Petersburg and who had made a good impression upon him. As prices in Archangel were proportionately higher, the only commodities which lent themselves to speculation there were tar and pitch. Taken in conjunction with the rate of exchange, the prices of these were so low that manufacturers in Russia could hardly make a living. Letters of 14th/27th January 1809 from R.Melvil, St.Petersburg, to Hope & Co., Amsterdam, and 22nd January/4th February 1809 from R.Melvil, St. Petersburg, to Matthiessen & Sillem, Hamburg.

PAGE 221

1 Letters of 6th and 9th January 1809 to R.Melvil, St.Petersburg, R., 37, 39.

2 Letter of 22nd January/4th February 1809 from R.Melvil, St.Petersburg, to Hope & Co., Amsterdam.

3 Letter of 15th/27th January 1809 from R.Melvil, St. Petersburg, to Hope & Co., Amsterdam. Letter of 29th January/9th February 1809 from R.Melvil, St.Petersburg, to Matthiessen & Sillem, Hamburg.

4 Letter of 15th/27th January 1809 from R.Melvil, St.Petersburg, to Hope & Co., Amsterdam.

5 Letter of 7th February 1809 from Matthiessen & Sillem, Hamburg, to Hope & Co., Amsterdam. Letter of 12th/24th February 1809 from R.Melvil, St.Petersburg, to Hope & Co., Amsterdam.

6 Letter of 15th/27th January 1809 from R.Melvil, St.Petersburg, to Hope & Co., Amsterdam.

PAGE 222

1 Letter of 5th/17th March 1809 from R.Melvil, St.Petersburg, to Hope & Co., Amsterdam.
We know from Voûte's visits in 1793 and 1794 that referring a matter to the czar or the empress was among the means employed to defer a decision or camouflage a refusal.

2 Letter of 26th February 1809 from Bethmann, Frankfurt, to P.C.Labouchère, Amsterdam.
Letter of 5th/17th March 1809 from R.Melvil, St.Petersburg, to Hope & Co., Amsterdam.
Bethmann had again raised the matter with Rumyantsev during the latter's visit to Frankfurt but, finding that he had many other things on his mind, had deemed it wise to arrange for a reminder from Hope after Rumiantsev's return to St.Petersburg. In all probability, Rumyantsev put Bethmann off with a few vague remarks.

3 Labouchère, who at this time was staying in Paris, asked Mollien, the French Treasury Minister, whether Hope & Co., would be involved in further drawings for the benefit of the French navy. Rumyantsev had mentioned a sum of fifteen million francs to the merchants. Mollien, however, knew nothing of such a development, and was disinclined to believe on the report. It may be that the purpose of this piece of wishful thinking was to discourage anti-French feeling in Russia (letter of 18th May 1809 from P.C.Labouchère, Paris, to Hope & Co., Amsterdam). Bethmann, Rumyantsev's friend, feared 'the activities of a class of men in St.Petersburg who indulge in intrigues in order to prove that the present political system is contrary to the interests of the Empire.'
Letter of 14th May 1809 from Bethmann Brothers, Frankfurt, to Hope & Co., Amsterdam.

PAGE 223

1 Hope urged Melvil (unnecessarily, since he had already done so on his own initiative) to profit from extremely low exchange rates by drawing on Amsterdam and using the proceeds to pay in advance for the purchases from Russian houses.
Letter of 14th March 1809 to R.Melvil, St.Petersburg, A XXVII, 45.
Letter of 23rd March/14th April 1809 from R.Melvil, St.Petersburg, to Matthiessen & Sillem, Hamburg.

2 Letters of 22nd and 25th April 1809 to Matthiessen & Sillem, Hamburg, A XXVII, 70, 78. Letter of 29th April 1809 to R.Melvil, St.Petersburg, R., 60.

3 Letters of 24th and 31st March 1809 from Matthiessen & Sillem, Hamburg, to Hope & Co., Amsterdam.
Matthiessen & Sillem stated that if vessels carrying a portion of the purchased goods were sent to the North Sea, Hamburg was an ideal port for hemp. Yellow tallow, in contrast to the white variety, was a welcome commodity in England. Flax could also be sent to England, but not to Scotland. Iron could only be shipped as ballast with light cargo such as flax and hemp. Potash was unsaleable in England, as were linen goods.
Letter of 20th June 1809 from Matthiessen & Sillem, Hamburg, to Hope & Co., Amsterdam.

PAGE 224

1 Letter of 23rd May 1809 to Matthiessen & Sillem, Hamburg, A XXVII, 90. Since the Russian Court had come down on the side of France (in fact, this was only a gesture), Hope dared not risk sending goods by sea, 'as it remains to be seen whether the Tyrants of the Seas will continue to respect their (i.e. the Russian–Ed.) navigation.' This is one of very few manifestly anti-British comments in Hope's correspondence.

2 Letters of 7th/19th and 19th/31st May 1809 from R.Melvil, St.Petersburg, to Hope & Co., Amsterdam.

3 Letter of 13th June 1809 to Matthiessen & Sillem, Hamburg, A XXVII, 102. Letter of 29th June 1809 from Melvil & Co., Amsterdam, to Hope & Co., Amsterdam. Crouzet, *Blocus continental*, II, 424.

4 Fears that the Baltic trade would be severely hampered by the arbitrary orders of the Privy Council in England were still felt by Bethmann at the beginning of May. Letter of 14th May 1809 from Bethmann Brothers, Frankfurt, to Hope & Co., Amsterdam.

5 Letters of 20th April/2nd May, 23rd April/5th May, 27th April/9th May, 1st/13th May, 4th/16th May, 7th/19th May, 11th/23rd May, 22nd May/4th June 1809 from R.Melvil, St.Petersburg and Riga, to Hope & Co., Amsterdam. Letter of 16th June 1809 from Matthiessen & Sillem, Hamburg, to Hope & Co., Amsterdam.

PAGE 225

1 Letters of 20th April/2nd May, 27th April/9th May, 19th/31st May 1809 from R.Melvil, St.Petersburg, to Hope & Co., Amsterdam. Letter of 27th May 1809 to Matthiessen & Sillem, Hamburg, A XXVII, 93. At the moment when Golubtsov informed Melvil that the transaction would not be cancelled, the rouble was valued at 16 *stuivers*. Cancellation would thus have resulted in a loss to the Russian government of 1¼ *stuivers* on every guilder paid out in Amsterdam. To Matthiessen & Sillem, the Company expressed fears that Melvil would not profit from the low exchange rate by drawing on Amsterdam. But, as we have seen (note 1, page 223), their anxiety was without foundation. 'R.M.'s vital fire is not equal to the goodness of his heart and who is a rare commercial character in the present state of the world, that of having too much prudence.'

2 Letter of 23rd March/4th April 1809 from R.Melvil, St.Petersburg, to Hope & Co., Amsterdam. Letter of 25th April 1809 to Matthiessen & Sillem, Hamburg, A XXVII, 78.

3 Letters of 19th/31st May and 22nd May/4th June 1809 from R.Melvil, Riga, to Hope & Co., Amsterdam. Letter of 4th July 1809 to Matthiessen & Sillem, Hamburg, A XXVII, 119. 10th July 1809: 'Papiers concernant l'opération R.M.'

4 Early in May the Company reported that the British had proclaimed a blockade of the coast from the Ems river to Bayonne. This, it was stated, was in reply to the American Non-Intercourse Act, which prohibited trade with England and also France. Letter of 2nd May 1809 to Matthiessen & Sillem, Hamburg, A XXVII, 80.

Crouzet, *Blocus continental*, II, 444.
Eli Heckscher, *The Continental System* (Oxford, 1922), 137.

PAGE 226

1 *Infra*, Appendix D-VIII.

2

Commodity	*Hope's price, quoted on 27.10.1808*	*Average price paid by Melvil*
Flax	50 roubles	Spot: 60–61 roubles Forward: 59–65 roubles
Potash	51 roubles	Forward: 43–46 roubles
Linseed	10–11 roubles	9–10 roubles
Yellow tallow	62 roubles	57 roubles

Thus, only in the case of flax did Melvil have to pay more than the price indicated by Hope; but his purchases of this commodity represented only 6% of the total.

3 In addition to brokerage, the houses which made purchases on Melvil's behalf received a commission of between 1% and 2%. The commission paid on a given commodity varied from one house to another. For example, Bothlingk received 2% on his purchase of linen fabrics, while Blessig was paid only 1% for the same article. *Vide* Cop. R, 'Notes diverses, etc.,' 'Notes,' 'M.' Melvil's travelling expenses, including the cost of the coach and the wages of his servant, totalled nearly cf 7,500. *Infra*, Appendix D-IX.

CHAPTER EIGHT

PAGE 227

1 Letter of 28th January 1809 to J. Williams Hope, London.
Letter of 21st February 1809 to R.Melvil, St.Petersburg, R., 47.
Letter of 23rd March 1809 to J.Williams Hope, London.
Letter of 4th July 1809 to the Committee for Foreign Loans, St.Petersburg, A XXVII, 120.

2 Letter of 11th April 1809 to the Committee for Foreign Loans, St.Petersburg, A XXVII, 61. Of the 4,109 bonds contracted in December 1808, only six or seven hundred had been sold by the following April.

PAGE 228

1 Letter of 1st June 1809 to J. Williams Hope, London.
Letter of 11th/23rd June 1809 from the Committee for Foreign Loans, St.Petersburg to Hope & Co. Amsterdam.
On 1st June 1809, 6,588 of the 13,109 bonds taken over had been sold, and 6,521 remained unsold. From the proceeds of the sale, cf 3,452,000 had been paid. Hope & Co. provisionally advanced cf 3,069,000.

2 Letter of 4th July 1809 to the Committee for Foreign Loans, St.Petersburg, A XXVII, 120.

3 Letters of 17th and 21st July 1809 from P.C.Labouchère, Bagnères, to Hope & Co., Amsterdam.
Letter of 10th August 1809, from P.C.Labouchère, Bordeaux, to Hope & Co., Amsterdam.
Letter of 8th September 1809 from P.C.Labouchère, Paris, to Hope & Co., Amsterdam.

PAGE 229

1 Letter of 12th September 1809 to the Committee for Foreign Loans, St.Petersburg, A XXVII, 161. Hope asked for flax, hemp, potash, tallow, linen fabrics, iron, copper and linseed–products which Melvil had also purchased. The Company opened discussions with Bergien concerning the purchase of 190,000 poods of P.S.F. iron from Yakovlev. It was willing to pay 180 kopecks per pood, at a rate of exchange of 15 *stuivers*, or another price at another rate of exchange, provided that the sum in guilders was the same. The Company reserved the freedom to meet the cost of purchase without resorting to drafts on St.Petersburg; in other words, with roubles provided by the Russian government.

Letter of 29th September 1809 to Bergien & Co., St.Petersburg, A XXVII, 170. Letters of 22nd September 1809 from P.C.Labouchère, Paris, to Hope & Co., Amsterdam, and of 12th/24th October 1809 from Bergien & Co., St.Petersburg, to Hope & Co., Amsterdam.

2 Letter of 1st/13th November 1809 from the Committee for Foreign Loans, St.Petersburg, to Hope & Co., Amsterdam.

3 It was reported that an attempt had been made in Genoa to obtain a loan of 6 million Genoese lire, and others in Paris, Hamburg and Frankfurt. It may be assumed that these were undertaken after 1st July 1809, the date on which the clause in the contract with the *entrepreneurs* which referred to competition lapsed. Letters of 13th March 1810 to Guryev, St.Petersburg, A XXVII, 318, and of 23rd May 1810 to Count Nesselrode, Paris, A XXVII, 357.

4 Letter of 6th January 1810 to the Committee for Foreign Loans, St.Petersburg, A XXVII, 249.

PAGE 230

1 The rate of exchange of the rouble kept roughly in step with the ratio between the paper rouble and the silver rouble. On 18th February 1810, Porter reported that 285 paper roubles could be obtained for 100 silver roubles. Taking the par value of the rouble at 40 *stuivers*, this does indeed give an exchange rate of 14 *stuivers* to the paper rouble. Letter of 18th February 1810 from W.Porter, St.Petersburg, to J.Williams Hope, London. Letter of 30th November 1809 to Nicolas Clary, Paris, A XXVII, 209. Letter of 16th December 1809 from Melvil & Co., Amsterdam, to Hope & Co., Amsterdam. Letter of 16th February 1810 to Bethmann Bros., Frankfurt, A XXVII, 298. Letter of 27th February 1810 to Guryev, St.Petersburg, A XXVII, 315.

2 Letters of 12th/24th January and 8th/20th February 1810 from Guryev, St.Petersburg, to Hope & Co., Amsterdam.
Amburger, *Geschichte Behördenorganisation*, 208, 210.
Letter of 13th March 1810 to Guryev, St.Petersburg, A XXVII, 318.
Letter of 23rd May 1810 from P.C.Labouchère, Amsterdam, to Count Nesselrode, Paris. The Company required a commission of 2½% on the operation which it had proposed.

3 Letter of 8th/20th May 1810 from Guryev, St.Petersburg, to Hope & Co., Amsterdam. The Court was willing to pay Hope & Co. the 2½% commission for which they had asked, and also to meet the stamp duty on the new vouchers relating to the bonds.

PAGE 231

1 Ukase of 27th May/8th June 1810 issued by Czar Alexander I, and concerning the loan in *assignats* opened in Russia. Land sales would be permitted for a period of five years. The principal sum would be one hundred million roubles, and this would be spread over five tranches of twenty million each. The first tranche would carry interest at 6% and be redeemed in 1817. It was a condition of the entire loan that interest and principal would be paid in silver roubles. Payment for the bonds could be effected in *assignats* or paper roubles and at the advantageous rate of two paper roubles for one silver rouble. Where land belonging to the State was sold, payment could be made in bonds; this facility was also extended to foreign buyers. The

assignats surrendered would be burnt, and the issue of new *assignats* would cease. Every Russian merchant who was a member of the First Guild (the association of large merchants) was permitted to purchase land on condition that payment was made in bonds of the new loan. This group, however, was prohibited from buying land from private individuals. The purchasers of State land were to enjoy manorial rights in respect of the estates so purchased, but remained in their own class and thus did not share the rights of the nobility. Payment for manorial assets purchased from the State could be effected in five annual instalments, interest being added. This provision was probably introduced in order to facilitate the purchase of land by noblemen. The first tranche, of 20 million roubles, was to be opened for subscription on 15th July 1810.

2 Letter of 13th March 1810 to Guryev, St.Petersburg, A XXVII, 318.
Letters of 8th/20th, 18th/30th May and 4th/16th July 1810 from Guryev, St.Petersburg, to Hope & Co., Amsterdam.
Letter of 6th June 1810 to R.Melvil, Amsterdam. During July and August, the rouble stood at about $11\frac{3}{4}$ *stuivers* in Amsterdam. The cf 863,000 was remitted from St.Petersburg by the house of Antoine Colombi. The temporary elimination of Rall must almost certainly be seen as a gesture to propitiate Hope & Co.

3 Letters of 17th June, 14th, 25th August, 8th and 25th September 1810 to Guryev. St.Petersburg, A XXVII, 382, 406, 415, 421, 437.
Vandal, *Napoleon Ier et Alexandre Ier*, II, Ch. XI, *passim.*

4 Letter of 14th August 1810 to Guryev, St.Petersburg, A XXVII, 406.

PAGE 232

1 Guryev agreed to Labouchère's terms, but he refused to extend payment of interest up to the end of the year to bonds which would be redeemed in the course of 1811 or subsequently. Letter of 24th August 1810 to Count Nesselrode, Paris, A XXVII, 416. Letter of 26th August/7th September 1810 from Guryev, St.Petersburg, to Hope & Co., Amsterdam. Letter of 24th September 1810 to the Prince Arch-Treasurer, Amsterdam, A XXVII, 438. Approval was given on 25th September.

2 Hope & Co. were on good terms with the Russian envoy to the Kingdom of Holland, Prince Sergei Dolgorukov. Letter of 28th September 1810 to Guryev, St.Petersburg, A XXVII, 445. Prince Alexander Kurakin had suffered serious injuries when fire broke out at a Court function which he was attending. The brother of Prince Alexander, Prince Alexei, who was just then in Paris for the purpose of conveying the czar's congratulations to Napoleon upon his second marriage, later took charge.

3 Letters of 28th September, 13th, 27th October, 3rd, 6th, 17th and 20th November 1810 to Guryev, St.Petersburg, A XXVII, 445, 468, 483, 490, 495, 497, 503.
Letter of 22nd November/4th December 1810 from Bergien & Co., St.Petersburg, to Hope & Co., Amsterdam.
Letter of 31st December 1810 to W.Borski, Amsterdam, A XXVII, 547. It is conceivable that, as previously, the balance of the bonds were sold to a consortium headed by Borski. However, no clear details are available.

4 Letter of 23rd November/5th December 1810 from Guryev, St.Petersburg, to Hope & Co., Amsterdam.

5 Crouzet, *Blocus continental*, II, 592–594.
Vandal, *Napoleon Ier et Alexander Ier*, II, 443–446.

PAGE 234

1 Crouzet, *ibid.*, 596–602. Vandal, *ibid.*, 489–490, 493–494, 510–511. The newly elected successor to the throne, the former French marshal Bernadotte, privately promised the English that Sweden would interpret very broadly indeed the application of the Continental System.

2 Vandal, *ibid.*, 530–531.

PAGE 235

1 Letter of 24th November 1810 from P.C.Labouchère, Amsterdam, to J.Sillem, Hamburg, A XXVII, 510.
Letter of 22nd January 1810 from P.C.Labouchère, Amsterdam, to Matthiessen & Sillem, Hamburg, A XXVII, 561.

2 Letter of 8th December 1810 to Guryev, St.Petersburg, A XXVII, 516, 524.
Letter of 8th January 1811 from P.C.Labouchère, Amsterdam, to Count von Stackelberg, Vienna, A XXVII, 555. The other Receivers were P.I.Hogguer and J.Hodshon. S.L.A.Keyzer and J.du Bois, of Amsterdam, also suspended payments. Labouchère attended to Von Stackelberg's private claims against De Smeth. Von Stackelberg was the Russian envoy in Vienna. In addition to the returned remittances, Rall & Severin had a claim of about cf 300,000 against De Smeth's estate. Letter of 5th January 1811 to Prince Kurakin, Paris, A XXVII, 552.

3 Letter of 3rd/15th December 1810 from Prince Alexei Kurakin, Paris, to Hope & Co., Amsterdam.
Letter of 22nd December 1810 to Guryev, St.Petersburg, A XXVII, 537.
Letter of 22nd December 1810 to Prince A.Kurakin, Paris, A XXVII, 535.
Letter of 28th December 1810 from Prince A.Kurakin, Paris, to Hope & Co., Amsterdam.
Letter of 31st December 1810/12th January 1811 from Guryev, St. Petersburg, to Hope & Co., Amsterdam.
Hope advanced Prince Kurakin a sum of cf 20,000 upon his personal responsibility pending official approval. Guryev allowed Hope to draw on Russian funds held by Matthiessen & Sillem. The Company was subsequently informed that Kurakin could draw up to cf 80,000.
Letter of 5th February 1811 to Guryev, St.Petersburg, A XXVII, 568.
Letter of 5th February 1811 to Prince A.Kurakin, Paris, A XXVII, 570.

PAGE 236

1 Letter of 29th December 1810 to Guryev, St.Petersburg, A XXVII, 542.

2 A number of bankruptcies in Riga were among the causes of Croese's difficulties. Rall was involved in Croese's bankruptcy to the extent of cf 220,000. Hope acted for Rall in these matters.
Letters of 24th January/5th February and 28th February/12th March 1811 from A.F.Rall, St.Petersburg, to Hope & Co., Amsterdam.

3 Letter of 18th May 1811 to Guryev, St.Petersburg, A XXVII, 5.
Letter of 20th May 1811 from P.C.Labouchère, Amsterdam (?), to Baguenault, Paris.
Letter of 20th June 1811 from P.C.Labouchère, Amsterdam, to John Hope, London. Following the death of Henry Hope, John Williams Hope ceased to use his second Christian name.

4 Letter of 11th June 1811 from Melvil & Co., Amsterdam, to P.C.Labouchère, Amsterdam.

PAGE 237

1 Letters of 22nd July and 19th August 1809 to Matthiessen & Sillem, Hamburg, A XXVII, 133, 146.
Letter of 20th August 1809 from Bethmann Bros., Frankfurt, to Hope & Co., Amsterdam.
Letter of 1st October 1809 from P.C.Labouchère, Paris, to Hope & Co., Amsterdam.
Meyer was appointed to a post in the Ministry of Finance in St.Petersburg in January 1811, whereupon he resigned from Meyer & Bruxner.
2 Letters of 25th July, 25th August and 19th September 1809 from Matthiessen & Sillem, to Hope & Co., Amsterdam.
3 Letter of 21st November 1809 from Matthiessen & Sillem, Hamburg, to P.C.Labouchère, Amsterdam.
Letter of 8th December 1809 from Matthiessen & Sillem, Hamburg, to Henry Hope & Co., London.
Letter of 5th December 1809 from P.C.Labouchère, Amsterdam, to Henry Hope & Co., London.

PAGE 238

1 'Notes diverses,' 'Notes,' 'M,' 'R.'
2 cf 137,287.8.0 in 1810, compared with cf 955,100.0.0, in 1809. 'Notes.'
Crouzet, *Blocus Continental*, II, 576, 634.
3 'Notes.' In the case of tar, 17% was added to the selling price to cover transport, storage, replenishment, registration fees (½% of the selling price), brokerage fees (also ½%), additional charges (1%), del credere (2%) and commission (2%). For tar, the charges were appreciably lower, totalling less than 10%. For iron, they represented only 3% of the selling price. The stock of linseed held by Meyer & Bruxner was sold at a loss of 5%. It had, however, suffered a decline in quality owing to overheating.

PAGE 239

1 Letter of 20th June 1811 from P.C.Labouchère, Amsterdam, to John Hope, London.
2 Letter of 11th June 1811 from Melvil & Co., Amsterdam, to P.C.Labouchère, Amsterdam.
3 Letter of 27th July/8th August 1811 from Meyer & Bruxner, St.Petersburg, to P.C.Labouchère, St.Petersburg.
Crouzet, *Blocus Continental*, II, 654–655, note 12, 655.
4 'Notes,' 'Notes diverses.'

PAGE 240

1 'State of Operation R.M. on 30th November 1811.' Labouchère placed an order with Brandt Rodde & Co. in Archangel for purchases within narrow margins. Because of its eccentric position, Archangel escaped the Russian government's strict control over foreign ships, and thus ample supplies of colonial produce could be relied upon there. Moreover, the difficulties surrounding onward transport to other European countries were greater there than, for example, in St.Petersburg or Riga. The Archangel house was unable to meet the limits laid down by Labouchère, namely 10,000 poods of top-

grade Georgian cotton at 10 roubles per pood, 100,000 poods of white Havana sugar at 20 roubles and 100,000 poods of brown Havana sugar at 14 roubles, the prices in all cases being based on the St.Petersburg rate of 10 *stuivers* to the rouble. Letters of 29th July/10th August and 6th/18th September 1811 from P.C.Labouchère, St.Petersburg, to Brandt & Rodde, Archangel. From the time of Labouchère's arrival in Russia, remittances totalling cf 270,000 had reached Amsterdam.

2 To meet the payment due on 1st January, a total of cf 1,450,000 could be remitted in the months of August to December 1811 without influencing the rate of exchange. The limits were cf 450,000 in August and September, cf 250,000 in October, cf 200,000 in November and cf 100,000 in December.

PAGE 241

1 Memorandum from P.C.Labouchère, enclosed with his letter to Guryev of 24th July/5th August 1811.

2 Note from the Russian minister of finance, undated.

3 Letter of 24th August/5th September 1811 from Guryev, St.Petersburg, to P.C.Labouchère, St.Petersburg.

PAGE 242

1 Letter of 25th August/6th September 1811 from P.C.Labouchère, St.Petersburg, to Guryev, St.Petersburg.
Letter of 1st/13th September 1811 from Guryev, St.Petersburg, to P.C. Labouchère, St.Petersburg.

2 Letter of 26th August/7th September 1811 from P.C.Labouchère, St.Petersburg, to John, Thomas and Henry Philip Hope, London.

3 Letter of 19th August 1812 from P.C.Labouchère, Kassel, to W.Borski, Amsterdam.

4 Letter of 11th/23rd September 1811 from P.C.Labouchère, Riga, to Hope & Co., Amsterdam.
Letter of 4th October 1811 from P.C.Labouchère, Berlin, to Hope & Co., Amsterdam.
Letter of 7th October 1811 from P.C.Labouchère, Leipzig, to Hope & Co., Amsterdam.
Letter of 11th December 1811 from P.C.Labouchère, Amsterdam, to Guryev, St.Petersburg.

5 Contract of 11th December 1811 between Willem Borski and Hope & Co.

PAGE 243

1 Letter of 25th December 1811 to W.Borski, Amsterdam, A XXVII, ii, 128.
Letter of 29th December 1811 to D.Berck and N.Entrop Muller, Amsterdam, A XXVII, ii, 129.
Letter of 16th/28th August 1812 from J.Sillem, St.Petersburg, to J.Hope, London.
Letter of 13th February 1812 from J.Hope, London, to P.C.Labouchère, Paris.
Borski bore no responsibility for the bonds transferred to him or for the five payment warrants which he had issued in favour of A.E.Hope.

2 Letter of 2nd January 1812 from P.C.Labouchère, Amsterdam, to De Ribeaupierre, St.Petersburg.

PAGE 244

1 Letter of 11th December 1811 from P.C.Labouchère, Amsterdam, to Nesselrode, St.Petersburg. Nesselrode had returned to Russia in October 1811. Waliszewski, *Règne d'Alexandre Ier*, I, 354.

2 The metallic bonds, which totalled 217,600 roubles, were divided as follows:
Ro. 15,000 in the name of P.C.Labouchère
Ro. 79,251 in the name of John Hope
Ro. 12,800 in the name of W. and J.Willink
Ro. 12,800 in the name of N. and J.P.van Staphorst
Ro. 38,400 in the name of D.J.Voombergh
Ro. 59,349 in the name of Willem Borski
Letter of 10th January 1812 to J.Sillem, Amsterdam, A XXVIII, 15. On 14th April 1812 – probably as a precaution – a redistribution of metallic bonds, totalling Ro. 219,178.8. (equivalent to cf 400,000 at a rate of exchange of 36½ *stuivers*) was made, namely:
Ro. 15,000 in the name of P.C.Labouchère
Ro. 79,251 in the name of David Berck
Ro. 12,800 in the name of W. and J.Willink
Ro. 47,749 in the name of W.Borski
Ro. 50,000 in the name of W.Borski, plus a balance of Ro. 1,578.8.
Letter of 14th April 1812 to Gouryev, St.Petersburg, A XXVIII, 65.

3 Vandal, *Napoleon Ier et Alexandre Ier*, III, 296, 412.

PAGE 245

1 *Ibid.*, 295–296.
Letter of 26th February 1812 from P.C.Labouchère, Paris, to Hope & Co., Amsterdam.

2 Talleyrand's financial straits were such that, among other steps, he was obliged to sell his books. He had had eighty works auctioned in April 1811. On 31st January 1812, Napoleon bought Talleyrand's house in the Rue de Varennes for Fr. 1,200,000. Thus, when Talleyrand sold his library to Labouchère, the worst of his financial problems were behind him. It is difficult to understand why he accepted Russian bonds as payment, since at that moment their value was largely speculative. Letters of 13th February and 24th June 1812 from J.Hope, London, to P.C. Labouchère, Paris and Amsterdam, A V, 119; of 15th May 1812 from P.C.Labouchère, Amsterdam, to J.Hope, London; of 18th August 1812 from Hottinguer & Co., Paris, to Harman & Co., London; of 23rd September and 28th October 1812 from Harman & Co., London, to J.Hope, London; and of 18th February 1813 from Hottinguer & Co., Paris, to Hope & Co., London. G.Lacour-Gayet, *Talleyrand*, II (Paris, 1930), 297, 300, 301, 304. Hottinguer, in Paris, was responsible for despatching the books. Talleyrand did not wish them to be sent in his name, since this would attract the attention of the newspapers in England. At his request, and against payment, Talleyrand received 52 volumes of the 'Annual Register' covering the years up to 1808.

PAGE 246

1 *Infra*, Appendix D-X.

2 Letter of 1st May 1812 from J.Sillem, Königsberg, to Hope & Co., Amsterdam.

Letter of 3rd May 1812 from J.Sillem, Königsberg, to Hope & Co., Amsterdam.
Letter of 8th May 1812 from J.Sillem, Danzig, to Hope & Co., Amsterdam.

3 Letter of 13th May 1812 from J.Sillem, Mitau, to Hope & Co., Amsterdam.
Letter of 7th/19th May 1812 from J.Sillem, Mitau, to Hope & Co., Amsterdam.
Letter of 11th/23rd May 1812 from J.Sillem, Riga, to Hope & Co., Amsterdam.
Letter of 17th/29th May 1812 from J.Sillem, St.Petersburg, to Hope & Co., Amsterdam.

4 Letters of 13th February and 8th May 1812 from J.Hope, London, to P.C.Labouchère, Paris.

PAGE 247

1 Letters of 15th May and 1st June 1812 from P.C.Labouchère, Amsterdam, to J.Hope, Paris. John Hope's aversion to continuing the business increased following the discovery that, by manipulating the entries of bonds and vouchers, the cashier, Elinck Sterck, had embezzled 240,000 guilders. In 1809, he had speculated with 5,000 Spanish vouchers, but just then the payment of interest on the bonds had been suspended, sending the price down. To cover his loss, he had speculated first in Dutch shares and later in Russian bonds. From the last of these malversations, there remained 61 bonds. Thanks to A. van der Hoop's keen eye, these frauds emerged when, under the new partnership, old and new business were separated for accounting purposes at the end of 1811. John Hope urged that the man be prosecuted, but Labouchère preferred to merely dismiss him in order to protect the name of the Company. A similar case, albeit on a smaller scale, had occurred at the house of Molière in The Hague. There, a clerk, who had meanwhile left, was found to have embezzled 10,000 guilders. Labouchère contributed one thousand guilders to a collection for the old Molière who, at the age of 77, lived in rooms with his daughter and had scarcely enough to eat.
Letter of 24th June 1812 from J.Hope, London, to P.C.Labouchère, Pyrmont, A v, 118.

2 Meyer & Bruxner had received a number of receipts and had already spied out the land. Letters of 19th/31st January 1812 from Meyer & Bruxner, St.Petersburg, to W.Borski, Amsterdam, and of 5th/17th March 1812 from Pichler & Co., St.Petersburg, to A.v.d.Hoop, Amsterdam.

3 Letters of 2nd, 16th and 20th May, and 16th June 1812 to J.Sillem, St.Petersburg, A XXVIII, 79, 86, 93, 116.
Letters of 17th/29th May and 29th May/10th June 1812 from J.Sillem, St.Petersburg, to Hope & Co., Amsterdam.
Letter of 1st August 1812 to John Hope, London.

PAGE 248

1 Letter of 18th/30th June 1812 from J.Sillem, St.Petersburg, to Hope & Co , Amsterdam

2 Letter of 25th June/7th July 1812 from J.Sillem, St.Petersburg, to P.C.Labouchère, Pyrmont.
Letters of 25th June/7th July and 28th June/10th July/from J.Sillem, St.Petersburg, to Hope & Co., Amsterdam. Sillem was able to send his report to Hope through the assistance of an ambassador who was leaving St.Petersburg following the declaration of hostilities.

3 H.T.Colenbrander, *Inlijving en opstand*, 2nd edition (Amsterdam, 1941), 251.
G.J.Renier, *Great Britain and the establishment of the Kingdom of the Netherlands 1813–1814: A study in British foreign policy* (The Hague, 1930), 223.
4 Letter of 5th/17th July 1812 from Guryev, St. Petersburg, to J.Sillem, St. Petersburg. Sillem carried evidence of ownership of cf 550,000 of the principal repayment of cf 800,000. Of this, cf 150,000 was to be paid in July, cf 200,000 in August and cf 200,000 in September.
5 Letter of 25th June/7th July 1812 from J.Sillem, St.Petersburg, to P.C.Labouchère, Pyrmont.

PAGE 249

1 Letter of 18th August 1812 from P.C.Labouchère, Kassel, to A.v.d.Hoop, Amsterdam.
Letter of 19th August 1812 fro, P.C.Labouchère, Kassel, to W.Borski, Amsterdam.

PAGE 250

1 Letter of 19th August 1812 from P.C.Labouchère, Kassel, to W.Borski, Amsterdam.
2 Letter of 5th September 1812 to John Hope, London.
3 Letters of 5th and 8th September 1812 from P.C.Labouchère, Frankfurt, to A.v.d.Hoop, Amsterdam.
Letter of 8th September 1812 from P.C.Labouchère, Frankfurt, to W.Borski, Amsterdam.

PAGE 251

1 Letters of 10th and 20th September 1812 from J.Hope, London, to J.Sillem, St.Petersburg, A v, 133, 139.
Letter of 24th September 1812 from J.Hope, London, to Guryev, St.Petersburg, A v, 140.
2 Letter of 25th September 1812 to J.Hope, London.
Letter of 19th September 1812 to J.Sillem, St.Petersburg, A XXVIII, 17.
3 'Speech given on behalf of Hope & Co. by A.v.d.Hoop at the meeting on 17th September 1812.' 'Resolutie van de algemeene vergadering van geïnteresseerden in de Russische leeningen,' held in the Doelen on 17th September 1812.

PAGE 252

1 Letter of 11th September 1812 from P.C.Labouchère, Frankfurt, to J.Sillem, St.Petersburg.
Letter of 22nd September 1812 from P.C.Labouchère, Frankfurt, to Hope & Co., Amsterdam.
Letter of 29th September 1812 to P.C.Labouchère, Frankfurt, A XXVIII, 176.
Letter of 7th November 1812 from W.Borski, Amsterdam, to Hope & Co., Amsterdam.
2 Letters of 22nd and 29th September 1812 from P.C.Labouchère, Frankfurt, to A.v.d.Hoop, Amsterdam.
Robert Voûte had been appointed Director of the Central Fund by Napoleon. In this post he was responsible to the Intendant of Finances, Gogel, who in turn was responsible to the Govenor-general, Lebrun.
Colenbrander, *Inlijving en Opstand*, 56.

Letter of 29th September 1812 to P.C.Labouchère, Frankfurt, A XXVIII, 177.
30th September 1812: requests to the Duke of Rovigo and the Emperor of the French, A XXVIII, 181, 183.

3 Letter of 14th/26th November 1812 from Guryev, St.Petersburg, to J.Sillem, St.Petersburg.
Letter of 15th/27th November 1812 from J.Sillem, St.Petersburg, to P.C.Labouchère, Frankfurt.
Letter of 31st December 1812 from P.C.Labouchère, Frankfurt, to A.v.d.Hoop, Amsterdam.

4 Letter of 31st December 1812 from P.C.Labouchère, Frankfurt, to Hope & Co., Amsterdam.
Letter of 9th January 1813 to P.C.Labouchère, Frankfurt, A XXVIII, 277. The managers decided not to publicize the fact that Labouchère had been refused a passport to enter Russia.

PAGE 253

1 Letters of 24th October, and 3rd, 14th and 28th November 1812 to J.Sillem, St.Petersburg, A XXVIII, 194, 209, 221, 232.
Letter of 29th October 1812 to J.Hope, London.

2 Letters of 12th and 21st November, and 1st December 1812 to Count von Stackelberg, Vienna, A XXVIII, 219, 229, 240.
Amburger, *Geschichte Behördenorganisation*, 446, 447.

3 Letter of 10th December 1812 from M.Bethmann, Frankfurt, to A.v.d.Hoop, Amsterdam.
Bethmann anticipated that the price would fall to 25–26 in January, and this he regarded as the limit. In fact, the price varied between 37 and 41 in January.

4 Letters of 10th July and 28th September 1812 from J.Hope, London, to Hope & Co., Amsterdam, A V, 123, 142.
Letter of 29th September 1812 from J.Hope, London, to D.Berck, Amsterdam, A V, 145.
Letter of 1st August 1812 to J.Hope, London.
Letter of 22nd September 1812 from P.C.Labouchère, Frankfurt, to A.v.d.Hoop, Amsterdam.

5 *Infra*, 426.
Letter of 28th February 1813 from D.Berck, Amsterdam, to J.Hope, London. Berck went so far as to say that, if necessary, he would draw on London.

PAGE 254

1 Letter of 28th February 1813 from D.Berck, Amsterdam, to J.Hope, London.

2 Letter of 28th February 1813 to J.Hope, London.
Labouchère also dissociated himself from any reimbursement of travelling expenses.
Letter of 1st March 1813 from W.Borski, Amsterdam, to Hope & Co., Amsterdam.

3 Letter of 18th February 1813 from Baring Bros., London, to Hope & Co., Amsterdam.
Letter of 21st February 1813 from S.P.Labouchère, Rotterdam, to A.v.d.Hoop, Amsterdam.
Letter of 27th February 1813 to Baring Bros., London, A XXVIII, 316.
Letter of 22nd March 1813 from Harman & Co., London, to Hope & Co., Amsterdam.

Letter of 31st March 1813 from Hottinguer & Co., Paris, to Hope & Co., Amsterdam.
Letter of 22nd June 1813 to Baron Voûte, Paris, A XXVIII, 372. The issue of the 'Moniteur' dated 31st March 1813 contained a report of the expulsion of Borski and S.P.Labouchère.

4 Letter of 11th/23rd October 1812 from J.Sillem, St.Petersburg, to Hope & Co., Amsterdam. Nevertheless, a further cf 93,239.4.0., representing sales of goods, was credited to the account H. of Melvil & Co. during the course of 1812.

PAGE 255

1 30th November 1812: Report on Operation R.M.Sillem succeeded in getting Wolff & Schlüsser to reduce their exhorbitant charges of Ro. 4,960.4 by Ro. 4,000 by threatening to publish their charge account alongside that of Blessig in a Dutch newspaper.
Letter of 8th/20th November 1812 from J.Sillem, St.Petersburg, to R.Melvil, Amsterdam.
The loss on the tar shipped by Becker amount ed to cf 56,030. Depreciation of cf 200,000 was applied to Operation R.M. during 1810. In 1812, cf 65,000 of this was restored under the head 'excess depreciation of profit and loss,' *grootboek* 1810: Account $^{7}/_{16}$, our account R.M., 199, *grootboek* 1812: Account $^{7}/_{16}$, our account R.M., 117. A further cf 93,239.4 was transferred via Melvil & Co. in 1812 (note 4, page 254). This represented remittances from Blessig, Meyer & Bruxner and Benecke & Co. of Hamburg; the last-named served as an intermediary for some remittances from Russia. In addition, Meyer & Bruxner remitted Ro. 69,757 to Baring Brothers in 1812. The former had also placed a sum of Ro. 29,120 at the disposal of Sillem upon his arrival in St.Petersburg. During 1812, this house sold 40,065 poods of Demidov's iron, the net proceeds totalling Ro. 171,505.89, and 141 bales, or 420,000 arshins, of crash, which netted Ro. 75,065. Of the stock of metal, 17,345 poods of Demidov's common bar old sable iron, 37,134 poods of Yakovlev's broad iron, 200,884 poods of P.S.F. common bar old sable iron and 1,438 poods of copper then remained. Sillem received a commission of 2% on the sums remitted to Holland since his arrival in Russia.

2 Letter of 28th November 1812 to J.Sillem, St.Petersburg, A XXVIII, 232.
Letter of 28th November 1812 to Guryev, St.Petersburg, A XXVIII, 237.
Letter of 17th/29 January 1813 from J.Sillem, St.Petersburg, to Hope & Co., Amsterdam.
It was not until 16th March 1813 that Guryev wrote to say that he recognized the duty to repay the cf 800,000 furnished in bonds; repayment, plus interest, was effected in twelve monthly instalments. Hope's connexions in England were of great value in this matter for, thanks to the English subsidies, it suited the Russian government to pay through Harman & Co.
Grootboek 1814: Russian Crown, 19.

3 Prince Dolgorukov was reported to be particularly concerned about the Dutch prisoners of war. As mentioned in note 2 on page 232, Prince Dolgorukov had been his country's envoy to the Kingdom of Holland until 1810. Among the persons about whom Sillem was asked to enquire were Von Kretschmar, Joseph Charles le Bas, Charles Augustin le Bas, Morard de Galles, Joachim Rendorp, Colonel Wagner, De Pontecoulant and De Noinville. In July 1813, Sillem wrote to say that the

correspondence concerning prisoners of war could better be entrusted to a Russian house because difficulty with the language hampered his contacts with the war and police departments.

4 *British and Foreign State Papers, edited by the Librarian of the Foreign Office*, I (London, 1838), 58, 63.

PAGE 256

1 O. Karmin, 'Autour des négociations financières Anglo-Prusso-Russes de 1813,' *Revue Historique de la Révolution et de l'Empire*, XI, 1917, 177–197, XII, 1917, 24–49, 216–252.
C. K. Webster, *The foreign policy of Castlereagh, 1812–1815*, I (London, 1931), 133.
F. de Martens, *Supplément au Recueil des Traités*, V, 1808–1814 (Göttingen, 1817), 568–570, 577–579. It was agreed at the Reichenbach Convention that paper money, to be known as 'argent fédératif,' would be issued to a value of 5 million pounds sterling. Half of this sum was to be repaid by England, $^{2}/_{6}$th by Russia and $^{1}/_{6}$th by Prussia. Of the 5 million pounds, Russia would receive two-thirds and Prussia one-third. Grave doubts concerning the ability of Russia and Prussia to repay this money, coupled with the insistence of the Prussian statesman Von Stein that England alone should guarantee the paper money (something which that country was unwilling to do), resulted in the 'argent fédératif' plan being dropped. Instead, England, in the supplementary convention of 30th September 1812, undertook to pay out half of the original sum, i.e. $2\frac{1}{2}$ million pounds sterling. This took the form of bills of credit which could later be exchanged for inscribed stock payable in cash, plus 6% interest. Two-thirds of the bills went to Russia and one-third to Prussia.
Memoir of the Public Life of the Right Hon. John Charles Herries, in the reigns of George III, George IV, William IV and Victoria, by his son Edward Herries, C.B., I (London, 1880), 88.

2 Letters of 26th November and 31st December 1812 to J.Hope, London.
Letters of 28th November 1812, and 9th January, 20th March, 1st June and 12th June 1813 to J. Sillem, St.Petersburg, A XXVIII, 232, 270, 332, 362, 365.
Letter of 17th January 1813 from P.C.Labouchère, Frankfurt, to A.v.d. Hoop, Amsterdam.

3 Letter of 17th January 1813 from P.C.Labouchère, Frankfurt, to A.v.d. Hoop, Amsterdam.
Letter of 12th June 1813 to J. Sillem, St.Petersburg, A XXVIII, 365.

4 Letter of 22nd June to Baron Voûte, Paris, A XXVIII, 372.

5 Letters of 4th and 14th August 1813 from Von Stackelberg, Vienna, to Hope & Co., Amsterdam.

6 Letters of 26th August and 9th September 1813 to Von Stackelberg, Vienna, A XXVIII, 411, 412.

PAGE 257

1 Letter of 10th November 1813 from Von Stackelberg, Vienna, to Hope & Co., Amsterdam.
Letter of 11th November 1813 from Von Stackelberg, Vienna, to P.C.Labouchère, Frankfurt.

2 1st November 1813: Confidential report by the prefect of the Zuyderzee *département* to the minister for home affairs. H.T.Colenbrander, *Gedenkstukken*, VI (The Hague,

1911), 478–479. The Rothschilds had been similarly watched by the French secret police in 1812, because they were suspected of having connexions with a relative, Nathan Mayer Rothschild, in London; Mollien, however, had protected them. E.C.Conte Corti, *Der Aufstieg des Hauses Rothschild* (Leipzig, 1927), 131–132. After Holland had been liberated, Labouchére, in company with Bethmann, made efforts to persuade the new government of the Netherlands to adopt a conciliatory policy which would include allowing those who had served Napoleon to continue in office and, if possible, reaching a compromise with the emperor himself. These semi-diplomatic attempts at mediation aroused the same sort of irritation and suspicion in the agent of the future King William I, Hans von Gagern – who had discussed the matter with Labouchère and Bethmann in Frankfurt in late November and early December 1813 – as they had aroused in De Celles a month earlier. H.T.Colenbrander, *Gedenkstukken*, VI, 1981; *Gedenkstukken*, VII (The Hague, 1914), 371, 388.

3 Letter of 23rd November 1813 from P.C.Labouchère, Frankfurt, to Von Stackelberg, Vienna.
Letter of 1st December 1813 from Von Stackelberg, Vienna, to P.C.Labouchère, Frankfurt.
Letter of 10th December 1813 from P.C.Labouchère, Mannheim, to Von Stackelberg, Vienna.
Letter of 15th March 1814 to A.Baring, London. Sillem was somewhat surprised by the unexpected draft.
Letter of 4th/16th November 1813 from J. Sillem, St.Petersburg, to Hope & Co., Amsterdam.

PAGE 258

1 Waliszewski, *Règne d'Alexandre Ier*, II, 203.
Letter of 13th November 1813 from P.C.Labouchère, Frankfurt, to Guryev, St.Petersburg.
Letter of 15th November 1813 from P.C.Labouchère, Frankfurt, to J.Sillem, St.Petersburg.
Letter of 28th November 1813 from P.C.Labouchère, Mannheim, to Hope & Co., Amsterdam.
Napoleon had also stayed with Bethmann in 1813.
Conte Corti, *Aufstieg Rothschild*, 453.
2 Letter of 15th January 1814 to Guryev, St.Petersburg, A XXVIII, 454.
Letter of 1st January 1814 to J.Sillem, St.Petersburg, A XXVIII, 452.
3 Letter of 25th March 1814 from J.Sillem, St.Petersburg, to Hope & Co., Amsterdam.

PAGE 259

1 Letter of 7/19th February 1814 from Guryev, St.Petersburg, to Hope & Co., Amsterdam.
Letter of 11th February 1814 from M.v. Bethmann, Frankfurt, to Hope & Co., Amsterdam.
Letter of 25th March 1814 from J. Sillem, St.Petersburg, to Hope & Co., Amsterdam.
Letter of 18th March 1814 from De Gervais, Amsterdam, to P.C.Labouchère, London.
Karmin, 'Autour des négociations,' 251–252. De Gervais was to work under the

supervision of Nesselrode. Under Article 4 of the supplementary convention of 30th September 1813, the Russian and Prussian representatives were made responsible for ensuring that the credit of their respective countries was not harmed by the issue of the bills of credit. Prussia sent the well-known classicist and historian Barthold Niebuhr to Amsterdam as its representative. He had tried unsuccessfully to negotiate a loan for Prussia with Hope & Co. in 1808, and since then had demonstrated a clear dislike of the Company, and especially of P.C.Labouchère.

2 Letter of 24th February 1814 from P.C.Labouchère, London, to De Gervais, Amsterdam.
Letter of 25th February 1814 from P.C.Labouchère, London, to Hope & Co., Amsterdam.
Letter of 26th February 1814 to J. Sillem, St.Petersburg, A XXVIII, 478.

3 Letter of 22nd February 1814 from P.C.Labouchère, London, to Hope & Co., Amsterdam.

PAGE 260

1 Letter of 25th February 1814 from P.C.Labouchère, London, to Hope & Co., Amsterdam.
Letter of 4th March 1814 to D.Berck and N.A.Entrop Muller, Amsterdam, A XXVIII, 481.

2 Letter of 22nd February 1814 from P.C.Labouchère, London, to Hope & Co., Amsterdam.

3 Letter of 23rd February 1814 from S.P.Labouchère, Rotterdam, to A.v.d. Hoop, Amsterdam.
Letter of 24th February 1814 from S.P.Labouchère, Rotterdam, to A.v.d. Hoop, Amsterdam.

4 Letter of 12th March 1814 to De Gervais, Amsterdam, A XXVIII, 489.
Letter of 1st March 1814 to Bethmann Bros., Frankfurt, A XXVIII, 481.

5 *Memoir Herries*, 85.
Letter of 10th/11th March 1814 from P.C.Labouchère, London, to Hope & Co., Amsterdam.

PAGE 261

1 Letter of 7th/8th March 1814 from P.C.Labouchère, London, to Hope & Co., Amsterdam.
After 1807 the Mint in Utrecht became the official Mint. Enno van Gelder, *De Nederlandse Munten*, 165, 167.

2 Letter of 7th/8th March 1814 from P.C.Labouchère, London, to Hope & Co., Amsterdam.

3 Letters concerning purchases of money: of 28th February, 4th, 8th, 12th, 18th and 24th March, 1st, 4th, 9th and 20 th April 1814 to De Gervais, Amsterdam, A XXVIII, 480, 483, 486, 489, 491, 493, 494, 495, 496–498, 507; of 12th May 1814 to De Gervais, Paris, A XXVIII, 519.

4 Letter of 25th February 1814 from P.C.Labouchère, London, to Hope & Co., Amsterdam.

5 Letter of 7th March 1814 from P.C.Labouchère, London, to D.Voombergh, Amsterdam. Labouchère felt that the machinations of the speculators could be brought to an end by making it compulsory to produce the covering bond when making a payment in matured vouchers.

PAGE 262

1 Letters of 25th March, and 5th April 1814 from J.Sillem, St.Petersburg, to Hope & Co., Amsterdam.
Letter of 18th March 1814 from De Gervais, Amsterdam, to P.C.Labouchère, London.
Letter of 1st April 1814 from P.C.Labouchère, London, to Hope & Co., Amsterdam.
Letter of 23rd April 1814 to J. Sillem, St.Petersburg, A XXVIII, 509.

2 Letter of 9th April 1814 from De Gervais, Amsterdam, to Hope & Co., Amsterdam.
Letter of 9th April 1814 to De Gervais, Amsterdam, A XXVIII, 498.
Letter of 12th April 1814 from P.C.Labouchère, London, to Hope & Co., Amsterdam.
Memoir Herries, 87, 89. Conte Corti, *Aufstieg Rothschild*, 139–140.

3 Letters of 22nd March and 5th April 1814 from P.C.Labouchère, London, to Hope & Co., Amsterdam.

PAGE 263

1 Letter of 29th April 1814 to De Gervais, Amsterdam, A XXVIII, 515.
Letter of 7th May 1814 to J.Sillem, St.Petersburg, A XXVIII, 517.
Letter of 26th April 1814 from P.C.Labouchère, London, to Hope & Co., Amsterdam.
Memoir Herries, 89, 237.

2 *Ibid.*, 238, 239.

3 Letter of 17th May 1814 from P.C.Labouchère, Paris, to De Gervais, Paris.
Letter of 17th May 1814 from De Gervais, Paris, to P.C.Labouchère, Paris.
Memoir Herries, 90, 240.

PAGE 264

1 Letter of 19th June 1814 from P.C.Labouchère, London, to Nesselrode(?)
Letter from G. Harrison, Secretary to the Treasury, to William Hamilton, Under-Secretary of Foreign Affairs, in reply to Count Nesselrode's note of 14th May 1814. Although this letter is only a reply to a note from Nesselrode, Harrison requests Hamilton to make its contents known to Castlereagh, who had passed notes from both the Russian and Prussian governments to the Lords Commissioners. We may assume that the notes from the governments were almost identical. It is scarcely conceivable that the Lords Commissioners would have agreed to general measures relating to the bills of credit of the Russian and Prussian requests had differed widely. *Memoir Herries*, 92, 240.

2 The documents ratifying the peace treaty were exchanged prior to 15th June, and thus redemption of the bills of credit would have had to commence on 15th July at the latest. Letter of 7th June 1814 from De Gervais, Amsterdam, to P.C.Labouchère, London.

3 Letters of 31st May and 7th June 1814 from De Gervais, Amsterdam, to P.C.Labouchère, London. De Gervais announced in a Frankfurt journal that, during a period of two months, facilities would be provided in Berlin and Königsberg whereby the *assignats* could either be exchanged for payment orders on the Russian Treasury, or for the first one-third in cash at the rate of 29 Prussian talers to 100 roubles or for 2-month drafts on London; for the second one-third in 9-month, 7% bonds in Prussian talers at the rate of 30 talers to 100 roubles; and for

the final one-third in similar bonds with a life of 18 months and bearing interest at 7%. *Assignats* in circulation in Germany were not allowed to be sent to Russia, lest this caused a further decline in the value of the rouble. *Memoir Herries*, 95. The low rate of exchange of the rouble produced such a demand for drafts on London that the exchange rate of the rouble there was adversely affected.

PAGE 265

1 Letters of 7th, 10th and 14th June 1814 from P.C.Labouchère, London, to Hope & Co., Amsterdam.
2 Letter of 17th June 1814 from De Gervais, Amsterdam, to P.C.Labouchère, London. Herries, representing the British Treasury, subsequently took over the agreement between Rothschild and the Russian government providing for accelerated payment of the first six monthly instalments, and also a second transaction relating to the last eight instalments. The assignment brought the British government a sizeable financial advantage, but we may assume that Rothschild also fared well. *Memoir Herries*, 93. R. Ehrenburg, *Grosse Vermögen, ihre Entstehung und ihre Bedeutung* (Jena, 1902), 65. Conte Corti, *Aufstieg Rothschild*, 151–152.
3 Letters of 26th and 28th July 1814 from P.C.Labouchère, London, to Hope & Co., Amsterdam.
Letter of 8th October 1814 from P.C.Labouchère, Paris, to A.v.d. Hoop, Amsterdam.
Letter of 22nd October 1814 to J.Sillem, St.Petersburg, A XXVIII, 583.

PAGE 266

1 Letter of 23rd July 1814 from De Gervais, Amsterdam, to Hope & Co., Amsterdam.
Letter of 25th July 1814 from Sir Geo. Burgmann, Amsterdam, to Hope & Co., Amsterdam. This concerned the monthly instalment due on 15th January 1815. This was paid through Rothschild.
Letter of 13th December 1814 to Salomon Mayer Rothschild, Amsterdam, A XXVIII, 616.
Letter of 17th December 1814 to De Gervais, Berlin, A XXVIII, 617.
2 Letter of 26th July 1814 from P.C.Labouchère, London, to Hope & Co., Amsterdam. Labouchère's disappointment over the cf 500,000 advance is understandable. However, during their meeting in Paris in May, De Gervais had made it clear that he did not intend to repay this advance with bills of credit.
Letter of 17th May 1814 from P.C.Labouchère, Paris, to Hope & Co., Amsterdam.
3 Letter of 22nd October 1814 to J.Sillem, St.Petersburg, A XXVIII, 583.
4 Letter of 27th December 1812/8th January 1813 from J.Sillem, St.Petersburg, to Hope & Co., Amsterdam.
5 Letters of 17th/29th June, 22nd July/3rd August and 9th/21st September 1813 from J.Sillem, St.Petersburg, to Hope & Co., Amsterdam. Sillem sold a further 300 ravenducks in September 1813, but apart from these the market was totally dead.
6 Letter of 4/16th November 1813 from J.Sillem, St.Petersburg, to Hope & Co., Amsterdam.

PAGE 267

1 Letters of 18th February/2nd March and 10th/22nd April 1814 from J.Sillem, St.Petersburg, to P.C.Labouchère, London. During Sillem's absence, his brother, Johann, took charge of affairs.

2 Letter of 21st April/3rd May 1814 from J.Sillem, St.Petersburg, to Hope & Co., Amsterdam.
Letter of 24th May 1814 from J.Sillem, Altona, to Hope & Co., Amsterdam.
Letters of 7th and 10th June 1814 from P.C.Labouchère, London, to Hope & Co., Amsterdam.
Letter of 13th June 1814 from De Gervais, Amsterdam, to P.C.Labouchère, London.
3 Letters of 14th and 21st June 1814 from P.C.Labouchère, London, to Hope & Co., Amsterdam. On 19th June, Labouchère had a meeting with Nesselrode, who repeated his assurance that the Dutch investors could fully rely upon the loyalty of the czar. Guryev had said something similar to Sillem, but he had not elaborated on this.
Concerning the festivities in London: H. Nicholson, *The Congress of Vienna, a study in allied unity 1812–1822* (New York, 1946), 113–116.

PAGE 268

1 Letter of 5th July 1814 to Guryev, St.Petersburg, A XXVIII, 540. To meet the czar's expenses during his stay in Holland, Hope & Co. advanced 6,000 ducats at cf 5.14 to the ducat. *Grootboek* 1814: Russian Crown, 19. Renier, *Great Britain*, 198.
2 Letter of 11th July 1814 from P.C.Labouchère, London, to Hope & Co., Amsterdam.
3 H.T.Colenbrander, *Ontstaan der Grondwet*, II (RGP, Kleine Serie 7, The Hague, 1909), 32–33.
Colenbrander, *Gedenkstukken*, VII, 62, 79–82, 85–87, 90, 161.
H.T.Colenbrander, *Vestiging van het Koninkrijk, 1813–1815* (Amsterdam, 1927), 178–182, 186.
Renier, *Great Britain*, 260, 261, 295. The question of interest payments by Russia had arisen in negotiations between the allies prior to the first Peace of Paris (Cf. page 248). Russia had made it a condition of her signature to the treaty of Chaumont (9th March 1814), under which the allies entered into a 20-year pact to oppose France, that England and Holland should assume responsibility for her debt in Holland. Castlereagh had then rejected the ultimatum. Under the final clause of the protocol of 21st June 1814, Nesselrode could press the claim.
4 Letter of 1st August 1814 from P.C.Labouchère, Rotterdam, to Hope & Co., Amsterdam.
Letter of 4th/14th September 1814 from J.Sillem, St.Petersburg, to Hope & Co., Amsterdam.
Letter of 15th October 1814 to J. Sillem, St.Petersburg, A XXVIII, 579.

PAGE 269

1 Letter of 25th September/7th October 1814 from J. Sillem, St.Petersburg, to R.Melvil, Amsterdam. The deal concerned P.S.F. iron from Yakovlev. Michailov offered 40,000 roubles in cash and the balance in proportion to the deliveries of the iron, spread over 7 months and with interest at $\frac{1}{2}$% per month.
Letter of 8th/18th November 1814 to the widow of W.Borski, Matthiessen & Sillem and Bethmann Bros., A XXVIII, 605. The market revived following the sale of the 200,000 poods of iron. Sillem put this down to commercial jealousy. A more probable explanation is that others also commenced to speculate on a resumption of trade with America in the next shipping season.
2 6th/18th November 1814: Purchase and Sale Accounts of Schlüsser & Co.,

St.Petersburg, covering 2,950 pieces of raven-duck at Ro. 36 and 500 pieces of Flemish linen at Ro. 45¾. 12th/24th November: Sale Account of Cramer Bros., St.Petersburg, covering 1,930 pieces of raven-duck, of which 1,830 were sold at Ro. 36 and 100 at Ro. 34 (owing to deterioration of quality). 13th/25th November 1814: Sale Account of N.D.Bothlingk, covering 1,516 pieces of Flemish linen at Ro.45¾ and 1,904 pieces of raven-duck at Ro. 36.

3 The purchasing costs of 238,000 poods of Yakovlev's P.S.F. iron, 9,725 poods of Demidov's iron and 1,428 poods of copper totalled cf 395,518, converted at a rate of 17 *stuivers* to the rouble. The selling price, after deducting costs, was cf 403,223, based on the fixed rate of 10¼ *stuivers* to the rouble. Ignoring the loss of interest, the profit was thus 2%. The raven-duck and the Flemish linen had in 1809 together cost cf 135,116, based on a rate of 17 *stuivers*. In 1814, at a rate of 10 *stuivers*, they fetched cf 159,078, after deducting costs. The profit on these, ignoring loss of interest, was therefore 20%.

PAGE 270

1 Letters of 15th and 25th October 1814 to J.Sillem, St.Petersburg, A XXVIII, 579, 589. Letter of 27th October/8th November 1814 from J.Sillem, St.Petersburg, to Hope & Co., Amsterdam. The cf 800,000 was furnished in the form of a letter of credit from Salomon Mayer Rothschild on Braunsberg & Co. of Amsterdam. This was made out in favour of Guryev and transferred by his endorsement to Hope & Co. 30th December 1814: Acknowledgement of receipt of cf 800,000 from Braunsberg & Co. Sillem received letters of introduction to 12 houses, namely Meyer & Bruxner, Colombi Zea & Co., Livio Bros. & Co., Amburger & Son, Stieglitz & Co., Ph.Stieglitz, Bagge & Co., Blessig & Co., J.A.Krehmer and Messrs.J.Krause; J.D.Drachenhauer & Co. and B.J.Zuckerbäcker Klein & Co., in Riga were the only houses outside St.Petersburg Sillem characterized a number of these houses: J A.Krehmer bit off more than it could chew, and would have lost heavily in 1814; Ph.Stieglitz was not a businessman, and had no opportunity to do anything abroad; Zuckerbäcker Klein & Co. had been successful in recent years and was worth retaining by reason of the honesty, energy and intelligence of the manager; but it was necessary to keep a tight rein on the house because the partners still had the unfortunate habit of exceeding their capacity. Letter of 25th October 1814 to J.Sillem, St.Petersburg, A XXVIII, 589.

Letter of 10th/22nd November 1814 from J.Sillem, St.Petersburg, to Hope & Co., Amsterdam. Hope informed Sillem that there was little demand for linen goods in Holland, but that prices were high on account of the small stocks. Little linseed was being sold, but not much was arriving either. Significant quantities of copper had been sold to Belgium, Germany and France during 1814, but strong competition from the Hamburg market adversely influenced sales in Amsterdam. The broker whom the Company employed in this sector was not particularly active, and for a commodity such as copper, which was not sold every day, this was a considerable handicap. Letters of 25th October and 1st November 1814 to J.Sillem, St.Petersburg, A XXVIII, 589, 596.

2 Letters of 14th and 20th October 1814 from P.C.Labouchère, Bordeaux and Nantes, to A.v.d.Hoop, Amsterdam.
Letter of 15th October 1814 to J.Sillem, St.Petersburg, A XXVIII, 579.

3 Renier, *Great Britain*, 297. Colenbrander, *Vestiging*, 209–213.

PAGE 272

1 Renier, *ibid.*, 298. Colenbrander, *ibid.*, 213.
2 Letter of 28th April 1815 from P.F.Lestapis, Amsterdam, to P.C.Labouchère, London.
Letter of 4th May 1815 from P.C.Labouchère, London, to Count Lieven, London. In their calculation of 15th April 1815, the partners put the balance of the principal sum at cf 84,300,000. In fact, 2000 bonds out of the total of 88,300 had been redeemed in 1803 and a further 2,700 in the years 1811 and 1812, so that 83,600 remained. In calculating the principal sum, Weeveringh, *Geschiedenis Staatsschulden*, II, 673, took no account of the redemption of 2,000 bonds in 1803.
3 Letter of 9th May 1815 from P.C.Labouchère, London, to Hope & Co., Amsterdam.
4 Letter of 16th May 1815 from P.C.Labouchère, London, to Hope & Co., Amsterdam.
5 At this time Talleyrand, who was in Vienna, kept Labouchère informed about political developments. His letters contain no reference to the unreliability of the Belgians.
Letters of 6th, 9th and 23rd April 1815 from Talleyrand, Vienna, to P.C.Labouchère, London.
Letter of 31st March 1815 from P.C.Labouchère, London, to A.v.d.Hoop, Amsterdam.

PAGE 273

1 Letter of 13th/25th June 1815 from Count Lieven, London, to P.C.Labouchère, London.
Early in 1816, 2 million francs were remitted to Hope from Paris by Rothschild and Gontard; a further 2½ million francs followed in the second half of the year. From these funds, two drafts each of cf 456,250 were issued for the dowry of the Grand Duchess Anna Paulowna, who married the Crown Prince in 1816.
According to the marriage contract of 1815, the grand duchess received a gift of 1 million roubles (N.Japikse, *De geschiedenis van het Huis Oranje-Nassau*, II, The Hague, 1948, 164). Observing that the rate of exchange of the rouble was then about 10 *stuivers*, the sum remitted was nearly twice that referred to in the marriage contract. Letters of 24th January/5th February, 6th/18th March, 22nd April/4th May, 31st May/12th June, 1st/13th July, 5th/17th August and 30th September/12th October 1816 from Guryev, St.Petersburg, to Hope & Co., Amsterdam.
Letters of 2nd, 8th, 15th and 26th March 1816 from De Gervais, Paris, to Hope & Co., Amsterdam.
2 'Avis' dated 9th November 1815, issued by Hope & Co. Vouchers which had matured on 1st January 1813 participated in a ballot for cf 100,000, those maturing on 1st January 1814 in a ballot for cf 75,000, those which had matured on 1st January 1815 shared cf 50,000 and those which fell due on 1st January 1816 shared cf 25,000. At the request of a large numner of bondholders, the bonuses were divided into lots of cf 1,000 in order that as many holders as possible could benefit. Letter of 13th November 1815 from A.Brinkman, Amsterdam, to Hope & Co., Amsterdam.
Stamp duty on the 18,000 new bonds was limited to 9½ *stuivers*. The 'Conseiller de Collège,' Perovsky, visited Amsterdam, for the purpose of countersigning the bonds. Because they were given in the form of bonds, the bonuses served to increase Russia's debt to cf 101,600,000. The sums of interest capitalized were:

Over 1812 at 5% cf	4,104,000 interest on interest from 1.1.13 to 1.1.16	cf	615,600
Over 1813 at 5% cf	4,180,000 interest on interest from 1.1.14 to 1.1.16	cf	418,000
Over 1814 at 5% cf	4,180,000 interest on interest from 1.1.15 to 1.1.16	cf	209,000
Over 1815 at 5% cf	4,180,000 interest on interest	cf	– –
cf	16,644,000	cf	1,242,600
Total to be converted plus bonus		cf	17,886,600
		cf	250,000
		cf	18,136,600

Of this sum, cf 18,000,000 was met by the issue of 18,000 new bonds. The Russian Court also had at its disposal 1,307 bonds which, with interest on interest, arrears of interest and two bonuses, were worth cf 1,576,135. (The ballot on 1st June 1811 had reduced the number to 1,289). After the payment of the balance of cf 136,600 plus Hope's commission of 6½% on cf 18,000,000, i.e. cf 1,170,000, there remained cf 269,535 or 269 bonds plus cf 535. 'Compte Général,' enclosed with Hope's letter of 15th June 1816 to Guryev, St.Petersburg

3 Letter of 11th December 1815 from J.v.d.Poll, C.v.d.Oudermeulen, J.Bondt, J.de Burlett and J.v.d.Mandele, to Hope & Co., Amsterdam.

4 Letter of 12th December 1815 from A.v.d.Hoop, Amsterdam, to J.v d.Poll, *cum suis*, Amsterdam.

PAGE 274

1 Weeveringh, *Geschiedenis Staatsschulden*, II, 872–873.

CHAPTER NINE

PAGE 279

1 J.Vicens Vives, *An Economic History of Spain* (Princeton, 1969), 475–476.

2 *Ibid.*, 484, 486, 507, 547.
Richard Herr, *The Eighteenth-Century Revolution in Spain* (Princeton, 1958), 11.

3 Vicens Vives, *Economic History*, 576–578 Herr, *Revolution*, 121–122

4 Vicens Vives, *Economic History*, 585–586 Herr, *Revolution*, 146.
Earl J.Hamilton, *War and Prices in Spain* (Harvard Economic Studies, LXXXXI), Cambridge, Mass., 1947, 78–79.
According to Hamilton, a syndicate of Spanish, French and Dutch merchants provided funds for an issue of *vales*. The Hope archives reveal no evidence that the Company was concerned in this.

PAGE 280

1 Concerning De Cabarrus as a promulgator of enlightened ideas: Jean Sarrailh, *L'Espagne éclairée de la seconde moitié du XVIII siècle* (Paris, 1954), *passim.*
Concerning the Bank of San Carlos: Earl.J.Hamilton, 'The foundation of the Bank of Spain,' *The Journal of Political Economy*, LIII (1945), 101.

2 G.A. Amsterdam, Not. Arch., 12441–719, 12444–796, 12454–592.
In *War and Prices in Spain* Hamilton points to loans totalling more than two million guilders for Spanish account in Amsterdam in the period 1778–1880 (p. 78). It is possible that he was referring to the three canal loans; but it is also conceivable that the reference was to a number of royal 'warrants' decreeing loans which in fact were not negotiated.
Herr, *Revolution*, 132–133.
Vicens Vives, *Economic History*, 515, 586.

3 The loans concerned were furnished by Badin & Co. on 1st March 1770 and 1st March 1773. The king of Spain gave a permanent guarantee in respect of the loans obtained from Echenique Sanchez & Co.

4 G.A. Amsterdam, Not. Arch., 12464–558, 559.
The issuing houses received commission of 2% on interest payments and 1% on repayments of principal Although the loan was repaid in accordance with the terms, a large number of bonds were not tendered by the prescribed date. On 19th May 1797, Paulus Taay, who was then a manager of Hope & Co., arranged for the official cancellation of 434 bonds; at the same time, Hogguer Grand & Co tendered 325 bonds for cancellation. On 19th May 1801 Hogguer Grand & Co. had a further 79 bonds cancelled.

PAGE 281

1 E.J.Hamilton, 'The Foundation of the Bank of Spain,' 165.
Grootboek 1783: 225, 352.
2 *Grootboek* 1789: 38, 304.
Grootboek 1790: 60.
Grootboek 1791: 337.
Grootboek 1792: 81.
3 Labouchère's judgement, as expressed in his instructions to William Gordon Coesvelt, 22nd July 1807. W.G.C. I.
4 G.A. Amsterdam, Not. Arch., 17984–95, 96.
Of the 6,000 bonds, the following numbers were cancelled on the dates shown: 24th October 1800: 1,193; 15th July 1801: 601; 4th March 1802: 592; 8th December 1802: 500; 9th March 1803: 89; 7th October 1803: 16; 7th December 1803: 2; 5th January 1804: 499; 8th February 1804: 63; 9th April 1804: 21; 18th July 1804: 4; 28th September 1804: 1; 5th October 1804: 1; 21st November 1804: 411; 6th December 1804: 85; 4th January 1805: 38; 8th February 1805: 36; 4th April 1805: 18; 8th August 1805: 7; 15th October 1805: 3; 4th November 1805: 2; 21st November 1805: 427; 10th January 1806: 67.

PAGE 282

1 Letter from P.C.Labouchère to W.G.Coesvelt. W.G.C. I.
R.Altamira, *A History of Spain* (New York, 1949), 514. Herr, *Revolution*, 286–287.
2 Herr, *Revolution*, 310, 314, 317, 323, 335.
Altamira, *History of Spain*, 515.
3 Vicens Vives, *Economic History*, 586–587.
Hamilton, *War and Prices*, 85.

PAGE 283

1 Letters of 13th January, 3rd, 20th February, 6th, 17th March, 26th May, 20th October 1798 from H.A.Insinger, Amsterdam, to Hope & Co., London.
2 J A.Sillem, *Het leven van Mr.Johan Valckenaer*, II (Amsterdam, 1876), 143, 144.
Letter from P.C.Labouchère, Amsterdam, to W.G.Coesvelt, W.G.C. I.
3 G.A. Amsterdam, Not. Arch., 18001–285, 286. Five drafts on the Mexican Treasury, totalling 1,319,000 piastres, were to be given as additional security.
4 G.A. Amsterdam, Not. Arch., 18007–103, 104.
5 G.A. Amsterdam, Not. Arch., 18009–375, 376. Additional security was provided in the form of drafts on the Mexican Treasury totalling 1,319,000 piastres.

PAGE 284

1 G.A. Amsterdam, Not. Arch., 18012–385, 386. Five drafts on the Mexican Treasury, totalling 1,800,000 piastres, were given as additional security.
Letter of 22nd July 1807 from P.C.Labouchère, Amsterdam, to W.G.Coesvelt, W.G.C. I.
2 Letter of 22nd July 1807 to W.G.Coesvelt, Paris, W.G.C. I.
3 A.Fugier, *Napoléon et l'Espagne*, 1799–1808, I (Paris, 1930), 197–245.
4 Letter of 22nd July 1807 from P.C.Labouchère, Amsterdam, to W.G.Coesvelt, W.G.C. I.

Letter of 4th March 1803 from P.C.Labouchère, Amsterdam, to Sir F.Baring, London.
Letter of 2nd August 1804 to the Marquis de la Colonilla, Paris, A II, 308.
5 Fugier, *Napoléon et l'Espagne*, I, 283.

PAGE 285

1 G.J.Ouvrard, *Mémoires sur sa vie et ses diverses opérations financières* (Paris, 1826), 75.
Arthur Lévy, *Un grand profiteur de guerre sous la Révolution, l'Empire et la Restauration; G.J.Ouvrard* (Paris, 1929), 94. Georges Weill, 'Le financier Ouvrard,' *Revue Historique*, XLIII, 127 (Paris, 1918), 38.
Otto Wolff, *Die Geschäfte des Herrn Ouvrard* (Frankfurt am Main, 1932), 104.
The majority of authors of works concerning Ouvrard have drawn on his memoirs for material. These memoirs are unreliable in terms of both facts and figures. An example of this is given in the text.
2 Gabriel Ramon, *Histoire de la Banque de France* (Paris, 1929), 58.
A.Thiers, *Histoire du Consulat et de l'Empire*, I (Brussels, 1845), 13–14; II (Brussels, 1846), 8–9.
Fugier, *Napoléon et l'Espagne*, I, 284.
3 Wolff, *Geschäfte Ouvrard*, 105.
Ouvrard, *Mémoires*, 78.
Thiers, *Histoire du Consulat*, I, 13.
Weill, 'Le financier Ouvrard,' 38.
4 *Ibid.*, 33.
Wolff, *Geschäfte Ouvrard*, 64–76.

PAGE 286

1 Arthur Lévy, *Un grand profiteur*, 82–83.
2 L.de Lanzac Laborie, *Le monde des affaires et du travail* (Paris, 1910), 14–15.
3 Manger, *Recherches*, 128, 130, 132.
4 Van Winter, *Aandeel*, II, 386.
Letters of 18th May, 1st June, 2nd, 30th July, 17th, 31st August, 14th September 1804 from Baguenault & Co., Paris, to P.C.Labouchère, Amsterdam.
Letters of 15th March, 5th, 19th July, 26th, 30th August, 13th September 1804 to Baguenault & Co., Paris, A II, 134, 261, 289, 330, 353, 377.

PAGE 287

1 Letter of 2nd August 1804 to Desprez, Paris, A II, 307.
2 Letters of 10th and 24th August 1804 from A.Baguenault & Co., Paris, to P.C.Labouchère, Amsterdam.
Letter of 19th July 1804 to Baguenault, Paris, A II, 289.
3 'Cedule Royale' issued by the King of Spain and his Council on 6th June 1804.
4 Letters of 10th and 24th May 1804 to the Marquis de la Colonilla, Paris, A II, 200, 218.
5 Letter of 2nd July 1804 to the Marquis de la Colonilla, Paris, A II, 252.
Letter of 28th July 1804 from P.C.Labouchère, Amsterdam, to A.Baring, London.

PAGE 288

1 Letters of 20th and 27th August, 17th and 24th September 1804 to the Marquis de la Colonilla, Paris, A II, 308, 338, 351, 385, 395.
Letters of 8th, 15th, 22nd and 25th October, 15th and 29th November 1804, and 4th March 1805 to the Marquis de la Colonilla, Paris, A II, 414, 420, 428, 437, 474, 493, 564. Fugier, *Napoléon et l'Espagne*, I, 316–317.

2 *Ibid.*, II, 9–10.
Wolff, *Geschäfte Ouvrard*, 110, 114.
Thiers, *Histoire du Consulat*, II, 12.

3 Fugier, *Napoléon et l'Espagne*, II, 10–11.
Wolff, *Geschäfte Ouvrard*, 115.

PAGE 289

1 *Ibid.*, Dokumente, II and III, p. 302. In Ouvrard's memoires it is made to appear that a covenant was entered into directly with the king on 26th November 1804 (Wolff, 115–117). The Hope archives contain a copy of an agreement between Espinosa and François Ouvrard, the terms of which differ widely from those of the covenant with the king, as quoted by Ouvrard. The latter refers only to a commission of 1 % on shipments of gold and silver. Only with the conclusion of the supplementary covenant on 4th December 1804 (of which Hope's version and the one in Ouvrard's memoirs are almost identical) were commissions for commercial transactions laid down. It appears more likely that Charles IV confirmed the monopoly granted to François Ouvrard & Co. in a decree, but had the actual partnership agreement between Ouvrard and Espinosa drawn up separately. According to the Hope version of the text of the covenant of 26th November, François Ouvrard & Co. were obliged to pay import and export duties to the Spanish Treasury (Art. 18).

2 Stuart Weems Bruchey, *Robert Oliver, Merchant of Baltimore, 1783–1819* (The John Hopkins University Studies in Historical and Political Science; Series LXXIV, No. 1, Baltimore, 1956), 263.
Vicens Vives, *Economic History*, 580.

3 Ouvrard, *Mémoires*, II, 338–342.
4th December 1804: supplementary articles relating to the covenant of 26th November 1804, which concerned trade with the colonies ruled by the Spanish king.

PAGE 290

1 Fugier, *Napoléon et l'Espagne*, II, 11–12.
Lanzac de Laborie, *Monde*, 200.

2 Fugier, *Napoléon et l'Espagne*, II, 15.
Ouvrard, *Mémoires*, 108–109.

3 Letter of 4th March 1805 to Hottinguer, Paris, A II, 570.
Letter of 4th March 1805 to Baguenault & Co., Paris, A II, 571.

4 Fugier, *Napoléon et l'Espagne*, I, 265–267.

PAGE 291

1 Letter of 4th March 1805 to Baguenault & Co., Paris, A II, 571.

PAGE 292

1 Ouvrard, *Mémoires*, 113.

Letter of 14th February 1805 to Desprez, Paris.
Nolte, *Fünfzig Jahre*, 79–80. Nolte asserts in his memoirs that he heard the story from the lips of Labouchère. Our story makes it abundantly clear that Labouchère was completely *au fait* with the situation when Ouvrard arrived, and had already laid the foundations for the transaction. Nolte's manuscript dates from round about 1850, which was 45 years later. It is conceivable that, wittingly or unwittingly, he borrowed the story from Ouvrard's memoirs.

PAGE 293

1 6th May 1805. Agreement between Hope & Co. of Amsterdam and François Ouvrard & Co. of Bordeaux (the latter represented by François Ouvrard, who was at that moment in Amsterdam) relating to trade with the Spanish colonies.
Letter of 22nd July 1807 from P.C.Labouchère, Amsterdam, to W.G.Coesvelt. During Ouvrard's stay in Amsterdam, Hope & Co. held exploratory discussions with persons who were being considered for the post of agent. The name of Parish already appeared in the supplementary agreement with Auguste Ouvrard dated 6th May 1805.

2 13th September 1805. Elaboration of Article 7 of the contract dated 6th May 1805. Cop. VI-fa-85.

3 This ensued from Article 8 of the agreement of 6th May 1805. Nolte, *Fünfzig Jahre*, 80, states that the commission on the piastres was 5%; this is incorrect.

PAGE 294

1 Letter of 22nd July 1807 from P.C.Labouchère, Amsterdam, to W.G.Coesvelt.

2 6th May 1805. Agreement between Hope & Co. and François Ouvrard & Co. In this it was stipulated that David Parish should receive a 'commission de gestion' equal to 15% of the sum of the nett profit on the Hope-Ouvrard account. Parish must therefore have formally accepted the post of general agent by 6th May.

3 Three letters from F. Ouvrard & Co., Amsterdam to Hope & Co., Amsterdam. Matters centred around 259 drafts on Don Lorenzo Angulo y Guardamino of Mexico, totalling 1,939,003 piastres. These had been received from Gardoqui Neveux & Co. of Madrid and were payable in Vera Cruz to the order of Don Manuel Sixto Espinosa, whose blank endorsement they bore.
On 8th May 1805 Hope & Co. received from François Ouvrard & Co. duplicate copies of the orders relating to trade with the Spanish colonies which the Spanish Court had issued to the Viceroy, the Governor and the Captain General of New Spain; the Viceroy, the Governor and the Captain General of Cuba; the Governor, the Captain General and the Intendant of the province of Venezuela; the Captain General and the Intendant of Buenos Aires; and the Spanish envoy to the United States.

CHAPTER TEN

PAGE 295

1 Letters of 10th and 11th May 1805 from P.C.Labouchère, Amsterdam, to Sir Francis Baring, London.
also: Bruchey, *Robert Oliver*, 274–275.
Philip G. Walters and Raymond Walters Jr., 'The American Career of David Parish,' *The Journal of Economic History*, IV, 1944, 151, note 4.
2 *Supra*, 294, note 2.

PAGE 296

1 *Supra*, 294, note 2.
Bruchey, *Robert Oliver*, 276.
2 Nolte, *Fünfzig Jahre*, 87–88.
Letters of 20th and 29th May 1805 from F. Ouvrard & Co., Paris, to Hope & Co., Amsterdam.
Letter of 27th May 1805 from D. Parish, Antwerp, to P.C.Labouchère, Amsterdam.
3 Nolte, *Fünfzig Jahre*, 90, 113.
Letter of 7th May 1805 from F. Ouvrard & Co., Amsterdam, to Hope & Co., Amsterdam.
4 Nolte, *Fünfzig Jahre*, 40, 44, 45.
Letter of 27th May 1805 from D. Parish, Antwerp to P.C.Labouchère, Amsterdam.
5 Nolte, *Fünfzig Jahre*, 90.
Letter of 10th June 1805 from D. Parish, Antwerp, to P.C.Labouchère, Amsterdam.
Letter of 26th June 1805 from F. Ouvrard & Co., Paris, to Hope & Co., Amsterdam.
Letter of 22nd June 1805 from P.C.Labouchère, Amsterdam, to A.Baring, London.
Labouchère made it appear to Alexander Baring that Nolte was travelling to America on behalf of his brother's firm, Trotreau & Labouchère of Nantes. However, Baring was informed of Parish's 'general superintendence' when the latter crossed to England late in September.
Letter of 18th September 1805 from P.C.Labouchère, Amsterdam, to A.Baring, London.

PAGE 297

1 Letters of 17th and 20th May, 4th, 14th, 18th and 26th June 1805 from F.Ouvrard & Co., Paris, to Hope & Co., Amsterdam.
2 Letters of 26th June and 12th July 1805 from F. Ouvrard & Co., Paris, to Hope & Co., Amsterdam.

3 Letter of 9th July 1805 from Walter Boyd, Paris, to Hope & Co., Amsterdam.
4 Letter of 15th July 1805 from P.C.Labouchère, Amsterdam, to W.Boyd, Paris.

PAGE 298

1 Letters of 16th, 20th and 31st August 1805 from W.Boyd, Paris, to Hope & Co., Amsterdam.
Letter of 1st August 1805 from P.C.Labouchère, Amsterdam, to W.Boyd, Paris.
2 Letters of 1st August 1805 from P.C.Labouchère, Amsterdam, to W.Boyd, Paris, and of 7th, 8th and 9th October 1805 to J.Ouvrard, Madrid, A IV, 21, 34.
3 G.A. Amsterdam, Not. Arch., 18022–482.
Translation from the Spanish of a royal patent issued by the King of Spain and the Gentlemen of the Council.
Letter of 4th October 1805 to Miguel Cajetano Soler, Minister of Finance and of the Indies, Madrid, A IV, 3.
Letter of 4th October 1805 to Manuel Sixto Espinosa, Director of the *Real Caja de Consolidacion de Vales*, Madrid, A IV, 7.
4 Letter of 4th November 1805 to J.Ouvrard, Madrid, A IV, 68.
Letter of 4th November 1805 to Vanlerberghe & Ouvrard, Paris, A IV, 62.

PAGE 300

1 Letter of 1st October 1805 from W.Boyd, Paris, to Hope & Co., Amsterdam.
2 Letter of 4th October 1805 to W.Boyd, Paris, A IV, 17. Both the 'plan' for the loan and the advertisement held out a prospect that bonds of the Croese conversion loan which had matured on 1st September would be accepted as payment up to a total of 600,000 guilders; 4½% bonds of the Hope loan of 1793, which had matured on 1st November 1806, up to a total of 600,000 guilders; and the remaining bonds of this loan, which were due for redemption on 1st November 1807, also up to a total of 600,000 guilders.
Letter of 4th November 1806 to Vanlerberghe & Ouvrard, Paris, A IV, 62.
3 Letters of 8/9th October and 4th November 1805 to Julien Ouvrard, Madrid, A IV, 34, 68.
Letters of 11th, 27th October 1805 from Vanlerberghe & Ouvrard, Paris, to Hope & Co., Amsterdam.
Letters of 17th, 28th October, 4th November (three letters) 1805 to Vanlerberghe & Ouvrard, Paris, A IV, 45, 53, 59, 62, 66.
Letters of 28th, 31st October 1805 to Baguenault & Co., Paris, A IV, 56, 58.
4 Letters of 7th October 1805 to Julien Ouvrard, Madrid, (two letters) A IV, 31, 32.

PAGE 301

1 Fugier, *Napoléon et l'Espagne*, II, 15.
2 *Ibid.*, 16.
Ramon, *Histoire de la Banque de France*, 66.
3 Fugier, *Napoléon et l'Espagne*, II, 17.
4 Comte Mollien, *Mémoires d'un ministre du Trésor Public, 1780–1815*, I (Paris, 1898), 410.

PAGE 302

1 Fugier, *Napoléon et l'Espagne*, II, 18.

2 Letter of 27th October 1805 from Barbé Marbois, Paris, to Hope & Co., Amsterdam.
Letter of 27th October 1805 from Desprez, Paris, to Hope & Co., Amsterdam.
Letter of 4th November 1805 to Desprez, Paris, A IV, 60.
Letter of 4th November 1805 to Barbé Marbois, Paris, A IV, 99.
Letters of 20th, 23rd November 1805 from P.C.Labouchère, Paris, to Hope & Co., Amsterdam.

PAGE 303

1 Letter of late January 1806 from Hope & Co., Amsterdam, to Baring Brothers & Co., London.
2 Letters of 27th and 31st December 1805 from Matthiesen & Sillem, Hamburg, to Hope & Co., Amsterdam.
Letter of 27th December 1805 from J. Osy, Hamburg, to Hope & Co., Amsterdam.
Letter of 6th January 1806 to Barbé Marbois, Paris, A IV, 123.
Letter of late January 1806 from Hope & Co., Amsterdam, to Baring Brothers & Co., London.
3 Fugier, *Napoléon et l'Espagne*, II, 41.
4 Letter of 24th December 1805 from Wed. E.Croese & Co., Amsterdam, to the Schepenen of the City of Amsterdam.
Letter of 30th December 1805 from P.C.Labouchère, Amsterdam, to H.Croese Edzn., Madrid.
Letter of 30th December 1805 from P.C.Labouchère, Amsterdam, to the Marquis de la Colonilla, Madrid.
5 Letters of 4th November 1805 and 24th February 1806 to Baguenault & Co., Paris, A IV, 78, 146.
Letter of 15th November 1805 to Vanlerberghe & Ouvrard, Paris, A IV, 109.
Letter of 6th December 1805 from Sir F.Baring, London, to Hope & Co., Amsterdam.
Letter of 20th January 1806 to Vanlerberghe & Ouvrard, Paris, A IV, 130. In Amsterdam, the wool was valued and sold by Willink & Co., on behalf of Hope & Co.

PAGE 304

1 Letter of late January 1806 from Hope & Co., Amsterdam, to Baring Brothers & Co., London.
2 *Ibid.*
3 *Ibid.*

PAGE 305

1 Wolff, *Geschäfte Ouvrard*, 132–134.
Arthur Lévy, *Un grand profiteur*, 160.
Ouvrard, *Mémoires*, 129–130.
Fugier, *Napoléon et l'Espagne*, II, 21.
2 *Ibid.*
3 Letter of 14th February 1806 from Vanlerberghe & Ouvrard, Paris, to Hope & Co., Amsterdam.
Letter of 21st February 1806 from Hope & Co., Amsterdam, to Mollien, Paris.
Letter of 22nd February 1806 from P.C.Labouchère, Amsterdam, to Auguste Ouvrard & Co., Paris.

Letter of 22nd February 1806 from Hope & Co., Amsterdam, to Auguste Ouvrard & Co., Paris.
Letter of 23rd February 1806 to Vanlerberghe & Ouvrard, Paris, A IV, 140, 145, 147.
Fugier, *Napoléon et l'Espagne*, II, 56.

PAGE 306

1 Letter of 22nd February 1806 from Hope & Co., Amsterdam, to Auguste Ouvrard & Co., Paris.
Letter of 22nd February 1806 from P.C.Labouchère, Amsterdam, to A.Baring, London.
2 Letter of 23rd February 1806 to Vanlerberghe & Ouvrard, A IV, 140.
3 Letter of 10th March 1806 from P.C.Labouchère, Amsterdam, to Mollien, Paris.
Also: VI fa-85: 'Offre de Vente.'

PAGE 307

1 Fugier, *Napoléon et l'Espagne*, II, 52–55.
2 *Ibid.*, 51, 59.
3 *Ibid.*, 55.

PAGE 308

1 *Ibid.*, 57, 58.
2 Letter of 10th May 1806 from Desprez, Paris, to Hope & Co., Amsterdam.
3 Letter of 10th May 1806 from W. Borski, Amsterdam, to P.C.Labouchère, Amsterdam.
Letter of 10th May 1806 to W.Borski, Amsterdam, A IV, 176.
Letter of 12th May 1806 from W.Borski, Amsterdam, to P.C.Labouchère, Amsterdam.
Letters of 12th and 19th May 1806 to Vanlerberghe & Ouvrard, Paris, A IV, 177, 191.
Letter of 12th May 1806 to J. Ouvrard, Paris, A IV, 188.
Letter of 28th May 1806 from W.Borski, Amsterdam, to Hope & Co., Amsterdam.

PAGE 309

1 Letter of 29th May 1806 to Michel Simons, Amsterdam, A IV, 194.
Letter of 29th May 1806 to Baguenault & Co., Paris, A IV, 201.
2 Letter of 30th May 1806 to Baguenault & Co., Paris, A IV, 203.
Michel Simons personally declared his willingness to take over 2,000 Spanish bonds on the terms accorded to Borski.
Letter of 9th June 1806 to Baguenault & Co., Paris, A IV, 304.
Letter of 16th June 1806 from Vanlerberghe & Ouvrard, Paris, to Hope & Co., Amsterdam.
Letter of 19th June 1806 to Espinosa, Madrid, A IV, 209.
Letter of 30th June 1806 to Vanlerberghe & Ouvrard, Paris, A IV, 214.

CHAPTER ELEVEN

PAGE 311

1 Walters and Walters, 'American Career,' 152.
Note, *Fünfzig Jahre*, 90, 94.
Nolte gives the date of Parish's arrival as mid-November 1805. Labouchère, however, states that Parish left Dover on 17th November. Letter of 5th December 1805 to D.Parish, New York, B.I. 1. According to Walters, the origin of the rumours concerning the piastre operation lay in indiscreet remarks made by Nolte and Lestapis. Ouvrard himself had approached American merchants in 1805, and thus his plans must have been known prior to the arrival of Hope's agents.

2 Hidy, *House of Baring*, 19–20, 48.
Bruchey, *Robert Oliver*, 277–278.

3 Herbert Lasky, in his treatise entitled: 'David Parish: A European in American Finance 1806–1816,' (unpublished Ph.d. dissertation, Ann Arbor, Michigan) questions whether Parish did in fact sell 3 or 4 licences to Gracie (p. 14, note 2). The consignment invoices show that he did indeed do so.

PAGE 312

1 Bruchey, *Robert Oliver*, 279–282.
Nolte, *Fünfzig Jahre*, 112. Parish had also approached others who were in correspondence with Hope, such as Willing & Francis in Philadelphia, and Robert Gilmor & Sons and James & Thomas G.Perkins in Boston. James Perkins had visited Holland during the summer of 1805 – as had also Nathaniel Amory of the house of Amory & Callender of New Orleans, in whose name the consignment of Silesian linen had been ordered in Hamburg, and to whose address this was shipped, to the relief of Matthiessen & Sillem. The willingness of the last-named to swear on oath that the linen was the bona fide property of Amory & Callender was made conditional upon Hope & Co. issuing a positive assurance that this was the case. Letters of 1st September 1805 from James Perkins, Rotterdam, to Hope & Co., Amsterdam; 13th September 1805 from James Perkins, London, to Hope & Co., Amsterdam; 10th October 1805 from Nathaniel Amory, London, to Hope & Co., Amsterdam; 22nd October and 5th November 1805, 1st and 11th April 1806 from Matthiessen & Sillem, Hamburg, to Hope & Co., Amsterdam.

2 John Craig died in June 1807. The Olivers continued the shipments, now for their own account.
Bruchey, *Robert Oliver*, 331.

PAGE 314

1 *Vide* consignment invoices and final accounts in the Hope archives. Bruchey, too, points to the random nature of the various dues (p. 307). The Olivers informed Parish by letter that they were frequently called upon to pay dues amounting to 50% of the proforma invoice value. They did not, however, mention that this figure included the commission of 6¼% on the gross proceeds in Vera Cruz. If the gross proceeds were equal to twice the value shown on the pro-forma invoice, the percentages, based on the pro-forma invoice, would naturally rise sharply.

2 Bruchey, *Robert Oliver*, 391–392.
The Olivers allowed 4,000 dollars for freight charges. As they carried the cargoes in their own vessels–fast schooners which were well able to excape from any pursuing British warships–the Olivers will have made a substantial profit on the operations.

3 *Ibid.*, 329, 331.

PAGE 315

1 33⅓% of the nett profit of 334,891 dollars, plus 5% of the nett value (76,810 dollars) = 411,701 dollars.

2 The gross profit on the two final shipments amounted to 181,273 dollars.

PAGE 316

1 Bruchey, *Robert Oliver*, 311. In the case of a shipment on behalf of Thomas Tenant of Baltimore, both the freight charges and the insurance premium for a voyage from Barcelona to Baltimore were quoted, thus clearly revealing that the cargo was of Spanish origin.

2 The consignment invoice values were as follows: McKim: 203,841 dollars; John Craig: 68,099 dollars; Archibald Gracie: 120,089 dollars: Amory & Callender: 184,181.05 dollars; James Brown: 112,924 dollars; Geo. T.Phillips: 38,882 dollars. Total 728,017 dollars. The amounts on the final accounts were: McKim: 424,603 dollars; John Craig: 151,095 dollars; Archibald Gracie: 245,996 dollars; Amory & Callender: 348,766 dollars; James Brown: 176,034 dollars; Geo. T.Phillips: 73,295 dollars. Total 1,419,790 dollars. The gross profit was thus 690,000 dollars and the nett profit, which may be estimated at ⅔rds, 460,000 dollars.
The pro-forma invoices relating to one expedition each by Archibald Gracie and John Craig and the four expeditions to Montevideo together totalled 283,357 dollars. The grand total of the pro-forma invoices was 1,031,374 dollars. Fifteen per cent of this sum is 154,760 dollars.

3 Hope & Co. returned a figure of 2,897,440.36 dollars to Auguste Ouvrard and the *Caja*. Documents in the Hope archives, however, show a figure of 2,913,688.31 dollars, a difference of just over ½%. In all, Hope's payments to the *Caja* totalled 709,400.14 dollars. This sum was included in the balance in Auguste Ouvrard & Co.'s account, from whence it was transferred to the general account 'X.' Auguste Ouvrard & Co. received 463,000 dollars.

4 Bruchey, *Robert Oliver*, 314–317.

PAGE 317

1 *Ibid.*, 304. The house of Matthiessen & Sillem in Hamburg had in 1806 complained of an overabundance of European textiles, which depressed the prices of Silesian linen. Losses in excess of 27,750 dollars were incurred on two shipments of Silesian

linen to New Orleans, together valued at 137,000 dollars.
2 *Ibid.*, 306.

PAGE 318

1 *Ibid.*, 287–292. At a nominal exchange rate of 50 *stuivers* and a discount of 21 %, Parish received 39½ *stuivers* for a piastre. The price of 3 frances 75 centimes per piastre agreed with the French Treasury was equal to about 36 *stuivers*, leaving a gross profit margin of 3½ *stuivers* per piastre. A discount of 17 % gave a gross profit of 5½ *stuivers* per piastre. Contracts were made with many other houses on the basis of a 15 % discount, which have a gross profit of 6½ *stuivers*.
2 The shipments concerned were each of 30,000 piastres from New Orleans to Liverpool in the vessels 'Joseph' and 'Wilhelm Tell.' The insurers paid 30,000 dollars in respect of the 'Joseph's' cargo, and this suggests that the vessel was either shipwrecked or captured.

PAGE 319

1 Remittances were occasionally made via Leghorn and Genoa. Some remittances to Paris were in the form of gold shipments.
2 Hidy, *House of Baring*, 22.
3 *Grootboek* 1792: 159, 268, 242.
Grootboek 1793: 46, 262, 371, 376.
Grootboek 1794: 170, 194, 196, 216, 226, 298, 320.
Grootboek 1801: 51, 63, 65, 38, 40.
4 *Grootboek* 1802: 27.
Grootboek 1803: 129, 132, 136.
Grootboek 1804: 116, 136, 157, 160, 163, 164, 182.
Grootboek 1805: 144, 148, 152, 168, 171, 175, 176, 178, 180, 185, 186, 187, 188, 194, 195, 196, 209.
Grootboek 1806: 124, 132, 135, 136, 158, 159, 167, 168, 174, 186, 187, 191, 192, 193, 194, 201, 202, 209, 210, 211, 213, 217, 219, 220, 223, 225, 226, 233, 243, 244.
Grootboek 1807: 112, 113, 114, 115, 116, 117, 118, 119, 120, 121, 122, 135, 138, 139, 152, 153, 161, 162, 163, 164, 165, 166, 167, 168, 193, 194, 203, 206, 207, 243, 244, 251, 252, 253, 258, 259, 260, 265, 266, 267, 272.

PAGE 320

1 In 1806 and 1807 Hope & Co. received twice as many consignments as W.&.J.Willink and Daniel Crommelin & Sons.
2 Bruchey, *Robert Oliver*, 298.
3 F.Crouzet, 'Groupes de pression et politique de blocus: remarques sur les origines des Ordres en Conseil de novembre 1807,' *Revue Historique*, 86, CCXXVIII (1962), 49. P.Hoekstra, *Thirty-Seven Years of Holland-American Relations, 1803 to 1840* (Grand Rapids, N.J., 1916), 57.

PAGE 321

1 Letters of 16th and 23rd July 1806 to D.Parish, Philadelphia, D.P. 1.
2 Letters of 3rd and 25th August 1806 to D.Parish, Philadelphia, D.P. 1.
3 Letters of 3rd and 16th September, 1st, 3rd and 4th October 1806 to D.Parish, Philadelphia, D.P. 1. According to Labouchère, the tobacco market was a shambles.

Numerous consignments had been sacrificed by panic-stricken brokers. It was common for consignments to be sold and then to be resold within an hour at a price which might be as much as half a *stuiver* per pound higher or lower. It was thus quite impossible to quote any firm prices.

4 Letters of 7th, 18th and 25th October, 3rd and 16th November 1806 to D.Parish, Philadelphia, D.P. I.

PAGE 322

1 Hoekstra, *Thirty-Seven Years*, 44, 46, 47.
Letters of 10th and 27th December 1806 to D.Parish, Philadelphia, D.P. I.

2 Letters of 26th February, 9th and 17th March, 12th and 20th April 1807 to D.Parish, Philadelphia, D.P. I.

3 Letter of 29th April 1807 to D.Parish, Philadelphia, D.P. I.
Letters of 16th and 19th May, 23rd June, 20th, 25th and 29th July 1807 to D.Parish, Philadelphia, D.P. II, VI-ha-35, 37, 44, 49, 50, 51.

4 Letters of 5th, 8th and 21st August 1807 to D.Parish, Philadelphia, D.P. II, VI-ha-52, 53, 56.
E.Channing, *A History of the United States*, IV (New York, 1917), 370–371.

PAGE 323

1 Hoekstra, *Thirty-Seven Years*, 51–52.

2 Letters of 11th and 18th September, 9th, 15th and 24th October, 3rd and 12th November 1807 to D.Parish, Philadelphia, D.P. II, VI-ha-60–72.
Hoekstra, *Thirty-Seven Years*, 52–53.
Hoekstra quotes reports from the Amsterdam merchant Backer who, in contrast to Labouchère, referred in optimistic terms to the sale of American produce.

3 *Ibid.*, 60.
Channing, *History*, IV, 376.
Crouzet, 'Groupes de pression,' 72.

4 Channing, *History*, IV, 380–381, 399.
Letters of 29th November 1807 and 8th January 1808 to D.Parish, Philadelphia, D.P. II.
Parish succeeded in obtaining from President Jefferson permits to collect piastres. According to Nolte, Gallatin, the Secretary of the Treasury, was involved in the issue of these. Parish states in a letter that the President had been influenced by 'my friend the general.' This officer, however, was not named.
Nolte, *Fünfzig Jahre*, 171.
Bruchey, *Robert Oliver*, 333.

5 Hoekstra, *Thirty-Seven Years*, 63.
Letter of 27th February 1808 to D.Parish, Philadelphia, D.P. II.
Grootboek 1808: 128, 132, 207, 131, 135, 165, 129, 225, 130, 167, 130, 133, 129, 132, 168, 235, 134, 198, 200, 166, 127, 136, 152, 166, 208.
Grootboek 1809: 123, 165, 168, 173, 180, 181, 191, 219, 220.
The turnover on the goods accounts totalled cf 5,651,849 in 1808. In 1809, the figure was cf 1,475,601.

PAGE 324

1 Letters of 15th April and 12th May 1808 to D.Parish, Philadelphia, D.P. II.

2 Letters of 15th/22nd September 1805 from P.C.Labouchère, Amsterdam, to Sir Francis Baring, London.
3 Letters of 22nd and 25th November 1805 from J.Richards, Amsterdam, to P.C.Labouchère, Paris.
Letter of 23rd November 1805 from P.C.Labouchère, Paris, to Hope & Co., Amsterdam.
4 'Investigations.'
25th November 1805: Memorandum concerning the possibilities for exporting piastres from Vera Cruz.
5 Memorandum concerning the Spanish piastres. Copy No. 2 (1st November 1805) and copy No. 3.

PAGE 325

1 Letter of 2nd December 1805 from J.Richards, Paris, to Hope & Co., Amsterdam.
Letter of 9th December 1805 from P.C.Labouchère, Paris, to Hope & Co., Amsterdam.
Letter of late January 1806 from Hope & Co., Amsterdam, to Baring Bros., London.
Letters of 13th December 1805 and 7th January 1806 from A.Baring, London, to Hope & Co., Amsterdam.
2 Letter of 18th February 1806 from A.Baring, London, to P.C.Labouchère, Amsterdam.
3 Fugier, *Napoléon et l'Espagne*, II, 74.
4 Letters of 7th and 15th March, 2nd April, 3rd May 1806 from P.C.Labouchère, Amsterdam, to A.Baring, London.
5 Letter of 4th July 1806 from A.Baring, London, to Hope & Co., Amsterdam.

PAGE 327

1 8th July 1806: draft contracts between Hope & Co. and Baring Bros. & Co. for the sale of piastres lying in Vera Cruz, and the collection thereof.
2 Letter of 8th July 1806 from A.Baring, Amsterdam, to Hope & Co., Amsterdam.
Adverse winds obliged Baring to stay in Den Helder for a week, awaiting a vessel to England. Letters of 9th, 11th, 13th and 15th July from A.Baring, Den Helder, to P.C.Labouchère, Amsterdam.
A sum of 1,000,000 piastres, representing the collected portion of the drafts for 1¼ million, did, however, appear on the final account rendered to the French Treasury.
3 Fugier, *Napoléon et l'Espagne*, II, 183. The story as told here by Fugier is not confirmed by material in the Hope archives. Louis did not arrive in Amsterdam until February 1807.
4 *Ibid.*, 184. Here, Fugier refers to a contract for piastres at a price of 3 francs and 55 centimes. The draft contracts of July 1806 and the contract of 12th March 1807 all embody a price of 3 francs 75 centimes. According to Fugier, the entire transaction was carried out at 3 francs 55 centimes per piastre; the account submitted to the French Treasury, however, shows that a price of 3 francs 75 centimes nett was maintained for the first five million piastres, and 3 francs 85 centimes for the second batch of drafts. It is conceivable that sticky fingers were at work in France, but the information in the Hope archives gives no hint as to where this might have occurred or who might have been responsible.

PAGE 328

1 Letter of 5th May 1807 from Sir Francis Baring, London, to Hope & Co., Amsterdam.
Another letter of the same date contained details of a contract between the London house of Thomas O'Gorman and Espinosa for the collection of three million piastres from Lima. This contract also provided for O'Gorman to import Spanish products such as quicksilver and stationery. The house issued drafts on itself for piastres at the rate of 177 pounds sterling for 1,000 piastres.
2 Letters of 6th March 1807 from Baring Bros., London, to Hope & Co., Amsterdam, and of 7th, 10th, 12th, 13th, 14th and 18th March from Sir Francis Baring, London, to Hope & Co., Amsterdam.
3 Letters of 14th, 16th, 18th, 19th, 20th and 23rd March 1807 to Louis, VII, 51, 55, 58, 61; A IV, 385, 386.
Letter of 23rd March 1807 from Louis, Amsterdam, to Hope & Co., Amsterdam.
4 *Reçu du Trésor Public;* also VI-fa-85, 25–26.
17th April 1807: Receipt for drafts from the Governor of the Castilian Council.
5 Letters of 18th and 29th May, 11th and 15th June 1807 from A.Baring, London, to Hope & Co., Amsterdam.
6 Letters of 27th May 1807 from Mollien, Paris, to Hope & Co., Amsterdam.
Letter of 5th June 1807 from Hope & Co., Amsterdam, to Mollien, Paris.
20th July 1807: supplementary contract between Hope & Co. and Baring Bros. & Co.

PAGE 329

1 Nolte, *Fünfzig Jahre*, 125.
General Account 'X' for the year 1808 in current money, or appendix to that of '1807.'
Compte B du Trésor Public de France, June 1807–23rd May 1808.
Le Trésor Public de France, *Compte des Piastres*, 25th October 1809.
2 Letters of 29th May, 11th June and 6th August 1807 from A. Baring, London, to Hope & Co., Amsterdam.
3 Letter of 20th October 1807 from Baring Bros., London, to P.C.Labouchère, Amsterdam.
'Account Sales of Dollars for account p. Diana, Frigate.'
Letter of 17th November 1809 from A.Baring, London, to Hope & Co., Amsterdam.
To the expenses was added a sum of 3,000 pounds sterling, which had been set aside for the medical treatment of James Richards, who liaised between Hope and Baring during the winter of 1805, and who had subsequently become insane.
4 Letter of 29th October 1807 from A.Baring, London, to Hope & Co., Amsterdam.
5 Letter of 3rd March 1808 to Mollien, Paris, VII, 324.

PAGE 330

1 Nolte, *Fünfzig Jahre*, 131.
2 *Ibid.*, 143.
3 *Ibid.*, 147.
4 *Ibid.*, 149 and Chapter VII (150–165).

PAGE 331

1 VI-fa-85, 37 and 38.
'Nouveaux avis sur le recouvrement à la Havane, transmis au Ministre.'

VI-fa-85, 40.
Nolte, *Fünfzig Jahre*, 189, 190.
Nolte makes it appear that the Intendant sought to get into Talleyrand's good books, and not to complain of his, Nolte's, conduct.

2 Letters of 23rd May, 9th June and 10th November 1808 to the Minister (Mollien), VI-fa-85, 42, 44, 47, 51.
VI-fa-86, 26.
This sum included 236,927.56 francs for expenses incurred in Havana.

3 Bruchey, *Robert Oliver*, 319–322.

CHAPTER TWELVE

PAGE 333

1 Letter of 26th June 1806 to Baguenault & Co., Paris, A IV, 212.

2 Letters of 26th June, 24th July and 25th August 1806 to Baguenault & Co., Paris, A IV, 212, 230, 245.
Letters of 9th and 19th June, and 14th July 1806 to Vanlerberghe & Ouvrard, Paris, A IV, 203, 206, 226.
Michel Simons at first agreed to take over 2,000 bonds, but later reduced this to 1,000. Borski thereupon assumed responsibility for the balance of the 3,900 bonds.
Letter of 16th June 1806 from Vanlerberghe & Ouvrard, Paris, to Hope & Co., Amsterdam.

2 Letter of 19th June 1806 to Espinosa, Madrid, A IV, 209.
Letter of 30th June 1806 to Vanlerberghe & Ouvrard, Paris, A IV, 214.

PAGE 334

1 Letter of 28th August 1806 to Baguenault & Co., Paris, A IV, 246.
5th September 1806: new plan for a loan to Spain, furnished by Izquierdo.
Letter of 9th September 1806 to Izquierdo, Paris, A IV, 265.

2 Fugier, *Napoléon et l'Espagne*, II, 175.

PAGE 335

1 Letters of 9th and 23rd September 1806 to Izquierdo, Paris, A IV, 265, 280.
Letters of 9th and 23rd September 1806 to Michel Simons, Paris, A IV, 272, 274, 281.

2 Letter of 12th January 1807 to J.B.Ouin, Amsterdam, A IV, 356.
Letter of 3rd November 1806 to J.Ouvrard, for Vanlerberghe & Ouvrard, Paris, A IV, 293.
Letters of 5th and 11th November 1806 to Michel Simons, Amsterdam, A IV, 297, 304.

3 Letter of 13th November 1806 to Roëll, Chancellor and Secretary of State, The Hague, A IV, 306.
13th November 1806: Petition to the King of Holland to approve the loan, A IV, 308.

PAGE 336

1 Letters of 29th November and 4th December 1806 to Izquierdo, Amsterdam, A IV, 321, 327.
28th February 1807: Summary of proposed loan for Spain's account handed to the king at his request in connexion with his approval of the loan.

2 Letters of 23rd September and 4th December 1806 to Michel Simons, Paris, A IV, 281, 326.
Simons reached agreement with Hope & Co. that they would come to a settlement with him regarding their share of the six months' additional interest. Hope's contracts with the *entrepreneurs*, however, provided for the extra interest, amounting to 2¾%, to go to the *entrepreneurs*. Godoy's memoirs make mention of Talleyrand receiving 2½% as 'pot-de-vin;' this figure almost corresponds with the extra interest. It is conceivable that Simons received ¼%. If this be so, the question arises where did the 2¾% for the *entrepreneurs* come from? Hope received a total commission of 7%, yet paid 5%+2¾%=7¾% to the *entrepreneurs*. There is, however, the point that the purchase price of 90% and the conversion at 100% of the bonds and vouchers surrendered (with the exception of the Echenique bonds, for which the conversion rate was 95%) left an appreciable margin.
Fugier, *Napoléon et l'Espagne*, II, 177, 178, note 2.
3 Letter of 19th November 1806 to Gogel, The Hague, A IV, 310.

PAGE 337

1 Letters of 28th and 29th November 1806 to Izquierdo, Amsterdam, A IV, 319, 321.
Letter of 8th December 1806 to Vanlerberghe & Ouvrard, Paris, A IV, 325, 329.
Letter of 29th November 1806 to Auguste Ouvrard & Co., Paris, A IV, 324.
Letter of 15th December 1806 to J.Ouvrard, Paris, A IV, 333.
2 1st January 1807: Deed, drawn up in Paris on this day, signed by Auguste Ouvrard & Co. and by Blanchard, on behalf of François Ouvrard & Co.
Letters of 3rd and 5th January 1807 from Desprez, Paris, to Hope & Co., Amsterdam.
Letters of 12th and 14th January 1807 to J.B.Ouin, Amsterdam, A IV, 356, 360.
Letter of 14th January 1807 to J.Ouvrard, Paris, A IV, 355. *Cf.* 14th January 1807, VI-fa-85.
3 Letters of 14th and 16th January, 5th February 1807 to Baguenault & Co., Paris, A IV, 363, 373, 377.
Cf. 8th February 1807, VI-fa-85, 25.

PAGE 338

1 30th March 1807: draft deed.
2nd April 1807. Declaration by Auguste Ouvrard & Co., J.B.Ouin, Desprez, J.Ouvrard and Vanlerberghe.
Letter of 28th March 1807 to Baguenault & Co., Paris, A IV, 390.
2 4th April 1807: Declaration in the name of Michel the Younger, given in the presence of the Amsterdam notary Chaussepié.
4th and 6th April 1807: Declaration by Fulchiron, Paris.
5th April 1807: Declaration by Michel the Younger, Paris.
Letters of 9th, 13th and 30th April to Baguenault & Co., Paris, A IV, 396, 400, 406.
3 Nolte, *Fünfzig Jahre*, 123.
Wolff, *Geschäfte Ouvrard*, 135.
Both authors aver that Louis visited Hope & Co. in 1806. The facts, however, point to the visit having taken place early in 1807.
Letter of 4th April 1807 from Louis, Paris, to P.C.Labouchère, Amsterdam.

4 Letters of 13th February, 9th, 15th and 20th March 1807 from Louis, The Hague, to Hope & Co., Amsterdam.

PAGE 339

1 Letter of 9th March 1807 from Louis, The Hague, to Hope & Co., Amsterdam.

2 Upon the initial repayment, on 1st April 1808, a premium of 3% was to be paid on each bond drawn. This premium was to be repeated at each repayment and to increase by 1% annually. The four million guilders allotted yearly to the sinking fund were transferred to the consortium, which used the monies for interest and principal payments. On 9th May 1807, King Louis decreed that the interest should be paid at half-yearly intervals.
28th February 1807: Summary of the proposed loan to Spain, written by P.C.Labouchère, The Hague.
9th March 1807: Correspondence and proposals, including a plan, concerning a loan of 40 million guilders to the debit of the Kingdom of Holland.
March 1807: Agreement between R. and Th.de Smeth, Hope & Co., W. and J.Willink, J.Hodshon & Son and W.van Brienen & Sons, as joint managers for the loan of 40 million guilders desired by the king, and the *entrepreneurs*.
A.R.A. The Hague, Decree issued by King Louis Napoleon on 31st March 1807, *Financiën* No. 7. Extract from the Register of Resolutions of the Legislative Body of the Kingdom of Holland, dated 31st March 1807.
1st April 1807: Report of a loan by the Kingdom of Holland, at 6% interest.
3rd April 1807: Extract from the Register of Orders issued by the Minister of Finance of His Majesty the King of Holland. Bethmann, in Frankfurt, and Matthiessen & Sillem, in Hamburg, proved not to be interested in the new Dutch loan.

3 Letters of 7th, 8th, 12th, 15th and 18th April, 4th, 5th, 6th, 8th and 11th May 1807 from P.C.Labouchère, Amsterdam, to Robert Voûte, The Hague.
Littledale & Dixon, with whom Hope & Co. were associated, reported that malcontents in Rotterdam viewed the loan as payment by the Amsterdammers for the permission granted to them to import goods from England. In a letter to King Louis dated 24th July 1807, Gogel reported that he had ordered the seizure of two vessels; their documents, he said, were almost certainly false. Their cargoes were consigned to Insinger & Co., the company through which, it was said, Hope carried on trade with England. Two others carried cargoes consigned to W.&J.Willink who, Gogel reported, had confessed almost openly to him that the vessels were carrying sugar from a British territory. It was generally believed that, since undertaking the 40 million guilder loan, Hope and Willink had been authorized by the king to import goods from England. This was the story which Dixon had put about at the beginning of April. Hope's reports to Parish concerning the arrival of American ships do not mention Insinger & Co. as consignees. This, of course, does not preclude the possibility that Gogel's story was true. Precisely because of their vulnerable position vis-à-vis old-style Patriots such as Gogel, Hope & Co. went to great lengths to comply with trading restrictions. H.T.Colenbrander, *Gedenkstukken*, v (The Hague, 1910), 306.
Letter of 2nd April 1807 from Littledale & Dixon, Rotterdam, to Hope & Co., Amsterdam.
Hoekstra, *Thirty-Seven Years*, 47–48.

4 Letter from M.Simons, Amsterdam, to Hope & Co., Amsterdam.

Letter of 12th May 1807 from P.C.Labouchère, Amsterdam, to Robert Voûte, The Hague.
Letter of 7th May 1807 to Michel Simons, 'of Paris,' A IV, 411.
19th May 1807: Decree by King Louis Napoleon.
On 29th October 1807 the consortium concerned with the Dutch loan transferred the balance of 12,000 bonds to the *entrepreneurs*, Willem Borski, Ketwich & Voombergh, Strockel Van Dijk and B.J.Weymar. The transfer price was 97. Payment for the bonds was to be effected between 31st October 1807 and 31st May 1808, the *entrepreneurs* enjoying interest from 1st October 1807. The agreement contained a provision for cancellation by the *entrepreneurs*, but the exercise by them of this option involved payment at 100% for all bonds which they had accepted at 97%.
5 Letter of 28th April 1807 from Councillor of State Louis, Paris, to P.C.Labouchère, Amsterdam.
Letters of 4th and 5th May 1807 from P.C.Labouchère, Amsterdam, to Robert Voûte, The Hague.

PAGE 340

1 Letter of 13th May 1807 to Gérardin, Amsterdam, VII, 79.
Letter of 13th May 1807 from Gérardin, Amsterdam, to Hope & Co., Amsterdam.
Letter of 14th May 1807 from P.C.Labouchère, Amsterdam, to Robert Voûte, The Hague.
2 20th May 1807: Agreement between Hope & Co., R.&Th.de Smeth and W.Borski.

PAGE 341.

1 25th May 1807: Agreement between Hope & Co. and W.Borski.
Letter of 25th May to Izquierdo, Paris, A IV, 425.
2 1st, 8th, 22nd June and 27th July 1807: Agreements between Hope & Co. and W.Borski.
Letters of 8th, 17th and 25th June, 27th July, 3rd August and 22nd October 1807 to Izquierdo, Paris, A IV, 436, 443, 453, 474, 478, 514.
3 Letters of 22nd October, 5th November, 10th and 31st December 1807, 4th and 29th February 1808 to Izquierdo, Paris, A IV, 514, 519; VII 232; OE II, 11, 24, 46.
4 Letters of 18th June and 23rd July 1807 to Mollien, Paris, A IV, 444, 469.
Letters of 6th and 20th August 1807 to Baguenault & Co., Paris, A IV, 482, 498.
Letter of 9th July 1807 to Izquierdo, Paris, A IV, 466.
Letter of 14th December 1807 to W.G.Coesvelt, Madrid, W.G.C. I.

PAGE 342

1 Fugier, *Napoléon et l'Espagne*, II, 216, 254.
2 *Ibid.*, 255–256.
3 Letter of 17th June 1807 to Izquierdo, Amsterdam, A IV, 442, 443.
19th June 1807: Receipt from R. & Th.de Smeth, Amsterdam, VI-ea-73, 150.

PAGE 344

1 Letter of 8th June 1807 from P.C.Labouchère, Amsterdam, to Louis, Paris.
Letter of 30th June 1807 from Hope & Co., Amsterdam, to Robert Voûte, The Hague.

2 Letter of 1st July 1807 from P.C.Labouchère, Amsterdam, to Robert Voûte, The Hague.
3 Letters of 23rd June and 11th July 1807 from Gérardin, Paris, to Hope & Co., Amsterdam.
Letter of 2nd July 1807 to Gérardin, Paris, VII, 117.
Letter of 2nd July 1807 to Roederer, Naples, VII, 120.
4 Letter of 30th June 1807 to the King of Holland, The Hague, VII, 113.
Letters of 30th June, 4th and 28th July to Robert Voûte, The Hague, VII, 114, 122, 147.
Letter of 11th July 1807 from Gérardin, Paris, to Hope & Co., Amsterdam.
17th July 1807: Approval by King Louis Napoleon for the loan of three million guilders to Naples.
Letter of 23rd July 1807 from P.C.Labouchère, Amsterdam, to Robert Voûte, The Hague.
Letters of 27th July and 13th August to Max H.F.Fréville, Tribun, Paris, VII, 142, 151.
Fréville had accompanied Gérardin to Amsterdam as his adviser.
Letter of 30th July 1807 from Robert Voûte, The Hague, to Hope & Co., Amsterdam.
Letters of 3rd and 21st August 1807 from Fréville, Paris, to Hope & Co., Amsterdam.

PAGE 345

1 Letter of 15th September 1807 from Roederer, Naples, to Hope & Co., Amsterdam.
Letters of 17th, 19th and 23rd September, 2nd, 5th, 7th, 8th, 10th and 12th October 1807 from P.C.Labouchère, Amsterdam to Robert Voûte, The Hague.
Letters of 30th September, 6th and 10th October 1807 to Robert Voûte, The Hague, VII, 175, 184, 191.
Letter of 1st October 1807 from Hope & Co., Amsterdam, to the King of Holland, The Hague.
Letter of 2nd October 1807 to Fréville, Paris, VII, 176.
Letters of 2nd and 8th October 1807 to Roederer, Naples, VII, 181, 188.
2 Letters of 14th, 15th and 21st October 1807 from P.C.Labouchère, Amsterdam, to Robert Voûte, The Hague.
Letters of 15th and 22nd October 1807 to Roederer, Naples, VII, 193, 203.
3 *Grootboek* 1808: 209. *Grootboek* 1809: 101.
Letter of 5th November 1807 to Roederer, Naples, VII, 212.
Letter of 6th November 1807 from Roederer, Naples, to Hope & Co., Amsterdam.
Letter of 9th November 1807 from P.C.Labouchère, Amsterdam, to Robert Voûte, Utrecht.
Letter of 19th November 1807 to Robert Voûte, Utrecht, VII, 217.
4 Letter of 24th December 1807 to Roederer, Naples, VII, 249.
Letter of 31st December 1807 to Baguenault & Co., Paris, VII, 256.
Lesage, *Napoléon I, créancier de la Prusse*, 274–275.
5 Letter of 14th January 1808 to Baguenault & Co., Paris, VII, 275.
Letter of 14th January 1808 to Roederer, Naples, VII, 270.
Grootboek 1809:101.
Letter of 19th February 1809 from Roederer, Naples, to Hope & Co., Amsterdam.
Letter of 18th March 1809 to Roederer, Naples, VII, 336.
6 15th May 1809: Report submitted to the king by the minister of finance.

20th May 1809: Decree issued by Joseph Napoleon, King of Naples and Sicily.
Letter of 2nd June 1809 from Roederer, Naples, to Hope & Co., Amsterdam.

PAGE 346

1 Letter of 25th June 1809 from Roederer, Naples, to Hope & Co., Amsterdam.
2 Letter of 10th June 1807 to Auguste Ouvrard & Co., Paris, VI-fa-85, 27.
3 Letters of 25th, 27th, 28th April and 5th June 1807 from Louis, Paris, to P.C.Labouchère, Amsterdam.
4 Letters of 21st and 25th May, 5th and 8th June 1807 from P.C.Labouchère, Amsterdam, to Louis, Amsterdam.

PAGE 347

1 Letters of 21st and 25th May 1807 from P.C.Labouchère, Amsterdam, to Louis, Paris.
Letters of 22nd May and 19th June 1807 from P.C.Labouchère, Amsterdam, to Baring Bros., London.
Letters of 15th and 29th May 1807 from Louis, Paris, to P.C.Labouchère, Amsterdam.
2 Letter of 2nd November 1807 from Cordier, Paris, to P.C.Labouchère, Amsterdam.
Letter of 30th November 1807 to Cordier, Paris, VII, 223, Wolff, *Geschäfte Ouvrard*, 145.
Arthur Lévy, *Un grand profiteur*, 170.
G. J. Ouvrard, *Mémoires*, 143.
3 Authorization, etc. from Auguste Ouvrard & Co., VI-fa-85, 36.
Letters, etc. of 1st and 19th October 1807, VI-fa-85, 31.
4 Letter of 19th June 1807 from P.C.Labouchère, Amsterdam, to Baring Bros., London.

PAGE 348

1 Letter of 22nd July 1807 to W.G.Coesvelt, Paris, W.G.C. I.
Fugier, *Napoléon et l'Espagne*, II, 55, 95–96.
Michel had obtained approval for the payment of his drafts on the *Caja* in March 1806, but Mollien had prevented this taking place. According to Fugier, Michel succeeded in having the drafts exchanged for others on Mexico in July 1806. Coesvelt's letter, however, reveals that, in Labouchère's view, this may well have happened during the second half of 1807. Michel the Younger sent drafts for $2\frac{1}{2}$ million piastres to Hope & Co. via Coesvelt, to be sold in London. Labouchère was anything but pleased about this, if only because the drafts bore the signatures of ministers in the government of Charles IV who had been replaced when Ferdinand VII acceded to the throne. It was a relief to him when, after a good deal of shilly-shallying, Michel the Younger gave instructions for the bills to be sent to his house in Paris where, he stated, Gordon & Murphy were willing to give a better rate of exchange.
Letters of 8th April, 5th and 19th May 1808 from Michel the Younger, Madrid, to Hope & Co., Amsterdam.
Letters of 18th April, 19th and 23rd May, 9th June 1808 to W.G.Coesvelt, Madrid, W.G.C. I.
Letters of 18th April, 23rd May, 2nd and 9th June 1808 to W.G.Coesvelt, Madrid, W.G.C. I.

Letters of 18th April, 23rd May, 2nd and 9th June 1808 to Michel the Younger, Madrid, VII, 352, 378, 386, 392.
Letters of 12th and 19th May, 9th June 1808 from W.G.Coesvelt, Madrid, to Hope & Co., Amsterdam, VI-fa-86, 24, 25, 25.

2 Letter of 8th August 1807 from W.G.Coesvelt, Paris, to Hope & Co., Amsterdam.
Letter of 6th September 1807 from W.G.Coesvelt, Paris, to Hope & Co., Amsterdam, VI-fa-86, 22.

3 Letter of 21st September 1807 from A.v.d. Hoop, Madrid, to the trustees of Croese & Co., Amsterdam.
Letters of 1st, 22nd and 29th October 1807 to W.G.Coesvelt, Madrid, W.G.C. I.

4 Letter of 5th November 1807 to W.G.Coesvelt, Madrid, W.G.C. I.

PAGE 349

1 Letter of 14th December 1807 to W.G.Coesvelt, Madrid, W.G.C. I.

2 Letters of 21st and 24th December 1807 to W.G.Coesvelt, Madrid, W.G.C. I.
Letter of 25th December 1807 to J. Dixon, VII, 250. In March 1808 Labouchère wrote to say that the price of tobacco in Amsterdam was exorbitant and that the article could not be shipped. Because of this, this he was making efforts via Barings. It is thus clear that, in spite of Hogguer's interest, Hope & Co. had not given up.
Letter of 3rd March 1808 to W.G.Coesvelt, Madrid, W.G.C. I.
Letter of 2nd March 1808 from Hope & Co., Amsterdam, to Baring Bros., London.

3 Letters of 25th and 27th January 1808 to W.G.Coesvelt, Madrid, W.G.C. I.

4 Letter of 8th February 1808 to Espinosa, Madrid, O.E. II, 38.

PAGE 350

1 Letter of 5th February 1808 to Henry Hope, London, O.E. II, 30.
Letter of 8th March 1808 from H.Hope, London, to Hope & Co., Amsterdam.

2 Fugier, *Napoléon et l'Espagne*, II, 260–262, Chapter VII, Part I, III.

3 Letters of 31st December 1807, and 8th February and 3rd March 1808 to W.G.Coesvelt, Madrid, W.G.C. I.

4 Fugier, *Napoléon et l'Espagne*, II, 416, 417, 435.
Letter of 3rd March 1808 to W.G.Coesvelt, Madrid, W.G.C. I.

PAGE 351

1 Fugier, *Napoléon et l'Espagne*, II, 436.
Letter of 14th March 1808 from W.G.Coesvelt, Madrid, to Hope & Co., Amsterdam, VI-fa-86, 23.

2 Fugier, *Napoléon et l'Espagne*, II, 442.

3 Letter of 23rd March 1808 from A.v.d. Hoop and W.G.Coesvelt, Madrid, to P.C.Labouchère, Amsterdam.

4 Letter of 11th April 1808 to W.G.Coesvelt, Madrid, W.G.C. I.

5 Letter of 11th April 1808 to W.G.Coesvelt, Madrid, W.G.C. I.

PAGE 352

1 Altamira, *History of Spain*, 527.

2 Letter of 24th March 1808 from Thomas de Foronda and Gabriel Filipe Melendez, Madrid, to Baguenault & Co., Paris.
Letter of 6th April 1808 from W.G.Coesvelt, Madrid, to Baguenault & Co., Paris.

3 Letter of 16th June 1808 to W.G.Coesvelt, Madrid, W.G.C. I.
Letter of 15th August 1808 to De Cabarrus, Madrid, VII, 469, and O.E. II, 72.

PAGE 353

1 G. de Grandmaison, *L'Espagne et Napoléon* (Paris, 1908), 317, 319.
Letters of 18th and 26th July 1808 from W.G.Coesvelt, Madrid, to Hope & Co., Amsterdam, VI-fa-86, 26, 26.
2 Letters of 15th and 29th August 1808 to De Cabarrus, Madrid, VII, 469, O.E. II, 72, O.E. II, 78.
Letter of 3rd September 1808 from W.G.Coesvelt, Madrid, to Hope & Co., Amsterdam, VI-fa-86, 27.
Letter of 3rd September 1808 from the Marquis de Fuerte Hisar, Madrid, to Hope & Co., Amsterdam.
Letter of 9th October 1808 from De Cabarrus, Vittoria, to Hope & Co., Amsterdam.
3 Letter of 9th December 1808 from J.G.de Villanueva, Philadelphia, to J.W.Hope, London.
Letter of 1st December 1808 from P.C.Labouchère, Amsterdam, to J.W.Hope, London.
Nolte, *Fünfzig Jahre*, 171. Nolte states that De Villanueva left for Philadelphia at the end of the summer, but he was frequently guilty of inaccuracy in regard to time.
Cf. Bruchey, *Robert Oliver*, 333, note 381.

PAGE 354

1 Letter of 3rd November 1808 to De Cabarrus, Vittoria, O.E. II, 97.
Letters of 1st-7th December 1808 from P.C.Labouchère, Amsterdam, to J.W.Hope, London.
Letter of 20th March 1809 from D.Parish, Philadelphia, to P.C.Labouchère, Amsterdam.
2 Letter of 1st December 1808 from Hope & Co., Amsterdam, to J.W.Hope, London.
31st October 1808: Approval by A.Ouvrard & Co., VI-fa-85, 51.
3 Letter of 9th October 1808 from De Cabarrus, Vittoria, to Hope & Co., Amsterdam.
Letters of 15th August, 26th September and 3rd November 1808 to De Cabarrus, Vittoria, O.E. II, 72, 84, 97.
4 Letter of 3rd November 1808 to De Cabarrus, Vittoria, O.E. II, 97.
5 Letter of 1st December 1808 from Hope & Co., Amsterdam, to J.W.Hope, London.
Letter of 5th January 1809 to W.G.Coesvelt, Madrid, W.G.C. II. 12.

PAGE 355

1 Letter of 15th November 1808 from the Marquis de Fuerte Hisar, Madrid, to Hope & Co., Amsterdam.
Letter of 3rd November 1808 to De Cabarrus, Vittoria, O.E. II, 97.
2 Letter of 2nd December 1808 from W.G.Coesvelt, Madrid, to Hope & Co., Amsterdam, VI-fa-86, 32.
3 Letter of 4th November 1808 from W.G.Coesvelt, Madrid, to Hope & Co., Amsterdam, VI-fa-86, 30.
4 Letter of 9th January 1809 from De Cabarrus, Madrid, to Hope & Co., Amsterdam.
Letter of 6th February 1809 to De Cabarrus, Madrid, O.E. II, 108.
5 Letters of 6th and 9th February 1809 to W.G.Coesvelt, Madrid, W.G.C. II, 16, 18.

Letter of 9th February 1809 to De Cabarrus, Madrid, O.E. II, 110.
De Grandmaison, *L'Espagne et Napoléon*, 445.
6 H. Baumgarten, *Geschichte Spaniens vom Ausbruch der französischen Revolution bis auf unsere Tage*, I (Leipzig, 1865), 377.

CHAPTER THIRTEEN

PAGE 357

1 Letters of 9th and 27th February, 9th March 1809 to W.G.Coesvelt, Madrid, W.G.C. II, 18, 19, 22.
Letter of 16th February 1809 from W.G.Coesvelt, Madrid, to Hope & Co., Amsterdam, VI-fa-86, 32.
2 Letters of 16th February and 2nd March 1809 from W.G.Coesvelt, Madrid, to Hope & Co., Amsterdam, VI-fa-86, 32, 33.
Letter of 16th March 1809 to W.G.Coesvelt, Madrid, W.G.C. II, 26.
3 Letters of 23rd March and 17th April 1809 to W.G.Coesvelt, Madrid, W.G.C. II, 27, 29.
Letter of 1st March 1808 to P.T.van Son, The Hague, VII, 324.
Letter of 16th June 1808 to W.G.Coesvelt, Madrid, W.G.C. I.
Labouchère's brother, Samuel, became 'Premier Successeur' of the house at Rotterdam, which bore the name S.Labouchère & Co.
Nolte, *Fünfzig Jahre*, 203.

PAGE 358

1 Letter of 16th March 1809 to De Cabarrus, Madrid, O.E. II, 111.
Letter of 20th March 1809 from W.G.Coesvelt, Madrid, to Hope & Co., Amsterdam, VI-fa-86, 36.
Letter of 17th April 1809 to W.G.Coesvelt, Madrid, W.G.C. II, 29.
2 Letter of 30th March 1809 from W.G.Coesvelt, Madrid, to Hope & Co., Amsterdam, VI-fa-86, 37.
Letter of 3rd April 1809 from W.G.Coesvelt, Madrid, to De Cabarrus, Madrid.
3 Letter of 11th April 1809 from De Cabarrus, Madrid, to Hope & Co., Amsterdam.
Letter of 11th April 1809 from W.G.Coesvelt, Madrid, to Hope & Co., Amsterdam, VI-fa-86, 39.
Letter of 11th April 1809 from the *Caja de Consolidacion*, Madrid, to Hope & Co., Amsterdam.
4 Letter of 12th April 1809 from John Murphy, Madrid, to Gordon & Murphy, London.

PAGE 359

1 Letter of 17th April 1809 to W.G.Coesvelt, Madrid, W.G.C. II, 29.
Letter of 11th May 1809 to Pedro de Cifuentes, Madrid.
Letter of 1st June 1809 to the *Caja de Consolidacion*, Madrid, O.E. II, 118.

2 Letter of 6th June 1809 from P.C.Labouchère, Poitiers, to D. Parish, Philadelphia.
Letters of 18th and 20th May 1809 from P.C.Labouchère, Paris, to Hope & Co., Amsterdam.
3 Letters of 18th and 20th May 1809 from P.C.Labouchère, Paris, to Hope & Co., Amsterdam.
4 Letter of 6th June 1809 from P.C.Labouchère, Orthez, to D.Parish, Philadelphia.
Letter of 28th May 1809 from P.C.Labouchère, Bordeaux, to Hope & Co., Amsterdam.
Letter of 3rd June 1809 from P.C.Labouchère, Orthez, to Hope & Co., Amsterdam.
5 Letter of 13th June 1809 from P.C.Labouchère, Orthez, to Hope & Co., Amsterdam.

PAGE 360

1 Letters of 22nd and 29th May 1809 from W.G.Coesvelt, Madrid, to P.C.Labouchère, Orthez.
Letter of 1st June 1809 to De Cabarrus, Madrid, O.E. II, 116.
Letter of 1st June 1809 to the *Caja de Consolidacion*, Madrid, O.E. II, 118.
2 Letter of 25th June 1809 from W.G.Coesvelt, Bayonne, to P.C.Labouchère, Bagnères.
Letter of 3rd July 1809 from P.C.Labouchère, Bagnères, to Hope & Co., Amsterdam.
Letter of 3rd July 1809 from P.C.Labouchère, Bagnères, to Henry Hope, London.
3 Letter of 1st June 1809 from De Cabarrus to the King, enclosing prospectus.
Letter of 15th July 1809 from P.C.Labouchère, Bagnères, to De Cabarrus, Madrid.
4 Letter of 6th August 1809 from W.G.Coesvelt, Rotterdam, to P.C.Labouchère.

PAGE 361

1 Letter of 11th August 1809 from Hope & Co., Amsterdam, to J.W.Hope, London.
2 Letter of 13th June 1809 from P.C.Labouchère, Orthez, to Hope & Co., Amsterdam.
3 Letter of 23rd June 1809 Hope & Co., Amsterdam, to J.W.Hope,London.
June 1809: Draft contract for the transfer to Willem Borski of 2,600 bonds at $5\frac{1}{2}$%.

PAGE 362

1 Letter of 28th June 1809 from Baring Bros., London, to Hope & Co., Amsterdam.
2 Letter of 6th August 1809 from W.G.Coesvelt, Rotterdam, to P.C.Labouchère.
Letter of 10th August 1809 from P.C.Labouchère, Bordeaux, to Hope & Co., Amsterdam.
Letter of 17th August 1809 from P.C.Labouchère, Nantes, to Hope & Co., Amsterdam.
Letter of 11th August 1809 to J.W.Hope, London.
3 Letter of 5th August 1808 from Falconnet & Co., Naples, to Hope & Co., Amsterdam.
Letter of 12th September 1808 to Falconnet & Co., Naples, VII, 476.
4 Letter of 29th November 1808 to Falconnet & Co., Naples, VII, 552.
The Hope archives contain details of a draft procedure relating to a speculative transaction in Neapolitan funds held by Willem Borski.
5 Letter of 3rd March 1809 from Prince de Gerace, Naples, to Hope & Co., Amsterdam.
6 Letter of 6th April 1809 to Prince de Gerace, Naples, A XXVII, 57.

PAGE 363

1 Letter of 26th June 1809 to Prince de Gerace, Naples, A XXVII, 112.
Letter of 26th June 1809 from P.C.Labouchère, Bagnères, to Hope & Co., Amsterdam.
2 Letter of 26th June 1809 to Prince de Gerace, Naples, A XXVII, 112.
Letter of 4th June 1815 from Falconnet & Co., Naples, to Hope & Co., Amsterdam.
Letter of 3rd July 1809 to Prince de Gerace, Naples, A XXVII, 115, 116.
3 Letter of 27th July 1809 from P.C.Labouchère, Toulouse, to Manuel Sanchez Toscano, Madrid, W.G.C. II, 31.
4 Letter of 3rd August 1809 from De Cabarrus, Madrid, to Hope & Co., Amsterdam.

PAGE 364

1 Letter of 19th September 1809 to Manuel Sanchez Toscano, Madrid, W.G.C. II, 33.
Letter of 15th September 1809 to the King of Spain, Madrid, O.E. II, 134.
Letters of 15th and 20th September, 6th October 1809 to De Cabarrus, Madrid, O.E. II, 137, 142, 148.
2 Letter of 27th September 1809 to De Cabarrus, Madrid, O.E. II, 144.
Letter of 6th October to De Cabarrus, Madrid, O.E. II, 146.
3 Letter of 4th December 1809 from De Cabarrus, Madrid, to Hope & Co., Amsterdam, VI-fa-86, 11.
4 Letter of 6th September 1809 from P.C.Labouchère, Paris, to Hope & Co., Amsterdam.

PAGE 365

1 Letter of 11th September 1809 from P.C.Labouchère, Paris, to Hope & Co., Amsterdam.
Letter of 14th May 1809 from Izquierdo, Paris, to Hope & Co., Amsterdam.
2 Nolte, *Fünfzig Jahre*, 207–208.
Letter of 30th October 1809 from P.C.Labouchère, Amsterdam, to Henry Hope, London.
Letter of 5th January 1810 from W.G.Coesvelt, Paris, to Hope & Co., Amsterdam.
3 Letters of 20th and 27th September, 6th October and 10th November 1809 to Cabarrus, O.E. II, 142, 144, 146, 148.
10th November 1809: Memorandum concerning the attitude of the Spanish government (in the handwriting of P.C.Labouchère).
Letter of 5th December 1809 from P.C.Labouchère, Amsterdam, to H. Hope & Co., London.
4 Letter of 5th December 1809 from P.C.Labouchère, Amsterdam, to H. Hope & Co., London.
Letter of 2nd January 1810 to W.G.Coesvelt, Paris, W.G.C. II, 35.
Letter of 28th January 1810 to De Cabarrus, Madrid, O.E. II, 155.

PAGE 366

1 Baumgarten, *Geschichte Spaniens*, I, 415.
2 Letter of 28th January 1810 to W.G.Coesvelt, Bayonne, W.G.C. II, 38, 42.
20th December 1809: Preliminary decree by Joseph Napoleon, King of Spain.
3 Letter of 12th January 1810 from W.G.Coesvelt, Bordeaux, to De Cabarrus, Madrid.
4 G.Labouchère, 'P.C.Labouchère, un financier diplomate au siècle dernier,' *Revue*

d'Histoire Diplomatique, XXVII (1913), 430–431.
Nolte, *Fünfzig Jahre*, 208–209.
Letter of 28th January 1810 to W.G.Coesvelt, Bayonne, W.G.C. II, 38, 42.

PAGE 367

1 Letters of 3rd, 5th, 8th, 9th, 18th and 22nd February, 5th, 6th, 11th, 20th, 26th and 30th March, 8th April 1810 from W.G.Coesvelt, Bayonne, to P.C.Labouchère, Amsterdam.
Letter of 20th February 1810 from W.G.Coesvelt, Bayonne, to De Cabarrus, Madrid.
Ramon, *Histoire de la Banque de France*, 94.
2 Letter of 22nd September 1809 from P.C.Labouchère, Paris, to Hope & Co., Amsterdam.
Letter of 30th September 1809 from P.C.Labouchère, Amsterdam, to Henry Hope, London.
Letter of 18th February 1810 from W.G.Coesvelt, Bayonne, to P.C.Labouchère, Amsterdam.
Letter of 6th March 1810 to Prince de Gerace, Naples, A XXVII, 317.
3 Letters of 26th and 30th March 1810 from W.G.Coesvelt, Bayonne, to P.C.Labouchère, Amsterdam.
4 Letter of 8th April 1810 from W.G.Coesvelt, Bayonne, to P.C.Labouchère, Amsterdam.
Letter of 14th April 1810 from W.G.Coesvelt, Vittoria, to P.C.Labouchère, Amsterdam.
Letter of 3rd May 1810 from W.G.Coesvelt, Madrid, to P.C.Labouchère, Amsterdam.

PAGE 368

1 Letter of 14th May 1810 from W.G.Coesvelt, Madrid, to P.C.Labouchère, Amsterdam.
2 Letters of 16th and 31st May, 6th, 17th and 28th July 1810 from W.G.Coesvelt, Madrid, to P.C.Labouchère, Amsterdam.
Letter of 18th May 1810 from W.G.Coesvelt, Madrid, to D'Almenara, Madrid.
Letter of 26th May 1810 from W.G.Coesvelt, Madrid, to Hope & Co., Amsterdam.
H.T.Colenbrander, *Schimmelpenninck en Koning Lodewijk* (Amsterdam, 1911), 212.
3 Letter of 28th July 1810 from W.G.Coesvelt, Madrid, to P.C.Labouchère, Amsterdam.
Letter of 15th September 1810 to W.G.Coesvelt, Madrid, W.G.C. II, 69.
4 Letters of 5th, 12th and 24th August, 25th September, 1810 from W.G.Coesvelt, Madrid, to P.C.Labouchère, Amsterdam.

PAGE 369

1 G.Labouchère, 'Un financier diplomate,' 437–442, 446–447.
Letter of 26th July 1810 from D.Parish, London, to J.W.Hope, London.
Letter of 22nd August 1810 to W.G.Coesvelt, Madrid, W.G.C. II, 68.
Letter of 17th July 1810 from W.G.Coesvelt, Madrid, to P.C.Labouchère, Amsterdam.
2 Letter of 16th July 1810 from D. Parish, London, to J.W.Hope, London.
Letter of 15th August 1810 from D.Parish, Antwerp, to P.C.Labouchère, Amsterdam.

14th September 1810: Letters of introduction for Parish to the Duke of Cadore, Mollien, Count Estève, Marquis d'Almenara, Prince de Benevento and Marquis de Santa Fé.
Letter of 15th September 1810 to W.G.Coesvelt, Madrid, W.G.C. II, 69.
3 Letter of 2nd October to D.Parish, Paris, W.G.C. II, 72.

PAGE 370

1 Letter of 11th October 1810 from D.Parish, Paris, to P.C.Labouchère, Amsterdam.
2 Letters of 2nd, 3rd and 4th October 1810 from D.Parish, Paris, to P.C.Labouchère, Amsterdam.
3 Letters of 12th, 13th and 15th October, 2nd and 17th November 1810 to D.Parish, Paris, W.G.C. II, 47, 83, 102.

PAGE 371

1 Letter of 2nd November 1810 to D.Parish, Paris, W.G.C. II, 83.
2 Letter of 2nd November 1810 to D'Almenara, Paris.
3 Letters of 12th November, 8th and 27th December 1810 from M.Simons, Paris, to P.C.Labouchère, Amsterdam.
Letter of 17th November 1810 to D.Parish, Paris, W.G.C. II, 102.
Letter of 1st December 1810 from D.Parish, Paris, to P.C.Labouchère, Amsterdam.
Letters of 8th and 14th December 1810 from Tourton Ravel & Co., Paris, to P.C.Labouchère, Amsterdam.
Letter of 14th December 1810 from R.&Th.de Smeth, Amsterdam, to Emperor Napoleon Bonaparte.
Letter of 27th December 1810 from P.C.Labouchère, Amsterdam, to D.Parish, Paris.
4 Letter of 20th March 1809 from D.Parish, Philadelphia, to P.C.Labouchère, Amsterdam.
Letter of 15th September 1809 to W.G.Coesvelt, Madrid, W.G.C. II, 69.
Nolte, *Fünfzig Jahre*, 234–235.

PAGE 372

1 *Ibid.*, 216–217.
Bruchey, *Robert Oliver*, 333.
2 Letter of 9th February 1809 from D.Parish, Philadelphia, to Hope & Co., Amsterdam.
Walters and Walters, 'American Career,' 154.
3 Letter of 3rd May 1810 from Charles W.Hare, Philadelphia, to D.Parish.
4 Walters and Walters, 'American Career,' 155.
5 July 1810: Questionnaire pertaining to the action brought against David Parish by the King of Spain, VI-ba-82. Replies VI-ba-83.

PAGE 373

1 Letter of 15th September 1810 to Baring Bros., London, A XXVII, 428.
2 18th June 1811: Statement prepared by P.C.Labouchère.
3 Letter of 17th January 1812 from Ch.W.Hare, E.Tilghmann, William Meredith and Joseph Hopkinson to D.Parish, Philadelphia.
4 Remarks by P.C.Labouchère concerning the letter of 17th January 1812 from Ch.W.Hare and others.

5 Letter of 10th March 1812 from Baring Bros., London, to P.C.Labouchère.
Letters of 27th March and 23rd April 1812 to Henry Hope & Co. and Baring Bros., London, A XXVIII, 54, 72.
6 Letter of 8th April 1812 to Baring Bros., London, A XXVIII, 62.
Letter of 8th April 1812 to Pedro de Echeverria, Vera Cruz, A XXVIII, 63.
Letter of 13th May 1812 from Baring Bros., London, to Hope & Co., Amsterdam.

PAGE 374

1 Letters of 3rd December 1812 and 13th January 1813 to D.Parish, Philadelphia, A XXVIII, 240, 281.
Letter of 20th August 1812 from P.C.Labouchère, Kassel, to A.v.d.Hoop, Amsterdam.
27th January 1813: Statement by David Baillie Wiordery, Consul General of the United States in Paris, concerning the receipt of two parcels from Hottinguer & Co., Paris.
2 Letter of 5th September 1812 to Baring Bros., London, A XXVIII, 158.
Letter of 4th January 1814 from Hope & Co., Amsterdam, to A.Baring, London.
Letter of 1st February 1814 to D.Parish, Philadelphia, A XXVIII, 469.
The visiting American was G.Emlen.
The case was, of course, brought before a higher court, but it would appear that Labouchère failed to recognize the distinction between the various courts.
3 Wolff, *Geschäfte Ouvrard*, 168.
Walters and Walters, 'American Career,' 155.
Letter of 15th February 1815 from J.Ouvrard, Paris, to the Chief Justice of the Supreme (?) Court of the United States, Philadelphia.
4 Letters of 15th and 28th December 1810 from W.G.Coesvelt, Madrid, to P.C.Labouchère, Amsterdam.
5 Letters of 28th December 1810, 15th, 21st and 27th January 1811 from W.G.Coesvelt, Madrid, to P.C.Labouchère, Amsterdam.

PAGE 375

1 Letter of 18th February 1811 from W.G.Coesvelt, Madrid, to P.C.Labouchère, Amsterdam.
2 Letters of 14th and 15th April 1811 from John Hope, London, to P.C.Labouchère, London.
3 Letters of 25th May and 20th June 1811 from P.C.Labouchère, Amsterdam, to J.Hope, London.
Circular from Hope & Co. dated 15th June 1811.
4 Letters of 12th June, 2nd, 26th and 30th August 1811 to Gennaro Francesconi, Naples, A XXVII 212, 240; A XXVII-ii, 52, 57.
Letter of 7th July 1811 from Gennaro Francesconi, Naples, to Hope & Co., Amsterdam.

PAGE 376

1 Letter of 3rd July 1810 to Prince de Gerace, Naples, A XXVII, 389.
Letter of 26th June 1811 to Prince de Gerace, Naples, A XXVII-ii, 19.
2 Letter of 18th December 1810 to Prince de Gerace, Naples, A XXVII, 532.
Letter of 9th February 1811 from P.F.Lestapis, Amsterdam, to P.C.Labouchère, Antwerp.

3 Letters of 22nd November 1811 and 31st January 1812 to Gennaro Francesconi & Co., Naples, A XXVII-ii, 101; A XXVIII, 26.
4 Letters of 20th and 22nd May 1809 from Hope & Co., Amsterdam, to Prince de Gerace, Naples.
Letters of 8th August 1810, and 8th January and 25th April 1811 to Prince de Gerace, Naples, A XXVII, 402, 549, 606.
5 Letters of 4th and 16th March, 21st October 1812 to Prince de Gerace, Naples, A XXVIII, 402, 549, 606.
6 Letters of 26th June and 14th August 1812 to Prince de Gerace, Naples, A XXVIII, 120, 151.
Letter of 6th July 1812 from P.C.Labouchère, Pyrmont, to A.v.d.Hoop, Amsterdam.

PAGE 378

1 Letter of 23rd March 1813 to Prince de Gerace, Naples, A XXVIII, 333.
2 Letters of 30th June, 6th, 9th, 22nd and 27th July, 10th, 13th and 25th August, 14th September, 11th and 22nd October 1813 to Prince de Gerace, Naples, A XXVIII, 385, 393, 394, 398, 399, 404, 405, 409, 416, 422, 427.
Letter of 1st July 1813 to Falconnet & Co., Naples, A XXVIII, 390.
G.A. Amsterdam, Not. Arch., 18034–163.
3 Letter of 1st November 1813 to Prince de Gerace, Naples, A XXVIII, 429. *Supra*, 256–257.
4 Letters of 12th and 22nd April 1814 to Prince de Gerace, Naples, A XXVIII, 500, 511.
5 Letter of 12th May 1814 from P.C.Labouchère, Paris, to Hope & Co., Amsterdam.
Letters of 7th and 17th June 1814 from P.C.Labouchère, London, to Hope & Co., Amsterdam.
Letter of 2nd July 1814 to Prince de Gerace, Naples, A XXVIII, 539.
6 Letter of 1st November 1814 to Prince de Gerace, Naples, A XXVIII, 597.
Letters of 3rd and 5th November 1814 from P.C.Labouchère, Paris, to A.v.d.Hoop.

PAGE 379

1 Letter of 13th November 1814 from P.C.Labouchère, Paris, to A.v.d.Hoop, Amsterdam.
Grootboek 1814: 22.
2 *Grootboek* 1816: 36.
G.A. Amsterdam, Not. Arch., 18035–315, 18035–2–82.
3 G.A. Amsterdam, Not. Arch., 18036–56.
Grootboek 1816: 32.
Grootboek 1817: 32.
Grootboek 1818: 30.
4 Letter of 28th January 1814 to the *Caja de Consolidacion*, A XXVIII, 467.
5 Letter of 11th March 1814 from P.C.Labouchère to Hope & Co., Amsterdam.

PAGE 380

1 Letter of 24th June 1814 from P.C.Labouchère, London, to Hope & Co., Amsterdam.
Letter of 17th September 1814 from J.C.Cambier, Paris, to Hope & Co., Amsterdam.
Letters of 8th October and 22nd December 1814 to J.C.Cambier, Madrid, A XXVIII, 576, 621.

Letters of 21st December 1814 and 2nd March 1815 from J.C.Cambier, Madrid, to Hope & Co., Amsterdam.

2 Letter of August 1815 from J.C.Cambier, Madrid, to Hope & Co., Amsterdam (via The Hague).

3 Weeveringh, *Geschiedenis Staatsschulden*, II, 730–731, 736–737.

An extensive but not very lucid story by J.A.Alting Bösken, *Over geldleeningen hier te lande door vreemde mogendheden aangegaan* (Utrecht, 1864), 81–88.

CHAPTER FOURTEEN

PAGE 383

1 H.Schäfer, *Geschichte von Portugal*, v (Gotha, 1854), 610–616. H.V.Livermore, *A New History of Portugal* (Cambridge, 1966), 245–246.

PAGE 384

1 C.R.Boxer, *The Portuguese Seaborne Empire* (London, 1969), 157. Schäfer, *Geschichte von Portugal*, v, 192, 193, 194.

2 Letter of 15th March 1765 from Barend Wessely, Copenhagen, to Hope & Co., Amsterdam.

PAGE 385

1 Letter of 22nd April 1777 from Thomas Mayne & Co., Lisbon, to Hope & Co., Amsterdam.

2 Letter of 1st April 1777 from Lewis Cantofer, Lisbon, to Hope & Co., Amsterdam. Cantofer estimated that the 60,000 carats about which he wrote would fetch cf 2,710,000 in Amsterdam. The carat prices which he maintained were identical to those maintained by Hope in 1800. The prices for small and large stones differed greatly, the former being calculated at cf 28 per carat and stones of between 40 and 79 grains at cf 100 per carat. A carat, which consists of four grains, may be put at about 0.2 grams. Robert Paisley & Co. of Lisbon, whom Cantofer introduced in an accompanying letter, felt that the estimated yield was too high. In Mayne's view, it was not necessary to take more than 40,000 carats annually, although a contract for larger quantities was to be preferred. Hope expressed the view that the Amsterdam market could absorb 50–60,000 carats annually. The newly appointed Inspector of the Treasury, the Marquis of Angeja, had informed Mayne of an offer by Cantofer to take 80,000 carats annually – 20,000 above the figure which he had indicated to Hope. Just who was guilty of an untruth is not clear from the correspondence, but it may be assumed that Cantofer planned to sell the 20,000 carats behind Hope's back. As will emerge, a considerable quantity of diamonds reached Amsterdam by way of London.

3 The contract was awarded to Paulo Jorge and Joao Ferreira of Lisbon, who, it was reported, proposed to appoint Van Brienen & Co. as their agents in Amsterdam. Letters of 10th and 17th April 1787 from Lewis Stephens, Lisbon, to Hope & Co., Amsterdam.

4 *Infra*, Appendix E-1. The *grootboeken* contain the names of the following London diamonds merchants: Aaron Goldsmid, Salomon Berend Gompertz, Benjamin and Abraham Goldsmid, Aaron and Salomon Norden, P.&S.Salomons & Co., Levy

Cohen, Meyer Asser & Co., Asser Asser, Ruben Harmsz. Kijzer and Eleasar Philip Salomons.

PAGE 386

1 The names of Joseph and Mordechai van Embden first appeared in the *grootboek* of 1785 (folio 263), and that of Hartog Eleasar Cohen in the *grootboek* of 1788 (folio 297).
2 *Infra*, Appendix E-II.
3 Letter of 19th June 1798 from H.A.Insinger, Amsterdam, to P.C.Labouchère, Hamburg.
4 Letter of 1st April 1800 from Hope & Co., London, to J.P.Quintella, Lisbon, VII, 171–172.
5 Letter of 1st April 1800 from Hope & Co., London, to J.P.Quintella, Lisbon, VII, 174. The specification of the diamonds deposited with the bank reads as follows:

4,000 carats of small stones	at cf	28 per carat	cf	112,000
4,000 stones of 2 grains	at cf	30 per carat	cf	120,000
4,000 stones of 3–4 grains	at cf	32 per carat	cf	128,000
4,000 stones of 5–6 grains	at cf	34 per carat	cf	136,000
4,000 stones of 7–8 grains	at cf	36 per carat	cf	144,000
3,500 stones of 9–10 grains	at cf	38 per carat	cf	133,000
3,500 stones of 11–12 grains	at cf	40 per carat	cf	140,000
3,500 stones of 13–16 grains	at cf	44 per carat	cf	154,000
3,500 stones of 17–20 grains	at cf	58 per carat	cf	203,000
3,500 stones of 21–40 grains	at cf	70 per carat	cf	245,000
2,500 stones of 41–79 grains	at cf	100 per carat	cf	250,000
			cf	1,765,000

PAGE 387

1 Letter of 27th May 1800 from Hope & Co., London, to J.P.Quintella, Lisbon, VII, 181.
2 Letter of March 1801 from J.Williams Hope, London, to Sampayo, Lisbon. John Williams Hope said that it would take three to six years to market the quantity offered. On the basis of the sales figures for previous years (20–30,000 carats annually), this indicates that between 100,000 and 120,000 carats were offered. Following the agreement negotiated with the Portuguese government by Labouchère in 1802, this stock did indeed come into the Company's hands.
3 Letters of 7th and 14th November 1801 from John Stanley, Lisbon, to F.Baring & Co., London.

PAGE 388

1 Letter of 14th November 1801: enclosure to letter of the same date from Bandeira.
2 Letter of 27th February 1802 from P.C.Labouchère, Lisbon, to Hope & Co., London. Labouchère maintained that the two houses had become involved in the Portuguese affair in order to gratify the wish of the British minister Addington, but in the light of the previous history this was, to say the least of it, a one-sided interpretation.
3 Letter of 7th December 1801 from J.Williams Hope, London, to P.C.Labouchère, Paris. In a letter of 5th December, John Williams Hope informed Labouchère that the Portuguese government had asked for a loan of twice the original sum. While he

considered this excessive, he was interested in cotton and sugar from the point of view of the re-establishment of the house in Amsterdam.

4 Letter of 8th December 1801 from J.Willems Hope, London, to P.C.Labouchère, Paris.

PAGE 389

1 Letter of 9th December 1801 from H.Hope, London, to Sir F.Baring, London.

2 It is also conceivable that Sir Francis Baring foresaw difficulty in placing this loan in England. As Hope had already pointed out, foreign loans were not popular there.

3 Letters of 15th and 29th December 1801 from J.Williams Hope, London to P.C. Labouchère, . . .
In Nantes, family matters awaited Labouchère's attention. In the margin against the passage concerning the chartering of a vessel there are notes: in pencil the word 'no,' and in ink the instruction 'I positively forbid, no hurry.' In all probability these remarks reveal concern on the part of Henry Hope, who did not wish to expose Labouchère to risks.

4 Letters of 21st and 23rd January 1802 from P.C.Labouchère, Madrid to J.Williams Hope, London.
Letter of 23rd February 1802 from R.Voûte, Amsterdam, to Henry Hope, London.
Letter of 20th January 1802 from J.Stanley, Lisbon, to Sir F.Baring, London.

PAGE 390

1 Letters of 5th, 18th, 25th and 26th January 1802 from J.Williams Hope, Bath, to P.C.Labouchère, Lisbon.

2 There were indeed others with an eye to the main chance. These were the house of Stephens in Lisbon and a partner in the firm of Wed. Croese & Co., of Amsterdam, both of whom attempted to thwart Labouchère's plan, but were forced to give up for lack of adequate funds. The partner concerned was probably H.Croese, who at that time was residing in Madrid in connexion with the Spanish 'conversion loans' (*supra*, 283–284). According to Labouchère, Croese was out to blacken the name of Hope & Co.
Letter of 17th February 1802 from P.C.Labouchère, Lisbon, to Hope & Co., London.

3 1st February 1802: the discussions which had taken place during the preceding days had been embodied in this 'Overture.'

4 This offer contained an element of 'sales talk.' The price of the bonds to which Labouchère referred was governed not only by the rate of interest which they bore, but also by the punctuality with which interest and principal instalments were paid. The prospects for the Portuguese bonds were decidedly favourable.

PAGE 391

1 If we add to this the 100,000 pounds sterling already advanced to De Souza Coutinho, we arrive at a total of 700,000 pounds sterling–the sum mentioned by John Williams Hope.

2 Hope & Co. made a further attempt to secure the stock of 55,722½ carats which had already been handed over to the French government, but they lost to two Jewish diamond merchants from London.
Letters of 9th March 1802 from Hope & Co., Amsterdam, to H.A.Insinger & Co.,

Amsterdam, and of 16th March 1802 from J.Williams Hope, London, to P.C.Labouchère, Lisbon.

PAGE 392

1 In his correspondence with Hope and Baring, Labouchère continued to work on a price of 90, even after the signing of the contract. He evidently viewed the price of 92 referred to in the contract as a sham concession. Letters of 4th and 6th February 1802 from P.C.Labouchère, Lisbon, to Sir F. Baring, London.
8th February 1802: Contract between Don Rodrigo de Souza Coutinho, Minister of Finance, and P.C.Labouchère, representing Baring & Co. and Hope & Co.

2 Labouchère described this issue as 'a mere nothing' in his correspondence with Hope & Co. Letter of 17th February 1802 from P.C.Labouchère, Lisbon, to Hope & Co., London.

3 Letter of 17th February 1802 from P.C.Labouchère, Lisbon, to Hope & Co., London.

PAGE 394

1 Letters of 26th February 1802 from P.C.Labouchère, Lisbon, to Hope & Co., London, and of 6th and 27th April 1802 from R. Voûte, The Hague, to J.Williams Hope, London.

2 Letter of 10th May 1802 from P.C.Labouchère, Paris, to R.de Souza Coutinho, Lisbon. Current Account Book relating to the Portuguese loan, 1802–1803. During Labouchère's discussions with Talleyrand, he was informed that France no longer required the funds in Lisbon, and that these should be transferred to Paris. Any exchange losses arising from the transfer were for Portuguese account. On 14th May 1802, Labouchère paid to Citizen Estève, *Trésorier du Gouvernement*, the three million livres demanded (Current Account Book, Portuguese loan, 1802–1803). This sum was furnished by Perregaux and Baguenault, who drew on Hope for the purpose. In all, the Company paid 20 million livres to Estève; the balance of 5 million livres (2 million crusados) had been paid by the Portuguese government in 1801.

3 The actual sum made available to the Portuguese government was 90% of cf 13,000,000 less commission at 5% = cf 11,050,000. Acting on instructions issued by the prince regent on 16th February 1802, Bandeira had already drawn on Barings for cf 2,400,000.
Letter of 30th March 1802 from R.Voûte, The Hague, to Hope & Co., London.

4 Letter of 19th March 1802 from J.Williams Hope, London, to H.A.Insinger & Co., Amsterdam.

5 Sales in 1802 totalled 33,069 $^{3}/_{16}$ carats, which fetched cf 821,390.4.0. In 1803 the totals were 36,228 $^{9}/_{16}$ carats and cf 936,383.0.8 respectively. In addition to these stocks, which came direct from Lisbon, Hope & Co. had managed to lay hands on 33,000 carats out of a parcel of 55,000 carats which the Portuguese government had surrendered to France. As explained in note 2 on page 391, these had come into the possession of two London diamond merchants. Upon reflection, these merchants, S.Salomons and L.de Symons, decided to sell the stones in Amsterdam and to employ Hope & Co. for this purpose. In June/July 1802, they received from the Company an advance of 40,000 pounds sterling on the sale.

PAGE 395

1 Letter of 9th March 1802 from R.Voûte, The Hague, to Hope & Co., London.

2 Letter of 30th March 1802 from R. Voûte, The Hague, to Hope & Co., London. Under the State Regulations of 1801, the Minister of Finance had been replaced by a Treasurer General and a Council of Finances.

3 Letters of 6th and 11th April 1802 from R.Voûte, The Hague, to Hope & Co., London. Henry Philip Hope had arrived in the Batavian Republic in March, and had been followed in June by Thomas Hope. Neither, however, was an active partner in the firm.

PAGE 396

1 Letter of 26th July 1802 from R.Voûte, Middagten, to Hope & Co., London.

2 Letter of 25th August 1802 from R.Voûte, Middagten, to Hope & Co., London. At a subsequent meeting with a deputation from the *Staatsbewind*, Bonaparte made some adverse comments concerning Spoors.
Colenbrander, *Bataafsche Republiek*, 280.

PAGE 397

1 Extract from *Het Register der Resolutien van Thesaurier-General en Raden van Finantieën der Bataafsche Republiek*, dated Wednesday, 14th July 1802, No. 4.

2 Letter of 26th July 1802 from R.Voûte, Middagten, to Hope & Co., London.

3 Letter of 21st July 1802 from R.Voûte, Middagten, to P.C.Labouchère, 'c/o 30 or 31, au Doelen du Gaarnalenmarkt,' Amsterdam.

4 Letter of 21st July 1802 from P.C.Labouchère, Amsterdam, to Van Son(?), The Hague.

PAGE 398

1 Letter of 3rd August 1802 from M.H.Van Son, The Hague, to P.C. Labouchère, (?).
Letter of 18th August 1802 from R.Voûte, Middagten, to Hope & Co., London.

2 While in Paris, Labouchère had also discussed the Portuguese affair with Schimmelpenninck, the Batavian envoy to France, who was greatly in favour with Bonaparte. Schimmelpenninck attributed the hesitant attitude on the part of the *Staatsbewind* to Hope's offer to pay $\frac{1}{4}\%$ tax on the loan, which, he said, had aroused suspicions of ulterior motives. The envoy promised to put in a good word for Hope & Co. in The Hague, but this had no effect. It was said of Schimmelpenninck that he had told his Portuguese counterpart that Portugal could have done better with another house, and that permission for the loan would then certainly have been forthcoming. Following the rejection of the request, Sir Francis Baring wrote to Talleyrand, asking him to instruct the new French envoy to the Batavian Republic, De Sémonville, to make a further appeal for the approval of the loan.
Letter of 25th August 1802 from R.Voûte, Middagten, to Hope & Co., London.

3 This was a misstatement. As we have already seen, the proposal to transfer the loan to Amsterdam emanated from Sir Francis Baring.

PAGE 399

1 Letter of 3rd August 1802 from Henry Hope, London, to P.C.Labouchère, Paris.

2 Mr.Th.L.Ingram, Archivist of Baring Brothers & Co. kindly allowed us to read a volume concerning the Portuguese loan which he has written and which is based on discoveries made by him in the Northbrook Papers, which are kept at the Company's offices in London. This reveals that Sir Francis Baring desired a far-reaching merger,

and indeed continued to hope for such a development right up to the enactment of the new deed of partnership in October 1802. Voûte had earlier referred to Sir Francis's plan for one of his sons to become a partner in Hope & Co. Letters of 4th and 22nd May 1802 from R.Voûte, Middagten, to J.W.Hope, London.

PAGE 400

1 Letter of 21st February 1803 from H. Hope, London, to J.Williams Hope,
2 Letter of 17th September 1802 from Hope & Co., London, to P. Taay, Amsterdam.
3 Letter of 6th November 1802 from Henry Hope, London, to J.Williams Hope, Norwich.
4 Letter of 4th September 1802 from R.Voûte, Middagten, to Hope & Co., London.
5 Letter of 13th September 1802 from R. Voûte, The Hague, to Hope & Co., London.
6 Letter of 29th September 1802 from R.Voûte, Middagten, to J.Williams Hope, London.

PAGE 402

1 Letter of 7th December 1802 from F. Baring, London, to J.Williams Hope, Amsterdam. Concerning Andries Pels & Sons: *Supra*, 5, 11, 13, 21.
2 Letter of 30th December 1802 from P.C.Labouchère, Amsterdam, to R.Voûte, The Hague.
3 Letter of 29th/30th December 1802 from R.Voûte, The Hague, to J.Williams Hope, Hope, Amsterdam. On 1st December 1802, Voûte had taken his seat on a committee set up to study the nature and shape of the trade with the Asiatic colonies and the administration of these. D.C.A.van Hogendorp, ed., *Mémoires du Général Dirk van Hogendorp* (The Hague, 1887), 131–132, 138.
4 The advertisement also appeared in London on 14th January 1803.

PAGE 403

1 Sir Francis Baring's reply to a letter from J.Stanley, Lisbon, dated 1st February 1803.
2 Letter of 24th December 1802 from Hottinguer, Paris, to P.C.Labouchère, Amsterdam.
Letter of 27th December 1802 from P.B.Babut, Paris, to P.C.Labouchère, Amsterdam.
3 To reach the total of 5,000 it was necessary to include the 610 bonds which belonged to the 'Concern' and had been redeemed at the end of 1802. Henry Hope had purchased his 3,000 bonds at 90%, and later 418 more at 95%. All the other bonds were sold at these rates. Voûte took 200, Insinger 50, A.P.Labouchère 20, S.P.Labouchère 23, W.G.Coesvelt 220 (of which he obtained 120 through Barings), Quintella 125, Bandeira 165 and J.M.de Souza 150. Labouchère himself took 19.
4 Controlling the sales in this manner also enabled the rate to be kept up. In fact, we are concerned here with receipts which could be exchanged for bonds at a convenient moment. During his stay in Lisbon in 1802, Labouchère had devised a plan for manipulating the market in such a manner that the bond price would gradually climb to the desired figure of 95. But the subsequent phase envisaged by him – 'throwing open' the market at that level – was not realized.
Letter of 17th February 1802 from P.C.Labouchère, Lisbon, to Hope & Co., London.'
5 Insinger took a further 25, Taay received 7, W.G.Coesvelt a further 43, and

Bandeira, Quintella and J.M.de Souza each acquired an additional 100.

6 The available details of the distribution of the bonds cover the period up to the end of 1805.
Infra, Appendix E-IV.

PAGE 404

1 Letters of 5th March 1803 from J.Stanley, Lisbon, and J.P.Quintella and J.F.Bandeira, Lisbon, to P.C.Labouchère, Amsterdam.
Letter of 18th March 1803 from J. Stanley, Lisbon, to P.C.Labouchère, Amsterdam.
Also the royal instruction dated 7th March 1803, transmitted by Don Rodrigo de Souza Coutinho and enclosed with the letter of 12th March 1803 from J.P.Quintella and J.F.Bandeira to Hope & Co., Amsterdam.

2 Letter of 1st April 1803 from Sir F.Baring, London, to Hope & Co., Amsterdam.

3 Letters of 29th March and 5th April 1803 from P.C.Labouchère, Amsterdam, to Sir F.Baring, London.

4 Extract from a letter of 22nd September 1802 from the Viceroy of Brazil to Don Rodrigo de Souza Coutinho, quoted in a letter of 5th April 1803 from J.Stanley, Lisbon, to P.C.Labouchère, Amsterdam.

5 Letter of 24th July 1802 from J.Stanley, Lisbon, to Sir F.Baring, London; 'Portugal Concern,' 31.

PAGE 405

1 The 'Amazone' carried 75,000 carats, and thus 90,000 carats in all reached England. At the auction of the seized diamonds. Hope's agent only managed to secure 1,200 carats, because his limits were too low. Other buyers included the house of Couderc in Amsterdam.
Letters of 23rd, 26th, 30th and 31st August 1803 from Sir Francis Baring, London, to Hope & Co., Amsterdam.

2 Letter of 25th August 1803 from Sir Francis Baring, London, to Don J.M.de Souza, Paris.

3 Letter of 13th October 1803 from J.M.de Souza, Paris, to Hope & Co., Amsterdam.

PAGE 406

1 Schäfer, *Geschichte von Portugal*, V, 620–621.
In letter book VI, 558: an effusive valedictory letter to Don Rodrigo de Souza Coutinho (which was not despatched). The letter which was sent, and which was couched in much calmer terms, will be found in A II, 2.

2 Letter of 13th December 1803 from F. Baring & Co., London, to J.F.Bandeira, Lisbon.
Letter of 26th January 1804 from Hope & Co., Amsterdam, to Don Louis de Vasconcellas, Lisbon.

3 Letter of 20th January 1804 to F.Baring & Co., London, A II, 72.

4 Letter of 22nd January 1804 from F.Baring & Co., London, to Hope & Co., Amsterdam. This letter may have reached Labouchère before he wrote to Don Louis; if so, this would explain his change of mind.

5 Letter of 29th June 1804 from Baguenault & Co., Paris, to P.C.Labouchère, Amsterdam.

PAGE 407

1 Letter of 18th May 1804 from Baguenault & Co., Paris, to Hope & Co., Amsterdam. Baguenault's interest in this matter was professional, for the payments in Paris were routed via the house which bore his name.
2 The first indication of this appears in a letter of 26th March 1804 to J.Stanley, Lisbon, A II, 161. Cf. 'Kasboek 1804–1806,' VI-ba-62.
3 'Kasboek 1804–1806,' VI-ba-62, 18–49.
4 Letter of 28th February 1805 to Francis Baring & Co., London, A II, 561.

PAGE 408

1 Letter of 21st October 1803 to John Stanley, Lisbon, VI, 581.
2 Letter of 28th October 1803 to John Stanley, Lisbon, VI, 586.
3 Letter of 28th October 1803 to John Stanley, Lisbon, VI, 586.
4 Letter of 13th February 1804 to John Stanley, Lisbon, A II, 94.
Letter of 13th February 1804 to J.F.Bandeira, Lisbon, A II, 95.

PAGE 409

1 Letters of 21st and 24th May 1804 to J.F.Bandeira, Lisbon, 208 et seq. Bandeira was not obliged to take more than two million pounds annually. The royal storehouse in Lisbon contained 600,000 pounds, and supplies in 1804 were expected to total 1,700,000 pounds. Labouchère took the view that if such a quantity were to materialize in 1804, imports in the ensuing year would have to be limited to 1–1.2 million pounds if a fall in prices was to be avoided.
2 Letter of 28th February 1805 to F. Baring & Co., London, A II, 561.
3 Letter of 13th February 1804 to J.F.Bandeira, Lisbon, A II, 96.
4 'Diversen Documenten laast 1700-begin 1800,' 511–513.

PAGE 410

1 Letter of 13th April 1804 to Voûte Bros., *en ville*, A II, 184. Barings participated in the brazilwood concern to the same extent as in Account F.R. and the entire Portuguese affair, namely one-quarter. The ratio of 5:2 in favour of Hope, to which reference was made on page 389, was thus subsequently altered.
2 There are no reports concerning the contract between Bandeira and Hope, but the settlement accounts show clearly that the Company acted simply as agents for Bandeira and that they paid him promptly for the quantities contracted with Voûte, having of course deducted insurance premiums, commission, etc. The quantities and prices are shown in Appendix E-V.
3 Letter of 13th June 1804 from Baguenault & Co., Paris, to P.C.Labouchère, Amsterdam.
4 Letter of 18th June 1804 to Talleyrand, Paris, A II, 230.
5 Letter of 18th June 1804 to J.M.de Souza, Paris, A II, 231.
6 Letter of 29th June 1804 from Baguenault & Co., Paris, to P.C.Labouchère, Amsterdam.
7 Hope & Co. were not concerned with these payments, for which Bandeira employed the house of Rougemont. When this house went bankrupt, in February 1803, the Portuguese government lost 450,000 livres. When it became clear that this loss would not have been sustained if De Souza had adhered to his instructions concerning the payments, he was held responsible for the consequences. His conduct in this matter set a pattern which was later to be emulated by the Spanish agent, Izquierdo.

PAGE 411

1 Letters of 25th June and 6th September 1804 from Baguenault & Co., Paris, to P.C.Labouchère, Amsterdam. Accounts relating to the Portuguese Loan, 1804–1806, 1–2. Talleyrand's distrust of De Souza was so intense that he sent a personal representative to attend a meeting between Baguenault and De Souza.
2 Letter of 29th June 1804 from Baguenault & Co., Paris, to P.C.Labouchère, Amsterdam.
3 Letter of 5th July 1804 to Baguenault & Co., Paris, A II, 259.
4 Letter of 13th July 1804 from Baguenault & Co., Paris, to P.C.Labouchère, Amsterdam. The plan provided for the undertaking to be signed by Bandeira, and it is probable that this occurred. The payments were not made at strict monthly intervals, but on 29th June, 6th July, 22nd August and 5th November 1804; 26th January, 12th March, 9th April, 21st May, 13th July, 20th September, 12th October and 24th December 1805; and 25th February, 27th May, 1st and 6th August 1806. According to another source, Hope & Co. were obliged to advance monies for the last two instalments. Fugier, *Napoléon et l'Espagne*, II, 65.
5 Letter of 17th August 1804 from Baguenault & Co., Paris, to P.C.Labouchère, Amsterdam. The Portuguese Court unjustly accused Hope and Baguenault of failing to make payment direct to the French Treasury. In fact, the houses followed the practice adopted in 1802 and 1803.
6 Letter of 6th September 1804 from Baguenault & Co., Paris, to P.C.Labouchère, Amsterdam.
7 The fact that De Souza's wife, the former Countess de Flahaut, had been one of Talleyrand's mistresses evidently did not save him. *Nouvelle Biographie Générale*, XLIV, 275.
8 'State of the Loan, as stated to the Minister,' 31st December 1803.
9 Letter of 2nd February 1804 to J.Stanley, Lisbon, A II, 85, 103.

PAGE 412

1 Letter of 9th March 1804 to J.P.Quintella, Lisbon, A II, 128.
2 Letter of 10th May 1804 to Don Louis de Vasconcellas, Lisbon, A II, 195 et seq.
3 Letter of 12th June 1804 J.P.Quintella, Lisbon, to P.C.Labouchère, Amsterdam.
4 Letter of 8th October 1804 to J. Stanley, Lisbon, A II, 413.
Letter of 10th January 1805 to Don Louis de Vasconcellas, A II, 526 et seq.

PAGE 413

1 Letter of 13th November from R.Voûte, Utrecht, to P.C.Labouchère, Amsterdam. Schäfer, *Geschichte von Portugal*, V, 627.
2 *Ibid.*, 629.
3 Letters of 15th January, 9th June, 11th August and 8th December 1808 to the Baron de Quintella and Jacinto Fernandes da Costa Bandeira, Lisbon, VII, 281, 390, 467, 564. On 8th December the Company wrote acknowledging receipt of the letters of 8th and 13th October.
Letters of 14th January, 8th April, 9th June, 11th August and 8th December 1808 to J.Stanley, Lisbon, VII, 267, 344, 391, 466, 563. The letter of 8th April was carried by G.J.Ouvrard, who visited Lisbon on business. Ouvrard had promised to take Stanley under his wing. Stanley wrote on 4th May 1808 to say that General Junot had recognized his naturalization and that of his son.

PAGE 414

1 Schäfer, *Geschichte von Portugal*, v, 664.
2 Letter of 24th January 1809 to the Département des Finances, Lisbon, A xxvii, 13.
Letter of 24th January 1809 to J.F.da Costa Bandeira, Lisbon, A xxvii, 2.
Letter of 24th January 1809 to Baron de Quintella, Lisbon, A xxvii, 7.
Hope drew on Bandeira and Quintella to the extent of their credit balances, which totalled cf 343,861.15.0 and cf 28,769.0.0. respectively. These balances remained frozen until the drafts were met.
3 Letter of 20th January 1810 to the Baron de Quintella and J.F.da Costa Bandeira, Lisbon, A xxvii, 206–207.
4 Schäfer, *Geschichte von Portugal*, v, 702, 703. Under the terms of a trade treaty dated 19th February 1810, the English paid only half the import duty levied on traders of other nationalities.

PAGE 415

1 Letter of 25th September 1809 from Baring Bros., London, to G.Kieckhoefer, Rio de Janeiro. Kieckhoefer saw in this measure the hand of the government in Brazil.
2 Letter of 20th January 1810 to the Département des Finances, Lisbon, A xxvii, 260.
Letter of 20th January 1810 to the Contractants de la Ferme Royale, Lisbon, A xxvii, 264.
Letter of 20th January 1810 to J.F.da Costa Bandeira, Lisbon, A xxvii, 271.
Letter of 20th January 1810 to Baron de Quintella, Lisbon, A xxvii, 275.
The method employed at the end of 1808 was thus followed here. This time, a sum of cf 127,409.6.0. was drawn on the tobacco lessees.
3 Letter of 6th August 1809 from Baring, London, to J.Williams Hope, Harley Street, London.

PAGE 416

1 Letter of April 1808 from G. Kieckhoefer, Hamburg, to Hope & Co., Amsterdam.
2 Letter of 17th May 1808 to Matthiessen & Sillem, Hamburg, vii, 377.
Letter of 12th July 1808 to Baring Bros., London, vii, 435. Hope envisaged a 10-year investment with interest at 4% per annum, the capital being repaid in five equal instalments commencing at the end of the sixth year.
3 Letter of 20th February 1809 from G.Kieckhoefer, Falmouth, to Hope & Co., Amsterdam. Kieckhoefer wanted to export Silesian linen to Brazil. This could only be done via England, where the linen was subject to a heavy tax imposed under the Orders in Council, the British answer to Napoleon's Continental System. The Portuguese envoy promised to support the measures taken by Kieckhoefer to obtain exemption from the tax.
4 Letter of 30th April 1809 from G.Kieckhoefer, Rio de Janeiro, to Hope & Co., Amsterdam.
Letter of 3rd June 1809 from G.Kieckhoefer, Rio de Janeiro, to J.Williams Hope, East Sheen, Surrey.

PAGE 417

1 Letter of 14th August 1809 from A.Baring, London, to J.Williams Hope, London.
2 Letter of 6th September 1809 from P.C.Labouchère, Paris, to Hope & Co., Amsterdam.

3 Letters of 14th and 22nd September 1809 from P.C.Labouchère, Paris, to Hope & Co., Amsterdam.
4 Letter of 6th October 1809 from F.Baring, Stratton Park, Winchester, to Don Dom. de Souza Coutinho, London.
5 Letter of 6th October 1809 from F. Baring, Stratton Park, Winchester, to J.Williams Hope, East Sheen, Surrey.

PAGE 418

1 Letter of 11th October 1809 from A.Baring, Bishopsgate, London, to J.Williams Hope, East Sheen, Surrey.
Baring's calculations agree with the proceeds of the diamonds sold in 1808, after the deduction of commission at 4%, del credere, etc. The average price obtained during 1809, however, works out at cf 26.50, which, at a rate of exchange of cf 9.6–9.8 to the pound sterling, was still less than the three pounds which Don Domingo demanded.
2 Letter of 6th October 1809 from F.Baring, Stratton Park, Winchester, to Don Domingo de Souza Coutinho, London.
3 Letter of 17th October 1809 from A.Baring, London, to Don Domingo de Souza Coutinho, London.
4 Letter of 20th October 1809 from Don Domingo de Souza Coutinho, London, to Sir F.Baring, London.
5 Letters of 20th and 21st October 1809 from A.Baring, London, to J.Williams Hope, London. Don Domingo persisted in addressing his letters to Sir Francis even though the replies came from Alexander Baring.
6 Letter of 3rd November 1809 from A.Baring, Carshalton, to J.Williams Hope, East Sheen, Surrey.
7 According to Kieckhoefer, this house bought between 22,000 and 25,000 carats at three pounds sterling per carat.
8 Letter of 9th January 1810 from J.Williams Hope, London, to Lord Liverpool, London.
9 Letters of 2nd and 13th January 1810 from A.Baring, London, to Don Dom.de Souza Coutinho, London.

PAGE 419

1 Letter of 13th January 1810 from G.Kieckhoefer, Rio de Janeiro, to J.Williams Hope, London. Don Domingo's authority to negotiate with Baring and Hope was vested in him by a decree issued by the prince regent on 16th December 1809. Letter of 8th June 1810 from B.I.Targini, Rio de Janeiro, to Baring and Hope, London.
2 Letter of 7th May 1810 from G.Kieckhoefer, Rio de Janeiro, to A.Baring, London.
3 Letter of 25th September 1809 from A.Baring, Banchurch, to J.Williams Hope, London.

PAGE 420

1 Letter of 29th May 1810 from G. Kieckhoefer, Rio de Janeiro, to A.Baring, London.
2 Letter of 2nd June 1810 from G.Kieckhoefer, Rio de Janeiro, to A.Baring, London.
3 Letter of 8th June 1810 from G.Kieckhoefer, Rio de Janeiro, to A. Baring, London.
4 Labouchère, 'Un financier diplomate,' 427.

PAGE 421

1 Letter of 24th April 1810 from A.Baring, London, to J.Williams Hope, London.
2 Letter of April 1810 from Sir Francis Baring, London, to Don Domingo de Souza Coutinho, London. It is not clear from the text whether Sir Francis was thinking also of the repayment of the loan from the British government, though it is probable that he was.
3 Letter of 6th August 1810 from Don Domingo de Souza Coutinho, London, to A.Baring, London.
4 Letter of 4th July 1810 from John Stanley Jevons, Lisbon, to A.Baring, London.
5 Letter of 17th March 1810 from Baron de Quintella, Lisbon, to Hope & Co., Amsterdam.

PAGE 422

1 Letter of May 1810 from P.C.Labouchère, . . ., to the Count of Montalivet, Paris.
2 Letter of 14th August 1810 from A.Baring, London, to Don Domingo de Souza Coutinho, London.
14th August 1810: Proposal to Don Domingo de Souza Coutinho concerning the Portuguese Loan.
3 Schäfer, *Geschichte von Portugal*, v, 668–677.
4 Letter of 15th October 1810 from A.Baring, London, to P.C.Labouchère, . . .

PAGE 423

1 'Portugal Concern,' 39 et seq. J.E.Lucena and M.S.de Paiva, Portuguese government agents in London, acted as witnesses. It is probable that the payment of the 30,000 pounds sterling was made through them. Barings did not participate in the advance of 50,000 pounds sterling. This house had had no part in the advancing of funds at the end of 1808 and 1809. In contrast to Henry Hope & Co., Barings had no financial interest in the loan. When the diamonds were sold, however, they resumed their one-fourth share.
2 Letter of 14th December 1810 from A.Baring, London, to P.C.Labouchère, . . .
3 1,607 bonds were to remain unredeemed on 31st December 1811, from which date they bore interest at 5%.
4 Letter of 26th December 1810 to The Prince Arch-Treasurer etc., A XXVII, 539.

PAGE 424

1 Letter of 27th December 1810 from P.C.Labouchère, Amsterdam, to D.Parish, Paris.
2 Letters of 13th, 14th, 15th and 18th February 1811 from D.Parish, Paris, to P.C.Labouchère, Antwerp.
Labouchère, 'Un financier diplomate,' 435–447.
Letter of 11th March 1811 from Jean François le Bras, Morlaix, to Hope & Co., Amsterdam.
3 Labouchère, 'Un financier diplomate,' 453–454.
4 Letter of 2nd May 1811 from P.C.Labouchère, Paris, to The Duke of Gaeta, Paris.

PAGE 425

1 Letter of 20th June 1811 from P.C.Labouchère, Amsterdam, to John Hope, London. Hope had approached the Lieutenant General at the end of 1810 with a request that

supplementary duty be waived in the case of the diamonds. Letter of 26th December 1810 to The Prince Arch-Treasurer, etc., A XXVII, 539.
Letter of 12th July 1811 from the Count of Montalivet, Paris, to W.G.Coesvelt, Amsterdam.
Letter of 26th August 1811 from Baring Bros. & Co., London, to Hope & Co., Amsterdam.

2 'Compte de Vente d'une boîte de diamants bruts du Brésil, vendu d'ordre de Son Excellence Monsr. le Chevalier de Souza Coutinho et pour compte de la Couronne de Portugal' and 'Invoice of a parcel of Brazil diamonds, purchased on joint account with Mrs.Hope & Co. of Amsterdam and delivered to W.G.Coesvelt Esq.' Both documents show that the parcel totalled 24,220 carats gross. From this, however, 29 carats had to be deducted for false stones and a further 121 carats (½%) for reduced weight, a sort of tare. The remaining 24,070 carats were sold at 47 shillings per carat, yielding 56,564.10 pounds sterling gross. After the deduction of brokerage, sorting costs, etc., a nett balance of 54,528.8 pounds remained. Insinger's account shows that this house settled with Hope for 24,089 1/16 carats which fetched cf 569,086.11.8 nett, indicating an average price of just over cf 23.50 per carat. At a rate of exchange of cf 10, the two houses thus made a profit of about cf 24,000 on the deal.
Grootboek 1812: 77.

3 Letter of 18th October 1811 from Hope & Co., Amsterdam, to Baring Bros., London.
Letter of 10th January 1812 from Insinger & Co., Amsterdam, to Baring Bros. & Co., London.
Letter of 10th January 1812 from Hope & Co., Amsterdam, to Baring Bros. & Co., London.

4 Any lengthy interruption in supplies produced a reduction in the number of cleavers and polishers. To offset the drain, Hope had taken timely steps to subsidize the training of diamond polishers. In the *grootboek* for 1805, the Account relating to the Portuguese Crown contains the following entries: 31st July, 'Paid to Keyzer for 7 apprentice diamond polishers at f 150: f 1,050;' 31st August, 'Ditto for three apprentices: f 450;' 30th September, 'Ditto for 4 apprentices: f 600;' 31st December, 'Ditto for 2 apprentices: f 300.'
The export of diamonds to Turkey had also ceased.

PAGE 426

1 Letter of 8th January 1812 to the Département des Finances, Lisbon, A XXVIII, 6.
Letter of 8th January 1812 to Baring Bros. & Co., London, A XXVIII, 8. Hope drew on Baring for the sum paid in Amsterdam.

2 Letter of 21st January 1812 from P.C.Labouchère, Paris, to Hope & Co., Amsterdam. In Paris he visited the Ministers of Home Affairs, Finance and Police.

3 Letter of 8th March 1812 from P.C.Labouchère, Paris, to John Hope, London.

4 Letter of 28th August 1812 from Baring Bros. & Co., London, to Hope & Co., Amsterdam. Don Domingo's successor proved to be opposed to the export of diamonds to Holland, and under the terms of the contract of 13th December 1810 the decision rested with him. Baring thereupon disposed of the stones to Goldsmith. The proceeds, 53,400 pounds sterling, were handed to the envoy, 'Mrs.Baring not having received any money for that object.' The size of the parcel will have been of the order of 22–23,000 carats.

5 Letter of 29th October 1812 from P.C.Labouchère, Amsterdam, to John Hope, London.

6 Letter of 23rd February 1813 from H.J.Swarth, Amsterdam, to John Hope, London.
7 Letter of 20th October 1812 from John Hope, London, to D.Berck, Amsterdam, A v, 151.
8 Letter of 14th October 1813 from Baring Bros. & Co., London, to Hope & Co., Amsterdam.

PAGE 427

1 Letter of 24th November 1815 from Baring Bros. & Co., London, to Hope & Co., Amsterdam.
2 The first parcel was of 19,751 5/8 carats and fetched cf 540,597.17.0 nett; the second, of 19,898¼ carats, fetched cf 587,669.17.0 nett. The mean price per carat for the first parcel was just over cf 29.50. *Grootboek* 1815: 249; *grootboek* 1816: 220. The loan sum was reduced by cf 1,055,208.8.0 at the end of 1816. *Grootboek* 1816: 215.
3 The exact quantity was 19,767 carats, which fetched cf 562,562.7.0, an average of just under cf 28.50 per carat. *Grootboek* 1817: 271.
4 At the end of 1819, settlement was made in respect of 25,863 7/8 carats. These fetched cf 825,851.12.0., an average of cf 30.50 per carat. *Grootboek* 1819: 274. This was the nett figure after the deduction of various expenses. The market price was approximately one guilder per carat higher.
5 Letter of 8th January 1819 to the Département des Finances, Lisbon, A XXIX, 462. Confirmation of this will be found in H.Heertje, *De Diamantbewerkers van Amsterdam* (Amsterdam, 1936), 25.

CHAPTER FIFTEEN

PAGE 431

1 Letter of 9th August 1787 to Laborde de Méréville, Paris, 'Private Correspondence begun 19th June, ended 31st Dec. 1787' (hereafter abbreviated to P.C. '87), 82.

2 Letter of 9th August 1787 to Laborde de Méréville, Paris, P.C. '87, 84.

3 Letter of 21st February 1788 to Bohl Bros., Cadiz, 'Private Correspondence 1788' (hereafter abbreviated to P.C. '88), 190.

PAGE 432

1 In his letters to Laborde, Hope made it appear that he was inpossession of detailed information.

2 Letter of 7th August 1787 to J.&F.Baring, London, P.C. '87, 81. Cochineal prices in Amsterdam had indeed declined steadily since 1770, albeit a mild recovery took place during the years of the American War of Independence. Since December 1786 the monthly average had been f 7.80 per pound. The yearly averages since 1770 had been as follows: 1770: f 13.83; 1771: f 14.99; 1772: f 13.68; 1773: f 11.41; 1774: f 11.14; 1775: f 10.28; 1776: f 8.62; 1777: f 9.74; 1778: f 10.06; 1779: f 10.08; 1780: f 10.55; 1781: f –.–; 1782: f 10.56; 1783: f 9.15; 1784: f 7.62; 1785: f 7.96; 1786: f 7.91. N.W.Posthumus, *Nederlandsche Prijsgeschiedenis*, I (Leiden, 1943), 422. Hope was also counting on a new arrangement for official trade with the West Indies delaying future imports of cochineal. Letter of 5th February 1788 to J.&F.Baring, London, P.C. '88, 131.

3 Laborde, Hope's correspondent, became well known for his advanced political views. He was among the architects of the Declaration of Human Rights, and he swore the Oath of the Tennis Court. He will certainly have been on the side of the Patriots in the party conflicts in the Republic. This was evidently no impediment to a friendly exchange of letters with Henry Hope. *Nouvelle Biographie Générale*, XXVII (Paris, 1858), 381–384.

4 Letter of 7th August 1787 to J.&F.Baring, London, P.C. '87, 80. On 28th July, Henry Hope wrote to the Swedish Minister of Finance, Ruuth, complaining of 'the thanklessness of the political circumstances in this country, which has a dominant influence on business, especially at the present time, when the Stock Exchange is feeling the effects of bankruptcies which add to the discomfort and mistrust.' Letter of 28th July 1787 to Baron de Ruuth, Stockholm, P.C. '87, 61.

PAGE 433

1 Concerning Voûte: *Nieuw Nederlandsch Biographisch Woordenboek*, II, 1508–1510.

Transactions between merchants, such at took place in Rouen, were viewed by Hope as unusual: 'We find that in Rouen everything is traded between the merchants and not thro' brokers, by which means a great deal of time is required and more skill than generally falls to the share of merchants in the detail of selling and buying.' Letter of 9th October 1787 to J.&F.Baring, London, P.C. '87, 189.

2 Voûte was subsequently to render valuable services to the Company during two missions to St.Petersburg in connexion with Russian and Polish loans (*supra*, Chapter Five, *passim*, 158–172). Voûte had written to Hope on 9th April 1787 concerning the potential market for cochineal in Russia. By then, however, Hope had already written to Ryan on the matter.

3 Hope fixed the arroba at $23^1/_8$ Amsterdam pounds (of 494 grams) and the suron or seroon at just under $8^7/_{10}$ arrobas. A seroon thus weighed 200 Amsterdam pounds, or nearly 98.8 kilograms. Letters of 16th and 18th April 1788 to Thos. Littledale, Rotterdam, P.C. '88, 347, 349. W.C.H.Staring, *De binnen- en buitenlandsche maten, gewichten van vroeger en tegenwoordig, met hunne onderlinge vergelijkingen en herleidingen* (Schoonhoven, 1902), 91, 106. The par value of the ducat can be put at $2\frac{1}{2}$ guilders; at the rate of exchange ruling when the speculation was set up, it was worth f 2.30. Staring, *Maten en gewichten*, 146. Posthumus, *Prijsgeschiedenis*, I, 585. The two Paris houses concerned were Boyd Kerr & Co and Vandenyver Frères & Co.

4 Letter of 17th August 1787 to J.&F.Baring. London, P.C. '87, 97. As Henry Hope had not referred to these two centres in his original plan, we may assume that he was influenced by Baring.

PAGE 434

1 Letter of 30th August 1787 to Bournissien Despreaux & Fils, Rouen, P.C. '87, 116.

2 Letter of 31st August 1787 to J.&F.Baring, London, P.C. '87, 126. Posthumus, in his *Prijsgeschiedenis*, states that the average price for cochineal in August 1787 was f 7.80 or 26 shillings per pound.

3 At the rate of exchange ruling in August 1787, the livre can be put at f 0.45. The limits in Marseilles thus lay between f 6.75 and f 6.98, and those in Rouen between f 9.00 and f 9.45. Bournissien and Councler also received letters of credit; these were drawn on Cottin & Fils and Jauge in Paris, because drawing too heavily on a single house might have attracted attention. Like Ryan, they could not draw on the credits until the purchases had been completed.

4 Bournissien replied to the letter of 30th August on 6th September (P.C. '87, 140). Councler's reply was sent on 10th September (P.C. '87, 149). Ryan replied to Hope's letter of 17th August on 7th September. These dates show that the estimated transmission times were correct (P.C. '87, 187). A normal letter took 3–4 days longer to reach Cadiz.

5 Sutherlands & Bock were given a price limit of 165 roubles per pood for cash, or 180 roubles for 12 months' credit. One pood can be put at 16.38 kilograms. If we assume that the rouble at that time was worth f 1.85, we arrive at a price of f 9.25 or thereabouts per Amsterdam pound for cash. Letter of 21st August 1787 to Sutherlands & Bock, St.Petersburg, P.C. '87, 102. The house was also authorized to buy up cochineal in Moscow.

6 Letter of 21st August 1787 to R.Sutherland, St.Petersburg, P.C. '87, 99. The preparations for the war against the Turks had greatly increased Russia's financial commitments abroad.

PAGE 435

1 Letters of 1st and 8th September 1787 to B.Roosen, Hamburg, P.C. '87, 129, 136. Hope estimated the stock in Hamburg to be between 50 and 100 seroons. Roosen put the figure at 20–25, but he was later obliged to revise this figure. This instance shows how difficult it was for even a local merchant to accurately assess the quantity available.

2 Letter of 17th September 1787 to Bournissien Despreaux & Fills, Rouen, P.C. '87, 145.

3 Letter of 1st October 1787 to Bournissien Despreaux, Rouen, P.C. '87, 166–167.

PAGE 436

1 These averaged 65 ducats per arroba for seroons, and $63\frac{3}{4}$ ducats for sobernales. Letter of 18th October 1787 to Th.Ryan, Cadiz, P.C. '87, 200.

2 The Five Gremios asked 66 ducats per arroba for cash.
Letter of 4th October 1787 to J.&F.Baring, London, P.C. '87, 180.

3 Letters of 10th and 18th October 1787 to Th.Ryan, Cadiz, P.C. '87, 194, 201.
Letter of 12th October 1787 to J.&F.Baring, London, P.C. '87, 196.

4 On 4th October 1787 Hope wrote to Baring, advising him of the arrival in Marseilles of 25 seroons from Cadiz. On 28th September, 65 seroons had arrived in London (P.C. '87, 177). On 13th November, two vessels carrying 90 seroons arrived in London, and later a further 50 seroons reached Amsterdam. Letters of 23rd November and 4th December to J.&F.Baring, London, P.C. '87, 269, 303. In addition, small quantities continued to arrive from Mexico – in all some 280 seroons, in three ships – a portion of which was bought by Ryan on a rising market, at prices up to 68 ducats per arroba. Letter of 19th October 1787 to J.&F.Baring, London, P.C. '87, 207.

5 This report from Ryan did not reach Hope until 27th November. The breakdown, according to quality, was as follows:

300 seroons 1st superior } black and grey, for London
260 seroons 2nd superior }
300 seroons for Marseilles and Amsterdam
145 seroons extraordinary good, for Amsterdam
1,005 seroons

24 sobernales 1st superior } principally grey, suitable for London
48 sobernales 2nd superior }
39 sobernales suitable for Marseilles or Amsterdam
111 sobernales

The colour, i.e. black or grey, was determined by the method of treatment of the cochineal insects after collection. Heating them in an oven caused them to turn grey, while contact with hot iron turned them black. Letter of 30th November 1787 to J.&F.Baring, London, P.C. '87, 291.

6 Letter of 27th November 1787 to J.&F.Baring, London, P.C. '87, 287.

PAGE 437

1 Letters of 7th and 11th September 1787 to J.&F.Baring, London, P.C. '87, 134, 137. De Bruyn had bought 244 seroons on 11th September. The information available

indicated that a further 243 seroons were held by other houses. On 7th September the stock which had not been purchased was described as 'not in our way,' but by 11th September opinions had changed. The price paid for the 244 seroons averaged 26 *schellingen* (f 7.80) per pound.

2 Letters of 25th and 28th September, and 9th and 12th October 1787 to J.&F.Baring, London, P.C. '87, 152, 158, 189, 195.

3 Since 30th October the price had remained at 30 *schellingen* (f 9.00) per pound. The gaps in the monthly quotations in Posthumus's *Prijsgeschiedenis* for the months of October and November can be filled in with figures of f 8.40 and f 9.00 respectively.

4 Letters of 4th and 28th September 1787 to J.&F.Baring, London, P.C. '87, 130, 160–163. By 28th September, Hope's brokers had succeeded in purchasing only 393 seroons. At the end of November, Baring's stock totalled 798 seroons. The price rose from 14 shillings and 8 pence in early September to about 17 shillings in October and November.

5 Letters of 24th and 27th September 1787 to Vve Councler & Fils Ainé, Marseilles, P.C. '87, 149, 158, and 25th September 1787 to J.&F.Baring, London, P.C. '87, 152. By the end of the 15-day purchasing period, Councler held 159 seroons. In Amsterdam some saw it as an (unsuccessful) operation on the part of English speculators. Others had earlier burned their fingers on cochineal.

PAGE 438

1 Letter of 1st October 1787 to Vve Councler & Fils Ainé, Marseilles, P.C. '87, 168.

2 Councler was thus free to go to 18–18½ livres per pound, but in fact he bought only 6 seroons at 18 livres. During November and December he went no higher than 17.1 livres. By the end of November his purchases totalled 265 seroons.

3 Letters of 17th, 20th and 27th September 1787 to Bournissien Despreaux & Fils, Rouen, P.C. '87, 145, 147, 153, and 28th September 1787 to J.&F.Baring, London, P.C. '87, 158. Hope had authorized Bournissien to pay up to 24 livres for small parcels. Bournissien also bought up parcels in Le Havre and others which were en route to that port.

4 Letters of 17th and 27th September 1787 to Bournissien Despreaux & Fils, Rouen, P.C. '87, 145, 154, and 21st September to J.&F.Baring, London, P.C. '87, 148. In the last of these, Hope wrote: 'We have found that a house here (i.e. in Amsterdam) has started up as a buyer.' He thereupon raised the price to 26½–27 *schellingen* per pound, but only managed to secure 20 seroons. By the end of November, Bournissien had bought 108 seroons.

5 Letters of 8th November 1787 to Bournissien Despreaux & Fils, Rouen, P.C. '87, 239–240, and 9th November to J.&F.Baring, London, P.C. '87, 241. Baring had informed Hope about a counterspeculation involving 90 seroons. Hope ultimately accepted 27 seroons at between 24.5 and 25.1 livres per pound, but declined a further 40. Bournissien's reply to Hope's 'insinuations of suspicion of unfair dealings' struck Hope as 'plausible.' Letter of 1st January 1788 to J.&F.Baring, London, P.C. '88, 2.

PAGE 439

1 The original limits were 165 roubles per pood for cash, or 180 roubles for 12 months credit. The ruling price, however, was 180–185 roubles for 12 months credit. Hope therefore consented to an increase to 185 roubles for credit, or 170–175 for cash. Letter of 5th October 1787 to Sutherlands & Bock, St.Petersburg. P.C. '87, 176. On

the same day, however, Sutherlands & Bock wrote to say that the price for 12 months credit had risen to 195–200 roubles, and the cash price to 180–185 roubles. Upon receipt of this news, Hope authorized the house to go to 180–190 roubles for cash, or 200–210 with credit, but in such a manner as to produce averages of 185 roubles for cash or 205 for credit. Letter of 19th October 1787 to Sutherlands & Bock, St.Petersburg, P.C. '87, 203. In his correspondence with Baring, Hope made no reference to suspicions of bad faith on the part of Sutherland. But as a *quid pro quo* he asked to be allowed to discount payments against credit at the low rate of exchange ruling at the time.

2 Letter of 18th December 1787 to Sutherlands & Bock, St.Petersburg, P.C. '87, 350. The average price for credit sales was just under 200 roubles per pood.

3 The rules prescribed in the Koran related to kermes, a dyestuff obtained in the Mediterranean region by drying the bodies of scale insects of the same name. Cochineal, however, had secured a firm place in the Moslim countries because of its fine bright red colour.

4 Letter of 6th November 1787 to J.&F.Baring, London, P.C. '87, 233.

5 Letters of 9th and 16th November 1787 to J.&F.Baring, London, P.C. '87, 240, 247.

PAGE 440

1 It was Hope's intention to have the cochineal sent to Amsterdam via Lyons and Strasbourg. As 'compact and valuable goods' were involved, the transport costs would not exceed 4% *ad valorem*, and the journey would not take more than four weeks. The cochineal would have to be packed in barrels, each of which could hold six seroons. If the full barrels were too heavy for the carts, the contents could be reduced to four seroons. When filling the barrels, the cochineal was to be consolidated in order to prevent powdering as a result of friction. Letters of 22nd October 1787 to Vve Councler & Fils Ainé, Marseilles, P.C. '87, 211, and 16th November 1787 to J.&F.Baring, London, P.C. '87, 247.

2 Hope also considered chartering a vessel in Leghorn, or arranging for a British silk carrier to call at Marseilles. Letter of 7th November 1787 to J.&F.Baring, London, P.C. '87, 281.

3 Letters of 16th November 1787 to J.&F.Baring, London, P.C. '87, 247, and 23rd November to Vve Councler & Fils Ainé, Marseilles, P.C. '87, 265. On 17th December 1787, Hope enquired of Councler concerning the composition and powers of the Chamber of Commerce in Marseilles. His action was prompted by questions put to him in connexion with a plan to establish a similar body in Amsterdam with the aim of finding the causes of the decline in Holland's trade and proposing suitable remedies. Hope viewed the plan as 'une idée bizarre de quelques individus ambitieux.' The date given by Westermann for the draft Articles of Association, i.e. 1786, thus appears to be too early. Letter of 17th December 1787 to Vve Councler & Fils Ainé, Marseilles, P.C. '87, 343; J.C.Westermann, *Kamer van Koophandel en Fabrieken voor Amsterdam, Gedenkboek*, I (Amsterdam, 1936), 3–4, Appendix I.

4 Letter of 24th December 1787 to Vve Councler & Fils Ainé, Marseilles, P.C. '87, 366.

5 Letters of 3rd and 10th December 1787 to Bournissien Despreaux & Fils, Rouen, P.C. '87, 293, 326, and 11th December to J.&F.Baring, London, P.C. '87, 334–335. Even after giving permission for these sales, Hope did not entirely abandon the idea of 'keeping up a circulation.'

6 Letter of 1st January 1788 to J.&F.Baring, London, P.C. '88, 2. On 17th December

1787 Hope instructed Ryan to send 600 seroons to Rotterdam, but on the 31st he issued amended orders providing for 300 seroons to go to Rotterdam and 200 to London. The Rotterdam consignment was subsequently increased by 100 seroons. The 400 seroons were accepted in Rotterdam by Thos. Littledale & Co., on behalf of Hope, at the end of April 1788 and provisionally placed in their warehouse. Littledales were requested to complete the inward clearance with the minimum of fuss, 'in an easy and satisfactory manner,' Letter of 18th April 1788 to Thos. Littledale & Co., Rotterdam, P.C. '88, 349.

PAGE 441

1 Letter of 4th December 1787 to J.&F.Baring, London, P.C. '87, 305.

2 Letters of 14th December 1787 to J.&F.Baring, London, P.C. '87, 337–338; 17th December to Thos. Ryan & Co., Cadiz, P.C. '87, 344, and 17th December to Bournissien Despreaux & Fils, Rouen, P.C. '87, 344.

3 Letters of 24th December 1787 to Vve Councler & Fils Ainé, Marseilles, P.C. '87, 368, and 17th December to Bournissien Despreaux & Fils, Rouen, P.C. '87, 344.

PAGE 442

1 Councler was frightened by a rumour concerning the arrival of 1,000 seroons in January 1788. Hope attributed the rumour to regret and anger on the part of sellers and outsiders, but privately those concerned were none too sure of their ground in view of 'Ryan's defective information.'
Letters of 24th December 1787 to Vve Councler & Fils Ainé, Marseilles, P.C. '87, 367; 30th November, 21st and 28th December 1787 to J.&F.Baring. London, P,C. '87, 290, 363, 374; 1st, 15th and 22nd January, 5th, 12th and 19th February 1788 to J.&F.Baring, London, P.C. '88, 1, 60, 96, 131, 145, 179; 18th February 1788 to Vve Councler & Fils Ainé, Marseilles, P.C. '88, 164; and 10th and 24th January 1788 to Bournissien Despreaux & Fils, Rouen, P.C. '88, 37, 105.

2 Letters of 31st December 1787 to Thos. Ryan & Co., Cadiz, P.C. '87, 378; and 4th and 8th January 1788 to J.&F.Baring, London, P.C. '88, 13, 31. Bohl Bros. & Co. was a German house.

3 The 63 seroons shipped to London in the 'Hesther' proved to have come from owners who had sold other parcels to Ryan. Hope was informed that no export duty had been paid on the consignment. Baring succeeded in laying hands on 50 of the 63 seroons. Hope complained to Baring about the 'defective conduct of our factor' (i.e. Ryan). Letters of 1st, 4th, 15th and 22nd January 1788 to J.&F.Baring, London P.C. '88, 1, 13, 62, 96; and 21st February to Bohl Bros. & Co., Cadiz, P.C. '88, 192.

4 Letter of 7th January 1788 to Bohl Bros. & Co., Cadiz, P.C. '88, 20. Hope made it appear to Bohl that the Company was acting on behalf of third parties.

5 Hope wrote to Bohl on 7th January; the four ships together carried 516 seroons and 29 sobernales.
Letters of 1st and 5th February 1788 to J.&F.Baring, London, P.C. '88, 121, 131.

PAGE 443

1 Letter of 21st February 1788 to Bohl Bros. & Co., Cadiz, P.C. '88, 189–190. The order to Bohl to implement Instruction Number One was given on 31st January 1788 (P.C. '88, 119). On the same day, Ryan was given permission to purchase the bulk of the new stock at 70 ducats. He was also authorized to take an option on large parcels

at 75–78 ducats per arroba and, if necessary, to give a bonus of 1 ducat. For the stock as a whole, Ryan's buying limits were competitive with those imposed on Bohl; for smaller parcels, they were less favourable. After all that had happened, this order can scarcely be taken seriously; in all probability it served as a 'safety net' beneath Bohl.

2 Letter of 21st February 1788 to Bohl Bros. & Co., P.C. '88, 193.

3 Hope assured Bohl that Ryan's purchases were not made on behalf of the speculators. Ryan had probably secured some of the parcels which had changed hands at 72 ducats. At the same time, Ryan was addressed in an encouraging tone in order to prevent large-scale sales–and with them a decline in prices. The order given to Ryan on 31st January was cancelled in a letter dated 31st March (P.C. '88, 224). Letters of 14th and 21st February, and 3rd March 1788 to Thos. Ryan, Cadiz, P.C. '88, 154, 189, 221.

4 On 14th March, Hope reported to Baring that the purchase by Bohl of 48 seroons had served to raise the price of current grades to 78–80 ducats, and that of the highest grades to 85–88 ducats. By then, the 500 seroons which had arrived in January had practically disappeared from the market.

PAGE 444

1 Letters of 29th February and 4th March 1788 to J.&F.Baring, London, P.C. '88, 212, 226.

2 The 'parr of the market' for Marseilles had originally been fixed at 98 ducats. This was subsequently lowered, first to 85–90 and then to 74–84 ducats. Letters of 21st, 24th and 31st January, and 14th February 1788 to Vve Councler & Fils Ainé, Marseilles, P.C. '88, 88, 101, 115, 148.

3 Letter of 14th February 1788 to Vve Councler & Fils Ainé, Marseilles, P.C. '88, 150.

4 Letter of 14th March 1788 to J.&F.Baring, London, P.C. '88, 260.

PAGE 445

1 Letter of 31st March 1788 to Vve Councler & Fils Ainé, Marseilles, P.C. '88, 306.

2 Letters of 28th February and 6th March 1788 to Bournissien Despreaux & Fils, Rouen, P.C. '88, 208, 232.

3 Letters of 27th March and 7th April 1788 to Bournissien Despreaux & Fils, Rouen, P.C. '88, 290, 328.

PAGE 446

1 Letters of 18th and 28th March 1788 to Sutherlands & Bock, St.Petersburg, P.C. '88, 269, 295; and 14th March to J.&F.Baring, London, P.C. '88, 263–264.

2 Letter of 8th April 1788 to J.&F.Baring, London, P.C. '88, 330. The fact that Barings had only a one-fourth share in the purchases will certainly have contributed to their optimism and boldness. The purchases up to this date totalled just over $5\frac{1}{2}$ million guilders.

3 Letter of 8th April 1788 to J.&F.Baring, London, P.C. '88, 331. The same guarded tone is discernible in the letter of 28th March 1788 to J.&F.Baring, London, P.C. '88, 296. Voûte had again been abroad in March. He returned on the 21st, but it was the 26th before he found time to discuss the cochineal affair with Hope. Letter of 25th March 1788 to J.&F.Baring, London, P.C. '88, 288.

4 Bohl wrote to Hope on 18th March. Hope's letter of 21st February had reached him round about mid-March. Letter of 10th April 1788 to Bohl Bros. & Co., Cadiz, P.C.

'88, 335. Hope was not willing to take over any cochineal which Ryan might buy. Letter of 10th April 1788 to Thos. Ryan & Co., Cadiz, P.C. '88, 333, 335.

PAGE 447

1 Letter of 24th March 1788 to Bohl Bros. & Co., Cadiz, P.C. '88, 281. Bohl was authorized to buy a further 50–100 seroons; Hope was anxious that the price should not drop below 75 ducats, preferring to see it rise to 80. On 10th April, Hope confirmed to Bohl the receipt of the latter's letter of 18th March. Letter of 10th April 1788 to Bohl Bros. & Co., Cadiz, P.C. '88, 335. On 11th April Hope wrote to Baring: 'By letters from Cadiz we have advice of the arrival of The Confidence from Vera Cruz with 295 surons cochineal & that The Mentor & St.Raphael were daily expected with about 400 surons more.' (P.C. '88, 339). When a letter dated 18th March refers to 'daily expected,' one of 24th March which takes three weeks to reach its destination cannot be in time.

2 Letter of 11th April 1788 to J.&F.Baring, London, P.C. '88, 339, 340.

3 For Hope, with a three-fourths share, this meant a loss of cf 1,588,194.8.0. Of this sum, cf 400,000 was written off.

4 The figures quoted here were obtained from the 'Cochineal Account' which appears in 'Balance of Several Accounts Anno 1793,' folios 8–24. *Infra*, Appendix F-I-II-III.

5 The selling prices are expressed in guilders and cents (in conformity with Posthumus's *Prijsgeschiedenis*) and in *schellingen*. No distinction is made between the terms 'bale' and 'seroon' in these accounts.

PAGE 448

1 Between 1790 and 1794 a total of 518 seroons were exported to Russia.

2 In 1788, 62 seroons were sold at a profit of cf 0.22 per pound. From then on, losses were suffered: in 1789, cf 0.27 per pound on 211 seroons; in 1790, cf 0.94 per pound on 142 seroons; in 1791, cf 0.67 per pound on 52 seroons; in 1792, cf 1.99 per pound on 104 seroons; and in 1793, cf 3.15 per pound on 2 seroons. The 2 seroons in 1793 were cochineal dust and thus of lower value.

3 In 1788, Hope's average selling price was cf 0.10 above the mean of the quotations over the year. In 1789, it was cf 0.19 below, in 1790 cf 0.55 below, in 1791 cf 0.49 below and in 1792 cf 1.70 below.

4 In September 1787 De Bruyn had purchased 244 seroons at an average price of 26 *schellingen*, or cf 7.80 per pound. This corresponded to the average of the quotations for the months January to September 1787 inclusive. Posthumus, *Prijsgeschiedenis*, I, 422.

5 The profit on the remaining 40% was no more than cf 0.15 per pound.

6 The low selling prices achieved by the speculators show that their stock was indeed 'dead stock' and that the demand at that time was little greater than the normal supply. It is unlikely that the steady decline in selling prices was caused by reduction in quality, for the article had good storage properties.

7 38 seroons went to Paul Thoron & Co. and M.A.Qm.Salomon Fua in Constantinople, 22 to J.J.Guérin in Aleppo and 6 to Alexandria.

PAGE 449

1 *Supra*, 123. In view of the fact that, according to the account of 1793, 198 seroons and 61 sobernales were held by Sutherland, a claim by Hope relating to the speculation

must have existed. A further 75 seroons were consigned to Wm.Porter & Co. in 1793.

2 Labouchère sold the claim to Lawrence C.Brown, the former partner of William Porter, for cf 25,000. Brown was in financial difficulties, partly as a result of errors in speculation and partly because of the Russian government's anti-British attitude. Letters of 6th/18th September 1811 from P.C.Labouchère, St.Petersburg, to G.Thomson Rowand & Co., Moscow, and 6/18th September 1811 from P.C.Labouchère, St.Petersburg, to Lawr.C.Brown, St.Petersburg.

INDEX

Wulff,J., Russian Councillor of State, 178, 190, 191, 201, 202, 208, 599, 601

Yakovlev, Russian owner of iron works, 604, 609, 619, 625, 626
Yeames, cashier of Sutherland & Co., 149
Yrujo, Marquis de, Spanish envoy to the United States, 312

Zablukov,A., Imperial Treasurer of the Russian government, 130, 575
Zakharev & Rebinin, merchant house in Moscow, 501
Zakrevsky, President of the College of Medicine in St.Petersburg, 149
Zenyavin,N.I., Russian admiral, 206, 215
Zhigarev, merchant in Moscow, 502
Zubov, Platon, favourite of Catherine II, 129, 134, 135, 137, 142, 145, 148, 150–153, 183
Zuckerbäcker Klein & Co.,B., merchant house in Riga, 216, 510, 626

LIST OF ILLUSTRATIONS
AND
TABLE OF CONTENTS

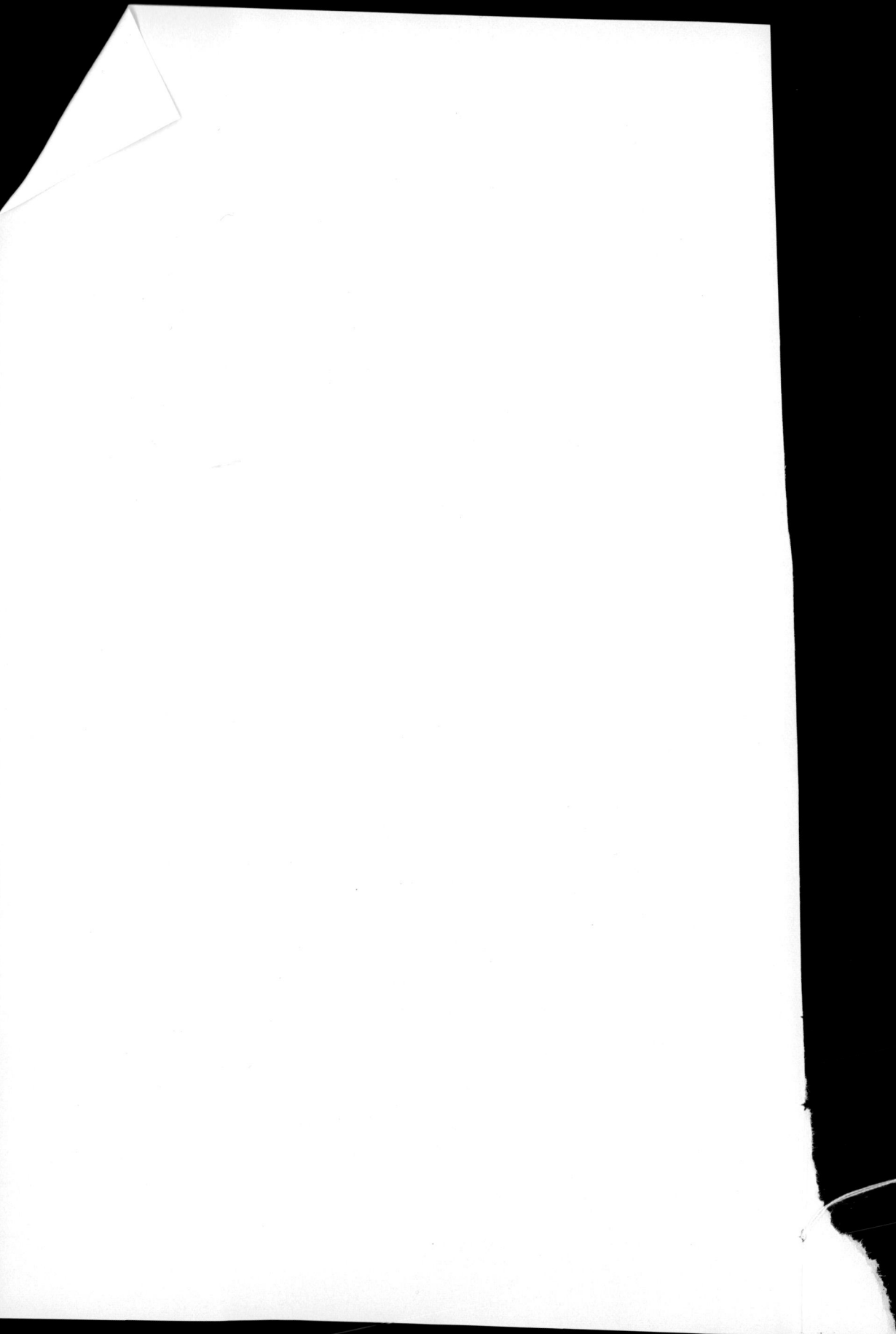